THE PHILOSOPHY OF SEX

Also by Alan Soble

Pornography, Sex, and Feminism

The Philosophy of Sex and Love: An Introduction

Sexual Investigations

The Structure of Love

Pornography: Marxism, Feminism, and the Future of Sexuality

Sex from Plato to Paglia: A Philosophical Encyclopedia (editor)

Sex, Love, and Friendship (editor)

Eros, Agape, and Philia: Readings in the Philosophy of Love (editor)

THE PHILOSOPHY OF SEX

Contemporary Readings

FIFTH EDITION

EDITED BY
ALAN SOBLE
AND
NICHOLAS POWER

ROWMAN & LITTLEFIELD PUBLISHERS, INC.
Lanham • Boulder • New York • Toronto • Plymouth, UK

ROWMAN & LITTLEFIELD PUBLISHERS, INC.

Published in the United States of America
by Rowman & Littlefield Publishers, Inc.
A wholly owned subsidiary of The Rowman & Littlefield Publishing Group, Inc.
4501 Forbes Boulevard, Suite 200, Lanham, Maryland 20706
www.rowmanlittlefield.com

Estover Road
Plymouth PL6 7PY
United Kingdom

British Library Cataloguing in Publication Information Available

Library of Congress Cataloging-in-Publication Data

The philosophy of sex : contemporary readings / [edited by] Alan Soble &
  Nicholas Power.
    p. cm.
  Includes index.
  ISBN-13: 978-0-7425-4798-8 (pbk. : alk. paper)
  ISBN-10: 0-7425-4798-1 (pbk. : alk. paper)
  1. Sex. 2. Sexual ethics. I. Soble, Alan. II. Power, Nicholas (Nicholas P.)
HQ12.P47 2008
306.7—dc22

                                                        2007012305

Printed in the United States of America

♾™ The paper used in this publication meets the minimum requirements of
American National Standard for Information Sciences—Permanence of Paper for
Printed Library Materials, ANSI Z39.48–1984.

For Sylvia and William Soble
spouses for sixty-five years

To Hannah Rachel Power and Molly Emma Power

CONTENTS

PART 2: HOMOSEXUALITY AND REPRODUCTION

PART 3: USE, OBJECTIFICATION, AND CONSENT— THE THEORY

PREFACE

The second edition of *The Philosophy of Sex* (1991) was an 80 percent revision of the first edition (1980); the third edition (1997) was an 80 percent revision of the second; the fourth edition (2002) was about a quarter or so revision of the third; and the current edition, the fifth in slightly over 25 years, is a 50 percent revision of the fourth. The first edition contained 20 essays; the second 19, the third 25, the fourth 31, and the fifth 30. The number of pages in the various editions, of course, also changed (although, in light of the contingency of font size, word count is a more significant figure): there were 412 pages in the first, 338 in the second, 376 in the third, 513 in the fourth, and 552 in the fifth. What these statistics fully mean, mundanely or cosmically, we haven't a clue. But we are pleased that *The Philosophy of Sex: Contemporary Readings* is alive and well and will continue to guide students who are being formally introduced to conceptual and normative questions that arise about sexuality.

This edition contains not only a different set of essays for students to read (although central papers in contemporary philosophy of sex remain) but also new "interstitial" matter, as we have learned to call it, something that earlier editions never attempted. Each essay is preceded by its own introductory paragraph prepared by the editors, and appended to each essay is a set of "study questions" for students to think about. We believe that the introductions and the study questions will help students master the material. Some technical terms in the study questions might have to be explained to students by the instructor—for example, "family resemblance," "individuation," "referential opacity," and the "doctrine of double effect." The suggested readings section at the end of the book has been expanded to take into account material that appeared in print after the 2002 fourth edition as well as older material that should be included in any comprehensive list of the significant work in contemporary philosophy of sex. The bibliography has been increased by nearly 100 percent—that's a statistic over which we need not scratch our heads. (All the topics discussed in *Philosophy of Sex* are covered in detail in *Sex from Plato to Paglia: A Philosophical Encyclopedia*

[Greenwood Press, 2006], edited by Alan Soble. Teachers of courses in the philosophy of sex would do well to encourage students to consult the encyclopedia; essays or term papers written for such a course will benefit. The encyclopedia also includes many more bibliographic entries than a teaching anthology could.)

This edition of *The Philosophy of Sex* is divided into four sections: (I) Analysis and Perversion, (II) Homosexuality and Reproduction, (III) Use, Objectification, and Consent—the Theory, and (IV) Use, Objectification, and Consent—Applied Topics. The section on conceptual analysis focuses on what sexual desire and sexual activity are, and investigates in what sense(s) some sexual desires and acts might be unnatural or perverted. (This question is also discussed by John Corvino in part II, and elsewhere.) Part I begins with a chapter that is designed to provide students with a general introduction to the conceptual and normative questions that pertain to sexuality. (This chapter is a revision of "The Fundamentals of the Philosophy of Sex," which served as the introduction to the fourth edition.) The section also includes Greta Christina's lively essay that demonstrates that defining "having sex" is not so easy; the classic essays by Thomas Nagel, Janice Moulton, and Alan Goldman; essays by Alan Soble and Christopher Hamilton that explore the classic pieces and other foundational writings in the philosophy of sex; and a new essay by Louise Collins on the ontology of cybersex.

The issues discussed in part II include the morality of homosexual behavior and the wisdom of same-sex marriage. The juxtaposition of the essays is meant to provoke questions about the logical connections between views about homosexual behavior and views about the use of contraception during heterosexual coitus. (Both same-sex sexual acts and contracepted heterosexual coitus fail to be procreative.) Essays by John Finnis and Stanley Kurtz criticize homosexual behavior and marriage; those by Andrew Koppelman, John Corvino, and Cheshire Calhoun present the other side. The essays by Karol Wojtyla (Pope John Paul II) and Koppelman address reproductive issues: periodic continence (or the "rhythm method") and infertility. Jerome Neu asks questions about the usefulness of thinking in terms of sexual identity or sexual orientation. The analytic essays of part I of this volume, on the nature of sexuality and perversion, have implications for these disagreements over homosexuality and same-sex sexual activity, as they do for all the other topics discussed in the book.

Part III is devoted to analytic and theoretical questions that derive from approaching sexuality within a Kantian framework, a topic that is broached by Goldman in his essay "Plain Sex" in part I. Thomas Mappes, Howard Klepper, and Alan Soble provide or explore Kantian accounts of sexual morality, explaining concepts such as use, objectification, and exploitation and applying them to sexual contexts. The essays by Alan

Wertheimer, Robin West, and David Benatar study the role and normative power of consent in sexual interactions, and Raja Halwani relies on virtue ethics in taking another look at sexual objectification. Moving beyond theory, the essays by both Benatar and Halwani are also concerned with applying ethical theory to particular sexual practices—pedophilia, rape, and casual sex—thereby providing a transition from part III to part IV.

The conceptual and theoretical discussions of sexual use, sexual objectification, and consent in part III supply the background for the applications in part IV. The topics covered in this section include prostitution, pornography, student-teacher sexual relationships, and date rape, all of which can be examined from a Kantian perspective in terms of use and objectification, but not only from that perspective, as the readings show. Prostitution is the subject of the essays by Martha Nussbaum (a liberal, at least in this essay) and Yolanda Estes (a Kantian, Fichtean, and phenomenologist), authors who arrive at different conclusions. Various features of pornography are discussed by Joan Mason-Grant (a feminist who hones the insights of Andrea Dworkin and Catharine MacKinnon), Sallie Tisdale (an observer of the pornographic genre), and Alan Soble (who is concerned with the presuppositions of research into the causal effects of pornography). Deirdre Golash investigates teacher-student sexual relationships and finds them lacking. Finally, Alan Soble and Eva Feder Kittay square off over Antioch University's "sexual offense policy," an attempt to reduce the incidence of acquaintance and date rape on its campus.

The editors thank Ross Miller and Ruth Gilbert of Rowman & Littlefield for their able and sustained counsel. Alan Soble thanks his parents for housing and feeding him for four months late in 2006, and Abington College for allowing him to teach in a gentle environment, 2006–2007, while this fifth edition was planned and prepared. Nick Power thanks his secretary Joulanda Garber for her superb assistance and the College of Arts and Sciences, University of West Florida, for financial support. Sarah Hoffman made excellent suggestions for study questions. We also thank authors and publishers who granted permission to reprint their material, and authors who generously wrote new essays for this edition of *Philosophy of Sex*.

PART 1
ANALYSIS AND PERVERSION

Chapter 1

THE ANALYTIC CATEGORIES OF THE PHILOSOPHY OF SEX

Alan Soble

*In this introductory essay, **Alan Soble** exhibits the range of topics that are studied—analytic, normative, and metaphysical—in the philosophy of sex. Analytic questions have to do with defining the central concepts in the field: sexual desire, sexual activity, and sexual pleasure. The goal of this analysis is to define each concept separately from each other (to avoid circularity) or, alternatively, to demonstrate that all the concepts can be defined in terms of just one of them, which would then be the basic concept in the philosophy of sex. Of particular interest is the analysis of the concept of sexual perversion and laying out the difference between the sexually natural and the unnatural. The analysis of sexual perversion requires that we be able to state what makes a desire, activity, or pleasure sexual to begin with, and then to identify the specific features of sexual desires, activities, or pleasures that make them perverted. Other concepts that are important to analyze in the philosophy of sex, such as consent and coercion, are important in other areas of philosophy as well, for example, social and political philosophy and the philosophy of law.*

The fact that the philosophy of sex often speaks about the natural and the unnatural and utilizes the concepts of consent and coercion means that normative issues also make up a large part of the philosophy of sex. Natural Law ethics asserts that there are significant connections between the naturalness of a desire or act and its morality; this is denied by philosophies that emphasize, for moral judgments, the presence of consent and the absence of coercion. When we throw in the ethics of Immanuel Kant, which focuses on the wrongs

3

*of using people and treating them as objects, sexual ethics becomes very com-
plicated territory. Sexual behaviors and practices that are scrutinized morally
include the use of contraception, masturbation, adultery, casual sex, rape,
harassment, prostitution, and pornography.*

This essay, a longer version of which appeared as "The Fundamentals of the Philosophy of Sex" in *The Philosophy of Sex*, 4th edition (xvii–xlii), is descended from several pieces: "Philosophy of Sexuality," in *Internet Encyclopedia of Philosophy*, ed.
James Fieser (www.utm.edu/research/iep); "Sexuality and Sexual Ethics," in *Encyclopedia of Ethics*, 1st edition, ed. Lawrence Becker and Charlotte Becker (Garland,
1992), 1141–47, and 2nd edition (Routledge, 2001), 1570–77; "La morale et la sex-
ualité," in *Dictionnaire d'éthique et de philosophie morale*, ed. Monique Canto-
Sperber (Presses Universitaires de France, 1996), 1387–91; and "Sexuality, Philosophy of," in *Routledge Encyclopedia of Philosophy*, ed. Edward Craig (London:
Routledge, 1998), 8: 717–30.

Among the topics explored by the philosophy of sex are procreation, contraception, celibacy, marriage, adultery, casual sex, flirting, prostitution, homosexuality, masturbation, seduction, rape, sexual harassment, sadomasochism, pornography, bestiality, and pedophilia.[1] What do all these things have in common? All are related to the vast domain of human sexuality, that is, they are related, on the one hand, to the human desires and activities that involve the search for and attainment of sexual pleasure or satisfaction and, on the other hand, to the human desires and activities that involve the creation of new human beings. It is a natural feature of human beings that certain sorts of behaviors and certain bodily organs are and can be employed either for pleasure or for reproduction, or for both.

The philosophy of sexuality explores these topics both conceptually and normatively. Conceptual analysis is carried out in the philosophy of sex in order to clarify fundamental notions, including *sexual desire* and *sexual activity*. Defining these concepts is no easy task. What are the distinctive features of an act that make it a sexual act instead of some other kind of act? Conceptual analysis is also carried out to arrive at satisfactory definitions of specific sexual practices, such as adultery, rape, and prostitution. In what ways does seduction differ from rape? Is it conceptually right to say that the women who model for pornography are prostitutes?

Normative philosophy of sexuality inquires about the value of sexual activity and sexual pleasure and of the various forms they take. It is concerned with the perennial questions of sexual morality and constitutes a large branch of applied ethics. Normative philosophy of sex studies what contribution is made to the good or virtuous life by sexuality, and tries to determine what moral duties we have to refrain from performing certain sexual acts and what moral permissions we have to engage in others. Moral issues surrounding homosexuality, abortion, date rape, harassment, pornography, and prostitution, among other things, have been widely discussed.

Sexual Metaphysics

Our moral evaluations of sexual activity are often affected by our views about the nature of the sexual impulse, or of sexual desire. In this regard there is a deep divide between those philosophers whom we might call the metaphysical sexual "optimists" and those we might call the metaphysical sexual "pessimists."

The pessimists in the philosophy of sexuality, such as St. Augustine, Immanuel Kant, and, sometimes, Sigmund Freud, perceive the sexual impulse and acting on it to be something nearly always, if not necessarily, unbefitting the dignity of the human person. They see the essence and the results of the sexual drive to be incompatible with more significant and lofty goals and aspirations of human existence. They fear that the power and demands of the sexual impulse make it a danger to harmonious civilized life. And they find in a person's sexuality a severe threat not only to his or her proper relations with, and moral treatment of, other persons, but also a threat to his or her own humanity.

On the other side are the metaphysical sexual optimists—Plato, in some of his works, sometimes Sigmund Freud, Bertrand Russell, and Albert Ellis—who perceive nothing especially obnoxious in the sexual impulse. They frequently view human sexuality as just another and mostly innocuous dimension of our existence as embodied or animal-like creatures (like the impulse to eat and find shelter). They judge that sexuality, which in unignorable measure has been given to us by evolution, cannot but be conducive to our well-being. And they applaud rather than fear the power of an impulse that can lift us to high forms of happiness.

The particular metaphysics of sex one holds will likely influence one's subsequent judgments about the value and role of sexuality in the good or virtuous life and about which sexual activities are morally wrong or morally permissible. An extended version of metaphysical pessimism might make the following claims.

(1) In virtue of the nature of sexual desire, a person who sexually desires another person objectifies that other person, both before and during sexual activity. Sex, says the German philosopher Immanuel Kant, "makes of the loved person an Object of appetite. . . . Taken by itself it is a degradation of human nature."[2] Our sexual desire for another person tends to make us view him or her merely as a thing, as a sexual object.

And when one person sexually desires another, the other person's body is primarily desired, distinct from the person.

(2) Further, certain types of mild deception seem required prior to engaging in sex with another person. We go out of our way to make ourselves look more physically attractive and socially desirable to the other person than we think we really are, and we go to great lengths to conceal our physical and personality defects. We are never our true selves on a first date, trying to make a good and hence misleading impression. While it might be the case that men sexually objectify women more than women objectify men, it is undeniable that both men and women engage in deception in trying to elicit a positive response from other people.

(3) The sexual act itself is peculiar, with its uncontrollable arousal, involuntary jerkings, and its yearning to master and consume the other person's body. This is part of what Augustine had in mind when he wrote, "lust . . . is the more shameful in this, that the soul does neither rule itself . . . nor the body either."[3] During the act, a person both loses control of himself or herself and loses regard for the humanity of the other person. Our sexuality is a threat to the other's personhood; but the one who is in the grip of desire is also on the verge of losing his or her personhood.

(4) Moreover, a person who gives in to another's sexual desire makes a tool of himself or herself. As Kant makes the point, "For the natural use that one sex makes of the other's sexual organs is *enjoyment*, for which one gives oneself up to the other. In this act a human being makes himself into a thing."[4] Those engaged in sexual activity make themselves into objects for each other merely for the sake of sexual pleasure. Both persons are reduced to the level of an animal.

(5) Finally, due to the insistent nature of the sexual impulse, once things get going it is often hard to stop them in their tracks, and as a result we often end up doing things sexually that we had never planned or wanted to do. Sexual desire is also powerfully inelastic, one of the passions most likely to challenge reason, compelling us to seek satisfaction even when doing so involves obvious physical and psychological dangers. The one who desires depends on the whims of another person to gain satisfaction, and thereby becomes susceptible to the demands of the other. People who are caught up in sexual desire can be easily exploited and manipulated.

Given this pessimistic metaphysics of human sexuality, one might conclude that acting on the sexual impulse is always morally wrong, or that for purely prudential reasons one would do best by being celibate. That might be precisely the right conclusion to draw, even if it implies the end of *Homo sapiens*. (This result is also implied by St. Paul's praising sexual celibacy as the ideal state; see 1 Cor. 7.) More often, however, the pessimistic metaphysicians of sexuality conclude that sexual activity is morally permissible and prudentially wise only within lifelong, monogamous, heterosexual marriage and should be engaged in only or primarily for the purpose of procreation. Regarding bodily acts that are both procreative and produce sexual pleasure, it is their procreative potential that is singularly significant and bestows value on these activities; seeking pleasure for its own sake, apart from procreation, is an impediment to morally virtuous sexuality, and should not be undertaken deliberately. Sexual pleasure at most has instrumental value, in inducing us to engage in an act that has procreation as its main purpose. Such views have been common among Christians, for example, Augustine: "A man turns to good use the evil of concupiscence, and is not overcome by it, when he bridles and restrains its rage . . . and never relaxes his hold upon it except when intent on offspring, and then controls and applies it to the carnal generation of children . . . , not to the subjection of the spirit to the flesh in a sordid servitude."[5]

Metaphysical sexual optimists suppose that sexuality is a natural bonding mechanism that joins people together both sexually and nonsexually. Sexual activity involves pleasing the self and the other at the same time, and these exchanges of pleasure generate both gratitude and affection, which in turn deepen human relationships and make them more satisfying and emotionally substantial. Further, and this may be the most important point, sexual pleasure is, for a metaphysical optimist, a valuable thing in its own right, something to be cherished and promoted because it has intrinsic and not merely instrumental value. Hence the pursuit of sexual pleasure does not require much intricate justification; sexual activity surely need not be confined to marriage or directed at procreation. The good and virtuous life, while including much else, can also include plentiful sexual relations.[6] Irving Singer is a contemporary philosopher of sexuality who expresses metaphysical optimism: "For though sexual interest resembles an appetite in some respects, it differs from hunger or thirst in being an *interpersonal* sensitivity, one that enables us to delight in the mind and character of other persons as well as in their flesh. Though at times people may be used as sexual objects and cast aside once their utility has been exhausted, this is [not] . . . definitive of sexual desire. . . . By awakening us to the living presence of someone else, sexuality can enable us to treat this other being as just the person he or she happens to be. . . . There is nothing in the nature of sexuality as such that necessarily . . . reduces persons to things. On the contrary, sex may be seen as an instinctual agency by which persons respond to one another *through* their bodies."[7]

Moral and Nonmoral Evaluations of Sexuality

We often evaluate sexual activity *morally*: we inquire whether a sexual act—either a particular occurrence of a sexual act (the act we are doing or want to do right now) or a general type of sexual act (say, all instances of homosexual fellatio)—is morally good or right or morally bad or wrong. More specifically, we evaluate or judge sexual acts to be morally obligatory, morally permissible, morally wrong, or even morally supererogatory. For example: a spouse might have a moral obligation to engage in sex with the other spouse; it might be morally permissible for married couples to employ contraception while engaging in coitus; rape, prostitution, and some forms of incest are commonly thought to be morally wrong (or immoral); and one person's agreeing to have sexual relations with another person when the former has no sexual desire of his or her own but only wants to please the other might be supererogatory. "Morally supererogatory" sexual activity is a category that is infrequently discussed by sexual ethicists. Raymond Belliotti has this to say about it: "We cannot fully describe this type of sex, but we can say generally that it goes above and beyond the call of moral duty. It is sex that is not merely morally permissible, but morally exemplary. It would involve some extraordinary moral benefits to others not attainable in merely morally permissible sex."[8]

Note that if a specific type of sexual act is immoral (say, homosexual fellatio), then every instance of that type of act will be morally wrong. However, from the fact that the particular sexual act we are now doing or contemplate doing is morally wrong, it does not follow that the specific type of act we are performing is morally wrong, in all cases; the sexual act that we are contemplating might be wrong for lots of reasons having nothing to do with the type of sexual act it is. For example, suppose we are engaging in heterosexual coitus, and that this particular sexual act is wrong because it is adulterous. The wrongfulness of our sexual activity does not imply that heterosexual coitus in general, as a type of sexual act, is morally wrong. In some cases, of course, a particular sexual act will be wrong for several reasons at once: not only is it wrong because it is of a specific type (say, it is an instance of homosexual fellatio), but it is also wrong because at least one of the participants is married to someone else (it is wrong also because it is adulterous).

In addition to evaluating sexual acts morally, we can also evaluate sexual activity (again, either a particular occurrence of a sexual act or a specific type of sexual activity) *nonmorally*. "Nonmorally good" sex is sexual activity that provides pleasure to the participants or is physically or emotionally satisfying, while "nonmorally bad" sex is unexciting, tedious, boring, unenjoyable, or even unpleasant. (Be careful: "nonmoral" is not the same as "immoral," and "nonmorally bad sexual activity" does not mean "immoral sexual activity.") An analogy will clarify the difference between morally evaluating something as good or bad and nonmorally evaluating it as good or bad. This radio on my desk is a good radio, in the nonmoral sense, because it does what I expect from a radio: it consistently provides clear tones. If, instead, the radio hissed and crackled most of the time, it would be a bad radio, nonmorally speaking, and it would be senseless for me to blame the radio for its faults and threaten it with a trip to hell if it did not improve its behavior. Similarly, sexual activity can be nonmorally good if it provides for us what we expect sexual activity to provide, which is usually sexual pleasure, and this fact has no necessary moral implications.

The fact that a sexual activity is nonmorally good, by abundantly satisfying both persons, does not necessarily mean that the act is morally good: some adulterous sexual activity might be pleasing to the participants yet be morally wrong. Further, the fact that a sexual activity is nonmorally bad, does not produce pleasure for the persons engaged in it, does not mean that the act is morally bad. Unpleasant sexual activity might occur between persons who have little experience engaging in sexual activity (they do not yet know how to do sexual things, or have not yet learned what their likes and dislikes are), but their failure to provide pleasure for each other does not mean that they are performing morally wrongful acts.

So the moral evaluation of sexual activity is distinct from the nonmoral evaluation of sexual activity, even if there are important connections between them. For example, the fact that a sexual act provides pleasure to both participants, and is thereby nonmorally good, might be taken (especially by a metaphysical sexual optimist) as a strong, but only prima facie good, reason for thinking that the act is morally good or has some moral value. (A Utilitarian moral philosopher, such as Jeremy Bentham and John Stuart Mill, would say that, in general, the nonmoral goodness of sexual activity goes a long way toward justifying it.) Another example: if one person never attempts to provide sexual pleasure for his or her partner, but selfishly insists on experiencing only his or her own pleasure, that person is behaving in a morally suspicious way. But that judgment might not rest simply on the fact that he or she did not provide pleasure for the other person, that is, on the fact that the sexual activity was for the other person nonmorally bad. The moral judgment might rest, more precisely, on his or her motives for not providing any pleasure, for not making the experience nonmorally good for the other person.

It is one thing to point out that as evaluative categories, moral goodness/badness is distinct from nonmoral goodness/badness. It is another thing to wonder, nonetheless, about the psychological connections between the moral quality of sexual activity and its nonmoral quality. Perhaps morally good or right sexual activity tends also to be the most satisfying sexual activity, in the nonmoral sense. Whether that is true likely depends on what we mean by morally "good" or "right" sexuality and on certain features of human moral psychology. What would our lives be like if there were always a neat correspondence between the moral quality of a sexual act and its nonmoral quality? Examples that violate such a neat correspondence are easy to come by. A sexual act might be morally good and nonmorally bad: consider the routine, bland sexual acts of a couple married for ten years ("bedroom death"). Further, a sexual act might be morally bad yet nonmorally good: one spouse in that couple, married for ten years, commits adultery with another married person and finds the sexual activity to be extraordinarily satisfying. A world in which there was little or no discrepancy between the moral quality and the nonmoral quality of sexual activity might be a better world than ours, or it might be a worse world. I would refrain from making such a judgment unless I were pretty sure what the moral goodness and badness of sexual activity amounted to in the first place, and until I knew a lot more about human psychology. Sometimes that a sexual activity is acknowledged to be morally wrong by its participants actually contributes to its being, for them, nonmorally good, that is, exciting. In this sense, the metaphysical sexual pessimists, by issuing moral prohibitions against sexual activity, might, ironically, be keeping our sexual lives happy or satisfying.

Dangerous Sex

Whether a particular sexual act, or type of sexual act, provides pleasure is not the only factor in judging its nonmoral quality: pragmatic considerations also figure into whether a sexual act, all things considered, has a preponderance of nonmoral goodness or badness. Many sexual activities can be physically or psychologically harmful, risky, or dangerous. Anal coitus, for example, whether carried out by a heterosexual couple or by two gay males, can damage tissues and is a mechanism for the potential transmission of pathogens (as can heterosexual genital intercourse). Thus in evaluating whether a sexual act will be overall nonmorally good or bad, not only its anticipated pleasure must be counted, but also all sorts of negative or undesired side effects: whether the sexual act is likely to damage the body, as in some sadomasochistic acts, or transmit a venereal disease, or result in an unwanted pregnancy, or even whether one might feel regret, anger, or guilt afterward. All these pragmatic and prudential factors can also figure into the moral evaluation of sexual activity: intentionally causing unwanted pain or discomfort to one's partner, or not taking adequate precautions against the possibility of pregnancy, or not informing one's partner of a suspected case of genital infection, might very well be morally wrong.[9] Depending on the particular sexual moral principles one holds, the myriad ingredients that constitute the nonmoral quality of sexual acts can influence one's moral judgments.

Sexual Perversion

In addition to inquiring about the moral and nonmoral quality of sexual acts, we can also ask whether the act or type is natural or unnatural ("perverted"). Natural sexual acts—to provide a broad definition—are acts that either flow naturally from human sexual nature or do not frustrate, counteract, or interfere with sexual tendencies that flow naturally from human sexual desire. An account of what is natural in human sexuality is part of a philosophical account of human nature in general (philosophical anthropology), which is a large undertaking.

Evaluating a particular sexual act or type of sexual activity as being natural or unnatural can be distinct from evaluating the act or type either as being morally good/bad or as being nonmorally good/bad. Suppose we assume, for the sake of discussion only, that heterosexual coitus is a natural human sexual activity and that homosexual fellatio is not natural. Even so, it does not follow from these judgments that all heterosexual coitus is morally good or right (some might be adulterous, or constitute rape); nor does it follow that all homosexual fellatio is morally bad or wrong (e.g., if engaged in by consenting adults, it might be morally permissible). Further, from the fact that heterosexual coitus is natural, it does not follow that acts of heterosexual coitus are nonmorally good, that is, pleasurable; nor does it follow from the fact that homosexual fellatio is unnatural that it cannot produce sexual pleasure for those who engage in it. Of course, both natural and unnatural sexual acts can be medically or psychologically risky or dangerous. There is no reason to assume that natural sexual acts are in general more safe than unnatural sexual acts; for example, unprotected (*sans* condom) heterosexual intercourse is more dangerous, in several ways, than mutual homosexual masturbation.

Since there are no necessary links between the naturalness/unnaturalness of sexual activity and moral and nonmoral quality, why would we wonder about the sexually unnatural? (Many philosophers suggest that we abandon the term "perversion" in talking about sexuality.)[10] One reason for continuing the discussion of the natural/unnatural is that understanding what is sexually natural and unnatural helps complete our picture of human nature in general, and allows us to understand our species more fully. With such deliberations, human self-reflection—which is the heart of philosophy—about humanity and the human condition becomes more complete. A second reason is that an account of the difference between the natural and the unnatural in human sexuality might be useful for the discipline of psychology, if we assume that a desire or tendency to engage in unnatural sexual activities is a sign or symptom of underlying mental pathology. (By the way, the American Psychiatric Association no longer considers homosexuality to be a "mental disorder.")[11] A third reason: even though natural sexual activity is not on that score alone morally good or right, and unnatural sexual activity is not necessarily morally bad or wrong, it is still possible to argue that whether a sexual act is natural or unnatural does influence, to a greater or lesser extent, whether the act is morally good or bad. Just as whether a sex act is nonmorally good, that is, produces pleasure for the participants, may be a factor, sometimes an important one, in our evaluating the act morally, whether a sexual act or type of sexual expression is natural or unnatural may also play a role, sometimes a large one, in deciding whether the act is morally good or bad. Roman Catholic sexual ethics certainly thinks so.

Natural Law

A comparison of the sexual philosophy of the medieval Catholic theologian St. Thomas Aquinas with that of the contemporary secular philosophy Thomas Nagel is, in this matter, instructive. Both Aquinas and Nagel make the innocuous assumptions that what is unnatural in human sexual behavior is perverted, and that what is unnatural in human sexuality is that which does not conform with or is inconsistent with natural human sexuality. But beyond these trivial areas of agreement, deep differences between Aquinas and Nagel exist.

Based on a comparison of the sexualities of humans and lower animals (birds, dogs, etc.), Aquinas concludes that what is natural in human sexuality is the impulse toward heterosexual coitus, which is the mechanism designed by God to insure the preservation of animal species, including the human species. Hence engaging in this activity is the primary natural expression of human sexual nature. Further, this God designed each of the parts of the human body to carry out specific functions and, on Aquinas's view, God designed the male's penis to implant sperm into the female's vagina to effect procreation. It follows, for Aquinas, that ejaculation elsewhere than inside a human female's vagina is unnatural: it violates God's sagacious design. For this reason alone, on Aquinas's view, such activities are immoral, a grave offense to the Almighty.

Sexual intercourse with lower animals (bestiality), sexual activity with members of one's own sex (homosexuality), and masturbation, for Aquinas, are unnatural sexual acts and immoral exactly because unnatural. If they are committed intentionally, they disrupt deliberately the natural order of the world as created by God and which He commanded to be respected.[12] In none of these activities is there any possibility of procreation, and the sexual and other organs are used, or misused, for purposes other than that for which they were designed. Although Aquinas does not say so explicitly, but only hints in this direction, it follows from his philosophy of sexuality that fellatio, even when engaged in by heterosexuals, is also perverted and morally wrong. At least in those cases in which orgasm occurs by means of this act, the sperm is not being placed where it should be placed and procreation is therefore not possible.[13] If the penis entering the vagina is the paradigmatic natural act, then any other combination of anatomical connections will be unnatural and hence immoral—for example, the penis, mouth, or fingers entering the anus. Aquinas's criterion of a sexually natural act, that it must be procreative in form or potential, and hence must involve a penis inserted into a vagina, makes no mention of human psychology. Aquinas's line of thought yields an anatomical or physiological criterion of natural and perverted sexuality that refers only to bodily organs, to where they are, or are not, put in relation to each other, and what they might accomplish as a result.

Thomas Nagel denies Aquinas's presupposition that in order to discover what is natural in human sexuality we should emphasize what is *common* sexually between humans and lower animals.[14] Applying this formula, Aquinas concludes that the purpose of sexual activity and the sexual organs in humans is procreation. Everything else in Aquinas's sexual philosophy follows more or less logically from this. Nagel, by contrast, argues that to discover what is distinctive about natural human sexuality, and hence what is unnatural or perverted, we should focus, instead, on what humans and lower animals do *not* have in common. We should emphasize the ways in which humans are different from animals, the ways in which humans and their sexuality are special. Thus Nagel argues that sexual perversion in humans should be understood as a psychological phenomenon rather than, as in Aquinas, an anatomical/physiological phenomenon. For it is human psychology that makes us different from other animals, and hence an account of natural human sexuality must acknowledge the role of human psychology in sexuality.

Nagel proposes that sexual interactions in which each person responds with sexual arousal to noticing the sexual arousal of the other person exhibit the psychology that is natural to human sexuality. In such an encounter, each person becomes aware of himself or herself and the other person as both the subject and the object of their joint sexual experiences. I am sexually aroused not only by your physical attractiveness or your touch, but also by the fact that you are aroused by me and my touches; we become sexually aroused by recognizing that we are aroused. Nothing as complex as this occurs among the lower animals. Perverted sexual encounters are, on Nagel's view, those in which this mutual recognition of arousal is absent, and hence in which a person remains fully a subject or fully an object of the sexual interaction. Sexual perversion, then, is a departure from or a truncation of a psychologically "complete" pattern of arousal.[15] Nothing in Nagel's psychological account of the natural and perverted refers to bodily organs or physiological processes. So, for a sexual encounter to be natural, it need not be procreative in form, as long as the requisite psychology of mutual recognition is present. Whether a sexual activity is natural or perverted does not depend, on Nagel's view, on what organs are used or where they are put, but only on the character of its psychology. Thus Nagel disagrees with Aquinas that homosexuality is unnatural, for homosexual fellatio and anal intercourse can be accompanied by the mutual recognition of and response to the other person's sexual arousal.

Note that Aquinas and Nagel agree about other things; for example, that fetishism is unnatural. But they disagree about the grounds of that evaluation. For Aquinas, masturbating while fondling shoes or undergarments is unnatural because the sperm is not deposited where it should be; the act has no procreative potential. For Nagel, masturbatory fetishism is perverted for a different reason: there is no possibility of one persons' noticing and being aroused by the arousal of another person. In this example, there is one more difference between Aquinas and Nagel: Aquinas would judge the sexual activity of the fetishist to be immoral precisely because it is unnatural, while Nagel would not conclude that it is morally wrong even though it is unnatural—after all, a fetishistic sexual act can be done harmlessly and be pleasurable. The move historically and socially away from a Thomistic moralistic account of sexual perversion toward a morality-free psychological account such as Nagel's represents a more widespread trend: the gradual replacement of moral or religious judgments, about all sorts of deviant behavior, by medical, psychiatric, or psychological judgments and interventions.[16] And, as we have seen, even psychiatry has lately been narrowing the scope of "perverted."

A different kind of disagreement with Aquinas is registered by Christine Gudorf, a Christian theologian who otherwise has much in common with Aquinas. Gudorf agrees that the study of human anatomy and physiology yields insights into God's plan and design, and that human sexual behavior should conform with God's creative intentions. Gudorf's philosophy is, therefore, squarely within the Thomistic Natural Law tradition. But Gudorf argues that if we take a more careful look at the anatomy and physiology of the female sexual organs, and especially the clitoris, instead of focusing exclusively on the sexual role of the male's penis (which is what Aquinas did), we can arrive at very different conclusions about God's plan and design and, as a result, Christian sexual ethics turns out to be less restrictive. In particular, Gudorf claims that the female's clitoris is an organ whose only purpose is the production of sexual pleasure and, unlike the mixed or dual function of the penis, has no connection with procreation. Gudorf concludes that the existence of the clitoris in the female body suggests that God intended that the purpose of sexual activity was as much for sexual pleasure *for its own sake* as it was for procreation. Hence, according to Gudorf, pleasurable sexual activity apart from procreation does not violate God's design, is not unnatural, and so is not necessarily morally wrong, as long as it occurs in the context of a monogamous marriage (including, even, a homosexual monogamous marriage).[17] Gudorf, it seems, is advancing a Christian semi-optimistic sexual metaphysics. Today we are not as confident as Aquinas was that God's plan and design can be discovered by a straightforward examination of human and animal bodies; but this healthy skepticism about our ability to discern God's intentions from facts of the natural world applies to Gudorf's proposal as well. That the clitoris, through its ability to provide pleasure, plays a crucial role in leading to procreative heterosexual sexual activity, is not obviously false.

Debates in Sexual Ethics

The ethics of sexual behavior, as a branch of applied ethics, is no more and no less contentious than the ethics of anything else within the area of applied ethics. Think of the notorious debates over euthanasia, welfare entitlements, capital punishment, abortion, environmental pollution, and our treatment of animals for food, clothing, entertainment, and scientific research. It should come as no surprise than even though a discussion of sexual ethics might remove some confusions and clarify the issues, few final or absolute answers to questions about the morality of sexual activity are likely to be forthcoming from the philosophy of sex. Of course, all parties, except maybe the Marquis de Sade, agree that rape is seriously morally wrong. Yet debates remain here: what exactly is a case of rape? How can its occurrence be reliably identified? And *why* is it wrong? Most ethical systems conclude that adultery is morally wrong or at least morally suspect. But, again, what counts as adultery? Is it merely having lustful thoughts, as claimed by Jesus in Matthew 5:28?

There are several major topics that have received much attention by philosophers of sex and provide arenas for continual debate. We have already encountered one of them: the dispute between a Natural Law approach to sexual morality and a liberal-secular outlook that denies a tight connection between what is unnatural and what is immoral. Secular liberal philosophers emphasize the values of autonomous choice, self-determination, and pleasure in arriving at moral judgments about sexual behavior, in contrast to the Thomistic tradition that justifies a more restrictive sexual ethics by invoking a divinely imposed scheme to which human action must conform. For a secular-liberal philosopher of sexuality, rape is the paradigmatically morally wrong sexual act, in which one person forces himself or herself on another or uses threats to coerce another to engage in sexual activity. By contrast, for the liberal, anything done voluntarily or consensually between two or more people is generally morally permissible. Thus a sexual act is morally wrong only if it is coercive, dishonest, or manipulative. Natural Law theory would agree, except to add, importantly, that a sexual act's being unnatural is another, independent reason for condemning it morally. Kant, for example, held that masturbation "is abuse of the sexual faculty. . . . By it man sets aside his person and degrades himself below the level of animals. . . . Intercourse between *sexus homogenii* . . . too is contrary to the ends of humanity."[18] The sexual liberal, however, usually finds nothing morally wrong or nonmorally bad about either masturbation or homosexual activity. These activities might be unnatural, and perhaps in some ways prudentially unwise, but in many if not most cases they can be carried out without harm being done either to anyone else or to the participants. Natural Law is alive and well today among some philosophers of sex, even if the details do not precisely match Aquinas's original version.[19]

Consent

When no harm is done to third parties (nonparticipants), is the fact that two people engage in sexual activity voluntarily, with their own free and informed consent, necessary and sufficient for making their interaction morally permissible? The Natural Law tradition denies that consent is sufficient, since on that view willingly engaging in unnatural sexual acts is morally wrong, but it is not alone in reducing the moral significance of consent. Sexual activity between two persons might be harmful to one or both participants, and a moral paternalist or perfectionist would claim that it is wrong for one person to harm another, or for the latter to allow the former to engage in harmful behavior, even when both persons provide free and informed consent to their joint activity. Consent in this case is not sufficient, and some forms of sadomasochism are morally wrong. That consent is not sufficient is also frequently asserted by philosophers who claim that only in a committed relationship is sexual activity between two people morally permissible. The free and informed consent of both parties may be a necessary condition for the moral goodness of their sexual activity, but in the absence of some other magical ingredient (love, marriage, devotion, and the like) their sexual activity remains mere mutual use or objectification and hence morally objectionable.

About casual sex, for example, it might be said that two people are merely using each other for their own separate sexual pleasure; even when genuinely consensual, these mutual sexual uses do not yield a virtuous sexual act. Kant and Karol Wojtyla (Pope John Paul II) take this position: willingly allowing oneself to be used sexually by another person makes an object of oneself. Hence mutual consent is not sufficient for the moral rightness of sexual acts. For Kant, sexual activity avoids treating a person merely as a means only in marriage, since in such a state both persons have surrendered their bodies and souls to each other.[20] For Wojtyla, "only love can preclude the use of one person by another," since love is a unification of persons resulting from a mutual gift of their selves.[21] Note, however, that the thought that a unifying love is the ingredient that justifies sexual activity (beyond consent) has an interesting implication: gay and lesbian sexual relations would seem to be permissible if they occur within homosexual marriages that are loving, committed, and monogamous. At this point, defenders of the view that sexual activity is justifiable only in marriage commonly appeal to Natural Law to rule out homosexual marriage.

On another view of these matters, the fact that sexual activity is carried out voluntarily by all persons involved means (assuming no harm to third parties), that the sexual activity is morally permissible. In defending the sufficiency of consent for the moral goodness of sexual activity, Thomas Mappes writes that "respect for persons entails that each of us recognize the rightful authority of other persons (as rational beings) to conduct their individual lives as they see fit."[22] Allowing the other person's consent to control when the other engages in sexual activity with me is to respect that person by taking seriously his or her autonomy, his or her ability to reason and make choices, while not to allow the other to make the decision about when to engage in sexual activity with me is disrespectful. According to such a view of the power of consent, there can be no moral objection in principle to casual sexual activity, to sexual activity with strangers, or to promiscuity, as long as the persons involved genuinely agree to engage in their chosen sexual acts.

Even if Mappes's free and informed consent criterion is correct, several difficult questions still remain. How *specific* must consent be? When one person agrees vaguely, and in the heat of the sexual moment, with another person, "yes, let's have sex," has the speaker consented to every type of sexual caress or coital position the other person has in mind? How *explicit* must consent be? Can consent be reliably implied by involuntary behavior (moans, for example), and do nonverbal cues (erection, lubrication) decisively show that another person has consented to sex? Some insist that consent must be exceedingly specific as to the sexual acts to be carried out, and some would permit only explicit verbal consent, denying that body language can do an adequate job of expressing desires and intentions.[23]

Another debate concerns the meaning of "free" (or "voluntary") in the expression "free and informed consent." Whether consent is only necessary for the moral goodness of sexual activity, or also sufficient, any principle that relies on consent to make moral judgments assumes a clear understanding of the "voluntary" nature of consent. Participation in sexual activity ought not to be physically forced on one person by another. But this obvious truth leaves matters wide open. The philosopher Onora O'Neill, for example, believes that much or most casual sex is morally wrong because the consent it involves is not likely to be sufficiently voluntary, in light of subtle pressures people commonly put on each other to engage in sexual activity. On her view, people who engage in casual sex are merely using each other, not treating each other with respect as persons in a Kantian sense.[24]

One moral ideal is that genuinely voluntary participation in sexual activity requires not a hint of coercion or pressure of any sort.[25] Because engaging in sexual activity can be risky or dangerous in many ways (physically, psychologically, metaphysically), we would like to be sure, according to this moral ideal, that anyone who engages in sexual activity does so with perfectly voluntarily consent. Some philosophers have argued that this ideal can be realized only when there is substantial economic and social equality between the persons involved in a given sexual encounter. For example, a society that exhibits disparities in income or wealth is one in which some people will be exposed to economic coercion. If some groups of people (women and members of ethnic minorities, in particular) have less economic and social power than others, members of these groups will be exposed to sexual coercion, among other kinds. One immediate application of this thought is that prostitution, which to many sexual liberals is a business bargain made by a provider of sexual services and a client and is largely characterized by adequately free and informed consent, may be morally wrong, if the economic situation of the prostitute acts as a kind of pressure that negates the voluntary nature of his or her participation. Further, women with children who are economically dependent on their husbands may find themselves in the position of having to engage in sexual activity whether they want to or not, for fear of being abandoned; these women, too, may not be engaging in sexual activity fully voluntarily. The woman who allows herself to be nagged into sex by her husband worries that if she says "no" too often, she will suffer economically, if not also physically and psychologically.

The view that the presence of any kind of pressure is coercive negates the voluntary nature of participation in sexual activity, and hence is morally objectionable has been expressed by, among others, Charlene Muehlenhard and Jennifer Schrag.[26] They list—to provide just two of their examples—"status coercion" (women are coerced into sexual activity or marriage by a man's occupation) and "discrimination against lesbians" (which compels women into having sexual relationships only with men) as forms of coercion that undermine the voluntary nature of participation by women in sexual activity with men. But depending on the kind of case we have in mind, it might be more accurate to say either that some pressures are not coercive and do not appreciably undermine voluntariness, or that some pressures are coercive but are nevertheless not morally objectionable. Is it true that the presence of any kind of pressure put on one person by another amounts to coercion that negates the voluntary nature of consent, so that subsequent sexual activity is morally wrong? I wonder whether a woman who says to her husband, "buy me that mink coat or you will sleep on the couch for a month," is engaging in any objectionable behavior.

Study Questions

1. How can one go about deciding whether sexual desires and sexual acts are natural or unnatural? Do you think that if a sexual desire or a sexual act is unnatural—goes against human sexual nature—that fact is (always, often, not often, never) an important consideration in judging the desire or the act morally? Why or why not?

2. How can one go about deciding whether sexual acts have been performed with consent or have been coerced? Does the presence of coercion always mean that the act was not performed with consent; does the absence of coercion always mean that the act was done consensually? Do we not often *legitimately* coerce or put pressure on people to do things they prefer not to do?

3. To what extent and in what ways do the nonmoral, pragmatic, and legal evaluations of sexual acts make a difference in evaluating sexual acts morally? If they do, and do so frequently, what might this mean about the difficulty of making judgments in sexual ethics? Should we conclude that to be morally safe, we should never engage in sex unless every single moral consideration points in its favor?

4. Does the marital status, age, sex or gender, species, or race or ethnicity of one's sexual partner make a difference to the morality of sexual acts carried out with that partner? Why or why not? What other features of potential partners might be added to this list? Their physical attractiveness? Income? Aspects of their biography?

5. In a legal case decided by the U.S. Supreme Court (*Rose v. Locke*, 423 U.S. 48 [1975]), the defendant was accused of forcing a woman, at knife point, "to submit to his twice performing

cunnilingus upon her." What are the analytic criteria for indi-
viduating and counting sexual acts, such that it is possible and
makes sense to say that X performed cunnilingus once, twice,
or N times? In this case, the defendant was not charged with
rape but only of violating a Tennessee "crimes against nature"
statute (by now, abandoned). Did he commit an unnatural act?
Should unnatural acts be illegal? Can you surmise why he was
not charged with rape?

Notes

1. See Alan Soble, ed., *Sex from Plato to Paglia: A Philosophical Encyclopedia*
(Westport, Conn.: Greenwood Press, 2006). Nearly all the writers, philosophies,
and sexual topics mentioned in this essay are covered in that two-volume work.

2. Immanuel Kant, *Lectures on Ethics*, trans. Louis Infield (New York: Harper
and Row, 1963), 163.

3. Augustine, *The City of God*, trans. John Healey (London: J. M. Dent, 1945),
vol. 2, bk. 14, sect. 23.

4. Immanuel Kant, *The Metaphysics of Morals*, trans. Mary Gregor (Cambridge: Cambridge University Press, 1996), 62.

5. Augustine, *On Marriage and Concupiscence*, in *The Works of Aurelius Augustine, Bishop of Hippo*, ed. Marcus Dods (Edinburgh: T. & T. Clark, 1874), vol. 12,
bk. 1, chap. 9.

6. See Russell Vannoy's spirited defense of the value of sexual activity for its
own sake, in *Sex Without Love: A Philosophical Exploration* (Buffalo, N.Y.:
Prometheus, 1980).

7. Irving Singer, *The Nature of Love, vol. 2: Courtly and Romantic* (Chicago:
University of Chicago Press, 1984), 382.

8. Raymond Belliotti, *Good Sex: Perspectives on Sexual Ethics* (Lawrence, Kan.:
University Press of Kansas, 1993), 210. For a review of *Good Sex*, see my "Book
Note," *Ethics* 105:2 (1995): 447–48.

9. The philosopher David Mayo is possibly unique in arguing that we do not
necessarily have a moral obligation to reveal our HIV status to potential sexual
partners. See his provocative essay "An Obligation to Warn of HIV Infection?" in
A. Soble, ed., *Sex, Love and Friendship* (Amsterdam: Rodopi, 1997), 447–53.

10. Michael Slote argues that "sexual perversion" is an "inapplicable concept"
("Inapplicable Concepts and Sexual Perversion," in *Philosophy and Sex*, 1st edition, Robert Baker and Frederick Elliston, eds. [Buffalo, N.Y.: Prometheus,
1975], 261–67, at 266); Graham Priest also calls it "inapplicable" and adds that
"the notion of sexual perversion makes no sense" any longer ("Sexual Perversion," *Australasian Journal of Philosophy* 75:3 [1997]: 360–72, at 370–71); Igor Primoratz thinks that "sexual perversion" is "a concept best discarded" (*Ethics and
Sex* [London: Routledge, 1999], 63–66); Linda LeMoncheck wants to replace
"sexual perversion" with "sexual difference" (*Loose Women, Lecherous Men: A Feminist Philosophy of Sex* [New York: Oxford University Press, 1997], 72, 80, 82–83);
and Robert Gray submits that "sexual perversion" should "be dropped from our

sexual vocabulary altogether" ("Sex and Sexual Perversion," *Journal of Philosophy* 75:4 [1978]: 189–99, at 199).

11. See *Diagnostic and Statistical Manual of Mental Disorders*, 4th edition (Washington, D.C.: American Psychiatric Association, 1994), 493–538. For discussion of the *DSM* on sexual disorders, see my "Paraphilia and Distress in *DSM-IV*," in Jennifer Radden, ed., *The Philosophy of Psychiatry: A Companion* (New York: Oxford University Press), 54–63.

12. See Thomas Aquinas, *Summa Theologiae* [1265–1273] (Cambridge: Blackfriars, 1964-1976), 43:2a2ae, questions 153–154.

13. Aquinas condemns sexual acts in which "the natural style of intercourse is not observed, as regards the proper organ or according to rather beastly and monstrous techniques" (question 154, article 11). He might have meant this claim to apply to oral and anal sex.

14. On the advantages and pitfalls of employing an animal model to understand human sexuality, see Jeffrey Hershfield, "Animal Sexuality," in Soble, *Sex from Plato to Paglia*, 45–50.

15. See Thomas Nagel's "Sexual Perversion," in this volume, chap. 3.

16. See my *Sexual Investigations* (New York: New York University Press, 1996), chap. 4; and Peter Conrad and Joseph W. Schneider, *Deviance and Medicalization: From Badness to Sickness* (St. Louis, Mo.: C. V. Mosby, 1980), especially "Homosexuality: From Sin to Sickness to Life-Style," 172–214.

17. Christine Gudorf, *Sex, Body, and Pleasure: Reconstructing Christian Sexual Ethics* (Cleveland, Ohio: Pilgrim Press, 1994), 65. For another Christian defense of homosexual marriage, see Patricia Jung and Ralph Smith, *Heterosexism: An Ethical Challenge* (Albany, N.Y.: State University of New York Press, 1993).

18. Kant, *Lectures on Ethics*, 170.

19. See, for example, John Finnis, "Law, Morality, and 'Sexual Orientation,'" *Notre Dame Law Review* 69:5 (1994): 1049–76.

20. For the details, see my "Sexual Use," chapter 18 in this volume.

21. Karol Wojtyla, *Love and Responsibility* (New York: Farrar, Straus and Giroux, 1981), 30.

22. Thomas Mappes, "Sexual Morality and the Concept of Using Another Person," in this volume, chap. 16. Also defending the sufficiency of consent is Bernard Baumrin's "Sexual Immorality Delineated," in *Philosophy and Sex*, 2nd edition, Robert Baker and Frederick Elliston, eds. (Buffalo, N.Y.: Prometheus, 1984), 300–11; and Igor Primoratz, "Sexual Morality: Is Consent Enough?" *Ethical Theory and Moral Practice* 4:3 (2001): 201–18.

23. See my "Antioch's 'Sexual Offense Policy': A Philosophical Exploration" and the reply by Eva Feder Kittay, "Ah! My Foolish Heart" (in this volume, chapters 29 and 30).

24. Onora O'Neill, "Between Consenting Adults," in her *Constructions of Reason: Explorations of Kant's Practical Philosophy* (Cambridge: Cambridge University Press, 1989), 105–25.

25. See my "Ethics, Sexual," in *Sex From Plato to Paglia*, 273–79.

26. Charlene Muehlenhard and Jennifer Schrag, "Nonviolent Sexual Coercion," in *Acquaintance Rape: The Hidden Crime*, Andrea Parrot and Laurie Bechhofer, eds. (New York: John Wiley, 1991), 115–28.

Chapter 2

ARE WE HAVING SEX NOW OR WHAT?

Greta Christina

*Though sex, and the philosophy of sex, is often a serious if not solemn affair, it pays to approach them with a sense of humor, as **Greta Christina** demonstrates. The philosophical topic at hand—what are the necessary and sufficient conditions for an act or encounter to be* sexual—*occupies much of part I (see also the essays by Alan Goldman and Alan Soble, in particular), and views about how to define "sex" properly are implicated in many other issues, for example, rape and sexual harassment. While laying out commonsensical definitions of sexual activity (say, that it must include penis-in-vagina coitus; that it requires that the participants be naked; that it involves sexual pleasure for all concerned), Christina reveals counterexamples, often from her own experience. This reflective exercise might lead us to be, as Christina is, skeptical about ever finding a final definition of sexual activity. But her essay has the virtue of forcing us to ask the analytic question and to realize that everyday understandings of "sex" are not very satisfying.*

Christina's essay was reprinted by the magazine Ms. *in its 1995 "Feminism and Sex" issue (November/December, 60–62). The essay's last two paragraphs are missing from that reprint, and there is no editorial warning that the essay had been abridged. Those paragraphs are perhaps the most provocative in Christina's essay: she admits to finding some sadomasochism "tremendously erotic," and she relates that when working as a nude dancer inside a peep show booth she had a "fabulous time" with one of her quarter-laden customers. These examples are valuable to think about, both conceptually and normatively.*

Christina is the author of *Bending,* an erotic novella edited by Susie Bright and published as part of a three-novella collection, *Three Kinds of Asking for It* (Simon & Schuster, 2005), and has edited *Paying for It: A Guide by Sex Workers for Their Clients* (Greenery Press, 2004). The editor of "Best Erotic Comics," an annual anthology series published by Last Gasp, she blogs at gretachristina.typepad.com and her web site is gretachristina.com.

When I first started having sex with other people, I used to like to count them. I wanted to keep track of how many there had been. It was a source of some kind of pride, or identity anyway, to know how many people I'd had sex with in my lifetime. So, in my mind, Len was number one, Chris was number two, that slimy awful little heavy metal barbiturate addict whose name I can't remember was number three, Alan was number four, and so on. It got to the point where, when I'd start having sex with a new person for the first time, when he first entered my body (I was only having sex with men at the time), what would flash through my head wouldn't be "Oh, baby, baby you feel so good inside me," or "What the hell am I doing with this creep," or "This is boring, I wonder what's on TV." What flashed through my head was "Seven!"

Doing this had some interesting results. I'd look for patterns in the numbers. I had a theory for a while that every fourth lover turned out to be really great in bed, and would ponder what the cosmic significance of the phenomenon might be. Sometimes I'd try to determine what kind of person I was by how many people I'd had sex with. At eighteen, I'd had sex with ten different people. Did that make me normal, repressed, a total slut, a free-spirited bohemian, or what? Not that I compared my numbers with anyone else's—I didn't. It was my own exclusive structure, a game I played in the privacy of my own head.

Then the numbers started getting a little larger, as numbers tend to do, and keeping track became more difficult. I'd remember that the last one was *seventeen* and so this one must be *eighteen,* and then I'd start having doubts about whether I'd been keeping score accurately or not. I'd lie awake at night thinking to myself, well, there was Brad, and there was that guy on my birthday, and there was David and . . . no, wait, I forgot that guy I got drunk with at the social my first week at college . . . so that's seven, eight, nine . . . and by two in the morning I'd finally have it figured out. But there was always a nagging suspicion that maybe I'd missed someone, some dreadful tacky little scumball that I was trying to forget about having invited inside my body. And as much as I maybe wanted to forget about the sleazy little scumball, I wanted more to get that number right.

It kept getting harder, though. I began to question what counted as sex and what didn't. There was that time with Gene, for instance. I was pissed off at my boyfriend, David, for cheating on me. It was a major crisis, and Gene and I were friends and he'd been trying to get at me for weeks and I hadn't exactly been discouraging him. I went to see him that night to gripe about David. He was very sympathetic of course, and he gave me a backrub, and we talked and touched and confided and hugged, and then we started kissing, and then we snuggled up a little closer, and then we started fondling each other, you know, and then all heck broke loose, and we rolled around on the bed groping and rubbing and grabbing and smooching and pushing and pressing and squeezing. He never did actually get it in. He wanted to, and I wanted to too, but I had this thing about being faithful to my boyfriend, so I kept saying, "No, you can't do that, Yes, that feels so good, No, wait that's too much, Yes, yes, don't stop, No, stop that's enough." We never even got our clothes off. Jesus Christ, though, it was some night. One of the best, really. But for a long time I didn't count it as one of the times I'd had sex. He never got inside, so it didn't count.

Later, months and years later, when I lay awake putting my list together, I'd start to wonder: Why doesn't Gene count? Does he not count because he never got inside? Or does he not count because I had to preserve my moral edge over David, my status as the patient, ever-faithful, cheated-on, martyred girlfriend, and if what I did with Gene counts then I don't get to feel wounded and superior?

Years later, I did end up fucking Gene and I felt a profound relief because, at last, he definitely had a number, and I knew for sure that he did in fact count.

Then I started having sex with women, and, boy, howdy, did *that* ever shoot holes in the system. I'd always made my list of sex partners by defining sex as penile-vaginal intercourse—you know, screwing. It's a pretty simple distinction, a straightforward binary system. Did it go in or didn't it? Yes or no? One or zero? On or off? Granted, it's a pretty arbitrary definition, but it's the customary one, with an ancient and respected tradition behind it, and when I was just screwing men, there was no compelling reason to question it.

But with women, well, first of all there's no penis, so right from the start the tracking system is defective. And then, there are so many ways women can have sex with each other, touching and licking and grinding and fingering and fisting—with dildoes or vibrators or vegetables or whatever happens to be lying around the house, or with nothing at all except human bodies. Of course, that's true for sex between women and men as well. But between women, no one method has a centuries-old tradition of being the one that counts. Even when we do fuck each other there's no dick, so you don't get that feeling of This Is What's Important, We Are Now Having Sex, objectively speaking, and all that other stuff is just foreplay or afterplay. So when I started having sex with women the binary system had to go, in favor of a more inclusive definition.

Which meant, of course, that my list of how many people I'd had sex with was completely trashed. In order to maintain it I would have had to go back and reconstruct the whole thing and include all those people I'd necked with and gone down on and dry-humped and played touchy-feely games with. Even the question of who filled the all-important Number One slot, something I'd never had any doubts about before, would have to be re-evaluated.

By this time I'd kind of lost interest in the list anyway. Reconstructing it would be more trouble than it was worth. But the crucial question remained: What counts as having sex with someone?

It was important for me to know. You have to know what qualifies as sex because when you have sex with someone your relationship changes. Right? *Right*? It's not that sex itself has to change things all that much. But knowing you've had sex, being conscious of a sexual connection, standing around making polite conversation with someone while thinking to yourself, "I've had sex with this person," that's what changes things. Or so I believed. And if having sex with a friend can confuse or change the friendship, think how bizarre things can get when you're not sure whether you've had sex with them or not.

The problem was, as I kept doing more kinds of sexual things, the line between *sex* and *not-sex* kept getting more hazy and indistinct. As I brought more into my sexual experience, things were showing up on the dividing line demanding my attention. It wasn't just that the territory I labeled sex was expanding. The line itself had swollen, dilated, been transformed into a vast gray region. It had become less like a border and more like a demilitarized zone.

Which is a strange place to live. Not a bad place, just strange. It's like juggling, or watchmaking, or playing the piano—anything that demands complete concentrated awareness and attention. It feels like cognitive dissonance, only pleasant. It feels like waking up from a compelling and realistic bad dream. It feels like the way you feel when you realize that everything you know is wrong, and a bloody good thing too, because it was painful and stupid and it really screwed you up.

But, for me, living in a question naturally leads to searching for an answer. I can't simply shrug, throw up my hands, and say, "Damned if I know." I have to explore the unknown frontiers, even if I don't bring back any secret treasure. So even if it's incomplete or provisional, I do want to find some sort of definition of what is and isn't sex.

I know when I'm *feeling* sexual. I'm feeling sexual if my pussy's wet, my nipples are hard, my palms are clammy, my brain is fogged, my skin is tingly and super-sensitive, my butt muscles clench, my heartbeat speeds up, I have an orgasm (that's the real giveaway), and so on. But feeling sexual with someone isn't the same as having sex with them. Good Lord, if I called it sex every time I was attracted to someone who returned the favor I'd be even more bewildered than I am now. Even *being* sexual with someone isn't the same as *having* sex with them. I've danced and flirted with too many people, given and received too many sexy, would-be-seductive backrubs, to believe otherwise.

I have friends who say, if you thought of it as sex when you were doing it, then it was. That's an interesting idea. It's certainly helped me construct a coherent sexual history without being a revisionist swine: redefining my past according to current definitions. But it really just begs the question. It's fine to say that sex is whatever I think it is; but then what do I think it *is*? What if, when I was doing it, I was *wondering* whether it counted?

Perhaps having sex with someone is the conscious, consenting, mutually acknowledged pursuit of shared sexual pleasure. Not a bad definition. If you are turning each other on and you say so and you keep doing it, then it's sex. It's broad enough to encompass a lot of sexual behavior beyond genital contact/orgasm; it's distinct enough *not* to include every instance of sexual awareness or arousal; and it contains the elements I feel are vital—acknowledgment, consent, reciprocity, and the pursuit of pleasure. But what about the situation where one person consents to sex without really enjoying it? Lots of people (myself included) have had sexual interactions that we didn't find satisfying or didn't really want and, unless they were actually forced on us against our will, I think most of us would still classify them as sex.

Maybe if *both* of you (or all of you) think of it as sex, then it's sex whether you're having fun or not. That clears up the problem of sex that's consented to but not wished-for or enjoyed. Unfortunately, it begs the question again, only worse: now you have to mesh different people's vague and inarticulate notions of what is and isn't sex and find the place where they overlap. Too messy.

How about sex as the conscious, consenting, mutually acknowledged pursuit of sexual pleasure of *at least one* of the people involved. That's better. It has all the key components, and it includes the situation where one person is doing it for a reason other than sexual pleasure—status, reassurance, money, the satisfaction and pleasure of someone they love, etc. But what if *neither* of you is enjoying it, if you're both doing it because you think the other one wants to? Ugh.

I'm having trouble here. Even the conventional standby—sex equals intercourse—has a serious flaw: it includes rape, which is something I emphatically refuse to accept. As far as I'm concerned, if there's no consent, it ain't sex. But I feel that's about the only place in this whole quagmire where I have a grip. The longer I think about the subject, the more questions I come up with. At what point in an encounter does it *become* sexual? If an interaction that begins nonsexually turns into sex, was it sex all along? What about sex with someone who's asleep? Can you have a situation where one person is having sex and the other isn't? It seems that no matter what definition I come up with, I can think of some real-life experience that calls it into question.

For instance, a couple of years ago I attended (well, hosted) an all-girl sex party. Out of the twelve other women there, there were only a few with whom I got seriously physically nasty. The rest I kissed or hugged or talked dirty with or just smiled at, or watched while they did seriously physically nasty things with each other. If we'd been alone, I'd probably say that what I'd done with most of the women there didn't count as having sex. But the experience, which was hot and sweet and silly and very, very special, had been created by all of us, and although I only really got down with a few, I felt that I'd been sexual with all of the women there. Now, when I meet one of the women from that party, I always ask myself: Have we had sex?

For instance, when I was first experimenting with sadomasochism, I got together with a really hot woman. We were negotiating about what we were going to do, what would and wouldn't be ok, and she said she wasn't sure she wanted to have sex. Now we'd been explicitly planning all kinds of fun and games—spanking, bondage, obedience—which I strongly identified as sexual activity. In her mind, though, *sex* meant direct genital contact, and she didn't necessarily want to do that with me. Playing with her turned out to be a tremendously erotic experience, arousing and stimulating and almost unbearably satisfying. But we spent the whole evening without even touching each other's genitals. And the fact that our definitions were so different made me wonder: Was it sex?

For instance, I worked for a few months as a nude dancer at a peep show. In case you've never been to a peep show, it works like this: the customer goes into a tiny, dingy black box, kind of like a phone booth, puts in quarters, and a metal plate goes up; the customer looks through a window at a little room/stage where naked women are dancing. One time, a guy came into one of the booths and started watching me and masturbating. I came over and squatted in front of him and started masturbating too, and we grinned at each other and watched each other and masturbated, and we both had a fabulous time. (I couldn't believe I was being paid to masturbate—tough job, but somebody has to do it. . . .) After he left I thought to myself: Did we just have sex? I mean, if it had been someone I knew, and if there had been no glass and no quarters, there'd be no question in my mind. Sitting two feet apart from someone, watching each other masturbate? Yup, I'd call that sex all right. But this was different, because it was a stranger, and because of the glass and the quarters. Was it sex?

I still don't have an answer.

Study Questions

1. Christina rejects her friends' "subjectivist" definition of sex—"if you thought of it as sex, then it was"—as being, in part, "revisionist." We seem to have objective, solid definitions of such things as chairs, dogs, asparagus. Why should defining "sex" be any different? Further, in conceding that her own experiences with women led her to redefine sex, for herself at least, is Christina embracing or practicing the subjectivist's definition? Why or why not?

2. Are there any differences between "having sex," "sexual act," and "sex"? Would being more careful about these three expressions help Christina solve or overcome some of her worries about finding a definition? Genital kisses might not be, on some plausible definition, "having sex," yet it is still a "sexual act," and if your spouse committed only oral sex with a stranger, would you not be upset at his or her *sexual* infidelity? If not, why not?

3. Many of Christina's examples are sexual acts that cannot be procreative. What makes nonprocreative acts sexual—*if* they are sexual? That is, can you find one single feature that is shared by all sexual acts? Note that there is a difference in the way that contracepted heterosexual intercourse is not procreative and the way in which sadomasochist sexuality is not.

4. Would you count as "sex," as "having sex," or as a "sexual activity" (or none of these) the masturbatory encounter described by Christina at the end of her essay? (On what kind of masturbation the event involved, see chapter 6.) What judgment would you make about the morality of that sexual encounter? Why?

5. What are some possible explanations for the abridgement of Christina's essay by the editors of *Ms.*? Was it merely a pragmatic matter of constraints on space, which often plagues editors, or might there have been political reasons for the exclusion of touchy material?

Chapter 3

SEXUAL PERVERSION

Thomas Nagel

The contribution of **Thomas Nagel** *to the philosophy of sex cannot be exaggerated. From his opening claim—"there is something to be learned about sex from the fact that we have a concept of sexual perversion"—to his final conclusion—that bad sex is preferable to no sex at all—the essay is chock-full of controversial claims bravely asserted and defended. The essay brought rigorous, analytic philosophy into the bedroom, invited existentialism along to help, and deepened our understanding of the distinction between the natural and the perverted that is central to the subsequent development of the philosophy of sex. Nagel offers a psychological account of the unnatural sex, or sexual perversion, which many see as a refreshing departure from theological and biological approaches. Moving away from moralistic accounts of sexual perversion, Nagel focuses on its phenomenology—on what "it is like to have a perverted sexual desire-arousal system." For Nagel, a natural (psychologically "complete") sexual encounter for humans results in the increasing mutual embodiment of both persons through a reciprocal awareness of their emotional responses. "Truncated" versions of this pattern constitute sexual perversion, as in sex with inanimate objects, animals, and young children. Using the same formula, Nagel argues that homosexual sexual acts are not perverted, since they can be as psychologically complete as heterosex. Consistently with contemporary psychiatry, Nagel insists that perversion lies not in the act performed, but in the psychology of the person who performs it, and that an important part of sexual perversion resides in his* preferring *certain truncated acts.*

Nagel is professor of philosophy and law at New York University and the author of *The Possibility of Altruism* (Oxford University Press, 1970), *Mortal Questions* (Cambridge

University Press, 1979), *The View from Nowhere* (Oxford University Press, 1986), and
Concealment and Exposure and Other Essays (Oxford University Press, 2002).

There is something to be learned about sex from the fact that we possess a concept of sexual perversion. I wish to examine the idea, defending it against the charge of unintelligibility and trying to say exactly what about human sexuality qualifies it to admit of perversions. Let me begin with some general conditions that the concept must meet if it is to be viable at all. These can be accepted without assuming any particular analysis.

First, if there are any sexual perversions, they will have to be sexual desires or practices that are in some sense unnatural, though the explanation of this natural/unnatural distinction is of course the main problem. Second, certain practices will be perversions if anything is, such as shoe fetishism, bestiality, and sadism; other practices, such as unadorned sexual intercourse, will not be; about still others there is controversy. Third, if there are perversions, they will be unnatural sexual *inclinations* rather than just unnatural practices adopted not from inclination but for other reasons. Thus contraception, even if it is thought to be a deliberate perversion of the sexual and reproductive functions, cannot be significantly described as a *sexual* perversion. A sexual perversion must reveal itself in conduct that expresses an unnatural *sexual* preference. And although there might be a form of fetishism focused on the employment of contraceptive devices, that is not the usual explanation for their use.

The connection between sex and reproduction has no bearing on sexual perversion. The latter is a concept of psychological, not physiological, interest, and it is a concept that we do not apply to the lower animals, let alone to plants, all of which have reproductive functions that can go astray in various ways. (Think of seedless oranges.) Insofar as we are prepared to regard higher animals as perverted, it is because of their psychological, not their anatomical, similarity to humans. Furthermore, we do not regard as a perversion every deviation from the reproductive function of sex in humans: sterility, miscarriage, contraception, abortion.

Nor can the concept of sexual perversion be defined in terms of social disapprobation or custom. Consider all the societies that have frowned upon adultery and fornication. These have not been regarded as unnatural practices, but have been thought objectionable in other ways. What is regarded as unnatural admittedly varies from culture to culture, but the classification is not a pure expression of disapproval or distaste. In fact, it is often regarded as a *ground* for disapproval, and that suggests that the classification has independent content.

I shall offer a psychological account of sexual perversion that depends on a theory of sexual desire and human sexual interactions. To approach this solution I shall first consider a contrary position that would justify skepticism about the existence of any sexual perversions at all, and perhaps even about the significance of the term. The skeptical argument runs as follows:

"Sexual desire is simply one of the appetites, like hunger and thirst. As such it may have various objects, some more common than others perhaps, but none in any sense 'natural.' An appetite is identified as sexual by means of the organs and erogenous zones in which its satisfaction can be to some extent localized, and the special sensory pleasures which form the core of that satisfaction. This enables us to recognize widely divergent goals, activities, and desires as sexual, since it is conceivable in principle that anything should produce sexual pleasure and that a nondeliberate, sexually charged desire for it should arise (as a result of conditioning, if nothing else). We may fail to empathize with some of these desires, and some of them, like sadism, may be objectionable on extraneous grounds, but once we have observed that they meet the criteria for being sexual, there is nothing more to be said on *that* score. Either they are sexual or they are not: sexuality does not admit of imperfection, or perversion, or any other such qualification—it is not that sort of affection."

This is probably the received radical position. It suggests that the cost of defending a psychological account may be to deny that sexual desire is an appetite. But insofar as that line of defense is plausible, it should make us suspicious of the simple picture of appetites on which the skepticism depends. Perhaps the standard appetites, like hunger, cannot be classed as pure appetites in that sense either, at least in their human versions.

Can we imagine anything that would qualify as a gastronomical perversion? Hunger and eating, like sex, serve a biological function and also play a significant role in our inner lives. Note that there is little temptation to describe as perverted an appetite for substances that are not nourishing: we should probably not consider someone's appetite *perverted* if he liked to eat paper, sand, wood, or cotton. Those are merely rather odd and very unhealthy tastes: they lack the psychological complexity that we expect of perversions. (Coprophilia, being already a sexual perversion, may be disregarded.) If on the other hand someone liked to eat cookbooks, or magazines with pictures of food in them, and preferred these to ordinary food—or if when hungry he sought satisfaction by fondling a napkin or ashtray from his favorite restaurant—then the concept of perversion might seem appropriate (it would be natural to call it gastronomical fetishism). It would be natural to describe as gastronomically perverted someone who could eat only by having food forced down his throat through a funnel, or only if the meal were a living animal. What helps is the peculiarity of the desire itself, rather than the inappropriateness of its object to the biological function that the desire serves. Even an appetite can have perversions if in addition to its biological function it has a significant psychological structure.

In the case of hunger, psychological complexity is provided by the activities that give it expression. Hunger is not merely a disturbing sensation that can be quelled by eating; it is an attitude toward edible portions of the external world, a desire to treat them in rather special ways. The method of ingestion: chewing, savoring, swallowing, appreciating the texture and smell, all are important components of the relation, as is the passivity and controllability of the food (the only animals we eat live are helpless mollusks). Our relation to food depends also on our size: we do not live upon it or burrow into it like aphids or worms. Some of these features are more central than others, but an adequate phenomenology of eating would have to treat it as a relation to the external world and a way of appropriating bits of that world, with characteristic affection. Displacements or serious restrictions of the desire to eat could then be described as perversions, if they undermined that direct relation between man and food which is the natural expression of hunger. This explains why it is easy to imagine gastronomical fetishism, voyeurism, exhibitionism, or even gastronomical sadism and masochism. Some of these perversions are fairly common.

If we can imagine perversions of an appetite like hunger, it should be possible to make sense of the concept of sexual perversion. I do not wish to imply that sexual desire is an appetite—only that being an appetite is no bar to admitting of perversions. Like hunger, sexual desire has as its characteristic object a certain relation with something in the external world; only in this case it is usually a person rather than an omelet, and the relation is considerably more complicated. This added complication allows scope for correspondingly complicated perversions.

The fact that sexual desire is a feeling about other persons may encourage a pious view of its psychological content—that it is properly the expression of some other attitude, like love, and that when it occurs by itself it is incomplete or subhuman. (The extreme Platonic version of such a view is that sexual practices are all vain attempts to express something they cannot in principle achieve: this makes them all perversions, in a sense.) But sexual desire is complicated enough without having to be linked to anything else as a condition for phenomenological analysis. Sex may serve various functions—economic, social, altruistic—but it also has its own content as a relation between persons.

The object of sexual attraction is a particular individual, who transcends the properties that make him attractive. When different persons are attracted to a single person for different reasons—eyes, hair, figure, laugh, intelligence—we nevertheless feel that the object of their desire is the same. There is even an inclination to feel that this is so if the lovers have different sexual aims, if they include both men and women, for example. Different specific attractive characteristics seem to provide enabling conditions for the operation of a single basic feeling, and the different aims all provide expressions of it. We approach the sexual attitude toward the person through the features that we find attractive, but these features are not the objects of that attitude.

This is very different from the case of an omelet. Various people may desire it for different reasons, one for its fluffiness, another for its mushrooms, another for its unique combination of aroma and visual aspect; yet we do not enshrine the transcendental omelet as the true common object of their affections. Instead we might say that several desires have accidentally converged on the same object: any omelet with the crucial characteristics would do as well. It is not similarly true that any person with the same flesh distribution and way of smoking can be substituted as object for a particular sexual desire that has been elicited by those characteristics. It may be that they recur, but it will be a new sexual attraction with a new particular object, not merely a transfer of the old desire to someone else. (This is true even in cases where the new object is unconsciously identified with a former one.)

The importance of this point will emerge when we see how complex a psychological interchange constitutes the natural development of sexual attraction. This would be incomprehensible if its object were not a particular person, but rather a person of a certain *kind*. Attraction is only the beginning, and fulfillment does not consist merely of behavior and contact expressing this attraction, but involves much more.

The best discussion of these matters that I have seen appears in part III of Sartre's *Being and Nothingness*.[1] Sartre's treatment of sexual desire and of love, hate, sadism, masochism, and further attitudes toward others depends on a general theory of consciousness and the body which we can neither expound nor assume here. He does not discuss perversion, and this is partly because he regards sexual desire as one form of the perpetual attempt of an embodied consciousness to come to terms with the existence of others, an attempt that is as doomed to fail in this form as it is in any of the others, which include sadism and masochism (if not certain of the more impersonal deviations) as well as several nonsexual attitudes. According to Sartre, all attempts to incorporate the other into my world as another subject, i.e. to apprehend him at once as an object for me and as a subject for whom I am an object, are unstable and doomed to collapse into one or other of the two aspects. Either I reduce him entirely to an object, in which case his subjectivity escapes the possession or appropriation I can extend to that object; or I become merely an object for him, in which case I am no longer in a position to appropriate his subjectivity. Moreover, neither of these aspects is stable; each is continually in danger of giving way to the other. This has the consequence that there can be no such thing as a *successful* sexual relation, since the deep aim of sexual desire cannot in principle be accomplished. It seems likely, therefore, that the view will not permit a basic distinction between successful or complete and unsuccessful or incomplete sex, and therefore cannot admit the concept of perversion.

I do not adopt this aspect of the theory, nor many of its metaphysical underpinnings. What interests me is Sartre's picture of the attempt. He says that the type of possession that is the object of sexual desire is carried out by "a double reciprocal incarnation" and that this is accomplished, typically in the form of a caress, in the following way: "I make myself flesh in order to impel the Other to realize *for herself* and *for me* her own flesh, and my caresses cause my flesh to be born for me in so far as it is for the Other *flesh causing her to be born as flesh*" (*Being and Nothingness*, p. 391; Sartre's italics). This incarnation in question is described variously as a clogging or troubling of consciousness, which is inundated by the flesh in which it is embodied.

The view I am going to suggest, I hope in less obscure language, is related to this one, but it differs from Sartre's in allowing sexuality to achieve its goal on occasion and thus in providing the concept of perversion with a foothold.

Sexual desire involves a kind of perception, but not merely a single perception of its object, for in the paradigm case of mutual desire there is a complex system of superimposed mutual perceptions—not only perceptions of the sexual object, but perceptions of oneself. Moreover, sexual awareness of another involves considerable self-awareness to begin with—more than is involved in ordinary sensory perception. The experience is felt as an assault on oneself by the view (or touch, or whatever) of the sexual object.

Let us consider a case in which the elements can be separated. For clarity we will restrict ourselves initially to the somewhat artificial case of desire at a distance. Suppose a man and a woman, whom we may call Romeo and Juliet, are at opposite ends of a cocktail lounge, with many mirrors on the walls which permit unobserved observation, and even mutual unobserved observation. Each of them is sipping a martini and studying other people in the mirrors. At some point Romeo notices Juliet. He is moved, somehow, by the softness of her hair and the diffidence with which she sips her martini, and this arouses him sexually. Let us say that X *senses* Y whenever X regards Y with sexual desire. (Y need not be a person, and X's apprehension of Y can be visual, tactile, olfactory, etc., or purely imaginary; in the present example we shall concentrate on vision.) So Romeo senses Juliet, rather than merely noticing her. At this stage he is aroused by an unaroused object, so he is more in the sexual grip of his body than she of hers.

Let us suppose, however, that Juliet now senses Romeo in another mirror on the opposite wall, though neither of them yet knows that he is seen by the other (the mirror angles provide three-quarter views). Romeo then begins to notice in Juliet the subtle signs of sexual arousal, heavy-lidded stare, dilating pupils, faint flush, etc. This of course intensifies her bodily presence, and he not only notices but senses this as well. His arousal is nevertheless still solitary. But now, cleverly calculating the line of her stare without actually looking her in the eyes, he realizes that it is directed at him through the mirror on the opposite wall. That is, he notices, and moreover senses, Juliet sensing him. This is definitely a new development, for it gives him a sense of embodiment not only through his own reactions but through the eyes and reactions of another. Moreover, it is separable from the initial sensing of Juliet; for sexual arousal might begin with a person's sensing that he is sensed and being assailed by the perception of the other person's desire rather than merely by the perception of the person.

But there is a further step. Let us suppose that Juliet, who is a little slower than Romeo, now senses that he senses her. This puts Romeo in a position to notice, and be aroused by, her arousal at being sensed by him. He senses that she senses that he senses her. This is still another level of arousal, for he becomes conscious of his sexuality through his awareness of its effect on her and of her awareness that this effect is due to him. Once she takes the same step and senses that he senses her sensing him, it becomes difficult to state, let alone imagine, further iterations, though they may be logically distinct. If both are alone, they will presumably turn to look at each other directly, and the proceedings will continue on another plane. Physical contact and intercourse are natural extensions of this complicated visual exchange, and mutual touch can involve all the complexities of awareness present in the visual case, but with a far greater range of subtlety and acuteness.

Ordinarily, of course, things happen in a less orderly fashion— sometimes in a great rush—but I believe that some version of this overlapping system of distinct sexual perceptions and interactions is the basic framework of any full-fledged sexual relation and that relations involving only part of the complex are significantly incomplete. The account is only schematic, as it must be to achieve generality. Every real sexual act will be psychologically far more specific and detailed, in ways that depend not only on the physical techniques employed and on anatomical details, but also on countless features of the participants' conceptions of themselves and of each other, which become embodied in the act. (It is a familiar enough fact, for example, that people often take their social roles and the social roles of their partners to bed with them.)

The general schema is important, however, and the proliferation of levels of mutual awareness it involves is an example of a type of complexity that typifies human interactions. Consider aggression, for example. If I am angry with someone, I want to make him feel it, either to produce self-reproach by getting him to see himself through the eyes of my anger, and to dislike what he sees—or else to produce reciprocal anger or fear, by getting him to perceive my anger as a threat or attack. What I want will depend on the details of my anger, but in either case it will involve a desire that the object of that anger be aroused. This accomplishment constitutes the fulfillment of my emotion, through domination of the object's feelings.

Another example of such reflexive mutual recognition is to be found in the phenomenon of meaning, which appears to involve an intention to produce a belief or other effect in another by bringing about his recognition of one's intention to produce that effect. (That result is due to H. P. Grice,[2] whose position I shall not attempt to reproduce in detail.) Sex has a related structure: it involves a desire that one's partner be aroused by the recognition of one's desire that he or she be aroused.

It is not easy to define the basic types of awareness and arousal of which these complexes are composed, and that remains a lacuna in this discussion. In a sense, the object of awareness is the same in one's own case as it is in one's sexual awareness of another, although the two awarenesses will not be the same, the difference being as great as that between feeling angry and experiencing the anger of another. All stages of sexual perception are varieties of identification of a person with his body. What is perceived is one's own or another's *subjection* to or *immersion* in his body, a phenomenon which has been recognized with loathing by St. Paul and St. Augustine, both of whom regarded "the law of sin which is in my members" as a grave threat to the dominion of the holy will.[3] In sexual desire and its expression the blending of involuntary response with deliberate control is extremely important. For Augustine, the revolution launched against him by his body is symbolized by erection and the other involuntary physical components of arousal. Sartre too stresses the fact that the penis is not a prehensile organ. But mere involuntariness characterizes other bodily processes as well. In sexual desire the involuntary responses are combined with submission to spontaneous impulses: not only one's pulse and secretions but one's actions are taken over by the body; ideally, deliberate control is needed only to guide the expression of those impulses. This is to some extent also true of an appetite like hunger, but the takeover there is more localized, less pervasive, less extreme. One's whole body does not become saturated with hunger as it can with desire. But the most characteristic feature of a specifically sexual immersion in the body is its ability to fit into the complex of mutual perceptions that we have described. Hunger leads to spontaneous interactions with food; sexual desire leads to spontaneous interactions with other persons, whose bodies are asserting their sovereignty in the same way, producing involuntary reactions and spontaneous impulses in *them*. These reactions are perceived, and the perception of them is perceived, and that perception is in turn perceived; at each step the domination of the person by his body is reinforced, and the sexual partner becomes more possessible by physical contact, penetration, and envelopment.

Desire is therefore not merely the perception of a pre-existing embodiment of the other, but ideally a contribution to his further embodiment which in turn enhances the original subject's sense of himself. This explains why it is important that the partner be aroused, and not merely aroused, but aroused by the awareness of one's desire. It also explains the sense in which desire has unity and possession as its object: physical possession must eventuate in creation of the sexual object in the image of one's desire, and not merely in the object's recognition of that desire, or in his or her own private arousal.

Even if this is a correct model of the adult sexual capacity, it is not plausible to describe as perverted every deviation from it. For example, if the partners in heterosexual intercourse indulge in private heterosexual fantasies, thus avoiding recognition of the real partner, that would, on this model, constitute a defective sexual relation. It is not, however, generally regarded as a perversion. Such examples suggest that a simple dichotomy between perverted and unperverted sex is too crude to organize the phenomena adequately.

Still, various familiar deviations constitute truncated or incomplete versions of the complete configuration, and may be regarded as perversions of the central impulse. If sexual desire is prevented from taking its full interpersonal form, it is likely to find a different one. The concept of perversion implies that a normal sexual development has been turned aside by distorting influences. I have little to say about this causal condition. But if perversions are in some sense unnatural, they must result from interference with the development of a capacity that is there potentially.

It is difficult to apply this condition, because environmental factors play a role in determining the precise form of anyone's sexual impulse. Early experiences in particular seem to determine the choice of a sexual object. To describe some causal influences as distorting and others as merely formative is to imply that certain general aspects of human sexuality realize a definite potential whereas many of the details in which people differ realize an indeterminate potential, so that they cannot be called more or less natural. What is included in the definite potential is therefore very important, although the distinction between definite and indeterminate potential is obscure. Obviously a creature incapable of developing the levels of interpersonal sexual awareness I have described could not be deviant in virtue of the failure to do so. (Though even a chicken might be called perverted in an extended sense if it had been conditioned to develop a fetishistic attachment to a telephone.) But if humans will tend to develop some version of reciprocal interpersonal sexual awareness unless prevented, then cases of blockage can be called unnatural or perverted.

Some familiar deviations can be described in this way. Narcissistic practices and intercourse with animals, infants, and inanimate objects seem to be stuck at some primitive version of the first stage of sexual feeling. If the object is not alive, the experience is reduced entirely to an awareness of one's own sexual embodiment. Small children and animals permit awareness of the embodiment of the other, but present obstacles to reciprocity, to the recognition by the sexual object of the subject's desire as the source of his (the object's) sexual self-awareness. Voyeurism and exhibitionism are also incomplete relations. The exhibitionist wishes to display his desire without needing to be desired in return; he may even fear the sexual attention of others. A voyeur, on the other hand, need not require any recognition by his object at all: certainly not a recognition of the voyeur's arousal.

On the other hand, if we apply our model to the various forms that may be taken by two-party heterosexual intercourse, none of them seem clearly to qualify as perversions. Hardly anyone can be found these days to inveigh against oral-genital contact, and the merits of buggery are urged by such respectable figures as D. H. Lawrence and Norman Mailer. In general, it would appear that any bodily contact between a man and a woman that gives them sexual pleasure is a possible vehicle for the system of multilevel interpersonal awareness that I have claimed is the basic psychological content of sexual interaction. Thus a liberal platitude about sex is upheld.

The really difficult cases are sadism, masochism, and homosexuality. The first two are widely regarded as perversions and the last is controversial. In all three cases the issue depends partly on causal factors: do these dispositions result only when normal development has been prevented? Even the form in which this question has been posed is circular, because of the word "normal." We appear to need an independent criterion for a distorting influence, and we do not have one.

It may be possible to class sadism and masochism as perversions because they fall short of interpersonal reciprocity. Sadism concentrates on the evocation of passive self-awareness in others, but the sadist's engagement is itself active and requires a retention of deliberate control which may impede awareness of himself as a bodily subject of passion in the required sense. De Sade claimed that the object of sexual desire was to evoke involuntary responses from one's partner, especially audible ones.

The infliction of pain is no doubt the most efficient way to accomplish this, but it requires a certain abrogation of one's own exposed spontaneity. A masochist on the other hand imposes the same disability on his partner as the sadist imposes on himself. The masochist cannot find a satisfactory embodiment as the object of another's sexual desire, but only as the object of his control. He is passive not in relation to his partner's passion but in relation to his nonpassive agency. In addition, the subjection to one's body characteristic of pain and physical restraint is of a very different kind from that of sexual excitement: pain causes people to contract rather than dissolve. These descriptions may not be generally accurate. But to the extent that they are, sadism and masochism would be disorders of the second stage of awareness—the awareness of oneself as an object of desire.

Homosexuality cannot similarly be classed as a perversion on phenomenological grounds. Nothing rules out the full range of interpersonal perceptions between persons of the same sex. The issue then depends on whether homosexuality is produced by distorting influences that block or displace a natural tendency to heterosexual development. And the influences must be more distorting than those which lead to a taste for large breasts or fair hair or dark eyes. These also are contingencies of sexual preference in which people differ, without being perverted.

The question is whether heterosexuality is the natural expression of male and female sexual dispositions that have not been distorted. It is an unclear question, and I do not know how to approach it. There is much support for an aggressive-passive distinction between male and female sexuality. In our culture the male's arousal tends to initiate the perceptual exchange, he usually makes the sexual approach, largely controls the course of the act, and of course penetrates whereas the woman receives. When two men or two women engage in intercourse they cannot both adhere to these sexual roles. But a good deal of deviation from them occurs in heterosexual intercourse. Women can be sexually aggressive and men passive, and temporary reversals of role are not uncommon in heterosexual exchanges of reasonable length. For these reasons it seems to be doubtful that homosexuality must be a perversion, though like heterosexuality it has perverted forms.

Let me close with some remarks about the relation of perversion to good, bad, and morality. The concept of perversion can hardly fail to be evaluative in some sense, for it appears to involve the notion of an ideal or at least adequate sexuality which the perversions in some way fail to achieve. So, if the concept is viable, the judgment that a person or practice or desire is perverted will constitute a sexual evaluation, implying that better sex, or a better specimen of sex, is possible. This in itself is a very weak claim, since the evaluation might be in a dimension that is of little interest to us. (Though, if my account is correct, that will not be true.)

Whether it is a moral evaluation, however, is another question entirely—one whose answer would require more understanding of both morality and perversion than can be deployed here. Moral evaluation of acts and of persons is a rather special and very complicated matter, and by no means all our evaluations of persons and their activities are moral evaluations. We make judgments about people's beauty or health or intelligence which are evaluative without being moral. Assessments of their sexuality may be similar in that respect.

Furthermore, moral issues aside, it is not clear that unperverted sex is necessarily *preferable* to the perversions. It may be that sex which receives the highest marks for perfection *as sex* is less enjoyable than certain perversions; and if enjoyment is considered very important, that might outweigh considerations of sexual perfection in determining rational preference.

That raises the question of the relation between the evaluative content of judgments of perversion and the rather common *general* distinction between good and bad sex. The latter distinction is usually confined to sexual acts, and it would seem, within limits, to cut across the other: even someone who believed, for example, that homosexuality was a perversion could admit a distinction between better and worse homosexual sex, and might even allow that good homosexual sex could be better sex than not very good unperverted sex. If this is correct, it supports the position that, if judgments of perversion are viable at all, they represent only one aspect of the possible evaluation of sex, even *qua sex*. Moreover it is not the only important aspect: sexual deficiencies that evidently do not constitute perversions can be the object of great concern.

Finally, even if perverted sex is to that extent not so good as it might be, bad sex is generally better than none at all. This should not be controversial: it seems to hold for other important matters, like food, music, literature, and society. In the end, one must choose from among the available alternatives, whether their availability depends on the environment or on one's own constitution. And the alternatives have to be fairly grim before it becomes rational to opt for nothing.

Study Questions

1. Try to provide examples of sexual acts that would be judged perverted on Nagel's model yet are not usually considered perverted, and of psychologically complete sexual events that may, nonetheless, be considered perverted by many people. If you can

find such examples, what would this mean, for you, about the accuracy of Nagel's theory?

2. On what grounds does Nagel argue against sexual desire's being an appetite, such as hunger (or the desire to eat food)? How does sexual desire differ from, and how is it similar to, the desire for pizza? How do these comparisons or contrasts affect Nagel's argument? We can stay alive without eating pizza; we cannot stay alive if we do not eat at all. Can we stay alive without engaging in some sexual activities? Can we stay alive *well*, i.e., flourish, if we are totally abstinent?

3. Nagel claims that a person could become sexually aroused by someone who is "purely imaginary" (or fantasized), for example, during solitary masturbation. Explore the implications of this observation for Nagel's account. Indeed, consider also both "deviant" Nagelian patterns (a person is sexually aroused not by the sexual arousal of the other person, but by the other's fear or disgust), and "degenerate" Nagelian patterns (in which one person is aroused not by the genuine arousal of the other person, but by the other person's feigned or pretended arousal).

4. Why does Nagel claim that "bad" sex may be better than none at all? Granted, he does not seem to mean that "morally bad" sex may be better than none. Still, does he claim that perverted sex (a kind of nonideal sex) may be better—more arousing? more satisfying?—than either having no sex at all, or at least better than nonperverted, psychologically complete sex?

5. Nagel proposes that we need an account of the "distorting influences" that cause some people to have unusual sexual preferences. He also admits that this theoretical requirement has the potential of leading any model of sexual perversion into failure. Explain. And what are the implications of this problem for a science of sexual perversion, or a medical/psychiatric account of sexual mental health and illness?

Notes

1. Jean-Paul Sartre, *L'Etre et le Néant* (Paris: Gallimand, 1943), translated by Hazel E. Barnes (New York: Philosophical Library, 1956).

2. H. P. Grice, "Meaning," *Philosophical Review* LXVI, no. 3 (July 1957), 377–88.

3. See Romans 7:23; and the *Confessions*, bk VIII, pt v.

Chapter 4

SEXUAL BEHAVIOR:
ANOTHER POSITION

Janice Moulton

*In this essay, **Janice Moulton** criticizes, among others, Thomas Nagel's model of sexual perversion (see chapter 3). Against Nagel, she argues that although the reciprocal awareness of increasing levels of mutual arousal and embodiment may characterize flirtation, seduction, and the anticipation present in novel sexual encounters, it does not accurately characterize everyday or more ordinary sexual relations or those between partners in longstanding relationships. As a result, "incompleteness" falls short as a general account of sexual perversion. Moulton professes a skeptical view of the conceptual enterprise in which Nagel and other philosophers engage, and proposes instead the psychological or sociological thesis that we label as perverted whatever sexual acts strike us as bizarre.*

Moulton is professor of philosophy at Smith College and coauthor, with George M. Robinson, of *The Organization of Language* (Cambridge University Press, 1981), *Ethical Problems in Higher Education* (Prentice-Hall, 1985), and *Scaling the Dragon* (Cross Cultural Publications, 1994), a whimsical story of her adventures while teaching in the People's Republic of China.

Reprinted, with the permission of Janice Moulton and the *Journal of Philosophy*, from *Journal of Philosophy* 73, no. 16 (1976): 537–46.

We can often distinguish behavior that is sexual from behavior that is not. Sexual intercourse may be one clear example of the former, but other sexual behaviors are not so clearly defined. Some kissing is sexual; some is not. Sometimes looking is sexual; sometimes *not* looking is sexual. Is it possible, then, to *characterize* sexual behavior?

Thomas Nagel in "Sexual Perversion"[1] and Robert Solomon in "Sexual Paradigms"[2] each offer an answer to this question. Nagel analyzes sexual desire as a "complex system of superimposed mutual perceptions." He claims that sexual relations that do not fit his account are incomplete and, consequently, perversions. Solomon claims that sexual behavior should be analyzed in terms of goals rather than feelings. He maintains that "the end of this desire is interpersonal communication" and not enjoyment. According to Solomon, the sexual relations between regular partners will be inferior to novel encounters because there is less remaining to communicate sexually.

I believe that sexual behavior will not fit any single characterization; that there are at least two sorts of sexual behavior to characterize. Both Nagel and Solomon have interesting things to say about one sort of sexual behavior. However, both have assumed that a model of flirtation and seduction constitutes an adequate model of sexual behavior in general. Although a characterization of flirtation and seduction can continue to apply to a relationship that is secret, forbidden, or in which there is some reason to remain unsure of one's sexual acceptability, I shall argue that most sexual behavior does not involve flirtation and seduction, and that what characterizes flirtation and seduction is not what characterizes the sexual behavior of regular partners. Nagel takes the development of what I shall call "sexual anticipation" to be characteristic of all sexual behavior and gives no account of sexual satisfaction.[3] Solomon believes that flirtation and seduction are different from regular sexual relationships. However, he too considers only characteristics of sexual anticipation in his analysis and concludes that regular sexual relationships are inferior to novel ones because they lack some of those characteristics.

Flirtation, seduction, and traditional courtship involve sexual feelings that are quite independent of physical contact. These feelings are increased by anticipation of success, winning, or conquest. Because what is anticipated is the opportunity for sexual intimacy and satisfaction, the feelings of sexual satisfaction are usually not distinguished from those of sexual anticipation. Sexual satisfaction involves sexual feelings which are increased by the other person's knowledge of one's preferences and sensitivities, the familiarity of their touch or smell or way of moving, and not by the novelty of their sexual interest.

It is easy to think that the more excitement and enthusiasm involved in the anticipation of an event, the more enjoyable and exciting the event itself is likely to be. However, anticipation and satisfaction are often divorced. Many experiences with no associated build-up of anticipation are very satisfying, and others, awaited and begun with great eagerness, produce no feelings of satisfaction at all. In sexual activity this dissociation is likely to be frequent. A strong feeling of sexual anticipation is produced by the uncertainty, challenge, or secrecy of novel sexual experiences, but the tension and excitement that increase anticipation often interfere with sexual satisfaction. The comfort and trust and experience with familiar partners may increase sexual satisfaction, but decrease the uncertainty and challenge that heighten sexual anticipation. Given the distinction between anticipation and satisfaction, there is no reason to believe that an increase of trust and love ought to increase feelings of sexual anticipation or that sexual anticipation should be a prerequisite for any long-term sexual relationship.

For some people the processes that create sexual anticipation, the exchange of indirect signals, the awareness of the other person's sexual interest, and the accompanying sexual anticipation may be *all* that is valued in sexual behavior. Satisfaction is equated with release, the end of a good time, and is not considered a process in its own right. But although flirtation and seduction are the main objects of sexual fantasy and fiction, most people, even those whose sexual relations are frequently casual, seek to continue some sexual relationships after the flirtation and seduction are over, when the uncertainty and challenge are gone. And the motives, goals, and feelings of sexual satisfaction that characterize these continued sexual relations are not the same as the motives, goals, and feelings of sexual anticipation that characterize the novel sexual relations Nagel and Solomon have tried to analyze. Let us consider their accounts.

Nagel's account is illustrated by a tale of a Romeo and a Juliet who are sexually aroused by each other, notice each other's arousal and become further aroused by that:

> He senses that she senses that he senses her. This is still another level of arousal, for he becomes conscious of his sexuality through his awareness of its effect on her and of her awareness that this effect is due to him. Once she takes the same step and senses that he senses her sensing him, it becomes difficult to state, let alone imagine, further iterations, though they may be logically distinct. If both are alone, they will presumably turn to look at each other directly, and the proceedings will continue on another plane. Physical contact and intercourse are natural extensions of this complicated visual exchange, and mutual touch can involve all the complexities of awareness present in the visual case, but with a far greater range of subtlety and acuteness.
>
> Ordinarily, of course, things happen in a less orderly fashion—sometimes in a great rush—but I believe that some version of this overlapping system of distinct sexual perceptions and interactions is the basic framework of any full-fledged sexual relation and that relations involving only part of the complex are significantly incomplete.

Nagel then characterizes sexual perversion as a "truncated or incomplete version" of sexual *arousal,* rather than as some deviation from a standard of subsequent physical interaction.

Nagel's account applies only to the development of sexual anticipation. He says that "the proliferation of levels of mutual awareness . . . is . . . a type of complexity that typifies human interactions," so he might argue that his account will cover Romeo and Juliet's later relationship as well. Granted that levels of mutual awareness exist in any close human relationship. But it does not follow that the development of levels of awareness *characterize* all human relationships, particularly sexual relationships between familiar partners. In particular, the sort of awareness Nagel emphasizes—"a desire that one's partner be aroused by the recognition of one's desire that he or she be aroused"—does not seem essential to regular sexual relationships. If we accept Nagel's account for sexual behavior in general, then we must classify as a perversion the behavior of an intimate and satisfying sexual relation begun without any preliminary exchange of multilevel arousals.[4]

Sexual desire can be generated by many different things—a smell, a phrase in a book, a familiar voice. The sexual interest of another person is only on occasion novel enough to be the main cause or focus of sexual arousal. A characterization of sexual behavior on other occasions should describe the development and sharing of sexual pleasure—the creation of sexual satisfaction. Nagel's contribution lies in directing our attention to the analysis of sexual behavior in terms of its perceptions and feelings. However, he characterizes only a limited sort of sexual behavior, flirtation and seduction.

Solomon characterizes sexual behavior by analogy with linguistic behavior, emphasizing that the goals are the same. He says:

> Sexual activity consists in speaking what we might call "body language." It has it own grammar, delineated by the body, and its own phonetics of touch and movement. Its unit of meaningfulness, the bodily equivalent of a sentence, is the *gesture.* . . . [B]ody language is essentially expressive, and its content is limited to interpersonal attitudes and feelings.

The analogy with language can be valuable for understanding sexual behavior. However, Solomon construes the goals of both activities too narrowly and hence draws the wrong conclusions. He argues that the aim of sexual behavior is to communicate one's attitudes and feelings, to express oneself, and further, that such self-expression is made less effective by aiming at enjoyment:

> That is why the liberal mythology has been so disastrous, for it has rendered unconscious the expressive functions of sex in its stress on enjoyment. . . .

It is thus understandable why sex is so utterly important in our lives, and why it is typically so unsatisfactory.

Does stress on enjoyment hinder self-expression? Trying to do one thing, *X*, may interfere with trying to do another, *Y*, for some *X*s and *Y*s. For example, trying to eat peanut butter or swim under water may interfere with vocal self-expression. But enjoyment is a different sort of goal. One isn't trying to do both *Y* and something else when aiming at *Y* and enjoyment, but to do one sort of thing, *Y*, a certain way. Far from interfering, one is more likely to be successful at a venture if one can manage to enjoy oneself during the process.

Solomon claims to refute that enjoyment is the essential aim of sexual activity, but he erroneously identifies enjoyment with orgasm:[5]

> No one would deny that sex is enjoyable, but it does not follow that sexuality is the activity of "pure enjoyment" and that "gratification," or "pure physical pleasure," that is, orgasm, is its end.

Consequently he shows merely that orgasm is not the only aim of sexual activity. His main argument is:

> If sex is pure physical enjoyment, why is sexual activity between persons far more satisfying than masturbation, where, if we accept recent physiological studies, orgasm is at its highest intensity and the post-coital period is cleansed of its interpersonal hassles and arguments?

One obvious answer is that, even for people who have hassles and arguments, interpersonal sexual activity is more enjoyable, even in the "pure physical" sense.[6] Solomon's argument does not show that enjoyment is not the appropriate aim of sexual activity, only that maximum-intensity orgasm is not. As those recent physiological studies pointed out, participants report interpersonal sexual activity as more enjoyable and satisfying even though their orgasms are less intense.[7] Only someone who mistakenly equated enjoyment with orgasm would find this paradoxical.

One need not claim that orgasm is always desired or desirable in sexual activity. That might be like supposing that in all conversations the participants do, or should, express their deepest thoughts. In sexual, as in linguistic, behavior, there is great variety and subtlety of purpose. But this is not to say that the desire for orgasm should be ignored. The disappointment and physical discomfort of expected but unachieved orgasm is only faintly parallel to the frustration of not being able to "get a word in edgewise" after being moved to express an important thought. It is usually rude or boorish to use language with indifference to the interests and cares of one's listeners. Sexual behavior with such indifference can be no better.

Solomon does not need these arguments to claim that enjoyment is not the only or the essential goal of sexual behavior. His comparison of sexual behavior with linguistic (or other social) behavior could have been used to do the job. The same social and moral distinctions and evaluations can be applied to both behaviors: hurting and humiliating people is bad; making people happy is good; loyalty, kindness, intelligence, and wit are valued; stupidity, clumsiness, and insincerity are not. The purpose of contact, sexual or otherwise, with other people is not just to produce or receive enjoyment—there are times of sadness, solace, and anguish that are important and meaningful to share, but not enjoyable.

Is self-expression, then, the essential goal of sexual behavior? Solomon lists a number of feelings and attitudes that can be expressed sexually:

> love, tenderness and trust, "being-with," mutual recognition
> hatred, indifference, jealousy, conflict
> shyness, fear, lack of confidence, embarrassment, shame
> domination, submissiveness, dependence, possessiveness, passivity

He claims "some attitudes, e.g., tenderness and trust, domination and passivity, are best expressed sexually," and says his account

> makes it evident why Nagel chose as his example a couple of strangers; one has far more to say, for one can freely express one's fantasies as well as the truth, to a stranger. A husband and wife of seven years have probably been repeating the same messages for years, and their sexual activity now is probably no more than an abbreviated ritual incantation of the lengthy conversations they had years before.

A glance at the list of feelings and attitudes above will show that its items are not independent. Shame, for example, may include components of embarrassment, lack of confidence, fear, and probably mutual recognition and submissiveness. To the extent that they can be conveyed by sexual body language,[8] a mere grunt or whimper would be able to express the whole range of the attitudes and feelings as well, if not better, than sexual gestures. Moreover, it is not clear that some attitudes are best expressed sexually. Tenderness and trust are often expressed between people who are not sexual partners. The tenderness and trust that may exist between an adult and a child is not best expressed sexually. Even if we take Solomon's claim to apply only to sexual partners, a joint checking account may be a better expression of trust than sexual activity. And domination, which in sadomasochistic sexual activity is expressed most elaborately with the cooperation of the partner, is an attitude much better expressed by nonsexual activities[9] such as beating an opponent, firing an employee, or mugging a passerby, where the domination is real, and does not require the cooperation of the other person. Even if some attitudes and feelings (for example, prurience, wantonness, lust) are best expressed sexually, it would be questionable whether the primary aim of sexual activity should be to express them.

The usual conversation of strangers is "small talk": cautious, shallow, and predictable because there has not been time for the participants to assess the extent and nature of common interests they share. So too with sexual behavior; first sexual encounters may be charged with novelty and anticipation, but are usually characterized by stereotypic physical interactions. If the physical interaction is seen as "body language," the analogy with linguistic behavior suggests that first encounters are likely to consist of sexual small talk.

Solomon's comparison of sexual behavior with linguistic behavior is handicapped by the limited view he has about their purposes. Language has more purposes than transmitting information. If all there were to sexual behavior was the development of the sexual anticipation prominent in flirtation and seduction, then Solomon's conclusions might be correct. The fact that people will continue sexual relations with the same partners even after the appropriate attitudes and feelings from Solomon's list have been expressed indicates that sexual behavior, like linguistic behavior, has other functions that are important. Solomon's analogy with linguistic behavior is valuable not because communication is the main goal of sexual behavior but because he directs attention to the social nature of sexual behavior. Solomon's analogy can be made to take on new importance by considering that sexual behavior not only transmits information about feelings and attitudes—something any activity can do—but also, like language, it has a *phatic* function to evoke feelings and attitudes.

Language is often used to produce a shared experience, a feeling of togetherness or unity. Duets, greetings, and many religious services use language with little information content to establish or reaffirm a relation among the participants. Long-term sexual relationships, like regular musical ensembles, may be valued more for the feelings produced than the feelings communicated. With both sexual and linguistic behavior, an interaction with a stranger might be an enjoyable novelty, but the pleasures of linguistic and sexual activity with good friends are probably much more frequent and more reliable. Solomon's conclusion that sexually one should have more to "say" to a stranger and will find oneself "repeating the same messages for years" to old acquaintances,[10] violates the analogy. With natural language, one usually has more to say to old friends than to strangers.

Both Nagel and Solomon give incomplete accounts because they assume that a characterization of flirtation and seduction should apply to sexual behavior in general. I have argued that this is not so. Whether we analyze sexual behavior in terms of characteristic perceptions and feelings, as Nagel does, or by a comparison with other complex social behavior, as Solomon does, the characteristics of novel sexual encounters differ from those of sexual relationships between familiar and recognized partners.

What about the philosophical enterprise of characterizing sexual behavior? A characterization of something will tell what is unique about it and how to identify a standard or paradigm case of it. Criteria for a standard or paradigm case of sexual behavior unavoidably have normative implications. It is my position that normative judgments about sexual behavior should not be unrelated to the social and moral standards that apply to other social behavior. Many people, in reaction to old standards, avoid disapproving of sexual behavior that involves deceit or humiliation to another, but will condemn or ridicule sexual behavior that hurts no one yet fails to conform to a sexual standard. Both Nagel and Solomon classify sexual behavior that does not fit their characterizations as perversion, extending this strong negative judgment to behavior that is neither morally nor socially condemned (i.e., sex without multilevel awareness of arousal; sex without communication of attitudes and feelings). Yet perversion can be more accurately accounted for as whatever makes people frightened or uncomfortable by its bizarreness.[11]

Sexual behavior differs from other behavior by virtue of its unique feelings and emotions and its unique ability to create shared intimacy. These unique features of sexual behavior may influence particular normative judgments, but they do not justify applying *different* normative principles to sexual behavior.

Study Questions

1. Even if we agree with Moulton that the psychologies of flirtation, seduction, and anticipation differ in important ways from the psychology of more routine sexual events, does this entail that Nagel is wrong to think that the reciprocal awareness of embodiment that deepens arousal is significantly absent from more routine sexual events? Similarly, is it possible that much routine sex also involves, even if in a brief or rudimentary way, some of the elements of flirtation, seduction, or anticipation?

2. How does Moulton account for the fact that we (apparently) prefer engaging in sexual activity with other people as opposed to solitary masturbation, even at the cost of a less intense orgasm? Explore the implications of her explanation. What might be more important in producing sexual satisfaction, the novelty or newness of a touch or partner's body, or their familiarity?

3. Philosophers have been trying to understand the nature of sexuality, and to provide convincing analyses of concepts such as "sexual activity," "sexual desire," and so forth. Moulton's contribution to this ongoing discussion might be summarized in her claim, "sexual behavior differs from other behavior by virtue of its unique feelings and emotions and its unique ability to create shared intimacy." Are you able to state clearly the several sorts of uniqueness that Moulton attributes to sexuality?

4. Identify some advantages and disadvantages of Moulton's account of sexual perversion in terms of the "bizarre." Think about this after reading Alan Goldman's remarks on sexual perversion (chapter 5).

5. Moulton is a woman; Nagel is a man (see chapter 3). Might it be argued plausibly that sex/gender has influenced their differing views not only about sexuality but also in the philosophy of sex? Provide specific examples from each essay that might support (or refute) the idea that their ideas are gender-related.

Notes

This paper has been greatly improved by the discussions and careful criticisms of G. M. Robinson and Helen Heise, the suggestions of Tim Binkley and Jay Rosenberg that it be expanded, and the comments from audiences of The Society for Women in Philosophy and the American Philosophical Association.

1. *Journal of Philosophy* 66, no. 1 (1969): 5–17. (In this volume, chapter 3.)

2. *Journal of Philosophy* 71, no. 11 (1974): 336–45.

3. Satisfaction includes the good feelings of intimacy, warm friendship, the pleasure of being appreciated and of giving pleasure. "Satisfaction" is not intended as a euphemism for orgasm, although the physical and social discomforts of the absence of orgasm often make a feeling of satisfaction impossible.

4. This was first pointed out to me by Sara Ketchum.

5. Solomon also claims that aiming at *orgasm* "overwhelms or distorts whatever else is being said sexually." In this case there might be interference. However, if one is trying to express feelings and attitudes through the giving or having of an orgasm, then "aiming at self-expression" and "aiming at orgasm" will describe the same activity and there will be no interference. It should be pointed out that whatever else is being said sexually should have been said before orgasm is imminent or should be postponed because one will not do a very good job of transmitting or receiving any other communication during orgasm. Instead of an objection to aiming at orgasm, the potential interference raises an objection to aiming at self-expression during the time that orgasm is the goal.

6. Several theories of motivation in psychology (e.g., McClelland's) easily incorporate this fact: Creatures find moderate discrepancies from predicted

sensation more pleasurable than sensations that are completely expected. Sensations produced by a sexual partner are not as adequately predicted as auto-erotic stimulation.

7. William Masters and Virginia Johnson, *Human Sexual Response* (Boston: Little, Brown, 1966), 113.

8. More than gestures must be employed to communicate such feelings as love, trust, hatred, shame, dependence, and possessiveness. I doubt that jealousy or a distinction between "one's fantasies [and] the truth" (Solomon) can be communicated by sexual body language at all.

9. In her comments on a relative of this paper at the 1976 Pacific Division APA meetings, Sara Ketchum pointed out that I have completely overlooked one sort of sexual activity in which the domination *is* real and the cooperation of the other person is not required: rape.

10. Repeated messages about one's feelings are not merely redundant; they convey new information: the continuation, renewal, or salience of those feelings.

11. See Mary Douglas, *Purity and Danger* (London: Routledge & Kegan Paul, 1966).

Chapter 5

PLAIN SEX

Alan Goldman

Whereas most accounts of human sexuality link, in some way or another, sexual activity with love or marriage and progeny, **Alan Goldman** *believes emphasizing these contingent ends or purposes of sexual desire and activity as either conceptually or morally central for understanding sexuality is a mistake. His title, "Plain Sex," is meant to alert us that if we want to capture the lowest common denominator of all sexuality, that if we want to expose what is analytically central to sexuality per se, we had better ignore these variable concomitants of sexuality. His proposal is that sexual desire is simply the desire for certain sensations or pleasures that are produced by physical, bodily contact, and that sexual activity is activity that "tends to fulfill" this desire for pleasurable contact. Goldman provides arguments that his definition of sexual desire is neither overly broad (i.e., does not include desires that are not sexual) nor too narrow (i.e., does not include desires that should be counted as sexual). Goldman then explores what his conceptual analysis implies or allows regarding sexual morality and the notion of sexual perversion. In particular he advances an interesting interpretation of Immanuel Kant's ethics as applied to sexual behavior, which should be kept in mind when the reader gets to parts III and IV, below.*

Goldman is Kenan Professor of Philosophy at the College of William and Mary. He is the author of *Moral Knowledge* (Routledge, 1988), *Aesthetic Value* (Westview, 1995), and *Practical Rules: When We Need Them and When We Don't* (Cambridge University Press, 2001).

Alan Goldman, "Plain Sex," *Philosophy and Public Affairs* 6, 3 (1977): 267–87. © 1977, Princeton University Press. Reprinted by permission of the publisher, Blackwell, Oxford, UK.

I.

Several recent articles on sex herald its acceptance as a legitimate topic for analytic philosophers (although it has been a topic in philosophy since Plato). One might have thought conceptual analysis unnecessary in this area; despite the notorious struggles of judges and legislators to define pornography suitably, we all might be expected to know what sex is and to be able to identify at least paradigm sexual desires and activities without much difficulty. Philosophy is nevertheless of relevance here if for no other reason than that the concept of sex remains at the center of moral and social consciousness in our, and perhaps any, society. Before we can get a sensible view of the relation of sex to morality, perversion, social regulation, and marriage, we require a sensible analysis of the concept itself; one which neither understates its animal pleasure nor overstates its importance within a theory or system of value. I say "before," but the order is not quite so clear, for questions in this area, as elsewhere in moral philosophy, are both conceptual and normative at the same time. Our concept of sex will partially determine our moral view of it, but as philosophers we should formulate a concept that will accord with its proper moral status. What we require here, as elsewhere, is "reflective equilibrium," a goal not achieved by traditional and recent analyses together with their moral implications. Because sexual activity, like other natural functions such as eating or exercising, has become embedded in layers of cultural, moral, and superstitious superstructure, it is hard to conceive it in its simplest terms. But partially for this reason, it is only by thinking about plain sex that we can begin to achieve this conceptual equilibrium.

I shall suggest here that sex continues to be misrepresented in recent writings, at least in philosophical writings, and I shall criticize the predominant form of analysis which I term "means-end analysis." Such conceptions attribute a necessary external goal or purpose to sexual activity, whether it be reproduction, the expression of love, simple communication, or interpersonal awareness. They analyze sexual activity as a means to one of these ends, implying that sexual desire is a desire to reproduce, to love or be loved, or to communicate with others. All definitions of this type suggest false views of the relation of sex to perversion and morality by implying that sex which does not fit one of these models or fulfill one of these functions is in some way deviant or incomplete.

The alternative, simpler analysis with which I will begin is that sexual desire is desire for contact with another person's body and for the pleasure which such contact produces; sexual activity is activity which tends to fulfill such desire of the agent. Whereas Aristotle and Butler were correct in holding that pleasure is normally a byproduct rather than a goal of purposeful action, in the case of sex this is not so clear. The desire for another's body is, principally among other things, the desire for the pleasure that physical contact brings. On the other hand, it is not a desire for a particular sensation detachable from its causal context, a sensation which can be derived in other ways. This definition in terms of the general goal of sexual desire appears preferable to an attempt to more explicitly list or define specific sexual activities, for many activities such as kissing, embracing, massaging, or holding hands may or may not be sexual, depending upon the context and more specifically upon the purposes, needs, or desires into which such activities fit. The generality of the definition also represents a refusal (common in recent psychological texts) to overemphasize orgasm as the goal of sexual desire or genital sex as the only norm of sexual activity (this will be hedged slightly in the discussion of perversion below).

Central to the definition is the fact that the goal of sexual desire and activity is the physical contact itself, rather than something else which this contact might express. By contrast, what I term "means-end analyses" posit ends which I take to be extraneous to plain sex, and they view sex as a means to these ends. Their fault lies not in defining sex in terms of its general goal, but in seeing plain sex as merely a means to other separable ends. I term these "means-end analyses" for convenience, although "means-separable-end analysis," while too cumbersome, might be more fully explanatory. The desire for physical contact with another person is a minimal criterion for (normal) sexual desire, but is both necessary and sufficient to qualify normal desire as sexual. Of course, we may want to express other feelings through sexual acts in various contexts; but without the desire for the physical contact in and for itself, or when it is sought for other reasons, activities in which contact is involved are not predominantly sexual. Furthermore, the desire for physical contact in itself, without the wish to express affection or other feelings through it, is sufficient to render sexual the activity of the agent which fulfills it. Various activities with this goal alone, such as kissing and caressing in certain contexts, qualify as sexual even without the presence of genital symptoms of sexual excitement. The latter are not therefore necessary criteria for sexual activity.

This initial analysis may seem to some either over- or underinclusive. It might seem too broad in leading us to interpret physical contact as sexual desire in activities such as football and other contact sports. In these cases, however, the desire is not for contact with another body per se, it is not directed toward a particular person for that purpose, and it is not the goal of the activity—the goal is winning or exercising or knocking someone down or displaying one's prowess. If the desire is purely for contact with another specific person's body, then to interpret it as sexual does not seem an exaggeration. A slightly more difficult case is that of a baby's desire to be cuddled and our natural response in wanting to cuddle it. In the case of the baby, the desire may be simply for the physical contact, for the pleasure of the caresses. If so, we may characterize this desire, especially in keeping with Freudian theory, as sexual or protosexual. It will differ nevertheless from full-fledged sexual desire in being more amorphous, not directed outward toward another specific person's body. It may also be that what the infant unconsciously desires is not physical contact per se but signs of affection, tenderness, or security, in which case we have further reason for hesitating to characterize its wants as clearly sexual. The intent of our response to the baby is often the showing of affection, not the pure physical contact, so that our definition in terms of action which fulfills sexual desire *on the part of the agent* does not capture such actions, whatever we say of the baby. (If it is intuitive to characterize our responses as sexual as well, there is clearly no problem here for my analysis.) The same can be said of signs of affection (or in some cultures polite greeting) among men or women: these certainly need not be homosexual when the intent is only to show friendship, something extrinsic to plain sex although valuable when added to it.

Our definition of sex in terms of the desire for physical contact may appear too narrow in that a person's personality, not merely her or his body, may be sexually attractive to another, and in that looking or conversing in a certain way can be sexual in a given context without bodily contact. Nevertheless, it is not the contents of one's thoughts per se that are sexually appealing, but one's personality as embodied in certain manners of behavior. Furthermore, if a person is sexually attracted by another's personality, he or she will desire not just further conversation, but actual sexual contact. While looking at or conversing with someone can be interpreted as sexual in given contexts it is so when intended as preliminary to, and hence parasitic upon, elemental sexual interest. Voyeurism or viewing a pornographic movie qualifies as a sexual activity, but only as an imaginative substitute for the real thing (otherwise a deviation from the norm as expressed in our definition). The same is true of masturbation as a sexual activity without a partner.

That the initial definition indicates at least an ingredient of sexual desire and activity is too obvious to argue. We all know what sex is, at least in obvious cases, and do not need philosophers to tell us. My preliminary analysis is meant to serve as a contrast to what sex is not, at least not necessarily. I concentrate upon the physically manifested desire for another's body, and I take as central the immersion in the physical aspect of one's own existence and attention to the physical embodiment of the other. One may derive pleasure in a sex act from expressing certain feelings to one's partner or from awareness of the attitude of one's partner, but sexual desire is essentially desire for physical contact itself. It is a bodily desire for the body of another that dominates our mental life for more or less brief periods. Traditional writings were correct to emphasize the purely physical or animal aspect of sex; they were wrong only in condemning it. This characterization of sex as an intensely pleasurable physical activity and acute physical desire may seem to some to capture only its barest level. But it is worth distinguishing and focusing upon this least common denominator in order to avoid the false views of sexual morality and perversion which emerge from thinking that sex is essentially something else.

II

We may turn then to what sex is not, to the arguments regarding supposed conceptual connections between sex and other activities which it is necessary to conceptually distinguish. The most comprehensible attempt to build an extraneous purpose into the sex act identifies that purpose as reproduction, its primary biological function. While this may be "nature's" purpose, it certainly need not be ours (the analogy with eating, while sometimes overworked, is pertinent here). While this identification may once have had a rational basis which also grounded the identification of the value and morality of sex with that applicable to reproduction and childrearing, the development of contraception rendered the connection weak. Methods of contraception are by now so familiar and so widely used that it is not necessary to dwell upon the changes wrought by these developments in the concept of sex itself and in a rational sexual ethic dependent upon that concept. In the past, the ever-present possibility of children rendered the concepts of sex and sexual morality different from those required at present. There may be good reasons, if the presence and care of both mother and father are beneficial to children, for restricting reproduction to marriage. Insofar as society has a legitimate role in protecting children's interests, it may be justified in giving marriage a legal status, although this question is complicated by the fact (among others) that children born to single mothers deserve no penalties. In any case, the point here is simply that these questions are irrelevant at the present time to those regarding the morality of sex and its potential social regulation. (Further connections with marriage will be discussed below.)

It is obvious that the desire for sex is not necessarily a desire to reproduce, that the psychological manifestation has become, if it were not always, distinct from its biological roots. There are many parallels, as previously mentioned, with other natural functions. The pleasures of eating and exercising are to a large extent independent of their roles in nourishment or health (as the junk-food industry discovered with a vengeance). Despite the obvious parallel with sex, there is still a tendency for many to think that sex acts which can be reproductive are, if

not more moral or less immoral, at least more natural. These categories
of morality and "naturalness," or normality, are not to be identified with
each other, as will be argued below, and neither is applicable to sex by
virtue of its connection to reproduction. The tendency to identify reproduction as the conceptually connected end of sex is most prevalent
now in the pronouncements of the Catholic church. There the assumed
analysis is clearly tied to a restrictive sexual morality according to which
acts become immoral and unnatural when they are not oriented toward
reproduction, a morality which has independent roots in the Christian
sexual ethic as it derives from Paul. However, the means-end analysis
fails to generate a consistent sexual ethic: homosexual and oral-genital
sex is condemned while kissing or caressing, acts equally unlikely to lead
in themselves to fertilization, even when properly characterized as sexual according to our definition, are not.

III

Before discussing further relations of means-end analyses to false or inconsistent sexual ethics and concepts of perversion, I turn to other examples of these analyses. One common position views sex as essentially
an expression of love or affection between the partners. It is generally
recognized that there are other types of love besides sexual, but sex itself
is taken as an expression of one type, sometimes termed "romantic"
love.[1] Various factors again ought to weaken this identification. First,
there are other types of love besides that which it is appropriate to express sexually, and "romantic" love itself can be expressed in many other
ways. I am not denying that sex can take on heightened value and meaning when it becomes a vehicle for the expression of feelings of love or
tenderness, but so can many other usually mundane activities such as
getting up early to make breakfast on Sunday, cleaning the house, and
so on. Second, sex itself can be used to communicate many other emotions besides love, and, as I will argue below, can communicate nothing
in particular and still be good sex.

On a deeper level, an internal tension is bound to result from an identification of sex, which I have described as a physical-psychological desire, with love as a long-term, deep emotional relationship between two
individuals. As this type of relationship, love is permanent, at least in intent, and more or less exclusive. A normal person cannot deeply love
more than a few individuals even in a lifetime. We may be suspicious that
those who attempt or claim to love many love them weakly if at all. Yet,
fleeting sexual desire can arise in relation to a variety of other individuals one finds sexually attractive. It may even be, as some have claimed,
that sexual desire in humans naturally seeks variety, while this is obvi-

ously false of love. For this reason, monogamous sex, even if justified, almost always represents a sacrifice or the exercise of self-control on the part of the spouses, while monogamous love generally does not. There is no such thing as casual love in the sense in which I intend the term "love." It may occasionally happen that a spouse falls deeply in love with someone else (especially when sex is conceived in terms of love), but this is relatively rare in comparison to passing sexual desires for others; and while the former often indicates a weakness or fault in the marriage relation, the latter does not.

If love is indeed more exclusive in its objects than is sexual desire, this explains why those who view sex as essentially an expression of love would again tend to hold a repressive or restrictive sexual ethic. As in the case of reproduction, there may be good reasons for reserving the total commitment of deep love to the context of marriage and family—the normal personality may not withstand additional divisions of ultimate commitment and allegiance. There is no question that marriage itself is best sustained by a deep relation of love and affection; and even if love is not naturally monogamous, the benefits of family units to children provide additional reason to avoid serious commitments elsewhere which weaken family ties. It can be argued similarly that monogamous sex strengthens families by restricting and at the same time guaranteeing an outlet for sexual desire in marriage. But there is more force to the argument that recognition of a clear distinction between sex and love in society would help avoid disastrous marriages which result from adolescent confusion of the two when sexual desire is mistaken for permanent love, and would weaken damaging jealousies which arise in marriages in relation to passing sexual desires. The love and affection of a sound marriage certainly differs from the adolescent romantic variety, which is often a mere substitute for sex in the context of a repressive sexual ethic.

In fact, the restrictive sexual ethic tied to the means-end analysis in terms of love again has failed to be consistent. At least, it has not been applied consistently, but forms part of the double standard which has curtailed the freedom of women. It is predictable in light of this history that some women would now advocate using sex as another kind of means, as a political weapon or as a way to increase unjustly denied power and freedom. The inconsistency in the sexual ethic typically attached to the sex-love analysis, according to which it has generally been taken with a grain of salt when applied to men, is simply another example of the impossibility of tailoring a plausible moral theory in this area to a conception of sex which builds in conceptually extraneous factors.

I am not suggesting here that sex ought never to be connected with love or that it is not a more significant and valuable activity when it is. Nor am I denying that individuals need love as much as sex and perhaps emotionally need at least one complete relationship which encompasses both. Just as sex can express love and take on heightened significance when it does, so love is often naturally accompanied by an intermittent desire for sex. But again love is accompanied appropriately by desires for other shared activities as well. What makes the desire for sex seem more intimately connected with love is the intimacy which is seen to be a natural feature of mutual sex acts. Like love, sex is held to lay one bare psychologically as well as physically. Sex is unquestionably intimate, but beyond that the psychological toll often attached may be a function of the restrictive sexual ethic itself, rather than a legitimate apology for it. The intimacy involved in love is psychologically consuming in a generally healthy way, while the psychological tolls of sexual relations, often including embarrassment as a correlate of intimacy, are too often the result of artificial sexual ethics and taboos. The intimacy involved in both love and sex is insufficient in any case in light of previous points to render a means-end analysis in these terms appropriate.

IV

In recent articles, Thomas Nagel and Robert Solomon, who recognize that sex is not merely a means to communicate love, nevertheless retain the form of this analysis while broadening it. For Solomon, sex remains a means of communicating (he explicitly uses the metaphor of body language), although the feelings that can be communicated now include, in addition to love and tenderness, domination, dependence, anger, trust, and so on.[2] Nagel does not refer explicitly to communication, but his analysis is similar in that he views sex as a complex form of interpersonal awareness in which desire itself is consciously communicated on several different levels. In sex, according to his analysis, two people are aroused by each other, aware of the other's arousal, and further aroused by this awareness.[3] Such multileveled conscious awareness of one's own and the other's desire is taken as the norm of a sexual relation, and this model is therefore close to that which views sex as a means of interpersonal communication.

Solomon's analysis is beset by the same difficulties as those pointed out in relation to the narrower sex-love concept. Just as love can be communicated by many activities other than sex, which do not therefore become properly analyzed as essentially vehicles of communication (making breakfast, cleaning the house, and so on), the same is true of the other feelings mentioned by Solomon. Domination can be communicated through economic manipulation, trust by a joint savings account. Driving a car can be simultaneously expressing anger, pride, joy, and so on. We may, in fact, communicate or express feelings in anything we do, but this does not make everything we do into language. Driving a car is not to be defined as an automotive means of communication, although with a little ingenuity we might work out an automotive vocabulary (tailgating as an expression of aggression or impatience; beating another car away from a stoplight as expressing domination) to match the vocabulary of "body language." That one can communicate various feelings during sex acts does not make these acts merely or primarily a means of communicating.

More importantly, to analyze sex as a means of communication is to overlook the intrinsic nature and value of the act itself. Sex is not a gesture or series of gestures, in fact not necessarily a means to any other end, but a physical activity intensely pleasurable in itself. When a language is used, the symbols normally have no importance in themselves; they function merely as vehicles for what can be communicated by them. Furthermore, skill in the use of language is a technical achievement that must be carefully learned; if better sex is more successful communication by means of a more skillful use of body language, then we had all better be well schooled in the vocabulary and grammar. Solomon's analysis, which uses the language metaphor, suggests the appropriateness of a sex-manual approach, the substitution of a bit of technological prowess for the natural pleasure of the unforced surrender to feeling and desire.

It may be that Solomon's position could be improved by using the analogy of music rather than that of language, as an aesthetic form of communication. Music might be thought of as a form of aesthetic communicating, in which the experience of the "phonemes" themselves is generally pleasing. And listening to music is perhaps more of a sexual experience than having someone talk to you. Yet, it seems to me that insofar as music is aesthetic and pleasing in itself, it is not best conceived as primarily a means for communicating specific feelings. Such an analysis does injustice to aesthetic experience in much the same way as the sex-communication analysis debases sexual experience itself.[4]

For Solomon, sex that is not a totally self-conscious communicative act tends toward vulgarity,[5] whereas I would have thought it the other way around. This is another illustration of the tendency of means-end analyses to condemn what appears perfectly natural or normal sex on my account. Both Solomon and Nagel use their definitions, however, not primarily to stipulate moral norms for sex, as we saw in earlier analyses, but to define norms against which to measure perversion. Once again, neither is capable of generating consistency or reflective equilibrium with our firm intuitions as to what counts as subnormal sex, the problem being that both build factors into their norms which are extraneous to an unromanticized view of normal sexual desire and activity. If perversion represents a breakdown in communication, as Solomon maintains, then any unsuccessful or misunderstood advance should count as perverted.

Furthermore, sex between husband and wife married for several years, or between any partners already familiar with each other, would be, if not perverted, nevertheless subnormal or trite and dull, in that the communicative content would be minimal in lacking all novelty. In fact, the pleasures of sex need not wear off with familiarity, as they would if dependent upon the communicative content of the feelings. Finally, rather than a release or relief from physical desire through a substitute imaginative outlet, masturbation would become a way of practicing or rehearsing one's technique or vocabulary on oneself, or simply a way of talking to oneself, as Solomon himself says.[6]

Nagel fares no better in the implications of his overintellectualized norm. Spontaneous and heated sex between two familiar partners may well lack the complex conscious multileveled interpersonal awareness of which he speaks without being in the least perverted. The egotistical desire that one's partner be aroused by one's own desire does not seem a primary element of the sexual urge, and during sex acts one may like one's partner to be sometimes active and aroused, sometimes more passive. Just as sex can be more significant when love is communicated, so it sometimes be heightened by an awareness of the other's desire. But at other times this awareness of an avid desire of one's partner can be merely distracting. The conscious awareness to which Nagel refers may actually impede the immersion in the physical of which I spoke above, just as may concentration upon one's "vocabulary" or technique. Sex is a way of relating to another, but primarily a physical rather than intellectual way. For Nagel, the ultimate in degeneration or perversion would have to be what he calls "mutual epidermal stimulation"[7] without mutual awareness of each other's state of mind. But this sounds like normal, if not ideal, sex to me (perhaps only a minimal description of it). His model certainly seems more appropriate to a sophisticated seduction scene than to the sex act itself,[8] which according to the model would often have to count as a subnormal anticlimax to the intellectual foreplay. While Nagel's account resembles Solomon's means-end analysis of sex, here the sex act itself does not even qualify as a preferred or central means to the end of interpersonal communication.

V .

I have now criticized various types of analysis sharing or suggesting a common means-end form. I have suggested that analyses of this form relate to attempts to limit moral or natural sex to that which fulfills some purpose or function extraneous to basic sexual desire. The attempts to brand forms of sex outside the idealized models as immoral or perverted fail to achieve consistency with intuitions that they themselves do not directly question. The reproductive model brands oral-genital sex a deviation, but cannot account for kissing or holding hands; the communication account holds voyeurism to be perverted but cannot accommodate sex acts without much conscious thought or seductive nonphysical foreplay; the sex-love model makes most sexual desire seem degrading or base. The first and last condemn extramarital sex on the sound but irrelevant grounds that reproduction and deep commitment are best confined to family contexts. The romanticization of sex and the confusion of sexual desire with love operate in both directions: sex outside the context of romantic love is repressed; once it is repressed, partners become more difficult to find and sex becomes romanticized further, out of proportion to its real value for the individual.

What all these analyses share in addition to a common form is accordance with and perhaps derivation from the Platonic-Christian moral tradition, according to which the animal or purely physical element of humans is the source of immorality, and plain sex in the sense I defined it is an expression of this element, hence in itself to be condemned. All the analyses examined seem to seek a distance from sexual desire itself in attempting to extend it conceptually beyond the physical. The love and communication analyses seek refinement or intellectualization of the desire; plain physical sex becomes vulgar, and too straightforward sexual encounters without an aura of respectable cerebral communicative content are to be avoided. Solomon explicitly argues that sex cannot be a "mere" appetite, his argument being that if it were, subway exhibitionism and other vulgar forms would be pleasing.[9] This fails to recognize that sexual desire can be focused or selective at the same time as being physical. Lower animals are not attracted by every other member of their species, either. Rancid food forced down one's throat is not pleasing, but that certainly fails to show that hunger is not a physical appetite. Sexual desire lets us know that we are physical beings and, indeed, animals; this is why traditional Platonic morality is so thorough in its condemnation. Means-end analyses continue to reflect this tradition, sometimes unwittingly. They show that in conceptualizing sex it is still difficult, despite years of so-called revolution in this area, to free ourselves from the lingering suspicion that plain sex as physical desire is an expression of our "lower selves," that yielding to our animal natures is subhuman or vulgar.

VI

Having criticized these analyses for the sexual ethics and concepts of perversion they imply, it remains to contrast my account along these lines. To the question of what morality might be implied by my analysis, the answer is that there are no moral implications whatever. Any analysis of sex which imputes a moral character to sex acts in themselves is wrong for that reason. There is no morality intrinsic to sex, although general moral rules apply to the treatment of others in sex acts as they apply to all human relations. We can speak of a sexual ethic as we can speak of a business ethic, without implying that business in itself is either moral or immoral or that special rules are required to judge business practices which are not derived from rules that apply elsewhere as well. Sex is not in itself a moral category, although like business it invariably places us into relations with others in which moral rules apply. It gives us opportunity to do what is otherwise recognized as wrong, to harm others, deceive them, or manipulate them against their wills. Just as the fact that an act is sexual in itself never renders it wrong or adds to its wrongness if it is wrong on other grounds (sexual acts toward minors are wrong on other grounds, as will be argued below), so no wrong act is to be excused because done from a sexual motive. If a "crime of passion" is to be excused, it would have to be on grounds of temporary insanity rather than sexual context (whether insanity does constitute a legitimate excuse for certain actions is too big a topic to argue here). Sexual motives are among others which may become deranged, and the fact that they are sexual has no bearing in itself on the moral character, whether negative or exculpatory, of the actions deriving from them. Whatever might be true of war, it is certainly not the case that all's fair in love or sex.

Our first conclusion regarding morality and sex is therefore that no conduct otherwise immoral should be excused because it is sexual conduct, and nothing in sex is immoral unless condemned by rules which apply elsewhere as well. The last clause requires further clarification. Sexual conduct can be governed by particular rules relating only to sex itself. But these precepts must be implied by general moral rules when these are applied to specific sexual relations or types of conduct. The same is true of rules of fair business, ethical medicine, or courtesy in driving a car. In the latter case, particular acts on the road may be reprehensible, such as tailgating or passing on the right, which seem to bear no resemblance as actions to any outside the context of highway safety. Nevertheless, their immorality derives from the fact that they place others in danger, a circumstance which, when avoidable, is to be condemned in any context. This structure of general and specifically applicable rules describes a reasonable sexual ethic as well. To take an extreme case, rape is always a sexual act and it is always immoral. A rule against rape can therefore be considered an obvious part of sexual morality which has no bearing on nonsexual conduct. But the immorality of rape derives from its being an extreme violation of a person's body, of the right not to be humiliated, and of the general moral prohibition against using other persons against their wills, not from the fact that it is a sexual act.

The application elsewhere of general moral rules to sexual conduct is further complicated by the fact that it will be relative to the particular desires and preferences of one's partner (these may be influenced by and hence in some sense include misguided beliefs about sexual morality itself). This means that there will be fewer specific rules in the area of sexual ethics than in other areas of conduct, such as driving cars, where the relativity of preference is irrelevant to the prohibition of objectively dangerous conduct. More reliance will have to be placed upon the general moral rule, which in this area holds simply that the preferences, desires, and interests of one's partner or potential partner ought to be taken into account. This rule is certainly not specifically formulated to govern sexual relations; it is a form of the central principle of morality itself. But when applied to sex, it prohibits certain actions, such as molestation of children, which cannot be categorized as violations of the rule without at the same time being classified as sexual. I believe this last case is the closest we can come to an action which is wrong *because* it is sexual, but even here its wrongness is better characterized as deriving from the detrimental effects such behavior can have on the future emotional and sexual life of the naive victims, and from the fact that such behavior therefore involves manipulation of innocent persons without regard for their interests. Hence, this case also involves violation of a general moral rule which applies elsewhere as well.

Aside from faulty conceptual analyses of sex and the influence of the Platonic moral tradition, there are two more plausible reasons for thinking that there are moral dimensions intrinsic to sex acts per se. The first is that such acts are normally intensely pleasurable. According to a hedonistic, utilitarian moral theory they therefore should be at least prima facie morally right, rather than morally neutral in themselves. To me this seems incorrect and reflects unfavorably on the ethical theory in question. The pleasure intrinsic to sex acts is a good, but not, it seems to me, a good with much positive moral significance. Certainly I can have no duty to pursue such pleasure myself, and while it may be nice to give pleasure of any form to others, there is no ethical requirement to do so, given my right over my own body. The exception relates to the context of sex acts themselves, when one partner derives pleasure from the other and ought to return the favor. This duty to reciprocate takes us out of the domain of hedonistic utilitarianism, however, and into a Kantian moral framework, the central principles of which call for such reciprocity in human relations. Since independent moral judgments regarding sexual activities constitute one area in which ethical theories are to be tested, these observations indicate here, as I believe others indicate elsewhere, the fertility of the Kantian, as opposed to the utilitarian, principle in reconstructing reasoned moral consciousness.

It may appear from this alternative Kantian viewpoint that sexual acts must be at least prima facie wrong in themselves. This is because they invariably involve at different stages the manipulation of one's partner for one's own pleasure, which might appear to be prohibited on the formulation of Kant's principle which holds that one ought not to treat another as a means to such private ends. A more realistic rendering of this formulation, however, one which recognizes its intended equivalence to the first universalizability principle, admits no such absolute prohibition. Many human relations, most economic transactions for example, involve using other individuals for personal benefit. These relations are immoral only when they are one-sided, when the benefits are not mutual, or when the transactions are not freely and rationally endorsed by all parties. The same holds true of sexual acts. The central principle governing them is the Kantian demand for reciprocity in sexual relations. In order to comply with the second formulation of the categorical imperative, one must recognize the subjectivity of one's partner (not merely by being aroused by her or his desire, as Nagel describes). Even in an act which by its nature "objectifies" the other, one recognizes a partner as a subject with demands and desires by yielding to those desires, by allowing oneself to be a sexual object as well, by giving pleasure or ensuring that the pleasures of the acts are mutual. It is this kind of reciprocity which forms the basis for morality in sex, which distinguishes right acts from wrong in this area as in others. (Of course, prior to sex acts one must gauge their effects upon potential partners and take these longer-range interests into account.)

VII

I suggested earlier that in addition to generating confusion regarding the rightness or wrongness of sex acts, false conceptual analyses of the means-end form cause confusion about the value of sex to the individual. My account recognizes the satisfaction of desire and the pleasure this brings as the central psychological function of the sex act for the individual. Sex affords us a paradigm of pleasure, but not a cornerstone of value. For most of us it is not only a needed outlet for desire but also the most enjoyable form of recreation we know. Its value is nevertheless easily mistaken by being confused with that of love, when it is taken as essentially an expression of that emotion. Although intense, the pleasures of sex are brief and repetitive rather than cumulative. They give value to the specific acts which generate them, but not the lasting kind of value which enhances one's whole life. The briefness of the pleasures contributes to their intensity (or perhaps their intensity makes them necessarily brief), but it also relegates them to the periphery of most rational plans for the good life.

By contrast, love typically develops over a long-term relation; while its pleasures may be less intense and physical, they are of more cumulative value. The importance of love to the individual may well be central in a rational system of value. And it has perhaps an even deeper moral significance relating to the identification with the interests of another person, which broadens one's possible relationships with others as well. Marriage is again important in preserving this relation between adults and children, which seems as important to the adults as it is to the children in broadening concerns which have a tendency to become selfish. Sexual desire, by contrast, is desire for another which is nevertheless essentially self-regarding. Sexual pleasure is certainly a good for the individual, and for many it may be necessary in order for them to function in a reasonably cheerful way. But it bears little relation to those other values just discussed, to which some analyses falsely suggest a conceptual connection.

VIII

While my initial analysis lacks moral implications in itself, as it should, it does suggest by contrast a concept of sexual perversion. Since the concept of perversion is itself a sexual concept, it will always be defined relative to some definition of normal sex; and any conception of the norm will imply a contrary notion of perverse forms. The concept suggested by my account again differs sharply from those implied by the means-end analyses examined above. Perversion does not represent a deviation from the reproductive function (or kissing would be perverted), from a loving relationship (or most sexual desire and many heterosexual acts would be perverted), or from efficiency in communicating (or unsuccessful seduction attempts would be perverted). It is a deviation from a norm, but the norm in question is merely statistical. Of course, not all sexual acts that are statistically unusual are perverted—a three-hour continuous sexual act would be unusual but not necessarily abnormal in the requisite sense. The abnormality in question must relate to the *form of the desire* itself in order to constitute sexual perversion; for example, desire, not for contact with another, but for merely looking, for harming or being harmed, for contact with items of clothing. The concept of sexual abnormality is that suggested by my definition of normal sex in terms of its typical desire. However, not all unusual desires qualify either, only those with the typical physical sexual effects upon the individual who satisfies them. These effects, such as erection in males, were not built into the original definition of sex in terms of sexual desire, for they do not always occur in activities that are properly characterized as sexual, say, kissing for the pleasure of it. But they do seem to bear a closer relation to the definition of activities as perverted. (For those who consider only genital sex sexual, we could build such symptoms into a narrower definition, then speaking of sex in a broad sense as well as "proper" sex.)

Solomon and Nagel disagree with this statistical notion of perversion. For them the concept is evaluative rather than statistical. I do not deny that the term "perverted" is often used evaluatively (and purely emotively for that matter), or that it has a negative connotation for the average speaker. I do deny that we can find a norm, other than that of statistically usual desire, against which all and only activities that properly count as sexual perversions can be contrasted. Perverted sex is simply abnormal sex, and if the norm is not to be an idealized or romanticized extraneous end or purpose, it must express the way human sexual desires usually manifest themselves. Of course not all norms in other areas of discourse need be statistical in this way. Physical health is an example of a relatively clear norm which does not seem to depend upon the numbers of healthy people. But the concept in this case achieves its clarity through the connection of physical health with other clearly desirable physical functions and characteristics, for example, living longer. In the case of sex, that which is statistically abnormal is not necessarily incapacitating in other ways, and yet these abnormal desires with sexual effects upon their subject do count as perverted to the degree to which their objects deviate from usual ones. The connotations of the concept of perversion beyond those connected with abnormality or statistical deviation derive more from the attitudes of those likely to call certain acts perverted than from specifiable features of the acts themselves. These connotations add to the concept of abnormality that of *sub*normality, but there is no norm against which the latter can be measured intelligibly in accord with all and only acts intuitively called perverted.

The only proper evaluative norms relating to sex involve degrees of pleasure in the acts and moral norms, but neither of these scales coincides with statistical degrees of abnormality, according to which perversion is to be measured. The three parameters operate independently (this was implied for the first two when it was held above that the pleasure of sex is a good, but not necessarily a moral good). Perverted sex may be more or less enjoyable to particular individuals than normal sex, and more or less moral, depending upon the particular relations involved. Raping a sheep may be more perverted than raping a woman, but certainly not more condemnable morally.[10] It is nevertheless true that the evaluative connotations attaching to the term "perverted" derive partly from the fact that most people consider perverted sex highly immoral. Many such acts are forbidden by long-standing taboos, and it is sometimes difficult to distinguish what is forbidden from what is immoral. Others, such as sadistic acts, are genuinely immoral, but again not at all because of their connection with sex or abnormality. The principles which condemn these acts would condemn them equally if they were common and nonsexual. It is not true that we properly could continue to consider acts perverted which were found to be very common practice across societies. Such acts, if harmful, might continue to be condemned properly as immoral, but it was just shown that the immorality of an act does not vary with its degree of perversion. If not harmful, common acts previously considered abnormal might continue to be called perverted for a time by the moralistic minority; but the term when applied to such cases would retain only its emotive negative connotation without consistent logical criteria for application. It would represent merely prejudiced moral judgments.

To adequately explain why there is a tendency to so deeply condemn perverted acts would require a treatise in psychology beyond the scope of this paper. Part of the reason undoubtedly relates to the tradition of repressive sexual ethics and false conceptions of sex; another part to the fact that all abnormality seems to disturb and fascinate us at the same time. The former explains why sexual perversion is more abhorrent to many than other forms of abnormality; the latter indicates why we tend to have an emotive and evaluative reaction to perversion in the first place. It may be, as has been suggested according to a Freudian line,[11] that our uneasiness derives from latent desires we are loath to admit, but this thesis takes us into psychological issues I am not competent to judge. Whatever the psychological explanation, it suffices to point out here that the conceptual connection between perversion and genuine or consistent moral evaluation is spurious and again suggested by misleading means-end idealizations of the concept of sex.

The position I have taken in this paper against those concepts is not totally new. Something similar to it is found in Freud's view of sex, which of course was genuinely revolutionary, and in the body of writings deriving from Freud to the present time. But in his revolt against romanticized and repressive conceptions, Freud went too far—from a refusal to view sex as merely a means to a view of it as the end of all human behavior, although sometimes an elaborately disguised end. This pansexualism led to the thesis (among others) that repression was indeed an inevitable and necessary part of social regulation of any form, a strange consequence of a position that began by opposing the repressive aspects of the means-end view. Perhaps the time finally has arrived when we can achieve a reasonable middle ground in this area, at least in philosophy if not in society.

Study Questions

1. Goldman defines "sexual activity" as acts that "tend to fulfill" sexual desire. Devise counterexamples to this definition that turn either on (a) the vagueness of "tends to fulfill" or, instead, (b) the purported link between activity and desire. Do these counterexamples deal a decisive blow to Goldman's conceptual analysis?

2. Suppose that the ancient Greek philosopher Aristotle was right that "every art and inquiry" has an aim. Does Goldman run afoul of Aristotle's insight by understanding sexual desire as, at root, the desire for the pleasure of physical contact, and not in terms of other goals, such as the expression of love or procreation? Review what Goldman says about the appropriateness of his "means-ends" terminology.

3. Though disagreeing with Nagel (chapter 3) on several counts, Goldman identifies, as Nagel does, another person (or person's body) as the locus, object, or source of sexual pleasure. What are the drawbacks, if any, to the conceptual requirement that sexuality is, ontologically, a relation between two people? Or does this requirement make all the sense in the world to you? If so, how do you understand solitary masturbation (see chapter 6)?

4. Goldman admits that if sexual desire is merely the desire for the pleasure of contact with another person's body, then sexual desire and its generated sexual activity at least prima facie involve treating the other person, in a negative moral sense, as an object or instrument. Thus sexual desire and activity seem to violate the ethics of Immanuel Kant, according to which it is morally wrong to treat other people merely as means or tools. Goldman tries to escape this conclusion. Explain how he does so and evaluate the sexual morality that he espouses. (For some discussion of this question, see chapter 18—after trying the question on your own.)

5. There may be some tension between Goldman's analysis of sexual desire and his account of sexual perversion as "statistically abnormal desire." Consider voyeurism, for example. On Goldman's view, is voyeurism a sexual perversion, because it involves an unusual sexual desire (to watch from a distance), or is it not even sexual to begin with, because it does not involve the desire for physical contact? What about gay sex for having the wrong *form*?

Notes

1. Even Bertrand Russell, whose writing in this area was a model of rationality, at least for its period, tends to make this identification and to condemn plain sex in the absence of love: "sex intercourse apart from love has little value, and is to be regarded primarily as experimentation with a view to love." *Marriage and Morals* (New York: Bantam, 1959), 87.

2. Robert Solomon, "Sex and Perversion," in Robert Baker and Frederick Elliston, eds., *Philosophy and Sex*, 1st ed. (Buffalo, N.Y.: Prometheus, 1975), 268–87.

3. Thomas Nagel, "Sexual Perversion," *Journal of Philosophy* 66, no. 1 (1960): 5–17 (in this volume, chap. 3).

4. Sex might be considered (at least partially) as communication in a very broad sense in the same way as performing ensemble music, in the sense that there is in both ideally a communion or perfectly shared experience with another. This is, however, one possible ideal view whose central feature is not necessary to sexual acts or desire per se. And in emphasizing the communication of specific feelings by means of body language, the analysis under consideration narrows the end to one clearly extrinsic to plain and even good sex.

5. Solomon, "Sex and Perversion," 284–85.

6. Ibid., 283. One is reminded of Woody Allen's rejoinder to praise of his technique: "I practice a lot when I'm alone."

7. Nagel, "Sex and Perversion," 15 [original page number; this passage is not in the later version of Nagel's essay that is reprinted in this volume].

8. Janice Moulton made the same point in a paper at the Pacific APA meeting, March 1976 (in this volume, chapter 4).

9. Solomon, "Sex and Perversion," 285.

10. The example is like one from Sara Ruddick, "Better Sex," in *Philosophy and Sex*, ed. Baker and Elliston, 96.

11. See Michael Slote, "Inapplicable Concepts and Sexual Perversion," in *Philosophy and Sex*, ed. Baker and Elliston, 261–67.

Chapter 6

MASTURBATION, AGAIN

Alan Soble

This essay on masturbation by **Alan Soble** *discusses both conceptual and normative questions. Fixing on the "correct" meaning of the word "masturbation" is complicated by the fact that there are at least three types: solitary, dual, and mutual masturbation. It turns out—which is not surprising, since we are doing philosophy—that defining "masturbation" is more difficult than we might have thought. Some of the problems in doing so might be avoided by acknowledging that "mutual masturbation" is perhaps a misnomer, not really being a case of masturbation at all. Moral questions about masturbation arise primarily because some philosophies of sex, in particular the Roman Catholic, insist that to be morally acceptable, sexual acts must bear some relation to procreation. On this score, not only masturbation but also same-sex sexual acts fail the moral test. Masturbation, as the author writes, "is queer." But, as the essay demonstrates, not even liberal philosophies of sex have been hospitable to masturbation, either ontologically or normatively. Why a harmless act that brings pleasure, and is engaged in by most human beings at some time or another, continually requires defense is an intriguing question.*

This vice, which shame and timidity find so convenient, has a particular attraction for lively imaginations. It allows them to dispose, so to speak, of the whole female sex at their will, and to make any beauty who tempts them serve their pleasure without the need of first obtaining her consent.

Jean-Jacques Rousseau[1]

If your right hand causes you to sin, cut it off and throw it away. It is better
for you to lose one part of your body than for your whole body to go into
hell.

    Jesus (Matthew 5:30)

Masturbation is queer. Like sex I've had with an admired and intimate lover, it is sex with someone I care about, whose satisfaction
and welfare are important to me. It is incestuous, since I am a blood-
member of my own family. When I was married, it was adulterous, because it was sex with someone who was not my spouse. It is gay: a man (in
my case) sexually pleases a man. It was pederastic, when I did it as a
youngster. It is sex I might fall into inadvertently ("if you shake it more
than twice, you're playing with it"); at those times I do not fully consent
to it, but it is also not against my will. When I do it while fantasizing, it is,
says Rousseau, the promiscuous rape of every man, woman, beast, or
doorknob to which I take a fancy. No wonder, then, that we advertise our
marriages and brag about our affairs, but keep silent about our masturbatory acts. The sexual revolution (is it over, *already*?) made sexual activity outside matrimony socially acceptable; it encouraged the liberal
toleration and the postmodernist celebration of homosexual lifestyles; it
breathed respectable life into the colorful practices of the sons and
daughters of the Marquis de Sade.[2] But to call a man a "jerk off" is still
strongly derogatory, and an accusation that masturbating women,
throughout history, have avoided. Masturbation, at least the male variety, is the black sheep of the family of sex. Women have no seed so easy
to waste.

The Concept

How to define "masturbation," or get at its essence? A paradigm case
gives us something to start with: a person in a private place manually
rubs the penis or clitoris and eventually reaches orgasm (perhaps aided
by fantasy or pornography). But one could masturbate in public, on a
bus, although that will get you into legal trouble. Your hands do not have
to be used, if the sexually sensitive areas of the body can be pressed
against the back of a horse, the seat of a bicycle or motorcycle, rugs, or
pillows. Further, orgasm need not be attained, nor need it be the goal.
Prolonged sexual pleasure itself is often the point of masturbation, and
that might be curtailed by orgasm. Not even the clitoris or penis need receive the most attention (the anus and nipples can be the target body
parts). What remains in the paradigm case? Perhaps this: the person
who, by touching the sexually sensitive areas of the body causally produces the sensations, is the same person who experiences them. The

rubber is the rubbed. Masturbation is, then, the "solitary vice" of "self-abuse."

But *mutual* masturbation would be conceptually impossible if masturbation were logically solitary, and we have a paradigm case of mutual masturbation: two people rubbing each other between the legs. Now, if it is conceptually possible for two persons X and Y to masturbate each other, it must also be conceptually possible for X to masturbate Y, while Y simply relaxes and receives this attention, not doing anything to or for X. To give to another person, or to receive from another person, what is sometimes called a "hand job" is to engage in half of a mutual masturbation. "To masturbate," then, is both transitive and intransitive. Similarly, I can both respect or deceive myself and respect or deceive another person. Reflexivity, then, may be sufficient, but it does not seem to be necessary, for a sexual act to be masturbatory.

But, if so, an analytic problem arises: why is mutual masturbation masturbation? (*Dual* masturbation, in which X masturbates X and Y masturbates Y in each other's presence, or while talking on the telephone, does not present this problem.) Saying—call this Attempt One—that the paradigm case of mutual masturbation is masturbatory just because it involves the hands and genitals is awkward. It entails that all solitary sex acts are masturbatory, even those that do not involve the hands and genitals, while paired sexual acts are masturbatory exactly when they do involve the hands and the genitals. So X's tweaking her own nipples when she is alone would be masturbatory, Y's doing it to X when they are together is *not* masturbatory, yet Y's manually tweaking X's clitoris *is* masturbatory. These implications of Attempt One are chaotic; there must be (we optimistically hope) a better way to distinguish paired masturbatory from paired nonmasturbatory sexual acts, if there is a distinction at all.

Another way (Attempt Two) to distinguish paired masturbatory sexual acts, or mutual masturbation, from paired nonmasturbatory sexual acts is to contrast sexual acts that do not involve "insertion" and those that do. The idea is that without the bodily insertion of something, somewhere, no mixing of two fleshes occurs, and the participants remain physically isolated (the way the solitary masturbator is physically isolated). On this view, the paradigm case of mutual masturbation, in which the persons rub each other between the legs, and the hand job, are both masturbatory because no insertion occurs. Male-female coitus and male-male anal coitus are not masturbatory because they involve insertion. Further, X's fellating Y is not masturbatory (which seems correct), and the view plausibly implies that coitus between a human male and a female sheep, or between a human female and a male dog, is not masturbatory—assuming that the man or woman is not engaged in a *solitary* activity if an animal is involved. These sexual acts are not masturbatory because insertion occurs. The view also implies that frottage in a

crowded subway car is masturbatory, even though it requires the presence of another person, the unwilling victim, and that tribadism is a mutually masturbatory, because no insertion occurs in either case. But distinguishing between paired masturbatory and paired nonmasturbatory
sexual activity by relying on insertion is inadequate. In mutual masturbation, insertion of one person's fingers into the other's vagina might
occur, and that some insertion takes place should not imply that the act
is not mutual masturbation. Further, to claim that cunnilingus is masturbatory when and only when it does not involve the insertion of the
tongue into the vagina implies that one continuous act of cunnilingus
changes from not masturbatory to masturbatory and back again often
within a few minutes. Attempt Two also has chaotic and counterintuitive
implications. What about a male who punctures a hole in a watermelon
to make room for his penis, or a female who reaches for her g-spot with
a zucchini inside her vagina? These acts are masturbatory yet involve "insertion."

Some of these problems can be avoided by narrowing what counts as
"insertion" (Attempt Three). Masturbation might be characterized as
sexual activity not involving the insertion of a real penis into a hole of a
living being. Then the watermelon and zucchini cases are solved. But it
seems to follow that paired lesbian sexuality, which does not involve a
penis, is masturbatory,[3] while paired sexual acts (fellatio and anal intercourse) engaged in by male homosexuals are not. This conclusion
doesn't make any sense at all.

Were we to decide, for which some reason exists, that a male having
intercourse with a sheep is, after all, engaging in a masturbatory act—if
we perceive no difference between this bestiality and his rubbing his penis on a rug or woman's panties (using "solitary" to mean being away
from other *people*)—we could define masturbation even more specifically (Attempt Four) as activity not involving the insertion of a real penis
into a hole of a human being. This refined, scholastic account of masturbation is phallocentric in characterizing sexual acts with reference to
the male organ. As a result, the analysis implies an implausible *conceptual*
double standard: fellatio, oral sex done on a male (whether by a male or
female), is not masturbatory, but cunnilingus, oral sex done on a female
(by a male or female), is always masturbatory. An *evaluative* double standard looms when to this analysis the usual disparagement of masturbation is added: fellatio is "real sex," cunnilingus is a masturbatory fraud.
This refined view is sexist but not heterosexist; its point does not depend
on the sex or gender of the fellator. It is similar to the claim, which is heterosexist but not necessarily sexist, that the paradigm case of a natural,
normal, or proper sexual act is male-female coitus. What is conceptually
and normatively emphasized in another view, Attempt Five—the most
specific we can get about "insertion"—is the insertion of a real penis not

into a particular hole of a human being, the vagina. This view suggests that masturbation be understood as any sexual act that is not procreative in its form or potential, whether solitary or paired. "Useless" sexual acts, those that do not have the potential to perpetuate the species, and whose purpose is only to yield pleasure for the participant(s), are masturbatory. If so, our sexual lives contain a *lot* more masturbation than we had thought. *Maybe* this is the right conclusion, that most of our paired sexual acts (plus our solitary acts) are masturbatory, but we would like convincing grounds for it. *Maybe*, though, we should abandon the task to distinguish paired masturbatory from paired nonmasturbatory acts, and jettison the notion of "mutual masturbation" from our sexual discourse as being an archaic, misleading misnomer. But let us stubbornly press forward.

Consider that under certain physical descriptions of paired sexual activity, no difference exists between paired sex and solitary masturbation. The young, precocious, helpful Alexander Portnoy offered his cheating father an exculpating redescription of adultery: "What after all does it consist of? You put your dick some place and moved it back and forth and stuff came out the front. So, Jake, what's the big deal?"[4]

Adulterous coitus is redescribed as solitary masturbation: you put your penis someplace—in your fist—and move it back and forth until it ejaculates. Portnoy's sarcasm has a wider implication: there is no difference between mutual masturbation and heterosexual genital or homosexual (or heterosexual) anal intercourse. *Every* paired sexual act is masturbatory because the rubbing of sensitive areas, the friction of skin against skin, that occurs during mutual masturbation is, from a physical perspective, the same as the rubbing of skin that occurs during intercourse. The only difference is that different parts of the body or patches of skin may be involved, but no one patch of skin has any sexual-ontological privilege over any other. Further, there is only one difference between solitary masturbation and paired masturbation or any paired sexual activity: the number of people who accomplish these physical rubbings. We might have a good reason for concluding that *all* sex is masturbatory.

Further, suppose X engages in some sexual activity with another person Y, and X's arousal is sustained during this physical interaction by X's having private fantasies. This sexual act is solitary and hence masturbatory in the sense that Y is absent from X's sexual consciousness. It is as if X were alone. That which would be arousing X during solitary masturbation (X's fantasies) is doing the same thing for X while X rubs his penis or clitoris on or with Y's body instead of with X's hand. Paired sex, then, even heterosexual genital intercourse, might be seen as masturbation, depending on certain "mental" components of the sexual act. Perhaps, then, "mental" aspects of sexual activity are that which distinguish masturbation from nonmasturbatory sex, even though they are physically the same.

Quite ordinary interpersonal considerations might help here. We might say (Attempt Six) that a sexual act between two people who are concerned not only (or not at all) with her or his own pleasure but also (or only) with the sexual pleasure of the other person is not masturbatory (no matter what physical acts they engage in), while sexual activity in which a person is concerned solely with her or his own pleasure is masturbatory. This view implies that inconsiderate husbands and rapists are the authors of masturbatory acts. It also implies that mutual masturbation is not masturbatory, as long as the touches are meant to produce sexual pleasure not only for the toucher but also for the one being touched. This view is plausible because what might lie at the heart of solitary masturbation is the effort to cause sexual pleasure for the self. So it is not exactly relevant that solitary masturbation is reflexive. For the attempt to produce sexual pleasure for the self can involve other people, animals, the whole universe. Or we might say that acting on and for oneself does not exclude acting on oneself, ultimately, by acting on others. To be sure, in light of the kind of physical creatures we are, attempting to please the self by acting on oneself is easy, because our own bodies are handy, more accessible than the bodies of others. As a result, though, we misleadingly associate masturbation entirely with one form of it, the case in which X touches and sexually pleases X. But producing one's own pleasure can involve other people. Solitary and paired sexual acts are masturbatory, then, to the extent that the actor produces pleasure for the actor; paired sexual activity is not masturbatory when one person tries to produce pleasure for the other.

Note that this notion of masturbation is conceptual, not normative. By itself, it neither praises nor condemns masturbation. That's because we have defined masturbation as sexual activity in which a person is out to provide his or her own sexual pleasure, without adding that such behavior is immoral. We could embrace that moral judgment, but it would be an addition to the conceptual analysis, not a logical implication of it.

Fulfilling Desire

Three contemporary philosophical accounts of sexuality, proffered by thinkers within the sexually liberal tradition, yield the conclusions that solitary masturbation is not a sexual activity at all (Alan Goldman), is perverted sexuality (Thomas Nagel), or is "empty" sexuality (Robert Solomon). These conclusions are surprising, given the pedigree of these philosophers.[5] Let's begin with Alan Goldman's[6] definitions of "sexual desire" and "sexual activity": "Sexual desire is desire for contact with another person's body and for the pleasure which such contact produces; sexual activity is activity which tends to fulfill such desire of the agent."

On Goldman's view, sexual desire is the desire for the pleasure of physical contact itself, nothing else; it does not include a component desire for, say, love, communication, emotional expression, or progeny. Goldman takes himself to be offering a liberating analysis of sexuality that does not tether sex normatively or conceptually to those other things. But while advocating the superiority of his notion of "plain sex," Goldman apparently forgot that masturbation needed protection from the same (conservative) philosophy that requires sexual activity to occur within a loving marriage or to be procreative for it to be morally acceptable. On Goldman's analysis, solitary masturbation is not a sexual activity to begin with, for it does not "tend to fulfill" sexual desire, that is, the desire for contact with another person's body. Solitary masturbation, on this view, is different from mutual masturbation, which does tend to fulfill the desire for contact, since it involves that contact. Goldman seems not to be troubled that on his view solitary masturbation is not a sexual act. But it is funny that masturbation is, for Goldman, not sexual, for the conservative philosophy that he rejects could reply to his account like this: by *reducing* sexuality entirely to the meaningless desire for the pleasure of physical contact ("meaningless" since divorced from love, marriage, and procreation), what Goldman has analyzed as *being* sexual is merely a form of masturbation, even if it occurs between two people.

"Tends to fulfill" in Goldman's analysis of sexual activity presents problems. Goldman intended, I think, a narrow causal reading of this phrase: actually touching another person's body is a sexual act just because by the operation of a simple mechanism the act fulfills the desire for that contact and its pleasure. The qualification "tends to" functions to allow, for example, bungled kisses to count as sexual acts, even though they did not do what they were intended to do. Kisses "tend to fulfill" desire in the sense that they normally and effectively produce pleasure, prevented from doing so only by the odd interfering event (the braces get tangled; the hurrying lips land on the chin). The qualification also allows disappointing sexual activity, which does not bring what anticipation promised, to count as sex. In this sense of "tends to fulfill," solitary masturbation is not sex. Suppose that X sexually desires Y, but Y declines X's invitations, and so X masturbates thinking about Y. Goldman's view is not that X's masturbation satisfies X's desire for contact with Y at least a little bit and hence is a sexual act, even if an inefficient one. X's solitary masturbation is not a sexual act at all, despite the sexual pleasure it yields, unlike the not pleasurable but still sexual bungled kiss that does involve the desired contact.

Suppose we read "tends to fulfill" in a causally broader way. Then giving money to a prostitute—the act of taking bills out of a wallet and handing them to her—might be a sexual act (even if no sexual arousal accompanies the act), because doing so allows the client to (tend to) fulfill his desire for contact with her body. Handing over $100 would be a *more efficient* sexual act than handing over $10. Even on this broader reading, however, solitary masturbation would not be a sexual activity; despite the causal generosity, masturbation is still precluded from fulfilling sexual desire in Goldman's sense. (For similar reasons, masturbating while looking at erotic photographs is not a sexual act.) Indeed, solitary masturbation would be a *contrasexual* act if the more X masturbates, the less time, energy, or interest X has for fulfilling the desire for contact with someone's body.

Goldman does acknowledge one sense in which solitary masturbation is a sexual activity: "Voyeurism or viewing a pornographic movie qualifies as a sexual activity, but only as an imaginative substitute for the real thing. . . . The same is true of masturbation as a sexual activity without a partner." As I read him, Goldman is claiming that masturbation done for its own sake, done only for the specific pleasure it yields, is *not* sexual, since it is not connected with a desire for contact with another's body. (Nor would masturbation be a sex act were it done to produce a sperm sample.) Masturbation is a sexual act only when done as a substitute for the not available "real thing." Even so, on what grounds could Goldman claim that masturbation's being an "imaginative substitute" for a sexual act makes it a sexual act? Being a *substitute for* a kind of act does not generally make something an act of that kind: to eat soyburger as a beef substitute is not to eat hamburger, even if the soyburger tastes exactly like hamburger. Eating a hamburger as a substitute for the sex I want but cannot have does not make my going to Burger Queen a sexual event. At best it is *compensation.*

Given Goldman's analyses of sexual desire and activity, the claim that masturbation done for its own sake is not sexual makes sense. If the solitary masturbator desires the pleasure of physical contact, and masturbates trying (in vain) to get that pleasure, the act, by a stretch, is sexual, because it involves genuine sexual desire. By contrast, if the masturbator wants only to experience pleasurable genital sensations, the masturbator does not experience sexual desire in Goldman's sense, and activity engaged in to fulfill this (on his view) nonsexual desire is not sexual activity. Now we have a different problem: what are we to call the act of this masturbator? In what category does it belong, if not the sexual? Goldman argues, along the same lines, that if a parent's desire to cuddle a baby, to have physical contact with it, is only a desire to show affection and not a desire for the pleasure of physical contact, then the parent's act is not sexual. Goldman assumes that if the *desire* that leads to an act is not sexual, then neither is the *act* sexual. But if so, a woman who performs fellatio on a man just for the money she gets from doing so is not performing a sexual act. It does not fulfill the sexual desire "of the agent," for, like the baby-cuddling parent, she has no sexual desire to begin with. The prostitute's fellatio must be called, instead, a "rent paying" or "food gathering" act, since it tends to fulfill her desires to have shelter and eat. That we should classify an act in part by its motive and not only in terms of its physical characteristics is an interesting idea. Still, what Goldman's account implies about a prostitute's participation in a sexual act—it is not sexual, because it is not tied to the appropriate desire—is counterintuitive, flying in the face of common definitions of prostitution as having sex in exchange for money. What the prostitute does is to pay the rent *by* engaging in sex.

Completeness

Thomas Nagel designed his theory of sexuality in order to distinguish between the humanly natural and unnatural (or the perverted.)[7] Human sexuality differs from animal sexuality in the role played by a spiral phenomenon that depends on our consciousness. Suppose (1) X looks at Y or hears Y's voice or smells Y's hair—that is, X "senses" Y—and as a result becomes sexually aroused. Also suppose (2) Y senses X, too, and as a result becomes aroused. X and Y are at the earliest or lowest stage of human sexual interaction: the animal level of awareness and arousal. But if (3) X becomes aroused further by noticing ("sensing") that Y is aroused by sensing X, and (4) Y becomes further aroused by noticing that X is aroused by sensing Y, then X and Y have reached a level of distinctively naturally psychological human sexuality. Higher iterations of the pattern are also characteristic of human sexuality: (5) X is aroused even further by noticing (4), i.e., that Y has become further aroused by noticing that X has been aroused by sensing Y. We might express Nagel's view of human sexuality this way: when X senses Y at the purely animal stage of sexual interaction, X is in X's own consciousness a subject and only a subject of a sexual experience; while Y is for X at this stage only an object of sexual attention. When X advances to the distinctively human level of sexuality, by noticing that Y is aroused by sensing X, X then becomes in X's own consciousness also an object (X sees himself through the eyes—through the desire and arousal—of Y), and so at this level X experiences X as both subject and object. If Y, too, progresses up the spiral, Y also recognizes Y as both subject and object. For Nagel, consciousness of oneself as *both subject and object* in a sexual interaction marks it as "complete," as psychologically natural.

Nagel's theory, because it is about natural sexuality and not about the essence of the sexual, does not entail that masturbation is not sexual. However, the judgment that solitary masturbation is unnatural *seems* to follow. Mutual masturbation can, but solitary masturbation cannot, exhibit the completeness of natural sexuality; it lacks the combination of an awareness of the embodiment of another person and an awareness of being sensed as embodied, in turn, by that person. This explains, apparently, why Nagel claims that "narcissistic practices"—which for him seem to include solitary masturbation—are "stuck at some primitive version of the first stage" of the spiral of arousal; "narcissistic practices" are perverted because they are "truncated or incomplete versions of the complete configuration." However, there is a world of difference between narcissism in some special, technical sense and solitary masturbation, so even if looking on one's own body in a mirror with delight is a sexual perversion, a theorist of sex should not feel compelled for that reason to judge perverted the prosaic practice of solitary masturbation. Nagel also claims that shoe fetishism is perverted: "intercourse with . . . inanimate objects" is incomplete. But just because shoe fetishism might be a sexual perversion that involves masturbation, a theory of sex need not conclude that shoeless masturbation is perverted.

A case can be made that sexual fantasy allows masturbation to be complete enough to be natural in Nagel's sense and not a sexual perversion. Consider someone who is masturbating while looking at erotic photographs. This sexual act avoids incompleteness insofar as the person is aroused not only by sensing the model's body (the animal level), but by being aware of the model's intention to arouse the viewer or by sensing her real or feigned arousal (the human level), as much as these things are captured by the camera (or read into the photograph by the masturbator). Completeness seems not to require that X's arousal as a result of X's awareness of Y's arousal occur at the same time as Y's arousal. Nor does completeness require that X and Y be in the same place: X and Y can cause each other pleasure by talking over the telephone, ascending without any trouble into the spiral of arousal. Further, if X masturbates while fantasizing, *sans* photograph, about another person, X might be aroused by the intentions expressed or arousal experienced by the imagined partner. (Nagel does say that X might become aroused in response to a "purely imaginary" Y, but does not explain this observation or explore its implications.) A masturbator can imagine, conjure up, these details and experience heightened arousal and pleasure as a result. If the masturbator is aroused not only by sensing, in imagination, the other's body, but aroused also by noticing (having created the appropriate fantasy) that the other is aroused by sensing X, then X can be conscious of X as both subject and object, which is the mark of complete, and hence not perverted, sexuality.

This argument that masturbation can be psychologically complete exposes a complication in Nagel's account. Consider a sexual encounter between a man and a female prostitute. The woman, in order to spend as little time as possible engaging in coitus with her client (she is a businessman, for whom time is money; besides, she might be repulsed by him), would like the client to achieve his orgasm quickly, so she can be done with him. She knows, by intuition or experience, that her feigning arousal both at the animal level and at Nagel's human level will greatly increase the sexual arousal of her client and thereby instigate his orgasm. She knows, equivalently, that failing to express arousal—lying mute and motionless on the bed—will impede his becoming aroused and delay or prevent his orgasm. The smart prostitute pretends, first, to be aroused at the animal level and then pretends to enter the spiral of arousal, while her client really does enter the spiral of arousal. The client is not responding with arousal to her being aroused, but only to his false belief that she is aroused. (She must fake it credibly, without histrionics.) He experiences himself as both subject and object of the sexual encounter, even though the prostitute remains altogether a sexual object. Thus, in order for one person *X* to ascend in the spiral of arousal, it need not be the case that the other person ascend as well; *X* need only *believe* that the other person is ascending. Whether this phenomenon (which is not confined to prostitution, but occurs as well during marital sex) confirms Nagel's account of human sexual psychology, or shows that his notion of psychological completeness is incomplete, is unclear.

Communication

Robert Solomon, as does Nagel, thinks it crucial to distinguish between animal and human sexuality.[8] On Solomon's view, human sexuality is differentiated by its being "primarily a means of communicating with other people" (*SAP*, 279). Sensual pleasure is important in sexual activity, but pleasure is not the main point of sexual interaction or its defining feature (SAP, 277–79). Sexuality is, instead, "first of all language" (*SAP*, 281). As "a means of communication, it is . . . *essentially* an activity performed with other people" (*SAP*, 279). Could such a view of human sexuality be kind to solitary masturbation? Apparently not:

> If sexuality is essentially a language, it follows that masturbation, while not a perversion, is a deviation. . . . Masturbation is not "self-abuse" . . . but it is . . . self-denial. It represents an inability or a refusal to say what one wants to say. . . . Masturbation is . . . essential as an ultimate retreat, but empty and without content. Masturbation is the sexual equivalent of a Cartesian soliloquy. (*SAP*, 283)

If sexuality is communicative, as Solomon claims, solitary masturbation can *be* a sexual activity, for conversing with oneself is not impossible, even if not the paradigm case of communication. The distinctive flaw of masturbation, for Solomon, is that communicative intent, success, or content is missing from masturbation. Hence solitary masturbation is "empty" and a "deviation," a conclusion that seems to follow naturally from the proposition that sexuality is "essentially" a way persons communicate *with each other*.

Solomon's denouncing masturbation as a "refusal to say what one wants to say," however, slights the fact that a person might not have, at a given time, something to say to someone else (without thereby being dull); or that there might be nothing worthy of being said, and so silence toward another person is appropriate. Solomon's communication model of sexuality seems to force people to have sexual activity with each other, to talk with each other—in order to avoid the "deviation" of masturbation—even when they have nothing special to say (*that* looks like "empty" sex). Further, even if the masturbator is merely babbling to himself or herself, he or she still enjoys this harmless pastime as much as does the baby who, for the pure joy if it, makes noises having no communicative intent or meaning. This is not to say that the masturbator is just an infant, in some derogatory sense. The point is that just as the baby who babbles confirms and celebrates its own existence, the person who masturbates can accomplish the same valuable thing, at the same time that he or she experiences the sheer physical pleasure of the act. Thus for Solomon to call masturbation "self-denial" is wrong. (It would be self-denial only if the masturbator had something to say to another person, and fled the opportunity to do so.) At least the accusation is a change from the popular conservative criticism of masturbation as being a *failure* of self-denial, as being a giving-in to distracting temptations, an immersing of the self in the hedonistic excess of self-gratification.

There is little warrant to conclude, within a communicative model of sexuality, that masturbation is inferior.[9] Solomon meant his analogy between masturbation and a "Cartesian soliloquy" to reveal the shallowness of solitary sex. But Rene Descartes' philosophical soliloquies are hardly uninteresting. Even if we reject the foundationalism of Cartesian epistemology, we must admit the huge significance of Descartes' project. I suspect that many people would be proud to masturbate as well as the *Meditations* does philosophy. Diaries—also analogous to masturbation—are often not masterpieces of literature, but that does not make them "empty." Indeed, some of the most fruitful discussions one can have are precisely with oneself, not as a substitute for dialogue with another person, and not as compensation for lacking conversation with another person, but exactly to explore one's mind, to get one's thoughts straight. This is the stuff from which intellectual integrity emerges, and is not necessarily just a preparation for polished public utterances. Woody Allen's answer to the question, "Why are you so good in bed?"—"I practice a lot when I'm alone"—is not the only way to diffuse the communicative critique of masturbation.

Solomon acknowledges that not only "children, lunatics, and her-
mits" talk to themselves; "poets and philosophers" do so, too (*SAP*, 283).
This misleading concession has obvious derogatory implications for
solitary masturbation. It plays on the silly notion that philosophers and
poets are a type of lunatic. Where are the bus drivers, the cooks, and the
accountants? Solomon's abuse of solitary masturbation trades unfairly
on the fact that talking to oneself has always received undeservedly bad
publicity—unfair because we all do it, lips moving and heads bouncing,
without thereby damning ourselves.

Solomon admits, given the fact that philosophers and others talk to
themselves—which is a counterexample to his argument that "sexuality
is a language . . . and primarily communicative" and, hence, masturbation must be deviant—that "masturbation might, *in different contexts*,
count as wholly different extensions of language" (*SAP*, 283; italics
added). This crucial qualification implies that Solomon's negative judgment of masturbation is, after all, unjustified. Sometimes we want to con-
verse with another person; sometimes we want to have that conversation
sexually. In other contexts—in other moods, with other people, in different settings—we want only the pleasure of touching the other's body
or of being touched, without communicating serious messages. To turn
around one of Solomon's points: sometimes pleasure alone *is* the goal
of sexual activity, and even though communication might occur it is not
the desired or intended result but only an unremarkable or curious side
effect. In still other contexts or moods, we will not want to talk with anyone at all, but spend time alone. We might want to avoid intercourse, of
all types, with human beings, those hordes from whose noisy prattle we
try to escape by running off to Montana—not an "ultimate retreat," but
a blessed haven, a sanctuary.

Men's Liberation

One curiosity of the late twentieth century and early twenty-first century
is that deciding who is liberal and who is conservative is no longer easy.
Consider, for example, the views of John Stoltenberg, a student of the
feminist writers Catharine MacKinnon and Andrea Dworkin. Stoltenberg
rightly complains about our "cultural imperative" that asserts that men in
our society must "fuck" in order to *be* men, and he rightly calls "baloney"
the idea that "if two people don't have intercourse, they have not had real
sex."[10] Stoltenberg also observes that "sometimes men have coital sex . . .
not because they particularly feel like it but because they feel they *should*
feel like it." This is a reasonable philosophy of men's liberation and men's
feminism. But from these observations Stoltenberg fails to draw the almost obvious conclusion about the value of men's solitary masturbation.

Indeed, it is jolting to behold him, in an argument reminiscent of religious objections to contraception (viz., it makes women into sexual objects), laying a guilt trip on men who masturbate with the aid of pornography:

> Pay your money and imagine. Pay your money and get real turned on. Pay your money and jerk off. That kind of sex helps . . . support an industry committed to making people with penises believe that people without are sluts who just want to be ravished and reviled—an industry dedicated to maintaining a sex-class system in which men believe themselves sex machines and men believe women are mindless fuck tubes. (35–36)

In light of Stoltenberg's criticism of the obnoxious social imperative that men must fuck women to be men, surely *something* can be said on behalf of men's solitary masturbation. The men's movement attack on oppressive cultural definitions of masculinity, in hand with feminist worries about the integrity of sexual activity between unequally empowered men and women, suggests that men's masturbation is at least a partial solution to a handful of problems. A man pleasing himself by masturbating is not taking advantage of economically and socially less powerful women; he is not refurbishing the infrastructure of his fragile ego at the expense of womankind. He is, instead, flouting cultural standards of masculinity that instruct him that he must perform sexually with women in order to be a man.

Yet, for Stoltenberg, fantasizing and the heightened sexual pleasure that the imagination makes possible (44), the things I mentioned while arguing that masturbation is psychologically complete, in Nagel's sense, constitutes wrongful sexual objectification. Stoltenberg does not merely condemn masturbating with pornography (35–36, 42–43, 49–50). Fantasy per se is at fault: Stoltenberg condemns men's masturbating with memories of and passing thoughts about women, even when these fantasies are not violent (41–44). A man's conjuring up a mental image of a woman, her body, or its various parts, is to view the woman as an object, as a thing. Stoltenberg thus takes Jesus and Immanuel Kant *very* seriously. He answers Robert Nozick's deconstructive or sarcastic question—"In getting pleasure from seeing an attractive person go by, does one use the other solely as a means? Does someone so use an object of sexual fantasies?"—with "yes."[11]

The mental sexual objectification involved in sexual fantasy is both a cause and a result of "male supremacy," according to Stoltenberg (51, 53–54). Further, mental sexual objectification makes its own contribution to violence against women (54–55). Stoltenberg's reason for thinking this is flimsy. He supposes that when a man fantasizes sexually about women, he reduces them from persons to objects. Further, when a man thinks of women as things, he has given himself *carte blanche* in his behavior toward them, including violence: regarding an object, "you can do anything to it you want" (55). The last claim is obviously false. There are innumerable lifeless objects to which I would never lay a hand, because other people value them, and I value these people, or because I myself dearly value the objects. Therefore, reducing a woman to a thing—or, to describe it more faithfully to men's experiences than Stoltenberg is willing to do: emphasizing for a while the beauty of only one aspect of a person's existence—does not mean that she can or will be tossed around the way a young girl slings her Barbie.

Stoltenberg underestimates the nuances of men's fantasies about women. His phenomenological account of what occurs in the minds of fantasizing men—the purported reduction of persons to things—is crude. Her smile, the way she moves down the stairs, the bounce of her tush, the sexy thoughts in her own mind, her lusty yearning for me—these are mere parts of her. But fantasizing or imagining them while masturbating, or driving my car, or having coffee, need not amount to, indeed is *the opposite of,* my reducing her to plastic. These are fantasies about people, not things, and they remain people during the fantasy. My fantasy of her (having a) fantasy of me (or of her having a fantasy of my [having a] fantasy of her) is structurally too sophisticated to be called objectification. The fantasizer makes himself in his consciousness both subject and object and imagines his partner as both subject and object. Recognizing the imagined person ontologically as a person is hardly a superfluous component of men's—or women's—fantasies. That Stoltenberg overlooks the complex structure of men's fantasies about women is not surprising. The primitive idea that men vulgarly reduce women to objects in their fantasies is precisely what would occur to someone (Stoltenberg) who has already objectified men, who has reduced men from full persons having intricate psychologies to robots with penises.

Conjugal Union

The "New Natural Law" philosopher and legal scholar John Finnis claims, plausibly, that there are morally worthless sexual acts in which "one's body is treated as instrumental for the securing of the experiential satisfaction of the conscious self."[12] Out of context, this claim seems to be condemning rape, the use of a person and his or her body by another person for mere "experiential satisfaction." But rape is the farthest thing from Finnis's mind, for he is talking not about coerced sex, but that which is voluntary. When is sex instrumental, and hence worthless, even though consensual? Finnis immediately mentions, implying that these sexual act are his primary targets, that "in masturbating, as in being . . . sodomized," the body is merely a tool of satisfaction. As a result of one's body being

used, a person undergoes "disintegration": in masturbation and homosexual anal intercourse "one's choosing self [becomes] the quasi-slave of
the experiencing self which is demanding gratification." We should ask—
since Finnis sounds remarkably like the Immanuel Kant who claims that
sex by its nature is instrumental and objectifying—how sexual acts other
than masturbation and sodomy avoid this problem. Finnis's answer is that
they don't: the worthlessness and disintegration of masturbation and
sodomy attach to "all extramarital sexual gratification." The physical nature of the act is not the decisive factor, after all; the division between the
sexually wholesome and the worthless is between potentially procreative
"conjugal activity" and everything else. Finnis's notion of masturbation is
broad, which explains why he mentions that practice as his first example
of a disintegrating, worthless sexual act. For Finnis, a married couple that
performs anal intercourse or fellatio (nonprocreative sexual acts) are engaging in *masturbatory* sex.[13]

The question arises: what is so special about the conjugal bed that allows marital sex to avoid promoting disintegration? Finnis replies that
worthlessness and disintegration attach to masturbation and sodomy in
virtue of the fact that in these activities "one's conduct is not the actualizing and experiencing of a real common good." Marriage, on the other
hand,

> with its double blessing—procreation and friendship—is a real common
> good . . . that can be both actualized and experienced in the orgasmic
> union of the reproductive organs of a man and a woman united in com-
> mitment to that good.

Being married is, we can grant, often conducive to the value of sexual activity. But what is objectionable about sexual activity between two single
consenting adults who care about and enjoy pleasing each other? Does
not this mutual pleasing avoid worthlessness? No: the friends might only
be seeking pleasure for its own sake, as often occurs in sodomy and masturbation. And although Finnis thinks that "pleasure is indeed a good,"
he qualifies that concession with "when it is the experienced aspect of
one's participation in some intelligible good." For Finnis's argument to
work, however, he must claim that pleasure is a good *only when* it is an aspect of the pursuit or achievement of some other good. This is not what
Finnis says. Perhaps he does not say it because he fears his readers will
reject such an extreme reservation about the value of pleasure. Or, perhaps, he doesn't say it because he realizes it's false: the pleasure of tast-
ing food is good in itself, regardless of whether eating is part of the
goods of securing nutrition or sharing table.

What if the friends say that they do have a common good, their friendship, the same way a married couple has the common good that is their

marriage? If "their friendship is not marital . . . activation of their reproductive organs cannot be, in reality, an . . . actualization of their friendship's common good," replies Finnis. The claim is obscure. Finnis tries to explain, and in doing so reveals the crux of his sexual philosophy:

> the common good of friends who are not and cannot be married (man and man, man and boy, woman and woman) has nothing to do with their having children by each other, and their reproductive organs cannot make them a biological (and therefore a personal) unit.

Finnis began with the Kantian intuition that sexual activity involves treating the body instrumentally, and he concludes with the Kantish intuition that sex in marriage avoids disintegrity since the couple is a biological "unit," or insofar as "the orgasmic union of the reproductive organs of husband and wife really unites them biologically." In order for persons to be part of a genuine union, their sexual activity must be both marital and procreative. The psychic falling apart each person would undergo in nonmarital sex is prevented in marital sex by their joining into one; this bolstering of the self against a metaphysical hurricane is gained by the tempestuous potentially procreative orgasm, of all things.

At the heart of Finnis's philosophy is a scientific absurdity, if not also an absurdity according to common sense, and further conversation with him becomes difficult. But Finnis's argument, even if it shows the worthlessness of sterile homosexuality and solitary masturbation, seems to have no relevance for heterosexual friends, for those who are not, but could be, married. After all, if marriage has the "double blessing" of procreation and friendship, the same double blessing is available to heterosexual friends. Would Finnis want to claim that if these friends are committed to each other and plan to, or do, have children with each other, they are in effect *married* and hence their sexual interactions are fine? That claim might be true, but others in Finnis's school of thought make it clear that marriage requires more than an informal agreement between people to spend their lives together indefinitely. No genuine commitment (or love, or union) exists without a formal compact; a promise too easily fled is no promise at all.

Transcendental Illusions

For Finnis, the self is so fragile metaphysically that engaging in sexual activity for the sheer pleasure of it threatens to burst it apart. For Roger Scruton, another conservative who condemns masturbation, the ephemeral self is in continual danger of being exposed as a fraud: "In my [sexual] desire [for you] I am gripped by the illusion of a transcendental unity behind the opacity of [your] flesh."[14] We are not transcendental selves but fully material beings, which is why "excretion is the final 'no' to all our transcendental illusions" (151). We are redeemed only through "a metaphysical illusion residing in the heart of sexual desire" (95). Our passions make it *appear* that we are ontologically more than we really are. Sexuality must be treated with kid gloves, then, lest we lose the spiritually uplifting and socially useful reassurance that we humans are the ontological pride of the universe, the crown of creation.

The requirement that human sexuality be approached somberly translates, for Scruton, not only into the ordinary claim that the sexual impulse must be educated or tamed to be the partner of heterosexual love, but also into a number of silly judgments. While discussing the "obscenity" of masturbation, Scruton offers this example:

> Consider the woman who plays with her clitoris during the act of coition. Such a person affronts her lover with the obscene display of her body, and, in perceiving her thus, the lover perceives his own irrelevance. She becomes disgusting to him, and his desire may be extinguished. The woman's desire is satisfied at the expense of her lover's, and no real union can be achieved between them. (319)

The obvious reply is to say that without the woman's masturbation, *her* desire might be extinguished and *his* desire satisfied at the expense of hers, and still no union is achieved. Further, her masturbating can help the couple attain the union Scruton hopes for as the way to sustain the metaphysical illusion, by letting them experience and recognize the mutual pleasure, perhaps the mutual orgasm, that results. Scruton's claim is false, I think, that most men would perceive a woman's masturbating during coitus as "disgusting." But even if there is some truth in this, we could, instead of blessing this disgust, offer the pastoral advice to the man who "perceives his own irrelevance" that he become more involved in his partner's pleasure by helping her massage her clitoral region or doing the rubbing for her. When they are linked together coitally, he will find the arms long and the body flexible.

Why does Scruton judge the woman's masturbation an "obscene display"? Here is one part of his thought. When masturbation is done in public (a bus station), it is obscene; it "cannot be witnessed without a sense of obscenity." Scruton then draws the astounding conclusion that *all* masturbation is obscene, even when done privately, on the grounds that "that which cannot be witnessed without obscene perception is itself obscene" (319). But Scruton's argument proves too much: it implies that coitus engaged in by a loving, heterosexual, married couple in private is also obscene, because this act "cannot be witnessed" in public "without obscene perception." The fault lies in the major premise of Scruton's syllogism. Whether an act is obscene might turn exactly on whether it is done publicly or privately. Scruton fails to acknowledge the difference between exposing oneself to anonymous spectators and opening oneself to the gaze of a lover.

All masturbation is obscene, for Scruton, also because the act "involves a concentration on the body and its curious pleasures" (319). Obscenity is an "obsession . . . with the organs themselves and with the pleasures of sensation" (154), and even if the sexual acts that focus on the body and its pleasures are paired sexual acts, they are nonetheless "masturbatory." (Recall how the religious conservative criticized Goldman's "plain sex.") "In obscenity, attention is taken away from embodiment towards the body" (32), and there is "a 'depersonalized' perception of human sexuality, in which the body and its sexual function are uppermost in our thoughts" (138). A woman's masturbation during coitus is obscene since it leads the couple to focus too sharply on physical features. She is a depersonalized body instead of a person-in-a-body. Thus, for Scruton, this obscene masturbation threatens the couple's metaphysical illusion. But if her masturbating during coitus is greeted with delight by her male partner, rather than disgust, and increases the pleasure they realize and recognize in the act together, then, contrary to Scruton, either not all masturbation is obscene (the parties have not been reduced altogether to flesh) or obscenity, all things considered, is not a sexual, normative, or metaphysical disaster.

Two Models of Sexuality

It is not be surprising that the conservatives, Finnis and Scruton, are suspicious about the value and morality of masturbation. But liberal philosophers, who are unconventional enough to reject traditional or religious views about sexuality, have also scorned masturbation. Why? Here is a diagnosis. Even as they reject particular conservative or religious judgments about sexual behavior, these liberal thinkers still hold the deepest global assumption of their ideological foes. Their accounts of sexuality exemplify a *binary model*: reference to an interaction between two persons occurs in their accounts of the essence of sexuality or in their description of the best sex or its paradigm case. They thereby bestow normative, logical/conceptual, or ontological primacy on paired sexual activity and evaluate the rest of sexuality from this perspective. The sexually conservative or religious theorist embraces a binary model either by taking seriously Genesis, in which God created the human pair, or by assimilating human sexuality to that of the animal kingdom, where they find paired sex galore. But there is no reason why liberal theorists must embrace a binary model. Because both Solomon and Nagel want to distinguish sharply between animal and human sexuality, it is disappointing that they construed human sexuality as only a variant of the paired, albeit less sophisticated, sexuality of animals.

The binary model is plainly exhibited in Goldman's definition of "sexual desire" as the "desire for contact with another person's body." He claims that sexual desire is directed at and hence depends, conceptually, on another *body*. In Nagel, sexual desire is directed at another *person*: it is "a feeling about other persons"; the sexual "has its own content as a relation between persons." (Nagel's use of the word "intercourse," in his phrase "intercourse with . . . inanimate objects," to talk about masturbation engaged in by the shoe fetishist, illustrates how his use of a binary model has colored his view of the sexual.) Solomon, too, assumes a binary model: sex "is essentially an activity performed with other people" (*SAP*, 279). While for Solomon, sexual desire is a binary desire to talk with other people, for Goldman it is a binary desire to touch them.

Binary accounts of sexuality cannot illuminate the full range of human sexuality. Ordinary, everyday sexuality includes a desire for physical contact with another person. And, we know, much paired sexual activity occurs. But we should still ask: *why* is paired sexual activity commonly practiced and commonly desired? In trying to fathom these facts, we formulate a theory of sex. But a theory that presupposes a binary model will not help. It is trivial to say that people commonly behave in a paired sexual way because sexuality by its essence is paired, in the same way that the dormative power of morphine does not explain why it knocks us out. An alternative account of sexuality is worth exploring, a *unitary model*, in which sexuality is not by its nature a relation between persons and sexual desire does not attach necessarily to other persons or bodies. On this view, sexual desire is the desire for certain pleasurable sensations, period. Hence a unitary model does not entail that solitary masturbation is logically secondary or peripheral in the domain of sexual acts. If a theorist of sexuality wanted to distinguish sharply between the instinctual, routine paired sexuality of animals and the endlessly varied behaviors of human sexuality, presupposing a unitary model seems an effective way to achieve that. Further, a unitary model leaves room for constructing interesting explanations of the desire to engage in paired sex acts that refer to the desire of persons for pleasurable sensations. The development of that desire within specific social and cultural contexts would be invoked to explain why people want, even prefer, physical contact with persons of the other biological sex, or the same sex, or contact with both, or contact with neither. The value of a unitary model is that it encourages the exploration of the etiology of our sexual preferences. It is a drawback of a binary model that it tends to obscure these questions.

How are we to decide whether the deep nature of sexuality is "really" captured by a unitary or a binary model? Is Freud right that infants desire pleasure and discover that the mother and her breast provide that pleasure; or are the object-relations psychoanalysts right that infants have a primitive desire for contact with the mother and her breast and discover willy-nilly that satisfying that desire yields pleasure? This puzzle is a kind of chicken-and-egg conundrum. But it can be ignored. The central question concerns the research advantages of the competing models. A unitary model seems better suited for studying, in the various empirical disciplines, all the manifestations of human sexuality.

Within a unitary model, the desire for pleasurable sensations is logically primary, and the task is to explain the common paired pattern of sexuality as well as other behaviors. Whatever it is that we as individuals or as societies eventually cathect is open to explanation: all aims, objects, and targets of sexual desire, and the means of satisfying it, are seen as contingent facts requiring investigation. By contrast, within Nagel's binary model, for example, the "psychologically complete configuration" is taken as logically primitive and as part of human nature; hence the common paired pattern does not *require* explanation, indeed is not *susceptible* of explanation. In this approach, only deviations from the complete configuration require explanation. Of course, when we ask for an explanation of valium's calming effect, we are disappointed if we are told it is an anti-anxiety agent. We are let down because we think that the calming nature of valium is explainable in terms of the *deeper nature* of the drug, its chemistry, and the biological system with which it interacts. This kind of "deep nature" of human sexuality is what Nagel is attempting to provide in his account of the psychological completeness. I think, however, that Nagel candidly recognizes the problem that this causes. Given that the complete configuration is primitively natural, the task is to explain the existence of deviations, patterns of sexuality that result from factors that interfere with the normal or automatic blossoming of the natural, paired pattern of sexuality. Speaking about this task, Nagel writes, "We appear to need an independent criterion for a distorting influence, and we do not have one."[15] A unitary model, by contrast, needs no such criterion: it does not claim that departures from the paired pattern are necessarily "deviations" or that factors that influence their development are "distorting." As a result, the unitary model yields a more empathetic clinical psychology of sexual deviance.

Study Questions

1. Define "solitary masturbation," "dual masturbation," and "mutual masturbation." In what situations might it be difficult to decide whether a sexual act falls into one category instead of another, or into none of them at all? Does it matter?

2. Is solitary masturbation a *sexual* act? If it is, what about it, what feature of the act, makes it a sexual act? If it is not a sexual act, why not? What does it lack that sexual acts possess or exhibit? And if it is not a sexual act, what *kind* of act is it? Is a male's rubbing his penis to produce a sperm sample for donation or medical analysis count as masturbation? Only if the room supplied by the physician or donor bank contains a tableful of *Playboy*?

3. Employ the conceptual framework from "The Analytic Categories of the Philosophy of Sex" (chapter 1) to discuss solitary masturbation. Is it, or when is it, moral/immoral, nonmorally good/nonmorally bad, pragmatically useful/counterproductive, and natural/perverted? Given your answers, what is your overall assessment of solitary masturbation?

4. What are the various roles of fantasy in solitary masturbation? What do they imply about the morality or naturalness of solitary masturbation? What *is* a sexual fantasy—a fantasy that has sexual content, or a fantasy, regardless of its content, that produces sexual arousal or pleasure? What would fantasy-less masturbation look like—sperm donation?

5. If Roman Catholic sexual ethics were altered to agree that the use of contraceptive devices by a married heterosexual couple to avoid procreation was morally licit in at least some circumstances, would Roman Catholic sexual ethics also have to abandon its claim that both solitary masturbation and same-sex sexual acts are sinful? You might want to think about this question, or think about it again, after reading John Finnis (chapter 9), Andrew Koppelman (chapter 10), and Karol Wojtyla (chapter 11).

Notes

The first piece I wrote on masturbation, "Sexual Desire and Sexual Objects," was a paper presented at the Pacific Division meetings of the American Philosophical Association (San Francisco, March 1978). I then published an essay, "Masturbation," in *Pacific Philosophical Quarterly* 61 (1980): 233–44. (That essay was reprinted, unchanged, in Igor Primoratz, ed., *Human Sexuality* [Dartmouth, 1997], 139–50.) A greatly revised, mostly new, version of the early essay, "Masturbation and Sexual Philosophy," was included in the second edition of *Philosophy of Sex* (1991). I continued to read and think about masturbation and the results of my additional research emerged in chapter 2 of *Sexual Investigations* (New York University Press, 1996). Part of that chapter became "Masturbation" in the third edition of *Philosophy of Sex* (1997), which was reprinted in David Benatar, ed., *Ethics for Everyday* (McGraw-Hill, 2002), 180–96. That version was further changed in various ways to form "Philosophies of Masturbation," in Martha Cornog, ed., *The Big Book of Masturbation: From Angst to Zeal* (Down There Press, 2003, 149–66). Yet another version, "Masturbation: Conceptual and Ethical Matters," was included in the fourth edition of *Philosophy of Sex* (2002). The essay included in this fifth edition of *Philosophy of Sex* is a pastiche of all this work, including the entry "Masturbation" in my *Sex from Plato to Paglia: A Philosophical Encyclopedia* (2006).

1. Jean-Jacques Rousseau, *The Confessions* (New York: Penguin, 1979), book 3, 109.

2. The mainstreaming of sadomasochism is suggested by this letter a woman wrote to Irma Kurtz's "Agony Column" (*Cosmopolitan*, January 1997, 34): "I'm thirty-four, successful, smart, independent . . . and *obsessed* by the bizarre fantasy of being spanked by a lover. What's *wrong* with me?" Kurtz replies: "Nothing's bizarre about your fantasy or wrong with you. . . . For some women *and* men, simply thinking about tushy slapping is extremely arousing. . . . When erotic fantasies become reality, they sometimes lose their power, but I see no harm in giving this one a try. . . . Next time you and a beau are getting intimate, why not confess you've been a naughty girl? Then climb over his knee . . . and savor your punishment." See also Daphne Merkin's spanking confessional, "Unlikely Obsession: Confronting a Taboo," *New Yorker* (February 26 & March 4, 1996), 98–115. For explorations and defenses of more intense sadomasochism, see Samois, ed., *Coming to Power*, 2nd edition (Boston, Mass.: Alyson Publications, 1982), and especially the writings of Pat Califia: "Feminism and Sadomasochism" (in Stevi Jackson and Sue Scott, eds., *Feminism and Sexuality: A Reader* [New York: Columbia University Press, 1996], 230–37), *Public Sex: The Culture of Radical Sex* (Pittsburgh, Penn.: Cleis Press, 1994), and *Macho Sluts* (Los Angeles: Alyson Books, 1988).

3. About problems in defining "sex" for lesbians, see the wonderful essay by Marilyn Frye, "Lesbian 'Sex,'" in her *Willful Virgin: Essays in Feminism 1976–1992* (Freedom, Calif.: Crossing Press, 1992), 109–19.

4. Philip Roth, *Portnoy's Complaint* (New York: Random House, 1969), 88.

5. A notable contrast is Russell Vannoy's humanist treatment of masturbation in *Sex without Love: A Philosophical Exploration* (Buffalo, N.Y.: Prometheus, 1980), 111–17.

6. Alan Goldman, "Plain Sex," *Philosophy and Public Affairs* 6 (1977): 267–87; in this volume, chap. 5.

7. Thomas Nagel, "Sexual Perversion," *Journal of Philosophy* 66 (1969): 5–17; in this volume, chap. 3.

8. Robert Solomon, "Sex and Perversion" [*SAP*], in Robert Baker and Frederick Elliston, eds., *Philosophy and Sex*, 1st ed. (Buffalo, N.Y.: Prometheus, 1975), 268–87. See also his "Sexual Paradigms," *Journal of Philosophy* 71 (1974): 336–45.

9. See Hugh Wilder, "The Language of Sex and the Sex of Language," in Alan Soble, ed., *Sex, Love, and Friendship* (Amsterdam: Rodopi, 1997), 23–31.

10. John Stoltenberg, *Refusing to Be a Man* (Portland, Ore.: Breitenbush Books, 1989), 39.

11. Robert Nozick, *Anarchy, State, and Utopia* (New York: Basic Books, 1974), 32. Martha Nussbaum has recently issued Stoltenberg's "yes." See her "Feminism,

Virtue, and Objectification," in Raja Halwani, ed., *Sex and Ethics: Essays on Sexuality, Virtue, and the Good Life* (New York: Palgrave/Macmillan, 2007), 49–62.

12. John Finnis, "The Wrong of Homosexuality," *New Republic* (November 15, 1993), 12–13; in this volume, chap. 9. All quotes are from this essay unless otherwise indicated.

13. Finnis, "Law, Morality, and 'Sexual Orientation,'" *Notre Dame Law Review* 69, no. 5 (1994): 1049–76, at 1068.

14. Roger Scruton, *Sexual Desire: A Moral Philosophy of the Erotic* (New York: Free Press, 1986), 130.

15. On the implications of this comment by Nagel, see Arnold Davidson, "Conceptual History and Conceptions of Perversion," in Robert Baker, Kathleen Wininger, and Frederick Elliston, eds., *Philosophy and Sex*, 3rd ed. (Amherst, N.Y.: Prometheus, 1998), 476–86, at 479–80.

Chapter 7

SEX

Christopher Hamilton

If we overlook that this essay inexplicably ignores American philosophy of sex, **Christopher Hamilton**'s *"Sex" is otherwise extremely erudite, bringing a wide-ranging discussion from both philosophy and literature to bear on various attempts to bottle the strangeness of sex. Focusing on, for example, the sexually conservative Roger Scruton and his nemesis, the sexually liberal Igor Primoratz, Hamilton extracts from these accounts a tension between shallow and deep aspects of sexuality. The utility of sex can be both prosaic and profound; sexual desire can be experienced as both wanton and wonderment. Unlike Alan Goldman (chapter 5), Hamilton is sympathetic to understanding sexuality teleologically, by linking sex to procreation, the natural cycles of life, and even to the transcendent escape from the body (even if he is not a traditional Roman Catholic). Some such account—some acknowledgment that the joyful pleasures of sex alone do not explain everything about sex—is required, Hamilton argues, for illuminating the significance of sex. Further, he suspects that analytic philosophy of sex cannot solve the central problems it has set for itself—defining sexual desire and sexual activity—and settles for a "family resemblance" framework derived from the later work of Ludwig Wittgenstein. Nonetheless, Hamilton does not keep himself from using loose expressions such as "telephone sex," which phrase raises all sorts of interesting technical questions (see chapter 8). Throughout, Hamilton provides a number of perceptive insights tying together sexuality and various provocative theological themes.*

Hamilton is lecturer in philosophy of religion at King's College, London, and author of *Living Philosophy: Reflections on Life, Meaning, and Morality* (Edinburgh University Press, 2001). He has also published on Nietzsche, Simone Weil, and Kierkegaard.

I

Ever since Socrates, philosophy has been interested in asking such questions as: What is art? What is morality? What is love? and the hope has been to find a definition of such areas of human concern, delineating each such form of attention to the world from other forms. Philosophers have often been attracted to such a procedure because it seems to hold out the prospect of genuine understanding and insight, and to promise to provide a method for settling disputes. Thus, if we take ourselves to be in possession of a definition of what, say, art is, then we shall be able to take any object and decide whether it does or does not have the properties which make it a work of art. This will allow us to sort out the real from the bogus, something which seems these days an especially great problem in the art world when a common reaction to many objects on display in public galleries is that they are not works of art at all and should not be there.

Some philosophers and others have adopted such an approach with respect to sexual desire. They have wanted to provide a definition of such desire, and one of the things that has motivated them to do so is the hope that, armed with a definition of what sexual desire is, they will be able to indicate which kinds of sexual activity, if any, express perversions of sexual desire or otherwise unacceptable forms of it. For example, Roman Catholicism bases its teaching concerning the morality of sex on a notion of what Nature, as an expression of God's design, intends. But what Nature intends, so it is said, is that sex shall be between a man and a woman, and that it shall issue in the birth of children. The raising of children is, however, a long and arduous process, and what the person engaging in sex commits himself or herself to is seeing this through to completion. This requires the stable institution of monogamous marriage. Further, such a marriage flourishes if it is an expression of love between two people on the model of God's love for human beings. Hence, Roman Catholic teaching confines morally decent sex to that which takes place between a man and woman in marriage for the purposes of procreation and the expression of the love that exists between them.

As I have noted, such a view of sex purports to tell us *what sex is* and hence which kinds of sexual activity are morally permitted: those that do not accord with such a definition will be in various ways unacceptable, and some will be perverted. Few people these days accept the Catholic view, and even many who call themselves Catholic would reject it, for it is extremely restrictive in its sense of what counts as acceptable sexual activity. But there are other views which have similar ambitions to provide a definition of what sexual desire is. Thus Roger Scruton, in what is certainly by a long way the most interesting and insightful philosophical account of sexual desire produced by modern analytic philosophy, has argued that any instance of sexual desire possesses an individualizing intentionality. By this he means that sexual desire is founded upon the thought of the other as the specific individual he or she is.[1] Hence, according to this account, if a man desires two women at the same time, he will be experiencing two different desires, each of which will be a desire for one of the two women. From this account is also follows that there cannot be any such sexual desire as an unfocused desire for no particular man or woman. Scruton considers the case of the sailor storming ashore with the thought "woman" in his mind: he might be thought to desire a woman, but no particular woman. Scruton claims that this is not so: until the sailor actually meets a specific woman he desires, he desired no woman; he was rather in the condition of desiring to desire.[2]

Such a view of sexual desire has to find an adequate response to such phenomena as that of Casanova, described by Stefan Zweig:

> His passion, flowing away at the purely erotic level, knows nothing of the ecstasy of uniqueness. We need have no anxiety, therefore, when he seems reduced to despair because Henriette or the beautiful Portuguese lady has left him. We know that he will not blow out his brains; nor are we surprised to find him, a day or two later, amusing himself in the first convenient brothel. If the nun C. C. is unable to come over from Murano, and the lay-sister M. M. arrives in her place, Casanova is speedily consoled. After all, one woman is as good as another![3]

Scruton writes: "If John is frustrated in his pursuit of Mary, there is something inapposite in the advice 'Take Elizabeth, she will do just as well.'"[4] Not, apparently, if one is Casanova! It seems, then, that Scruton has two options. Either he could insist that he has provided a true account of sexual desire, in which case Zweig has totally misunderstood and misdescribed the case of someone like Casanova, and, indeed, that a lot of what looks like sexual desire where what is desired is *someone or other* is not really sexual desire after all since it does not display an individualizing intentionality; or he could say that such cases display sexual desire all right, but a perverted or otherwise morally unacceptable form. In fact, Scruton seems to waver between the two, for, although, as we have seen, he claims that in cases such as that of the sailor the man in question experiences no sexual desire until he comes into contact with the woman he desires, he also grants, at the end of his book, and looking over his argument as a whole, that "my analysis has included a large prescriptive component."5 In other words, he seems to concede that his analysis is not an analysis of sexual desire as such but a moral view about the best form that sexual desire can take.

Actually, it seems to me that, whatever the weaknesses of his account, what Scruton is offering is a picture of sexual desire which helps to make sense of the fact that there can be deeper and shallower ways of understanding and experiencing our sexuality. I am sure that the Catholic view attempts the same. Some accounts, it seems, do not. Thus Igor Primoratz has argued that sexual desire "is sufficiently defined as the desire for certain bodily pleasures, period."6 It is hard to see how such a view can make sense of the fact that sexual desire is capable of finding deeper forms of expression in human life, let alone the fact that it often seeks to do so. For it seems to assimilate sexual desire to something like the desire to scratch an itch, and the possibilities of a deepened understanding of itch-scratching are severely limited, to say the least. This is not to say that only deepened forms of expression of sexual desire are morally legitimate, or anything like that: it is merely to say that any account of sexual desire must be able to make sense of the possibility of those deeper forms of expression.

In any case, Primoratz's account of sexual desire has some odd consequences. It leads, he argues, to the conclusion that any putative sexual act which is devoid of pleasure for the person engaged in that act is not, after all, a sexual act at all. Thus he claims that a prostitute who gains no pleasure from intercourse with a customer is not engaged in a sexual act (whereas the customer is). Further:

> As for the couple who have lost sexual interest in each other but still engage in routine coitus, the less pleasurable it gets, the less valuable it is as sex. If, at some point, it becomes utterly bereft of sexual pleasure, would it be so odd to say that they were performing acts that for most people ordinarily involve at least a modicum of sexual pleasure, but that *they* were merely going through the motions, that *for them* there was no sex in it any longer?7

One might suspect that Primoratz is not, after all, just trying to tell us what sex is, but prescribing a particular form of it, that is, one through which one experiences as much pleasure as possible. For he clearly believes that the less pleasurable sex is, the less valuable it is. Still, leaving that aside, it does, surely, seem odd to suppose that the bored couple in Primoratz's example are not actually engaged in a sexual act. One might as well say that what it is to feel hunger is to have a desire for certain bodily pleasures so that if one eats something utterly bland which fails to fill the stomach (modern mass-produced strawberries, for example) one is not really eating at all.

In fact, I do not think that Primoratz need deny on his account that the prostitute or the bored couple are engaged in sex even if they get no pleasure from such acts. His view expresses a confusion between sexual desire and sexual acts. One is, after all, still eating if there is no pleasure in doing so. The prostitute might not, indeed, possess any sexual desire for her clients, but it does not follow from that that she is not engaged in sexual acts with them. The same may be the case for the bored couple. In the same way, I might for some reason have no hunger, no desire for food, yet still be eating. It is possible to defend the "pleasure view" of sex and grant that sexual acts which involve no pleasure are still genuinely sexual acts.

Still, even if Primoratz's account can be repaired in the way suggested, it is still exposed to the earlier criticism that it cannot make sense of the possibility of a deepened understanding of sex. Scruton's view, as we have seen, also has weaknesses. They are both questionable because, however much they differ from each other, they share the same fundamental aspiration which I mentioned at the outset, namely, the desire to provide a definition of sexual desire, to find some feature which any and every experience of sexual desire possesses. And it seems to me that what is mistaken about this is that it is far too restrictive. Sexual desire is a huge, sprawling phenomenon, which casts its shadow over almost every aspect of our inner life and can find expression in a fantastic variety of acts. It seems unlikely that we shall ever be able to define it. Wittgenstein suggested that if we consider the concept of a game we should not assume that there must be some feature or features which they all—football, patience, ring-a-ring-a-roses, chess, noughts and crosses, and so on—share in common. He suggested, rather, that as we compare one game with another, and then with another, and so on, we shall see that there is "a complicated network of similarities overlapping and criss-crossing: sometimes overall similarities, sometimes similarities of detail."[8] And he goes on:

> I can think of no better expression to characterize these similarities than "family resemblances"; for the various resemblances between members of a family: build, features, colour of eyes, gait, temperament, etc. etc. overlap and criss-cross in the same way.—And I shall say: "games" form a family.[9]

I would say the same about sexual desire. We are not going to get far, I think, if we try to provide a definition of sexual desire or of what constitutes a sexual act, for we shall in such a case always end up ruling out some desire or act which, in the absence of the definition, we should have no difficulty in regarding as sexual. The different acts and kinds of desire which one can think of as sexual resemble one another in the way members of a family resemble one another, with overlapping and criss-crossing characteristics, as Wittgenstein puts it. The desire some adult men have to dress up in nappies and be mothered by a woman is a sexual desire, but whatever it is that makes this a sexual desire has little to do with the sexual desire which finds expression in the wish to make love to one's partner whom one cherishes. They are connected as being both sexual by bearing family resemblances to each other and to other forms of sexual desire. Or again, consider the following passage from Heinrich Böll's story "Im Tal der donnernden Hufe" ("In the Valley of the Thundering Hooves"). Paul is waiting in church to go to confession. A woman tells him that it is his turn. He shakes his head and indicates that his turn is after hers. Böll writes:

> [T]he intensity with which he desired her tormented him; he had not even seen her face; the gentle smell of lavender, a young voice, the soft and yet hard noise of her high-heels as she walked the four paces to the confessional: this rhythm of the high-heels, hard and yet so soft, was only a fragment of the unending melody which raged all day and night in his ears. In the evenings, he would lie awake, the window open, and would hear them walking along the asphalt of the pavement: shoes, heels, hard, soft, unsuspecting; he heard voices, whispering, laughter under the chestnut trees. There were too many of them, and they were too lovely: some opened their handbag, in the tram, at the box-office in the cinema, on the counter in the shop; they left their handbags lying around in cars and he could look inside: lipstick, handkerchiefs, loose change, crumpled up tickets, packets of cigarettes, powder compacts.[10]

This wonderful evocation of adolescent sexuality, of the time when the entire world seems to take on a sexual hue and everything seems to have some sexual aspect; of a time when, for a boy at least, more or less any object associated with the opposite sex can take his breath away and make him yearn—this nameless, glorious, tormenting, fear-filled, anxious longing has little in common with, say, the cynical, brutal dehumanized forms of the sexual desire of the pimps, prostitutes, murderers, and queens which Jean Genet describes in his *Our Lady of the Flowers*. What links them is, once again, a series of family resemblances. And such resemblances are not just interpersonal ones, but intrapersonal: they have to do with the way in which, later in life and reflecting on the changes to which our own sexual desires have been subject, we see that what makes all of them sexual desires is that they bear family resemblances to one another. For what one finds sexually appealing or exciting at the age of, say, forty, may be utterly unlike that which one found sexually appealing at the age of fifteen; and the fifteen-year-old would have been, perhaps, uncomprehending about the forty-year-old's pattern of desires. Yet, at the same time, one can see how the one type of desires developed into the other; and one might think that it is only through telling the story of the changes in one's desires that one could come to see how it is that *these* things later in life could be sexually exciting at all.

None of this is to say, however, that the accounts of sexual desire offered by Roman Catholic teaching or by Scruton or Primoratz have nothing to be said for them. On the contrary, the very amorphousness of sexual desire is such that these accounts certainly do latch onto part of that to which any sensitive understanding of sexual desire should draw our attention.

Consider again the Catholic emphasis on the relation between sexual desire and procreation. To many people, such an emphasis seems absurd, and it is easy to find arguments to criticize the idea that every sexual act not "by nature" aimed at procreation is morally suspect.[11] But it by no means follows from this that an adequate understanding of sexual desire may leave out the notion of procreation as, for example, the accounts of both Scruton and Primoratz do. We can see this by the simple reflection that a species of creature which had all our experiences of sexual desires but in whom sexual desire had no connection with procreation would have a profoundly different understanding of sexual desire from the one we have. As so often in philosophy, the real problem is to find a way of expressing this point which does not fall foul of some unhelpful generalization, such as that which the Catholic view involves.

At one point D. H. Lawrence writes: "Sex is the balance of male and female in the universe, the attraction, the repulsion, the transit of neutrality, the new attraction, the new repulsion, always different, always new. The long neuter spell of Lent, when the blood is low, and the delight of the Easter kiss, the sexual revel of the spring, the passion of midsummer, the slow recoil, revolt, and grief of autumn, greyness again, then the sharp stimulus of long winter nights. Sex goes through the rhythm of the year, in man and woman, ceaselessly changing: the rhythm of the sun in his relation to the earth."[12] It goes without saying that many, if not most, do not share this view of sex, wonderful though it is. And there are lots of ways in which one might pursue or develop or respond to the thoughts Lawrence articulates. For our purposes what is important is that Lawrence connects sex to the natural cycle of life, and does so in such a way as to express a sense of the wonder and mystery of sex. But if we ask ourselves how it is possible to see sex in this way, then I think that we shall not be able long to resist the thought that it is the fact that sex is related to conception and procreation that allows us to do this. For it is *this* fact about it which most immediately and forcefully connects it to the notions of corruption and regeneration and hence allows it to be brought into contact with our sense of the natural cycle of the seasons. And if, as we do, we can wonder at that cycle, at its utter familiarity together with the strangeness that each spring green shoots sprout from what looks like dead wood, we can also see why it is that we can wonder at sex, at the strangeness of a force at once so familiar and yet *unheimlich*—this incomparable German word, which means "uncanny" or "spooky" or "frightening," captures the sense of something's not being like that which one meets with at home (*Heim*), that which is unfamiliar or upsets one's ingrained and habitual ways of dealing with things.

We could perhaps get at the significance of procreation for an understanding of sexual desire in another way. Many people experience a sense of wonder and mystery at the birth of a child. And this very sense can cast in a certain light the sexual act which directly led to this birth, can remind us of the strangeness and mystery of sex. But to speak here of a reminder is not to suggest that anyone might actually have forgotten anything, for we are all familiar with the fact that sexual desire has its own demands and needs which well up and grip us in ways we cannot fully fathom, and that it attaches us to people in ways we cannot properly comprehend. We all know that sex, where what is craved is so clear and yet weirdly elusive, seems at once completely natural and an intrusion from another world into our daily activities. The issue is rather that of such knowledge becoming deeper and more alive as an object of wonder in a person, much as, say, suffering but surviving a dreadful accident might be said to remind one of one's mortality. Thus the connection with sex of reproduction and all it involves casts its shadow over sex in the kind of way that mortality casts its shadow over human life. And this is so even if a given person never thinks of procreation (except, perhaps, to prevent his or her sexual acts leading to conception), just as it is so even if a person never thinks of his own mortality (except to suppress or ridicule the thought). For the kinds of thoughts I have said people have about the birth of a child and those that people have who have survived death form part of the collective experience of mankind, of the wisdom concerning what it is to be a human being and thus of our sense of who and what we are.

I am not claiming, of course, that reflection on the connection of sex with reproduction is the only way in which it is possible for one to come to a deepened understanding of human sexuality. I am just saying that it is a central or permanent way in which this can happen for creatures such as we are, and thus that any account of sexual desire which leaves it out must be inadequate.

II

I earlier suggested that the view that sexual desire is a desire for pleasure and nothing else is misleading because it seeks to reduce the variety of desires which are correctly understood to be sexual desires to one type. But some have suggested that the idea is absurd for other reasons. Thus, in a brilliant discussion of the nature of sexual desire, Jean-Paul Sartre argued that sexual desire cannot be understood to be a desire merely for pleasure, for this view would not allow us to make sense of how it is that such desire could come to "attach" itself to an object: why would masturbation not be enough?[13] Roger Scruton[14] and Thomas Nagel[15] have echoed Sartre's claim. Is this view correct? The basic problem with it seems to me this: even if it is true that not all sexual desire can be understood to be a desire for pleasure, it does not follow from this that sexual desire is never simply desire for pleasure. And if a particular person understands his own sexual desire to be nothing more than a desire for pleasure we can, *pace* Sartre, account for the way in which his desire attaches itself to an object, for the pleasure which comes from having sex with a person might seem to him greater or to offer more variety or the like than does masturbation.[16] I do not think, therefore, that Sartre is right to say that sexual desire *cannot* be a desire simply for pleasure or orgasm. No purely philosophical thesis can legislate out of existence a particular experience of, and attitude toward, sex, however much one might judge it to be inhuman or thoughtless or shallow or degrading (if one does).

Still, the fact remains that for most people sexual desire is much more than a desire for pleasure, though it is also at least that. As Stuart Hampshire has put it:

> It is unhistorical, and contrary to experience, a Manichean error, to think of erotic feeling as comparable with hunger and thirst, as a primitive need. . . . [O]ur sexual desires and practices vividly express individual natures as well as something of the customs of a particular culture. They are penetrated by thought, by symbolism and by imagery, and therefore by that kind of thought which is called imagination.[17]

This very complexity of sexual desire, and the way in which it expresses something of one's very nature as a person—as Freud put it with exaggeration but point: "The sexual behavior of a human being often *lays down the pattern* for all his other modes of reacting to life"[18]—this very complexity gives a reason for thinking that the pleasure which sex affords must itself be complex. And, indeed, as others have pointed out, the pleasure that sex brings is peculiar among our many pleasures in often being experienced as strangely hollow. Of course, all of our pleasures can fail to bring satisfaction: nothing is more common than to satisfy a desire and remain unsatisfied oneself. But the point about sexual desire goes deeper than this: it is that it seems in some way doomed to frustration, as Sartre in his account proposes. Why should this be so? Here is a suggestion: sexual desire seems to be a deeply unstable desire. On the one hand, it is roving, largely undiscriminating about the individuals to whom it attaches itself, restless: one wants "woman" or "man." On the other, it can be especially excited by, and become fixated upon, a specific individual. This lends sexual desire a strange fragility: for, in desiring a given individual, one also desires him or her as man or woman, as a representative of the male or the female sex. There accordingly seems to me to be a way in which what one wants in the sexual act is two things that one cannot have: one wants this individual man or woman and one wants *all* men or *all* women. That is, one wants all men or all women in and through this one individual. But this is impossible. Yet this is why it is that one of the most recurrent sexual fantasies is that of not knowing who one's sexual partner is.

Roger Scruton holds a similar view, and he traces sexual jealousy to the very fact that if one is desired, one is desired as an example of one's sex, for this means that one is always in principle replaceable by another as an object of desire.[19] This understanding of jealousy comes out well in Büchner's great play *Woyzeck* (from which Berg made an opera and Herzog a film), his study, based on real sources, of the sexual jealousy of the eponymous downtrodden soldier who murders his common-law wife when he discovers she has been sleeping with the Drum-Major. The scene in which Woyzeck confronts her with this is extraordinary:

Woyzeck (staring at her, shaking his head): Hm! I don't see anything, I don't see anything. Oh, you think you'd see it—you'd think you could catch hold of it.

Marie (frightened): What's up, Franz? You're raving, Franz.

Woyzeck: A sin so big and so fat. It stinks so you'd think it'd smoke the angels out of Heaven. You've got a red mouth, Marie. No blisters on it? Goodbye, Marie, you're as beautiful as sin. Can mortal sin be so beautiful?

Marie: Franz, you're talking like you were mad.

Woyzeck: To hell with it!—Did he stand like that or like this?

Marie: As the day is long and the world old lots of people can stand in the same place, one after the other.

Woyzeck: I saw him.

Marie: You can see a lot if you've got two eyes and aren't blind and the sun's shining.[20]

The whole scene expresses in a wonderfully economical fashion—and, it must be said, in language which cannot be adequately captured in translation—horror at the thought that in sexual desire one person can be replaced by another. When in Herzog's film of the play Woyzeck, played by Klaus Kinski, asks "Did he stand like that or like this?" Kinski places himself right in front of Marie and thrusts his pelvis now this way, now that, into her groin, and this gesture perfectly captures the horror at the replaceability of individuals in sexual desire.

Yet it captures more than horror, for there is disgust in Woyzeck's reaction. This is why he immediately associates Marie's infidelity with disease. And the disgust is also captured in Kinski's portrayal of the soldier: during the scene, he bends down and buries his nose in the turned-back sheets and blankets of the bed, smelling for the animal-like scent of the sex act. (Büchner was very influenced by Shakespeare, and one cannot help thinking in this connection of Hamlet's "Nay, but to live / In the rank sweat of an enseamed bed, / Stew'd in corruption, honeying and making love / Over the nasty sty!"[21] and Kinski—or Herzog—may have had this in mind.) There is an important connection between disgust and sexual jealousy.

In a valuable essay, David Pole has analyzed the concept of disgust.[22] He argues that disgust always carries a charge of attraction, and I think that this attraction is evident in Woyzeck's reaction to Marie: witness the association of her beauty with sin and the emphasis on the diseased redness of her mouth, dreadful yet enticing. Pole also suggests that we get our central notion of disgust from organic matter that is decomposing in some way, which would help explain why such things as slugs—to take one of Pole's examples—are experienced as disgusting: for the slug's slimy body, which it appears to be losing as it crawls along, seems to be caught in a process of decay and corruption. One of the most disgusting things I have ever seen was the neck of an otherwise healthy horse, gashed wide open by barbed wire, into which had buried themselves thousands of maggots which were feeding on the blood oozing in clots from the wound. A friend told me of his disgust on seeing a frog which has a loose back like a string vest into which the young flee to seek shelter and are carried for safety. Organic decay, then, or what looks like it, or smells of it, is perhaps the core of disgust.

Consider now the sexual act. In this act the bodies of those involved undergo profound changes: the flushing of the face, the erection of the penis, the tumescence of the nipples, the secretions of the vagina. One is overwhelmed in desire by one's body, as Sartre puts it: one's will is here in abeyance. All of these things can, of course, be received as an expression of excitement. But there is no doubt that they can be seen as disgusting, and often have been so seen. For, by their very nature, and in their triumph over the will, they are redolent of a body in decay. This is why desire for the other in his or her flesh can so easily, in certain persons, tip over into disgust with his or her flesh. And in sexual jealousy such disgust is to the fore: for the sexually exciting transformations of the beloved's body resemble nothing so much as the disgusting decay of that body when they are provoked by, and express desire for, a rival. Yet the transformations of one's beloved's body, even when they are connected with one's rival, remain exciting, and they do so even partly because they disgust, for that which is disgusting is appealing, as we have already noted. Disgust, one might say, adapting a Sartrean idiom from another context, lies coiled like a worm at the heart of desire, and it is brought to the light of day by betrayal. Sexual jealousy may begin in the recognition of one's dispensability as a sexual partner, but once it has been evoked it feeds upon the primordial disgust which lies hidden in all sexual acts. It is *this* recognition which animates the brilliance of Büchner's treatment of Woyzeck's jealousy and Kinski's portrayal of it.

It might be said that the idea that disgust lies at the heart of sexual desire is absurd. And it is, of course, true that not everyone will be susceptible to the sense that the transformations of the body in sexual excitement are redolent of a body in decay, however latent this might be. But there are other reasons for supposing that disgust is inherent in sexual desire. For example, it just seems to be the case that sexual desire (especially male desire?) is often ignited and intensified by a sense of doing something which involves disgust. This is connected with the fact that in sex we suspend or overcome our normal sense of disgust. As William Ian Miller says:

> [S]exual desire depends on the idea of a prohibited domain of the disgusting. A person's tongue in your mouth could be experienced as a pleasure or as a most repulsive and nauseating intrusion depending on the state of relations that exist or are being negotiated between you and the person. But someone else's tongue in your mouth can be a sign of intimacy *because* it can also be a disgusting assault.[23]

But can it be right to say that modern sexual desire, whose expression is so free in comparison with that of previous ages, carries a sense of disgust at its core? Perhaps the idea is not as absurd as it might seem, for A. Béjin has argued that

> present day [sexual] norms tend to provoke a conflict between immediate surrender to the demands of the senses, and an increased conscious mastery of the organic processes. . . . One must . . . abandon oneself to sensation, without ceasing to submit one's actions to a rational calculation of "sexual expedience."[24]

The claim is that we have done a great deal to subsume our sexual practices under the same kind of cost-benefit calculus that applies in so many other areas of our life. If this is right, then modern sexual desire, for all its seeming liberation from older forms of control, may be thought to express a powerful asceticism which itself testifies to a sense of disgust with sex.

III

I mentioned earlier Sartre's thought that in desire one is overwhelmed by the body. He makes this point in the context of his discussion of the caress which expresses sexual desire. Such a caress—it may be a caress of the hand or the eye—constitutes an attempt to *incarnate* the other. The other, he says, is born as flesh under my caress, whence the idea that I want him or her to be overwhelmed by his or her body: "Desire is the attempt to strip the body of its movements as of its clothing and to make it exist as pure flesh."[25] If the other responds to my caress then this person will experience his or her arousal as "troubling," as "clogging" consciousness. Yet, at the same time, my experiencing my own desire is felt by me in the same way, and I, too, in responding to the caress of the other, am born as flesh for him or her.

This process of mutual incarnation leads Sartre to speak of a "world of desire": "If my body . . . is lived as flesh, then it is as a reference to my flesh that I apprehend the objects in the world. This means that I make myself passive in relation to them and that they are revealed to me from the point of view of this passivity. . . . Objects then become the transcendent ensemble which reveals my incarnation to me. A contact with them is a *caress;* that is, my perception is not the *utilization* of the object, but to perceive an object when I am in the desiring attitude is to caress myself with it. Thus I am sensitive not so much to the form of the object and to its instrumentality, as to its matter (gritty, smooth, tepid, greasy, rough, etc.). In my desiring perception I discover something like a *flesh* of objects."[26] This passage, typical in both its insight and incantatory quality of the whole of Sartre's discussion, could be read as a philosophical explication of Heinrich Böll's description of the adolescent boy's sexual excitement at the objects he associates with women. But it is more than that. For it helps provide an explanation of why it is that in desire the lovers can want the entire world to become sexualized, made over in the image of their desire: there is in desire a hostility to that which does not support and feed the desire itself. The lovers attempt to discover, so to speak, the sexual qualities of the objects around them. This is why there is an ancient connection between sex and food. For it is not just that we like eating and associate its pleasures with those of sex, as if we were dealing here with two intense forms of pleasure and wanted to have them both simultaneously. Rather, because we like eating anyway, and because when we eat we are profoundly aware of the *matter* of what we eat (its smoothness, greasiness, and so on), we seek in sex to co-opt the experience of food to that of sex, to sexualize our food, discover its flesh, which is why a shared meal is so often a desired prelude to the sex act. Or again, fashion itself, which helps construct our sense of gender as men and women, is, amongst other things, the construction of a style through which, in the world of desire, one can be aware of the fleshliness of the material of one's clothes not simply as clothes but as representations of one's existence as man or woman. One's clothes, after all, are things constantly in contact with one's flesh, and they are therefore the first objects to whose fleshliness one responds in the world of desire: it is thus gratifying that they should be invested in such a moment with the imagery and symbolism of gender. Even the act of love itself does not rest content until it discovers to itself the flesh of objects. This is why especially manufactured sex toys are readily incorporated into the sex act itself. Such toys discover to the lovers the fleshliness of the world around them, and help preserve the fantasy that the world itself can be made over in the image of their desire, that the world is compliant to their will. Similar things may be said about the kind of fantasy clothing that typically serves to raise sexual excitement and about the materials from which it is made: leather, plastic, rubber, fur. The lovers want to discover the fleshliness of such materials which is one reason why the clothing made from such fabric is often conceptualized as a "second skin": for in this way it can subserve the desire to be both the skin of the lover and partake of the nature of the inanimate world, thus discovering to the lovers both their own nature as flesh and the flesh of the world around them.

I referred just now to the lovers' imposition of their will on the world in the wish in desire that the world itself cooperate in supporting and feeding that desire. There is something apposite about this way of speaking. For, as we have seen, in desire one is overwhelmed by one's body: the will is cancelled, especially in one's properly sexual parts. Thus we might speculate that the attempt to make the world over in the image of one's desire can be interpreted as an attempt to impose one's will at one site (the world) which has been put in abeyance at another site (the body). And this itself, if correct, deepens our understanding of the seemingly inevitable frustration of sexual desire, discussed earlier: for such an attempt is, of course, futile.

I have suggested, following Sartre, that such stratagems of desire involve an attempt to sexualize material objects. But this very attempt contains within itself its own mirror image: the desire to turn the object of sexual interest into a material object. This is clear from a great deal of pornography, for example, where the individuals presented often appear "dollified." Hence it is that the deeper meaning ("project," as Sartre would say) of pornography is not that of its being a substitute for a sexual partner, though, it may, of course, serve this purpose, but of its being the object of a distinctive kind of sexual desire: that, once again, of sexualizing the entire world. This reaches its apotheosis, perhaps, in such wonderfully bizarre phenomena of the modern world as telephone sex, where the very emptiness of the sexual encounter—merely auditory, and devoid of tactile, olfactory, visual, and gustatory qualities—together with the insistence of topic awakens the fantasy that the world of objects is a world of sexual objects, for there is no object in the world which does not subserve a sexual purpose, all other objects having been destroyed. That is, there is in this fantasy only one object—and it is a sexual object—the voice of the other person on the end of the line, and this object is omnipresent, emanating from every person because it emanates from no particular person one knows. Perhaps we should see in this some version of the Christian conception of God: for the caller speaks to the voice at the end of the line as the person in prayer speaks to God, that is, by speaking into the ether. And it is, as I have said, an omnipresent voice. Moreover, it is an omniscient voice, for it knows one's desire through and through; and omnipotent, since it can give one what one wants. There is even a kind of supplication in both the masturbator on the telephone and the believer. But, in the end, the voice is an inversion of God: for he required that one bend one's desires to his will; the voice exists merely to satisfy one's desire.

IV

I spoke earlier of the possibility of a deepened understanding of sex. I have also spoken of the disgust which is implicit in sex. These two ways of thinking can certainly pull us in different directions, making us think of sex as now something full of grace and light, now as something mean and shabby. But they can pull in the same direction. For the experience of sex can be deeply consoling. If we ask why this is so, then a key part of the answer is surely that, given the wretchedness of the human heart and its potential to fill one with disgust, it can seem little short of a miracle that one person should consent to the intimacy with another that making love involves. In other words, in some moods it can seem that when two people make love this act will depend upon, and involve, mutual forgiveness. Responding to such a thought, some have seen in sex the possibility of a quasi-religious act. Such an idea is certainly blasphemous, but it helps us see that, in an age of decay of religious belief, there may lie secretly in the modern obsession with sex a kind of longing for a redemption no longer available in traditional terms.

There is, for some people, something melancholy in the fact that sex can be both a source of the kind of consolation I have mentioned, as well as being rampant and imperious in the way I have also discussed. We often long for it to express only the most tender of feelings. Yet one can also be glad of this discrepancy in our experience of what sex is, since it makes of sex one of those mysteries of the human condition which help us hold onto the sense that life is worth living because what it offers us is inexhaustibly rich and varied.

Study Questions

1. Hamilton discusses and disagrees with a view that he attributes to Igor Primoratz: that if an activity occurring between two people produces no sexual pleasure for them, it is not, or is no longer, a *sexual* act. Suppose a woman and a man have received doses of local anesthesia and can feel no sexual pleasure in their genitals and other sexual parts, and they then proceed to engage in coitus. Are they performing a sexual act? Why or why not? Further, what should we say about rape in which the man experiences pleasure but the woman none at all?

2. When—in what circumstances or as the result of what causes—is sex disgusting, or when does it become disgusting to at least one participant? Does this happen only or mostly in the performance or contemplation of perverted sexual acts? Are disgust and powerful arousal mutually exclusive? Might love conquer disgust and allow desire to be victorious? Hamilton finds a connection between disgust and sexual jealousy. He also finds connections between sexual jealously and both "replaceability" and "dispensability." Are the latter two even the same? How do they link with disgust? Are you able to state clearly all these "connections" Hamilton finds?

3. Illustrate, with a variety of examples, how both "sexual activity" and "sexual desire" might be family resemblance concepts. Then consider whether "sexual activity" might be a family resemblance concept because (a) sexual activity is a game (perhaps only through a family resemblance to "game"?) and (b) "game" itself is a family resemblance concept.

4. Explain what Hamilton means when he suggests that "in an age of decay of religious belief, there may lie secretly in the modern obsession with sex a kind of longing for a redemption no longer available in traditional terms." If God is dead, is that missing piece of the supernatural replaced by our beloveds toward whom we have a head-over-heels, if not obsessive, romantic experience? Is the thunderbolt of sexual passion and any subsequent sexual ecstasy the closest we can come to spiritual bliss and transcendence?

5. Compare what Hamilton claims about telephone sex and, by extrapolation, other forms of cybersex, with Louise Collins's concerns about and insights into these phenomena (chapter 8).

Notes

1. Roger Scruton, *Sexual Desire: A Moral Philosophy of the Erotic* (London: Weidenfeld and Nicolson, 1986), chap. 4.

2. Scruton, *Sexual Desire*, 89–90.

3. Stefan Zweig, *Casanova: A Study in Self-Portraiture*, trans. Eden Paul and Cedar Paul (London: Pushkin Press, 1998 [1928]), 88–89.

4. Scruton, *Sexual Desire*, 76.

5. Scruton, *Sexual Desire*, 362–63. Cf. also Igor Primoratz's discussion of Scruton's views in *Ethics and Sex* (London: Routledge, 1999), chap. 3.

6. Primoratz, *Ethics and Sex*, 46.

7. Primoratz, *Ethics and Sex*, 49.

8. Ludwig Wittgenstein, *Philosophical Investigations I*, trans. G. E. M. Anscombe (Oxford, UK: Blackwell, 1983 [1953]), §66.

9. Wittgenstein, *Philosophical Investigations I*, §67.

10. Heinrich Böll, "Im Tal der donnernden Hufe," in *Als der Krieg ausbrach: Erzählungen* (Köln, Ger.: Deutscher Taschenbuch Verlag, 1971), 140–41; my translation.

11. Many of them are offered by Primoratz in *Ethics and Sex*, chap. 2.

12. D. H. Lawrence, "A Propos of 'Lady Chatterley's Lover,'" in *Phoenix II*, ed. Warren Roberts and Harry T. Moore (New York: Viking Press, 1970), 504.

13. Jean-Paul Sartre, *Being and Nothingness*, trans. Hazel Barnes (London: Methuen, 1984 [1943]), II, iii, 2.

14. Scruton, *Sexual Desire*, 74.

15. Thomas Nagel, "Sexual Perversion" in *Mortal Questions* (in this volume, chapter 3).

16. This point is made by Primoratz, *Ethics and Sex*, 47.

17. Stuart Hampshire, *Innocence and Experience* (Harmondsworth, UK: Penguin, 1989), 125–26.

18. Sigmund Freud, "'Civilized' Sexual Morality and Modern Nervous Illness," in *Civilization, Society, and Religion*, trans. Angela Richards (Harmondsworth, UK: Penguin, 1991 [1908]), 50.

19. Scruton, *Sexual Desire*, 163.

20. Georg Büchner, *Woyzeck*, in *Werke und Briefe*, ed. K. Pörnbecher, G. Schaub, H.-J. Simm, and E. Ziegler (München, Ger.: Deutscher Taschenbuch Verlag, 1988), scene 7; my translation. (Büchner left behind four unfinished versions of the play when he died, and since no one knows what final order of the scenes he intended this scene appears in a different place in the play in some published editions.)

21. William Shakespeare, *Hamlet*, ed. Harold Jenkins (London: Arden, 1997 [1603]), III, iv, 91–94.

22. David Pole, "Disgust and Other Forms of Aversion," in George Roberts, ed., *Aesthetics, Form, and Emotion* (London: Duckworth, 1983), 219–31.

23. William Ian Miller, *An Anatomy of Disgust* (Cambridge, Mass.: Harvard University Press, 1997), 137.

24. A. Béjin, "The Influence of the Sexologists," in P. Ariès and A. Béjin, eds., *Western Sexuality: Practice and Precepts in Past and Present Times* (Oxford: Basil Blackwell, 1985), 201–17, at 211.

25. Sartre, *Being and Nothingness*, 389.

26. Sartre, *Being and Nothingness*, 392.

Chapter 8

IS CYBERSEX SEX?

Louise Collins

In this provocative essay that discusses a host of unusual practices and philosophical ideas, **Louise Collins** *exposes us to the various forms of cybersex and leads us through a forest of analytic and normative tangles. What is fascinating and seductive about the topic of cybersex is that reflecting on it raises questions in, seemingly, all branches of philosophy, including epistemology (What can we know about our sex partners, both real-life and virtual, and does it matter?), metaphysics (What is the "self"? Do we have one, or are we one, or is there any such thing?), and, of course, ethics. What Collins writes about cybersex and the massive deception it allows should be read in the context of the Kantian approach to sexual morality advanced by Thomas Mappes (below, chapter 16) and discussed by Alan Soble (chapter 18). Further, readers should not forget the sexual temptations and dangers for young users of the Internet.*

Collins is associate professor of philosophy at Indiana University, South Bend. Her areas of interest are feminist theory, ethics, and social philosophy. She has published on gossip, human cloning, cybersex, and teaching philosophy.

Consider these two scenarios:

(1) Your beloved has moved overseas. To maintain your erotic relationship, you arrange to don virtual reality suits, as imagined by Howard Rheingold:

> [After] you put on your 3D glasses, you slip into a lightweight . . . bodysuit.
> . . . Embedded in the inner surface of the suit . . . is an array of intelligent

sensor-effectors—a mesh of tiny tactile detectors coupled to vibrators of varying degrees of hardness, hundreds of them per square inch, that can receive and transmit a realistic sense of tactile presence, the way the audio and visual displays transmit a realistic sense of visual and auditory presence. . . . Now, imagine plugging your whole sound-sight-touch telepresence system into the telephone network. You see a lifelike but totally artificial visual representation of your own body and your partner's. . . . Your partner(s) can move independently in the cyberspace, and your representations are able to touch each other, even though your physical bodies might be continents apart.[1]

One night, you agree to go all the way in virtual reality sex. Afterward, you are exhilarated but confused: are you still virgins? You had vowed to give yourself to your one true love: have you now consummated your relationship?

(2) You surprise your spouse at the computer, who is typing feverishly and breathing heavily. Over your spouse's shoulder, you read on the screen: "LuvBunni: Oh baby, do me now." Scrolling up, you read: "Pocket-Rocket: I'm hot, hard, and ready to launch." You feel upset and betrayed, but have you been sexually betrayed? Is your spouse an adulterer?

Even when we have filled in the details in each of these scenarios—the disposition of body parts and technical devices, the beliefs and desires of those involved—a residual confusion remains. Clearly something was going on in each case, but was it sex?

According to the dominant account in our culture, the paradigm case of what counts as sex is heterosexual intercourse, where a man and woman engage in a particularly intimate form of physical contact, in which a penis penetrates a vagina (or where a vagina engulfs a penis). This case is paradigmatic in that it organizes social judgments about which other activities count as sexual, and also connects to dominant views about what sex is normal, natural, and good.

Some activities get counted as sexual because they are seen as relevantly similar to the paradigm case in some respect, or because they are assumed to be causally connected to moments in the paradigm case. Reading pornography and purchasing phone sex are classed as sexual activities because they are usually undertaken to produce pleasures similar to those assumed to be characteristic of intercourse. Flirting counts as sexual activity because it is seen as loosely causally connected to finding a partner for intercourse.

The two cybersex scenarios above clearly differ from the paradigm case. The virtual-reality sex lovers are physically separated, not in flesh-to-flesh contact, and the same is true of the lusty correspondents. The correspondents have at most carnal knowledge-by-description of each other, not the multisensory knowledge-by-acquaintance typical of paradigmatic sex. It is hard to say whether the virtual-reality sex lovers literally sense each other, which is rarely a question in the standard case of sex. During paradigmatic sex, mistakes about one's partner's anatomical sex, number, and existence are unusual, while participants in the scenarios above may be mistaken about all these attributes. In cybersex, the risk of an unplanned pregnancy or of contracting a sexually transmitted disease is significantly lower than in paradigmatic sex.

This paper comprises four parts. Before tackling the main question, it is useful to recognize the range of information-technology-mediated erotic activities labeled as cybersex, and the challenge each type poses to the culturally dominant account of sex (I, II). In search of further insight, we then turn to three philosophical attempts to define sex (III). These accounts offer different approaches to deciding whether cybersex is sex, but require further philosophical work to be conclusive. Finally (IV), we turn to underlying normative questions about what is at stake in determining whether any activity is properly classed as sex.

I. Species of Cybersex

The term "cybersex" is sometimes construed broadly, to refer to a growing array of erotically charged activities mediated by new information technology, which range from accessing sexually explicit videos online, to text-messaging flirtatious comments to a high-school classmate or Congressional page, and from posting a personal profile on a web site in search of an offline date, to bartering with an international sex trafficker.

More often, "cybersex" is construed to refer more narrowly, to "[A] social interaction between at least two people who are exchanging real-time digital [video, audio, but, typically, text-based] messages in order to become sexually aroused. People send provocative and erotic messages to each other, with the purpose of bringing each other to orgasm as they masturbate in real time."[2] Less restrictively, cybersex can be defined as "[A] computer mediated interpersonal interaction in which the participants are sexually motivated, meaning they are seeking sexual arousal and satisfaction."[3] This definition encompasses both virtual reality-based cybersex, like the first scenario above, and text-based cybersex, like the second.

In "virtual reality-based cybersex," a person employs a bodysuit and helmet that transmit data to create a three-dimensional sensory (audio-visual, tactile) virtual reality, as described by Rheingold in the first scenario. Though such equipment was not available very early in the twenty-first century, prototype computer-mediated, remote-controlled sex toys were.[4] Participants in "video-based cybersex" engage in online video conferences during which they remove their clothing, show each other their bodies, including their genitals, and commonly look at each other as they masturbate. In commercial video-based cybersex, a model is viewed by paying clients over a livecam; the clients can use a telephone or send an e-mail message to tell the model what to do.[5]

"Text-based cybersex" involves the real-time exchange of explicit text messages, short or long, in which the parties describe body parts and features, elaborate sexual actions and reactions to them, and may pretend that these "virtual" events are really happening. Text-based cybersex requires a networked computer with suitable software; many of the participants are sexually imaginative, write eloquently, and read and type quickly. Text-based cybersex includes TinySex and Hot Chat. TinySex occurs in a multi-user domain/dimension/dungeon (MUD), which is a computer-generated, interactive text environment with a particular theme in which many persons can interact simultaneously. Once logged on a MUD, a person is represented by a virtual character, established in a fictional self-description.

> MUDs put you in virtual spaces in which you are able to navigate, converse and build. . . . For example, if I am playing the character named ST . . . any words I type after the command "say" will appear on all players' screens as "ST says." Any actions I type after the command "emote" will appear after my name just as I type them, as in "ST waves hi" or "ST laughs uncontrollably." I can "whisper" to a designated character and only that character will be able to see my words.[6]

The MUD program converts a character's first-person comments and actions into third person reports on others' screens. Hot Chat is a popular form of text-based cybersex that uses a chat program. Chat forums can be found on online services such as AOL and Compuserve as well as on the Internet, using Internet Relay Chat channels (which allow multiple users to connect to a live discussion). In chatting, one posts real-time messages to a virtual meeting place, where others are present and conversing. At some point, one person typically withdraws to a private venue with direct person-to-person connections in order to exchange more explicit sexual messages with others (see the second scenario, above).

II. Is Cybersex Sex? A First Pass

Some features of cybersex (narrowly defined) raise the conceptual question: Is cybersex really sex? Hot Chat lacks direct bodily contact between participants. Though cyberers often use real-time messaging, some use e-mail that involves significant time delays between sending and receiving erotic messages. TinySex in MUDs sharpens the question whether writing first-person descriptions of the sexual activities of a virtual character or persona is tantamount to one's engaging in sexual activity. The possibility of virtual reality bodysuits, which would allow lovers to feel as well as see each other's body through an atypical electronic pathway, raises questions about the boundaries of the body and the locus of sexual union. Thus, cybersex suggests a host of questions: What is sex, really? What is good sex? What is the relationship between imagined and real acts in general, and between imagined and real sexual acts, in particular? What is the relationship between one's personae in various venues and one's "genuine" self?

As noted above, paradigmatic sex requires direct physical contact between lovers. Since there is no physical contact in Hot Chat, perhaps it belongs with the exchange of erotic letters, or phone sex, and not sex proper. Or, Hot Chat might be classed as coauthored pornography about the sex lives of virtual personae, individuated by online tags such as "HotLips," and not as sex between the authors. However, participants report that Hot Chat can be as physically and emotionally compelling as paradigmatic sex, despite the absence of normal multisensory cues.[7] Further, Hot Chat sometimes leads to later offline trysts, so it might be classed as "foreplay" (as in "seductive activity anticipatory of penetration").

If one also rejects the heteronormative defining of the boundaries of sexual episodes by relation to penetration,[8] then Hot Chat might be classed as sex proper. Whether the participants touch each other directly, what matters is that each is sexually aroused by the other's response. Thus phone sex and Hot Chat can be real sex. The conceptual question then becomes, what is distinctive about sexual arousal?

TinySex raises more complex questions about the attribution of erotic acts and agency. In a MUD, one assumes a named, fictional persona ("Pooh") by posting a self-description that need not match one's actual appearance, character, or species ("a stout and reliable bear"). I type speech, actions, and reactions that are meant to be attributed to my persona, "Pooh," not to me, "the author of the Pooh character." For the sake of erotic arousal, I may initiate an encounter in the MUD between "Pooh" and another persona, "Piglet," scripted by another pseudonymous author. As Elizabeth Reid comments, "Who it is that is communicating becomes unclear, and whether passion is being simulated or transmitted through the MUD becomes truly problematic."[9] According to Sherry Turkle and Julian Dibbell, that MUD-players find such encounters sexually arousing confirms the postmodern claims that the self is multiple, fragmentary, and constituted by language, and that sex is an exchange of signifiers.[10]

One might object that the question, "Has the author of Pooh had sex with Piglet?" commits a category mistake similar to "Did Shakespeare kill Macduff?" We can say that "Pooh had sex with Piglet" if the transcripts of the MUD support this interpretation, just as we can say "Macbeth killed Macduff" if the text of *Macbeth* supports that reading. No real sex took place in the MUD, any more than real killing occurs on stage at Stratford. Pooh's actions in the MUD do not reflect on the author's character any more than Macbeth's actions in the play reflect on the actor playing Macbeth.

However, this reply does not capture the fact that I (the author of Pooh) derived actual erotic pleasure, perhaps masturbated, in response to "what Pooh said and did to Piglet" on the screen. As herrup comments, "[W]hen this cyberspace self becomes the vehicle for real-life sexual arousal, what you think of as your 'real-life self' becomes implicated in whatever sexuality you experience on-line. Even if this cyberspace self is entirely fantastical . . . there is always some kind of 'real self' that is implicated insofar as you believe you had a role in deciding which fantasy persona to take on."[11]

Perhaps TinySex, too, should be classed as a kind of collaborative pornography and not as sex proper. Even if TinySex may be closer to a game or artistic improvisation than real sex, how we play games and improvise together may reflect on our actual tastes and moral personalities. For example, Dibbell and Turkle discuss a "virtual rape" in which a MUD player (or players) hijacks other players' characters and makes them perform violent sexual acts, greatly distressing the characters' respective authors and many onlookers. In the context of this case, the original decision (to hijack a character) and subsequent indifference to the distress so caused both count against the virtue of the hijacking player.

Alternatively, perhaps reflection on TinySex should displace the traditional paradigm of sex as flesh-to-flesh. It is not clear that direct fleshly contact is necessary for sex, for sexual activity that involves using a dental dam or a condom is no less sex for being safer by excluding direct contact. Sex between two people swathed in Saran wrap is still sex.[12] Related questions will recur below when we look at the writings of Thomas Nagel and Alan Goldman.

Virtual reality suits raise other issues. Imagine that you are in a virtual reality bodysuit, and your senses are being stimulated by the actions of someone in a bodysuit elsewhere. You respond not to a verbal description of the other's arousal, but to a panoply of sensory stimuli originating from the other's body, through a long and nonstandard causal chain. Should the virtual reality suit be seen as a prosthesis that extends the reach of one's body or, to the contrary, as a complex barrier contraceptive that keeps lovers' bodies safely apart? Or, does virtual reality sex merely simulate sex, without being sex?

To throw some light on these issues, let us turn to three leading philosophers' attempts to define sex.

III. Three Philosophers Define Sex

Alan Goldman's analysis of "plain sex" tries to free the concept of sex from what he takes as the distortions of residual Platonic-Christian moralizing. According to Goldman, such moralizing motivates "means-ends" accounts of sex, which build a further purpose (communication, procreation, love) into the very definition of sex, as part of a crusade to redeem the base physicality of sex. Goldman regards such attempts as unnecessary and confused. That sex is rooted in our physical natures should simply be acknowledged without shame or obfuscation: "Sexual desire lets us know that we are physical beings and, indeed, animals."[13] Sex as such is morally neutral, while particular sexual activities are subject to the same moral standards that govern any other activities.

According to Goldman, "Sexual desire is desire for contact with another person's body and for the pleasure which such contact brings; sexual activity is activity which tends to fulfill such desire of the agent. . . . [Sexual desire] is not a desire for a particular sensation detachable from its causal context, a sensation which can be derived in other ways."[14] Thus, on his view, cybersex (like sexual experiences involving pornography) qualifies only as "an imaginative substitute for the real thing."[15]

Goldman's account, however, relies on an unexplicated notion of physical contact. Is half as much sex going on if the participants are semi-naked (or semi-clothed)? Is safe sex that prevents direct physical contact an oxymoron? If you can have sex wearing spectacles, why can't you have sex by using videocams?

Let us overlook these problems and grant to Goldman some "commonsense" test of physical contact. Since there is no direct contact between bodies, what happens in cybersex isn't sex, even if I think it is, and even if it is both enjoyable and morally admirable. Goldman claims that "sexual desire . . . is not a desire for a particular sensation detachable from its causal context, a sensation which can be derived in other ways." The case of virtual-reality sex heightens a question. If I believe that my desire for physical contact and the pleasures caused by physical contact have been satisfied, why exactly does it matter if, unbeknownst to me, the pleasures I have experienced have a nonstandard cause and my belief is false? For Goldman's account, the problem here is ontological, not moral or epistemological. Recall that sex matters because it" lets us know that we are . . . indeed animals." But what kind of animal does Goldman think sex tells us we are?

Perhaps for Goldman we are animals whose bodily boundaries are fixed by our brute biology. Our technologies and cultural ideologies do not touch this aspect of our physical nature. Then cybersex may let us know that we are pleasure-seeking, tool-using animals, but it cannot change the bounds of our bodies. Ironically, Goldman may share, with the Platonic-Christians he opposes, the belief that our physical nature is fixed.

However, cybersex may teach a different view of our natures. Perhaps we are animals whose nature it is to remake not just our environment, but our own bodies through biotechnology and information technologies. Sadie Plant argues that "the digital machines of the late twentieth century are not add-on parts that serve to augment an existing human form. Quite beyond their own perceptions and control, bodies are continually engineered by the processes in which they engage."[16] Thus virtual-reality sex should not be assimilated to sex with a discrete tool (for example, a dildo); rather, the immersive multimedia technology of virtual-reality sex changes the very boundaries of our bodies.

Thomas Nagel takes a different approach to Goldman. He defines human sex in terms of a normative psychological structure, rather than in relation to procreation, because he sees this psychological dimension as what is distinctively human in sex. Nagel analyses "natural" (or "complete") human sex in terms of escalating psychological attitudes: Romeo is aroused by noticing and sensing Juliet's arousal at her awareness of Romeo's arousal, and Juliet is aroused by sensing Romeo's arousal at his awareness of her arousal. "[S]exual desire leads to spontaneous interactions with other persons, whose bodies are asserting their sovereignty . . . producing involuntary reactions and spontaneous impulses in *them*. These reactions are perceived, and the perception of them is perceived, and that perception is in turn perceived."[17] In his original argument, Nagel illustrates this escalation with the case of two strangers who flirt indirectly, via their reflections in the mirrored walls of a cocktail lounge.

Hot Chat probably produces physiological arousal qualitatively similar to that of conventional sex, and its erotic e-mails likely express the psychological escalation described by Nagel. However, the causal route from stimulus to arousal is different in the case of mirrors and typed text on a screen. When observing the object of one's desire in a mirror, though the glance is mediated by a technological device (the mirror), the observer's arousal is triggered by a visual cue (the image in the mirror) that operates by a similar causal route as in direct perception (a direct look at the other). In the case of Hot Chat, the desirer's response is triggered by a visual cue (the typed text on screen) through a different route: illuminated pixels have to be interpreted by the reader as meaningful symbols and decoded before the erotic imagination kicks in and produces arousal.

As Sandy Stone suggests about commercial phone sex, Hot Chat might be arousing just because of the dearth of sensory cues given: "In phone sex, once the signifiers begin to 'float' loose from their moorings in a particularized physical experience, the most powerful attractor becomes the client's idealized fantasy. In this circumstance narrow bandwidth becomes a powerful asset, because extremely complex fantasies can be generated from a small set of cues."[18]

Hot Chat may not meet Nagel's requirement that "at each step the domination of the person by his body is reinforced, and the sexual partner becomes more possessible by physical contact, penetration, and envelopment."[19] As to the "domination of the person by his body," for the text to produce arousal at all, the reader's mental skills of interpretation and imagination must be actively engaged. Further, the typist must maintain control over at least one keyboarding hand. Thus, Nagel might classify Hot Chat as a sexual perversion, since it requires this resistance to one's own bodily surrender.

Long-distance erotic trysts employing virtual reality bodysuits would also raise questions for Nagel. Virtual reality suits in cybersex play a causal role closer to the lounge mirrors' role in Juliet and Romeo's dalliance than does the typed text of Hot Chat. The sensors and effectors in Rheingold's fantasy deal in the currency of sensations and perceptions, unmediated by the cognitive labor of decoding literal text. Unnervingly, virtual-reality sex with another person might be qualitatively indistinguishable from "asymmetrical" virtual-reality sex, where the suit itself generates stimuli rather than transmitting them between persons.[20] For all one knows, the other party to the escalating psychological attitudes expressed in Hot Chat may be a computer program. (See the "Julia" case described below.)

According to Nagel, natural human sexuality involves a pleasurable oscillation between awareness of oneself as the object of the other's desire and my awareness, as a desiring subject, of the other as desirable to me. The proper target of sexual desire is a nonfungible person, and persons are embodied subjectivities, capable of perceiving and being perceived. Thus, the interleaving psychological attitudes constitutive of sexual arousal, such as "Juliet's desire to arouse Romeo's desire," should be interpreted as desires *de re*, not *de dicto*. If this is correct, then cybersex with bots is, at most, perverse sex. However, until Nagel is clearer on what he means by sex making lovers "more possessible by physical contact," it is uncertain whether other kinds of cybersex are sex.

Robert Solomon criticizes what he sees as liberal platitudes, according to which, given informed consent between adults, any kind of sex is as good as another, and that the right measure of sex is pleasure. He claims that sex is (or is at its best) a form of communication between people employing body language and yields pleasure only as an accidental byproduct. "Sexual activity consists in speaking what we might call 'body language.' It has its own grammar, delineated by the body." The content of this communication is a range of "interpersonal attitudes and feelings" best expressed in gestures, "the bodily equivalent of a sentence."[21]

Applying these claims to cybersex again opens some new questions. It is unclear why Solomon thinks that some messages are most efficiently or appropriately expressed through body language rather than, say, sentences of English. Most of us have received some training in making ourselves understood in English; perhaps only choreographers are trained to articulate self-expression through bodily movement. While mass-marketed pornography and erotica may have imposed stability on the meanings of intimate bodily gestures in the bedroom, there is a broader and deeper social consensus on what words mean. If sex is essentially for communication, Hot Chat may offer less risk of miscommunication than paradigmatic bodily based sex, with a comparable possibility of erotic pleasure as a by-product.

A further question arises from the possibility of being erotically aroused by a computer program. Turkle records the case of a student who flirts with the intelligent agent, Julia, which is programmed to generate appropriate e-mail responses to syntactic and semantic cues in incoming e-mails.[22] For example, when asked "Do you like X?" Julia generates a response governed by transformation rules, replacing "you" with "I" and question formats with answer formats, "Yes, I love doing X." The student falsely believes he is seducing a real woman.

If sexual behavior is essentially communicative, then, if one's partner cannot understand the meaning of your communications, the sex is defective. It is interesting whether Solomon could here draw on a difference between genuine and fake (e.g., Chinese-box) communications to argue that a bot cannot really understand the meaning of your typed symbols and hence that sex with a bot is either impossible or horribly semantically deviant (perhaps, in a Solomonesque way, perverted). However, on a commonsense account, sex with a foreign human sex-worker is still sex, even if the prostitute has merely memorized rote seductive phrases from the john's language. So perhaps genuine understanding is necessary only for good sex.

Solomon asserts that bodily gestures lose something vital when translated into sentences. Perhaps the semantic density of body language is lost when it is reduced to a string of words. Thus Hot Chat is just talk about sex, not equivalent to sex, just as a description of a painting is not equivalent to the painting itself. On the other hand, virtual-reality cybersex in a sensor-effector-rich bodysuit might present a different case. Spectacles help myopics read the fine nuances of bodily gestures; perhaps a virtual reality bodysuit should be classed as a prosthetic device for preserving the semantic density of body language in sex.

Analysis of cybersex shows up lacunae in all three philosophers' accounts of sex. This may show that their accounts are flawed or simply incomplete. Rather than speculate further how each account might be extended to handle the varieties of cybersex, let us survey how practical, metaphysical, and epistemic features of participation in text-based and virtual reality cybersex may raise some novel moral questions.

IV. Cybersex and Values

Cybersex carries no risk of unwanted pregnancy or of contracting venereal diseases. On the other hand, cybersex cannot yield the benefit of wanted children. For a consequentialist, such practical costs and benefits should be factored into the moral evaluation of cybersex. Procreation cannot result from cybersex and thus, for a Thomistic Natural Law theorist, cybersex is unnatural and hence immoral. Other practical features of cybersex may matter morally. In text-based cybersex (without livecams), access to the other's body is always mediated by a textual representation under the other's control. As noted above, for such cybersex to continue, at least one participant must continue typing, thus that person's experience of immersion in sexual embodiment is constrained. These features of cybersex may raise normative questions about authenticity, spontaneity, and alienation from one's own and the other's body. On the other hand, text-based cybersex gives participants an opportunity to establish preferences, give consent, and announce and document promises and intentions, all of which play a key role in libertarian sexual ethics.

Cyberspace offers anonymous, discreet access to many potential cybersexual partners with a wide array of proclivities. That cybersex may be anonymous or pseudonymous also leads to questions about accountability and personal integrity (although these concerns arise in offline contexts, too). Sexual libertarians welcome the broadening of opportunities online for safe, sexual experimentation, particularly for members of stigmatized sexual minorities, and favor expanding access to and reduced censorship of cyberspace. Just such opportunities are regarded with moral suspicion by sexual conservatives. Feminist theorists articulate a wide range of views about practical features of cyberspace and women's empowerment.[23]

Tricky conceptual and metaphysical questions recur in moral debates about interpersonal relationships and cybersex. If one holds that the proper occasion for sex is within a committed relationship, and that cybersex really is sex, then one must also resolve the conceptual question whether a relationship conducted wholly online can count as a committed relationship.[24] Similarly, if one thinks that sex is permissible if and only if it is an expression of love, one must then determine whether love requires only the virtual meeting of two minds, or whether it requires living together. Again, if sex is morally valuable just as an expression of profound trust, can virtual sex, which limits mutual physical vulnerability, be good sex?

Cybersex underlines difficult questions about the relation between sex and gender, particularly for those who believe sex is only permissible between a woman and a man.[25] If your cybersexual partner (who, unbeknownst to you, is anatomically male) consistently and convincingly described himself to you as female, while you (also anatomically male) described yourself to him as male, have you engaged in immoral gay cybersex or morally permissible heterosexual cybersex? What if your cybersexual partner, when challenged, sincerely claims to be a woman trapped inside a man's body? Is her online self-presentation as female an expression of authenticity or culpably deceptive?

For those who believe that sex properly belongs within monogamous relationships, it is important to determine whether cybersex is indeed sex, and hence whether cybersex outside one's real-life partnership is adulterous and wrong. If the key wrong in adultery is a matter of promise-breaking or deception, then we might ask whether we should accept a monogamy contract prohibiting cybersex. It can be argued that we should not, for occasional virtual-reality cybersex with others may benefit one's real life partnerships, by providing a safe venue "like a flight simulator" to practice transferable skills.[26] Moderate indulgence in Hot Chat with others may benefit real life relationships in some cases.[27]

Even if text-based cybersex is merely collaborative writing of pornography and not really sex, a question remains whether it is wrong to share sexual fantasies with someone other than one's real-life partner.[28] Reflection on cybersex thus leads into broader debates about the moral status of imagination.[29] Laura Kipnis cautions that the law may conflate imagined and enacted erotic fantasies, when fantasies are mediated by internet communication.[30]

The epistemic features of cybersex allow profound deceptions that go beyond the familiar offline artifices that enhance one's appeal (cosmetics, elevator shoes, fibs about one's wealth, and so on). Cybersex allows thoroughgoing deception about one's physical attributes, including anatomical sex, physical ability, and age, and about socially conferred attributes such as status. In one much-discussed case from the early 1980s, when bulletin boards were novel, a shy male psychiatrist, Alex, passed online as a feisty disabled woman, "Joan," who gave out lots of advice and also seduced several of her online friends.[31] Some of "Joan's" friends were devastated by this betrayal; others were less upset. Sorting out what the virtue of honesty requires is made more complicated by the variety of contexts and expectations online. In a realm where people know that deception is both commonplace and easy, deception may lose some of its immoral zing. Indeed, part of the appeal of TinySex for some people is that it allows deceptive but consensual role-playing. For example, in FurryMuck players engage in sex games in character as nonhuman animals.

One might dismiss cybersex as the pursuit of merely simulated plea-sures, and as a repudiation of the risks and responsibilities of real rela-tionships with actual, embodied others. However, cybersex may, in some cases, be an attempt to resist or escape the unfair and unchosen limits the real world imposes. If, as a matter of bad luck, one happens to be ugly by conventional standards of beauty, in a society that treats the ugly as sexual pariahs, one might find in cyberspace a virtual community where beauty is defined differently, or where one can fictionally present oneself as conventionally attractive. If sex has an important place in a flourishing life, we should not dismiss cybersex as trivial.

We might think that the novel possibilities for erotic play offered by cybersex will not affect our cultural paradigms of sex and good sex. How-ever, the invention of the contraceptive pill, a novel biotechnology, played a role in displacing procreation from its central role in how we define sex. Perhaps, as new information technologies increasingly per-meate our lives, our conceptions of everyday activities will change, and experience with cybersex will reshape how we think about sex.

Study Questions

1. How might reading this essay by Louise Collins have helped Greta Christina (chapter 2) answer her own questions about either the meaning or extension of "sex"? Or vice versa: how might have reading Christina helped Collins? Or even: how might have read-ing Collins made Christina's task more difficult for her, and con-firmed her suspicion that the analytic task is unsolvable? Recon-sider, too, Christopher Hamilton's (chapter 7) invoking Ludwig Wittgenstein's notion of "family resemblance" to understand sex.

2. Goldman explicitly defines "sexual desire" and "sexual activity" (see chapter 5). Do Thomas Nagel (chapter 3) and Robert Solomon also do so? If not, what difference does this make to Collins's discussion of the latter two philosophers within the framework of her wondering whether cybersex is sexual activity? Collins argues that cybersex exposes "lacunae" in the views of Goldman, Nagel, and Solomon. Might it be, instead, that cyber-sex has less going for it, in various ways, than Collins claims—that, for example, it is marginal as sex, and will always be mar-ginal and hence not philosophically interesting? Does Collins show us, perhaps unwittingly, both the happy and the sad truths contained in Nagel's "bad sex may be better than none at all"?

3. What is the distinction, if any, between "directly" having physi-cal contact with another person, and having "indirect" physical

contact? Does touch involve direct contact, but not sight or smell? Is there any important difference between holding hands while both people are wearing silk gloves and while both hands are encased in mittens made of inflexible, impermeable glass or metal?

4. Discuss: "If I (an anatomic male) get aroused knowingly by a (pre-op) transsexual, am I gay?"

5. Collins claims that "it is important to determine whether cybersex is indeed sex, and hence whether cybersex outside one's real-life partnership is adulterous and wrong." Might not cybersex still be wrong in this situation, even if it is not sex and is not technically adulterous, or even if neither party in the real-life relationship would agree that it is sex? If a lap dance is not really sex, does that matter much to the partner who sits at home while her spouse is at the bar? Do you agree with "No French, no foul?" That is, is it permissible to kiss another person, not one's partner (say, at an office Christmas party), as long as tongues are not involved?

Notes

1. Howard Rheingold, *Virtual Reality* (New York: Simon & Schuster, 1992), 346.

2. Aaron Ben-Ze'ev, *Love Online: Emotions on the Internet* (Cambridge: Cambridge University Press, 2004), 5.

3. Nicola Döring, "Feminist Views of Cybersex: Victimization, Liberation and Empowerment." *CyberPsychology and Behavior* 3, no. 5 (2000): 863–84.

4. Joel Stein, "Will Cybersex Be Better than Real Sex?" *Time* 155, no. 25 (June 19, 2000), 62, 64.

5. See Robert Rossney, "The Next Best Thing to Being There." *Wired* 3, no. 5 (May 1995); Donna M. Hughes, "The Use of New Communications and Information Technologies for Sexual Exploitation of Women and Children," *Hastings Women's Law Journal* 13, no. 1 (Winter 2002): 129–48, at 143–44.

6. Sherry Turkle, *Life on the Screen: Identity in the Age of the Internet* (New York: Simon & Schuster, 1995), 11.

7. Ben-Ze'ev, *Love Online*, chap. 1.

8. See Diana Richardson, "Constructing Lesbian Sexualities," in Stevi Jackson and Sue Scott, eds., *Feminism and Sexuality: A Reader* (Edinburgh, Scot.: Edinburgh University Press, 1996), 267–86; Marilyn Frye, "Lesbian 'Sex,'" in *Willful Virgin: Essays in Feminism, 1976–1992* (Freedom, Calif.: Crossing Press, 1992), 102–19.

9. Elizabeth M. Reid, "Text-Based Virtual Realities: Identity and the Cyborg Body," in Peter Ludlow, ed., *High Noon on the Electronic Frontier: Conceptual Issues in Cyberspace* (Cambridge, Mass.: MIT Press, 1996), 327–45, at 341.

10. Turkle, *Life on the Screen*, 14–15; Julian Dibbell, "A Rape in Cyberspace; or How an Evil Clown, a Haitian Trickster Spirit, Two Wizards, and a Cast of Dozens Turned a Database into a Society," in Ludlow, *High Noon*, 375–95.

11. mocha jean herrup, "Virtual Identity," in Rebecca Walker, ed., *To Be Real: Telling the Truth and Changing the Face of Feminism* (New York: Doubleday, 1995), 239–51, at 245.

12. Nigel Warburton, "Virtual Fidelity," *Cogito* (November 1998), 193–99.

13. Alan Goldman, "Plain Sex," in Alan Soble, ed., *The Philosophy of Sex: Contemporary Readings*, 4th ed. (Savage, Md.: Rowman & Littlefield, 2002), 39-55, at 49. (In this volume, chap. 5; all page references are to the reprint in POS4.)

14. Goldman, "Plain Sex," 40.

15. Goldman, "Plain Sex," 42.

16. Sadie Plant, *Zeros + Ones: Digital Women + the New Technoculture* (London: Fourth Estate, 1997), 182.

17. Thomas Nagel, "Sexual Perversion," in Alan Soble, ed., *The Philosophy of Sex: Contemporary Readings*, 4th ed. (Savage, Md.: Rowman & Littlefield, 2002), 9–20, at 16. (In this volume, chap. 3; all page references are to the reprint in POS4.)

18. Sandy [Allucquère Rosanne] Stone, *The War of Desire and Technology at the Close of the Mechanical Age* (Cambridge, Mass.: MIT Press, 1995), 94–95.

19. Nagel, "Sexual Perversion," 16.

20. See Warburton, "Virtual Fidelity"; and Douglas Adeney, "Evaluating the Pleasures of Cybersex," *Australasian Journal of Professional and Applied Ethics* 1, no. 1 (June 1999): 69–79.

21. Robert Solomon, "Sexual Paradigms," in Alan Soble, ed., *The Philosophy of Sex: Contemporary Readings*, 4th ed. (Savage, Md. Rowman & Littlefield, 2002), 21–29, at 27.

22. Turkle, *Life on the Screen*, 88ff.

23. These are usefully summarized by Döring.

24. See Louise Collins, "Emotional Adultery: Cybersex and Commitment," *Social Theory and Practice* 25, no. 2 (Summer 1999): 243–70; and Hubert L. Dreyfus, *On the Internet* (London: Routledge, 2001).

25. See Amy S. Bruckman, "Gender Swapping on the Internet," in Ludlow, *High Noon*, 317–25.

26. See Warburton, "Virtual Fidelity."

27. See Ben-Ze'ev, *Love Online.*

28. See Collins, "Emotional Adultery."

29. See Ben-Ze'ev, *Love Online*, chap. 4, "Online Imagination."

30. Laura Kipnis, *Bound and Gagged: Pornography and the Politics of Fantasy in America* (New York: Grove Press, 1996).

31. See Stone, *War of Desire*; and Lindsy Van Gelder, "The Strange Case of the Electronic Lover," in Rob Kling, ed., *Computerization and Controversy*, 2nd ed. (San Diego, Calif.: Academic Press, 1996), 533–46.

PART 2

HOMOSEXUALITY AND REPRODUCTION

Chapter 9

THE WRONG OF HOMOSEXUALITY

John Finnis

Relying on the thought (from Immanuel Kant; see part III) that using the self and others, treating the body and person of oneself and other people instrumentally, is morally wrong in sexuality (and elsewhere), **John Finnis** *builds a case against same-sex sexual behavior and masturbation, indeed, against any sexual activity that is not heterosexual and conjugal. Finnis, well known as a contemporary scholar and proponent of the philosophy of Thomas Aquinas and a developer of what is called "New Natural Law," thereby defends a sexual ethics that is strikingly like that of Roman Catholicism. The interesting project of combining Kantian and Catholic sexual morality is attempted also by Karol Wojtyla (see chapter 11).*

Finnis is professor of law, Oxford University, and the author of *Natural Law and Natural Rights* (Oxford University Press, 1980), *Moral Absolutes: Tradition, Revision, and Truth* (Catholic University of America Press, 1991), and *Aquinas: Moral, Political, and Legal Theory* (Oxford University Press, 1998).

The underlying thought is on the following lines. In masturbating, as in being masturbated or sodomized, one's body is treated as instrumental for the securing of the experiential satisfaction of the conscious self. Thus one disintegrates oneself in two ways, (1) by treating one's body as a mere instrument of the consciously operating self, and (2) by making one's choosing self the quasi-slave of the experiencing self which is demanding gratification. The worthlessness of the gratification, and the disintegration of oneself, are both the result of the fact that, in these sorts of behavior, one's conduct is not the actualizing and experiencing of a real common good. Marriage, with its double blessing—procreation and friendship—is a real common good. Moreover, it is a common good that can be both actualized and experienced in the orgasmic union of the reproductive organs of a man and a woman united in commitment to that good. Conjugal sexual activity, and—as Plato and Aristotle and Plutarch and Kant all argue—*only* conjugal activity is free from the shamefulness of instrumentalization that is found in masturbating and in being masturbated or sodomized.

At the very heart of the reflections of Plato, Xenophon, Aristotle, Musonius Rufus, and Plutarch on the homoerotic culture around them is the very deliberate and careful judgment that homosexual *conduct* (and indeed all extramarital sexual gratification) is radically incapable of participating in, or actualizing, the common good of friendship. Friends who engage in such conduct are following a natural impulse and doubtless often wish their genital conduct to be an intimate expression of their mutual affection. But they are deceiving themselves. The attempt to express affection by orgasmic nonmarital sex is the pursuit of an illusion. The orgasmic union of the reproductive organs of husband and wife really unites them biologically (and their biological reality is part of, not merely an instrument of, their *personal* reality); that orgasmic union therefore can actualize and allow them to experience their real common good—their marriage with the two goods, children and friendship, which are the parts of its wholeness as an intelligible common good. But the common good of friends who are not and cannot be married (man and man, man and boy, woman and woman) has nothing to do with their having children by each other, and their reproductive organs cannot make them a biological (and therefore a personal) unit. So their genital acts together cannot do what they may hope and imagine.

In giving their considered judgment that homosexual conduct cannot actualize the good of friendship, Plato and the many philosophers who followed him intimate an answer to the questions why it should be considered shameful to use, or allow another to use, one's body to give pleasure, and why this use of one's body differs from one's bodily participation in countless other activities (e.g., games) in which one takes and/or gets pleasure. Their response is that pleasure is indeed a good, when it is the experienced aspect of one's participation in some intelligible good, such as a task going well, or a game or a dance or a meal or a reunion. Of course, the activation of sexual organs with a view to the pleasures of orgasm is sometimes spoken of as if it were a game. But it differs from real games in that its point is not the exercise of skill; rather, this activation of reproductive organs is focused upon the body precisely as a source of pleasure for one's consciousness. So this is a "use of the body" in a strongly different sense of "use." The body now is functioning not in the way one, as a bodily person, acts to instantiate some other intelligible good, but precisely as providing a service to one's consciousness, to satisfy one's desire for satisfaction.

This disintegrity is much more obvious when masturbation is solitary. Friends are tempted to think that pleasuring each other by some forms of mutual masturbation could be an instantiation or actualization or promotion of their friendship. But that line of thought overlooks the fact that if their friendship is not marital . . . activation of their reproductive organs cannot be, in reality, an instantiation or actualization of their friendship's common good. In reality, whatever the generous hopes and dreams with which the loving partners surround their use of their genitals, *that use* cannot express more than is expressed if two strangers engage in genital activity to give each other orgasm, or a prostitute pleasures a client, or a man pleasures himself. Hence, Plato's judgment, at the decisive moment of the *Gorgias*, that there is no important distinction in essential moral worthlessness between solitary masturbation, being sodomized as a prostitute, and being sodomized for the pleasure of it. . . .

Societies such as classical Athens and contemporary England (and virtually every other) draw a distinction between behavior found merely (perhaps extremely) offensive (such as eating excrement) and behavior to be repudiated as destructive of human character and relationships. Copulation of humans with animals is repudiated because it treats human sexual activity and satisfaction as something appropriately sought in a manner that, like the coupling of animals, is divorced from the expressing of an intelligible common good—and so treats human bodily life, in one of its most intense activities, as merely animal. The deliberate genital coupling of persons of the same sex is repudiated for a very similar reason. It is not simply that it is sterile and disposes the participants to an abdication of responsibility for the future of humankind. Nor is it simply that it cannot *really* actualize the mutual devotion that some homosexual persons hope to manifest and experience by it; nor merely that it harms the personalities of its participants by its disintegrative manipulation of different parts of their one personal reality. It is also that it treats human sexual capacities in a way that is deeply hostile to the self-understanding of those members of the community who are willing to commit themselves to real marriage [even one that happens to be sterile] in the understanding that its sexual joys are not mere instruments or accompaniments to, or mere compensation for, the accomplishments of marriage's responsibilities, but rather are the *actualizing and experiencing* of the intelligent commitment to share in those responsibilities. . . .

This pattern of judgment, both widespread and sound, concludes as follows. Homosexual orientation—the deliberate willingness to promote and engage in homosexual acts—is a standing denial of the intrinsic aptness of sexual intercourse to actualize and give expression to the exclusiveness and open-ended commitment of marriage as something good in itself. All who accept that homosexual acts can be a humanly appropriate use of sexual capacities must, if consistent, regard sexual capacities, organs, and acts as instruments to be put to whatever suits the purposes of the individual "self" who has them. Such an acceptance is commonly (and in my opinion rightly) judged to be an active threat to the stability of existing and future marriages; it makes nonsense, for example, of the view that adultery is per se (and not merely because it may involve deception), and in an important way, inconsistent with conjugal love. A political community that judges that the stability and educative generosity of family life is of fundamental importance to the community's present and future can rightly judge that it has a compelling interest in denying that homosexual conduct is a valid, humanly acceptable choice and form of life, and in doing whatever it properly can, as a community with uniquely wide but still subsidiary functions, to discourage such conduct.

Study Questions

1. Finnis claims that solitary masturbation involves a kind of metaphysical or ethical shamefulness ("instrumentalization") that is absent from conjugal sexual activity. Does Finnis think that young children should be taught by their parents that masturbating is a very bad thing to do, thereby instilling psychological shamefulness into the act as well?

2. Finnis is not content to repudiate promiscuity and casual sex (see chapter 22); he also rejects, as morally wrong, sexual activity between two people who are close friends, if they are not married. He states, "The attempt to express affection by orgasmic nonmarital sex is the pursuit of an illusion." Do you agree or disagree? Why? Does Finnis do a good job of supporting this claim? What does he mean by "illusion"?

3. At the end of his essay, Finnis asserts that it is permissible (if not mandatory?) for a "political community" to discourage homosexual behavior by doing "whatever it properly can." Does he provide any guidelines for distinguishing between "proper" and

"improper" measures? Would "proper" measures include the use of the criminal law to prohibit same-sex sexual activity? (The U.S. Supreme Court ruled in 2003 that laws prohibiting private, consensual homosexual conduct are unconstitutional; see *Lawrence v. Texas* 539 U.S. 558.) Because Finnis lumps solitary masturbation and homosexuality together as equally morally wrong, should he not also claim that a "political community" should do "whatever it properly can" to discourage masturbation?

4. Finnis makes a number of claims about the views of the philosopher Plato. Consult the following essay in trying to decide whether Finnis accurately represented Plato's views: Martha Nussbaum, "Platonic Love and Colorado Law: The Relevance of Ancient Greek Norms to Modern Sexual Controversies," *Virginia Law Review* 80, no. 7 (1994): 1515–1651.

5. Read or review the essays by Alan Soble (chapter 6, on masturbation) and Andrew Koppelman (chapter 10, on homosexuality and infertile heterosexual relations), both of which contain criticisms of Finnis's sexual ethics. Try to devise defenses of Finnis's position and arguments against these criticisms.

Chapter 10

HOMOSEXUALITY AND INFERTILITY

Andrew Koppelman

Many of the popular considerations against homosexuality and gay/lesbian liberation start from the perceived or perhaps imagined negative consequences of recurrent same-sex sexual activity or a nontraditional lifestyle: this sort of sexual behavior is unhealthy (while pursuing heterosex is worry-free), gay and lesbian parents damage their children, even if not intentionally (while few heterosexual parents need to be much concerned about this), and so forth. These anti-homosexuality positions live or die by the best available medical, psychological, and sociological evidence that we have. (See John Corvino's essay, chapter 12.) However, as we've seen, the arguments offered by John Finnis (chapter 9) rest on deeper ethical and metaphysical grounds derived from Thomas Aquinas and Immanuel Kant. In what follows, **Andrew Koppelman** *takes Finnis's and similar arguments head-on. Koppelman starts by reviewing the "New Natural Law" (NNL) moral theory of Finnis and his ideological colleagues, which Koppelman sees as "the most sophisticated . . . case for the view that homosexual conduct is intrinsically immoral" and not merely contingently questionable. NNL theory is attractive because many of its claims about human nature and what choices are good for us as humans rest on or support widely shared intuitions and firmly held beliefs, viz., that sex is supposed to be procreative, that heterosexuality and marriage are natural for humans, that something as significant as one's personal integrity can be at stake in sexuality, and that unhappiness is often the wage of seeking mere pleasure. In a largely Christian society, such attitudes carry great rhetorical if not normative force, and for that reason Koppelman believes that they deserve especially careful and pointed challenge.*

Koppelman, professor of law and political science at Northwestern University, has written *Antidiscrimination Law and Social Equality* (Yale University Press, 1996), *The Gay Rights Question in Contemporary American Law* (University of Chicago Press, 2002), and *Same Sex, Different States: When Same-sex Marriages Cross State Lines* (Yale University Press, 2006).

The arguments developed by the theologian Germain Grisez and the legal scholar and philosopher John Finnis, and further elaborated by Robert George, Gerard Bradley, and Patrick Lee, constitute the most sophisticated philosophical case for the view that homosexual conduct is intrinsically immoral. Consistent with the religious (usually Catholic) tradition from which it emerges, their position, generally known as "New Natural Law" (NNL), condemns ubiquitous sexual behaviors that are widely regarded in the West as morally innocuous, such as contracepted heterosexual coitus and masturbation. But NNL theorists also defend many popular moral intuitions, including the condemnation of homosexual activity.

A foundational theme of NNL is that particular identifiable goods are intrinsically and not merely instrumentally worthy of being pursued. These "basic goods" are intelligible ends, valuable in themselves, and capable of motivating us to act. Such goods are worth pursuing even at the price of discomfort or pain. In the early work of Grisez and Finnis, the "reasons for acting which need no further reason" include life, health, knowledge, aesthetic experience, excellence in work and play, friendship, inner peace, peace of conscience, and peace with God.[1] Each good, as an end, can provide a sufficient explanation of human action: being told that an action is done for the sake of these goods is answer enough.[2] Note that bodily pleasure for its own sake is not a basic good.[3] Declining to acknowledge the intrinsic value of pleasure makes it easier for NNL to reject nonprocreative sexuality like masturbation and homosexual relations.

The basic goods are incommensurable: none is reducible to any other or to a common factor, such as utility, that they essentially share. Further, as incommensurable "[n]o basic good considered precisely as such can be meaningfully said to be better than another."[4] Hence they cannot be arranged hierarchically.[5] It follows from this that it can never be morally justified to act in a way directly contrary to one of the basic goods. For Finnis, a

> proposed destroying, damaging, or blocking of some basic aspect of some person's reality provides, of itself, a reason not to choose that option. . . . [T]hat reason could be set aside . . . only if one could . . . identify some rationally preferable reason for choosing that option: that is, some greater good . . . promised by that option than is . . . promised by the options which

do not include that choice to destroy, damage, or block a basic human good. But . . . such a commensurating of goods is rationally impossible.[6]

Basic goods may never be sacrificed for less valuable advantages or states of affairs, and this is how NNL grounds the wrongness of, for example, contraception, "acts whose exclusive intention is to impede the coming-to-be of a human life."[7] Life is a basic good, and sexual acts employing contraception impede this good: "the choice to exclude the possibility of procreation while engaging in intercourse is always, and in an obvious and unambiguous way (which it requires no Christian weighting of the value of procreation to see), a choice directly and immediately against a basic value."[8] Similarly, for NNL, casual sex, masturbation, and homosexual acts are wrong, because they, too, damage or block basic goods.

The integrity of the self, "harmony among all the parts of a person which can be engaged in freely chosen action,"[9] is a basic good; it is better to be a single, coherent self rather than a heap of conflicting desires and impulses. Integrity is violated when one acts for the sake of bodily pleasure in, for example, masturbating or using psychoactive drugs. In these cases, "one separates in one's choice oneself as bodily from oneself as an intentional agent. The content of such a choice includes the disintegration attendant upon a reduction of one's bodily self to the level of an extrinsic instrument."[10] Similarly, Finnis claims that "in masturbating, as in being . . . sodomized," the body is a mere tool of satisfaction. As a result, a person undergoes disintegration. In these activities "one's choosing self [becomes] the quasi-slave of the experiencing self which is demanding gratification."[11] The danger of disintegration is especially prominent in sexuality, since sexual conduct aims at bodily pleasure.

For NNL, the only morally permissible sexual acts are those of married couples (even here there are many restrictions). In their more recent work, Grisez and Finnis add another basic good to those enumerated above, claiming that marriage is among them.[12] Marriage is a basic good because it constitutes "a full communion of persons: a communion of will by mutual covenantal commitment, and of organism by the generative act they share in."[13] Communion of will consists of a mutual commitment to an exclusive and indissoluble partnership, while organic communion consists in the fact that, when husband and wife engage in procreative marital intercourse, they become a single organism.

For NNL "each animal is incomplete, for a male or a female . . . is only a potential part of the mated pair, which is the complete organism . . . capable of reproducing sexually. This is true also of men and women: as mates who engage in sexual intercourse suited to initiate new life, they complete each other and become an organic unit. In doing so, it is literally true that 'they become one flesh' (Gn 2.24)."[14] For the married couple, sexual union is not extrinsic to their mutual friendship. It is not merely a means to their experience of bodily pleasure, and so does not violate their integrity the way other sexual acts would. On the contrary, according to Lee and George, sexual union preserves their integrity:

> In sexual intercourse they unite (become one) precisely in that respect in which their community is distinct and naturally fulfilled. So this bodily unity is not extrinsic to their emotional and spiritual unity. The bodily, emotional, and spiritual are the different levels of a unitary, multi-leveled personal communion. Therefore, in such a community sexual intercourse actualizes the multi-leveled personal communion.[15]

Nonmarital sexual acts, whether homosexual or heterosexual, cannot achieve this bodily unity. At best, they achieve the *illusory experience* of unity.[16] "For a truly common good, there must be more than experience; the experiences must be subordinated to a truly common act that is genuinely fulfilling."[17] When gay couples (or heterosexual couples, for that matter) achieve sexual satisfaction by means other than marital intercourse, the act "is really an instance of mutual masturbation, and is as self-alienating as any other instance of masturbation." Thus Finnis writes about sex between unmarried people that

> their reproductive organs cannot make them a biological (and therefore personal) unit.... Because their activation of ... their reproductive organs cannot be an actualizing and experiencing of the *marital* good ... it can do no more than provide each partner with an individual gratification. For want of a *common good* that could be actualized ... *by and in this bodily union*, that conduct involves the partners in treating their bodies as instruments to be used in the service of their consciously experiencing selves; their choice to engage in such conduct thus dis-integrates each of them precisely as acting persons.[18]

Homosexual acts are wrong not only because they violate integrity, but also because they "violate the good of marriage."[19] Choosing nonmarital sex "damages the body's capacity for the marital act as an act of self-giving which constitutes a communion of bodily persons."[20] This damage is "a damage to the person as an integrated, acting being; it consists principally in that disposition of the will which is initiated by the choice to engage in" such sexual activity.[21] Consider a married man who has never committed adultery, but who might be willing to do so if, say, his wife were unavailable when he felt strong sexual desire. The exclusivity of the man's sex with his wife is not an expression of commitment, because conditional willingness to commit adultery precludes commitment. He is thus motivated even in marital intercourse by something other than the good of marriage. This is why Finnis claims that the "complete exclusion of nonmarital sex acts from the range of acceptable and valuable human options is existentially, if not logically, a precondition for the truly marital character of one's intercourse as and with a spouse."[22] When one damages that precondition, one damages marriage, since "to damage an intrinsic and necessary condition for attaining a good is to damage that good itself."[23]

Thus, the NNL case against sexual acts that are not of the procreative kind (including masturbation, homosexual sex, and any marital sex involving male ejaculation outside the vagina) can be summarized as follows:

1. It is always wrong to act directly contrary to a basic good.

2. Performing sex acts not of the procreative kind is always directly contrary to the basic good of integrity.

3. Performing sex acts not of the procreative kind is always directly contrary to the basic good of marriage.

4. Therefore, it is always wrong to perform sex acts not of the procreative kind.

For the conclusion to follow, all three premises must be true. There is, however, reason to think that none of them is.

First, from NNL's claim that the basic goods are incommensurable, it does not follow that acting directly contrary to a basic good is always wrong. Even if there is no airtight argument that can justify any particular trade-off of incommensurable goods, it might still be possible to compare these goods intuitively and to feel reasonably confident of one's conclusions. NNL concedes that, even after honoring the rule against "doing evil that good might come of it," there are still choices to be made between goods, for example, between pursuing graduate programs in psychology or in medicine.[24] The choice against a basic good might rest on just this kind of intuitive weighing. NNL, which constrains choice regardless of the consequences, might in some circumstances require one to endure very bad consequences. For example, one might be required to surrender to a totalitarian state if the only defense against that state is the use of nuclear weapons, which is prohibited because doing so directly targets the innocent, contrary to the basic good of life. Charles Larmore has argued that deontology's indifference to consequences is acceptable only if we have theological guarantees, so that we are assured that the damage we tolerate or suffer will be corrected, ultimately, by divine providence.[25] NNL theorists are divided over whether their moral theory makes sense without this theology. Finnis places great weight on faith in providence,[26] while Grisez suggests that the theory holds together without such faith, that "a generous and reasonable love of human goods will lead one to act in a way compatible with this ideal."[27]

The second premise is also weak. Even if nonmarital sex acts cannot realize the good of marriage, it does not follow that such acts "can do no more than provide each partner with an individual gratification."[28] Weithman, for one, thinks that homosexual activity "provides the occasion of, and thus serves the function of, promoting emotional intimacy."[29] In this way, loving homosexual activity could fail to damage and even support integrity. If so, loving homosexual activity is a counterexample to the second premise. There are other reasons the premise fails.

NNL claims that it is always wrong to manipulate one's body, or another's, for the sole purpose of pleasure, in part because doing so involves disintegration. Hence NNL concludes, in effect, that most sexual activity engaged in by human beings is wrong. Were bodily pleasure a basic good, this conclusion could be avoided. Of course, we often do act solely for the sake of pleasure, and it is extraordinarily difficult to comprehend how this is morally problematic. Many would agree that "bodily pleasure is itself an important human good" and that "absolutely nothing [is] wrong with using one's body for the purpose of getting pleasure."[30] Finnis admits that pleasure is a good but he qualifies that concession: "when it is the experienced aspect of one's participation in some intelligible good."[31] This piggybacking of pleasure onto other goods underestimates the value of pleasure.

Further, and perhaps more to the point, it is not obvious that pursuing pleasure for its own sake always disrupts integrity. The pursuit of pleasure is often a response to a bodily need. In scratching an itch, I am not abusing my body or regarding it as "a lower form of life with its own dynamism."[32] I am tending to its needs, which are *my* needs, the needs of an integrated person, not the needs of a body detached from or distinct from me. And when *A* gives *B* sexual pleasure, *A* is tending to the needs of at least *B*'s body (if not also *B*'s mind), which are *B*'s needs, the needs of a similarly integrated person. Such considerations seem not to move NNL. Even a married couple, according to NNL, might fail to achieve unity if their sexual pleasure is divorced from marital acts. "If Susan, for example, masturbates John to orgasm or applies oral stimulation to him to bring him to orgasm, no real unity has been effected."[33] But a case can be made that their joint sexual activity, even if neither coital nor procreative, can still deepen their union and preserve their integrity. One might even suggest that solitary masturbation, too, involves no disintegration: "An experience of masturbation . . . is not an experience of a conscious self but of a whole person. . . . There is no existential alienation from the body."[34]

Seeking pleasure for its own sake in sexuality also runs counter, for NNL, to the basic good of marriage. What about a young married couple that has intercourse when and only when it gives them pleasure to do so—is their intercourse morally licit? On Finnis's sympathetic account of Aquinas's sexual ethics, "there is nothing wrong at all with our welcoming assent to such pleasure in the marital act, nor in our being motivated towards such an act by the prospect of giving and sharing in that delight as token of our marital commitment."[35] Moreover, it is appropriate for spouses to refrain from intercourse when, for example, "either of them is disinclined or unwell."[36] But it is morally illicit for spouses to desire coitus solely for its pleasure, even if they are wholly unwilling to have sex with anyone else.[37] What is wrong is one's having an attitude in which "one is not interested in or concerned with anything about one's spouse other than what one would be concerned with in a prostitute."[38]

Some pretty fine line-drawing seems at work here. How could one tell whether the young married couple is engaging in sex for the sake of the good of marriage, or as a token of their commitment (in which case the pleasure of the act is innocent), or just for the sake of their mutual pleasure? Probably not even the couple will know. Another implication is that an elderly married couple that no longer experiences pleasure in intercourse still has reason, for NNL, to engage in it—in order to actualize their unity.[39] It is a curious view that blesses "unitive" intercourse without pleasure but condemns pleasure for its own sake even within marriage.

The phenomenon of infertility within heterosexual marriage presents a foundational challenge to NNL's theory of sexuality. Many object to NNL's prohibition of contraception not only because the purported harm done to the basic goods seems strained, but also because the emphasis placed on the value of procreative coitus would seem to rule out, in addition to contraception, not just masturbation and homosexual activity but any coitus engaged in by infertile heterosexual couples (whether due to advanced age or a medical condition).

Sterile heterosexual couples too, one might argue, are incapable of becoming one procreative organism, because it is impossible that in them sperm and egg could be united. If "the organic complementarity of man and woman in respect to reproduction is the necessary condition for the very possibility of marriage,"[40] then the infertile heterosexual couple would seem to lack that complementarity in the same way as the homosexual couple. They may differ from the homosexual couple in that they *seem* to the untrained observer to be capable of becoming a "complete organism that is capable of reproducing sexually,"[41] but medical science can show that this is an illusion and that they are *in fact* like the homosexual couple in lacking that capacity. If "two persons can become one flesh in marriage only because they are a male and a female *who can join together as a single principle of reproduction*,"[42] then one might infer that persons who cannot so join together cannot marry.

What Finnis says of the homosexual couple might equally be said of the sterile heterosexual couple: "*[I]n reality*, whatever the generous hopes and dreams and thoughts of *giving* with which some same-sex partners may surround their sexual acts, those acts cannot express or do more than is expressed or done if two strangers engage in such activity to give each other pleasure, or a prostitute pleasures a client to give him pleasure in return for money, or (say) a man masturbates to give himself pleasure and a fantasy of more human relationships after a grueling day on the assembly line."[43]

Moreover, this argument would imply, a fertile person ought not to choose a sterile spouse, particularly when a fertile partner is also available. The illusion of marital communion would have been chosen instead of the reality. Finnis does not draw these conclusions, of course, but other natural law theorists have been less diffident. Philo, a Judaeo-Platonist philosopher of the early Christian period, condemned as "unnatural" not only homosexuality and masturbation, but also celibacy and failure to divorce a barren wife.[44] "Those who woo women who have been shown to be barren with other husbands are simply mounting them in the manner of pigs or goats and should be listed among the impious as enemies of God."[45]

The proponents of NNL, of course, take an altogether different line. "If a couple know or come to learn that they will never be able to have children, their marital communion is no less real and no less fulfilling as a communion of complementary persons, even though it always will lack the fulfillment of parenthood."[46] But this line is equally applicable to the homosexual couple. Although the good of procreation is unavailable to them, they may find marriage "fulfilling for them in itself, apart from the fruitfulness of their cooperation."[47] Their sexual acts would not be merely instrumental, or the choice of appearance over reality; rather, they would be integrated with their commitments. "The willing of a good leads to the integration of acts with it, and the full integration of sexual acts in marriage with the good of marriage makes those acts reasonable and worthy."[48] But then, it appears that the unitary good of marriage is realizable even when the one-flesh communion of a single reproductive organism cannot be achieved. Moreover, the possibility of adoption or artificial insemination means that they, like sterile heterosexual couples, can become parents. "For parenthood is far more a moral than a biological relationship: its essence is not so much in begetting and giving birth as in readiness to accept the gift of life, commitment to nurture it, and faithful fulfillment of that commitment through many years."[49] All the evidence we now have indicates that children raised by gay couples turn out as well as those raised by heterosexual couples.[50] In short, if the basic good of marriage is available to, and thereby can make intelligible and appropriate the sexual activity of, the sterile heterosexual couple, the same seems true of the gay couple. No distinction between the two kinds of couple seems capable of bearing the weight that the NNL theorists want to place upon it.

The proponents of NNL have tried to defend the distinction by focusing on the capacity of the heterosexual couple to engage in acts of the reproductive *kind*. Even when a heterosexual couple cannot reproduce, Finnis writes, the "union of the reproductive organs of husband and wife really unites them biologically (and their biological reality is part of, not merely an instrument of, their *personal* reality)."[51] The gay couple is different: "their reproductive organs cannot make them a biological (and therefore personal) unit." Finnis also writes that the infertile married couple

> who unite their reproductive organs in an act of sexual intercourse which, so far as they can make it, is of a kind suitable for generation, do function as a biological (and thus personal) unit and thus can be actualizing . . . the two-in-one-flesh common good and reality of marriage, even when some biological condition happens to prevent that unity resulting in generation of a child. Their conduct thus differs radically from the acts of a husband and wife whose intercourse is . . . sodomitic or by fellatio or coitus interruptus.[52]

The *radical* difference here is difficult to discern. That sterile heterosexual coitus could have been procreative in some other possible world does not distinguish it from homosexual sex.

The NNL distinction turns on the *form* of the act, about which Lee and George write:

> People who are not temporarily or permanently infertile could procreate by performing exactly the same type of act which the infertile married couple perform and by which they consummate or actualize their marital communion. The difference between sterile and fertile married couples is not a difference in what they do. Rather it is a difference in a distinct condition which affects what may result from what they do.[53]

What sense, however, does it make to say that heterosexual intercourse is an act of a reproductive type or kind even if reproduction cannot be intended and is known to be impossible? It would seem to be equally plausible to say that all acts of seminal ejaculation are reproductive in kind (even masturbatory acts) or even that no ejaculatory acts are reproductive in kind (since no mere ejaculation, by itself, results in procreation). Reproduction would then be merely an accidental effect that occurs only under certain conditions. Nothing in nature dictates that the lines should be drawn one way or another.

The distinctive good of marriage that NNL advocates appears to be incoherent. Gareth Moore has argued that the idea of a "two-in-one-flesh" cannot do the necessary work in NNL's argument unless it is understood literally (since even gay and lesbian couples might unite metaphorically). But it cannot be so understood, because a heterosexual couple does not in fact unite biologically: "We might at a pinch speak of male and female reproductive organs as incomplete, if by that is meant that one cannot achieve reproduction without the other, but the male and female animals are in no sense incomplete. So neither is a mating pair a single complete organism: it is simply two organisms cooperating in a joint activity of mating."[54]

NNL's argument might be salvaged by presupposing an Aristotelian metaphysics in which infertile heterosexual married couples participate imperfectly in the *idea* of one-flesh unity but same-sex couples do not participate at all. The infertile heterosexual couple does become one organism, albeit a handicapped organism that cannot do what a normally functioning organism can do. The heterosexual couple is only accidentally infertile, while the same-sex couple is essentially so. In what sense, however, is an infertile couple one flesh, since in them procreative unity is not realized? Their unity, if it exists outside the symbolic community in which they participate, and in which the same-sex couple could also participate, consists in their membership in a class, a natural kind composed of those who ideally *could* procreate. But why think that this natural kind is a real thing, rather than a construct? An unloaded but otherwise functional gun remains a gun, a device designed for and capable of shooting. In contrast, the genital organs of a sterile man cannot be called reproductive organs at all. They are not fit for reproduction. They are more like a gun with a busted firing pin that is, as a result, unfit for shooting.

Finnis recognizes that not every ejaculation of normal male genitalia will successfully lead to conception, and perhaps this is meant to minimize the difference between the organs of normal and infertile males. "Biological union between humans is the inseminatory union of male genital organ with female genital organ; in most circumstances it does not result in generation, but it is the behavior that unites biologically because it is the behavior which, as behavior, is suitable for generation."[55] But whether such behavior "is suitable for generation" depends on whether the organs are in fact suitable for generation. A sterile person's genitals are no more suitable for generation than a gun with a broken firing pin is suitable for shooting. The gun's pin might be repairable, perhaps not; perhaps medicine can in some cases cure infertility. It is, however, a conceptual stretch to insist that the sexual acts of the incurably infertile are of the same kind as the sexual acts of fertile organs that occasionally fail to deliver the goods.

NNL might, finally, appeal to the essentialism implied by the ordinary meaning of words. A dead man's heart, which will never beat again, is still a heart, and his stomach is still a digestive organ. (So to speak! Don't put lasagna in it.) So the penis of a sterile man is still a reproductive organ. But the only aspect of reproductiveness relevant to NNL's argument—the reproductive power of the organ—does not inhere in this particular organ. It is not reproductive in the sense of power or potential, even if it is a reproductive organ in the taxonomic sense. It is mysterious why its being taxonomically a reproductive organ should have any moral significance.

The claims of NNL theorists may sometimes be obscure, but they are significant. Only NNL theorists, among defenders of traditional views about the morality of homosexuality, justify those views without invoking false factual claims about gay people. They alone recognize that their task is to identify some valuable characteristic that is present even in infertile heterosexual couples but absent from gay couples.

The failure of the NNL argument is important, because it was the last intellectually respectable stronghold of the beliefs that homosexual conduct is intrinsically wrong and that marriage is inherently heterosexual. Those beliefs remain politically potent by virtue of being widely held. In this respect, however, they do not differ from other widely held beliefs, such as astrology or abduction by aliens.

Study Questions

1. Explore whether NNL as a moral theory requires "theological guarantees." Does a full defense of NNL's approach to sexual questions require faith in providence (Finnis) or only a "generous and reasonable love of human goods" (Germain Grisez)? What difference does this make?

2. If health is a basic good, and it is morally wrong to act directly against a basic good, is overeating *morally* wrong (and not merely pragmatically dumb)? What about eating fried food? Many people do this, despite believing that they could eat better. Can we also say, by analogy, "Many people masturbate, despite believing that they would be better off engaging in coitus"? Why or why not?

3. Suppose we eventually find definitive scientific evidence for a genetic origin of homosexuality. Would this have any implications for the debate between Koppelman and NNL? If homosexuality were found to be genetic, we would still have to decide whether it is like some diseases (sickle-cell anemia), or innocuously genetic like eye color. So?

4. What role does the "incommensurability thesis"—basic human goods cannot be ranked in relative importance nor reduced to

any more basic good—play in NNL? Independent of the theory, is it plausible?

5. Defend the NNL contention that a heterosexual infertile couple is only accidentally infertile, while a same-sex couple is essentially infertile.

Notes

This essay began as, and is partly derived from, "Homosexual Conduct: A Reply to the New Natural Lawyers," in John Corvino, ed., *Same Sex: Debating the Ethics, Science, and Culture of Homosexuality* (Lanham, Md.: Rowman & Littlefield, 1997), 44–57; and "Is Marriage Inherently Heterosexual?" *American Journal of Jurisprudence* 42 (1997), 51-95. Other versions appeared as "The Decline and Fall of the Case against Same-Sex Marriage," *University of St. Thomas Law Journal* 2, no. 1 (2004): 5-32; and "Natural Law (New)," in Alan Soble, ed., *Sex from Plato to Paglia: A Philosophical Encyclopedia* (Westport, Conn.: Greenwood Press, 2006), 702-11.

1. Germain Grisez, Joseph Boyle, and John Finnis, "Practical Principles, Moral Truth, and Ultimate Ends," *American Journal of Jurisprudence* 32 (1987): 99-151, 107-108; John M. Finnis, *Natural Law and Natural Rights* (Oxford, UK: Clarendon Press, 1980), 85-90. For variations of this list in Finnis, see Sabina Alkire, "The Basic Dimensions of Human Flourishing: A Comparison of Accounts," in Nigel Biggar and Rufus Black, eds., *The Revival of Natural Law: Philosophical, Theological, and Ethical Responses to the Finnis-Grisez School* (Aldershot, UK: Ashgate, 2000), 76.

2. Robert P. George, *In Defense of Natural Law* (Oxford, UK: Oxford University Press, 1999), 45-48.

3. Finnis, *Natural Law*, 95-96; see Rufus Black, "Introduction: The New Natural Law Theory," in Biggar and Black, *Revival*, 11-12.

4. Grisez et al., "Practical Principles," 110.

5. Finnis, *Natural Law*, 92.

6. Finnis, *Moral Absolutes: Tradition, Revision, and Truth* (Washington, D.C.: Catholic University of America Press, 1991), 54-55.

7. Finnis, *Moral Absolutes*, 87.

8. Finnis, "Natural Law and Unnatural Acts," *Heythrop Journal* 11 (1970): 365-87, at 384.

9. Germain Grisez, *The Way of the Lord Jesus*, vol. 1: *Christian Moral Principles* (Chicago: Franciscan Herald Press, 1983), 124.

10. Patrick Lee and Robert P. George, "What Sex Can Be: Self-Alienation, Illusion, or One-Flesh Union," *American Journal of Jurisprudence* 42 (1997): 135-57, at 139.

11. John M. Finnis and Martha C. Nussbaum, "Is Homosexual Conduct Wrong? A Philosophical Exchange," *The New Republic* (November 15, 1993): 12–13. [See John Finnis, in this volume, chap. 9.]

12. Grisez, *The Way of the Lord Jesus*, vol. 2: *Living a Christian Life* (Quincy, Ill.: Franciscan Press, 1993), 556; Finnis, "Law, Morality, and 'Sexual Orientation,'" *Notre Dame Law Review* 69 (1994): 1049, 1064-65.

13. Grisez, *The Way*, vol. 2, 580.

14. Grisez, *The Way*, vol. 2, 570.

15. Lee and George, "What Sex Can Be," 144.

16. On this see Michael J. Perry, "The Morality of Homosexual Conduct: A Response to John Finnis," *Notre Dame Journal of Law, Ethics, and Public Policy* 9, no. 1 (1995): 41-74; Paul J. Weithman, "A Propos of Professor Perry: A Plea for Philosophy in Sexual Ethics," *Notre Dame Journal of Law, Ethics, and Public Policy* 9, no. 1 (1995): 7592.

17. Lee and George, "What Sex Can Be," 146.

18. Finnis, "Law, Morality, and 'Sexual Orientation,'" 1066-67.

19. Grisez, *The Way*, vol. 2, 633.

20. Grisez, *The Way*, vol. 2, 650.

21. Finnis, "The Good of Marriage and the Morality of Sexual Relations: Some Philosophical and Historical Observations," *American Journal of Jurisprudence* 42 (1997): 97-134, at 119.

22. Finnis, "The Good of Marriage," 123.

23. Grisez, *The Way*, vol. 2, 650-51.

24. George, *In Defense of Natural Law*, 117-18.

25. See Charles Larmore, *Patterns of Moral Complexity* (Cambridge, UK: Cambridge University Press, 1987), 134-39.

26. Finnis, *Moral Absolutes*, 9-20; Finnis, *Aquinas: Moral, Political, and Legal Theory* (Oxford, UK: Oxford University Press, 1998), 315-19.

27. Grisez, *The Way*, vol. 1, 186.

28. Finnis, "Law, Morality, and 'Sexual Orientation,'" 1066.

29. Weithman, "A Propos," 87; Weithman, "Natural Law, Morality, and Sexual Complementarity," in David M. Estlund and Martha C. Nussbaum, eds., *Sex, Preference, and Family: Essays on Law and Nature* (New York: Oxford University Press, 1997), 239-40.

30. Martha C. Nussbaum and Kenneth J. Dover, "Appendix 4: Dover and Nussbaum Reply to Finnis," in Martha C. Nussbaum, "Platonic Love and Colorado Law: The Relevance of Ancient Greek Norms to Modern Sexual Controversies," *Virginia Law Review* 80, no. 7 (1994): 1515-1651, at 1649; see Nigel Biggar, "Conclusion," in *The Revival*, 286-87.

31. Finnis and Nussbaum, "Is Homosexual Conduct Wrong?"

32. Grisez, *The Way*, vol. 1, 139.

33. Lee and George, "What Sex Can Be," 146.

34. Gareth Moore, "Natural Sex: Germain Grisez, Sex, and Natural Law," in Biggar and Black, *Revival*, 232; Andrew Koppelman, *The Gay Rights Question in Contemporary American Law* (Chicago: University of Chicago Press, 2002), 85-86.

35. Finnis, *Aquinas*, 147; see also Finnis, "The Good of Marriage," 102.

36. Finnis, *Aquinas*, 151n86; Finnis, "The Good of Marriage," 109n47.

37. Finnis, *Aquinas*, 148-49.

38. Finnis, "The Good of Marriage," 103.

39. Robert P. George and Gerard V. Bradley, "Marriage and the Liberal Imagination," *Georgetown Law Journal* 84, no. 2 (1995): 301-20, at 310.

40. Grisez, *The Way*, vol. 2, 634.

41. Grisez, *The Way*, vol. 2, 570.

42. Grisez, *The Way*, vol. 2, 618; emphasis added.

43. Finnis, "Law, Morality, and 'Sexual Orientation,'" 1067; emphasis in original.

44. See John Boswell, *Christianity, Social Tolerance, and Homosexuality: Gay People in Western Europe from the Beginning of the Christian Era to the Fourteenth Century* (Chicago: University of Chicago Press, 1980), 148.

45. Philo, *De specialibus legibus* 3.36, translated and quoted in Boswell, *Christianity*, 155.

46. Grisez, *The Way*, vol. 2, 572.

47. Grisez, *The Way*, vol. 2, 572-73.

48. Grisez, *The Way*, vol. 2, 637.

49. Grisez, *The Way*, vol. 2, 689.

50. See Judith Stacey and Timothy J. Biblarz, "(How) Does the Sexual Orientation of Parents Matter?" *American Sociological Review* 66 (2001): 159-83; Charlotte J. Patterson, "Children of Lesbian and Gay Parents," *Child Development* 63 (1992): 1025-42.

51. Finnis, "Law, Morality, and 'Sexual Orientation,'" 1066.

52. Finnis, "Law, Morality, and 'Sexual Orientation,'" 1068.

53. Lee and George, "What Sex Can Be," 150.

54. Moore, "Natural Sex," 225-26.

55. Finnis, "Law, Morality, and 'Sexual Orientation,'" 1066n46.

Chapter 11

PERIODIC CONTINENCE

Karol Wojtyla

Karol Wojtyla *was born in Poland in 1920 and was Pope John Paul II from 1978 until his death in 2005. After obtaining the Ph.D. in philosophy, he held the Chair of Ethics at the Catholic University of Lublin. His lectures covered, among other things, sexual ethics, some of which material was incorporated, in 1960, into his book* Love and Responsibility. *In this compendium, Wojtyla, an active philosopher, attempted to carry out an ambitious project: to weld together Kantian ethics, phenomenology, and Catholicism. He argued that the "personalist norm," a moral principle reminiscent of the Second Formulation of Immanuel Kant's Categorical imperative, was identical to or at least followed from the Christian Love Commandment. Throughout the book he employs the personalist norm to defend various pieces of Catholic sexual ethics, including the prohibition against married couples utilizing artificial methods of contraception during intercourse. In the section of* Love and Responsibility *reproduced here, Wojtyla explains in detail why the use of contraception is wrong and, further, tackles the perennially difficult issue of why the use of condoms, say, is illicit but refusing to engage in sexual intercourse during the fertile segment of a woman's reproductive cycle is permissible—or, more precisely, under what conditions restricting intercourse according to her cycle is allowed.*

This philosophical-theological treatise was originally published in Polish in 1960. The unnamed editors of the volume may have been members of the communist party, or at least worked under its influence, for to Wojtyla's straightforward historical claim (see the selection, below), "According to 'Malthusian' doctrine the limitation of births is an economic necessity, since the means of subsistence, which increase by arithmetic progression, cannot keep up with the population, which naturally increases by geometric progression," the editorial staff appended an endnote (not included in the selection): "This [Malthus's thesis] is obviously not entirely correct. The birth of a new human being is the birth not only of 'another stomach to fill' but of another worker, perhaps even an inventor and a creator of the technical means for increasing many times over the productivity of labour" (309n68). This irrelevant, wishful-thinking endnote injects a Marxist spin into Wojtyla's text. Note that it can also be read, conveniently, in unsophisticated Catholic terms: it is always a mistake to abort a fetus or to interfere with the reproductive potential of sexual intercourse, because the baby-person who does not, as a result, exist might have become the next winner of the Nobel Peace Prize.

Reprinted from "Periodic Continence: Method and Interpretation," from *Love and Responsibility* by Karol Wojtyla, translated by H. T. Willetts (New York: Farrar, Straus and Giroux, 1981; 2nd printing, 1994), pp. 237–44, with the permission of Farrar, Straus and Giroux, LLC. Translation copyright © 1981 by Farrar, Straus and Giroux, Inc., and William Collins and Sons, & Co, Ltd.

From our discussion so far it follows that sexual intercourse between husband and wife has the value of love, that is to say of a true union of persons, only when neither of them deliberately excludes the possibility of procreation, only when in the mind and will of husband and wife respectively it is accompanied by acceptance of the possibility of paternity or maternity. In the absence of this the man and the woman should refrain from intercourse. They should refrain from it also when they "are unwilling to" or "must not" become father and mother. The words in inverted commas cover many different situations. But whenever a man and a woman ought to abstain from intercourse, and from the erotic experiences of a sensual and sexual character which accompany it, continence is the obvious course, for continence is a condition of love, the only attitude toward a partner in marriage, and particularly toward a wife, compatible with affirmation of the value of the person. Let us recall that the question of continence was discussed in the previous chapter in connection with the virtue of moderation (*temperantia*). This is a peculiarly difficult virtue to practice, for it is often necessary to master not only the promptings of sensuality, in which a powerful instinct makes itself felt, but also those emotional reactions which are such an intimate part of love between man and woman, as we saw in our analysis of marital love.

Marital continence is so much more difficult than continence outside marriage because the spouses grow accustomed to intercourse, as befits the state which they have both consciously chosen. Once they begin to have sexual intercourse as a habit, and a constant inclination is created, a mutual need for intercourse comes into being. This need is a normal manifestation of love, and not only in the sensual-sexual sense but in the personal sense too. In matrimony the man and the woman belong to each other in a special way, they are "one flesh" (Genesis 2:24). The mutual need of the two persons for each other expresses itself also in the need for sexual intercourse. This being so, the idea of refraining from intercourse inevitably runs into certain difficulties and objections. On the other hand, a couple who do not sometimes refrain from sexual intercourse may see their family increase excessively. This problem is an extremely important one in our time. In the conditions of modern life we find that the family in its old traditional form—the large family relying on the father as the breadwinner, and sustained internally by the mother, the heart of the family—has reached a state of crisis. The fact that married women must or at any rate are able to take up regular employment seems to be the main symptom of the crisis, but it is obviously not an isolated symptom: several distinct factors combine to create this situation.

To discuss this question at length would take us away from the main theme of our book, although it is undoubtedly relevant. Let us simply note here that the circumstances mentioned above are often put forward as strong arguments for the limitation of births. As was mentioned in chapter 1, such demands are linked with the name of Thomas Malthus, an Anglican clergyman, author of *Essay on the Principle of Population*. According to "Malthusian" doctrine the limitation of births is an economic necessity, since the means of subsistence, which increase by arithmetic progression, cannot keep up with the population, which naturally increases by geometric progression. This idea took root in intellectual ground cultivated by sensualist empiricism and the utilitarianism which goes with it, and the fruit which it bore there was what is called "neo-Malthusianism." We met in chapter 1 (section on the "Critique of Utilitarianism") the view that reason's task is to help man to calculate how to combine throughout his life the maximum of pleasure with the minimum of pain—this combination being synonymous with "happiness," superficially understood. Since sexual intercourse gives men and women so much pleasure, so much intense enjoyment, means must be found to spare them the need to refrain from it even when they do not want offspring, when they 'cannot' become father and mother ("cannot" in the sense defined above). We are here at the source of the various "methods" recommended by neo-Malthusians. For human intelligence, since it is able to see the process of intercourse and the attendant possibility of procreation as a whole, can devise a variety of means for the deliberate avoidance of procreation. Neo-Malthusianism points particularly to those means which in one way or another interfere with the normal, "natural" course of the whole process of the sexual act.

Obviously if we resort to such means we find ourselves in conflict with the principle formulated in the previous paragraph of this chapter

("Reproduction and Parenthood"). Sexual intercourse in marriage takes place at the level of a union of loving persons only if they do not deliberately exclude the possibility of procreation and parenthood. When the idea that "I may become a father"/"I may become a mother" is totally rejected in the mind and will of husband and wife nothing is left of the marital relationship, objectively speaking, except mere sexual enjoyment. One person becomes an object of use for another person, which is incompatible with the personalistic norm. Man is endowed with reason not primarily to "calculate" the maximum of pleasure obtainable in his life, but above all to seek knowledge of objective truth, as a basis for absolute principles (norms) to live by. This he must do if he is to live in a manner worthy of what he is, to live justly. Human morality cannot be grounded in "utility" alone, it must sink its roots in "justice." Justice demands recognition of the supra-utilitarian value of the person: and in this the contrast between "justice" and mere "utility" is most clearly evident. In sexual matters in particular it is not enough to affirm that a particular mode of behavior is expedient. We must be able to say that it is "just." Now if we wish to take our stand firmly on the dictates of justice and the personalistic norm which goes with it, the only acceptable "method" of regulating conception in marital relations is continence. Those who do not desire the consequence must avoid the cause. Since sexual intercourse is the biological cause of conception spouses who wish to avoid conception must abstain from intercourse. From the moral point of view the principle is absolutely clear. It remains for us to deal with the practice known as "periodic continence."

It is a matter of common knowledge that biological fertility in woman is cyclical. She has natural periods of infertility, and it is fairly easy to formulate general rules for determining them. Difficulties arise when the general rules are applied to a particular woman. This is a special question, to which we shall revert in the concluding chapter. For the moment we are concerned with the purely ethical problem: if a man and a woman time their periods of continence to coincide with the above-mentioned periods of fertility, and so have sexual intercourse only as and when they expect procreation to be biologically impossible, can it be said that they bring to the marital act that readiness for parenthood, that acceptance of the idea that "I may become a father," "I may become a mother," of which we have spoken? After all, they have intercourse in the expectation that they will not become parents: it is precisely for that reason that they have chosen the period during which the woman is supposed to be infertile. Are they, then, not deliberately excluding the possibility of procreation? Why should the natural method be morally superior to artificial methods, since the purpose is the same in each case—to eliminate the possibility of procreation from sexual intercourse?

To answer this we must rid ourselves of some of the associations of the word "method." We tend to approach "the natural method" and "artificial methods" from the same point of view, to derive them from the same utilitarian premises. Looked at like this, the natural method is just another means to ensure the maximum pleasure, differing from artificial methods only in the direction it takes. But this is where the fundamental error resides. It is clearly not enough to speak of a method without going on to interpret it correctly. Only then shall we be able to answer the question asked above. Periodic continence as a means of regulating conception is, then, (1) permissible because it does not conflict with the demands of the personalistic norm and (2) permissible only with certain qualifications.

To take (1) first, in marital relations, as we have said before, the demands of the personal norm and those of the natural order are in agreement. The natural method, unlike artificial methods, seeks to regulate conception by taking advantage of circumstances in which conception cannot occur for biological reasons. Because of this the "naturalness" of sexual intercourse is not affected—whereas artificial methods do destroy the naturalness of intercourse. In the first case, infertility results from the natural operation of the laws of fertility; in the second it is imposed in defiance of nature. Let us add that this problem is closely bound up with that of justice to the Creator—which we shall examine later in order to reveal its personalistic significance. The personalistic value of periodic continence as a method of regulating conception is evident not only in the fact that it preserves the "naturalness" of intercourse, but even more in the fact that in the wills of the persons concerned it must be grounded in a sufficiently mature virtue. And this is where we see how important it is to interpret periodic continence correctly: the utilitarian interpretation distorts the true character of what we call the natural method, which is that it is based on continence as a virtue and this—as was shown in the previous chapter—is very closely connected with love of the person.

Inherent in the essential character of continence as a virtue is the conviction that the *love of man and woman loses nothing as a result of temporary abstention from erotic experiences, but on the contrary gains*: the personal union takes deeper root, grounded as it is above all in affirmation of the value of the person and not just in sexual attachment. *Continence as a virtue cannot be regarded as a "contraceptive measure."* The spouses who practice it are prepared to renounce sexual intercourse for other reasons (religious reasons for instance) and not only to avoid having children. Self-interested, calculating continence awakens doubts. Continence must, like all other virtues, be disinterested, and wholly concerned with "justice," not with "expediency." Otherwise there will be no place for it in a genuine love of persons. Continence, unless it is a virtue, is alien to love. The love of man and woman must ripen to the point where continence is possible, and continence must acquire a constructive significance for them, become one of the factors which give shape to their love. Only then is the "natural method" congruent with the nature of the person: its secret lies in the practice of virtue—technique alone is no solution here.

We have noted above (point 2) that the natural method is permissible only with certain reservations. The most important concerns attitudes to procreation. If continence is to be a virtue and not just a "method" in the utilitarian sense, it must not serve to destroy readiness for parenthood in a husband and wife, since acceptance that "I may become a father"/"I may become a mother" is what justifies the marital relationship and puts it on the level of a true union of persons. We cannot therefore speak of continence as a virtue where the spouses take advantage of the periods of biological infertility exclusively for the purpose of avoiding parenthood altogether, and have intercourse only in those periods. To apply the "natural method" in this way would be contrary to nature—both the objective order of nature and the essential character of love are hostile to such a policy.

So, then, if periodic continence can be regarded as a "method" at all, it is a method of regulating conception and not of avoiding a family. Until we realize the true significance of the family we shall not understand the relevant moral rules. The family is an institution created by procreation within the framework of marriage. It is a natural community, directly dependent on the parents for its existence and functioning. The parents create the family as a complement to and extension of their love. To create a family means to create a community, since the family is a social unit or else it is not a family. To be a community it must have a certain size. This is most obvious in the context of education. For the family is an educational institution within the framework of which the personality of a new human being is formed. If it is to be correctly formed it is very important that this human being should not be alone, but surrounded by a natural community. We are sometimes told that it is easier to bring up several children together than an only child, and also that two children are not a community—they are two only children. It is the role of the parents to direct their children's upbringing, but under their direction the children educate themselves, because they develop within the framework of a community of children, a collective of siblings.

Those who set about regulating conception must consider this aspect of the matter before all else. The larger social unit—the state or nation within which the family happens to live—must see to it that the family is a genuine social unit. At the same time, parents themselves must be careful, when they limit conception, not to harm their families or society at large, which has an interest of its own in the optimum size of the family. A determination on the part of husband and wife to have as few children as possible, to make their own lives easy, is bound to inflict moral damage both on their family and on society at large. Limitation of the number of conceptions must in any case not be another name for renunciation of parenthood. From the point of view of the family, *periodic continence as a method of regulating conception is permissible insofar as it does not conflict with a sincere disposition to procreate.* There are, however, circumstances in which this disposition itself demands renunciation of procreation, and any further increase in the size of the family would be incompatible with parental duty. A man and a woman moved by true concern for the good of their family and a mature sense of responsibility for the birth, maintenance, and upbringing of their children will then limit intercourse, and abstain from it in periods in which this might result in another pregnancy undesirable in the particular conditions of their married and family life.

Acceptance of parenthood also expresses itself in not endeavouring to avoid pregnancy at all costs, readiness to accept it if it should unexpectedly occur. This acceptance of the possibility of becoming a father or a mother must be present in the mind and the will even when the spouses do not want a pregnancy, and deliberately choose to have intercourse at a period when it may be expected not to occur. This acceptance, in the context of any particular occasion of intercourse, together with a general disposition to parenthood in the broader context of the marriage as a whole, determines the moral validity of periodic continence. There can be no question here of hypocrisy, of disguising one's true intentions—it cannot be said that the man and the woman, in defiance of the Creator, are unwilling to become father and mother, since they themselves do nothing definitively to preclude this possibility (though of course they obviously could). They do not apply all means to this end, and in particular not those which are incompatible with a disposition to parenthood, and therefore deprive marital intercourse of the value of love and leave it only the value of "enjoyment."

Study Questions

1. Wojtyla claims that once a married couple begins to engage in sexual intercourse, it is difficult for them to resist engaging in it on a regular basis, repeatedly ("a constant inclination is created"). Others have claimed that being married kills sexual desire ("bedroom death"). Who is right? Qualified—hedged—answers are acceptable.

2. Wojtyla tries to distinguish between "periodic continence" (sometimes called, perhaps misleadingly, "the rhythm method")

as an acceptable procedure for limiting family size (the number of children born into a family) and unacceptable techniques and technologies such as condoms and oral contraceptive pills. How successful is he is drawing a firm and coherent distinction between them? (This line-drawing was also attempted by Pope Paul VI in his 1968 encyclical *Humanae vitae,* in which he reiterated and reemphasized the Catholic prohibition of artificial contraception.)

3. Wojtyla asserts two conditions that must be satisfied for periodic continence to be morally permissible. What are they? He also claims that periodic continence is acceptable only if limiting family size is not the only reason for engaging in periodic continence. What other reasons must there be? Does this imply that Wojtyla is here appealing to the Doctrine of Double Effect?

4. Wojtyla's provocative emendation of Vatican doctrine—periodic continence is permissible only if the couple has other reasons for abstaining from sexual intercourse—is missing from his 1995 encyclical *Evangelium vitae,* which discusses this question again, among many other similar questions. Wojtyla's *Love and Responsibility* was written well before he became pope; he wrote the encyclical as John Paul II. Speculate why his position changed in the direction of being more (if not entirely) consistent with standard Catholic doctrine.

5. Wojtyla claims that a genuine union, and hence love, exists between the married couple only if they leave every act of sexual intercourse open to procreation. Try to discern how this claim fits into a dispute between John Finnis (chapter 9) and Andrew Koppelman (chapter 10). Wojtyla also claims that genuine union, and hence love, exists when the couple refrains from sexual intercourse, when they practice sexual continence together. Is he being consistent? What do you think of Wojtyla's definition of love in terms of "union"?

Chapter 12

IN DEFENSE OF HOMOSEXUALITY

John Corvino

In this comprehensive essay, **John Corvino** *states clearly the most likely grounds for the common moral compunction against homosexual acts and homosexuality in general—viz., they are unnatural, and/or harmful, and/ or run afoul of biblical pronouncement about homosexuality—and argues against all three considerations. Questioning not only whether there exists a morally relevant sense of "natural" that is helpful in moral discussions, Corvino challenges derivations of moral evaluations of sexuality from natural or biological facts (or purported facts). Corvino also doubts the wisdom of viewing sexual orientation as completely or even mostly a matter of lifestyle choice. (He asks readers the rhetorically powerful question whether they chose to have the sexual feelings they found themselves having when they became conscious of their sexuality.) As a result of these deliberations, Corvino deems irrelevant the "nature vs. nurture" debate over the origins of sexual prefer- ence, and points out that sexuality and sex organs can have multiple func- tions beyond the procreative. (See also Andrew Koppelman's essay, chapter 10.) Corvino, further, questions that there are reliable correlations between homosexual activities or lifestyles, on the one hand, and emotional distress and disease, on the other. Homosex may be no more and no less dangerous than heterosex. Corvino's careful analysis and criticism of biblical condem- nations of homosexuality is perhaps that part of his essay that speaks directly to the most popular moral concern about homosexuality, that it violates Scripture, the Word of the Lord.*

Corvino teaches philosophy at Wayne State University in Detroit, Michigan. He is the editor of *Same Sex: Debating the Ethics, Science, and Culture of Homosexuality*

(Rowman & Littlefield, 1997), a member of the Independent Gay Forum, http://www
.indegayforum.org, and a frequent lecturer on gay rights issues.

This is a slightly modified version of "Why Shouldn't Tommy and Jim Have Sex?" from
John Corvino, ed., *Same Sex: Debating the Ethics, Science, and Culture of Homosexuality* (Lanham, Md.: Rowman & Littlefield, 1997), pp. 3–16. Reprinted by permission
of John Corvino and Rowman & Littlefield.

Tommy and Jim are a homosexual couple I know. Tommy is an ac-
countant; Jim is a botany professor. They are in their forties and
have been together for fourteen years, the last five of which they have
lived in a Victorian house that they lovingly restored. Although their relationship has had its challenges, each has made sacrifices for the sake of
the other's happiness and the relationship's long-term success.

I assume that Tommy and Jim have sex with each other (although I've
never bothered to ask). Furthermore, I suspect that they probably *should*
have sex with each other. For one thing, sex is pleasurable. But it is also
much more than that: a sexual relationship can unite two people in a
way that virtually nothing else can. It can be an avenue of growth, of communication, and of lasting interpersonal fulfillment. These are reasons
why most heterosexual couples have sex even if they don't want children, don't want children yet, or don't want additional children. And if
these reasons are good enough for most heterosexual couples, then they
should be good enough for Tommy and Jim.

Of course, having a reason to do something does not preclude there
being an even better reason for not doing it. Tommy might have a good
reason for drinking orange juice (it's tasty and nutritious) but an even
better reason for not doing so (he's allergic). The point is that one
would need a pretty good reason for denying a sexual relationship to
Tommy and Jim, given the intense benefits widely associated with such
relationships. The question I shall consider in this paper is thus quite
simple: Why shouldn't Tommy and Jim have sex?

Homosexual Sex Is "Unnatural"

Many contend that homosexual sex is "unnatural." But what does that
mean? Many things that people value—clothing, houses, medicine, and
government, for example—are unnatural in some sense. On the other
hand, many things that people detest—disease, suffering, and death, for
example—are "natural" in the sense that they occur in nature. If the unnaturalness charge is to be more than empty rhetorical flourish, those
who levy it must specify what they mean. Borrowing from Burton Leiser,
I will examine several possibilities of what "unnatural" means.[2]

What Is Unusual or Abnormal Is Unnatural. One meaning of "unnatural" refers to that which deviates from the norm, that is, from what most people do. Obviously, most people engage in heterosexual relationships. But does it follow that it is wrong to engage in homosexual relationships? Relatively few people read Sanskrit, pilot ships, play the mandolin, breed goats, or write with both hands, yet none of these activities is immoral simply because it is unusual. As the Ramsey Colloquium, a group of Jewish and Christian scholars who oppose homosexuality, write, "The statistical frequency of an act does not determine its moral status."[3] So while homosexuality might be unnatural in the sense of being unusual, that fact is morally irrelevant.

What Is Not Practiced by Other Animals Is Unnatural. Some people argue, "Even animals know better than to behave homosexually; homosexuality must be wrong." This argument is doubly flawed. First, it rests on a false premise. Numerous studies—including Anne Perkins's study of "gay" sheep and George and Molly Hunt's study of "lesbian" seagulls—have shown that some animals do form homosexual pair-bonds.[4] Second, even if that premise were true, it would not prove that homosexuality is immoral. After all, animals don't cook their food, brush their teeth, attend college, or drive cars; human beings do all of these without moral censure. Indeed, the idea that animals could provide us with our standards—especially our sexual standards—is simply amusing.

What Does Not Proceed from Innate Desires Is Unnatural. Recent studies suggesting a biological basis for homosexuality have resulted in two popular positions. One side proposes that homosexual people are "born that way" and that it is therefore natural (and thus good) for them to form homosexual relationships. The other side maintains that homosexuality is a lifestyle choice and therefore unnatural (and thus wrong). Both sides assume a connection between the origin of homosexual orientation, on the one hand, and the moral value of homosexual activity, on the other. And insofar as they share that assumption, both sides are wrong.

Consider first the pro-homosexual side, which assumes that all innate desires are good ones (i.e., that they should be acted upon). But that assumption is clearly false. Research suggests that some people are born with a predisposition toward violence, but such people have no more right to strangle their neighbors than anyone else. So while people like Tommy and Jim may be born with homosexual tendencies, it doesn't follow that they ought to act on them. Nor does it follow that they ought *not* to act on them, even if the tendencies are not innate. I probably do not have any innate tendency to write with my left hand (since I, like everyone else in my family, have always been right-handed), but it doesn't follow that it would be immoral for me to do so. So simply asserting that homosexuality is a lifestyle choice will not show that it is an immoral lifestyle choice.

Do people "choose" to be homosexual? People certainly don't seem to choose their sexual *feelings*, at least not in any direct or obvious way. (Do you? Think about it.) Rather, they find certain people attractive and certain activities arousing, whether they "decide" to or not. Indeed, most people at some point in their lives wish that they could control their feelings more—for example, in situations of unrequited love—and find it frustrating that they cannot. What they *can* control to a considerable degree is how and when they act upon those feelings. In that sense, both homosexuality and heterosexuality involve lifestyle choices. But in either case, determining the origin of the feelings will not determine whether it is moral to act on them.

What Violates an Organ's Principal Purpose Is Unnatural. Perhaps when people claim that homosexual sex is unnatural they mean that it cannot result in procreation. The idea behind the argument is that human organs have various natural purposes: eyes are for seeing, ears are for hearing, genitals are for procreating. According to this argument, it is immoral to use an organ in a way that violates its particular purpose.

Many of our organs, however, have multiple purposes. Tommy can use his mouth for talking, eating, breathing, licking stamps, chewing gum, kissing women, or kissing Jim; and it seems rather arbitrary to claim that all but the last use are "natural."[5] (And if we say that some of the other uses are "unnatural, but not immoral," we have failed to specify a morally relevant sense of the term "natural.")

Just because people can and do use their sexual organs to procreate, it does not follow that they should not use them for other purposes. Sexual organs seem very well suited for expressing love, for giving and receiving pleasure, and for celebrating, replenishing, and enhancing a relationship—even when procreation is not a factor. Unless opponents of homosexuality are prepared to condemn heterosexual couples who use contraception or individuals who masturbate, they must abandon this version of the unnaturalness argument. Indeed, even the Roman Catholic Church, which forbids contraception and masturbation, approves of sex for sterile couples and of sex during pregnancy, neither of which can lead to procreation. The church concedes here that intimacy and pleasure are morally legitimate purposes for sex, even in cases where procreation is impossible. But since homosexual sex can achieve these purposes as well, it is inconsistent for the church to condemn it on the grounds that it is not procreative.

One might object that sterile heterosexual couples do not *intentionally* turn away from procreation, whereas homosexual couples do. But this distinction does not hold. It is no more possible for Tommy to procreate with a woman whose uterus has been removed than it is for him to procreate with Jim.[6] By having sex with either one, he is intentionally engaging in a non-procreative sexual act.

One might press the objection further and insist that Tommy and the woman *could* produce children if the woman were fertile: whereas homosexual relationships are essentially infertile, heterosexual relationships are only incidentally so. But what does that prove? Granted, it might require less of a miracle for a woman without a uterus to become pregnant than for Jim to become pregnant, but it would require a miracle nonetheless. Thus it seems that the real difference here is not that one couple is fertile and the other not, nor that one couple "could" be fertile (with the help of a miracle) and the other not, but rather that one couple is male-female and the other male-male. In other words, sex between Tommy and Jim is wrong because it's homosexual. But that, of course, is no argument at all.[7]

What Is Disgusting or Offensive Is Unnatural. It often seems that when people call homosexuality "unnatural" they really just mean that it's disgusting. But plenty of morally neutral activities—handling snakes, eating snails, performing autopsies, cleaning toilets, and so on—disgust people. Indeed, for centuries, most people found interracial relationships disgusting, yet that feeling—which has by no means disappeared—hardly proves that such relationships are wrong. In sum, the charge that homosexuality is unnatural, at least in its most common forms, is longer on rhetorical flourish than on philosophical cogency.

Homosexual Sex Is Harmful

A second common argument is that homosexuality is harmful. The Ramsey Colloquium, for instance, argues that homosexuality leads to the breakdown of the family and, ultimately, of human society, and points to the "alarming rates of sexual promiscuity, depression, and suicide and the ominous presence of AIDS within the homosexual subculture."[8] Thomas Schmidt marshals copious statistics to show that homosexual activity undermines physical and psychological health.[9] Such charges, if correct, would seem to provide strong evidence against homosexuality. But are the charges correct? And do they prove what they purport to prove?

One obvious (and obviously problematic) way to answer the first question is to ask people like Tommy and Jim. It would appear that no one is in a better position to judge the homosexual lifestyle than those who know it firsthand. Yet it is unlikely that critics would trust their testimony. Indeed, the more homosexual people try to explain their lives, the more critics accuse them of deceitfully promoting an agenda. (It's like trying to prove that you're not crazy. The more you object, the more people think, "That's exactly what a crazy person would say.")

One might instead turn to statistics. An obvious problem with this tack is that both sides of the debate bring forth extensive statistics and "expert" testimony, leaving the average observer confused. There is a more subtle problem as well. Because of widespread antigay sentiment, many homosexual people won't acknowledge their feelings to themselves, much less to researchers.[10] I have known a number of gay men who did not "come out" until their forties and fifties, and no amount of professional competence on the part of interviewers would have been likely to open their closets sooner. Such problems compound the usual difficulties of finding representative population samples for statistical study.

There are other problems with the statistical claims of gay rights opponents. First, as any good statistician realizes, correlation does not equal cause. Even if homosexual people were more likely to commit suicide, be promiscuous, or contract AIDS than the general population, it would not follow that their homosexuality causes them to do these things. An alternative—and very plausible—explanation is that these phenomena, like the disproportionately high crime rates among African Americans, are at least partly a function of society's treatment of the group in question. Suppose you were told from a very early age that the romantic feelings that you experienced were sick, unnatural, and disgusting. Suppose further that expressing these feelings put you at risk of social ostracism or, worse yet, physical violence. Is it not plausible that you would, for instance, be more inclined to depression than you would be without such obstacles? And that such depression could, in its extreme forms, lead to suicide or other self-destructive behaviors? (It is indeed remarkable that, in the face of such obstacles, couples like Tommy and Jim continue to flourish.)

A similar explanation can be given for the alleged promiscuity of homosexuals.[11] The denial of legal marriage, the pressure to remain in the closet, and the overt hostility toward homosexual relationships are all more conducive to transient, clandestine encounters than they are to long-term unions. As a result, that which is challenging enough for heterosexual couples—settling down and building a life together—becomes far more challenging for homosexual couples.

• Indeed, there is an interesting tension in the critics' position here. Opponents of homosexuality commonly claim that "marriage and the family . . . are fragile institutions in need of careful and continuing support."[12] And they point to the increasing prevalence of divorce and premarital sex among heterosexuals as evidence that such support is declining. Yet they refuse to concede that the complete absence of similar support for homosexual relationships might explain many of the alleged problems of homosexuals. The critics can't have it both ways: if heterosexual marriages are in trouble despite the various social, economic, and legal incentives for keeping them together, society should be little surprised that homosexual relationships—which not only lack such supports, but face overt hostility—are difficult to maintain.

One might object that if social ostracism were the main cause of homosexual people's problems, then homosexual people in more "tolerant" cities like New York and San Francisco should exhibit fewer such problems than their small-town counterparts; yet statistics do not seem to bear this out. This objection underestimates the extent of anti-gay sentiment in our society. By the time many gay and lesbian people move to urban centers, much damage has already been done to their psyches. Moreover, the visibility of homosexuality in urban centers makes gay and lesbian people there more vulnerable to attack (and thus more likely to exhibit certain difficulties). Finally, note that urbanites *in general* (not just homosexual urbanites) tend to exhibit higher rates of promiscuity, depression, and sexually transmitted disease than the rest of the population.

But what about AIDS? Opponents of homosexuality sometimes claim that even if homosexual sex is not, strictly speaking, immoral, it is still a bad idea, since it puts people at risk for AIDS and other sexually transmitted diseases. But that claim is misleading; it is infinitely more risky for Tommy to have sex with a woman who is HIV-positive than with Jim, who is HIV-negative. Obviously, it's not homosexuality that's harmful, it's the virus; and the virus may be carried by both heterosexual and homosexual people. It may be the case that in a given population a homosexual male is statistically more likely to carry the virus than a heterosexual female, but opponents of homosexuality need something stronger than this statistical claim. For if it is wrong for men to have sex with men because their doing so puts them at a higher AIDS risk than heterosexual sex, then it is also wrong for women to have sex with men because their doing so puts them at a higher AIDS risk than homosexual sex (lesbians as a group have the lowest incidence of AIDS). Purely from the standpoint of AIDS risk, women ought to prefer lesbian sex.

If this response seems silly, it is because there is obviously more to choosing a romantic or sexual partner than determining AIDS risk. And a major part of the decision, one that opponents of homosexuality consistently overlook, is considering whether one can have a mutually fulfilling relationship with the partner. For many people like Tommy and Jim, such fulfillment—which most heterosexuals recognize to be an important component of human flourishing—is only possible with members of the same sex.

Of course, the foregoing argument hinges on the claim that homosexual sex can only cause harm indirectly. Some would object that there are certain activities—anal sex, for instance—that for anatomical reasons are intrinsically harmful. But an argument against anal intercourse is by no means tantamount to an argument against homosexuality: neither all nor only homosexuals engage in anal sex. There are plenty of other things for both gay men and lesbians to do in bed. Indeed, for women, it appears that the most common forms of homosexual activity may be *less* risky than penile-vaginal intercourse, since the latter has been linked to cervical cancer.[13]

In sum, there is nothing *inherently* risky about sex between persons of the same gender. It is only risky under certain conditions: for instance, if they exchange diseased bodily fluids or if they engage in certain "rough" forms of sex that could cause tearing of delicate tissue. Heterosexual sex is equally risky under such conditions. Thus, even if statistical claims like those of Schmidt and the Ramsey Colloquium were true, they would not prove that homosexuality is immoral. At best, they would prove that homosexual people—like everyone else—ought to take great care when deciding to become sexually active.

Of course, there's more to a flourishing life than avoiding harm. One might argue that even if Tommy and Jim are not harming each other by their relationship, they are still failing to achieve the higher level of fulfillment possible in a heterosexual relationship, which is rooted in the complementarity of male and female. This argument just ignores the facts: Tommy and Jim are homosexual *precisely because* they find relationships with men (and, in particular, with each other) more fulfilling than relationships with women. Even evangelicals (who have long advocated "faith healing" for homosexuals) are beginning to acknowledge that the choice for most homosexual people is not between homosexual relationships and heterosexual relationships, but rather between homosexual relationships and celibacy.[14] What the critics need to show, therefore, is that no matter how loving, committed, mutual, generous, and fulfilling the relationship may be, Tommy and Jim would flourish more if they were celibate. This is a formidable—and, I suspect, impossible—task.

Thus far I have focused on the allegation that homosexuality harms those who engage in it. But what about the allegation that homosexuality harms other, non-consenting parties? Here I will briefly consider two claims: that homosexuality threatens children and that it threatens society.

Those who argue that homosexuality threatens children may mean one of two things. First, they may mean that homosexual people are child molesters. Statistically, the vast majority of reported cases of child sexual abuse involve young girls and their fathers, stepfathers, or other familiar (and presumably heterosexual) adult males.[15] But opponents of homosexuality argue that when one adjusts for relative percentage in the population, homosexual males appear more likely than heterosexual males to be child molesters. As I argued above, the problems with obtaining reliable statistics on homosexuality render such calculations difficult. Fortunately, they are also unnecessary.

Child abuse is a terrible thing. But when a heterosexual male molests a child (or rapes a woman or commits assault), the act does not reflect upon all heterosexuals. Similarly, when a homosexual male molests a child, there is no reason why that act should reflect upon all homosexuals. Sex with adults of the same sex is one thing; sex with *children* of the same sex is quite another. Conflating the two not only slanders innocent people, it also misdirects resources intended to protect children. Furthermore, many men convicted of molesting young boys are sexually attracted to adult women and report no attraction to adult men.[16] To call such men "homosexual," or even "bisexual," is probably to stretch such terms too far.[17]

Alternatively, those who charge that homosexuality threatens children might mean that the increasing visibility of homosexual relationships makes children more likely to become homosexual. The argument for this view is patently circular. One cannot prove that doing *X* is bad by arguing that it causes people to do *Y*, which is bad. One must first establish independently that *X* is bad. That said, there is not a shred of evidence to demonstrate that exposure to homosexuality leads children to become homosexual.

But doesn't homosexuality threaten society? A Roman Catholic priest once put the argument to me as follows: "Of course homosexuality is bad for society. If everyone were homosexual, there would be no society." Perhaps it is true that if everyone were homosexual, there would be no society. But if everyone were a celibate priest, society would collapse just as surely, and my friend the priest didn't seem to think that he was doing anything wrong simply by failing to procreate. Jeremy Bentham made the point somewhat more acerbically roughly 200 years ago: "If then merely out of regard to population it were right that [homosexuals] should be burnt alive, monks ought to be roasted alive by a slow fire."[18]

● From the fact that the continuation of society requires procreation, it does not follow that *everyone* must procreate. Moreover, even if such an obligation existed, it would not preclude homosexuality. At best, it would preclude *exclusive* homosexuality: homosexual people who occasionally have heterosexual sex can procreate just fine. And given artificial insemination, even those who are exclusively homosexual can procreate. In short, the priest's claim—if everyone were homosexual, there would be no society—is false; and even if it were true, it would not establish that homosexuality is immoral. ●

The Ramsey Colloquium commits a similar fallacy.[19] Noting (correctly) that heterosexual marriage promotes the continuation of human life, it then infers that homosexuality is immoral because it fails to accomplish the same.[20] But from the fact that procreation is good, it does not follow that childlessness is bad—a point that the members of the colloquium, several of whom are Roman Catholic priests, should readily concede.

I have argued that Tommy and Jim's sexual relationship harms neither them nor society. On the contrary, it benefits both. It benefits them because it makes them happier—not merely in a short-term, hedonistic sense, but in a long-term, "big picture" sort of way. And, in turn, it benefits society, since it makes Tommy and Jim more stable, more productive, and more generous than they would otherwise be. In short, their relationship—including its sexual component—provides the same kinds of benefits that infertile heterosexual relationships provide (and perhaps other benefits as well). Nor should we fear that accepting their relationship and others like it will cause people to flee in droves from the institution of heterosexual marriage. After all, as Thomas Williams points out, the usual response to a gay person is not, "How come he gets to be gay and I don't?"[21]

Homosexuality Violates Biblical Teaching

At this point in the discussion, many people turn to religion. "If the secular arguments fail to prove that homosexuality is wrong," they say, "so much the worse for secular ethics. This failure only proves that we need God for morality." Since people often justify their moral beliefs by appeal to religion, I will briefly consider the biblical position.

At first glance, the Bible's condemnation of homosexual activity seems unequivocal. Consider, for example, the following two passages, one from the Old Testament and one from the New:[22]

You shall not lie with a male as with a woman; it is an abomination (Lev. 18:22)

For this reason God gave them up to degrading passions. Their women exchanged natural intercourse for unnatural, and in the same way also the men, giving up natural intercourse with women, were consumed with passion for one another. Men committed shameless acts with men and received in their own persons the due penalty for their error (Rom. 1:26–27)

Note, however, that these passages are surrounded by other passages that relatively few people consider binding. For example, Leviticus also declares, "The pig . . . is unclean for you. Of their flesh you shall not eat, and their carcasses you shall not touch; they are unclean for you" (11:7–8). Taken literally, this passage not only prohibits eating pork, but also playing football, since footballs are made of pigskin. (Can you believe that the University of Notre Dame so flagrantly violates Levitical teaching?)

Similarly, St. Paul, author of the Romans passage, also writes, "Slaves, obey your earthly masters with fear and trembling, in singleness of heart, as you obey Christ" (Eph. 6:5)—morally problematic advice if there ever

were any. Should we interpret this passage (as Southern plantation owners once did) as implying that it is immoral for slaves to escape? After all,
God himself says in Leviticus,

> [Y]ou may acquire male and female slaves . . . from among the aliens re-
> siding with you, and from their families that are with you, who have been
> born in your land; and they may be your property. You may keep them as a
> possession for your children after you, for them to inherit as property.
> (25:44–46)

How can people maintain the inerrancy of the Bible in light of such passages? The answer, I think, is that they learn to interpret the passages *in
their historical context.*

Consider the Bible's position on usury, the lending of money for interest (for *any* interest, not just excessive interest). The Bible condemns
this practice in no uncertain terms. In Exodus God says that "if you lend
money to my people, to the poor among you . . . you shall not exact interest from them" (22:25). Psalm 15 says that those who lend at interest
may not abide in the Lord's tent or dwell on his holy hill (1–5). Ezekiel
calls usury "abominable"; compares it to adultery, robbery, idolatry, and
bribery; and states that anyone who "takes advanced or accrued interest
. . . shall surely die; his blood shall be upon himself" (18:13).[23]

Should believers therefore close their savings accounts? Not necessarily. According to orthodox Christian teaching, the biblical prohibition
against usury no longer applies. The reason is that economic conditions
have changed substantially since biblical times, such that usury no
longer has the same negative consequences it had when the prohibitions
were issued. Thus, the practice that was condemned by the Bible differs
from contemporary interest banking in morally relevant ways.[24]

Yet are we not in a similar position regarding homosexuality? Virtually
all scholars agree that homosexual relations during biblical times were
vastly different from relationships like Tommy and Jim's. Often such relations were integral to pagan practices. In Greek society, they typically
involved older men and younger boys. If those are the kinds of features
that the biblical authors had in mind when they issued their condemnations, and such features are no longer typical, then the biblical condemnations no longer apply. As with usury, substantial changes in cultural context have altered the meaning and consequences—and thus
the moral value—of the practice in question. Put another way, using the
Bible's condemnations of homosexuality against contemporary homosexuality is like using its condemnations of usury against contemporary
banking.

Let me be clear about what I am *not* claiming here. First, I am not
claiming that the Bible has been wrong before and therefore may be

wrong this time. The Bible may indeed be wrong on some matters, but for the purpose of this argument, I am assuming its infallibility. Nor am I claiming that the Bible's age renders it entirely inapplicable to today's issues. Rather, I am claiming that when we do apply it, *we must pay attention to morally relevant cultural differences between biblical times and today.* And, as the above argument shows, that claim is not very controversial. To deny it is to commit oneself to some rather strange views on slavery, usury, women's roles, astronomy, evolution, and the like.

Here, one might also make an appeal to religious pluralism. Given the wide variety of religious beliefs (e.g., the Muslim belief that women should cover their faces, the Orthodox Jewish belief against working on Saturday, the Hindu belief that cows are sacred and should not be eaten), each of us inevitably violates the religious beliefs of others. But we normally don't view such violations as occasions for moral censure, since we distinguish between beliefs that depend on particular revelations and beliefs that can be justified independently (e.g., that stealing is wrong). Without an independent justification for condemning homosexuality, the best one can say is, "My religion says so." But in a society that cherishes religious freedom, that reason alone does not normally provide grounds for moral or legal sanctions. That people still fall back on that reason in discussions of homosexuality suggests that they may not have much of a case otherwise.

Conclusion

As a last resort, opponents of homosexuality typically change the subject: "But what about incest, polygamy, and bestiality? If we accept Tommy and Jim's sexual relationship, why shouldn't we accept those as well?" Opponents of interracial marriage used a similar slippery-slope argument in the 1960s when the Supreme Court struck down anti-miscegenation laws.[25] It was a bad argument then, and it is a bad argument now.

Just because there are no good reasons to oppose interracial or homosexual relationships, it does not follow that there are no good reasons to oppose incestuous, polygamous, or bestial relationships. One might argue, for instance, that incestuous relationships threaten delicate familial bonds, or that polygamous relationships result in unhealthy jealousies (and sexism), or that bestial relationships—do I need to say it?— aren't really "relationships" at all, at least not in the sense we've been discussing.[26] Perhaps even better arguments could be offered (given much more space than I have here). The point is that there is no logical connection between homosexuality, on the one hand, and incest, polygamy, and bestiality, on the other.

Why, then, do critics continue to push this objection? Perhaps it's because accepting homosexuality requires them to give up one of their favorite arguments: "It's wrong because we've always been taught that it's wrong." This argument—call it the argument from tradition—has an obvious appeal: people reasonably favor tried-and-true ideas over unfamiliar ones, and they recognize the foolishness of trying to invent morality from scratch. But the argument from tradition is also a dangerous argument, as any honest look at history will reveal.

I conclude that Tommy and Jim's relationship, far from being a moral abomination, is exactly what it appears to be to those who know them: a morally positive influence on their lives and on others. Accepting this conclusion takes courage, since it entails that our moral traditions are fallible. But when these traditions interfere with people's happiness for no sound reason, they defeat the very point of morality: promoting individual and communal well-being. To put the argument simply, Tommy and Jim's relationship makes them better people. And that's not just good for Tommy and Jim: that's good for everyone.

Study Questions

1. There is a line of thought (expressed by, among others, Sir Patrick Devlin in his 1965 book *The Enforcement of Morals*) that claims: "Most people find homosexual sex disgusting, and this disgust is a reliable compass for making moral judgments." How might Corvino reply to this argument?

2. Suppose homosexuality is found by science to be similar to some obesity, alcoholism, or depression, in that a certain percent of the condition is attributable to genetic heritage. What policy implications might follow (or not follow) from such a finding?

3. Corvino's couple, Tommy and Jim, seem typical of those gay men who have known of their orientation from a relatively early age. (Consult, for one gay author, Andrew Sullivan, *Virtually Normal.*) Are Tommy and Jim typical of homosexuals in general? Does this matter to any of Corvino's arguments? Would it be helpful here to consider Will's childhood on the television program "Will and Grace"?

4. Do you think that Corvino has convincingly put to rest the objections to homosexual sexual activity arising from Roman Catholic ethics? Try to answer this question after taking seriously the views of John Finnis (chapter 9) and Karol Wojtyla (chapter 11).

5. The questions of early Christian condemnation of homosexuality and the exact meaning of biblical passages that apparently criticize homosexuality have been much debated in scholarly journals. One famous treatise that discusses these issues is John Boswell's 1980 book, *Christianity, Social Tolerance, and Homosexuality*. A more recent text that covers the territory in less technical fashion is Patricia Jung and Ralph Smith, *Heterosexism* (1993). Consult these texts while studying and evaluating Corvino's views about the relationship between religion and the morality of homosexuality.

Notes

This paper grew out of a lecture, "What's (Morally) Wrong with Homosexuality?" which I first delivered at the University of Texas in 1992 and have since delivered at numerous other universities around the country. I am grateful to countless audience members, students, colleagues, and friends for helpful dialogue over the years. I would especially like to thank the following individuals for detailed comments on recent drafts of the paper: Edwin B. Allaire, Daniel Bonevac, David Bradshaw, David Cleaves, Mary Beth Mader, Richard D. Mohr, Jonathan Rauch, Robert Schuessler, James Sterba, Alan Soble, and Thomas Williams. I dedicate this paper to Carlos Casillas.

1. Although my central example in the paper is a gay male couple, much of what I say will apply mutatis mutandis to lesbians as well, since many of the same arguments are used against them. This is not to say gay male sexuality and lesbian sexuality are largely similar or that discussions of the former will cover all that needs to be said about the latter. Furthermore, the fact that I focus on a long-term, committed relationship should not be taken to imply any judgment about homosexual activity outside of such unions. If the argument of this paper is successful, then the evaluation of homosexual activity outside of committed unions should be largely (if not entirely) similar to the evaluation of heterosexual activity outside of committed unions.

2. Burton M. Leiser, *Liberty, Justice, and Morals: Contemporary Value Conflicts* (New York: Macmillan, 1986), 51–57.

3. The Ramsey Colloquium, "The Homosexual Movement," *First Things* (March 1994): 15–20.

4. For an overview of some of these studies, see Simon LeVay, *Queer Science* (Boston, Mass.: MIT Press, 1996), chap. 10.

5. I have borrowed some items in this list from Richard Mohr's pioneering work *Gays/Justice* (New York: Columbia University Press, 1988), 36.

6. I am indebted to Andrew Koppelman and Stephen Macedo for helpful discussions on this point. See Andrew Koppelman's argument [chap. 10 of this volume], and Stephen Macedo's article "Homosexuality and the Conservative Mind," *Georgetown Law Journal* 84, no. 2 (1995): 261–300.

7. For a fuller explication of this type of natural law argument, see John Finnis, "Law, Morality, and 'Sexual Orientation,'" *Notre Dame Law Review* 69, no. 5

(1994): 1049–76. For cogent and well-developed responses, see Koppelman and Macedo.

8. Ramsey Colloquium, "Homosexual Movement," 19.

9. Thomas Schmidt, "The Price of Love," in *Straight and Narrow? Compassion and Clarity in the Homosexuality Debate* (Downers Grove, Ill.: InterVarsity Press, 1995), chap. 6.

10. Both the American Psychological Association and the American Public Health Association have conceded this point: "Reliable data on the incidence of homosexual orientation are difficult to obtain due to the criminal penalties and social stigma attached to homosexual behavior and the consequent difficulty of obtaining representative samples of people to study" (*Amici Curiae* Brief in *Bowers v. Hardwick*, Supreme Court No. 85–140 [October Term 1985]).

11. It is worth noting that allegations of promiscuity are probably exaggerated. The study most commonly cited to prove homosexual male promiscuity, the Bell and Weinberg study, took place in 1978, in an urban center (San Francisco), at the height of the sexual revolution—hardly a broad sample. See Alan P. Bell and Martin S. Weinberg, *Homosexualities* (New York: Simon and Schuster, 1978). The far more recent and extensive University of Chicago study agreed that homosexual and bisexual people "have higher average numbers of partners than the rest of the sexually active people in the study," but it concluded that the differences in the mean number of partners "do not appear very large." See Edward O. Laumann et al., *The Social Organization of Sexuality: Sexual Practices in the United States* (Chicago: University of Chicago Press, 1994), 314, 316. I am grateful to Andrew Koppelman for drawing my attention to the Chicago study.

12. Ramsey Colloquium, "Homosexual Movement," 19.

13. See S. R. Johnson, E. M. Smith, and S. M. Guenther, "Comparison of Gynecological Health Care Problems between Lesbian and Bisexual Women," *Journal of Reproductive Medicine* 32 (1987): 805–11.

14. See, for example, Stanton L. Jones, "The Loving Opposition," *Christianity Today* 37, no. 8 (July 19, 1993).

15. See Danya Glaser and Stephen Frosh, *Child Sexual Abuse*, 2nd ed. (Houndmills, UK: Macmillan, 1993), 13–17, and Kathleen Coulbourn Faller, *Understanding Child Sexual Maltreatment* (Newbury Park, Calif.: Sage, 1990), 16–20.

16. See Frank G. Bolton Jr., Larry A. Morris, and Ann E. MacEachron, *Males at Risk: The Other Side of Child Sexual Abuse* (Newbury Park, Calif.: Sage, 1989), 61.

17. Part of the problem here arises from the grossly simplistic categorization of people into two (or, at best, three) sexual orientations: heterosexual, homosexual, and bisexual. Clearly, there is great variety within (and beyond) these categories. See Frederick Suppe, "Explaining Homosexuality: Philosophical Issues, and Who Cares Anyhow?" in Timothy F. Murphy, ed., *Gay Ethics: Controversies in Outing, Civil Rights, and Sexual Science* (New York: Harrington Park Press, 1994), esp. 223–68, published simultaneously in *Journal of Homosexuality* 27, nos. 3–4 (1994): 223–68.

18. "An Essay on 'Paederasty,' " in Robert Baker and Frederick Elliston, eds., *The Philosophy of Sex* (Buffalo, N.Y.: Prometheus, 1984), 360–61. Bentham uses the word "paederast" where we would use the term "homosexual." The latter term was not coined until 1869, and the term "heterosexual" was coined a few years after that. Today, "pederasty" refers to sex between men and boys—a different phenomenon from the one Bentham was addressing.

19. Ramsey Colloquium, "Homosexual Movement," 17–18.

20. The argument is a classic example of the fallacy of denying the antecedent: if X promotes procreation, then X is good; X does not promote procreation, therefore X is not good. Compare: if X is president, then X lives in the White House; Chelsea Clinton is not president, therefore Chelsea Clinton does not live in the White House.

21. Actually, Williams makes the point with regard to celibacy, while making an analogy between celibacy and homosexuality. See "A Reply to the Ramsey Colloquium," in John Corvino, ed., *Same Sex: Debating the Ethics, Science, and Culture of Homosexuality* (Lanham, Md.: Rowman and Littlefield, 1997), 69–80.

22. All biblical quotations are from the New Revised Standard Version.

23. See also Deut. 23:19, Lev. 25:35–37, Neh. 5:7–10, Jer. 15:10, Ezek. 22:12, and Luke 6:35. For a fuller explication of the analogy between homosexuality and usury, see John Corvino, "The Bible Condemned Usurers, Too," *Harvard Gay and Lesbian Review* 3, no. 4 (Fall 1996): 11–12.

24. See Richard P. McBrien, *Catholicism*, study ed. (San Francisco: Harper & Row, 1981), 1020.

25. *Loving v. Virginia*, 388 U.S. 1967.

26. One might object here that I am equivocating on the term "relationship," since throughout the paper I have been discussing acts, not relationships. But I maintain that Tommy and Jim's sexual act is *relational* in a way that Tommy and Fido's simply could not be. Even apart from their love for each other, Tommy and Jim have capacities for mutual communication and respect that Tommy and Fido simply do not have. Thus, one can approve of Tommy and Jim's sexual act without implying anything about Tommy and Fido's: the two are fundamentally different.

Chapter 13

BEYOND GAY MARRIAGE:
THE ROAD TO POLYAMORY

Stanley Kurtz

Though the U.S. Census Bureau reports difficulties in identifying "married" couples, there can be little doubt that the profile of marriage has been changing: same-sex/gender households now make up about one-sixth of all households with unmarried partners. Still, gay and lesbian couples are a small minority of the nontraditional alternatives to marriage found in America today, yet **Stanley Kurtz** *perceives a gay-lesbian tail wagging this pluralistic dog. On his view, at the forefront of many recent debates in family law is the gay and lesbian agenda, the key item of which may well be the eventual abolition of marriage as an institution. In this socially conservative essay, Kurtz provides a sustained, detailed account of why contemporary American society should resist same-sex marriage. One of his concerns is revealed in his polemical slippery-slope argument against same-sex marriage: it will lead to polygamy and its latest incarnation, polyamory ("having many lovers"). Whereas other theorists might see the increasing legal frameworks for alternatives to marriage as a good thing because, for example, they add to people's options, Kurtz weighs in on the negative side, forecasting only doom.*

Kurtz was formerly a research fellow at the Hoover Institution of Stanford University. In addition to being a contributing editor to the *National Review*, he is a senior fellow at the Ethics and Public Policy Center, Washington, D.C.

Reprinted from the *Weekly Standard* 8, no. 45 (August 4–11, 2003). © Copyright 2006, News Corporation, *Weekly Standard*.

After gay marriage, what will become of marriage itself? Will same-sex matrimony extend marriage's stabilizing effects to homosexuals? Will gay marriage undermine family life? A lot is riding on the answers to these questions. But the media's reflexive labeling of doubts about gay marriage as homophobia has made it almost impossible to debate the social effects of this reform. Now with the Supreme Court's ringing affirmation of sexual liberty in *Lawrence v. Texas*, that debate is unavoidable.

Among the likeliest effects of gay marriage is to take us down a slippery slope to legalized polygamy and "polyamory" (group marriage). Marriage will be transformed into a variety of relationship contracts, linking two, three, or more individuals (however weakly and temporarily) in every conceivable combination of male and female. A scare scenario? Hardly. The bottom of this slope is visible from where we stand. Advocacy of legalized polygamy is growing. A network of grass-roots organizations seeking legal recognition for group marriage already exists. The cause of legalized group marriage is championed by a powerful faction of family law specialists. Influential legal bodies in both the United States and Canada have presented radical programs of marital reform. Some of these quasi-governmental proposals go so far as to suggest the abolition of marriage. The ideas behind this movement have already achieved surprising influence with a prominent American politician.

None of this is well known. Both the media and public spokesmen for the gay marriage movement treat the issue as an unproblematic advance for civil rights. True, a small number of relatively conservative gay spokesmen do consider the social effects of gay matrimony, insisting that they will be beneficent, that homosexual unions will become more stable. Yet another faction of gay rights advocates actually favors gay marriage as a step toward the abolition of marriage itself. This group agrees that there is a slippery slope, and wants to hasten the slide down.

To consider what comes after gay marriage is not to say that gay marriage itself poses no danger to the institution of marriage. Quite apart from the likelihood that it will usher in legalized polygamy and polyamory, gay marriage will almost certainly weaken the belief that monogamy lies at the heart of marriage. But to see why this is so, we will first need to reconnoiter the slippery slope.

Promoting Polygamy

During the 1996 congressional debate on the Defense of Marriage Act, which affirmed the ability of the states and the federal government to withhold recognition from same-sex marriages, gay marriage advocates were put on the defensive by the polygamy question. If gays had a right to marry, why not polygamists? Andrew Sullivan, one of gay marriage's most intelligent defenders, labeled the question fear-mongering—akin to the discredited belief that interracial marriage would lead to birth defects. "To the best of my knowledge," said Sullivan, "there is no polygamists' rights organization poised to exploit same-sex marriage and return the republic to polygamous abandon." Actually, there are now many such organizations. And their strategy—even their existence— owes much to the movement for gay marriage.

Scoffing at the polygamy prospect as ludicrous has been the strategy of choice for gay marriage advocates. In 2000, following Vermont's enactment of civil unions, Matt Coles, director of the American Civil Liberties Union's Lesbian and Gay Rights Project, said, "I think the idea that there is some kind of slippery slope [to polygamy or group marriage] is silly." As proof, Coles said that America had legalized interracial marriage, while also forcing Utah to ban polygamy before admission to the union. That dichotomy, said Coles, shows that Americans are capable of distinguishing between better and worse proposals for reforming marriage.

Are we? When Tom Green was put on trial in Utah for polygamy in 2001, it played like a dress rehearsal for the coming movement to legalize polygamy. True, Green was convicted for violating what he called Utah's "don't ask, don't tell" policy on polygamy. Pointedly refusing to "hide in the closet," he touted polygamy on the Sally Jessy Raphael, Queen Latifah, Geraldo Rivera, and Jerry Springer shows, and on "Dateline NBC" and "48 Hours." But the Green trial was not just a cable spectacle. It brought out a surprising number of mainstream defenses of polygamy. And most of the defenders went to bat for polygamy by drawing direct comparisons to gay marriage.

Writing in the *Village Voice,* gay leftist Richard Goldstein equated the drive for state-sanctioned polygamy with the movement for gay marriage. The political reluctance of gays to embrace polygamists was understandable, said Goldstein, "but our fates are entwined in fundamental ways." Libertarian Jacob Sullum defended polygamy, along with all other consensual domestic arrangements, in the *Washington Times.* Syndicated liberal columnist Ellen Goodman took up the cause of polygamy with a direct comparison to gay marriage. Steve Chapman, a member of the *Chicago Tribune* editorial board, defended polygamy in the *Tribune* and in *Slate.* The *New York Times* published a "Week in Review" article juxtaposing photos of Tom Green's family with sociobiological arguments about the naturalness of polygamy and promiscuity.

The ACLU's Matt Coles may have derided the idea of a slippery slope from gay marriage to polygamy, but the ACLU itself stepped in to help Tom Green during his trial and declared its support for the repeal of all "laws prohibiting or penalizing the practice of plural marriage." There is of course a difference between repealing such laws and formal state recognition of polygamous marriages. Neither the ACLU nor, say, Ellen Goodman has directly advocated formal state recognition. Yet they give us no reason to suppose that, when the time is ripe, they will not do so. Stephen Clark, the legal director of the Utah ACLU, has said, "Talking to Utah's polygamists is like talking to gays and lesbians who really want the right to live their lives."

All this was in 2001, well before the prospect that legal gay marriage might create the cultural conditions for state-sanctioned polygamy. Can anyone doubt that greater public support will be forthcoming once gay marriage has become a reality? Surely the ACLU will lead the charge.

Why is state-sanctioned polygamy a problem? The deep reason is that it erodes the ethos of monogamous marriage. Despite the divorce revolution, Americans still take it for granted that marriage means monogamy. The ideal of fidelity may be breached in practice, yet adultery is clearly understood as a transgression against marriage. Legal polygamy would jeopardize that understanding, and that is why polygamy has historically been treated in the West as an offense against society itself.

In most non-Western cultures, marriage is not a union of freely choosing individuals, but an alliance of family groups. The emotional relationship between husband and wife is attenuated and subordinated to the economic and political interests of extended kin. But in our world of freely choosing individuals, extended families fall away, and love and companionship are the only surviving principles on which families can be built. From Thomas Aquinas through Richard Posner, almost every serious observer has granted the incompatibility between polygamy and Western companionate marriage.

Where polygamy works, it does so because the husband and his wives are emotionally distant. Even then, jealousy is a constant danger, averted only by strict rules of seniority or parity in the husband's economic support of his wives. Polygamy is more about those resources than about sex.

Yet in many polygamous societies, even though only 10 or 15 percent of men may actually have multiple wives, there is a widely held belief that men need multiple women. The result is that polygamists are often promiscuous—just not with their own wives. Anthropologist Philip Kilbride reports a Nigerian survey in which, among urban male polygamists, 44 percent said their most recent sexual partners were women other than their wives. For monogamous, married Nigerian men in urban areas, that figure rose to 67 percent. Even though polygamous marriage is less about sex than security, societies that permit polygamy tend to reject the idea of marital fidelity—for everyone, polygamists included.

Mormon polygamy has always been a complicated and evolving combination of Western mores and classic polygamous patterns. Like Western companionate marriage, Mormon polygamy condemns extramarital sex. Yet historically, like its non-Western counterparts, it de-emphasized romantic love. Even so, jealousy was always a problem. One study puts the rate of nineteenth-century polygamous divorce at triple the rate for monogamous families. Unlike their forebears, contemporary Mormon polygamists try to combine polygamy with companionate marriage— and have a very tough time of it. We have no definitive figures, but divorce is frequent. Irwin Altman and Joseph Ginat, who've written the most detailed account of today's breakaway Mormon polygamist sects, highlight the special stresses put on families trying to combine modern notions of romantic love with polygamy. Strict religious rules of parity among wives make the effort to create a hybrid traditionalist/modern version of Mormon polygamy at least plausible, if very stressful. But polygamy let loose in modern secular America would destroy our understanding of marital fidelity, while putting nothing viable in its place. And postmodern polygamy is a lot closer than you think.

Polyamory

America's new, souped-up version of polygamy is called "polyamory." Polyamorists trace their descent from the anti-monogamy movements of the sixties and seventies—everything from hippie communes, to the support groups that grew up around Robert Rimmer's 1966 novel *The Harrad Experiment*, to the cult of Bhagwan Shree Rajneesh. Polyamorists proselytize for "responsible non-monogamy"—open, loving, and stable sexual relationships among more than two people. The modern polyamory movement took off in the mid-nineties—partly because of the growth of the Internet (with its confidentiality), but also in parallel to, and inspired by, the rising gay marriage movement.

Unlike classic polygamy, which features one man and several women, polyamory comprises a bewildering variety of sexual combinations. There are triads of one woman and two men; heterosexual group marriages; groups in which some or all members are bisexual; lesbian groups, and so forth. (For details, see Deborah Anapol's *Polyamory: The New Love Without Limits*, one of the movement's authoritative guides, or Google "polyamory.")

Supposedly, polyamory is not a synonym for promiscuity. In practice, though, there is a continuum between polyamory and "swinging." Swinging couples dally with multiple sexual partners while intentionally avoiding emotional entanglements. Polyamorists, in contrast, try to establish stable emotional ties among a sexually connected group. Although the subcultures of swinging and polyamory are recognizably different, many individuals move freely between them. And since polyamorous group marriages can be sexually closed or open, it's often tough to draw a line between polyamory and swinging. Here, then, is the modern American version of Nigeria's extramarital polygamous promiscuity. Once the principles of monogamous companionate marriage are breached, even for supposedly stable and committed sexual groups, the slide toward full-fledged promiscuity is difficult to halt.

Polyamorists are enthusiastic proponents of same-sex marriage. Obviously, any attempt to restrict marriage to a single man and woman would prevent the legalization of polyamory. After passage of the Defense of Marriage Act in 1996, an article appeared in *Loving More*, the flagship magazine of the polyamory movement, calling for the creation of a polyamorist rights movement modeled on the movement for gay rights. The piece was published under the pen name Joy Singer, identified as the graduate of a "top ten law school" and a political organizer and public official in California for the previous two decades.

Taking a leaf from the gay marriage movement, Singer suggested starting small. A campaign for hospital visitation rights for polyamorous spouses would be the way to begin. Full marriage and adoption rights would come later. Again using the gay marriage movement as a model, Singer called for careful selection of acceptable public spokesmen (i.e., people from longstanding poly families with children). Singer even published a speech by Iowa state legislator Ed Fallon on behalf of gay marriage, arguing that the goal would be to get a congressman to give exactly the same speech as Fallon, but substituting the word "poly" for "gay" throughout. Try telling polyamorists that the link between gay marriage and group marriage is a mirage.

The flexible, egalitarian, and altogether postmodern polyamorists are more likely to influence the larger society than Mormon polygamists. The polyamorists go after monogamy in a way that resonates with America's secular, post-sixties culture. Yet the fundamental drawback is the same for Mormons and polyamorists alike. Polyamory websites are filled with chatter about jealousy, the problem that will not go away. Inevitably, group marriages based on modern principles of companionate love, without religious rules and restraints, are unstable. Like the short-lived hippie communes, group marriages will be broken on the contradiction between companionate love and group solidarity. And children will pay the price. The harms of state-sanctioned polyamorous marriage would extend well beyond the polyamorists themselves. Once monogamy is defined out of marriage, it will be next to impossible to educate a new generation in what it takes to keep companionate marriage intact. State-sanctioned polyamory would spell the effective end of marriage. And that is precisely what polyamory's new—and surprisingly influential—defenders are aiming for.

The Family Law Radicals

State-sanctioned polyamory is now the cutting-edge issue among scholars of family law. The preeminent school of thought in academic family law has its origins in the arguments of radical gay activists who once *opposed* same-sex marriage. In the early nineties, radicals like longtime National Gay and Lesbian Task Force policy director Paula Ettelbrick spoke out against making legal marriage a priority for the gay rights movement. Marriage, Ettelbrick reminded her fellow activists, "has long been the focus of radical feminist revulsion." Encouraging gays to marry, said Ettelbrick, would only force gay "assimilation" to American norms, when the real object of the gay rights movement ought to be getting Americans to accept gay difference. "Being queer," said Ettelbrick, "means pushing the parameters of sex and family, and in the process transforming the very fabric of society."

Promoting polyamory is the ideal way to "radically reorder society's view of the family," and Ettelbrick, who has since formally signed on as a supporter of gay marriage (and is frequently quoted by the press), is now part of a movement that hopes to use gay marriage as an opening to press for state-sanctioned polyamory. Ettelbrick teaches law at the University of Michigan, New York University, Barnard, and Columbia. She has a lot of company.

Nancy Polikoff is a professor at American University's law school. In 1993, Polikoff published a powerful and radical critique of gay marriage. Polikoff stressed that during the height of the lesbian feminist movement of the seventies, even many heterosexual feminists refused to marry because they believed marriage to be an inherently patriarchal and oppressive institution. A movement for gay marriage, warned Polikoff, would surely promote marriage as a social good, trotting out monogamous couples as spokesmen in a way that would marginalize non-monogamous gays and would fail to challenge the legitimacy of marriage itself. Like Ettelbrick, Polikoff now supports the right of gays to marry. And like Ettelbrick, Polikoff is part of a movement whose larger goal is to use legal gay marriage to push for state-sanctioned polyamory—the ultimate subversion of marriage itself. Polikoff and Ettelbrick represent what is arguably now the dominant perspective within the discipline of family law.

Cornell University law professor Martha Fineman is another key figure in the field of family law. In her 1995 book *The Neutered Mother, the Sexual Family, and Other Twentieth Century Tragedies*, she argued for the abolition of marriage as a legal category. Fineman's book begins with her recollection of an experience from the late seventies in politically radical Madison, Wisconsin. To her frustration, she could not convince even the most progressive members of Madison's Equal Opportunities

Commission to recognize "plural sexual groupings" as marriages. That failure helped energize Fineman's lifelong drive to abolish marriage.

But it is University of Utah law professor Martha Ertman who stands on the cutting edge of family law. Building on Fineman's proposals for the abolition of legal marriage, Ertman has offered a legal template for a sweeping relationship contract system modeled on corporate law. (See *Harvard Civil Rights and Civil Liberties Law Review*, Winter 2001.) Ertman wants state-sanctioned polyamory, legally organized on the model of limited liability companies.

In arguing for the replacement of marriage with a contract system that accommodates polyamory, Ertman notes that legal and social hostility to polygamy and polyamory are decreasing. She goes on astutely to imply that the increased openness of homosexual partnerships is slowly collapsing the taboo against polygamy and polyamory. And Ertman is frank about the purpose of her proposed reform—to render the distinction between traditional marriage and polyamory "morally neutral."

A sociologist rather than a professor of law, Judith Stacey, the Barbra Streisand Professor in Contemporary Gender Studies at USC, is another key member of this group. Stacey has long championed alternative family forms. Her current research is on gay families consisting of more than two adults, whose several members consider themselves either married or contractually bound.

In 1996, in the *Michigan Law Review*, David Chambers, a professor of law at the University of Michigan and another prominent member of this group, explained why radical opponents of marriage ought to support gay marriage. Rather than reinforcing a two-person definition of marriage, argued Chambers, gay marriage would make society more accepting of further legal changes. "By ceasing to conceive of marriage as a partnership composed of one person of each sex, the state may become more receptive to units of three or more."

Gradual transition from gay marriage to state-sanctioned polyamory, and the eventual abolition of marriage itself as a legal category, is now the most influential paradigm within academic family law. As Chambers put it, "All desirable changes in family law need not be made at once."

Finally, Martha Minow of Harvard Law School deserves mention. Minow has not advocated state-sanctioned polygamy or polyamory, but the principles she champions pave the way for both. Minow argues that families need to be radically redefined, putting blood ties and traditional legal arrangements aside and attending instead to the functional realities of new family configurations.

Ettelbrick, Polikoff, Fineman, Ertman, Stacey, Chambers, and Minow are among the most prominent family law theorists in the country. They have plenty of followers and hold much of the power and initiative within their field. There may be other approaches to academic family law, but none exceed the radicals in influence. In the last couple of years, there have been a number of conferences on family law dominated by the views of this school. The conferences have names like "Marriage Law: Obsolete or Cutting Edge?" and "Assimilation & Resistance: Emerging Issues in Law & Sexuality." The titles turn on the paradox of using marriage, seemingly a conservative path toward assimilation, as a tool of radical cultural "resistance."

One of the most important recent family law meetings was the March 2003 Hofstra conference on "Marriage, Democracy, and Families." The radicals were out in full force. On a panel entitled "Intimate Affiliation and Democracy: Beyond Marriage?" Fineman, Ertman, and Stacey held forth on polyamory, the legal abolition of marriage, and related issues. Although there were more moderate scholars present, there was barely a challenge to the radicals' suggestion that it was time to move "beyond marriage." The few traditionalists in family law are relatively isolated. Many, maybe most, of the prominent figures in family law count themselves as advocates for lesbian and gay rights. Yet family law today is as influenced by the hostility to marriage of seventies feminism as it is by advocacy for gay rights. It is this confluence of radical feminism and gay rights that now shapes the field.

Beyond Conjugality

You might think the radicals who dominate the discipline of family law are just a bunch of eccentric and irrelevant academics. You would be wrong. For one thing, there is already a thriving non-profit organization, the Alternatives to Marriage Project, that advances the radicals' goals. When controversies over the family hit the news, experts provided by the Alternatives to Marriage Project are often quoted in mainstream media outlets. While the Alternatives to Marriage Project endorses gay marriage, its longer-term goal is to replace marriage with a system that recognizes "the full range" of family types.

That includes polyamorous families. The Alternatives to Marriage Project's statement of purpose—its "Affirmation of Family Diversity"—is signed not only by Ettelbrick, Polikoff, and Stacey but by several polyamorists as well. On a list of signatories that includes academic luminaries like Yale historian Nancy Cott, you can find Barry Northrup of *Loving More* magazine. The Alternatives to Marriage Project, along with Martha Ertman's pioneering legal proposals, has given polyamory a foothold on respectability.

The first real public triumph of the family law radicals has come in Canada. In 1997, the Canadian Parliament established the Law Commission of Canada to serve Parliament and the Justice Ministry as a kind of advisory board on legal reform. In December 2001, the commission submitted a report to Parliament called "Beyond Conjugality," which stops just short of recommending the abolition of marriage in Canada.

"Beyond Conjugality" contains three basic recommendations. First, judges are directed to concentrate on whether the individuals before them are "functionally interdependent," regardless of their actual marital status. On that theory, a household consisting of an adult child still living with his mother might be treated as the functional equivalent of a married couple. In so disregarding marital status, "Beyond Conjugality" is clearly drawing on the work of Minow, whose writings are listed in the bibliography.

The second key recommendation "Beyond Conjugality" is that a legal structure be established allowing people to register their personal relationships with the government. Not only could heterosexual couples register as official partners, so could gay couples, adult children living with parents, and siblings or friends sharing a house. Although the authors of "Beyond Conjugality" are politic enough to relegate the point to footnotes, they state that they see no reason, in principle, to limit registered partnerships to two people.

The final recommendation of "Beyond Conjugality"—legalization of same-sex marriage—drew the most publicity when the report was released. Yet for the Law Commission of Canada, same-sex marriage is clearly just one part of the larger project of doing away with marriage itself. "Beyond Conjugality" stops short of recommending the abolition of legal marriage. The authors glumly note that, for the moment, the public is unlikely to accept such a step.

The text of "Beyond Conjugality," its bibliography, and the Law Commission of Canada's other publications unmistakably reveal the influence of the radical theorists who now dominate the discipline of family law. While Canada's parliament has postponed action on "Beyond Conjugality," the report has already begun to shape the culture. The decision by the Canadian government in June 2003 not to contest court rulings legalizing gay marriage is only the beginning of the changes that Canada's judges and legal bureaucrats have in mind. The simultaneity of the many reforms is striking. Gay marriage is being pressed, but in tandem with a registration system that will sanction polyamorous unions, and eventually replace marriage itself. Empirically, the radicals' hopes are being validated. Gay marriage is not strengthening marriage but has instead become part of a larger unraveling of traditional marriage laws.

Ah, but that's Canada, you say. Yet America has its rough equivalent of the Law Commission of Canada—the American Law Institute (ALI), an organization of legal scholars whose recommendations commonly shape important legal reforms. In 2000, ALI promulgated a report called "Principles of the Law of Family Dissolution" recommending that judges effectively disregard the distinction between married couples and long-time cohabitors. While the ALI principles do not go so far as to set up a system of partnership registration to replace marriage, the report's framework for recognizing a wide variety of cohabiting partnerships puts it on the same path as "Beyond Conjugality."

Collapsing the distinction between cohabitation and marriage is a proposal especially damaging to children, who are decidedly better off when born to married parents. (This aspect of the ALI report has been persuasively criticized by Kay Hymowitz, in the March 2003 issue of *Commentary*.) But a more disturbing aspect of the ALI report is its evasion of the polygamy and polyamory issues.

Prior to publication of the ALI Principles, the report's authors were pressed (at the 2000 annual meeting of the American Law Institute) about the question of polygamy. The authors put off the controversy by defining legal cohabitors as couples. Yet the ALI report offers no principled way of excluding polyamorous or polygamous cohabitors from recognition. The report's reforms are said to be based on the need to recognize "statistically growing" patterns of relationship. By this standard, the growth of polyamorous cohabitation will soon require the legal recognition of polyamory.

Although America's ALI Principles do not follow Canada's "Beyond Conjugality" in proposing either state-sanctioned polyamory or the outright end of marriage, the University of Utah's Martha Ertman has suggested (in the Spring/Summer 2001 *Duke Journal of Gender Law and Policy*) that the American Law Institute is intentionally holding back on more radical proposals for pragmatic political reasons. Certainly, the ALI Principles' authors take Canadian law as the model for the report's most radical provisions.

Further confirmation, if any were needed, of the mainstream influence of the family law radicals came with Al and Tipper Gore's 2002 book *Joined at the Heart*, in which they define a family as those who are "joined at the heart" (rather than by blood or by law). The notion that a family is any group "joined at the heart" comes straight from Harvard's Martha Minow, who worked with the Gores. In fact, the Minow article from which the Gores take their definition of family is also the article in which Minow tentatively floats the idea of substituting domestic partnership registries for traditional marriage ("Redefining Families: Who's In and Who's Out?" *University of Colorado Law Review* 62, no. 2 [1991]). So one of the guiding spirits of Canada's "Beyond Conjugality" report almost had a friend in the White House.

Triple Parenting

Polygamy, polyamory, and the abolition of marriage are bad ideas. But what has that got to do with gay marriage? The reason these ideas are connected is that gay marriage is increasingly being treated as a civil rights issue. Once we say that gay couples have a right to have their commitments recognized by the state, it becomes next to impossible to deny that same right to polygamists, polyamorists, or even cohabiting relatives and friends. And once everyone's relationship is recognized, marriage is gone, and only a system of flexible relationship contracts is left. The only way to stop gay marriage from launching a slide down this slope is if there is a compelling state interest in blocking polygamy or polyamory that does not also apply to gay marriage. Many would agree that the state has a compelling interest in preventing polygamy and polyamory from undermining the ethos of monogamy at the core of marriage. The trouble is, gay marriage itself threatens the ethos of monogamy.

The "conservative" case for gay marriage holds that state-sanctioned marriage will reduce gay male promiscuity. But what if the effect works in reverse? What if, instead of marriage reducing gay promiscuity, sexually open gay couples help redefine marriage as a non-monogamous institution? There is evidence that this is exactly what will happen.

Consider sociologist Gretchen Stiers's 1998 study "From this Day Forward." (Stiers favors gay marriage, and calls herself a lesbian "queer theorist.") "From this Day Forward" reports that while exceedingly few of even the most committed gay and lesbian couples surveyed believe that marriage will strengthen and stabilize their personal relationships, nearly half of the surveyed couples who actually disdain traditional marriage (and even gay commitment ceremonies) will nonetheless get married. Why? For the financial and legal benefits of marriage. And Stiers's study suggests that many radical gays and lesbians who yearn to see marriage abolished (and multiple sexual unions legitimized) intend to marry, not only as a way of securing benefits but as part of a self-conscious attempt to subvert the institution of marriage. Stiers's study suggests that the "subversive" intentions of the radical legal theorists are shared by a significant portion of the gay community itself.

Stiers's study was focused on the most committed gay couples. Yet even in a sample with a disproportionate number of male couples who had gone through a commitment ceremony (and Stiers had to go out of her research protocol just to find enough male couples to balance the committed lesbian couples) nearly 20 percent of the men questioned did not practice monogamy. In a representative sample of gay male couples, that number would be vastly higher. More significantly, a mere 10 percent of even this skewed sample of gay men mentioned monogamy as an important aspect of commitment (meaning that even many of those men who had undergone "union ceremonies" failed to identify fidelity with commitment). And these, the very most committed gay male couples, are the ones who will be trailblazing marital norms for their peers, and exemplifying gay marriage for the nation. So concerns about the effects of gay marriage on the social ideal of marital monogamy seem justified.

A recent survey of gay couples in civil unions by University of Vermont psychologists Esther Rothblum and Sondra Solomon confirms what Stiers's study suggests—that married gay male couples will be far less likely than married heterosexual couples to identify marriage with monogamy. Rothblum and Solomon contacted all 2,300 couples who entered civil unions in Vermont between June 1, 2000, and June 30, 2001. More than 300 civil union couples residing in and out of the state responded. Rothblum and Solomon then compared the gay couples in civil unions with heterosexual couples and gay couples outside of civil unions. Among married heterosexual men, 79 percent felt that marriage demanded monogamy, 50 percent of men in gay civil unions insisted on monogamy, while only 34 percent of gay men outside of civil unions affirmed monogamy.

While gay men in civil unions were more likely to affirm monogamy than gays outside of civil unions, gay men in civil unions were far less supportive of monogamy than heterosexual married men. That discrepancy may well be significantly greater under gay marriage than under civil unions. That's because of the effect identified by Stiers—the likelihood that many gays who do not value the traditional monogamous ethos of marriage will marry anyway for the financial benefits that marriage can bring. (A full 86 percent of the civil unions couples who responded to the Rothblum-Solomon survey live outside Vermont, and therefore receive no financial benefits from their new legal status.) The Rothblum-Solomon study may also undercount heterosexual married male acceptance of monogamy, since one member of all the married heterosexual couples in the survey was the sibling of a gay man in a civil union, and thus more likely to be socially liberal than most heterosexuals.

Even moderate gay advocates of same-sex marriage grant that, at present, gay male relationships are far less monogamous than heterosexual relationships. And there is a persuasive literature on this subject: Gabriel Rotello's "Sexual Ecology," for example, offers a documented and powerful account of the behavioral and ideological barriers to monogamy among gay men. The moderate advocates say marriage will change this reality. But they ignore, or downplay, the possibility that gay marriage will change marriage more than it changes the men who marry. Married gay couples will begin to redefine the meaning of marriage for the culture as a whole, in part by removing monogamy as an essential component of marriage. No doubt, the process will be pushed along by cutting-edge movies and TV shows that tout the new "open" marriages being pioneered by gay spouses. In fact, author and gay marriage advocate Richard Mohr has long expressed the hope and expectation that legal gay marriage will succeed in defining monogamy out of marriage.

Lesbians, for their part, do value monogamy. Over 82 percent of the women in the Rothblum-Solomon study, for example, insisted on monogamy, regardless of sexual orientation or marital status. Yet lesbian marriage will undermine the connection between marriage and monogamy in a different way. Lesbians who bear children with sperm donors sometimes set up de facto three-parent families. Typically, these families include a sexually bound lesbian couple, and a male biological father who is close to the couple but not sexually involved. Once lesbian couples can marry, there will be a powerful legal case for extending parental recognition to triumvirates. It will be difficult to question the parental credentials of a sperm donor, or of a married, lesbian nonbirth mother spouse who helps to raise a child from birth. And just as the argument for gay marriage has been built upon the right to gay adoption, legally recognized triple parenting will eventually usher in state-sanctioned triple (and therefore group) marriage.

This year, there was a triple parenting case in Canada involving a lesbian couple and a sperm donor. The judge made it clear that he wanted to assign parental status to all three adults but held back because he said he lacked jurisdiction. On this issue, the United States is already in "advance" of Canada. Martha Ertman is now pointing to a 2000 Minnesota case (*La Chapelle v. Mitten*) in which a court did grant parental rights to lesbian partners and a sperm donor. Ertman argues that this case creates a legal precedent for state-sanctioned polyamory.

Gay Marriages of Convenience

Ironically, the form of gay matrimony that may pose the greatest threat to the institution of marriage involves heterosexuals. A Brigham Young University professor, Alan J. Hawkins, suggests an all-too-likely scenario in which two heterosexuals of the same sex might marry as a way of obtaining financial benefits. Consider the plight of an underemployed and uninsured single mother in her early thirties who sees little real prospect of marriage (to a man) in her future. Suppose she has a good friend, also female and heterosexual, who is single and childless but employed with good spousal benefits. Sooner or later, friends like this are going to start contracting same-sex marriages of convenience. The single mom will get medical and governmental benefits, will share her friend's paycheck, and will gain an additional caretaker for the kids besides. Her friend will gain companionship and a family life. The marriage would obviously be sexually open. And if lightning struck and the right man came along for one of the women, they could always divorce and marry heterosexually.

In a narrow sense, the women and children in this arrangement would be better off. Yet the larger effects of such unions on the institution of marriage would be devastating. At a stroke, marriage would be severed not only from the complementarity of the sexes but also from its connection to romance and sexual exclusivity—and even from the hope of permanence. In Hawkins's words, the proliferation of such arrangements "would turn marriage into the moral equivalent of a Social Security benefit." The effect would be to further diminish the sense that a woman ought to be married to the father of her children. In the aggregate, what we now call out-of-wedlock births would increase. And the connection between marriage and sexual fidelity would be nonexistent.

Hawkins thinks gay marriages of convenience would be contracted in significant numbers—certainly enough to draw the attention of a media eager to tout such unions as the hip, postmodern marriages of the moment. Hawkins also believes that these unions of convenience could begin to undermine marriage's institutional foundations fairly quickly. He may be right. The gay marriage movement took more than a decade to catch fire. A movement for state-sanctioned polygamy-polyamory could take as long. And the effects of sexually open gay marriages on the ethos of monogamy will similarly occur over time. But any degree of publicity for same-sex marriages of convenience could have dramatic effects. Without further legal ado, same-sex marriages of convenience will realize the radicals' fondest hopes. Marriage will have been severed from monogamy, from sexuality, and even from the dream of permanence. Which would bring us virtually to the bottom of the slippery slope.

We are far closer to that day than anyone realizes. Does the Supreme Court's defense of sexual liberty last month in the *Lawrence v. Texas* sodomy case mean that, short of a constitutional amendment, gay marriage is inevitable? Perhaps not. Justice Scalia was surely correct to warn in his dissent that *Lawrence* greatly weakens the legal barriers to gay marriage. Sodomy laws, although rarely enforced, did provide a public policy basis on which a state could refuse to recognize a gay marriage performed in another state. Now the grounds for that "public policy exception" have been eroded. And as Scalia warned, *Lawrence*'s sweeping guarantees of personal autonomy in matters of sex could easily be extended to the question of who a person might choose to marry.

So it is true that, given *Lawrence*, the legal barriers to gay marriage are now hanging by a thread. Nonetheless, in an important respect, Scalia underestimated the resources for a successful legal argument against gay marriage. True, *Lawrence* eliminates moral disapprobation as an accept-able, rational basis for public policy distinctions between homosexuality and heterosexuality. But that doesn't mean there is no rational basis for blocking either same-sex marriage or polygamy.

There is a rational basis for blocking both gay marriage and polygamy, and it does not depend upon a vague or religiously based disapproval of homosexuality or polygamy. Children need the stable family environ-ment provided by marriage. In our individualist Western society, mar-riage must be companionate—and therefore monogamous. Monogamy will be undermined by gay marriage itself, and by gay marriage's usher-ing in of polygamy and polyamory.

This argument ought to be sufficient to pass the test of rational scrutiny set by the Supreme Court in *Lawrence v. Texas.* Certainly, the slippery-slope argument was at the center of the legislative debate on the federal Defense of Marriage Act, and so should protect that act from be-ing voided on the same grounds as Texas's sodomy law. But of course, given the majority's sweeping declarations in Lawrence, and the hostil-ity of the legal elite to traditional marriage, it may well be foolish to rely on the Supreme Court to uphold either state or federal Defense of Mar-riage Acts.

This is the case, in a nutshell, for something like the proposed Federal Marriage Amendment to the Constitution, which would define marriage as the union of a man and a woman. At a stroke, such an amendment would block gay marriage, polygamy, polyamory, and the replacement of marriage by a contract system. Whatever the courts might make of the slippery-slope argument, the broader public will take it seriously. Since *Lawrence,* we have already heard from Jon Carroll in the *San Francisco Chronicle* calling for legalized polygamy. Judith Levine in the *Village Voice* has made a plea for group marriage. And Michael Kinsley—no queer theorist but a completely mainstream journalist—has publicly called for the legal abolition of marriage. So the most radical proposal of all has now moved out of the law schools and legal commissions, and onto the front burner of public discussion.

Fair-minded people differ on the matter of homosexuality. I happen to think that sodomy laws should have been repealed (although legisla-tively). I also believe that our increased social tolerance for homosexu-ality is generally a good thing. But the core issue here is not homosexu-ality; it is marriage. Marriage is a critical social institution. Stable families depend on it. Society depends on stable families. Up to now, with all the changes in marriage, the one thing we've been sure of is that marriage means monogamy. Gay marriage will break that connection. It will do this by itself, and by leading to polygamy and polyamory. What lies be-yond gay marriage is no marriage at all.

Study Questions

1. Kurtz points out, "From Thomas Aquinas through Richard Posner, almost every serious observer has granted the incompatibility between polygamy and Western companionate marriage." What follows from the fact that all these writers make the same observation? Is this is a serious consideration, or a mere rhetorical device employed by Kurtz? Similar, consider (from chapter 9), John Finnis's claim, "At the very heart of the reflections of Plato, Xenophon, Aristotle, Musonius Rufus, and Plutarch . . . is the very deliberate and careful judgment that homosexual conduct . . . is radically incapable of . . . actualizing . . . the common good of friendship." Should we be impressed?

2. Kurtz claims that gay and lesbian marriages will "almost certainly weaken the belief that monogamy lies at the heart of marriage." He concedes, however, that lesbians value monogamy in their relationships (and might be naturally suited to it?), and even that gay men within civil unions affirm the value of monogamy more than do gay men outside such unions. Is Kurtz's position in this respect consistent?

3. Consider a triumvirate of which Kurtz speaks: a lesbian couple and the male sperm donor who is their child's biological father. Is this a "polygamous" relationship? Do you find it objectionable or a viable option in the expanding realm of possibilities?

4. Kurtz, apparently, would have us all be straight, monogamous, and married (as would John Finnis and Karol Wojtyla)—unless we committed ourselves to the celibate life. Which of these conditions tops his wish list? Which of these conditions tops *your* wish list, and why?

5. Kurtz asserts that polygamy, polyamory, and other variants that deviate from the pattern one man, one woman, are *not marriages at all.* Is there a cogent difference between "not a marriage at all" and "an improper or troublesome type of marriage" that we should acknowledge? Further, even if the variants are not marriages, in some technical sense, is that by itself a reason to judge these arrangements improper or troublesome?

Chapter 14

IN DEFENSE OF SAME-SEX MARRIAGE

Cheshire Calhoun

Why would gays and lesbians want any part of the institution of marriage, given its central role in the social standards and practices of heteronormativity and compulsory pairing, and the fact that nearly half of all heterosexual marriages end in divorce? Why are many people opposed to it, so that gay marriage has become a notoriously divisive issue in U.S. politics? **Cheshire Calhoun** *provides a sophisticated take on the topic that begins to answer these questions. She argues that the right to marry must be at the center of gay and lesbian liberation, but not for the usual reasons circulated in the debate. Gays and lesbians should not press for same-sex marriage on the typical utilitarian grounds of extending a set of benefits (economic, legal, social) to the partners; nor by claiming, on the grounds of equality, that marriage is a moral good that should be accessible to everyone; nor for the reason that same-sex marriage furthers the cause of breaking down gender conformity by rebuking sexist assumptions about male and female roles. Calhoun's rejection of these views leads us to consider homophobia, the social construction of queerness, legal sexism, and the basis of the perceived threat that same-sex marriage represents. Her positive argument in defense of same-sex marriage rests on the meaning of "marriage" as used by all parties to this dispute and what is done by discriminatory marriage laws in the political subordination of homosexuals.*

Calhoun received her Ph.D. from the University of Texas at Austin (long the home of the recently deceased and distinguished Robert C. Solomon, with whom she collaborated). Now Charles A. Dana Professor of Philosophy at Colby College, Calhoun is the author of *Feminism, the Family, and the Politics of the Closet: Lesbian and Gay Displacement* (Oxford University Press, 2000). She has also edited *What Is an Emotion?*

On September 21, 1996, President Clinton signed into law the Defense of Marriage Act (DOMA). That Act did two things. It amended the Full Faith and Credit Clause so that no state is required to honor same-sex marriages performed in another state. Second, it "defended" marriage by defining marriage for federal purposes as involving one man and one woman.

The immediate impetus behind the Defense of Marriage Act was the Hawaii Supreme Court's ruling in *Baehr v. Lewin* that absent a compelling state interest, the same sex-marriage bar would be deemed an unconstitutional form of sex discrimination. Court suits for the right of gays and lesbians to marry, however, are not new. They date from the 1970s. Gay men and lesbians now divide over the issue of same-sex marriage rights. Proponents point to both the practical benefits of legal marriage—such as immigration preference and spousal health insurance—and to the importance of securing gays' and lesbians' equal treatment under the law. Opponents argue that distributing benefits such as health insurance through marriage is itself unjust. They also argue that, rather than endorsing a sexist and normalizing institution like marriage, gay men and lesbians would be better off creating new intimate and familial arrangements outside the scope of the law.

My aim in this essay is to try to forge some common ground. I side with proponents of marriage rights in thinking that the right to marry is critical to gay and lesbian equality. But I side with opponents in thinking that some prominent arguments for marriage rights are bad ones. And I mean politically bad. What matters politically is not just which rights we strive for, but also which arguments get culturally circulated in the process.

In what follows, I examine three different arguments for same-sex marriage. The first defends marriage rights by appealing to the value of long-term, monogamous, sexually faithful intimacy. The second argues that same-sex marriage rights would reduce sexism. The third claims that denying same-sex marriage rights currently enables heterosexuals to claim for themselves a privileged political status as sustainers of culture, society, and civilization. I will critique the first two arguments. I will defend a variant of the third argument.

I. Marriage as Normative Ideal

For many, the legal institution of marriage rests on the moral ideal of an emotional and spiritual unity of two people. That unity is expressed in monogamy, long-term commitment, sexual fidelity, mutual economic support, procreation, and child-rearing. Marriage, in this sense, represents the normative ideal for how sexuality, companionship, affection, personal economics, and child-rearing should be organized. On this view, the fact that marriage is a moral ideal justifies state regulation of marriage. The state protects both the legal right to marry and marital privacy, provides unique benefits to marital couples, and regulates the dissolution of marriages because marriage is a basic personal and social good. Although state neutrality may require permitting other forms of intimate relationship, the state has a special obligation to promote valued ways of living. Thus the answer to the question, "Why should anyone have the right to marry?" is that committed, monogamous, sexually faithful relationships contribute to personal and social flourishing.

William Eskridge, Jr., author of *The Case for Same-Sex Marriage*, uses this argument to defend same-sex marriage rights. In his view, state promotion of long-term commitment in both heterosexual and same-sex couples is important because commitment both adds depth to a relationship and helps individuals maintain a stable sense of self within lives that are often fragmented by our occupying too many roles, by our geographical mobility, and often by our lack of stable employment.[1] Because a stable sense of self is such an important good to the individual, the law needs to protect both heterosexual and same-sex relationships from external intervention and internal dissolution.

Eskridge's argument dovetails with that of cultural conservatives.[2] Cultural conservatives often charge liberalism with overvaluing personal choice, self-expression, and lifestyle experimentation and undervaluing such personal and civic virtues as self-sacrifice, self-discipline, planning for the future, concern for others, responsible conduct, and loyalty.[3] What makes marriage important is precisely that it presupposes the value of these virtues. And because the virtues of loyalty, self-discipline, and self-sacrifice are good both for individuals and for society, the state should promote and to some extent coercively enforce long-term marriage. Eskridge himself points out that the costliness of dissolving a legal marriage is a prime benefit of legal marriage. People must enter *legal* marriage with a higher personal commitment than domestic partnerships require and, once married, have additional incentives to stay married. Such incentives, he hypothesizes, are especially important for sexually promiscuous gay men who have difficulty sustaining committed relationships.

Would it be a good thing to win same-sex marriage rights by using this argument? I do not think so. As I see it, the basic problem with this argument is that it is fundamentally anti-liberal. It assumes that it is the legitimate business of the state to promote one particular moral conception of marriage. It also elevates long-term commitment to such importance that the state is permitted to coercively enforce the continuance of marriages even though people may have very good reasons for not staying married. Of course, most states presently have no-fault divorce laws, and thus the coercive pressures exerted on couples to stay married are limited to the tax incentives and the costliness of divorce proceedings. But Eskridge's argument clearly would justify toughening divorce laws. And many, who like Eskridge value long-term commitment, have recommended less modestly coercive measures, such as re-stigmatizing divorce, toughening divorce laws for couples with children, enacting punitive welfare policies for poor women who have children out of wedlock, and returning to some form of gender structured marriage.[4] What is especially worrisome about Eskridge's argument, then, is not his specific argument but its natural place within a larger cultural conversation about the benefits of returning to a particular normative ideal of marriage and parenting. Returning to that ideal means using the law to dissuade individuals from pursuing a plurality of conceptions of how intimate relationships ought to be organized.

Eskridge's argument also plays into queer theorists' and lesbian feminists' worst fears about what advocating same-sex marriage might mean. Queer theorists worry that gays and lesbians who seek to marry are seeking simply to assimilate to mainstream culture. Now, I think this worry about assimilation is often misplaced. To claim that same-sex marriage would *necessarily* assimilate gays and lesbians to mainstream culture ignores the fact that many heterosexuals (who of course do have the right to marry) have been anything but assimilationists. Indeed, marriage law has evolved because of heterosexuals' resistance to legal and social conceptions of marriage.

However, when same-sex marriage rights are tied to the policy goal of promoting *one* normative ideal for intimacy, queer theorists are right to worry. Marriage rights, so construed, ought not to have priority in a gay/lesbian political agenda. Because gays and lesbians have also developed alternative families composed of friends rather than biological kin, it is important to secure legal rights for those who function as family members even if these families diverge from the conventional picture. Securing such rights requires abandoning the culturally conservative idea that there is only one normative ideal for intimacy. In short, tying same-sex marriage rights to state promotion of one normative conception of marriage and family means not critically rethinking which rights and benefits should be distributed to whom given a plurality of family forms.

Eskridge's argument also plays into lesbian-feminists' worst fears. Lesbian feminists worry that same-sex marriage rights would simply endorse patriarchal gender-structured marriage. I think this worry is often misplaced too. It ignores the fact that many heterosexuals have themselves resisted the gender structuring of marriage, producing substantial changes in marriage law that have included eliminating separate husband-wife roles, fault-based divorce, long-term alimony, and a required shared domicile.[5]

However, when same-sex marriage rights are tied to the policy goal of promoting one normative ideal for intimacy, lesbian feminists are right to worry. What gets put into cultural circulation is a particular style of thinking about marriage. It is a style that resists any thoroughgoing departure from the most traditional normative ideal of marriage and family. It is a style that links marital-familial arrangements so tightly to the public good that state neutrality with respect to conceptions of the intimate good cannot go all the way down. And it is a style whose terms—procommitment, profamily, antipromiscuity—are easily invoked to support moral norms and social policies that constrain women's reproductive, sexual, and relational liberty.

One last objection. To my mind, the greatest defect of this culturally conservative argument for same-sex marriage rights is that it doesn't explain why same-sex marriage rights belongs on a specifically *gay and lesbian* political agenda. For this, we would need a different sort of argument. In particular, we need a reason for thinking that the bar on same-sex marriage sustains heterosexual privilege. This is exactly what gender-based arguments claim to do.

II. Gender-Based Arguments

Gender-based arguments occur most commonly in legal literature and were central in the Hawaii case. In a nutshell, gender-based arguments claim that homophobia, including the bar on same-sex marriage, originates from a system of male domination over women. The bar on gay and lesbian marriage is thus really an instance of sex discrimination and should be eliminated for that reason.[6]

Gender-based arguments for same-sex marriage take two forms. Because one does a better job than the other of answering the question "Why should marriage rights be a political priority for gays and lesbians?" it is worth sorting them out.

The first view claims that there is cultural hostility to same-sex marriage because same-sex marriages are likely to be gender-free. A marriage between two women or two men cannot easily be organized around husband and wife roles. And were same-sex marriages held up as a possible model, heterosexual couples might be tempted to follow suit, modeling their own marriages on the already more egalitarian models adopted by lesbians and gay men. Thus legalizing same-sex marriage poses a threat to the gender system, because it would, in essence, declare that gendered husband and wife roles are inessential to any marriage, whether same-sex or opposite sex.

On this view, the bar on same sex-marriage is like earlier anti-miscegenation laws. The premise of interracial marriage bars was that there are two distinct races whose differences must be preserved. So, too, the premise of same-sex marriage bars is that there are two distinct genders whose differences must be preserved.[7] This means that the same-sex marriage bar is simply a specific expression of a general intolerance to the blurring of gender difference anywhere, by anyone, including by heterosexuals in heterosexual marriages. Thus the answer to the question, "Why should gays and lesbians have the right to marry?" is that same-sex marriage would make gender difference irrelevant within *all* marriages and would help bring about a gender-just society.

Would it be a good thing to win same-sex marriage rights by using this argument? I do not think so. While it is always desirable to culturally circulate arguments for gender justice, the central problem with this argument is that it gives *heterosexuals* a better reason to make same-sex marriage a political priority than it does for gays and lesbians to do so. After all, the primary beneficiaries on this view would be heterosexual couples, particularly heterosexual women. The argument assumes that lesbians and gay men *already* have gender-just relationships. Only heterosexuals persist in imagining that marriages require gendered husband and wife roles.

Equally troubling, this argument loses sight of the special animus visited upon lesbians and gay men. It does so because it assumes that there are only two kinds of persons—men and women. The fact that a lesbian is a *lesbian* turns out to be irrelevant. All that matters is that she is a gender deviant *woman*. Gender deviant heterosexual women and gender deviant lesbians are, on this view, in exactly the same boat; whatever hostility they may encounter is solely a result of their gender deviance, not their sexual orientation. But this seems false. Hostility to legal same-sex marriage runs high even though heterosexual marriages have already been de-gendered under the law. For example, the law no longer compels married women to adopt their husband's name, to share his domicile wherever he chooses it to be, to provide domestic services, and to submit to marital rape. Long-term alimony for wives was eliminated and alimony for needy ex-husbands was introduced when the law gave up the idea that only husbands are economic providers. In addition, antidiscrimination laws forbidding formal and informal enforcement of gender differences in the workplace, education, access to housing, and loans have helped de-gender the public sphere. These legal changes suggest that hostility to unsettling gender categories is much less when heterosexual women and men do the unsettling than when lesbians and gay men do it. Thus, hostility to same-sex marriage cannot adequately be explained by appeal to the fear that such marriages spell disaster for the gender structure of heterosexual marriages.

The second gender-based argument tries to explain the special animus directed at lesbians and gay men by rejecting the idea that there are just two kinds—men and women. Rather, the social construction of the homosexual and the lesbian at the turn of the century pluralized sex-gender categories beyond the original two. Both gay men and lesbians were described as a third sex, as men-women, as inverts, as the unsexed, the semi-women and semi-men, as men trapped in female bodies or women trapped in male bodies, as people with a touch of the hermaphrodite. Gays and lesbians were not *just* gender deviant men and women. For them, gender deviance was a uniquely constitutive and unavoidable part of their nature.

Hostility to this third sex derives from the view that the only normal, natural, healthy kinds of people are real women and real men, who at least by nature have the *capacity* to conform to gender norms. Heterosexuals have this capacity to conform to gender norms, even if they sometimes choose to violate gender norms. By contrast, gays and lesbians constitute a category of persons who are naturally unfit for incorporation into a society governed by gender norms because gender deviance is built into their very nature.

Lesbians and gays are thus singled out for special mistreatment and legal regulation not visited upon gender deviant heterosexuals. Nevertheless, the special opprobrium felt toward lesbians and gay men is ultimately rooted in gender ideology. Same-sex marriage bars may not be, precisely, sex discrimination, since they are not aimed at controlling all women. They are, nevertheless, of a piece with policies that discriminate on the basis of sex.

There is a good deal to be said for this second argument. It accounts for the special animus motivating mistreatment of gays and lesbians. It thus explains why gays and lesbians have a special political interest in challenging legal regulations that target them. In addition, this argument also accounts for the intimate connection between gay and lesbian oppression and male dominance.

Even so, I think this is the wrong argument for same-sex marriage rights—or at least it is seriously incomplete. All gender-based arguments start from an assumption that merits questioning. The assumption is that the fundamental inequality at stake in all gay rights issues is the inequality between men and women. On these arguments, male dominance alone accounts for both the oppression of women and the oppression of gays and lesbians. As a result, the possibility is never entertained that heterosexual domination might be a separable axis of oppression; nor is the possibility entertained that in maintaining same-sex marriage bars, in maintaining the liberty to discriminate against lesbians and gays, and in limiting gay and lesbian access to children, what is at stake is preserving heterosexuals' privileged sociopolitical status.

In addition, both gender-based arguments under-describe the ideological construction of "gay" and "lesbian" as stigmatized social identities. It *is* true that cross-genderization was the defining feature of the third sex at the turn of the century. It is also true that hostility to gender blurring continues to sustain the stigma attached to being gay or lesbian.

However, gender deviance does not fully exhaust the content of what it culturally means to be gay or lesbian. Equally important to the cultural construction of gay and lesbian identities is the idea that both gays' and lesbians' sexuality is dangerously uncontrolled, predatory, insatiable, narcissistic, and self-indulgent. This aspect of gay and lesbian identity came to particular cultural prominence during the 1930s through the 1950s—the era of both the sex crime panics and the formal exclusion of so-called "sex perverts" from all governmental service.[8] Imagined to possess an excessive and unregulated sexuality, both gays and lesbians allegedly posed a threat to heterosexual adults and to children, who might be either molested or seduced. Because of their sexual insatiability, gays and lesbians were also presumed psychologically unable to maintain stable intimate relationships.

Linking both the images of the gender deviant and the sex pervert is the culturally elaborated view that gays and lesbians are multiply unfit for marriage and family: they are unfit for assuming gendered familial roles and producing properly gendered children; they are incapable of sustaining long-term stable relationships; they pose a sexual threat to their own and others' children; and they risk reproducing their own defects in a second generation.

In sum, gender-based arguments for same-sex marriage take up only one theme in a historically complex construction of lesbian and gay identity. As a result, they fail to explain why hostility to homosexuality and lesbianism crystallizes around marital and familial issues in the way that it does. They also fail to explain the content of contemporary anti-gay discourse. If gender-based arguments were correct, the House and Senate debates over the Defense of Marriage Act should have focused on gays' and lesbians' unsuitability for fulfilling husband and wife roles, the possibility of their producing gender deviant children, the unnaturalness of men marrying men or women marrying women, and the importance of traditional gender structured marriage. The DOMA debates, however, are strikingly *devoid* of any references to gender.

I turn now to the DOMA debates and what I think the moral argument for same-sex marriage should be.

III. DOMA's Defense of Heterosexual Status

Let me begin with two observations. First, all anti-gay policies—including same-sex marriage bars, sodomy laws, bars to adoption or foster parenting, court denial of child custody, and the absence of anti-discrimination laws—are predicated on stereotypes about gays' and lesbians' difference from heterosexuals. Specifically they presuppose views about gays' and lesbians' gender deviance, lack of sexual control, and unfitness for family life. They thus assume that heterosexuals and nonheterosexuals are different kinds of people who can thus be treated differently under the law.

Second, anti-gay policies differ from racist or sexist policies. The aim of racist or sexist policies is to keep racial minorities and women *in their place*. Anti-gay policies, I think, have a different aim, namely, to *displace* gays and lesbians from civil society by refusing to recognize that lesbians and gay men belong in either the public or the private sphere.[9]

What I want to suggest is that same-sex marriage bars play an especially critical role in displacing gays and lesbians from civil society. And this is the reason why same-sex marriage rights belong at the center of a gay/lesbian political agenda.

The same-sex marriage bar works in a particularly powerful way to displace gays and lesbians because we, as a culture, assume that married couples play a unique role in sustaining civil society. Within both legal reasoning and broader cultural discourse, marriage and the family are typically taken to be the bedrock on which social and political life is built. Indeed, proponents of DOMA repeatedly emphasized the way marriages provide the foundation for civil society: "Marriage is the *foundation* of our society; families are built on it and values are passed through it."[10] Marriage is "the *keystone* in the arch of civilization."[11] "The time-honored and unique institution of marriage between one man and one woman is a *fundamental pillar* of our society and its values."[12] "[T]hroughout the annals of human experience, in dozens of civilizations and cultures of varying value systems, humanity has discovered that the permanent relationship between man and woman is a *keystone* to the stability, strength, and health of human society—a relationship worthy of legal recognition and judicial protection."[13] And "governments have recognized the traditional family as the *foundation* of prosperity and happiness, and in democratic societies, as the *foundation* of freedom."[14] (All italics mine.)

DOMA proponents clearly conceived of marriage as a prepolitical institution. Although states create the legal package of rights and benefits that attach to marriage and states set age, sex, biological relationship, and other restrictions on who may marry, the state does not create the institution of marriage itself. In addition, while a state might *choose* to legally recognize and protect a variety of voluntary relationships—for example, domestic partnerships—recognizing marriages is not a matter of choice. Since the very possibility of civil society depends on people entering marriages and forming families, the state *must* recognize marriages.

This conception of marriage as the prepolitical foundation of society has an important implication: It means that if a social group can lay claim to being inherently qualified or fit to enter into marriage and found a family, it can also claim a distinctive political status. Members of the group can claim that they play an essential role in sustaining the very foundation of civil society. Conversely, if a particular social group is deemed *un*fit to enter marriage and found a family, that group can then be denied this distinctive political status. Members of a group judged incapable of providing the necessary foundation for civil society become inessential citizens. Or at best, they are dependent citizens, because whatever social contribution they might make to civil society depends on the antecedent marital and familial labor of others.

For proponents of DOMA, the central question was "*Who* is entitled to the political status that comes with being deemed qualified for marriage and the family?"[15] The aim of proponents was to reaffirm, by constructing a federal definition of marriage, that only heterosexuals are entitled to this status.

Anxiety about what would happen to heterosexuals' status if same-sex marriages were legally recognized ran very close to the surface in these debates. Representative Smith, for example, asserted that "[s]ame-sex 'marriages' demean the fundamental institution of marriage. . . . And they trivialize marriage as a mere 'lifestyle choice.'"[16] Others echoed this sentiment: "[I]t is vital that we protect marriage against attempts to redefine it in a way that causes the family to lose its special meaning."[17] "Should the law express its neutrality between homosexual and heterosexual relationships? Should the law elevate homosexual unions to the same status as the heterosexual relationships on which the traditional family is based, a status which has been reserved from time immemorial for the union between a man and a woman?"[18] "Allowing for gay marriages would be the final straw, it would devalue the love between a man and a woman and weaken us as a Nation."[19]

But exactly why would same-sex marriages devalue heterosexual love, belittle marriage, and render it a mere lifestyle choice? The obvious answer is that homosexuality is immoral. To legally recognize same-sex marriages would place the sacred institution of marriage in the disreputable company of immoral, unnatural unions, thus cheapening its status. This was surely part of the thinking. But it is not the whole story. For if concern about giving the same state seal of approval to immoral same-sex unions as to honorable heterosexual marriages were the primary concern, then one would expect proponents of DOMA to also be adamantly opposed to any legal protection of same-sex unions. Yet Representative Lipinski, who thought that allowing gay marriages would be the final straw devaluing love between man and woman also observed that "gays can legally achieve the same ends as marriage through draft wills, medical powers of attorney, and contractual agreements in the event that the relationship should end."[20] Other proponents affirmed the importance of guaranteeing the right to privacy[21] and pointed out that the law protects a variety of unions outside of marriage law (which presumably might also include same-sex unions).[22] These sorts of remarks suggest that the immorality of homosexuality was not the only issue.

The central worry instead seemed to be that recognizing same-sex unions as marriages would *demote marriage from a naturally defined prepolitical institution to a state-defined contract.* Senators Gramm and Byrd clearly expressed this concern. According to Gramm, "[h]uman beings have always given traditional marriage a special sanction. Not that there cannot be contracts among individuals, but there is something unique about the traditional family in terms of what it does for our society and the foundation it provides."[23] Byrd articulated a similar distinction:

> Obviously, human beings enter into a variety of relationships. Business partnerships, friendships, alliances for mutual benefits, and team memberships all depend upon emotional unions of one degree or another. For that reason, a number of these relationships have found standing under the laws of innumerable nations. . . . However, in no case, has anyone suggested that these relationships deserve the special recognition or the designation commonly understood as "marriage."[24]

Reading between the lines, the underlying view seems to be this: Free, self-defining, sociable citizens may choose to enter a variety of voluntary relationships with each other. In deciding what legal protections might be in order for these relationships, a liberal political society that values freedom of association and the right to pursuit of happiness must adopt a position of neutrality. Rather than giving priority to some of these relationships on moral grounds, the state instead assumes that citizens may reasonably choose any of these relationships on the basis of their own conception of the good. Thus, such voluntary associations might reasonably be dubbed "lifestyle choices." To call them "lifestyle choices" is not to say that they are in fact morally equivalent. One might, for example, think that same-sex unions are immoral, but nevertheless think the state should adopt a neutral position, and it should offer legal protection for same-sex unions under domestic partnership laws. To say that a particular form of relationship is a "lifestyle choice," then, is simply to say that it falls within the category of relationships with respect to which *state* neutrality is appropriate.

What proponents of DOMA took pains to emphasize was that marriage falls in a different category. Marriage is not one among many voluntary associations that citizens might make a "lifestyle" choice to enter. Marriage constitutes the prepolitical foundation of society. In other words, societies depend for their functioning on marriages *and* the essential nature of marriage is fixed independently of liberal society—by God, or by human nature, or by the prerequisites for civilization. Consequently, state neutrality with respect to the definition of marriage involves a category mistake. State neutrality would involve treating a prepolitical institution as though it were a political institution, that is, as though it were an institution that must be compatible with multiple conceptions of the good. Since, on this view, marriage is not in fact a political institution, it is legitimate to insulate marriage against liberal revisions. This is what DOMA does.

In my view, then, what makes same-sex marriage rights so important is that marriage bars do not represent merely one among many ways that the state may discriminate against gays and lesbians by enacting laws based on stereotypes about lesbians' and gay men's gender deviance, undisciplined sexual desire, and unfitness for family life. Marriage bars specifically enact the view that *heterosexual* love, marriage, and family have a uniquely prepolitical, foundational status in civil society. Marriage bars assume that heterosexual relationships are not just morally superior, but that they have a uniquely privileged status beyond the reach of liberal political values. Marriage bars also enact the view that because only heterosexuals are fit to participate in this foundational marital institution, only heterosexuals are entitled to lay claim to a unique citizenship status: Heterosexuals are not just free, rational, self-defining persons. They are also naturally fit to participate in the one institution that all societies, liberal or otherwise, must presuppose. Thus they may lay claim to a citizenship status that exceeds what individuals are entitled to on the basis of being free, rational, self-defining persons. So, for example, in addition to the rights of free association, including intimate association, to which all citizens are entitled, heterosexuals may also lay claim to special state solitude for their private lives, a partial insulation of their legal privileges from liberal principles, and special entitlement to influence future generations.

Conclusion

So, what is my conclusion? What, given the backdrop of the DOMA debates, ought lesbians and gay men to want with respect to same-sex marriage rights? Here there are two options. On the one hand, one might agree, in part, with proponents of DOMA that marriage, even if not heterosexual marriage, is unlike other possible voluntary intimate arrangements—for example, it is unlike the families of choice described by Kath Weston—because some form of marriage is indeed a prepolitical, foundational institution meriting special legal treatment. One might then argue that heterosexuals are *not* the only ones qualified to enter this prepolitical institution. This option would, of course, take us back to some form of the argument based on a normative ideal for how persons should organize their intimate, affectional, personal economic, reproductive, sexual, and child-rearing lives. The legal task would then be to determine which forms of heterosexual and non-heterosexual intimacy would be dignified with the label "marriage" and the status of being regarded as foundational to civil society. Under this option, the bid for same-sex marriage rights would amount to a demand to be deemed fit to participate in the foundational social institution and thus to be deemed an essential citizen who is not dependent on the marital and familial work of others.

The second option is that one might reject the idea altogether that there are any prepolitical, foundational forms of intimacies. Civil societies depend only in the most general way on their citizens having the capacities for and interest in casting their personal lot with others, sharing, in voluntary private arrangements, sex, affection, reproduction, care for the young, the infirm, and the elderly, and economic support. But no one form or set of forms for doing so is foundational to civil society. Instead, one might envision a fully liberal society in which no private relationships are insulated from liberal principles and in which legal protection and support of the private sphere and the production of future generations is predicated on the assumption that persons might choose a plurality of intimate arrangements in accord with their own conceptions of the good. In this case, the bid for same-sex marriage rights would amount to a demand to be deemed equal citizens within a fully liberal society.

To many, the obviously correct option is the second one. Of course, the state should be neutral with respect to conceptions of the good. Of course, it is always a bad thing for the state to promote any normative ideal of intimate relations. While I agree, I also find the choice of option more difficult to make. Defending same-sex marriage on grounds of state neutrality requires only that same-sex marriages be legally permitted *regardless* of how they are morally viewed. Genuine equality for gays and lesbians, however, requires more than merely coming to be tolerated. It requires that we, as a culture, give up the belief that gays and lesbians are unfit to participate in normatively ideal forms of marriage, parenting, and family. Only the first option permits us to put into cultural circulation arguments that directly challenge the ideology sustaining gays' and lesbians' social inequality.

Study Questions

1. Explain the meaning and implications of Calhoun's mentioning that marriage is a "prepolitical institution." Explore a similar idea in the writings of such disparate political philosophers as John Rawls and Karl Marx.

2. Why, according to Calhoun, is a straightforward analogy to anti-miscegenation laws not a sufficient basis to oppose laws banning same-sex marriage? Read, to help you think about different kinds of discrimination, the 1967 U.S. Supreme Court decision, *Loving v. Virginia*, 388 U.S. 1, in which it was ruled that anti-miscegenation laws (which prohibit interracial marriage) are unconstitutional.

3. Evaluate the threat the supporters of the Defense of Marriage Act (DOMA) say that same-sex marriage holds for children. What are some other perceived threats to children spoken of within the larger cultural debate over same-sex marriage, and do they have any merit? Think about how same-sex couples and their children are portrayed in television programs and Hollywood films.

4. Debate the strengths and weaknesses of Calhoun's position in light of Stanley Kurtz's many arguments against same-sex marriage (chapter 13). Figure out how Calhoun might respond to this common sentiment: "But why must they demand the right to *marry*? Why can they not settle for domestic partnerships?" How would she respond to the other sentiment, that gays and lesbians should not even have recourse to civil unions? And to the radical sentiment that the institution of marriage is a disaster and should be done away with, not expanded?

5. What does the issue of same-sex marriage have to do with sexuality and sexual relations? Could there be same-sex marriages that do not include any sexual activity between the spouses? Are there heterosexual marriages that do not include much if any sexual activity between the partners? Is sex, or must sex be, one of the (main) points of marriage? If being married morally justi-

fies the sexual activity of a heterosexual couple, does being married also morally justify homosexual sexual activity?

Notes

1. William Eskridge, *The Case for Same-Sex Marriage: From Sexual Liberty to Civilized Commitment* (New York: The Free Press, 1996), 72.

2. Karen Struening, "Feminist Challenges to the New Familialism: Lifestyle Experimentation and the Freedom of Association," *Hypatia* 11 (1996): 135–54.

3. Stephen Macedo, "Sexuality and Liberty: Making Room for Nature and Tradition?" in *Sex, Preference, and Family*, ed. David M. Estlund and Martha C. Nussbaum (New York: Oxford University Press, 1996), 86–101. Struening surveys the main themes of cultural conservatives with respect to the family, focusing particularly on William Galston.

4. Struening, "Feminist Challenges."

5. Of course, not all of these changes have been salutary for women, since the beneficial consequences of eliminating the formal gender structure of marriage depends in large part on the *actual* de-gendering of marital practices as well as gender equity in the paid workforce.

6. See, for example, Sylvia Law, "Homosexuality and the Social Meaning of Gender," *Wisconsin Law Review* 1988 (1988):187-235; Cass R. Sunstein, "Homosexuality and the Constitution," in Estlund and Nussbaum, *Sex, Preference, and Family*, 208–26; Andrew Koppelman, "The Miscegenation Analogy: Sodomy Law as Sex Discrimination," *Yale Law Journal* 98 (1988): 145-164; Andrew Koppelman, "Why Discrimination Against Lesbians and Gay Men is Sex Discrimination," *NYU Law Review* 69 (1994): 197-287; Nan D. Hunter, "Marriage, Law, and Gender: A Feminist Inquiry," in Lisa Duggan and Nan D. Hunter, *Sex Wars: Sexual Dissent and Political Culture* (New York: Routledge, 1995), 107–22.

7. Sunstein, "Homosexuality."

8. I give a more detailed account of the multilayered construction of lesbians and gay men as unfit for family life in "Constructing Lesbians and Gay Men as Family's Outlaws," chapter 6 of my *Feminism, the Family, and the Politics of the Closet* (New York: Oxford University Press, 2000), 132–60.

9. Cheshire Calhoun, "Sexuality Injustice," *Notre Dame Journal of Law, Ethics, and Public Policy* 9 (1995): 241-74.

10. Representative Lipinski, *Congressional Record* 142, no. 103 (July 12, 1996), H7495.

11. William J. Bennett, "Not a Very Good Idea," quoted from the *Washington Post* (May 21, 1996) in *Congressional Record* 142, no. 103 (July 12, 1996), H7495.

12. Representative Ensign, ibid., H7493.

13. Senator Byrd, *Congressional Record*, vol. 142, no. 123 (September 10, 1996), p. S10109.

14. Senator Gramm, ibid., S10106.

15. Opponents clearly took the debate to be about something else, namely, about why, in practice, real families aren't doing very well. Completely bypassing

proponents' point, opponents instead focused on the misbehavior of heterosexual family members as well as inadequate health, education, and day care, unemployment, the absence of a livable minimum wage, inability to afford single-family homes, loss of pensions, and insufficient Medicare payments.

16. *Congressional Record* 123, no. 103 (July 12, 1996), H7494.

17. Representative Weldon, ibid., H7493

18. Representative Canady, ibid., H7491.

19. Representative Lipinski, ibid., H7495.

20. Ibid., H7495.

21. Senator Burns, *Congressional Record* 142, no. 123 (September 10, 1996), S10117.

22. Senator Byrd, ibid., S10109.

23. Senator Gramm, ibid., S10106.

24. Senator Byrd, ibid., S10109.

Chapter 15

SEXUAL IDENTITY AND
SEXUAL JUSTICE

Jerome Neu

In this critical essay-review of Morris Kaplan's Sexual Justice, **Jerome Neu** *points out that our current discourse about the liberation of gays and lesbians presumes that we know who gets liberated. In response to calls for equal treatment of lesbians and gays, such as Kaplan's, he wonders whether these sexual orientation categories fully capture the minority class that deserves recognition by straight society. What does it mean to be "homosexual"? What does it mean to identify one's self in terms of one's sexual desires (as opposed to other features humans possess)? Neu argues that the adoption of a discrete "queer" identity implies that queers are essentially different from members of the heterosexual majority. One (Freudian) alternative is that gays and lesbians merely occupy one locale on a sexual continuum from homosexual, at one end, to heterosexual, at the other. If so, there are no essentially different sexualities, since all locations on the continuum experience similar desires and pleasures. Neu suggests that essentialist sexual self-concepts exclude other sexual minorities, such as bisexuals and transsexuals, from benefiting from a liberatory political agenda, and he asks whether gays and lesbians might be better off rejecting the very sexual categories they are usually prone to use.*

Neu is professor of humanities at the University of California, Santa Cruz, and the author of *Emotion, Thought, and Therapy* (Routledge & Kegan Paul, 1977), *A Tear Is an Intellectual Thing: The Meanings of Emotion* (Oxford University Press, 2000), and *Sticks and Stones: The Philosophy of Insults* (Oxford University Press, forthcoming).

Reprinted with the permission of Jerome Neu from *Ethics* 108 (April 1998): 586–96.
© 1998 by The University of Chicago. All rights reserved.

We all have many identities. Some voluntarily adopted, some unconsciously internalized, others socially ascribed, indeed, sometimes
imposed. Who we are, who we think we are, and who others think we are
can come to matter very deeply in a world in which the headings under
which we are understood can have important social and economic consequences. We are discriminated against under certain headings, and to
achieve justice and equality, we may sometimes have to organize politically under those same headings. Hence, identity politics. "Black Pride,"
"Gay Pride," "Deaf Pride," and so on have emerged as transvaluations of
denigrated minority positions, as part of a process of achieving recognition and, ultimately, equal treatment. Morris Kaplan calls for "sexual justice" for lesbians and gays and, more generally, queers.

The argument is structured around readings of a number of central
texts (by Plato, Freud, Hannah Arendt, and Thoreau) and a line of
Supreme Court cases dealing with privacy. Kaplan's own readings are
very judicious (though one might sometimes wish the writing less poly-
syllabic and the vocabulary less ornate—e.g., "imbricated" occurs more
often than it has a right to in any book). So, for example, in filling in the
background to Plato's *Symposium* and to nineteenth-century idealization
of the Greeks, he brings out how, though the ancient Greeks were
clearly different in their sexual attitudes and in some ways were certainly
more accepting than many are today, they also drew their own lines—
rejecting, to cite one important example, phallic penetration of an adult
male citizen by another man as disgraceful sexual passivity, beneath the
status of a citizen (though of course natural to women and at least some
subordinate males). Modern sexual justice requires more than just toleration of a wide range of intimate associations, though that (including
decriminalization of private, consensual homosexual acts between
adults) is needed, for (aside from standard liberal arguments) much of
individual identity is formed in and through personal relationships.
Some of the social institutions that Kaplan discusses involve rather fleeting relationships (in gay male bathhouses and sex clubs, a one-night
stand might constitute a long-term relationship), but society often has
difficulty in accepting even the "more continuous forms of sexual intimacy, friendship, and family" that these relationships sometimes lead to
(p. 223). Kaplan, using his central authors in order to develop a picture
of the role of desire in self-making and in democratic politics, concludes
with an extended argument in favor of lesbian and gay marriage: "Full
equality for lesbian and gay citizens requires access to the legal and social recognition of our intimate associations" (p. 207). Also needed for

modern sexual justice is protection against particular forms of invidious discrimination "in employment, housing, education, and public accommodations" (p. 141).

In responding to Kaplan's thoughtful and stimulating book, I will refer only in passing to his careful readings of the many authors from whom he culls valuable insights, in order to focus on what I take to be an insufficiently acknowledged tension in the book and in reality between the personal and the political. It is a tension that emerges when one examines the notion of "identity" in identity politics and that becomes acute when one attempts to secure legal protections using such identities to pick out the relevant categories for protection.

I should first note that I agree with what I take to be the main thrust of the book: Kaplan's defense of a strong conception of rights, in particular rights of privacy and association, which come together in Justice Blackman's analysis of freedom of intimate association and Kaplan's Foucauldian notions of self-making, self-formation, and identity shaping. More is needed than simple toleration, the negative right to be left alone. There are indeed important connections between the personal and the political. Whether one *thinks* in terms of Arendt's "insistence on the ability to establish a private household as a precondition of political participation" (p. 151) or in terms of Kaplan's emphasis on the conditions for self-making, who we are and can be depends on social support and political possibilities, which are in turn shaped by what might seem to be private arrangements. Some radicals disparage the fight for conventional rights by gays and lesbians. (When I heard Kaplan present an early version of his argument for gay marriage at the University of California, Santa Cruz, he was indeed attacked from the left.) Why fight for gay marriage? Doesn't that just perpetuate and extend the despised patriarchal order? Kaplan argues that even if it does (which is doubtful), it extends needed protections and possibilities for organizing lives. It empowers. But it also transforms. The institutions themselves become different as they enlarge to encompass unconventional family structures. As Kaplan notes, conservative defenders of "traditional family values" understand this very well (pp. 234-35).

Some years ago I saw a Canadian movie about a man who is the father of a five-year-old child and who enters into a homosexual relationship. I cannot now recall the title, but as I recall the movie itself, there is a scene set at the little girl's kindergarten where the children describe their families: one boy announces that he has two mommies and one daddy. Another announces that he has two daddies and one mommy. A girl declares that she has two mommies and two daddies. The central child has three daddies and one mommy. Finally, a child reveals that he has *one* mommy and *one* daddy. The other children shake their heads and sympathetically note his deprivation, saying "too bad."

For the moment, we must live in the world that exists, and in that world, it is better to share rights and privileges accorded to others, be they health benefits or child custody, than not. And to change the world, experiments in living need social recognition and support in order to be sustained. These experiments reward that support by enriching life for all and by sometimes suggesting alternatives to too-rigid and stultifying aspects of the old order. I join Kaplan in the tradition that sees plural forms of life as a positive good and that embraces social diversity as a consequence of political equality (pp. 233-34).

But when minorities engage in identity politics, asking for themselves what society should accord to all—dignity and respect and the equal protection of the laws—can they speak for all? When we gays and lesbians ask for antidiscrimination laws and social recognition of our intimate associations, who are "we"? Kaplan tells us that Eve Kosofsky Sedgwick "marks a vacillation, within both homophobic and emancipatory discourses, between 'minoritizing' views of homosexuality that define a distinct group with a common identity and 'universalizing' views that link homosexuality to tendencies shared by all human beings. That vacillation, which is also enacted in the differences between Freud and the third sex theories of early homosexual rights activists, may be read as expressing in general theoretical terms an analogy with the social dilemmas of assimilation and divergence generated by Jewish emancipation" (p. 160).

Again I ask, who are "we"? Perhaps like the Danish king who put on a Star of David when the Nazis decreed that all Jews must wear the star in order to single them out for persecution, we should all be Jews in a world of anti-Semitism. But how do we get to a world where we are all in this together, where no one is oppressed? Gay Pride, like Black Pride, seeks to transvalue a previously despised identity category. Some think that one ought rather to question the divisions and classifications themselves. Sometimes this is a matter of pointing out the predominance of gray. Sexual preferences and sexual activities allow for all degrees of exclusivity and combination. The exclusive heterosexual, in deed and fantasy, may be as rare as the exclusive homosexual. And even who counts as "black," despite what might appear to be a simple visual criterion, is by no means always obvious. Lawrence Wright, in a *New Yorker* article entitled "One Drop of Blood," brings out how troubled the category is, in an interbreeding society, even for purposes of census taking (especially when tied to the distribution of social benefits).[1] This is before issues of cultural identification and self-identification are introduced to complicate matters—whether a black child who is adopted and brought up by white parents in a white neighborhood is somehow thereby denied the blackness conferred by "black culture." An interracial society leads to multiracial individuals. But there are problems with the socially constructed categories of invidious discrimination other than being sure who fits in them; the problem isn't just the existence of degrees of gray. Some would reject the categories even in the supposedly clear cases.

Foucault and some of his followers urge that a truly radical politics should emphasize resistance rather than liberation. Liberation involves accepting the categories of the powers that be, even when liberation insists on transvaluation (i.e., asserting the positive value of the denigrated, marginalized category). Resistance questions and rejects those categories. Thus, David Halperin writes: "The most radical reversal of homophobic discourses consists not in asserting, with the Gay Liberation Front of 1968, that "gay is good" (on the analogy with "black is beautiful") but in assuming and empowering a marginal positionality—not in rehabilitating an already demarcated, if devalued, identity but in taking advantage of the purely oppositional location homosexuality has been made to occupy."[2] The rejection of categories in this sort of "queer" politics, a politics of positionality (of opposition, contrast, resistance) rather than identity, obscures (deliberately) the identity of the group being defended; it objects to identity politics by attacking the terms of identity: "To shift the position of 'the homosexual' from that of object to subject is therefore to make available to lesbians and gay men a new kind of sexual identity, one characterized by its lack of a clear definitional content. The homosexual subject can now claim an identity without an essence."[3] But the lack of a clear essence makes the alternative politics of positionality rather unclear. In Halperin's version, "queer" politics (vs. "gay" politics) includes all sexually marginalized individuals: "anyone who is or who feels marginalized because of her or his sexual practices: it could include some married couples without children, for example, or even (who knows?) some married couples with children."[4] All that unites the group is its felt marginalization in relation to social norms—which seems rather too broad for an organized group politics. (Put differently, the "subject position" emphasized is perhaps too subjective—however that it may be that we are *all* gay, all women, all black, for we are all marginalized, denigrated, despised, under some heading or other some of the time.) Halperin acknowledges that the vast range of sexual outlaws (including sadomasochists, fetishists, pederasts) can have diverse and divergent interests.[5] There is another paradox here in a politics of positionality: aside from the fact that we are all somehow, in some aspect, outside the accepted norms, the supposed deessentialized subject position requires that one feel marginalized in terms of a norm that is the norm of society or of "the others," so those norms and their understanding—objectification—re-enter the picture; one's self-identity for oppositional purposes must depend on categories and norms provided from outside (at least if it is to count as "resistance" to those categories and norms), just as identity politics depends on those categories and norms before it undertakes its work of transvaluing them. Self-identification through desire may remain the best defense, as Leo Bersani has put it: "De-gaying gayness can only fortify homophobic oppression; it accomplishes in its own way the principal aim of homophobia: the elimination of gays. The consequence of self-pleasure is . . . self-pleasure. Even a provisional acceptance of the very categories elaborated by dominant identitarian regimes might more effectively undermine those forces than a simple disappearing act."[6]

Kaplan recognizes how a concept like Freud's notion of bisexuality depends on the bipolar terms that it is in some ways meant to question: subject and object bisexuality invoke contrasts between masculinity and femininity, activity and passivity, that the concept itself tends to undermine (p. 145). But, like Halperin, he states "I am drawn to the inclusiveness of 'queer' rather than 'lesbian and gay' politics. It seeks to embrace lesbians, gay men, bisexuals, transvestites, transsexuals, sadomasochists, boy-lovers, and any other 'others' who find themselves marginalized and abjected by the normalizing force of modern sexuality. A movement based on narrowly defined 'lesbian and gay' identities risks further marginalizing those who elude its terms" (p. 143, cf. p. 175). Fair enough and sympathetic enough, but does Kaplan seriously wish to propose civil rights legislation ensuring nondiscrimination in employment and housing for sadomasochists (of course both homosexual and heterosexual)? Why does that seem such an unpromising political agenda? (The notion of ensuring pedophiles the right to marry the boys they love raises further, special difficulties.) Must potential employers inquire about their employees' private sexual preferences in order to avoid unknowingly discriminating against them? (Is unknowing discrimination discrimination?) I will return to problems of "visibility" in a moment. At this point, the ideal of equal treatment for all seems increasingly appealing, and the notion of special categories of the despised and marginalized seems appalling. Kaplan sensibly notes, "Adding 'lesbian' and 'gay' to 'heterosexual' in the repertoire of acceptable identities in our society would be a real but limited accomplishment in the struggle for full equality" (p. 144). Anything short of equal treatment for all is rightly condemned as "limited," but civil rights for blacks were similarly "limited." The practices of discrimination, however, make some "limited" advances more pressing than others. (Are sadomasochists regularly discriminated against in employment and housing? Who would know?)

Whose oppression matters most? Here visibility plays a role, but it is multifaced. The possibility of invisibility can provide protection, protection that the law may deny. But the fact that one can hide one's sexual preferences, keep them private, is small consolation to those who regard those preferences as an important part of who they are, a part they do not wish to be obliged to conceal (especially given that there are advantages in being identifiable to those others who happen to share one's preferences). And of course, another side of the possibility of conceal-ment, of passing, is the possibility of mistaken identification, of misiden-tification. Suppose that someone was mistakenly identified as a member of a currently protected category (say of religion or race, e.g., an Epis-copalian was mistaken for a Catholic, or a very tan individual for an African American) by a potential employer or landlord and was im-properly discriminated against on the basis of that mistaken identifica-tion? Surely there is an intention to improperly discriminate. Would the victim have standing to sue under the statutes (given that he or she was not in fact a member of the protected category)? But then, in a world where sexual orientation was given specific protection, could anyone self-declare and then obtain legal redress? Transvestites are widely and mistakenly believed to all be homosexuals. Would a heterosexual trans-vestite who was mistakenly discriminated against as a homosexual have standing to sue under civil-rights laws that protected gays but not trans-vestites? Again one feels the push toward the universal. Who decides who is in what category? It is worth noting that there is at the moment a movement afoot among some Orthodox Jewish rabbis to denounce cer-tain branches of Judaism, Conservative and Reform, as not-Jewish. Again, who decides? Is it the discriminators? The issue of attempted dis-crimination points to the question of whether the wrong is the mistake or the treating of *anyone* as though they were a second-class citizen, mis-taken identification or correct notwithstanding? The question is whether antidiscrimination legislation can ultimately be understood as protecting individuals in certain categories, or all citizens. The rationale for such legislation turns on equal treatment for all, but the protections have had to be hard won in political contests, one despised category at a time.

Kaplan may wish to protect all marginalized sexual outlaws, but in practice, his argument has a narrower focus when he goes beyond An-drew Sullivan and those who would ask for no more than mere decrim-inalization of gay and lesbian sexual activity. Kaplan seeks specifically to add gays and lesbians to other protected categories (racial, religious, and ethnic groups, women, the physically and mentally handicapped, workers age forty and older) for purposes of protection against dis-crimination in employment, education, and housing. He argues: "The underlying rationale of the antidiscrimination provisions of civil rights legislation is the recognition that formal legal equality is inadequate to provide for equal citizenship under conditions of popular hostility and pervasive social inequality. It is precisely the intensity and extent of the prejudice against homosexuality that justifies the claims of lesbian and gay citizens to protection against discrimination" (p. 43). And here he must have in mind extended histories of mistreatment, which have, of course, depended on identification by others, the mistreaters. Kaplan insists that "the definition of protected classes does not construct personal or political identities but rather forbids employers, landlords, and other decision makers from using such categories as race, religion, or sex to *impose* an invidious identity on a person rather than treating her in terms of her individual character and qualities" (p. 45). He is certainly right about the point of such legislation. But if it is to be effectively enforced, it must specify the protected categories in a way that enables people to identify themselves under them for purposes of protection. And that risks the sort of rigidity and fixity that Kaplan wishes to avoid. I don't see how the law, for its purposes, which are indeed important, can avoid it. Moreover, the characteristics that are most significant, and so the ones most likely to be taken to be defining, are the very ones that decision makers (the discriminators and mistreaters) might be feared to improperly use—so perhaps it is the socially constructed categories, whatever the truth may be about essential characteristics, which become the most relevant ones. (As Arendt insisted: "If one is attacked as a Jew one must defend oneself as a Jew" [p. 160].) Again, it is a history of popular hostility that makes something more than formal legal equality necessary.

There is a tension in Kaplan's own account: he wants protective justice, and he wants sexual plasticity. But how can one insist on protection for people with a certain sexual identity if one denies the reality of such identities? Kaplan says, like Halperin, that Foucault's "analysis of sexuality as a mode of social control calls for a politics that contests the definition of the sexual identities it seeks to mobilize" (p. 173). So one must resist essentializing pseudoscience and medicine, the creation of false subspecies within the human. At the conclusion of a sensitive and complex reading of the drama in Plato's *Symposium*, Kaplan writes: "To the extent that lesbian and gay politics depends on the definition of homosexuals as a specific kind of person defined by an exclusive attraction to others of the same sex, it perpetuates fairly rigid terms of erotic and political identity. The dynamic of needy excess and creative transcendence described in Diotima's speech provides grounds for criticizing any such restriction of one's attention and sympathy" (p. 112). Of course Kaplan is right to see the complexity, variety, and malleability of sexual desire. What follows for politics? He writes, "A politics based on fixed identities may foreclose the openness to contestation and negotiation required by justice" (p. 112). That is surely a risk, but perhaps progress only gets made one step at a time. So far as Kaplan argues for antidiscrimination law, the groups to be protected must be defined in ways that make their members identifiable. A politics of legal reform must require the very "fixed identities" that Kaplan seems to wish to deny. Of course, they need not be fixed forever or for even a lifetime, but they need to be fixed for purposes of adjudication once one emerges from behind Rawls's veil of ignorance into a world where some are identified (by others, if not themselves) as gay or lesbian and discriminated against on that basis.

Kaplan warns against essentialist and naturalizing tendencies, noting that such views can be used y both progressives and reactionaries (pp. 171-72). They are, he points out, a "double-edged sword" (p. 176). And he emphasizes that it is important to "avoid the hazards of a politics of exclusive identification" (p. 175). Essentialized collective identities may be obviously false in terms of the multiplicity of identifications in any individual and the many factors that go into any one identity, but Kaplan's own arguments for legal protections, antidiscrimination law, and social recognition of unconventional relationships may have to invoke such identifications. He should perhaps be comforted by his own recognition that they can serve as double-edged swords, which means whatever the risks, they can serve progressive purposes.

It is difficult to see what one does differently when resisting a category rather than liberating or expressing an aspect of self-esteem under that category. And who one does it with is politically problematical. Is "queer" politics supposed to unite all who are nonmainstream sexually? The "we" here might include all sorts of folks who fit very uncomfortably with each other. Not that all gay folks are comfortable together. Our political views (like our actual sexual activities) cover as wide a spectrum as those of heterosexual folks. It is very difficult to see heterosexuals as a group with homogenized interests. The only reason it is easier for those who march under the banner of gay pride to be so seen is that they do have one important interest in common: sexual liberation and nondiscrimination on the basis of orientation—but they may not feel that way about all aspects of sexual expression ("sexual orientation" is doubtless the way the relevant category would be described for purposes of legislation, but what exactly would it cover?). Similarly, there are all sorts of political and social diversity among blacks—though all might agree that skin color is no proper ground for shame or discrimination. Political and social coalition among all racial and ethnic minorities has had a hard history—even if all might agree that skin color and place of origin and cultural background are no proper grounds for shame or discrimination. It also might become unclear who the opposed "majority" is. Coalitions should nonetheless always be possible, and perhaps that, and not the rejection of the very identity under which one is claiming protection, is all Kaplan is calling for when he writes: "Informed by the genealogy of its historical production, a democratic politics of sexuality must forgo the temptations of exclusive identification and forge alliances for common action from intersecting and multiple identifications and communities" (p. 176).

Of course, there are problems with traditional identity politics, some stemming from the admitted grayness of categories.[7] What and who is in the category? Even a category such as race, which might appear straight-forwardly biological, can be problematical—as noted, skin color may provide no sure index of anything, and we may all in the end be mul-tiracial. And again, gay behavior, desires and inclinations, and attitudes can all vary in more ways than are marked even by Kinsey's categories, and that before account is taken of the unconscious. Who are "we"? And if we think of the gay identified as excluding the repressed or closeted homosexual, we may be focusing too much on the voluntaristic aspects of identification where identification is self-identification. But where the political problem may arise from the identification and stigmatization by others, perhaps a politically relevant notion of identification must be broader (even if it risks objectification of individuals and reification of the categories of the others—after all, the struggle is with or against those very others). Even when one is not asked and doesn't tell, one may be discriminated against, one's life restricted.

So far as the politics of marginal positionalities is aimed at denying privileged valuations of either side of dichotomies, the message may ul-timately be the same as "Black is Beautiful" or "Gay is Good" or "Deaf Power." For the point, typically, is not to say that black is better than white or gay is better than straight or deaf is better than hearing but sim-ply to deny the denigration of the minority position. The point is to de-mand political equality, equal concern, and respect.

Who are "we" for purposes of political organization and activism, for purposes of demanding nondiscrimination, for purposes of demanding the right to marry, and so on? In a sense, of course, "we" is everyone, every citizen entitled to equal concern and respect, and equal treatment under the law.

But for purposes of the law, without denying or weakening the claim of anyone else, one can insist that experiencing same-sex desire or en-gaging in certain sexual practices with members of the same sex is no ground for invidious treatment, for discrimination in housing, educa-tion, or job opportunities. Perhaps one wants to say the same for other sexual minorities (and other nonsexual minorities as well). But so long as discrimination law singles out special categories for protection, one must be precise. If equal treatment for all is not enough to protect gays and lesbians, and we need to ask for specific protection, why should we be surprised if other sexual minorities need to do the same? Marginal-ized groups might wish to band together, but "queer" identity by itself may not do what is required.[8]

So the desire for legal protection may be in tension with the rejection of confining self-identities; personal rejection of confining sexual iden-tities may not work well with organizing politically to gain legal recognition. I should perhaps close by acknowledging once more the positive overlap between the personal and the political. *Sexual Justice* is pervaded and informed by the ideal of democratic equality. Kaplan writes in his introduction of Constant's distinction between the liberty of the ancients and the liberty of the moderns, and notes the equivocal nature of the advance from one to the other: "The protection of private liberty and enjoyment is accompanied by the restriction of most individuals to the domain of privacy" (p. 4). Kaplan insists, however, "that abstract rights can be vindicated only through collective political struggle and must be established in social and ethical institutions. The integrity of a private sphere of individual decision making will be protected only to the extent that it is recognized as such by political and legal authorities and respected by popular opinion" (p. 5).

At the end of his discussion of Plato's *Symposium*, Kaplan writes, "Love and politics meet in concrete contexts where each has the possibility of supporting or disrupting the other" (p. 111). This seems importantly right to me. The insight goes back at least to Pausanias, who pointed to a connection between political repression and sexual repression in the ancient world (an insight developed in our time by Marcuse and others).

Kaplan is against class and racial domination, compulsory heterosexuality, and gender hierarchy. He is for lesbian and gay and queer emancipation. I am with him. Nonetheless, I think there are more tensions between the personal and the political than he acknowledges, and they become especially disruptive and disturbing within the quest for legal reform through identity politics, sexuality, and gender hierarchy.

Study Questions

1. Despite the fact that racial categories are, ultimately, biologically arbitrary and do not represent discrete, essentialist identities, race still matters social and politically. Might Kaplan use a similar line of reasoning in replying to the "tension" Neu finds in his work? Explore further the analogy between racial and sexual discrimination. One area where a comparison might be revealing is marriage (see Calhoun, chapter 14). Note that one might claim that just as sexualities are mere locations on a continuum, racialities or ethnicities are also mere locations on a continuum, in which all locations share more important features in common. Does an emphasis on, say, black racial identity politics leave out from consideration and protection those persons who are various mixtures of various "races"—the analogues to the bisexuals or transsexuals?

2. Explain the notion of "self-identification through desire" and its significance in Neu's approach. Relate it to his comments about shame and self-love. Consider, also, the historical relationship between sexual and political repression. Does one necessarily or frequently follow the other?

3. Are there limits to "sexual plasticity" in a liberal society? What role does the private-public distinction play here?

4. In your experience, how "homogenized" are the interests (personal, sexual, social, and political) of all gay men? Of all lesbians? Are they more or less homogenized than other legally protected groups (women, the handicapped)?

5. Try your hand at defining "homosexual," "bisexual," and other purportedly distinct sexual orientations. You might want to do some research into scholarly attempts to define these terms. See, for example, John De Cecco, "Definition and Meaning of Sexual Orientation," *Journal of Homosexuality* 6, no. 4 (1981): 51–67; Michael Shively and John De Cecco, "Components of Sexual Identity," *Journal of Homosexuality* 3, no. 1 (1977): 41–48; and Michael Storms, "Theories of Sexual Orientation," *Journal of Personality and Social Psychology* 38, no. 4 (1980): 783–92. Think, again, about study question 4 in chapter 8. And keep in mind Thomas Nagel's claim (chapter 3) that merely performing a perverted act does not make one a "pervert"—more is needed. What is it?

Notes

This essay is a review of Morris B. Kaplan, *Sexual Justice: Democratic Citizenship and the Politics of Desire* (New York: Routledge, 1997), xix, 281. All parenthetical references in the text are to this work. A version of this review was presented in an "Author Meets Critics" session of the Pacific Division of the American Philosophical Association (Berkeley, Calif., March 1997).

1. Lawrence Wright, "One Drop of Blood," *New Yorker* (July 25, 1994), pp. 46 ff.

2. David Halperin, *Saint Foucault: Towards a Gay Hagiography* (Oxford: Oxford University Press, 1995). p. 61.

3. Ibid.

4. Ibid.

5. Ibid., p. 64.

6. Leo Bersani, *Homos* (Cambridge, Mass.: Harvard University Press, 1995). p. 5.

7. There are also deeper problems, stemming from what Freud referred to as the "narcissism of minor differences," with its underlying aggression, and the

role of rejection in self-definition by contrast and opposition. These I discuss in "Pride and Identity," *Midwest Studies in Philosophy* 22 (1998), 227–48.

8. There is actually some acknowledgment of the tensions in the book's introduction, when Kaplan speaks about Benjamin Constant's contrast between the liberty of the ancients and the liberty of the moderns, but especially when Kaplan writes about "queer" identity: "To the extent that 'queer politics' embraces the cause of transgendered and transsexual people, boy-lovers, bisexuals, consensual sadomasochists, leatherfolk, and other sexual minorities, it is an important reminder of the range of sexual discrimination and the realities of modern pluralism. To the extent that it becomes a means of effacing the specificities of lesbian and gay oppression or of subordinating the concerns of lesbians to an amorphous celebration of nonconformity, it may be misleading" (p. 6).

PART 3

USE, OBJECTIFICATION, AND CONSENT—THE THEORY

Chapter 16

SEXUAL MORALITY AND THE CONCEPT OF USING ANOTHER PERSON

Thomas A. Mappes

The Second Formulation of the German philosopher Immanuel Kant's (1724–1804) famous Categorical Imperative—"always treat humanity, whether in your own person or in the person of any other, never simply as a means, but always at the same time as an end"—continues to frame philosophical discussions of the moral value of rational autonomy and our contemporary thoughts about the moral power of consent. Its proper application to sexual relations is the nexus of most of the essays in part III of this volume, beginning with the contribution of Thomas A. Mappes, who sees Kant's views on objectification and using others for one's own goals as providing both necessary and sufficient conditions for licit sexual activity. On Mappes's perhaps "libertarian" reading of the Second Formulation, sexual relations are morally permissible just in case they occur with the free and informed consent of the participants (by the way, a view not dissimilar from that of the utilitarian John Stuart Mill), which is the way he interprets the Second Formulation. Mappes examines different ways in which misinformation or deception (outright lies) as well as pressure or coercion (as in rape, for example) can poison sexual relations, and brings up for our consideration a number of difficult or borderline cases. His remarks on the wrongness of sexual "exploitation" at the end of his essay are an interesting extension of his Kantian perspective.

In order to do competent exegetical work in this area (to comprehend Kantian ethics, and essays other than Mappes's in both Parts III and IV), one must study Kant's writings, especially his Lectures on Ethics *(trans. Peter Heath, ed. Peter Heath and J. B. Schneewind [Cambridge: Cambridge University Press, 1997]) and* The Metaphysics of Morals *(trans. Mary Gregor [Cambridge: Cambridge University Press, 1991, 1996]). Many other editions of these works are available, but these are undoubtedly currently the best.*

Mappes is professor of philosophy at Frostburg State University in Maryland. He is the editor, with David DeGrazia, of *Biomedical Ethics*, 6th edition (McGraw-Hill, 2006), and the editor, with Jane S. Zembaty, of *Social Ethics: Morality and Social Policy*, 6th edition (McGraw-Hill, 2002).

Reprinted with permission of the author from *Social Ethics: Morality and Social Policy*, 3rd edition (McGraw-Hill, 1987), pp. 248–62, edited by Thomas A. Mappes and Jane S. Zembaty. © 1985, Thomas A. Mappes.

The central tenet of *conventional* sexual morality is that nonmarital sex is immoral. A somewhat less restrictive sexual ethic holds that *sex without love* is immoral. If neither of these positions is philosophically defensible, and I would contend that neither is, it does not follow that there are no substantive moral restrictions on human sexual interaction. Any human interaction, including sexual interaction, may be judged morally objectionable to the extent that it transgresses a justified moral rule or principle. The way to construct a detailed account of sexual morality, it would seem, is simply to work out the implications of relevant moral rules or principles in the area of human sexual interaction.

As one important step in the direction of such an account, I will attempt to work out the implications of an especially relevant moral principle, the principle that it is wrong for one person to use another person. However ambiguous the expression "using another person" may seem to be, there is a determinate and clearly specifiable sense according to which using another person is morally objectionable. Once this morally significant sense of "using another person" is identified and explicated, the concept of using another person can play an important role in the articulation of a defensible account of sexual morality.

I. The Morally Significant Sense of "Using Another Person"

Historically, the concept of using another person is associated with the ethical system of Immanuel Kant. According to a fundamental Kantian principle, it is morally wrong for A to use B *merely as a means* (to achieve A's ends). Kant's principle does not rule out A using B as a means, only A using B *merely* as a means, that is, in a way incompatible with respect for B as a person. In the ordinary course of life, it is surely unavoidable (and morally unproblematic) that each of us in numerous ways uses others as a means to achieve our various ends. A college teacher uses students as a means to achieve his or her livelihood. A college student uses instructors as a means of gaining knowledge and skills. Such human interactions, presumably based on the voluntary participation of the respective parties, are quite compatible with the idea of respect for persons. But respect for persons entails that each of us recognize the rightful authority of other persons (as rational beings) to conduct their individual lives as they see fit. We may legitimately recruit others to participate in the satisfaction of our personal ends, but they are used merely as a means whenever we undermine the voluntary or informed character of their consent to interact with us in some desired way. A coerces B at knife point to hand over $200. A uses B merely as means. If A had requested of B a gift of $200, leaving B free to determine whether or not to make the gift, A would have proceeded in a manner compatible with respect for B as a person. C deceptively rolls back the odometer of a car and thereby manipulates D's decision to buy the car. C uses D merely as a means.

On the basis of these considerations, I would suggest that the morally significant sense of "using another person" is best understood by reference to the notion of *voluntary informed consent.* More specifically, A immorally uses B if and only if A intentionally acts in a way that violates the requirement that B's involvement with A's ends be based on B's voluntary informed consent. If this account is correct, using another person (in the morally significant sense) can arise in at least two important ways: via *coercion,* which is antithetical to voluntary consent, and via *deception,* which undermines the informed character of voluntary consent.

The notion of voluntary informed consent is very prominent in the literature of biomedical ethics and is systematically related to the much emphasized notion of (patient) autonomy. We find in the famous words of Supreme Court justice Cardozo a ringing affirmation of patient autonomy. "Every human being of adult years and sound mind has a right to determine what shall be done with his own body." Because respect for individual autonomy is an essential part of respect for persons, if medical professionals (and biomedical researchers) are to interact with their patients (and research subjects) in an acceptable way, they must respect individual autonomy. That is, they must respect the self-determination of the patient/subject, the individual's right to determine what shall be done with his or her body. This means that they must not act in a way that violates the requirement of voluntary informed consent. Medical procedures must not be performed without the consent of competent patients; research on human subjects must not be carried out without the consent of the subjects involved. Moreover, consent must be voluntary; coercion undermines individual autonomy. Consent must also be informed; lying or withholding relevant information undercuts rational decision making and thereby undermines individual autonomy.

To further illuminate the concept of using that has been proposed, I will consider in greater detail the matter of research involving human subjects. In the sphere of researcher-subject interaction, just as in the sphere of human sexual interaction, there is ample opportunity for immorally using another person. If a researcher is engaged in a study that involves human subjects, we may presume that the "end" of the researcher is the successful completion of the study. (The researcher may desire this particular end for any number of reasons: the speculative understanding it will provide, the technology it will make possible, the eventual benefit of humankind, increased status in the scientific community, a raise in pay, etc.) The work, let us presume, strictly requires the use (employment) of human research subjects. The researcher, however, immorally uses other people only if he or she intentionally acts in a way that violates the requirement that the participation of research subjects be based on their voluntary informed consent.

Let us assume that in a particular case participation as a research subject involves some rather significant risks. Accordingly, the researcher finds that potential subjects are reluctant to volunteer. At this point, if an unscrupulous researcher is willing to resort to the immoral using of other people (to achieve his or her own ends), two manifest options are available—deception and coercion. By way of deception, the researcher might choose to lie about the risks involved. For example, potential subjects could be explicitly told that there are no significant risks associated with research participation. On the other hand, the researcher could simply withhold a full disclosure of risks. Whether pumped full of false information or simply deprived of relevant information, the potential subject is intentionally deceived in such a way as to be led to a decision that furthers the researcher's ends. In manipulating the decision making process of the potential subject in this way, the researcher is guilty of immorally using another person.

To explain how an unscrupulous researcher might immorally use another person via coercion, it is helpful to distinguish two basic forms of coercion.[1] "Occurrent" coercion involves the use of physical force. "Dispositional" coercion involves the threat of harm. If I am forcibly thrown out of my office by an intruder, I am the victim of occurrent coercion. If, on the other hand, I leave my office because an intruder has threatened to shoot me if I do not leave, I am the victim of dispositional coercion. The victim of occurrent coercion literally has no choice in what happens. The victim of dispositional coercion, in contrast, does intentionally choose a certain course of action. However, one's choice, in the face of the threat of harm, is less than fully voluntary.

It is perhaps unlikely that even an unscrupulous researcher would resort to any very explicit measure of coercion. Deception, it seems, is less risky. Still, it is well known that Nazi medical experimenters ruthlessly employed coercion. By way of occurrent coercion, the Nazis literally forced great numbers of concentration camp victims to participate in experiments that entailed their own death or dismemberment. And if some concentration camp victims "volunteered" to participate in Nazi research to avoid even more unspeakable horrors, clearly we must consider them victims of dispositional coercion. The Nazi researchers, employing coercion, immorally used other human beings with a vengeance.

II. Deception and Sexual Morality

To this point, I have been concerned to identify and explicate the morally significant sense of "using another person." On the view proposed, A immorally uses B if and only if A intentionally acts in a way that violates the requirement that B's involvement with A's ends be based on B's voluntary informed consent. I will now apply this account to the area of human sexual interaction and explore its implications. For economy of expression in what follows, "using" (and its cognates) is to be understood as referring only to the morally significant sense.

If we presume a state of affairs in which A desires some form of sexual interaction with B, we can say that this desired form of sexual interaction with B is A's end. Thus A sexually uses B if and only if A intentionally acts in a way that violates the requirement that B's sexual interaction with A be based on B's voluntary informed consent. It seems clear then that A may sexually use B in at least two distinctive ways, (1) via coercion and (2) via deception. However, before proceeding to discuss deception and then the more problematic case of coercion, one important point must be made. In emphasizing the centrality of coercion and deception as mechanisms for the sexual using of another person, I have in mind sexual interaction with a fully competent adult partner. We should also want to say, I think, that sexual interaction with a child inescapably involves the sexual using of another person. Even if a child "consents" to sexual interaction, he or she is, strictly speaking, incapable of *informed* consent. It's a matter of being *incompetent* to give consent. Similarly, to the extent that a mentally retarded person is rightly considered incompetent, sexual interaction with such a person amounts to the sexual using of that person, unless someone empowered to give "proxy consent" has done so. (In certain circumstances, sexual involvement might be in the best interests of a mentally retarded person.) We can also visualize the case of an otherwise fully competent adult temporarily disordered by drugs or alcohol. To the extent that such a person is rightly regarded as

temporarily incompetent, winning his or her "consent" to sexual interaction could culminate in the sexual using of that person.

There are a host of clear cases in which one person sexually uses another precisely because the former employs deception in a way that undermines the informed character of the latter's consent to sexual interaction. Consider this example. One person, A, has decided, as a matter
of personal prudence based on past experience, not to become sexually
involved outside the confines of a loving relationship. Another person,
B, strongly desires a sexual relationship with A but does not love A. B,
aware of A's unwillingness to engage in sex without love, professes love
for A, thereby hoping to win A's consent to a sexual relationship. B's
ploy is successful; A consents. When the smoke clears and A becomes
aware of B's deception, it would be both appropriate and natural for A
to complain, "I've been used."

In the same vein, here are some other examples. (1) Mr. A is aware
that Ms. B will consent to sexual involvement only on the understanding
that in time the two will be married. Mr. A has no intention of marrying
Ms. B but says that he will. (2) Ms. C has herpes and is well aware that Mr.
D will never consent to sex if he knows of her condition. When asked by
Mr. D, Ms. C denies that she has herpes. (3) Mr. E knows that Ms. F will
not consent to sexual intercourse in the absence of responsible birth
control measures. Mr. E tells Ms. F that he has had a vasectomy, which is
not the case. (4) Ms. G knows that Mr. H would not consent to sexual involvement with a married woman. Ms. G is married but tells Mr. H that
she is single. (5) Ms. I is well aware that Ms. J is interested in a stable lesbian relationship and will not consent to become sexually involved with
someone who is bisexual. Ms. I tells Ms. J that she is exclusively homosexual, whereas the truth is that she is bisexual.

If one person's consent to sex is predicated on false beliefs that have
been intentionally and deceptively inculcated by one's sexual partner in
an effort to win the former's consent, the resulting sexual interaction involves one person sexually using another. In each of the above cases, one
person explicitly *lies* to another. False information is intentionally conveyed to win consent to sexual interaction, and the end result is the sexual using of another person.

As noted earlier, however, lying is not the only form of deception. Under certain circumstances, the simple withholding of information can be
considered a form of deception. Accordingly, it is possible to sexually
use another person not only by (deceptively) lying about relevant facts
but also by (deceptively) not disclosing relevant facts. If A has good reason to believe that B would refuse to consent to sexual interaction
should B become aware of certain factual information, and if A with-
holds disclosure of this information in order to enhance the possibility
of gaining B's consent, then, if B does consent, A sexually uses B via de-

ception. One example will suffice. Suppose that Mr. A meets Ms. B in a singles bar. Mr. A realizes immediately that Ms. B is the sister of Ms. C, a woman that Mr. A has been sexually involved with for a long time. Mr. A, knowing that it is very unlikely that Ms. B will consent to sexual interaction if she becomes aware of Mr. A's involvement with her sister, decides not to disclose this information. If Ms. B eventually consents to sexual interaction, since her consent is the product of Mr. A's deception, it is rightly thought that she has been sexually used by him.

III. Coercion and Sexual Morality

We have considered the case of deception. The present task is to consider the more difficult case of coercion. Whereas deception functions to undermine the *informed* character of voluntary consent (to sexual interaction), coercion either obliterates consent entirely (the case of occurrent coercion) or undermines the voluntariness of consent (the case of dispositional coercion).

Forcible rape is the most conspicuous, and most brutal, way of sexually using another person via coercion.[2] Forcible rape may involve either occurrent coercion or dispositional coercion. A man who rapes a woman by the employment of sheer physical force, by simply overpowering her, employs occurrent coercion. There is literally no sexual *interaction* in such a case; only the rapist performs an action. In no sense does the woman consent to or participate in sexual activity. She has no choice in what takes place, or rather, physical force results in her choice being simply beside the point. The employment of occurrent coercion for the purpose of rape "objectifies" the victim in the strongest sense of that term. She is treated like a physical object. One does not interact with physical objects; one acts upon them. In a perfectly ordinary (not the morally significant) sense of the term, we "use" physical objects. But when the victim of rape is treated as if she were a physical object, there we have one of the most vivid examples of the immoral using of another person.

Frequently, forcible rape involves not occurrent coercion (or not *only* occurrent coercion) but dispositional coercion.[3] In dispositional coercion, the relevant factor is not physical force but the threat of harm. The rapist threatens his victim with immediate and serious bodily harm. For example, a man threatens to kill or beat a woman if she resists his sexual demands. She "consents," that is, she submits to his demands. He may demand only passive participation (simply not struggling against him) or he may demand some measure of active participation. Rape that employs dispositional coercion is surely just as wrong as rape that employs occurrent coercion, but there is a notable difference in the mechanism by which the rapist uses his victim in the two cases. With occurrent coercion, the victim's consent is entirely bypassed. With dispositional coercion, the victim's consent is not bypassed. It is coerced. Dispositional coercion undermines the *voluntariness* of consent. The rapist, by employing the threat of immediate and serious bodily harm, may succeed in bending the victim's will. He may gain the victim's "consent." But he uses another person precisely because consent is coerced.

The relevance of occurrent coercion is limited to the case of forcible rape. Dispositional coercion, a notion that also plays an indispensable role in an overall account of forcible rape, now becomes our central concern. Although the threat of immediate and serious bodily harm stands out as the most brutal way of coercing consent to sexual interaction, we must not neglect the employment of other kinds of threats to this same end. There are numerous ways in which one person can effectively harm, and thus effectively threaten, another. Accordingly, for example, consent to sexual interaction might be coerced by threatening to damage someone's reputation. If a person consents to sexual interaction to avoid a threatened harm, then that person has been sexually used (via dispositional coercion). In the face of a threat, of course, it remains possible that a person will refuse to comply with another's sexual demands. It is probably best to describe this sort of situation as a case not of coercion, which entails the *successful* use of threats to gain compliance, but of *attempted* coercion. Of course, the moral fault of an individual emerges with the *attempt* to coerce. A person who attempts murder is morally blameworthy even if the attempt fails. The same is true for someone who fails in an effort to coerce consent to sexual interaction.

Consider now each of the following cases:

Case 1 Mr. Supervisor makes a series of increasingly less subtle sexual overtures to Ms. Employee. These advances are consistently and firmly rejected by Ms. Employee. Eventually, Mr. Supervisor makes it clear that the granting of "sexual favors" is a condition of her continued employment.

Case 2 Ms. Debtor borrowed a substantial sum of money from Mr. Creditor, on the understanding that she would pay it back within one year. In the meantime, Ms. Debtor has become sexually attracted to Mr. Creditor, but he does not share her interest. At the end of the one-year period, Mr. Creditor asks Ms. Debtor to return the money. She says she will be happy to return the money so long as he consents to sexual interaction with her.

Case 3 Mr. Theatregoer has two tickets to the most talked-about play of the season. He is introduced to a woman whom he finds sexually attractive and who shares his interest in the theater. In the course of their conversation, she expresses disappointment that the play everyone is talking about is sold out; she would love to see it. At this point, Mr. Theatregoer suggests that she be his guest at the theater. "Oh, by the way," he says, "I always expect sex from my dates."

Case 4 Ms. Jetsetter is planning a trip to Europe. She has been trying for some time to develop a sexual relationship with a man who has shown little interest in her. She knows, however, that he has always wanted to go to Europe and that it is only lack of money that has deterred him. Ms. Jetsetter proposes that he come along as her traveling companion, all expenses paid, on the express understanding that sex is part of the arrangement.

Cases 1 and 2 involve attempts to sexually use another person, whereas cases 3 and 4 do not. To see why this is so, it is essential to introduce a distinction between two kinds of proposals, viz., the distinction between *threats* and *offers*.[4] The logical form of a threat differs from the logical form of an offer in the following way. Threat: "If you *do not* do what I am proposing you do, I will bring about an *undesirable consequence* for you." Offer: "If you *do* what I am proposing you do, I will bring about a *desirable consequence* for you." The person who makes a threat attempts to gain compliance by attaching an undesirable consequence to the alternative of noncompliance. This person attempts to *coerce* consent. The person who makes an offer attempts to gain compliance by attaching a desirable consequence to the alternative of compliance. This person attempts not to coerce but to *induce* consent.

Since threats are morally problematic in a way that offers are not, it is not uncommon for threats to be advanced in the language of offers. Threats are represented as if they were offers. An armed assailant might say, "I'm going to make you an *offer*. If you give me your money, I will allow you to go on living." Though this proposal on the surface has the logical form of an offer, it is in reality a threat. The underlying sense of the proposal is this: "If you do not give me your money, I will kill you." If, in a given case, it is initially unclear whether a certain proposal is to count as a threat or an offer, ask the following question. Does the proposal in question have the effect of making a person *worse off upon noncompliance?* The recipient of an offer, upon noncompliance, is *not worse off* than he or she was before the offer. In contrast, the recipient of a threat, upon noncompliance, *is worse off* than he or she was before the threat. Since the "offer" of our armed assailant has the effect, upon noncompliance, of rendering its recipient worse off (relative to the preproposal situation of the recipient), the recipient is faced with a threat, not an offer.

The most obvious way for a coercer to attach an undesirable consequence to the path of noncompliance is by threatening to render the victim of coercion materially worse off than he or she has theretofore been. Thus a person is threatened with loss of life, bodily injury, damage to property, damage to reputation, etc. It is important to realize, however, that a person can also be effectively coerced by being threatened with the withholding of something (in some cases, what we would call a "benefit") to which the person is entitled. Suppose that A is mired in quicksand and is slowly but surely approaching death. When B happens along, A cries out to B for assistance. All B need do is throw A a rope. B is quite willing to accommodate A, "provided you pay me $100,000 over the next ten years." Is B making A an offer? Hardly! B, we must presume, stands under a moral obligation to come to the aid of a person in serious distress, at least when such assistance entails no significant risk, sacrifice of time, etc. A is entitled to B's assistance. Thus, in reality, B attaches an undesirable consequence to A's noncompliance with the proposal that A pay B $100,000. A is undoubtedly better off that B has happened along, but A is not rendered better off by *B's proposal.* Before B's proposal, A legitimately expected assistance from B, "no strings attached." In attaching a very unwelcome string, B's proposal effectively renders A worse off. What B proposes, then, is not an offer of assistance. Rather, B threatens A with the withholding of something (assistance) that A is entitled to have from B.

Since threats have the effect of rendering a person worse off upon noncompliance, it is ordinarily the case that a person does not welcome (indeed, despises) them. Offers, on the other hand, are ordinarily welcome to a person. Since an offer provides no penalty for noncompliance with a proposal but only an inducement for compliance, there is *in principle* only potential advantage in being confronted with an offer. In real life, of course, there are numerous reasons why a person may be less than enthusiastic about being presented with an offer. Enduring the presentation of trivial offers does not warrant the necessary time and energy expenditures. Offers can be both annoying and offensive; certainly this is true of some sexual offers. A person might also be unsettled by an offer that confronts him or her with a difficult decision. All this, however, is compatible with the fact that an offer is fundamentally welcome to a rational person in the sense that the *content* of an offer necessarily widens the field of opportunity and thus provides, in principle, only potential advantage.

With the distinction between threats and offers clearly in view, it now becomes clear why cases 1 and 2 do indeed involve attempts to sexually use another person whereas cases 3 and 4 do not. Cases 1 and 2 embody threats, whereas cases 3 and 4 embody offers. In case 1, Mr. Supervisor proposes sexual interaction with Ms. Employee and, in an effort to gain compliance, threatens her with the loss of her job. Mr. Supervisor thereby attaches an undesirable consequence to one of Ms. Employee's alternatives, the path of noncompliance. Typical of the threat situation, Mr. Supervisor's proposal has the effect of rendering Ms. Employee worse off upon noncompliance. Mr. Supervisor is attempting via (dispositional) coercion to sexually use Ms. Employee. The situation in case 2 is similar. Ms. Debtor, as *she* might be inclined to say, "offers" to pay Mr. Creditor the money she owes him *if* he consents to sexual interaction with her. In reality, Mrs. Debtor is threatening Mr. Creditor, attempting to coerce his consent to sexual interaction, attempting to sexually use him. Though Mr. Creditor is not now in possession of the money Ms. Debtor owes him, he is *entitled* to receive it from her at this time. She threatens to deprive him of something to which he is entitled. Clearly, her proposal has the effect of rendering him worse off upon noncompliance. Before her proposal, he had the legitimate expectation, "no strings attached," of receiving the money in question.

Cases 3 and 4 embody offers; neither involves an attempt to sexually use another person. Mr. Theatregoer simply provides an inducement for the woman he has just met to accept his proposal of sexual interaction. He offers her the opportunity to see the play that everyone is talking about. In attaching a desirable consequence to the alternative of compliance, Mr. Theatregoer in no way threatens or attempts to coerce his potential companion. Typical of the offer situation, his proposal does not have the effect of rendering her worse off upon noncompliance. She now has a new opportunity; if she chooses to forgo this opportunity, she is no worse off. The situation in case 4 is similar. Ms. Jetsetter provides an inducement for a man whom she is interested in to accept her proposal of sexual involvement. She offers him the opportunity to see Europe, without expense, as her traveling companion. Before Ms. Jetsetter's proposal, he had no prospect of a European trip. If he chooses to reject her proposal, he is no worse off than he has theretofore been. Ms. Jetsetter's proposal embodies an offer, not a threat. She cannot be accused of attempting to sexually use her potential traveling companion.

Consider now two further cases, 5 and 6, each of which develops in the following way. Professor Highstatus, a man of high academic accomplishment, is sexually attracted to a student in one of his classes. He is very anxious to secure her consent to sexual interaction. Ms. Student, confused and unsettled by his sexual advances, has begun to practice "avoidance behavior." To the extent that it is possible, she goes out of her way to avoid him.

Case 5 Professor Highstatus tells Ms. Student that, though her work is such as to entitle her to a grade of B in the class, she will be assigned a D unless she consents to sexual interaction.

Case 6 Professor Highstatus tells Ms. Student that, though her work is such as to entitle her to a grade of B, she will be assigned an A if she consents to sexual interaction.

It is clear that case 5 involves an attempt to sexually use another person. Case 6, however, at least at face value, does not. In case 5, Professor Highstatus *threatens* to deprive Ms. Student of the grade she deserves. In case 6, he *offers* to assign her a grade that is higher than she deserves. In case 5, Ms. Student would be worse off upon noncompliance with Professor Highstatus's proposal. In case 6, she would not be worse off upon noncompliance with his proposal. In saying that case 6 does not involve an attempt to sexually use another person, it is not being asserted that Professor Highstatus is acting in a morally legitimate fashion. In offering a student a higher grade than she deserves, he is guilty of abusing his institutional authority. He is under an obligation to assign the grades that students earn, as defined by the relevant course standards. In case 6, Professor Highstatus is undoubtedly acting in a morally reprehensible way, but in contrast to case 5, where it is fair to say that he both abuses his institutional authority and attempts to sexually use another person, we can plausibly say that in case 6 his moral failure is limited to abuse of his institutional authority.

There remains, however, a suspicion that case 6 might after all embody an attempt to sexually use another person. There is no question that the literal content of what Professor Highstatus conveys to Ms. Student has the logical form of an offer and not a threat. Still, is it not the case that Ms. Student may very well feel threatened? Professor Highstatus, in an effort to secure consent to sexual interaction, has announced that be will assign Ms. Student a higher grader than she deserves. Can she really turn him down without substantial risk? Is he not likely to retaliate? If she spurns him, will he not lower her grade or otherwise make it harder for her to succeed in her academic program? He does, after all, have power over her. Will he use it to her detriment? Surely he is not above abusing his institutional authority to achieve his ends; this much is abundantly clear from his willingness to assign a grade higher than a student deserves.

Is Professor Highstatus naive to the threat that Ms. Student may find implicit in the situation? Perhaps. In such a case, if Ms. Student reluctantly consents to sexual interaction, we may be inclined to say that he has *unwittingly* used her. More likely, Professor Highstatus is well aware of the way in which Ms. Student will perceive his proposal. He knows that threats need not be verbally expressed. Indeed, it may even be the case that he consciously exploits his underground reputation. "Everyone knows what happens to the women who reject Professor Highstatus's little offers." To the extent, then, that Professor Highstatus intends to convey a threat in case 6, he is attempting via coercion to sexually use another person.

Many researchers "have pointed out the fact that the possibility of sanctions for noncooperation is implicit in all sexual advances across authority lines, as between teacher and student."[5] I do not think that this consideration should lead us to the conclusion that a person with an academic appointment is obliged in all circumstances to refrain from attempting to initiate sexual involvement with one of his or her students.

Still, since even "good faith" sexual advances may be ambiguous in the eyes of a student, it is an interesting question what precautions an instructor must take to avoid unwittingly coercing a student to consent to sexual interaction.

Much of what has been said about the professor/student relationship in an academic setting can be applied as well to the supervisor/subordinate relationship in an employment setting. A manager who functions within an organizational structure is required to evaluate fairly his or her subordinates according to relevant corporate or institutional standards. An unscrupulous manager, willing to abuse his or her institutional authority in an effort to win the consent of a subordinate to sexual interaction, can advance threats and/or offers related to the managerial task of employee evaluation. An employee whose job performance is entirely satisfactory can be threatened with an unsatisfactory performance rating, perhaps leading to termination. An employee whose job performance is excellent can be threatened with an unfair evaluation, designed to bar the employee from recognition, merit pay, consideration for promotion, etc. Such threats, when made in an effort to coerce employee consent to sexual interaction, clearly embody the attempt to sexually use another person. On the other hand, the manager who (abusing his or her institutional authority) offers to provide an employee with an inflated evaluation as an inducement for consent to sexual interaction does not, at face value, attempt to sexually use another person. Of course, all of the qualifications introduced in the discussion of case 6 above are applicable here as well.

IV. The Idea of a Coercive Offer

In section III, I have sketched an overall account of sexually using another person *via coercion*. In this section, I will consider the need for modifications or extensions of the suggested account. As before, certain case studies will serve as points of departure.

Case 7 Ms. Starlet, a glamorous, wealthy, and highly successful model, wants nothing more than to become a movie superstar. Mr. Moviemogul, a famous producer, is very taken with Ms. Starlet's beauty. He invites her to come to his office for a screen test. After the screen test, Mr. Moviemogul tells Ms. Starlet that he is prepared to make her a star, on the condition that she agree to sexual involvement with him. Ms. Starlet finds Mr. Moviemogul personally repugnant; she is not at all sexually attracted to him. With great reluctance, she agrees to his proposal.

Has Mr. Moviemogul sexually used Ms. Starlet? No. He has made her an offer that she has accepted, however reluctantly. The situation would be quite different if it were plausible to believe that she was, before acceptance of his proposal, *entitled* to his efforts to make her a star. Then we could read case 7 as amounting to his threatening to deprive her of something to which she was entitled. But what conceivable grounds could be found for the claim that Mr. Moviemogul, before Ms. Starlet's acceptance of his proposal, is under an obligation to make her a star? He does not threaten her; he makes her an offer. Even if there are other good grounds for morally condemning his action, it is a mistake to think that he is guilty of coercing consent.

But some would assert that Mr. Moviemogul's offer, on the grounds that it confronts Ms. Starlet with an overwhelming inducement, is simply an example of a *coercive offer*. The more general claim at issue is that offers are coercive precisely inasmuch as they are extremely enticing or seductive. Though there is an important reality associated with the notion of a coercive offer, a reality that must shortly be confronted, we ought not embrace the view that an offer is coercive merely because it is extremely enticing or seductive. Virginia Held is a leading proponent of the view under attack here. She writes:

> A person unable to spurn an offer may act as unwillingly as a person unable to resist a threat. Consider the distinction between rape and seduction. In one case constraint and threat are operative, in the other inducement and offer. If the degree of inducement is set high enough in the case of seduction, there may seem to be little difference in the extent of coercion involved. In both cases, persons may act against their own wills.[6]

Certainly a rape victim who acquiesces at knifepoint is forced to act *against her will.* Does Ms. Starlet, however, act against her will? We have said that she consents "with great reluctance" to sexual involvement, but she does not act against her will. She *wants* very much to be a movie star. I might want very much to be thin. She regrets having to become sexually involved with Mr. Moviemogul as a means of achieving what she wants. I might regret very much having to go on a diet to lose weight. If we say that Ms. Starlet acts against her will in case 7, then we must say that I am acting against my will in embracing "with great reluctance" the diet I despise.

A more important line of argument against Held's view can be advanced on the basis of the widely accepted notion that there is a moral presumption against coercion. Held herself embraces this notion and very effectively clarifies it:

> . . . although coercion is not always wrong (quite obviously: one coerces the small child not to run across the highway, or the murderer to drop his weapon), there is a presumption against it. . . . This has the standing of a fundamental moral principle. . . .
>
> What can be concluded at the moral level is that we have a *prima facie* obligation not to employ coercion.[7] (all italics hers)

But it would seem that acceptance of the moral presumption against co-ercion is not compatible with the view that offers become coercive pre-cisely inasmuch as they become extremely enticing or seductive. Sup-pose you are my neighbor and regularly spend your Saturday afternoon on the golf course. Suppose also that you are a skilled gardener. I am anxious to convince you to do some gardening work for me and it must be done this Saturday. I offer you $100, $200, $300, . . . in an effort to make it worth your while to sacrifice your recreation and undertake my gardening. At some point, my proposal becomes very enticing. Yet, at the same time in no sense is my proposal becoming morally problematic. If my proposal were becoming coercive, surely our moral sense would be aroused.

Though it is surely not true that the extremely enticing character of an offer is sufficient to make it coercive, we need not reach the conclu-sion that no sense can be made out of the notion of a coercive offer. In-deed, there is an important social reality that the notion of a coercive of-fer appears to capture, and insight into this reality can be gained by simply taking note of the sort of case that most draws us to the language of "coercive offer." Is it not a case in which the recipient of an offer is in circumstances of genuine need, and acceptance of the offer seems to present the only realistic possibility for alleviating the need? Assuming that this sort of case is the heart of the matter, it seems that we cannot avoid introducing some sort of distinction between *genuine needs* and *mere wants*. Though the philosophical difficulties involved in drawing this distinction are not insignificant, I nevertheless claim that we will not achieve any clarity about the notion of a coercive offer, at least in this context, except in reference to it. Whatever puzzlement we may feel with regard to the host of borderline cases that can be advanced, it is never-theless true, for example, that I *genuinely need* food and that I *merely want* a backyard tennis court. In the same spirit, I think it can be acknowl-edged by all that Ms. Starlet, though she *wants* very much to be a star, does not in any relevant sense *need* to be a star. Accordingly, there is lit-tle plausibility in thinking that Mr. Moviemogul makes her a coercive of-fer. The following case, in contrast, can more plausibly be thought to embody a coercive offer.

Case 8 Mr. Troubled is a young widower who is raising his three chil-dren. He lives in a small town and believes that it is important for him to stay there so that his children continue to have the emotional sup-port of other family members. But economic times are tough. Mr. Trou-bled has been laid off from his job and has not been able to find an-other. His unemployment benefits have ceased and his relatives are in no position to help him financially. If he is unable to come up with the money for his mortgage payments, he will lose his rather modest house. Ms. Opportunistic lives in the same town. Since shortly after the death of Mr. Troubled's wife, she has consistently made sexual overtures in his direction. Mr. Troubled, for his part, does not care for Ms. Opportunistic and has made it clear to her that he is not interested in sexual involvement with her. She, however, is well aware of his present difficulties. To win his consent to a sexual affair, Ms. Opportunistic offers to make mortgage payments for Mr. Troubled on a continuing basis.

Is Ms. Opportunistic attempting to sexually use Mr. Troubled? The correct answer is yes, even though we must first accept the conclusion that her proposal embodies an offer and not a threat. If Ms. Opportunistic were threatening Mr. Troubled, her proposal would have the effect of rendering him worse off upon noncompliance. But this is not the case. If he rejects her proposal, his situation will not worsen; he will simply remain, as before, in circumstances of extreme need. It might be objected at this point that Ms. Opportunistic does in fact threaten Mr. Troubled. She threatens to deprive him of something to which he is entitled, namely, the alleviation of a genuine need. But this approach is defensible only if, before acceptance of her proposal, he is entitled to have his needs alleviated *by her*. And whatever Mr. Troubled and his children are entitled to from their society as a whole—they are perhaps slipping through the "social safety net"—it cannot be plausibly maintained that Mr. Troubled is entitled to have his mortgage payments made *by Ms. Opportunistic.*

Yet, though she does not threaten him, she is attempting to sexually use him. How can this conclusion be reconciled with our overall account of sexually using another person? First of all, I want to suggest that nothing hangs on whether or not we decide to call Ms. Opportunistic's offer "coercive." More important than the label "coercive offer" is an appreciation of the social reality that inclines us to consider the label appropriate. The label most forcefully asserts itself when we reflect on what Mr. Troubled is likely to say after accepting the offer. "I really had no choice." "I didn't want to accept her offer but what could I do? I have my children to think about." Both Mr. Troubled and Ms. Starlet (in our previous case) *reluctantly* consented to sexual interaction, but I think it can be agreed that Ms. Starlet had a choice in a way that Mr. Troubled did not. Mr. Troubled's choice was *severely constrained by his needs*, whereas Ms. Starlet's was not. As for Ms. Opportunistic, it seems that we might describe her approach as in some sense exploiting or taking advantage of Mr. Troubled's desperate situation. It is not so much, as we would say in the case of threats, that she coerces him or his consent, but rather that she achieves her aim of winning consent by taking advantage of the fact that he is already "under coercion," that is, his choice is severely constrained by his need. If we choose to describe what has taken place as a "coercive offer," we should remember that Mr. Troubled is "coerced" (constrained) by his own need or perhaps by preexisting factors in his situation rather than by Ms. Opportunistic or her offer.

Since it is not quite right to say that Ms. Opportunistic is attempting to coerce Mr. Troubled, even if we are prepared to embrace the label "coercive offer," we cannot simply say, as we would say in the case of threats, that she is attempting to sexually use him via coercion. The proper account of the way in which Ms. Opportunistic attempts to sexually use Mr. Troubled is somewhat different. Let us say simply that she attempts to sexually use him *by taking advantage of his desperate situation.* The sense behind this distinctive way of sexually using someone is that a person's choice situation can sometimes be subject to such severe prior constraints that the possibility of *voluntary* consent to sexual interaction is precluded. A advances an offer calculated to gain B's reluctant consent to sexual interaction by confronting B, who has no apparent way of alleviating a genuine need, with an opportunity to do so, but makes this opportunity contingent upon consent to sexual interaction. In such a case, should we not say simply that B's need, when coupled with a lack of viable alternatives, results in B being incapable of *voluntarily* accepting A's offer? Thus A, in making an offer which B "cannot refuse," although not coercing B, nevertheless does intentionally act in a way that violates the requirement that B's sexual interaction with A be based upon B's voluntary informed consent. Thus A sexually uses B.

The central claim of this paper is that A sexually uses B if and only if A intentionally acts in a way that violates the requirement that B's sexual interaction with A be based on B's voluntary informed consent. Clearly, deception and coercion are important mechanisms whereby sexual using takes place. But consideration of case 8 has led us to the identification of yet another mechanism. In summary, then, limiting attention to cases of sexual interaction with a fully competent adult partner, A can sexually use B not only (1) by deceiving B or (2) by coercing B but also (3) by taking advantage of B's desperate solution.

Study Questions

1. Some philosophers take the principle of free and informed consent so seriously that they apply it across the board, to all human activities. Thus, the moral considerations relevant to having sex with another person are no different from those that govern playing tennis. (A version of this thesis can be found in Alan Goldman's essay; see chapter 5.) Suppose someone says, by contrast, "Any comparison between the informed consent I give in a hospital setting to that I give for sexual relations must be flawed, because sexual relations are significantly different in nature from medical procedures." Do you agree? How is sex different— if it is different—from the other ways we submit our bodies to the

touch of others? (This question is posed in another context by study question 3 in chapter 23.)

2. Mappes says that it is possible to use another person sexually by not disclosing relevant facts to him or her prior to sex. What specific sorts of facts are "relevant" to the morality of the sexual use of someone? One possibility is that any fact is relevant if that fact is one that at least one party would want to now. Is this account morally adequate?

3. In the movie *Indecent Proposal*, actors Woody Harrelson ("David") and Demi Moore ("Diana") play a young married couple who gamble away all their savings in Las Vegas, and then encounter a billionaire, John Gage (played by Robert Redford). John sexually desires Diana and offers David one million dollars to spend an evening with her. David and Diana eventually decide to accept the offer. Who, if anyone, used whom here, according to Mappes? Who, if anyone, was morally culpable in this scenario? Would you take part in such an arrangement—as either David, John, or Diana?

4. On Mappes's view, should a client of a prostitute feel less guilt about hiring her, if he knows her to be hungry, than about hiring a prostitute he knows to be a drug addict? Try to get clear about Mappes's notion of "exploitation" and how it fits, logically, with the rest of his Kantian sexual ethics.

5. In Howard Klepper's "Case 2" (see chapter 17), Romeo brags to friends about his sexual adventures with Juliet. By Mappes's lights, does Romeo dispositionally coerce Juliet into having sex, or does he simply disrespect her? Is Case 2 a case of (impermissible) sexual use at all?

Notes

1. I follow here an account of coercion developed by Michael D. Bayles in "A Concept of Coercion," in J. Roland Pennock and John W. Chapman, eds., *Coercion: Nomos XIV* (Chicago: Aldine-Atherton, 1972), pp. 16–29.

2. Statutory rape, sexual relations with a person under the legal age of consent, can also be construed as the sexual using of another person. In contrast to forcible rape, however, statutory rape need not involve coercion. The victim of statutory rape may freely "consent" to sexual interaction but, at least in the eyes of the law, is deemed incompetent to consent.

3. A man wrestles a woman to the ground. She is the victim of occurrent coercion. He threatens to beat her unless she submits to his sexual demands. Now she becomes the victim of dispositional coercion.

4. My account of this distinction largely derives from Robert Nozick, "Coercion," in Sidney Morgenbesser, Patrick Suppes, and Morton White, eds., *Philosophy, Science, and Method* (New York: St. Martin's Press, 1969), 440–72, and from Michael D. Bayles, "Coercive Offers and Public Benefits," *The Personalist* 55, no. 2 (Spring 1974), 139–44.

5. The National Advisory Council on Women's Educational Programs, *Sexual Harassment: A Report on the Sexual Harassment of Students* (August 1980), 12.

6. Virginia Held, "Coercion and Coercive Offers," in Pennock and Chapman, *Coercion: Nomos XIV*, p. 58.

7. Ibid., pp. 61, 62.

Chapter 17

SEXUAL EXPLOITATION AND THE VALUE OF PERSONS

Howard Klepper

This essay by **Howard Klepper** *adds depth to Thomas Mappes's (chapter 16) take on Immanuel Kant's Second Formulation. Though Klepper concurs with Mappes on the centrality of free and informed consent in making moral judgments about sexual activity, he argues that obtaining the consent of the other prior to sex is not sufficient for morally proper sexual relations in a robust Kantian sense: a person can be treated sexually as a mere means (that is, wrongly) even if they have consented in a Mappesian way. In order to satisfy the Kantian requirement that we do not wrongly use another person sexually, we must— beyond getting their consent—be considerate of them and their needs. (See a similar thesis, stated briefly by Alan Goldman [chapter 5], as well as Karol Wojtyla's more stringent view [chapter 11] that if we really want to avoid using each other in sex, we must be married—a view nearly identical to Kant's.) Our cultural norms to treat sexual partners or lovers in a respectful and sensitive manner generate continuing obligations that extend to our subsequent treatment of them. Klepper also makes trenchant points about Kant's views on marriage and prostitution (on which, see also chapters 18 and 23).*

Klepper previously taught in the philosophy department and in the Strich School of Medicine of Loyola University, Chicago, and was a visting fellow in the Biomedical Ethics Program at Stanford University. Now living in Berkeley, California, he makes, by hand, one-of-a-kind guitars (see images of his art at www.klepperguitars.com).

Reprinted, with the permission of Howard Klepper and the publisher, Springer-SBM B.V., from the *Journal of Value Inquiry* 27, 3–4 (1993), pp. 479–86. © 1993 Kluwer Academic.

In his *Lectures on Ethics*,[1] Kant gives us an application of his ethical theory to human sexual relations. Much of what he says there seems irrelevant and puritanical to the modern reader. For example, Kant condemns all sex outside of marriage, and he calls masturbation an abominable crime against nature.[2] It is not my purpose to defend these positions. But I think that Kant's discussion of the wrongfulness of using another person as a sexual object helps explain the wrongfulness of some kinds of sexual relations. In this essay I develop a Kantian account of sexual exploitation and suggest how to apply it to other exploitative relationships.

Kant's second formulation of the categorical imperative (the "Formula of Humanity") is often taken to be equivalent to a requirement that in our transactions with others, we do not deprive them of the opportunity for voluntary informed consent to their own actions. In our teaching we may conveniently answer a student's query as to what it means to treat another as a mere means, and not at the same time as an end, by saying that we do this if we induce another to act by coercion or deceit. We usually add that coercion includes threats as well as force, and that deceit includes withholding relevant information as well as lying. The virtue of this account is that coercion and deceit, while problematic, are easier to define and detect than the vaguer notion of respect for moral personhood. But I argue that this reduction of the Kantian imperative is incomplete, by showing how a person may be treated as a mere means sexually and otherwise in the absence of coercion or deceit.

The shortcomings of a reduction of the imperative to a ban on coercion or deceit may be illustrated by Thomas Mappes's essay, "Sexual Morality and the Concept of Using Another Person."[3] Mappes considers what moral rules govern sexual behavior in the context of general moral principles, by analysis of using another person sexually as a mere means. He defines the immoral use of another person, sexually or otherwise, as intentionally acting in a way that deprives the other person of voluntary informed consent. He further defines this as using coercion or deception to induce another to consent to an action.

Examples offered of deception by lying include denying having herpes, or being married, in order to get another to consent to a sexual relationship. Examples of deception by withholding information include failing to inform another of having a venereal disease, or being married, when there is good reason to believe that consent to sexual relations would be refused if that information were divulged.

Mappes considers coercion to present more difficult problems than deception, and he devotes the bulk of his essay to distinguishing coercive from noncoercive behavior. He discusses the distinction between threats and mere offers, concluding that taking advantage of another's desperate situation is coercion, even if threats and deception are not involved. For example, if Tom, a single father of two children, loses his job and is unable to make his mortgage payments, and Jane offers to pay the mortgage if Tom will enter into a sexual relationship with her, her behavior should be considered as treating Tom as a mere means.

Mappes's analysis is useful and correct as far as it goes. However, the concept of using another person sexually as a mere means is much broader than what is included in Mappes's account, which ends with the parties' agreement to have sex.[4] This is a description of immoral means of obtaining "consent" to a sexual relationship, but our moral obligations to others in sexual relationships do not end there. A person may be used sexually as a mere means during and after sexual acts as well. Consider the following case:

Case 1. Romeo and Juliet have been out together on a few dates. They are sexually attracted to each other. Juliet willingly accepts Romeo's suggestion that they have sex together. During intercourse, Romeo makes no attempt to please or satisfy Juliet. After having an orgasm, he rolls over without a word and goes to sleep.

Case 1 is an uncontroversial instance, perhaps a paradigm instance, of using another person sexually, despite voluntary informed consent to engage in sex having occurred. Romeo has been selfish, rude, and inconsiderate. He has disregarded Juliet's value as a person and treated her as an object, a mere means to his ends. Our moral obligations to our sexual partners surely do not end with their voluntary informed consent. Closer to the truth is that they begin there. We have an ongoing obligation to be respectful and considerate of our sexual partners' needs. Like voluntary informed consent, this is not an obligation unique to sexual relationships. It applies to all our relationships with others, but the requirements imposed by this obligation increase with the intimacy of the relationship. The obligation applies with particular force to sexual relationships, because the intimacy of those relationships involves relinquishing defenses, which leaves people particularly vulnerable to feeling used. This obligation does not end with considerate lovemaking.

Case 2. Romeo and Juliet begin a sexual relationship as before, but in this case both are generous and affectionate lovers. The next day, however, Romeo brags to his friends of his seduction of Juliet and gives them a lurid and detailed account of her sexual technique.

Case 2 is another instance of using another person sexually. Although the wrongful acts take place subsequent to the sexual acts, as in Case 1 their wrongfulness is based on a lack of respect and consideration for a sexual partner. The sexual character of the relationship, together with cultural conventions regarding privacy, renders the acts wrongful. In Western culture one shows disrespect for another by revealing intimate facts about the other's sexual behavior. For Romeo to give his friends a

detailed account of the rest of his date with Juliet, exclusive of their sexual relations, would not be wrong. But the privacy of a person's sexual
acts is a legitimate end for that person to seek, and to disregard that end
does not respect the value of that person as an end in herself or himself.

A plausible response to the above cases is that they are instances of deceit. In Case 1 there was an implicit agreement on the part of Romeo to
be concerned with Juliet's pleasure and satisfaction, and in Case 2 there
was an implicit agreement to not make public intimate information that
is conventionally considered to be private. If these are instances of deceit, the conclusion might be drawn that Mappes is wrong to say that coercion presents the more difficult and interesting instances of using another person sexually. That claim results from his focus on pre-sexual
acts, in which implicit agreements as to how the partners will treat each
other during and after sex have not yet become relevant. Once we take
into our account the ways in which a person who has voluntarily consented to sex may be used sexually during and after the sexual acts, we
have moved into an area in which the more difficult and interesting
questions are those of deceit.

What would be the source of the implicit agreements in Cases 1 and
2? Juliet's having the relevant expectations about Romeo's conduct
would by itself be insufficient. One party's unspoken expectations do
not make for an implied agreement. For agreements to be implied in
these cases means that both parties were aware of norms or standards of
conduct, and that absent any explicit exclusion of these norms, it was
reasonable to assume that they were incorporated into the parties'
agreement. So, for implicit agreements to be binding, they must not be
only expected by one party; the expectation must in a relevant sense be
legitimate.

Does mutuality legitimate the expectation? An analogy to contract law
is appropriate. The general legal rule is that a contractual term is implied where a reasonable person would infer it to exist, on the basis of
the express agreements and observable behavior of the parties. A term
may be taken as implied if it is customary and usual to the kind of agreement being made, and each party may reasonably assume that the other
is aware of the custom and usage. That each party had the same unex-
pressed assumptions will not result in an implied agreement, despite the
mutuality of the expectation, if a reasonable objective observer would
not infer the agreement to exist under the circumstances. Thus, under
the "objective" standard in contract law, mutual expectation is neither
necessary nor sufficient to create an implied agreement. However, if neither party was aware of the custom and usage, no agreement occurred,
under the doctrine of "mutual mistake."

Should we take an implicit agreement to engage in sexual behavior to
morally legitimize that behavior? I think not. Our moral obligations are

broader in scope than our legal ones. In what follows I argue that not only an implicit agreement, but also an explicit, voluntary, and informed agreement may be insufficient to justify behavior that amounts to using another person sexually by treating that person as a mere means to an end.

Let's get back to cases. Case 1 involves a norm within contemporary Western culture that sexual partners will be mutually concerned with each other's pleasure and feelings. Both partners will usually be aware of this norm and will be justified in taking the awareness to be mutual without explicit mention. Their agreement to have sex together will thus include an implicit agreement to attend to their partner's sexual satisfaction. Failure to keep this implicit agreement is a form of deceit, and therefore a conventional case of using another as a mere means. Two other possibilities are to be considered. The first is where one of the parties is unaware of the norm. Perhaps Romeo is a visitor from a culture in which men customarily are not concerned with mutuality in sex but regard a woman's sexual pleasure as unnecessary or even undesirable. Nonetheless, if Romeo were to be aware Juliet's reasonable expectations and say nothing regarding his intent to honor those expectations, he would be deceitful by the standard we have set for implied agreements.

Second, let's suppose that Romeo is unaware of the sexual norms in Juliet's culture and that his unawareness is reasonable. In this case an objective reasonable observer would not take Romeo to have impliedly agreed to behave according to those sexual norms. In legal terms we might say that no agreement was made because of a mutual mistake of fact, that is, the parties did not agree as to the terms of their "contract," and this lack of agreement was not just subjective, but also would have been evident to an informed, objective observer. Does this mean that when Romeo behaves as in Case 1 he has not used Juliet sexually? I think he has, despite the lack of an implied agreement to honor her expectations. Using another person as a mere means is not a culturally relative notion. We should instead say that in Romeo's home culture the norm is that men use women sexually as mere means to their ends. This is just an instance of the familiar truism that wrongful conduct does not become moral if everybody does it.

Even in the case where Juliet is aware of the norms of Romeo's culture, or is herself a member of that culture, so that we may take her to have impliedly agreed to his actions, I think that we would be entirely justified to say that Romeo had used Juliet sexually as a mere means. This further illustrates the difference between moral and legal notions. Legality has a relativistic dimension that morality does not share. Cultural conventions may determine the content of a lawful agreement; they do not thereby morally legitimize it. Put another way, the question whether Romeo has treated Juliet immorally is not settled by Romeo's behavior having been lawful, and even agreed upon.

Just because Juliet knew Romeo isn't very nice doesn't mean he isn't using her as a means to an end

The point may be further illustrated by variations on our cases. Suppose that in Case 1, Juliet is aware that Romeo is a selfish and insensitive lover, but in spite of this (or, in a more perverse variant, because of it) chooses to have sex with him. Or, in Case 2, suppose that Juliet is aware of Romeo's propensity to kiss and tell. This would not change the fact that Romeo treats Juliet as a mere means in these cases and uses her sexually.

If I am right about these cases, we must reject the interpretation of Kant's second formulation of the categorical imperative that equates treating another person as a mere means with using coercion or deceit. Neither is present in the variations on our cases just considered. Juliet gives voluntary informed consent, yet is treated as a mere means, as a sexual object.

Quote

More generally, treating another as a mere means includes treating the other as an object, and not at the same time as an intrinsically valuable moral subject; this is not negated even by the other's explicit consent to such treatment. A familiar example is slavery. The slave's voluntary informed consent to enter into the slavery relationship does not provide a moral justification for it. Similarly, consent to being abused or degraded does not render the abuse or degradation moral. (Although, with some limitations, it may make it legal. For example, consent is a defense to battery and rape, but not to murder and mayhem.)

Another aspect of the above variations on Cases 1 and 2 is that both parties violate the Kantian imperative. This may be illustrated more clearly by examples involving prostitution relationships, where the behaviors of the parties are explicitly agreed to. Kant considered it to be "the depth of infamy"[5] to provide sexual services in exchange for money. He argues that a person's body is not property, which can be disposed of however that person wishes. The body is an inseparable part of a person, and because persons are priceless it cannot be treated as a mere thing that may be let out for hire.

are/how ideal that would be

Kant carried this idea further to claim that mutual satisfaction of sexual desire with no idea of material gain is also morally unacceptable. Here Kant's argument is that an agreement for mutual sexual satisfaction purports to be a contract to surrender only each person's body to the other, while retaining freedom over the other aspects of the person. But such a contract must necessarily be violated, because a part of the person cannot be separated from the whole; in a sexual relationship I necessarily use the whole person of my partner, thereby violating my agreement to use only a part, and making the person into a mere thing (which would be wrong even if it were agreed to).

Kant offers no justification for his claim that to have a right to use a part of a person is to have a right to use the whole person, though his argument depends on this claim. To surrender all of one's humanity to another, as in a relationship of slave to master, is wrong, but we have no good reason to see mutual consent to sexual relations as a surrender of the whole person, and thus contrary to the rational nature of humanity. Moreover, Kant's argument could extend, implausibly, to any agreement to sell one's labor to another. So we may reject Kant's claim that all sex outside of marriage is immoral. But I argue below that some kinds of prostitution relationships are immoral for Kantian reasons.

I am not claiming that all prostitution is necessarily exploitive or immoral. I leave that question open, as in some possible culture the sale of sexual services might not be either exploitive or degrading, and that even within contemporary Western culture a prostitution relationship might not involve treating another as a mere means to an end. I make here only the weaker claim that some prostitution agreements are cases of mutual exploitation. A typical example is Case 3.

Case 3. Romeo desires impersonal sex, in which he can use another person's body as a tool for his own pleasure. He meets Juliet, a prostitute, on a street corner. They negotiate an explicit agreement for the performance of sexual acts and go to a motel where they have sex in much the same fashion as in Case 1. Juliet dislikes being used as Romeo's sexual object, but performs according to their contract, and considers her payment to be sufficient compensation.

We saw above that Kant's claim, that an agreement which gives another rights over a part of a person is necessarily an agreement for the surrender of all of that person, might lead to the conclusion that all agreements to hire out one person's services to another are immoral. A typical employment relationship, in which the employee is paid to perform work that he or she may not enjoy doing, is not necessarily an instance of mutual exploitation or of mutual treatment of another person as a mere means. A principled distinction between Case 3 and other employment relationships is needed. What distinguishes Case 3 from a common employer-employee relationship is that in Case 3 it is Romeo's objective, a part of his ends or a second-order end, to treat another person as a mere means to his ends. Romeo might not want to find out that Juliet enjoyed her sexual acts with him; he may want a lack of mutuality. If in some employer-employee relationships the employee may feel used or degraded, that is normally incidental to such relationships, which could just as well (or better) exist without such feelings. But any employment relationship which has as the employer's purpose the denigration of the employee would similarly be wrongful regardless of the employee's voluntary informed consent, whether implicit or explicit.

We can also avoid the possibility that Case 3 might be explained by Juliet's being coerced, in Mappes's sense, by Romeo taking advantage of her desperate economic situation. Let's suppose that economic need has not driven Juliet to prostitution. Perhaps she is supplementing an otherwise adequate income in order to obtain some luxury item she desires.

By hypothesis, Romeo intends to treat Juliet as a mere means in Case 3. His purpose in hiring her is to treat her sexually as a mere object, and not as an end in herself. He exploits Juliet's willingness to be so treated. Juliet, for her part, has treated humanity *in her own person* as a mere means, by choosing, without necessity, to be so treated by Romeo. Kant might say that for a rational being to freely choose to be treated as a mere means and hence not as a free, rational being is contradictory. Moreover, a rational will would not voluntarily allow itself to be determined by the unfree, animal will of another. Juliet acts irrationally by Kantian standards. From a Kantian perspective such a choice must be motivated by sensuous inclination and hence be unfree.

Where Juliet is aware of the purpose that she be treated as a mere means by Romeo, her assent to that purpose determines that she is being treated as a mere means by both Romeo and herself. In such a case the exploitation is mutual. Juliet's end is to obtain money, and because Romeo's will is determined by irrational sensuous inclination he is unable to freely assent to her end. Juliet has used Romeo as a mere means to an end, by taking advantage of his lapse of rationality (in the Kantian sense).

We may now generalize the above conclusions. A person may be treated as a mere means not only by coercion and deceit, but also by any conduct intended to achieve the purpose of treating that person as an object and not at the same time an intrinsically valuable moral subject. The intention determines the treating as a mere means, not the success of the method by which it is carried out. Next, a person treats himself or herself as a mere means by voluntarily agreeing to be the object of conduct by which another intends to treat him or her as a mere means, where that intention is known. Last, such a relationship is mutually exploitative; a person who wishes to use another as a mere means cannot be acting from reason, in a Kantian sense, and therefore is in turn used as a mere means by another who consents to being so used.

These conclusions are drawn from cases of sexually using another as a mere means, but I see no problem in applying them elsewhere. They explain, for example, the wrongfulness many people intuitively saw in the dwarf-throwing contests that attracted media attention a few years ago.[6] Despite protests from the dwarfs involved that they were freely choosing to accept this employment as human projectiles, the sense shared by most observers, I think, was that a point of the game was that the dwarfs be treated as mere things. The dwarfs were being hired not just for the fact that they were projectiles of a desired shape or weight, but in order that human beings might be treated as non-rational, non-sentient objects. If those human projectiles did not see this, they did not do wrong, although we may be inclined to pity them. If they knew that their wrongful treatment was a purpose of the game, then they were wronging themselves and also exploiting their exploiters. This is explained by my interpretation of Kant's injunction against treating any person, including oneself, as a mere means to an end.

Study Questions

1. On what grounds does Klepper conclude that sexual relationships leave "people particularly vulnerable to feeling used"? What other sorts of relationships also or likely share these features? Does that make them wrong? Might sexual and other relationships have redeeming qualities that at least partially overcome these defects?

2. If, as Klepper claims, "intention determines the treating as a mere means," have I exploited a prostitute if my big-hearted intention is to enable her to buy food for her children? In general, do our intentions determine whether our actions are right or wrong, or are they relevant only in making judgments about our moral characters?

3. Consider the claim that "consent to being abused or degraded does not render the abuse or degradation moral." Would Mappes (chapter 16) or Kant agree or disagree (chapter 18)? Does the claim imply that consensual sadomasochistic sexual acts are immoral (if we assume they involve consensual degradation)? Similarly, does the claim imply that it is immoral for a person to consent to being sexually used? What is morally wrong, if anything, for two mutually consenting adults to use and be used by each other sexually? (See John Finnis, chapter 9.)

4. Klepper speaks about "our cultural norms" that obligate us to treat a lover "as an intrinsically valuable moral subject." Might we argue that these cultural norms are in need of revision? Are they somehow written in stone? Our society, or large segments of it, apparently accepts or tolerates casual sex, extramarital sex, promiscuity, and various kinds of sex work. Does this fact weaken Klepper's arguments that are grounded on his view of what "our" norms are?

5. If we were to agree with Klepper that our moral obligations to our sex partners only begin with free and informed consent, and must be supplemented with other considerations, where do our obligations to others (or to ourselves) in sexual contexts come to

an end? Why add *only* "show consideration" to the other person? Why not also add, as Karol Wojtyla does (chapter 11), that another necessary condition is that birth-control techniques not be employed? Or any number of other restrictive moral considerations?

Notes

1. Immanuel Kant, *Lectures on Ethics*, trans. L. Infield (London: The Century Co., 1930).

2. Ibid., pp. 166–67, 170.

3. Thomas Mappes, "Sexual Morality and the Concept of Using Another Person," in Thomas Mappes and Jane Zembaty, eds., *Social Ethics*, 4th ed. (New York: McGraw-Hill, 1992). (See chapter 16.)

4. Much philosophical writing on the subject of sex only discusses activity which precedes sexual acts. Thomas Nagel's seminal essay "Sexual Perversion," *Journal of Philosophy* 66 (1969), is typical in its focus on attraction and arousal. Nagel has been criticized for this truncated account (Janice Moulton, "Sexual Behavior: Another Position," *Journal of Philosophy* 73 [1976]). (See chapters 3 and 4.)

5. Kant, *Lectures on Ethics*, p.166.

6. "Little People Oppose Events in Which Dwarfs Are Objects," *The New York Times*, 3 July 1992, p. 8, col. 1.

Chapter 18

SEXUAL USE

Alan Soble

*If sexual desire is, by its nature, directed toward another person as an object; if the experience of sexual desire itself challenges a person's rationality and autonomy; and if while engaging in sexual activity, people are essentially making use of each other as instruments of their own pleasure—then sexuality seems, on account of its own nature, morally suspicious or even, in the absence of special overriding excuses that yield justifiable exceptions, morally wrong. This is what **Alan Soble** calls the "Kantian sex problem." It cannot be answered by saying merely that we must nevertheless engage in sex to keep the human population going. Not only does that answer ignore that Christians, including St. Paul and St. Augustine, were not persuaded that there was any religious or theological requirement—given the grand narrative story that comprises Christianity—to keep earthly humanity going, it also commits one to a teleological solution to what is a deontological ethical tangle. The task here is not to sidestep the problem by denying the Kantian account of the natures of sexual desire and sexual activity, by denying the validity of the Second Formulation of Kant's Categorical Imperative, or by denying his anthropology or ontology of the human person (our characteristic rational autonomy; our inherent worth or dignity), but to fashion a sexual ethics consistent with all three sets of assumptions that entail that sex is not, after all, as morally pernicious as these Kantian considerations suggest. Soble proposes a typology of various recently offered solutions and critically discusses each type, finding them lacking in some way or another. He also examines the writings of Kant, trying to understand the passages in which Kant himself tries to solve the problem.*

I begin by describing the hideous nature of sexuality, in virtue of which sexual desire and activity are morally suspicious, or what we have been told about the foulness of sex by Immanuel Kant.[1] I then explain, given Kant's metaphysics of sex, why sexual activity apparently conflicts with the Second Formulation of the Categorical Imperative. I propose a typology of solutions to this problem and critically discuss recent philosophical ethics of sex that fall within the typology. I conclude with remarks about Kant's own solution.

The Nature of Sex

On Kant's view, a person who sexually desires another person objectifies the other both before and during sexual activity. Manipulation and deception—primping, padding, making a good first impression—are so common as to seem natural to human sexual interaction.[2] The other's body, his or her lips, thighs, buttocks, and toes, are desired as the arousing parts they are, distinct from the person. As Kant says, about the genitals,

> sexuality is not an inclination which one human being has for another as such, but is an inclination for the sex of another. . . . [O]nly her sex is the object of his desires. . . . [A]ll men and women do their best to make not their human nature but their sex more alluring.[3]

Further, both the body and the compliant actions of the other person are tools—a means—one uses for one's own sexual pleasure, and to that extent the other person is a thing. Sexual activity itself is strange, not only by manifesting unwilled arousal and involuntary bodily movements, but also with its yearning to master, dominate, and consume the other's body. Sexual desire is a threat to the other's personhood, but the one under the spell of desire also loses hold of his or her own personhood. The person who desires another depends on the whims of that other for satisfaction, and becomes as a result a jellyfish, vulnerable to the other's demands and manipulations.[4] Merely being sexually aroused by another person can be experienced as coercive; similarly, a person who proposes an irresistible sexual offer may be exploiting another who has been made weak by sexual desire.[5] Moreover, a person who willingly complies with another person's request for a sexual encounter voluntarily makes an object of himself or herself. As Kant puts it, "For the natural use that one sex makes of the other's sexual organs is *enjoyment*, for which one gives oneself up to the other. In this act a human being makes himself into a thing."[6] And, for Kant, because those engaged in sexual activity make themselves into objects merely for the sake of sexual pleasure, both persons reduce themselves to animals. When a man wishes to satisfy his desire, and a woman hers, they stimulate each other's desire; their inclinations meet, but their object is not human nature but sex, and each of them dishonours the human nature of the other. They make of humanity an instrument for the satisfaction of their lusts and inclinations, and dishonour it by placing it on a level with animal nature.[7]

Finally, the power of the sexual urge makes it dangerous. Sexual desire is inelastic, relentless, the passion most likely to challenge reason and make us succumb to *akrasia*, compelling us to seek satisfaction even when doing so involves the risks of dark-alley gropings, microbiologically filthy acts, slinking around the White House, or getting married impetuously. Sexually motivated behavior easily destroys our self-respect.

The sexual impulse, then, is morally dubious and, to boot, a royal pain. Kant thought that humans would be delighted to be free of such promptings: "Inclinations . . . , as sources of needs, are so far from having an absolute value to make them desirable for their own sake that it must rather be the universal wish of every rational being to be wholly free from them."[8] I am not sure I believe all these claims about the nature of sexuality, but that is irrelevant, since many philosophers, with good reason, have taken them seriously. In some moods I might reply to Kant by muttering a Woody Allen joke: "Is sex an autonomy-killing, mind-numbing, subhuman passion? Yes, but only when it's good." In this essay, however, I want to examine how sexual acts could be moral, if Kant's description is right.

Sex and the Second Formulation

Michael Ruse has explained how a moral problem arises in acting on sexual desire:

> The starting point to sex is the sheer desire of a person for the body of another. One wants to feel the skin, to smell the hair, to see the eyes—one wants to bring one's own genitals into contact with those of the other. . . . This gets dangerously close to treating the other as a means to the fulfillment of one's own sexual desire—as an object, rather than as an end.[9]

We should add, to make Ruse's observation more comprehensively Kantian, that the desire to be touched, to be thrilled by the touch of the other, to be the object of someone else's desire, is just as much "the starting point" that raises the moral problem.

Because this sex problem arises from the intersection of Kant's view of the nature of sexuality and Kant's ethics, let us review the Second Formulation: "Act in such a way that you always treat humanity, whether in your own person or in the person of any other, never simply as a means, but always at the same time as an end." Or "man . . . *exists* as an end in himself, *not merely as a means* for arbitrary use by this or that will: he must in all his actions, whether they are directed to himself or to other rational beings, always be viewed *at the same time as an end.*"[10] The question arises: how can sexual desire be satisfied without merely using the other or treating the other as an object, and without treating the self as an object? How can sexual activity be planned and carried out while "at the same time" treating the other and the self as persons, treating their "humanity" as an end and confirming their autonomy and rationality? The Second Formulation directs us not to treat ourselves and others *merely* as means or objects. Permissible is treating another and ourselves as means as long as at the same time we are also treated as persons or our humanity is treated as an end. Can this be done?

A person's providing free and informed consent to interactions with other persons is, in general for Kant, a necessary condition for satisfying the Second Formulation. But it is not sufficient. In addition, treating someone as a person at least includes taking on the other's ends as if they were one's own ends: "the ends of a subject who is an end in himself must, if this conception is to have its *full* effect in me, be also, as far as possible, *my* ends."[11] I must take on the other's ends for their *own* sake, not because doing so is effective in advancing my own goals. It is further required, when I treat another as a means, that the other can take on my ends, my purpose, in so using him or her as a means:

> the man who has a mind to make a false promise to others will see at once that he is intending to make use of another man *merely as a means* to an end he does not share. For the man whom I seek to use for my own purposes by such a promise cannot possibly agree with my way of behaving to him, and so cannot himself share the end of [my] action."[12]

Given Kant's metaphysics of sexuality, can all these requirements of the Second Formulation be satisfied in sexual interaction? That is the Kantian sex problem.

It should be noted that even though Kant advances these two conditions in addition to free and informed consent—I must take on your ends, and you must take on my ends—he apparently relaxes his standard for some situations, allowing one person to use another just with the free and informed consent of the used person, as long as one allows the used person to *retain* personhood or one does *not interfere* with his or her retaining personhood. This weaker test for satisfying the Second Formulation may be important in Kant's account of the morality of work-for-hire and of sexual relations.[13]

I now proceed to display a conceptual typology of various solutions to the Kantian sex problem, and discuss critically whether solutions that occupy different logical locations in the typology conform with the Second

Formulation. There are five types of solution: behavioral internalism, psychological internalism, thin externalism, thick minimalist externalism, and thick extended externalism.

Internalist Solutions

Internalist solutions to the sex problem advise us to modify the character of sexual activity so that persons engaged in it satisfy the Second Formulation. For internalists, restraints on how sexual acts are carried out, or restraints on the expression of the impulse, are required. Consent, then, is not sufficient for the morality of sexual acts, even if necessary. Note that one might fix a sexual act internally so that *qua* sexual act the act is unobjectionable, but it still might be wrong for other reasons; for example, it might be adulterous. There are two internalisms: *behavioral* internalism, according to which the physical components of sexual acts make the moral difference, and *psychological* internalism, according to which certain attitudes must be present during sexual activity.

Behavioral Internalism

Alan Goldman defines "sexual desire" as the "desire for contact with another person's body and for the pleasure which such contact produces. . . . The desire for another's body is . . . the desire for the pleasure that physical contact brings."[14] Since sexual desire is a desire for one's own pleasure, it is understandable that Goldman senses a Kantian problem. Thus Goldman writes that sexual activities "invariably involve at different stages the manipulation of one's partner for one's own pleasure" and thereby, he notes, seem to violate the Second Formulation—which, on Goldman's truncated rendition, "holds that one ought not to treat another as a means to such private ends." (Kant would have said "subjective," "discretionary," or "arbitrary" ends, instead of "private," but he would be making the same point.) But Goldman suggests that from a Kantian perspective, "using other individuals for personal benefit," in sex or other interactions, is wrong "only when [the acts] are one-sided, when the benefits are not mutual." So, as a solution to the sex problem, Goldman proposes that "Even in an act which by its nature 'objectifies' the other, one recognizes a partner as a subject with demands and desires by yielding to those desires, by allowing oneself to be a sexual object as well, by giving pleasure or ensuring that the pleasures of the act are mutual." This sexual moral principle—make sure to provide sexual pleasure for your partner—seems plausible and least in spirit consistent with the Second Formulation.[15]

But *why* might one sexually please the other? (Pleasing the other person can be done, as Goldman recognizes, by actively doing something to the other, or by allowing the other person to treat us as an object, so that they do things as we passively acquiesce.) One answer comes from sexual egoism or hedonism: pleasing the other is *necessary for or contributes to one's own pleasure.* How so?—by inducing the other, through either the other's sexual arousal or gratitude, to furnish pleasure to oneself. Or because sexually pleasing the other satisfies one's desire to exert power or influence over the other. Or because in providing pleasure to the other we get pleasure by witnessing the effects of our exertions.[16] Or by causing the other to hold us in an esteem that heightens our arousal. Or because while giving pleasure to the other person we identify with his or her arousal and pleasure, which identification increases our own arousal and pleasure.[17] Or because pleasing the other alleviates or prevents guilt feelings, or doing so makes us feel good that we have kept a promise. Or. . . .

Another answer is that providing pleasure to the other can *and should* be done for the sake of pleasing the other, just because you know the other person has sexual needs and desires and hopes for their satisfaction. The sexual satisfaction of the other is an end in itself, is valuable in its own right, is not merely instrumentally valuable. It follows that in some circumstances you must be willing and ready to please the other person sexually when doing so does not contribute to your own satisfaction or even runs counter to it. (Kant likes to focus on this sort of scenario in the *Groundwork,* cases that single out the motive of benevolence or duty from motives based on inclination.)

I categorized Goldman as a behavioral internalist because all he insists on, in order to make sexual activity Kantianly morally permissible, is the *behavior* of providing pleasure for the other person. Goldman never claims that providing pleasure be done with a benevolent *motive* or purity of purpose. But this feature of his proposal is exactly why it fails, in its *own* terms. If providing pleasure to the other is a mechanism for attaining or improving one's own pleasure, providing pleasure to the other continues to treat the other merely as a means. Since giving pleasure to the other is instrumental in obtaining my pleasure, giving pleasure has not at all succeeded in internally *fixing* the nature of the sexual act. Providing pleasure can be a genuine internalist solution, by changing the nature of the sexual act, only if providing pleasure is an unconditional giving. Goldman's proposal thus fails to accommodate his own Kantian commitment. When Kant claims that we must treat the other as a person by taking on his or her ends as our own—by providing sexual pleasure, if that is his or her end—Kant does not mean that as a hypothetical, as if taking on the other's ends were a mechanism for getting the other person to allow us to treat him or her as a means. We must not take on the other's ends as our own simply because doing so is useful for us in generating our own pleasure or achieving our own sexual goals. Sharing the ends of the other person means viewing those ends as valuable in their own right.

Further, for Kant, we may take on the ends of the other as our own only if the other's ends are themselves morally permissible: I may "make the other's ends my ends provided only that these are not immoral."[18] Given the objectification and use involved in sexual activity, as conceded by Goldman, the moral permissibility of the end of seeking sexual pleasure by means of another person has not yet been established for *either* party. We are not to make the other's ends our own ends if the other's ends are not, in themselves, already morally permissible, and whether the sexual ends of the other person *are* permissible is precisely the question at issue. Thus, to be told by Goldman that it is morally permissible for one person to objectify another in sexual activity if the other also objectifies the first, with the first's allowance, does not answer the question. Goldman's internalist solution attempts to change the nature of the sexual act, from what it is essentially to what it might be were we to embrace *slightly* better bedroom behavior, by avoiding raw selfishness. But this doesn't go far enough to fix the nature of sexual activity, if all that is required is that both parties add the giving of pleasure to an act that is by its nature, and remains, self-centered. Finally (and *perhaps* most important), Goldman ignores, in Kant's statement of the Second Formulation, that we must also respect the humanity *in one's own person*. To make oneself voluntarily an object for the sake of the other person's sexual pleasure, as Goldman recommends, only multiplies the use; it does not eliminate it.

Goldman has, in effect, changed the problem from one of sexual objectification and use to one of distributive justice.[19] Sex is morally permissible, on his view, if the pleasure is mutual; the way to make sexual activity moral is to make it nonmorally good for both participants. Use and objectification remain, but they are permissible, on his view, because the objectification is reciprocal and the act is mutually beneficial. Even though in one sense Goldman makes sexual activity moral by making it *more* nonmorally good, for the *other* party, he also makes sexual activity moral by making it *less* nonmorally good, for the *self*, since one's sexual urgings must be restrained. What goes morally wrong in sexual activity, for Goldman, is that only one person experiences pleasure (or lopsidedly) and only one bears the burden of providing it. This is what Goldman means by saying that "one-sided" sexual activity is immoral. The benefits of receiving pleasure, and the burdens of the restraint of seeking pleasure and providing it to the other, must be passed around to everyone involved. This is accomplished, for Goldman, by a reciprocal distribution of being used as an object.

Suppose, instead, that both parties are expected to inject *unconditional* giving into an act that is essentially self-centered. Then both parties must buckle down more formidably, in order to restrain their impulses for their own pleasure and to provide pleasure to the other. But if altruistic giving were easy, given our natures, there would be less reason for thinking, to begin with, that sexual desire tends to use the other person in a self-interested way. To the extent that the sexual impulse is self-interested, as Goldman's definitions make clear, it is implausible that sexual urges could be controlled by a moral command to provide pleasure unconditionally. The point is not only that a duty to provide pleasure unconditionally threatens the nonmoral goodness of sexual acts, that it reduces the sexual excitement and satisfaction of both persons. Fulfilling such a duty, if we assume Goldman's account of sexual desire, may be impossible or unlikely.

Psychological Internalism

If Goldman wants to fix the sexual act internally, to change its nature, he must insist not merely on our performing behaviors that produce pleasure for the other, but on our producing pleasure for a certain reason. In this way, we move from behavioral to psychological internalism, which claims that sexual acts must be accompanied and restrained by certain attitudes, the presence of which ensure the satisfaction of the Second Formulation.

At one point in her essay "Defining Wrong and Defining Rape," Jean Hampton lays out a view that is similar to Goldman's, in which the occurrence of mutual pleasure alone solves the sex problem: "when sex is as much about pleasing another as it is about pleasing oneself, it certainly doesn't involve using another as a means and actually incorporates the idea of respect and concern for another's needs."[20] Providing sexual pleasure to the other person seems to Hampton to satisfy Kant's Second Formulation. But she goes beyond Goldman in attempting to understand the depth or significance of the sexual experience:

> one's humanity is perhaps never more engaged than in the sexual act. But it is not only present in the experience; more important, it is "at stake" in the sense that each partner puts him/herself in a position where the behavior of the other can either confirm it or threaten it, celebrate it or abuse it.[21]

This point is Kantian: sex is metaphysically and psychologically dangerous. Hampton continues:

> If this is right, then I do not see how, for most normal human beings, sexual passion is heightened if one's sexual partner behaves in a way that one finds personally humiliating or that induces in one shame or self-hatred or that

makes one feel like a "thing." . . . Whatever sexual passion is, such emotions seem antithetical to it, and such emotions are markers of the disrespect that destroys the morality of the experience. . . . [W]hat makes a sexual act morally right is also what provides the groundwork for the experience of emotions and pleasures that make for "good sex."[22]

If the wrongness of the act is a function of its diminishing nature, then that wrongness can be present even if, ex ante, each party consented to the sex. So . . . consent is *never by itself* that which makes a sexual act morally right. . . . Lovemaking is a set of experiences . . . which includes attitudes and behaviors that are different in kind from the attitudes and behaviors involved in morally wrongful sex.[23]

Hampton's thesis, as I understand it, is that sexual activity must be accompanied by certain humanity-affirming attitudes or emotions that manifest themselves in the sexual activity itself. Attitudes and emotions that repudiate humanity, that are disrespectful, are morally wrong and (because) destructive of mutual pleasure.[24] Hampton's psychological internalism seems fairly consistent with Kant's Second Formulation: for Hampton, consent may be necessary but it is not sufficient for behaving morally or respectfully toward another person sexually; giving pleasure to the other person, taking on their sexual ends, is required; and *why* the persons produce pleasure for each other is morally relevant. But Kant would still object to Hampton's view, even though he might admit that she is on the right track. The willingness to provide, selflessly, sexual pleasure for the other, for Kant, does not erase the fundamentally objectifying nature of sexual activity. And the nonmarital (even if humanity-affirming) sexual activity that is in principle justifiable by Hampton's criterion would be rejected by Kant as immoral.

Hampton's view apparently entails that casual sex, in which both parties are out to satisfy their own randiness, is morally wrong, along with prostitution, since these sexual acts are not likely to be, in some robust sense, humanity-affirming. Sadomasochism would also seem to be morally wrong, on her view, because they involve what Hampton sees as humanity-denying attitudes. Yet casual sex and prostitution, as objectifying and instrumental as they can be, and sadomasochistic sexual acts, as humiliating to one's partner as they can be, still often produce tremendous sexual excitement—contrary to what Hampton says about the coincidence of the moral and nonmoral goodness of sexual acts. For this reason I perceive a problem in Hampton's position. She believes, as does Goldman, that morally permissible sex involves mutual sexual pleasing, that the morality of sexual activity then depends on its nonmoral goodness, and, further, that disrespectful attitudes destroy this mutual pleasure. But are disrespectful attitudes morally wrong exactly because they destroy the other's sexual pleasure or because they are disrespectful? This question is important regarding Hampton's assessment of sado-masochism. For if her argument is that disrespectful attitudes that occur during sexual encounters are morally wrong because they are disrespect-ful, sadomasochistic sexual activities are morally wrong even if they do, *contra* Hampton's intuition, produce pleasure for the participants. (If so, Hampton may be what I later call an "externalist.") But if her argument is that disrespectful attitudes are wrong because or when they destroy the mutuality of the pleasure, then sadomasochism does not turn out to be morally wrong. (In this case, Hampton remains an internalist.)

Perhaps Hampton means that sexual activity is morally permissible only when it is *both* mutually pleasure-producing *and* incorporates humanity-affirming attitudes. This dual test for the morality of sexual en-counters prohibits casual sex between strangers, prostitution, as well as sadomasochistic sexuality, no matter how sexually satisfying these activi-ties are. In Hampton's essay, however, I could find no clear criterion of "humanity-affirming" other than "provides mutual pleasure." This is why she has trouble denying the permissibility of sadomasochism. Consider the lesbian sadomasochist Pat Califia on sadomasochism: "The things that seem beautiful, inspiring, and life-affirming to me seem ugly, hate-ful, and ludicrous to most other people."[25] As far as I can tell, Califia means "provides sexual pleasure" by "life-affirming." If so, no disagree-ment in principle exists between Hampton and Califia, if Hampton means "provides pleasure" by "humanity-affirming." What Hampton does not take seriously is Califia's point that brutal behaviors and hu-miliating attitudes that occur during sexual activity can make for mutu-ally exciting and pleasurable sex.

Externalist Solutions

According to *externalism*, morality requires that we place restraints on when sexual acts are engaged in, with whom sexual activity occurs, or on the conditions under which sexual activities are performed. Properly set-ting the background context in which sexual acts occur enables us to sat-isfy the Second Formulation. One distinction among externalisms is that between *minimalist* externalism, which claims that morality requires that only the context of the sexual activity be set, and the sexual acts may be whatever they turn out to be, and *extended* externalism, which claims that setting the context will also affect the character of the sexual acts. An-other distinction among externalisms is that between *thin* externalism, according to which free and informed consent is both necessary and suf-ficient for the moral permissibility of sexual acts (with a trivial *ceteris*

paribus clause), and *thick* externalism, which claims that something beyond consent is required for the morality of sexual activity.

Thin Externalism

Thomas Mappes argues that only weak contextual constraints are required for satisfying Kantian worries about sexual activity.[26] The giving
of free and informed consent by the persons involved in a sexual encounter is both necessary and sufficient for the morality of their sexual
activity, for making permissible the sexual use of one person by another
person.[27] Consent is not sufficient for the morality of sexual acts *sim-
pliciter*, because even though a sexual act might be morally permissible
qua sexual act, it still might be, for example, adulterous. Mappes's position is a thin minimalist externalism. Indeed, thin externalism, defined
as making consent both necessary and sufficient, must also be minimalist. This criterion of the morality of sexual activity is contentless, or fully
procedural: it does not evaluate the form or the nature of the sexual act
(what body parts are involved; in what manner the acts are carried out),
but only the antecedent and concurrent conditions or context in which
the sexual act takes place. In principle, the acts engaged in need not
even produce (mutual) pleasure for the participants, an implication that
differs from Goldman's behavioral internalism.

Mappes, while developing his theory of sexual ethics, begins by repeating a point made frequently about Kantian ethics: "According to a
fundamental Kantian principle, it is morally wrong for A to use B *merely
as a means* (to achieve A's ends). Kant's principle does not rule out A using B as a means, only A using B *merely* as a means, that is, in a way incompatible with respect for B as a person." Then Mappes lays out his
central thesis: "A immorally uses B if and only if A intentionally acts in a
way that violates the requirement that B's involvement with A's ends be
based on B's voluntary informed consent." For Mappes, the presence of
free and informed consent—there is no deception and no coercive force
or threats—satisfies the Second Formulation, since each person's providing consent ensures that the persons involved in sexual activity with
each other are not *merely* or *wrongfully* using each other as means.
Mappes intends that this principle be applied to any activity, whether
sexual or otherwise; he believes, along with Goldman, that sexual activity should be governed by moral principles that apply in general to human behavior.

Mappes spends almost all his essay discussing various situations that
might, or might not, involve violating the free and informed consent criterion. He discusses what acts are deceptive, coercive (by force or
threat), or exploitative, in which case sexual activity made possible by

such maneuvers would be morally wrong. Some of these cases are intriguing, as anyone familiar with the literature on the meaning and application of the free and informed consent criterion in the area of medical ethics knows. But, putting aside for now the important question of the sufficiency of consent, not everyone agrees that in sexual (or other) contexts free and informed consent is absolutely necessary. Jeffrie Murphy, for one, has raised some doubts:

> "Have sex with me or I will find another girlfriend" strikes me (assuming normal circumstances) as a morally permissible threat, and "Have sex with me and I will marry you" strikes me (assuming the offer is genuine) as a morally permissible offer. . . . We negotiate our way through most of life with schemes of threats and offers . . . and I see no reason why the realm of sexuality should be utterly insulated from this very normal way of being human.[28]

Both "Have sex with me or I will find another girlfriend" and "Marry me or I will never sleep with you again (or at all)" seem to be coercive yet permissible threats,[29] but sexual activity obtained by the employment of these coercions involves immoral use, on Mappes's criterion. Further, it is not difficult to imagine circumstances in which deception in sexual contexts is not morally wrong (even if we ignore the universal and innocuous practice of the deceptive use of cosmetics and clothing). Mappes claims that my *withholding* information from you, information that would influence your decision as to whether to have sexual relations with me, is deception that makes any subsequent sexual activity between us morally wrong. But if I withhold the fact that I have an extraordinarily large or minuscule penis, and withholding that fact about my sexual anatomy plays a role in your eventually agreeing to engage in sex with me, it is not obviously true that my obtaining sex through this particular deception-by-omission is morally wrong. I suspect that such cases tend to show that we cannot rely comprehensively on a consent criterion to answer all (or perhaps any of) our pressing questions about sexual morality. Does the other person have a *right* to know the size of my penis while deliberating whether to have sex with me? What types of coercive threat do we have a *right* to employ in trying to achieve our goals? These significant questions cannot be answered by a free and informed consent criterion; they also suggest that reading the Second Formulation such that consent by itself can satisfy the Second Formulation is questionable.

Indeed, Mappes provides little reason for countenancing his unKantian notion that the presence of free and informed consent is a sufficient condition for the satisfaction of the Second Formulation, for not treating another person merely as a means or not wrongfully using him or her. He does write that "respect for persons entails that each of us recognize the rightful authority of other persons (as rational beings) to conduct their individual lives as they see fit," which suggests the following kind of argument: Allowing the other's consent to control when the other may be used for my sexual ends is to respect that person by taking his or her autonomy, his or her ability to reason and make choices, seriously, while not to allow the other to make the decision about when to be used for my sexual ends is disrespectfully paternalistic. If the other's consent is acknowledged to be sufficient, that shows that I respect his or her choice of ends; or that even if I do not respect his or her particular choice of ends, at least I thereby show respect for his or her ends-making capacity or for his or her being a self-determining agent. And taking the other's consent as sufficient can be a way of taking on his or her sexual ends as my own ends, as well as his or her taking on my sexual ends in my proposing to use him or her. According to such an argument, perhaps the best way to read Kant's Second Formulation is as a pronouncement of moral libertarianism, or a quasi-libertarianism that also, as Mappes does, pays attention to situations that are ripe for exploitation.[30]

Even if the argument makes Kantian sense, Mappes's sexual principle seems to miss the point. The Kantian problem about sexuality is not, or is not only, that one person might make false promises, engage in deception, or employ force or threats against another person in order to gain sex. The problem of the objectification and use of both the self and the other arises for Kant even when, or especially when, both persons give perfectly free and informed consent. Thin externalism does not get to the heart of *this* problem. Perhaps no liberal philosophy that borders on moral libertarianism could even sense it as a problem; at any rate, no minimalist externalism could. The only sexual objectification that Mappes considers in his essay is that which arises with coercion, most dramatically in rape. Nothing in his essay deals with what Kant and other philosophers discern as the intrinsically objectifying nature of sexuality itself. As Goldman does, Mappes assimilates sexual activity to all other human activities, all of which should be governed by the same moral principles. Whether Mappes's proposal works will depend, then, in part on whether sex is not so different from other joint human activities that free and informed consent is not too weak a criterion in this area of life.

It is an interesting question why free and informed consent does not, for Kant, solve the sex problem. It seems so obvious to many today that Mappes's consent criterion solves the sex problem that we wonder what Kant was up to in his metaphysical critique of sexuality. Kant's rejection of Mappes's solution suggests that Kant perceived deeper problems in sexual desire and activity than Mappes and Goldman acknowledge. In

the *Lectures on Ethics*, Kant apparently accepts a Mappesian consent criterion regarding work-for-hire, but rejects it for sexual activity:

> Man [may], of course, use another human being as an instrument for his
> services; he [may] use his hands, his feet, and even all his powers; he [may]
> use him for his own purposes with the other's consent. But there is no way
> in which a human being can be made an Object of indulgence for another
> except through sexual impulse.[31]

For Kant, it seems that using another person in a work-for-hire situation
is permissible, just with free and informed consent, as long as one does
not undermine or deny the worker's humanity in any other way. But
Kant finds something problematic about sexual interaction that does
not exist during, say, a tennis game between two people (or in a work-
for-hire situation), while Mappes sees no moral difference between playing tennis with someone and playing with their genitals. This disagreement between philosophers who view sexual activity as something or as
somehow special, and philosophers who lump all human interactions together, requires further thought.

Thick Externalism

Thick externalism claims that more stringent contextual constraints, beyond free and informed consent, are required for the morality of sexual
activity. My central example is Martha Nussbaum's essay "Objectification," in which she submits that the Kantian sex problem is solved if sexual activity is confined to the context of an abiding, mutually respectful,
and mutually regarding relationship. However, Nussbaum advances
both a thick minimalist externalism and a thick extended externalism.
In her long and complex essay, we find at least two theses: (1) a background context of an abiding, mutually respectful relationship makes
noxious objectification during sexual activity morally *permissible*; and (2)
a background context of an abiding, mutually respectful relationship
turns what might have been noxious objectification into something *good*
or even "wonderful," a valuable type of objectification in which autonomy is happily abandoned, a thesis she derives from her reading of D. H.
Lawrence.

Thick Minimalist Externalism

In several passages, Nussbaum proposes a thick minimalist externalism,
according to which sexual objectification is morally permissible in the

context of an abiding, mutually respectful relationship. Consider this modest statement of her general thesis:

> If I am lying around with my lover on the bed, and use his stomach as a pillow, there seems to be nothing at all baneful about this [instrumental objectification], provided that I do so with his consent . . . and without causing him pain, provided, as well, that I do so in the context of a relationship in which he is generally treated as more than a pillow. This suggests that what is problematic is not instrumentalization per se but treating someone *primarily* or *merely* as an instrument [for example, as a pillow]. The overall context of the relationship thus becomes fundamental.[32]

We can modify this passage so that Nussbaum's general point about permissible instrumental objectification-in-context can be applied more directly to the sex problem:

> If I am lying around with my lover on the bed, and use his penis for my sexual satisfaction, there seems to be nothing at all baneful about this instrumental objectification, provided that I do so with his consent . . . and without causing him pain, provided, as well, that I do so in the context of a relationship in which he is generally treated as more than a penis. This suggests that what is problematic is not instrumentalization per se but treating someone *primarily* or *merely* as an instrument [for example, as a penis]. The overall context of the relationship thus becomes fundamental.

Other passages in Nussbaum's essay also express her thick minimalist externalism: "where there is a loss in subjectivity in the moment of lovemaking, this can be and frequently is accompanied by an intense concern for the subjectivity of the partner *at other moments.*"[33] Again: "When there is a loss of autonomy in sex, the context . . . can be . . . one in which, on the whole, autonomy is respected and promoted"[34] And "denial of autonomy and denial of subjectivity are objectionable if they persist throughout an adult relationship, but *as phases* in a relationship characterized by mutual regard they can be all right, or even quite wonderful."[35]

One of Nussbaum's theses, then, is that a loss of autonomy, subjectivity, and individuality in sex, and the reduction of a person to his or her sexual body or its parts, in which the person is or becomes a tool or object, are morally acceptable if they occur within the background context of a psychologically healthy and morally sound relationship, an abiding relationship in which one's personhood—one's autonomy, subjectivity, and individuality—is generally respected and acknowledged. This solution to the sex problem seems plausible. It confirms the common (even if sexually conservative) intuition that one difference between morally permissible sexual acts and those that are wrongful because they are merely mutual use is the difference between sexual acts that occur in the context of a loving or caring relationship and those that occur in the absence of love, mutual care, or concern. Further, it appeals to our willingness to tolerate, exculpate, or bless (as the partners' own private business) whatever nastiness that occurs in bed between two people *as long as* the rest, and the larger segment, of their relationship is morally sound. The lovers may sometimes engage in objectifying sexual games, by role-playing boss and secretary, client and prostitute, or teacher and student (phases of their relationship in which autonomy, subjectivity, and individuality might be sacrificed), since *outside* these occasional sexual games, they do display respect for each other and abidingly support each other's humanity.

But this solution to the sex problem is inconsistent with Kant's Second Formulation, for that moral principle requires that a person be treated as an end *at the same time* he or she is being treated as a means. On Nussbaum's thick minimalist externalism, small, sexually vulgar chunks of a couple's relationship, small pieces of noxious sexual objectification, are morally permissible in virtue of the larger or more frequent heavenly chunks of mutual respect that comprise their relationship. But it is not, in general, right (except, perhaps, for some utilitarians) that my treating you badly today is either *justified* or *excusable* if I treated you admirably the whole day yesterday and will treat you more superbly tomorrow and the next day. As Nussbaum acknowledges, Kant insists that we ought not to treat someone *merely* as means, instrumentally, or as an object, but by that qualification Kant does not mean that treating someone as a means, instrumentally, or as an object at *some* particular time is morally permissible as long as he or she is treated with respect as a full person at *other* particular times.[36] That Nussbaum's thick minimalist externalist solution to Kant's sex problem violates the Second Formulation in this way is not the fault of the details of her account of the proper background context; the problem arises whether the background context is postulated to be one of abiding mutual respect and regard, or love, or marriage, or something else. Any version of thick minimalist externalism violates Kant's prescription that someone who is treated as a means must be treated *at the same time* as an end. Thick minimalist externalism fails because, unlike behavioral or psychological internalism, it makes no attempt to improve or fix the nature of sexual activity itself. It leaves sexual activity exactly as it was or would be, as essentially objectifying or instrumental, although it claims that even when having this character, it is morally permissible.

Thick Extended Externalism

Thick extended externalism tries to have it both ways: to justify sexual activity when it occurs within the proper context *and* to fix the nature of the sexual acts that occur in that context. So Nussbaum's second proposal would seem to stand a better chance of conforming with the Second Formulation. In explaining the thesis that sexual objectification can be a wonderful or good thing in the proper context, Nussbaum says that in Lawrence's *Lady Chatterley's Lover,*

> both parties put aside their individuality and become identified with their bodily organs. They see one another in terms of those organs. And yet Kant's suggestion that in all such focusing on parts there is denial of humanity seems quite wrong. . . . The intense focusing of attention on the bodily parts seems an *addition,* rather than a subtraction.[37]

Nussbaum means that being reduced to one's body or its parts is an addition to one's personhood, not a subtraction from it, *as long as* the background context of an abiding, mutually respectful relationship exists, as she assumes it did between Constance Chatterley and Oliver Mellors. Nussbaum is claiming that sexual objectification, the reduction of a person to his or her flesh, and the loss of individuality and autonomy in sexual activity, can be a wonderful or good aspect of life and sexuality. Being reduced to one's flesh, to one's genitals, supplements, or is an expansion or extension of, one's humanity, as long as it happens in a psychologically healthy and morally sound relationship.

Nussbaum goes so far in this reasoning as to make the astonishing assertion that "In Lawrence, being treated as a cunt is a permission to expand the sphere of one's activity and fulfillment."[38] In the ablutionary context of an abiding relationship of mutual respect, it is permissible and good for persons to descend fully to the level of their bodies, to become "cock" and "cunt," to become identified with their genitals, because in the rest of the relationship they are treated as *whole* persons. Or, more precisely, the addition of the objectification of being sexually reduced to their flesh *makes* their personhoods whole (it is, as Nussbaum writes, not a "subtraction"), as if without such a descent into their flesh they would remain partial, incomplete persons. This is suggested when Nussbaum writes, "Lawrence shows how a kind of sexual objectification . . . , how the very surrender of autonomy in a certain sort of sex act can free energies that can be used to make the self *whole and full.*"[39] I suppose it is a metaphysical truth that to be whole and full, I must realize all my potential. But some of this potential, it is not unreasonable to think, should not be realized, just because it would be immoral or perversely and stupidly imprudent to do so. Shall I, a professor of philosophy, fulfill my humanity by standing on street corners in the Bronx and try homosexual tricking? Recall Kant: I may take on the other's ends only if those ends are themselves moral. Similarly, I may supplement or try to attain the fullness of my humanity only in ways that are moral. Whether adding to my personhood the identification of myself with my genitals is moral is precisely the question at issue. Merely because reducing myself to my genitals is an "expansion" of myself and of my "sphere of . . . activity" does little to justify it.

In any event, one implication of Nussbaum's requirement of a background context of an abiding, mutually respectful relationship worries me, whether this background context is part of a thick minimalist or a thick extended externalism: casual sex turns out to be morally wrong. In the sexual activity that transpires between strangers or between those who do not have much or any mutual regard for each other, sexual objectification and instrumentalization make those sexual acts wrong, because there is no background context of the requisite sort that would either justify the sexual objectification or transform it into something good. Casual sex is a descent to the level of the genitals with nothing for the persons to hang on to, nothing that would allow them to pull themselves back up to personhood when their sexual encounter is over. (This is, in effect, what Kant claims about prostitution and concubinage.)[40] Nussbaum explicitly states this sexually conservative trend in her thought, and does not seem to consider it a weakness or defect of her account. Sounding like Kant, she writes:

> For in the absence of any narrative history with the person, how can desire attend to anything else but the incidental, and how can one do more than use the body of the other as a tool of one's own states? . . . Can one really treat someone with . . . respect and concern . . . if one has sex with him in the anonymous spirit? . . . [T]he instrumental treatment of human beings, the treatment of human beings as tools of the purposes of another, is always morally problematic; if it does not take place in a larger context of regard for humanity, it is a central form of the morally objectionable.[41]

Now, it is one thing to point out that Nussbaum's thick externalism is inimical to casual sex, or sex in the "anonymous spirit," for many would agree with her. Yet there is another point to be made. If noxious sexual objectification is permissible or made into something good only in the context of an abiding, mutually respectful relationship, then it is morally impermissible to engage in sexual activity in getting a relationship *underway*. The two persons may not engage in sexual activity early in their acquaintance, before they know whether they will come to have such an abiding and respectful relationship, because the sexual objectification of that premature sex could not be redeemed or cleansed—the requisite background context is missing. But, as some of us know, engaging in sexual activity, even when the persons do not know each other very well, often reveals to them important information about whether to pursue a relationship, whether to attempt to ascend to the abiding level. This is another aspect of Nussbaum's conservative turn: the persons must *first* have that abiding, mutually respectful relationship before engaging in sexual activity. It would be unconvincing to argue, in response, that sexual objectification in the early stages of their relationship is morally permissible, after all, because that sexual activity might contribute to the formation of an abiding, mutually respectful and regarding relationship that does succeed, later, in eliminating or cleansing the sexual objectification of the couple's sexual activity. That argument simply repeats in another form the dubious claim that morally bad phases or segments of a relationship are justified or excused in virtue of the larger or more frequent morally good segments of that relationship.

A similar problem arises in Nussbaum's discussion of sadomasochism. In response to her own question, "can sadomasochistic sexual acts ever have a simply Lawrentian character, rather than a more sinister character?" she replies:

> There seems to be no . . . reason why the answer . . . cannot be "yes." I have no very clear intuitions on this point, . . . but it would seem that some narrative depictions of sadomasochistic activity do plausibly attribute to its consensual form a kind of Lawrentian character in which the willingness to be vulnerable to the infliction of pain . . . manifests a more complete trust and receptivity than could be found in other sexual acts. Pat Califia's . . . short story ["Jessie"] is one example of such a portrayal.[42]

This is unconvincing (it also sounds more like a Hamptonian psychological internalism than a thick externalism). Califia describes in this lesbian sadomasochistic short story a first sexual encounter between two *strangers*, women, who meet at a party, an encounter about which neither knows in advance whether it will lead to a narrative history or an abiding relationship between them. In the sexual encounter described by Califia, there is no background context of an abiding, let alone mutually respectful, relationship. This means that the nature of their sexual activity *as sadomasochism* is irrelevant; the main point is that each woman, as a stranger to the other, must, on Nussbaum's own account, be merely using each other in the "anonymous spirit." Something Califia writes in "Jessie" makes a mockery of Nussbaum's proposal: "I hardly know you—I don't know if you play piano, I don't know what kind of business it is you run, I don't know your shoe size—but I know you better than anyone else in the world."[43]

If Nussbaum wants to justify sadomasochistic sexual acts, she must say that, *in the context of an abiding, mutually regarding and respectful relationship*, either (1) sadomasochistic sexuality is permissible, no matter how humiliating or brutal the acts are to the participants (thick minimalist externalism), or (2) sadomasochistic sexuality is permissible because, in this background context, it can be a good or wonderful thing, an expansion of the couple's humanity (thick expanded externalism).

Kant's Solution

To provoke the reader's curiosity about Kant, I conclude with some preliminary remarks about Kant's solution to the sex problem.[44]
Kant argues in both the earlier *Lectures on Ethics* and the later *Metaphysics of Morals* that sexual activity is morally permissible only within a
heterosexual, lifelong, and monogamous legal marriage. Hence Kant
advances a thick externalism. (I will suggest that his externalism is minimalist.) Kant barely argues in these texts, or argues weakly, that marriage must be lifelong and heterosexual.[45] But Kant's argument that the
only permissible sexual activity is married sexual activity is distinctive and
presented forcefully. In the *Metaphysics of Morals*, he writes:

> There is only one condition under which this is possible: that while one per-
> son is acquired by the other *as if it were a thing*, the one who is acquired ac-
> quires the other in turn; for in this way each reclaims itself and restores its
> personality. But acquiring a member of a human being [i.e., access to or
> possession of the other's genitals and associated sexual capacities] is at the
> same time acquiring the whole person, since a person is an absolute unity.
> Hence it is not only admissible for the sexes to surrender and to accept
> each other for enjoyment under the condition of marriage, but it is possi-
> ble for them to do so *only* under this condition.[46]

Sexual activity, with its essential sexual objectification, is morally permissible only in marriage, because only in marriage can each of the persons engage in sexual activity *without losing* their own personhood or humanity. In a Kantian marriage, each person is "acquired" by the other
person (along with his or her genitals and sexual capacities) as if he or
she were an object, and hence, by being acquired, loses his or her humanity (autonomy, individuality). But because the acquisition in marriage is reciprocal, each person *regains* his or her personhood (and
hence does not lose it, after all). When I "surrender" myself to you, and
you thereby acquire me, but you also "surrender" yourself to me, and I
thereby acquire you, which "you" includes the "me" that you have acquired, we each surrender but then re-acquire ourselves. (I think this
means that "I do" must be said simultaneously.)
There are many puzzles in Kant's solution. One is that Kant does not
explicitly state in laying out his solution that through such a reciprocal
surrender and acquisition the persons in some robust sense treat each
other as persons or acknowledge each other's humanity as an end, in
bed or otherwise. That is, after laying out his relentless criticism of sexual desire and activity, Kant never poses the question, "How might two
people, married or not, treat themselves and each other as persons during sexual activity?" Kant is notorious for being stingy with examples, but

why here? In fact, in only one place that I could find, a footnote in *Meta-physics of Morals,* does Kant use the language of the Second Formulation to speak about marriage:

> if I say "my wife," this signifies a special, namely a rightful, relation of the possessor to an object as a *thing* (even though the object is also a person). Possession (*physical* possession), however, is the condition of being able to *manage* . . . something as a thing, even if this must, in another respect, be treated at the same time as a person.[47]

But in neither the footnote nor the text does Kant explain what "in an-other respect" being treated as a person amounts to. The language of the Second Formulation is plainly here, including the crucial "at the same time," but not its substance. Further, in the text, Kant refrains from using the language of the Second Formulation:

> What is one's own here does not . . . mean what is one's own in the sense of property in the person of another (for a human being cannot have prop-erty in himself, much less in another person), but means what is one's own in the sense of usufruct . . . to make direct use of a person *as of* a thing, as a means to my end, but still *without infringing* upon his personality.[48]

It is permissible in *some* contexts to use another person as a means or treat as an object, merely with the other's free and informed consent, as long as one does not violate the humanity of the other in some other way, as long as one allows him or her otherwise to retain intact his or her personhood. The reciprocal surrender and acquisition of Kantian mar-riage, which involves a contractual free and informed agreement to ex-change selves, *prevents* this (possibly extra) denial or loss of personhood. But this moral principle is far removed from the Second Formulation as Kant usually articulates it.

Kant's externalism, I submit, is minimalist: the objectification and in-strumentality that attach to sexuality remain even in marital sexual ac-tivity. Hence not even Kant abides by the "at the same time" requirement of the Second Formulation in his solution to the sex problem. Nussbaum seems to recognize Kant's minimalism when she writes, "sexual desire, according to his analysis, drives out every possibility of respect. This is so even in marriage."[49] Raymond Belliotti finds, instead, thick extended ex-ternalism in Kant:

> Kant suggests that two people can efface the wrongful commodification in-herent in sex and thereby redeem their own humanity only by mutually ex-changing "rights to their whole person." The *implication* is that a deep, abid-ing relationship of the requisite sort ensures that sexual activity is not separated from personal interaction which honors individual dignity.[50]

But the "implication" is something Belliotti illicitly reads into Kant's texts. Kant nowhere says that in marriage, which is for him a contractual relationship characterized by mutual acquisition of persons as if they were objects (hardly a "deep, abiding relationship"), sexual activity "honors individual dignity." Belliotti reads Kant as if Kant were Nussbaum. When Kant asserts in the *Metaphysics* that sexual activity is permissible only in marriage, he speaks about the *acquisition* or *possession* of the other person by each spouse, and never mentions benevolence, altruism, or love. For similar reasons, Robert Baker and Frederick Elliston's view must be rejected. They claim that, according to Kant, "marriage transubstantiates immoral sexual intercourse into morally permissible human copulation by transforming a manipulative masturbatory relationship into one of altruistic unity."[51] But Kant never says anything about "altruism" in his account of marriage or of sex in marriage; nowhere does he claim that married persons come to treat each other as ends and respect their humanity in sexual activity by unconditionally providing sexual pleasure for each other. Indeed, Kant writes in the *Metaphysics* that "benevolence . . . deter[s] one from carnal enjoyment."[52] Further, both these readings of Kant are insensitive to the sharp contrast between Kant's glowing account of male friendship, in the *Lectures* and the *Metaphysics*, as a morally exemplary and fulfilling balance of love and respect, and Kant's dry account of heterosexual marriage, which makes marriage look like a continuation, or culmination, of the battle of the sexes. Kant never says about marriage anything close to this: "Friendship . . . is the union of two persons through equal mutual love and respect. . . . [E]ach participat[es] and shar[es] sympathetically in the other's well-being through the morally good will that unites them."[53]

Of course, the virtue of Belliotti's reading, and that of Baker and Elliston, is that if sexual activity can indeed be imbued with Kantian respect or "altruism," then the "at the same time" requirement of the Second Formulation is satisfied. But there is good evidence that Kant's own view is minimalist. When Kant writes in the *Lectures* that

> If . . . a man wishes to satisfy his desire, and a woman hers, they stimulate each other's desire; their inclinations meet, but their object is not human nature but sex, and each of them dishonours the human nature of the other. They make of humanity an instrument for the satisfaction of their lusts and inclinations, and dishonour it by placing it on a level with animal nature.[54]

he intends this description to apply to sexual activity even in marriage, and not only to casual sex, prostitution, or concubinage. This point is confirmed by Kant's letter to C. G. Schütz, who had written to Kant to complain about Kant's similar treatment of sexuality in the later *Meta-*

physics. To this objection offered by Schütz, "You cannot really believe that a man makes an object of a woman just by engaging in marital cohabitation with her, and vice versa," Kant concisely replies: "if the cohabitation is assumed to be *marital,* that is, *lawful,* . . . the authorization is already contained in the concept."[55] Note that Kant does not deny that objectification still occurs in marital sex; he simply says it is permissible, or authorized. Schütz makes the point another way: "married people do not become *res fungibiles* just by sleeping together," to which Kant replies: "An enjoyment of this sort involves at once the thought of this person as merely *functional,* and that in fact is what the reciprocal use of each other's sexual organs by two people *is.*"[56]

Further, that marriage is designed and defined by Kant to be only about sexuality, about having access to the other person's sexual capacities and sexual body parts—for enjoyment or pleasure, not necessarily for reproduction—also suggests that his solution is minimalist. Consider Kant's definition of marriage in the *Metaphysics:* "Sexual union in accordance with principle is *marriage* (*matrimonium*), that is, the union of two persons of different sexes for lifelong possession of each other's sexual attributes."[57] There is no suggestion in this definition of marriage that Belliottian human, individual dignity will make its way into marital sexual activity (quite the contrary). Howard Williams tartly comments, about Kant's notion of marriage, that "sex, for Kant, seems simply to be a form of mutual exploitation for which one must pay the price of marriage. He represents sex as a commodity which ought only to be bought and sold for life in the marriage contract."[58] If sexual activity in marriage is, for Kant, a commodity, it has hardly been cleansed of its essentially objectionable qualities. Kant's view of marriage has much in common with St. Paul's (see 1 Corinthians 7; *Metaphysics,* 179–80), in which each person has power over the body of the other spouse, and each spouse has a "conjugal debt" to engage in sexual activity with the other nearly on demand. That marriage is defined by Kant to be only about access to sex is what is astounding, even incomprehensible, to the contemporary mind, and may explain why modern philosophers are quick to attribute to Kant more congenial solutions to the sex problem.

Finally, a commonly neglected aspect of the Second Formulation, that one must *also* treat the humanity in one's own person as an end, is important in understanding Kant's solution to the sex problem. Duties to self are important for Kant, a fact overlooked by those philosophers (e.g., Mappes and Goldman) who emphasize its treat-the-other-as-an-end part. Notice the prominence of Kant's discussion of the duties to self in the *Lectures.* They are elaborately discussed early in the text, well before Kant discusses moral duties to others, and Kant in the *Lectures* launches into his treatment of sexuality immediately after he concludes his account of duties to self in general and before he, finally, gets around to duties to others. Allen Wood is one commentator on Kant who gets this right:

> [Kant] thinks sexual intercourse is "a degradation of humanity" because it is an act in which "people *make themselves* into an object of enjoyment, and hence into a thing" (VE 27:346). He regards sex as permissible only within marriage, and even there it is in itself "a merely animal union" (MS 6:425).[59]

Kant makes it clear that a duty to treat the humanity in one's own person as an end is his primary concern in restricting sexual activity to marriage: "there ar[ises] from one's duty to oneself, that is, to the humanity in one's own person, a right (*ius personale*) of both sexes to acquire each other as persons *in the manner of things* by marriage."[60]

For Kant, then, the crux of the argument about sex and marriage does not turn on a duty to avoid sexually objectifying the other, but to avoid the sexual objectification of the self. It would be an ironic reading of Kant to say that he claims that *my right to use you* in sexual activity in marriage arises from *my duty to myself*. What Kant is saying, without irony, is that as a result of the duty toward myself, I cannot enter into sexual relations with you unless I preserve my personhood; you, likewise, cannot enter into sexual relations with me unless you are able to preserve your personhood. Each of us can accomplish that goal only by mutual surrender and acquisition, the exchange of rights to our persons, genitals, and sexual capacities that constitutes marriage. It is not the right to use you sexually that is my goal, although I do gain that right. My goal is to preserve my own personhood in the face of the essentially objectifying nature of sexuality. But preserving my own personhood, as admirable as that might be, is not the same thing as treating you with dignity (or altruism) during marital sexual activity. Kant has still done nothing to accomplish that. Nor was that his intention.

Metaphilosophical Finale

Howard Williams has made a shrewd observation about Kant's solution to the sex problem: "[A]n important premiss of Kant's argument is that sexual relations necessarily involve treating oneself and one's partner as things. . . . [T]o demonstrate convincingly that marriage is the only ethically desirable context for sex, Kant ought to start from better premises than these."[61]

Let me explain what is interesting here. Bernard Baumrin argues that if we want to justify sexual activity *at all*, we should start our philosophizing by conceding the worst: "I begin . . . by admitting the most damaging facts . . . that any theory of sexual morality must countenance," viz., that "human sexual interaction is essentially manipulative—physically, psychologically, emotionally, and even intellectually."[62] Starting with premises about sexuality any less ugly or more optimistic would make justifying sexual activity too easy. Williams's point is that if we want to justify the specific claim that sex is *permissible only in marriage*, starting with Kantian premises about the nature of sex makes *that* task too easy. If sex is in its essence wholesome, or if, as in Mappes and Goldman, sexual activity does not significantly differ from other activities that involve human interaction, then it becomes easier both to justify sexual activity and to justify sex outside of marriage. Those, including many Christian philosophers and theologians, who assume the worst about sexuality to begin with, gain an advantage in defending the view that sexuality must be restricted to matrimony.[63] This tactic is copied in a milder way by Nussbaum and Hampton, who reject casual sex. The convincing intellectual trick would be to assume the *best* about sex, that it is by its nature wholesome, and then argue, *anyway*, that it should be restricted to lifelong, monogamous matrimony and that casual sex is morally wrong. Perhaps the liberals Baumrin and Goldman are trying to pull off the reverse trick, in that they admit the worst about sexuality and still come out with a permissive sexual morality. But in admitting the worst, how do they avoid concluding, with Kant, that sexual activity is permissible only in the restrictive conditions of marriage? Perhaps they succeed, or think they do, only by reading the Second Formulation in a very narrow or easily satisfied way.

Study Questions

1. Explain Kantian doubts about the morality of sexuality, by invoking specifically the Second Formulation of the Categorical Imperative. Focus on two questions: (a) how does sexual desire, how does merely the experience of sexual urges, compromise the morality of the agent in whom they occur? What is the effect of sexual passion on the agent's rational autonomy? And (b), how does sexual activity, too, compromise the morality of the agent who engages in this behavior? Take into account both threats to the humanity of the person himself or herself as well as threats to the humanity of the agent's partner.

2. Be sure you understand Soble's criticisms of the attempts of several philosophers to solve the Kantian sex problem, including Alan Goldman (chapter 5), Jean Hampton, Thomas Mappes (chapter 16), and Martha Nussbaum. How might each of these

writers defend their proposals against the critical points made by Soble?

3. State and evaluate Kant's own solution to the Kantian sex problem, as well as interpretations of his solution offered on his behalf and in his name by other philosophers (e.g., Robert Baker and Frederick Elliston; Raymond Belliotti).

4. Already the "applied" topic of the morality of prostitution from a Kantian perspective is brought up in this theoretical and exegetical essay, both explicitly in several passages and implicitly between the lines. Dig out these remarks on prostitution and compare them with the views of Martha Nussbaum (chapter 24) and Yolanda Estes (chapter 23).

5. Take seriously the joke "Is sex an autonomy-killing, mind-numbing, subhuman passion? Yes, but only when it's good" and work out its personal, social, and ethical implications.

Notes

A short version of this essay ("Kant on Sex") was presented at a meeting of the Society for the Philosophy of Sex and Love, held with the Central Division meetings of the American Philosophical Association, New Orleans, May 8, 1999. Another version was presented at Washburn University as the Keynote Lecture of the 54th Mountain-Plains Philosophy Conference, October 13, 2000. It was published, revised, in *Essays in Philosophy* 2, no. 2 (June 2001; www.humboldt.edu/~essays), which granted permission to reprint further revisions in *Philosophy of Sex*, 4th edition, and in this volume.

1. Kant's views on sexuality are in his *Lectures on Ethics* [ca. 1780], trans. Louis Infield (Indianapolis, Ind.: Hackett, 1963), 162–71, and *The Metaphysics of Morals* [1797], trans. Mary Gregor (Cambridge: Cambridge University Press, 1996), 61–64, 126–28, 178–80.

2. Bernard Baumrin, "Sexual Immorality Delineated," in Robert Baker and Frederick Elliston, eds., *Philosophy and Sex*, 2nd ed. (Buffalo, N.Y.: Prometheus, 1984), 300–11, at 300–2.

3. Kant, *Lectures*, 164.

4. "In desire you are compromised in the eyes of the object of desire, since you have displayed that you have designs which are vulnerable to his intentions" (Roger Scruton, *Sexual Desire: A Moral Philosophy of the Erotic* [New York: Free Press, 1986], 82).

5. See Virginia Held, "Coercion and Coercive Offers," in J. Roland Pennock and John W. Chapman, eds., *Coercion: Nomos VIX* (Chicago: Aldine, 1972), 49–62.

6. Kant, *Metaphysics*, 62.

7. Kant, *Lectures*, 164. Kant also suggests that sexuality can reduce humans *below* the level of animals; animals in their instinctual innocence do not use each other sexually (122–23).

8. Kant, *Groundwork of the Metaphysic of Morals*, trans. H. J. Paton (New York: Harper Torchbooks, 1964), 95–96 (AK 4:428).

9. Michael Ruse, *Homosexuality: A Philosophical Inquiry* (Oxford: Blackwell, 1988), 185.

10. Kant, *Groundwork*, 96 (429); 95 (428).

11. Kant, *Groundwork*, 98 (430); see also *Metaphysics*, 199.

12. Kant, *Groundwork*, 97 (429). See Christine Korsgaard, "Creating the Kingdom of Ends: Reciprocity and Responsibility in Personal Relations," *Philosophical Perspectives* 6, *Ethics* (1992), 305–32.

13. C. E. Harris, Jr., seems to have this weaker version of the Second Formulation in mind when he claims that we are permitted to use another person in our interactions with him or her (e.g., a post office worker, doctor, professor) as long as, beyond using them for our purposes, we "do nothing to negate [their] status as a moral being," "do not deny him his status as a person," or "do not obstruct [their] humanity." Harris applies this principle to casual sex: as long as "neither person is overriding the freedom of the other or diminishing the ability of the other to be an effective goal-pursuing agent," it is permissible (*Applying Moral Theories*, 4th ed. [Belmont, Calif.: Wadsworth, 2002], 153–54, 164).

14. Alan Goldman, "Plain Sex," in this volume, chapter 5.

15. David Archard's position is similar to Goldman's. "If Harry has sex with Sue solely for the purpose of deriving sexual gratification from the encounter and with no concern for what Sue might get out of it, if Harry pursues this end single-mindedly and never allows himself to think of how it might be for Sue, then Harry treats Sue merely as a means to his ends. If, *by contrast*, Harry derives pleasure from his sex with Sue but also strives to attend to Sue's pleasure and conducts the encounter in a way that is sensitive to her needs, then Harry does not treat Sue merely as a means. . . . That the sexual relationship between Sue and Harry is consensual does not mean that neither one of them is treating the other merely as a means" (*Sexual Consent* [Boulder, Colo.: Westview, 1998], 41, italics added).

16. "The delight men take in delighting, is not sensual, but a pleasure or joy of the mind consisting in the imagination of the power they have so much to please" (Thomas Hobbes, "Human Nature, or the Fundamental Elements of Policy," in *The English Works of Thomas Hobbes*, vol. IV, ed. Sir William Molesworth [Germany: Scientia Verlag Aalen, 1966], chap. 9, sect. 15, p. 48).

17. See Thomas Nagel, "Sexual Perversion," in this volume, chapter 3.

18. Kant, *Metaphysics*, 199.

19. See "Orgasmic Justice," in my *Sexual Investigations* (New York: New York University Press, 1996), 53–57.

20. Jean Hampton, "Defining Wrong and Defining Rape," in Keith Burgess-Jackson, ed., *A Most Detestable Crime: New Philosophical Essays on Rape* (New York: Oxford University Press, 1999), 118–56, at 147.

21. Hampton, "Defining Wrong," 147.

22. Hampton, "Defining Wrong," 147–48.

23. Hampton, "Defining Wrong," 150.

24. Alan Donagan's view (*The Theory of Morality* [Chicago: University of Chicago Press, 1977] is similar. He praises "life-affirming and nonexploitative" sexuality; by contrast, "sexual acts which are life-denying in their imaginative significance, or are exploitative, are impermissible" (107, italics omitted). Donagan rejects sadomasochism, prostitution, and casual sex.

25. Pat Califia, "Introduction," *Macho Sluts* (Los Angeles, Calif.: Alyson Books, 1988), 9.

26. Thomas Mappes, "Sexual Morality and the Concept of Using Another Person," in this volume, chapter 16. Mappes's Kantian theory of sexual ethics counts as a solution to the Kantian sex problem, for he observes that "the domain of sexual interaction seems to offer ample opportunity for 'using' another person" (Mappes's introductory essay to chapter 4, "Sexual Morality," in Thomas A. Mappes and Jane S. Zembaty, eds., *Social Ethics: Morality and Social Policy*, 6th ed. [New York: McGraw-Hill, 2002], 157–64, at 160; or see the 4th edition, 1992, 192; or the 5th, 1997, 153).

27. For another Kantian consent view, see Raymond Belliotti, "A Philosophical Analysis of Sexual Ethics," *Journal of Social Philosophy* 10, no. 3 (1979): 8–11.

28. Jeffrie Murphy, "Some Ruminations on Women, Violence, and the Criminal Law," in Jules Coleman and Allen Buchanan, eds., *In Harm's Way: Essays in Honor of Joel Feinberg* (Cambridge: Cambridge University Press, 1994), 209–30, at 218.

29. Alan Wertheimer argues that "Have sexual relations with me or I will dissolve our dating relationship" is *not* "a coercive proposal" (although it might still be wrong). See his "Consent and Sexual Relations," in this volume, chap. 19.

30. Mappes's free and informed consent test seems to imply that prostitution is permissible if the prostitute is not exploited, taken advantage of in virtue of her economic needs. Baumrin's consent view seems to imply that prostitution is permissible, because either party may "discharge" the other's duty of providing sexual satisfaction ("Sexual Immorality Delineated," 303; see 305). But Goldman's position on prostitution is unclear. He does not advance a mere free and informed consent test, but lays it down that each person must make a sexual object of himself or herself for the sake of the pleasure of the other, or must provide sexual pleasure to the other so that their activity is mutually pleasurable. That seems to condemn prostitution, unless the client provides pleasure for the prostitute, or unless the prostitute's pleasure in receiving money makes their encounter "mutual" enough for Goldman.

31. Kant, *Lectures*, 163. In several places I replaced "can" in Infield's translation with "may"; Kant's point is moral, not about natural or conceptual possibility.

32. Martha Nussbaum, "Objectification," *Philosophy and Public Affairs* 24, no. 4 (1995): 249–91, reprinted in my *Philosophy of Sex*, 4th ed., 381–419 (passage is on 394; all references to "Objectification" are to POS4). In a slightly revised version of "Objectification" (*Sex and Social Justice* [New York: Oxford University Press, 1999], 213–39), Nussbaum changed "without causing him pain" to "without causing him unwanted pain" (223).

33. Nussbaum, "Objectification," 401, italics added.

34. Nussbaum, "Objectification," 401.

35. Nussbaum, "Objectification," 411, italics added.

36. There is a similar problem of Kant exegesis in Baumrin's "Sexual Immorality Delineated." He claims that what is morally wrong, for Kant, is treating a person in *every* respect as a means. What is permissible, for Baumrin (or Baumrin's Kant), then, is treating a person as a means as long as the person is treated in (at least and perhaps only) *one* respect *not* as a means (300). What this means and whether it is compatible with the Second Formulation are unclear. Baumrin's rendition of the Second Formulation (he quotes Lewis White Beck's translation) does not include the phrase "at the same time" (310n1).

37. Nussbaum, "Objectification," 400–1, italics added.

38. Nussbaum, "Objectification," 405.

39. Nussbaum, "Objectification," 402, italics added.

40. Kant, *Lectures*, 165–66.

41. Nussbaum, "Objectification," 409, 410, 411. I am not able to explore here the tension between Nussbaum's rejecting sexuality in the "anonymous spirit" and her legal and moral defense of prostitution ("'Whether from Reason or Prejudice.' Taking Money for Bodily Services," *Sex and Social Justice*, 276–98; in this volume, chap. 24). See my discussions of Nussbaum in *Pornography, Sex, and Feminism* (Amherst, N.Y.: Prometheus, 2002), 72–78, 163–74; and "Concealment and Exposure: A Mostly Temperate and Courageous Afterword," in Raja Halwani, ed., *Sex and Ethics: Essays on Sexuality, Virtue, and the Good Life* (New York: Palgrave/Macmillan, 2007), 229–52, at 248–51.

42. Nussbaum, "Objectification," 404. Nussbaum mistakenly calls Califia's short story "Jenny."

43. Pat Califia, "Jessie," in *Macho Sluts*, 28–62, at 60. This was said by the top, Jessie, to her bottom, Liz, the morning after their sexual encounter.

44. Important accounts of Kant on sex include Vincent M. Cooke, "Kant, Teleology, and Sexual Ethics," *International Philosophical Quarterly* 31, no. 1 (1991): 3–13; Onora O'Neill, "Between Consenting Adults," in *Constructions of Reason: Explorations of Kant's Practical Philosophy* (Cambridge: Cambridge University Press, 1989), 105–25; Susan Meld Shell, *The Embodiment of Reason: Kant on Spirit, Generation, and Community* (Chicago: University of Chicago Press, 1996) and *The Rights of Reason: A Study of Kant's Philosophy and Politics* (Toronto, Can.: University of Toronto Press, 1980); Irving Singer, *The Nature of Love*, vol. 2: *Courtly and Romantic* (Chicago: University of Chicago Press, 1984); and Keith Ward, *The Development of Kant's View of Ethics* (Oxford: Blackwell, 1972).

45. I examine Kant's philosophical objections to homosexuality and, a fortiori, to homosexual marriage, in "Kant and Sexual Perversion," *Monist* 86, no. 1 (2003): 57–92. See also Lara Denis, "Kant on the Wrongness of 'Unnatural' Sex." *History of Philosophy Quarterly* 16, no. 2 (1999), 225–48.

46. Kant, *Metaphysics*, 62; *Lectures*, 167.

47. Kant, *Metaphysics*, 126*n*.

48. Kant, *Metaphysics*, 127; italics added.

49. Nussbaum, "Objectification," 415, note 30.

50. Raymond Belliotti, *Good Sex: Perspectives on Sexual Ethics* (Lawrence: University Press of Kansas, 1993), 100, italics added.

51. Baker and Elliston, "Introduction," *Philosophy and Sex*, 1st ed. (Buffalo, N.Y.: Prometheus, 1975), 8–9; 2nd ed. (Buffalo, N.Y.: Prometheus, 1984), 17–18. Or see the "Introduction" in Robert B. Baker, Kathleen J. Wininger, and Fred-

erick A. Elliston, eds., *Philosophy and Sex*, 3rd ed. (Amherst, N.Y.: Prometheus, 1998), 23.

52. Kant, *Metaphysics*, 180. In her earlier translation of the *Metaphysics*, Gregor rendered this line "benevolence . . . stop[s] short of carnal enjoyment" (*The Doctrine of Virtue: Part II of the Metaphysic of Morals* [New York: Harper Torchbooks, 1964], 90).

53. Kant, *Metaphysics*, 215. Lara Denis attempts to rehabilitate Kant on marriage in "From Friendship to Marriage: Revising Kant," *Philosophy and Phenomenological Research* 63, no. 1 (2001): 1–28.

54. Kant, *Lectures*, 164.

55. Kant, *Philosophical Correspondence: 1759–99*, trans. Arnulf Zweig (Chicago: University of Chicago Press, 1967), letter dated July 10, 1797, p. 235.

56. Kant, *Philosophical Correspondence*, 235–36; italics added to "is."

57. Kant, *Metaphysics*, 62.

58. Howard Williams, *Kant's Political Philosophy* (New York: St. Martin's Press, 1983), 117.

59. Howard Williams, *Kant's Ethical Thought* (Cambridge: Cambridge University Press, 1999), 2; italics added. Here is the line in the *Metaphysics* to which Wood refers ("MS 6:425"): "even the permitted bodily union of the sexes in marriage . . . [is] a union which is in itself merely an animal union" (179). This is more evidence that Kant's solution is minimalist.

60. Kant, *Metaphysics*, 64.

61. Williams, *Kant's Political Philosophy*, 117.

62. Baumrin, "Sexual Immorality Delineated," 301, 300.

63. Mary Geach (an offspring of Peter Geach and Elizabeth Anscombe) claims, as did Augustine and Jerome, that Christianity "encourages men and women to recognize the whoredom in their own souls. It is a decline from Christianity to see oneself as better than a prostitute if one is . . . given to masturbatory fantasies, or if one defiles ones [*sic*] marriage with contraception." Mary, not surprisingly, limits sexual activity to marriage ("Marriage: Arguing to a First Principle in Sexual Ethics," in Luke Gormally, ed., *Moral Truth and Moral Tradition: Essays in Honour of Peter Geach and Elizabeth Anscombe* [Dublin, Ire.: Four Courts Press, 1994], 177–93, at 178).

Chapter 19

CONSENT AND SEXUAL RELATIONS

Alan Wertheimer

*It is often thought that moral questions about behavior, including sexual activity, can be appreciably if not finally answered by determining whether the participants consented. Although in this essay **Alan Wertheimer** does not reject the moral power of consent or deny that consent can be "morally transformative," he does raise fascinating questions about consent: its nature, when it is present and absent, and its ultimate moral force. Wertheimer argues that it is too simple to deal with all sexual moral questions by referring to consent alone, that other moral factors and deliberations play an essential role. He presents a number of conundrums about the use of fraud or deception in sex as well as about the use of coercion and other sorts of pressures. In an intriguing section of his essay, Wertheimer suggests that whether and when "yes" means "yes" is a more important question than whether and when "no" means "no." He also discusses the novel idea that persons might, in some circumstances, have a moral duty to give consent to sexual relations. The very wording of this inquiry shows that other factors, beyond consent, must be brought to bear on questions in sexual ethics.*

Wertheimer, professor emeritus of the University of Vermont, is the author of *Coercion* (Princeton University Press, 1987), *Exploitation* (Princeton University Press, 1996), and *Consent to Sexual Relations* (Cambridge University Press, 2003).

I. INTRODUCTION

This essay has two broad purposes. First, as a political philosopher who has been interested in the concepts of coercion and exploitation, I want to consider just what the analysis of the concept of consent can bring to the question, what sexually motivated behavior should be prohibited through the criminal law?[1] Put simply, I shall argue that conceptual analysis will be of little help. Second, and with somewhat fewer professional credentials, I shall offer some thoughts about the substantive question itself. Among other things, I will argue that it is a mistake to think that sexual crimes are about violence rather than sex and that we need to understand just why the violation of sexual autonomy is a serious wrong. I shall also argue that the principle that "no means no" does not tell us when "yes means yes," and that it is the latter question that poses the most interesting theoretical difficulties about coercion, misrepresentation, and competence. In addition, I shall make some brief remarks concerning two questions about consent and sexual relations that lie beyond the criminal law: What "consent compromising behaviors" should be regarded as indecent, although not criminal? When *should* someone consent to sexual relations within an enduring relationship?

[A word about notation. In what follows, A will represent a person who attacks B or makes a proposal to B, and it is B's consent that is at issue. A will always be male and B will always be female.]

II. CONSENT AND CONCEPTUAL ANALYSIS

A standard picture about this topic goes something like this. We start with the principle that the criminal law should prohibit behavior that seeks to obtain sexual relations without valid consent. To determine which specific behaviors should be prohibited by the criminal law, we must engage in a detailed philosophical analysis of the concept of consent (and related concepts). If such an analysis can yield the criteria of valid consent, we are then in a better position to identify the behaviors that should be prohibited.

I believe that this picture is mistaken. My central point in this section is that the questions (and their facsimiles)—What is consent? What is valid or meaningful consent?—are less important than they first seem. The concept of consent provides a useful template to organize many of the moral issues in which we are interested, but it cannot do much more than that. The question as to what behavior should be prohibited through the criminal law will be settled by moral argument informed by empirical investigation. Any attempt to resolve that question through an inquiry into the "essence" of consent or the conditions under which we can use the word "consent" will prove to be of only limited help.

A. Consent as Morally Transformative

Let us begin by noting that we are not interested in consent as a free-standing concept. Rather, we are interested in consent because consent is *morally transformative*, that is, it changes the moral relationship between A and B and between them and others.[2] B's consent may *legitimate* an action by A that would not be legitimate without B's consent, as when B's consent to surgery transforms A's act from a battery to a permissible medical procedure. B's consent to a transaction with A provides a reason for others not to interfere with that transaction, as when B's consent to let A put a tattoo on her arm gives C a reason to let them be. And B's consent may give rise to an *obligation*. If B consents to do X for A, B acquires an obligation to do X for A.

To say that B's consent is morally transformative is not to say that B's consent is either necessary or sufficient to change an "all things considered" moral judgment about A's or B's action. It may be legitimate for A to perform surgery on a delusional B without B's consent. It may be wrong for A to perform surgery on B with B's consent if the procedure is not medically indicated.[3] Similarly, we may think that exchanging money for sexual relations is wrong even if the prostitute consents to the exchange. But this does not show that the prostitute's consent is not morally transformative. After all, the prostitute's consent to sexual relations with A eliminates one very important reason for regarding A's behavior as wrong, namely, that A had sexual relations with B without her consent. B's consent is morally transformative because it provides a reason, although not a conclusive reason, for thinking that A's behavior is legitimate.

B. The Logic of Consent Arguments

To put the point of the previous section schematically, we are interested in the following sort of argument.

> *Major Premise:* If B consents to A's doing X to B, then it is legitimate for A to do X to B.
> *Minor Premise:* B has (has not) consented to A's doing X to B.
> *Conclusion:* It is (is not) legitimate for A to do X to B.

Given the major premise, it seems that we must determine when the *minor premise* is true if we are going to know when the conclusion is warranted.

For that reason, we may be tempted to think that an analysis of the concept of consent will identify the *criteria* or necessary and sufficient conditions of valid consent, and that empirical investigation can then (in principle) determine if those criteria are met. If the criteria are met, then the minor premise is true and the conclusion follows. If not, then the minor premise is false and the conclusion does not follow.

If things were only so simple. It is a mistake to think that we will be able to make much progress toward resolving the substantive moral and legal issues in which we are interested by philosophical resources internal to the concept of consent. In the final analysis, we are always going to have to ask: Given the facts that relate to issues of consent, how should we think about the moral and legal status of a transaction or relationship? In that sense, I am squarely in the camp that maintains that the concept of consent is fundamentally normative.

In suggesting that consent is essentially normative, I do not deny that it is possible to produce a morally neutral account of consent that would allow us to say when B consents by reference to specific empirical criteria. I do maintain that if we were to operate with a morally neutral account of consent, we would then have to go on to ask whether B's consent legitimates A's action, and that we will be unable to answer that question without introducing substantive moral arguments. A morally neutral account of consent would do little work in our moral argument. If we want consent to do more work in our moral argument, we must build some of our substantive moral principles into the account of consent that we deploy. We could say that B "really" consents only when B's consent token is morally transformative. In the final analysis, it does not matter much whether we adopt a thin, morally neutral, account of consent or a thick, morally laden, account of consent. Either way, the point remains that we will not be able to go from a morally neutral or empirical account of consent to moral or legal conclusions without introducing substantive moral arguments.

C. The Fallacy of Equivocation

Precisely because we can pack a lot or a little into our account of consent, it is all too easy for a "consent argument" to commit the fallacy of equivocation, in which the meaning of consent assumed by the major premise is not identical to the meaning of consent in the minor premise, and, thus, the conclusion does not follow even though both the major premise and minor premise may be true (given different meanings of consent). Consider a classic problem of political philosophy: Do citizens have a general (prima facie) obligation to obey the law? A standard argument goes like this:

Major Premise: One is obligated to obey the laws if one consents to do so.

Minor Premise (Version 1): One who remains in his society rather than leaves thereby gives his consent to that society (Plato).[4]

Minor Premise (Version 2): One who benefits from living in a society gives his consent to that society (Locke).[5]

Conclusion: One who does not leave his society or benefits from living in a society has an obligation to obey its laws.

Is either version of the minor premise true? The problem is this: There may be a linguistically plausible sense in which one who accepts the benefits of one's government has consented to that government or in which one who remains in one's society has consented to remain in that society. But, even if that were so, that will not resolve the problem of political obligation. We will have to determine if the type or strength of consent that figures in the major premise has been met in the minor premise. And it may not. Thus, we could agree with Plato that there is a sense in which one who does not leave his society gives his consent, while also agreeing with Hume that it is not the sort of *free* consent that would justify the ascription of a strong obligation to obey the law.[6] We can make a similar point about Locke's view.

The danger of equivocation arises with respect to two other concepts that will figure in our analysis: coercion and harm. Let us assume that one who is coerced into consenting does not give valid or morally transformative consent. When is consent coerced? Consider Harry Frankfurt's example:

> The courts may refuse to admit in evidence, on the grounds that it was coerced, a confession which the police have obtained from a prisoner by threatening to beat him. But the prisoner's accomplices, who are compromised by his confession, are less likely to agree that he was genuinely coerced into confession.[7]

Was the prisoner's confession coerced? There is no reason to think that there must be a single acceptable answer to this question. The answer to this question will depend on the sort of moral transformation that consent is meant to trigger. The sort of pressure to which the prisoner was subject may be sufficient to deprive his confession of legal validity. At the same time, and if there is anything like honor among thieves, the very same pressures may not be sufficient to excuse his betrayal of his accomplices. It will do no good to ask what appears to be a conceptual and empirical question: Was his confession coerced or not? Rather, we need to answer two moral questions: What sorts of pressures on prisoners to confess are sufficient to bar the introduction of the confession as evidence? What sorts of pressures on prisoners are sufficient to excuse the ascription of blame by those to whom the prisoner has obligations of silence?

A similar point can be made about the concept of harm. Suppose we start from the Millian principle that the state can justifiably prohibit only conduct that causes harm to others. The following questions arise: Does the psychic distress caused by offensive speech count as harmful? Does trespass that causes no physical damage to one's property constitute a harm? Does a Peeping Tom harm his target? Does he harm his target if she is unaware of his voyeurism? Clearly there is a sense in which psychic distress caused by offensive speech is harmful. As a matter of empirical psychology, it is simply untrue that "sticks and stones will break your bones, but names will never hurt you." And there is clearly a sense in which one has not been harmed by trespass that causes no physical damage, or by the Peeping Tom, particularly if the target is unaware of his voyeurism. But these observations will not tell us which activities can be legitimately prohibited by the state under the Millian principle.[8]

Once again, we have two choices. We could opt for a morally neutral or neurological account of harm, but then we will have to go on to ask whether harm so defined should or should not be prohibited, and whether some acts excluded by that definition can be legitimately prohibited. On the other hand, we could opt for a moralized account of harm, say, one in which one is harmed if one's rights are violated. On this view, we can maintain that the psychic distress caused by offensive speech does not count as a harm because it does not violate one's rights, whereas trespassing and voyeurism do count as harm because they violate one's rights to property and privacy. From this perspective, sexual offenses may cause a particularly serious harm because they violate an important right of the subject, not (solely) because they are physically or psychologically more damaging than nonsexual violence (although that may also be true).

III. A (BRIEF) THEORY OF CONSENT

With these anti-essentialist ruminations behind us, I shall sketch an account of consent in two stages. First, I shall consider the ontology of consent, the phenomena to which the template of consent calls our attention. Second, I shall consider what I shall call the "principles of consent," the conditions under which these phenomena are morally transformative.

A. The Ontology of Consent

First, morally transformative consent always involves a verbal or nonverbal action, some token of consent. Consent is performative rather than attitudinal. It might be objected that there is a plausible understanding of the word consent, in which mental agreement is sufficient to establish consent. I do not want to quibble over words. If one wants to insist that mental agreement is sufficient to establish consent, then I shall say that B's mental agreement to allow A to do X does not *authorize* or *legitimate* A's doing X in the absence of B's communication. If B has decided to accept A's business proposal and was about to communicate that decision to A when their call was disconnected, it would not be legitimate for A to proceed as if B had agreed. Similarly, that B actually desires sexual relations with A does not authorize A to have sexual relations with A if B has said "no."

Second, and to cover well-trod ground, B's consent token can be explicit or tacit, verbal or nonverbal. B gives verbal explicit agreement to A's proposal when B says "yes" or some equivalent. B may give nonverbal but explicit consent to A's proposal that they have sexual relations if B smiles and leads A into her bedroom. One gives tacit consent when silence or inaction is understood to constitute agreement. Thus if my department chair says, "Unless I hear from you, I'll assume that you can advise students at orientation," my silence is an indication that I am available. In general, it is of no fundamental importance whether consent is explicit or tacit, if it is understood that silence or inaction indicates consent, if there is a genuine opportunity for B to dissent, and if B's dissent will have moral force.

And that brings me to the third consideration. Consent will be valid or morally transformative only when certain conditions are met or, perhaps more helpfully, only in the absence of certain background defects. Those conditions will include, among other things, that B is competent to give consent, the absence of coercion, and also perhaps the absence of misrepresentation and concealment of important information. We could say that one who signs a contract at the point of a gun has not consented at all, or that her consent isn't sufficiently free to give rise to an obligation. Either way, her consent token will not be morally transformative.

B. The Principles of Consent

To put the argument in somewhat different terms, we do not start from the assumption that B's consent is morally transformative, in which case the question for philosophical analysis becomes whether B has or has not consented to A's action. Rather, the determination as to when consent is morally transformative is an *output* of moral theorizing rather than an *input*. Let us call the principles that define when a consent token is morally transformative the *principles of consent*.

The principles of consent may vary from context to context. To see this, consider four cases: (1) A physician tells his patient that she has breast cancer and that she should immediately undergo a mastectomy. He does not explain the risks of the procedure or other options. Because the patient trusts her physician, she signs a consent form. (2) A patient's leg is gangrenous and she must choose between amputation and death. She understands the alternatives, and, because she does not want to die, she signs the consent form. (3) A dance studio gets an elderly woman to contract to pay $20,000 for dance lessons by "a constant and continuous barrage of flattery, false praise, excessive compliments, and panegyric encomiums."[9] (4) A psychotherapist proposes that he and the patient have sexual relations. Because the patient has become sexually attracted to the psychotherapist, she enthusiastically agrees.

We might think that the woman's consent in (1) is not valid because the principles of consent for medical procedures require that the physician explain the risks and alternatives. In this case, valid or morally transformative consent must be *informed* consent. Yet, the principles of consent may also entail that the consent given in (2) is valid even though the patient reasonably believed that she had no choice but to agree, say, because the very real constraints on her decision were not the result of *illegitimate* pressures on her decision-making process. By contrast, the principles of consent might hold that the consent given in (3) is not valid or morally transformative because the dance studio acted illegitimately in procuring the woman's consent, even though she had more "choice" than in (2). And the principles of consent might hold that the consent given in (4) does not render it legitimate for the psychotherapist to have sexual relations with his patient, because he has a fiduciary obligation to refrain from sexual relations with his patient. Period.[10]

These are just intuitions. How do we determine the correct principles of consent for one context or another? At one level, the answer to these questions will ultimately turn on what is the best account of morality in general or the sorts of moral considerations relevant to this sort of problem. Somehow, I think we are unlikely to resolve that here. Suppose that the best account of the principles of consent reflect a commitment to impartiality, and that this commitment will be cashed out along consequentialist or contractarian lines. If we adopt a consequentialist outlook, we will want to examine the costs and benefits of different principles of consent and will adopt those principles that generate the best consequences—all things considered. From a contractarian perspective, we can think of the principles of consent as the outcome of a choice made under conditions of impartiality, perhaps as modeled by a Rawlsian veil of ignorance, although here, too, we will want to consider the costs and benefits of different principles (which is not to say that a contractarian will consider them in the way in which a consequentialist would). But the crucial and present point is that from either perspective, the point of moral theorizing is not to determine when one consents, per se. The task is to determine the principles for morally transformative consent.

IV. CRIMINAL OFFENSES

In this section, I want to bring the previous analysis to bear on the central question of this symposium: What sexually motivated behaviors should be regarded as criminal offenses? In considering this question, I shall bracket several related issues. First, I have nothing to say about the history of the law of rape. Second, I shall have little to say about problems of proof that arise because sexual offenses involve behavior that is frequently consensual, and because we operate in a legal context in which we are especially concerned to avoid the conviction of the innocent. Third, I shall not be concerned with questions as to the best interpretations of existing statutes. The question here is not, for example, whether Rusk was guilty under an existing statute if he caused his victim to fear being stranded in an unknown part of the city unless she engaged in sexual acts with him, but whether legislation should be designed so as to regard such behavior as a criminal offense.[11] Finally, I shall have little to say about questions of culpability, the sorts of issues raised in the (in)famous case of *Regina v. Morgan,* in which several men claimed to believe that the wife of a friend consented to sexual relations with them even though she strongly objected at the time.[12] I am concerned with the question as to what conduct should be criminal, and not the conditions under which one might be justifiably excused from liability for such conduct.

A. Criminal Elements

In considering the question so posed, it will be useful to disaggregate some of the ways in which sexually motivated behavior might be seriously wrong.

First, a sexual offense involves a nonconsensual touching or bodily contact, that is, the elements of a standard battery. Nonconsensual touchings need not be violent or painful or involve the penetration of a bodily orifice.

Second, a sexual offense may involve a violent assault or battery, that is, physical contact that involves overpowering restraint of movement or physical pain or harm to the victim's body that lasts beyond the duration of the incident.

Third, a sexual offense may involve *threats* of violence. The perpetrator puts the victim in fear of harm to her life or body, and then uses that fear to obtain sexual relations. As the victim in *Rusk* put it, "If I do want you want, will you let me go?"

Fourth, sexual offenses may often involve harm or the fear of harms that *flow from* penetration as distinguished from the penetration itself, for example, unwanted pregnancy and sexually transmitted diseases.

Fifth, and of greatest relevance to this essay, is the moral and psychological harm associated with the fact that a sexual offense involves unwanted and nonconsensual penetration, that it "violates the interest in exclusive control of one's body for sexual purposes."[13]

B. Seriousness

The seriousness of a sexual offense may vary with the way in which these elements are combined. We can distinguish at least five sorts of sexual offense. Although reasonable people may disagree about the precise ranking, one view of their relative seriousness, in descending order of seriousness, looks like this: (1) sexually motivated assault with penetration and where violence is actually used to inflict harm or overcome resistance; (2) sexually motivated assault with penetration where violence is threatened but not used; (3) sexually motivated assault (where violence is used or threatened) where penetration does not occur ("attempted rape"); (4) penetration of the victim in the face of the victim's refusal to have sexual relations or her inability to consent to sexual relations, but without the use or threat of violence; (5) sexual battery or sexual harassment, where the victim is touched without her consent, but where penetration does not occur.

Before going further, let me make several points about this list. First, this list makes no distinction between cases in which the penetrator and victim are strangers and those in which they are acquaintances (or married). Second, this ordering does not draw a fundamental distinction between the *use* and *threat* of violence, an important departure from the traditional law of rape, in which actual violence and resistance to that violence were sometimes required. It is clearly a mistake to minimize the importance of threats. Consider a case in which A says something like this (perhaps using cruder language):

> You and I are going to play a game. We are going to have sex and I want you to act like you want it and are enjoying it. If you play the game, you won't be hurt. Indeed, I will do everything I know how to do to make the sex as pleasurable as possible. Otherwise, I will kill you with this gun.

Because B regards A's threat as credible, B goes along with A's game. This example indicates that the mere utterance of a phrase that would constitute valid consent if uttered in the absence of such threats ("Please do it!") does not constitute any kind of valid consent in the presence of such threats.[14]

For the purposes of this essay, the most interesting questions concern cases (3) and (4). A sexual offense may involve assault without what Dripps calls the "expropriation" of the victim's body (as in (3)) and may involve expropriation without the use or threat of violence (as in (4)). It might be argued that (4) is a more serious offense than (3) because non-consensual sexual penetration is a greater harm than the use or threat of violence that does not result in penetration. If this is a plausible view, even if not the most widely held or correct view, we need to ask why non-consensual penetration is such a serious wrong. Second, if it should be criminal to have sexual relations with someone who has refused sexual relations, if "no means no," we still need to ask when "yes means yes." We have already described a case in which a consent token ("Please do it!") does *not* mean yes. Other cases are more difficult.

A currently fashionable view maintains that rape is about violence not sex. That view might be resisted in two ways. It might be argued that rape is about sex because sex itself is about violence (or domination).[15] I have little to say about that view, expect to note that even if there is a violent dimension to "ordinary" sex, there is still a distinction between the violence intrinsic to ordinary sex and the violence peculiar to what we have traditionally regarded as sexual crimes.

But I want to suggest that, for both empirical and moral reasons, it is crucial to see that sexual offense is at least partly about sex. First, there is considerable evidence that nonconsensual sexual relations are "a substitute for consensual sexual intercourse rather than a manifestation of male hostility toward women or a method of establishing or maintaining male domination."[16] Second, we cannot explain why the use or threat of violence to accomplish sexual penetration is more traumatic and a graver wrong than the use or threat of violence per se, except on the assumption that invasion of one's sexual being is a special sort of violation. Third, if women experience *non*violent but nonconsensual sex as a serious violation, this, too, can be explained only in the view that violation of a woman's sexual being is special. Consider, for example, the case in which A has sexual relations with an unconscious B. Some of the elements associated with a violent sexual assault would be lacking. There would be no fear, no overpowering of the will or experience of being coerced, and no experience of pain. Yet, even if B never discovers that A had sexual relations with her while she was unconscious, we might well think that B has been harmed or violated by A.[17]

The view that nonconsensual but nonviolent sex is a serious violation has been previously defended by several [authors]. Stephen Schulhofer argues that it should be a criminal offense to violate a person's sexual autonomy.[18] On Donald Dripps's "commodity" theory of sexual crime, the "expropriation" of another person's body for purposes of sexual gratification violates that person's interest in exclusive control over her body for sexual purposes.[19] Joan McGregor connects nonconsensual sexual relations to the invasion of privacy and the control of information about ourselves. She argues that nonconsensual sexual relations can be understood as violating an individual's right to control the "borders" of her relations with others.[20]

For present purposes, there is not much difference among these views. Although Dripps uses the avowedly "unromantic" language of commodity and expropriation, whereas Schulhofer and McGregor use the more philosophically respectable language of autonomy and control, these views are virtually extensionally equivalent.[21] They all maintain that it should be a criminal offense for A to engage in sexual penetration of B if B objects, whether or not A uses or threatens physical harm. It is true that Dripps would criminalize only the disregard of another's refusal to engage in sexual acts (except in cases in which the victim is unable to refuse) whereas Schulhofer and McGregor require a verbal or nonverbal yes. But this is of little practical import. If the law clearly states that B need only say "no" to render A liable to a criminal offense, then B's passivity will not be misunderstood.

Let us assume that this general view is correct. But why is it correct? Jeffrie Murphy suggests that it is not self-evident why the nonconsensual "penetration of a bodily orifice" is such a grave offense. He maintains that there is nothing that makes sexual assault "objectively" more serious than nonsexual assault, that the importance attached to penetration "is essentially cultural," and that if we did not "surround sexuality with complex symbolic and moral baggage," then nonconsensual sex would not be viewed as a particularly grave wrong.[22]

Murphy's science is probably wrong. A woman's abhorrence of nonconsensual sex may be at least partially hard-wired. Evolutionary psychologists have argued that because reproductive opportunities for women are relatively scarce, it is genetically costly for a woman to have sex with a man whose attributes she could not choose and who shows "no evident inclination to stick around and help provide for the offspring."[23] Thus, evolution would favor those women who were most disposed to abhor such sexual encounters. This is not to deny that there is great individual and cultural variability in the way in which people experience nonconsensual sexual relations. It is only to say that there is no reason to assume that culture is writing on a blank state.

Yet, for our purposes, it does not really matter whether the best explanation for a woman's aversion to nonconsensual penetration is cultural or biological. The important question for moral and legal theory is whether the seriousness of a violation should be understood as *experience-*

dependent or (at least partially) *experience-independent.* Although Murphy contrasts a "cultural" explanation of the wrongness of sexual crime with an "objective" explanation, what would an "objective" explanation look like? Murphy thinks that we need to explain why the penetration of an orifice is objectively more harmful than a punch in the nose. Fair enough. But then we also need to explain why physical injury is "objectively" worse than harm to our property or reputations or feelings or character. If the objective seriousness of harm is experience-*dependent*, there is nothing inherently special about physical injury, which Murphy takes to be the paradigm case of objective harm. After all, we could experience insults to our reputations as worse than physical injury and harm to our souls or character as a fate worse than death. On the other hand, if an objective account of harm is experience-*independent*, we would also need to explain why violations of sexuality are more serious than a punch in the nose. But here, once again, sexual harm is on a par with physical harm, for we would need to explain why harm to one's body is objectively more harmful than harm to one's property or reputation or soul.

I cannot produce an adequate account of the objective seriousness of sexual offense in this essay (and not just for lack of space), although the truth about that matter will affect the criminal penalties we are prepared to apply.[24] Although I am inclined to think that the character of this harm is at least partially experience-independent (that is, it would be a serious wrong even if it is not experienced that way), it should be noted that, even if it is experience-dependent, the criminal law is not designed to respond to the harm to the individual victim. Suppose, for example, that A rapes B, who, unbeknownst to A, actually embodies the alleged male fantasy: B wants to be raped. If the wrongness of a crime depends on the harm to the particular victim, then we might regard the rape of B as a lesser wrong. But, while the harm to a specific victim may affect the compensation owed to the victim in a civil action, the criminal law concerns harms to society and can be triggered even when there is no harm to a specific victim, as in an attempted crime in which no one is hurt. Similarly, even if the rape of a prostitute is a less serious offense because it does not involve the forcible taking of something that she regards as a "sacred and mysterious aspect of her self-identity," but merely the theft of a commodity that she normally trades for monetary gain, it does not follow that the criminal law should treat this rape as a less serious wrong.[25]

C. Defective Consent: When Does Yes Mean Yes?

Let us assume that the criminal law regards the disregard of a "no" (or the absence of a verbal or nonverbal "yes") as a basis for criminal liability. As we have seen, that would not resolve all of the problems. We have already seen that when B says "yes" in response to a threat of violence, her consent has no morally transformative power. The question arises, however, as to what other consent-eliciting behavior should be criminal. In this section, I want to focus on three ways in which B's consent token might be considered defective: (1) coercion; (2) misrepresentation or concealment; and (3) incompetence.

1. Coercion

Let us say that A coerces B to consent to engage in a sexual act when (a) A threatens to make B worse off if she does not perform that act and (b) it is reasonable to expect B to succumb to the threat rather than suffer the consequences.

It can be ambiguous as to whether condition (a) is met for two reasons. First, it can be ambiguous as to whether A threatens B at all. We do not say that a panhandler threatens B if he says, "Do you have any money to spare?" But does a large and tough-looking A threaten B when he says "I would appreciate it if you would give me your wallet," but issues no threat as to what he will do if B refuses? We are inclined to think that some nonverbal behaviors are reasonably understood as proposing to make B worse off if B refuses, and that it is also reasonable to expect A to understand this.

Let us assume that there is no misunderstanding as to the likely consequences of refusal. It can be ambiguous as to whether condition (a) is met because we must ask, "Worse off than what?" I have argued elsewhere that the crucial element in coercive proposals is that A proposes to make B worse off than she has a *right* to be vis-à-vis A or that A proposes to violate B's right, and not (as it might seem) that A proposes to make B worse off than her status quo.[26] Whereas the gunman's proposal—"Sign this contract or I will shoot you"—proposes to make B worse off than both her status quo baseline and her right-defined baseline, those baselines can diverge. If a drowning B has a right to be rescued by A, then A's proposal to rescue B only if she pays him $10,000 is a coercive proposal on this view because A proposes to make B worse off than her right-defined baseline, even though he proposes to make her better off than her status quo-defined baseline. On the other hand, A's proposal is not coercive on this view if A proposes to make B worse off than her status quo-defined baseline, but not worse off than her right-defined baseline ("Plead guilty to a lesser offense or I will prosecute you on the charge of which we both know you are guilty").

Consider six cases:

1. A says to B, "Have sex with me or I won't return your car keys and you will be left stranded in a dangerous area."

2. A says, "Have sexual relations with me or I will dissolve our dating relationship."

3. A, a professor, says, "Have sexual relations with me or I will give you a grade two grades lower than you deserve."

4. A, a professor, says, "Have sexual relations with me and I will give you a grade two grades higher than you deserve."

5. A, who owes B money, says, "Have sexual relations with me and I will repay the money that I owe you. Otherwise, ciao."

6. A, a jailer, says, "Have sexual relations with me and I will arrange your escape; otherwise you and I know that you will be executed by the state."[27]

On my view, A makes a coercive proposal in cases (1), (3), and (5), but not in cases (2), (4), and (6). In cases (1), (3), and (5), A proposes to make B worse off than she has a right to be if she refuses—to have her car keys returned, to receive the grade she deserves, to have her loan repaid. By contrast, in cases (2), (4), and (6), A does not propose to make B worse off than she has a right to be if she refuses. B has no right that A continue their dating relationship or a right to a higher grade than she deserves or not to be executed by the state (bracketing general objections to capital punishment).

To anticipate objections, I do not deny that it is wrong for A to make his proposal in (4) and (6) or (sometimes) in (2). A jailer violates his obligation to society if he helps a prisoner escape and commits an additional wrong if he trades that favor for sexual services. It is wrong for a professor to use his control over grades to obtain sexual favors. He violates his responsibility to his institution and to other students. Moreover, and perhaps unlike (6), A's proposal in (4) may entice B into accepting an arrangement that she will subsequently regret. In general, it is often wrong for A to make a "seductive offer" to B, that is, where A has reason to believe that it is likely that B will mistakenly perceive the (short-term) benefits of accepting the offer as greater than the (long-term) costs.

In any case, I do not say that A's proposals are coercive in (4) and (6) simply because, like (3), they create a choice situation in which B decides that having sexual relations with A is the lesser of two evils. After all, we could imagine that B, not A, initiates the proposals in (4) and (6) or is delighted to receive them, and it would be strange to maintain that B is coerced by a proposal that she initiates or is delighted to receive.

Now, consider (2) once again. B may regard the consequences of refusing A's proposal as devastating, as worse, for example, than receiving a lower grade than she deserves. It is also true that B's situation will be worse than her status quo if she refuses. Still, B cannot reasonably claim that she is the victim of "status coercion" or, more importantly, that her consent is not morally transformative.[28] And this [is] because A does not propose to violate B's rights if she refuses, for B has no right that A continue his relationship with B on her preferred terms.

The general point exemplified by (2) is that people make many decisions that they would not make if more attractive options were available to them. If I were independently wealthy, I might not choose to teach political philosophy for a living. If I were not at risk for losing my teeth, I would not consent to painful dental work. But it does not follow that I have been coerced into teaching or agreeing to have dental work performed. In principle, sex is no different. If B were wealthier or more attractive or more famous, she might not have to agree to have sexual relations with A in order to keep him in the relationship. Things being what they are, however, B might well decide that what she wants to do—all things considered—is to have sexual relations with A. It may be regrettable that people bargain with their sexuality, but there is no reason to regard bargaining *within the framework of one's rights* as compromising consent, at least in any way that should be recognized by the criminal law.

Let us now consider condition (b), which states that A coerces B only when it is reasonable to expect B to succumb to A's (admittedly coercive) threat rather than suffer the consequences or pursue a different course of action. Suppose that A proposes to tickle B's feet if she does not have sexual relations with him. I believe that A has made a coercive proposal to B, because A proposes to make B worse off than both her status quo baseline and her right-defined baseline. Still, if B decides to have sexual relations to avoid being tickled, I doubt that we would want to charge A with a criminal offense (unless, perhaps, A believed that B had an extreme aversion to being tickled). Here, we expect B to endure the consequences of A's coercive proposal rather than succumb to it.

Now, recall case (5). In my view, A has made a coercive proposal because A has proposed to violate B's right to be repaid if B refuses. But we might also say that B should sue A for breach of contract, and that we should not regard A's proposal as so compromising B's consent (because she has other legal options) that it should render A subject to a criminal charge.[29] We might disagree about this case. There are resources internal to the notion of coerced consent that allow us to go the other way. But it is moral argument, and not conceptual analysis, that will determine whether this is the sort of sexually motivated behavior that should be punished through the criminal law.

2. Fraud and Concealment

Suppose that A does not threaten B or propose to violate B's rights if she refuses to have sexual relations with A, but that B agrees to sexual relations with A only because B has certain beliefs about A that result from things that A has or has not said.

Consider:

7. A falsely declares that A loves B.

8. A falsely declares that he intends to marry B.

9. A falsely declares that he intends to dissolve the relationship if B does not consent (unlike (2), A is bluffing).

10. A fails to disclose that he has a sexually transmitted disease.

11. A fails to disclose that he has been having sexual relations with B's sister.

Has B given "valid" consent in these cases? We know that A has misrepresented or concealed important information in all of these cases. That is not at issue. The question is whether we should regard A's conduct as criminal.

There are several possibilities. If we were to extend the principle of *caveat emptor* to sexual relations, then there is arguably no problem in any of these cases. On the other hand, if we were to extend principles of criminal fraud or anything like the well-known medical principle of informed consent to the arena of sexual relations, then we could conclude that many representations that are now part and parcel of courtship should be illegal. I do not have anything close to a firm view about this matter. I think it entirely possible that, from either a contractualist or consequentialist perspective, we would choose a legal regime in which we treat the failure to disclose information about sexuality transmitted diseases as criminal, but that we would not want to treat misrepresentation or failure to disclose information about one's feelings or marital intentions or other relationships as criminal offenses.[30] But that is only a guess. For now, I want only to stress that the question as to whether A should be criminally liable in any of these cases will be resolved by moral argument as to what parties who engage in sexual relations owe each other by way of intentional falsehood and disclosure of information, and not by an analysis of the concept of consent.

3. Competence

B can give valid or "morally transformative" consent to sexual relations with A only if B is sufficiently competent to do so. It is uncontroversial that B cannot consent to sexual relations with A if she is unconscious.[31] It is also relatively uncontroversial that B cannot give valid or morally transformative consent if she does not possess the appropriate mental capacities, say, because B is below an appropriate age or severely retarded.

The most interesting *theoretical* questions about competence arise with respect to (otherwise) competent adults who consent to sexual relations because they are under the influence of voluntarily consumed alcohol or some other judgment-distorting substance. Consider two possible positions about this issue. It might be argued that if a competent adult allows herself to become intoxicated, her initial competence flows through to any decisions she makes while less than fully competent. In a second view, A should be liable for a criminal offense if he engages in sexual relations with B when B's first indication of consent is given while intoxicated, even if B is responsible for having put herself in that position.[32]

I do not have a firm view as to what position we should adopt about this matter. But we should not say that A should not be held liable just because B has acted imprudently, or even wrongly, in allowing herself to become intoxicated. Although B's behavior may put her on the moral hook, it does not take A off the moral hook. Although B acts imprudently if she leaves her keys in an unlocked car, A still commits a theft if he takes it. We could adopt a similar view about sexual relations with an intoxicated B.

D. Benefits and Costs

I have argued that the principle that society should make it criminal for individuals to engage in sexual acts without the consent of the other party is highly indeterminate, that we must decide under what conditions consent is morally transformative. Suppose that we were to consider a choice between what I shall call a *permissive legal regime* (LR$_P$), under which A commits a sexual crime only when he uses violence or the threat of violence against B, and a *rigorous legal regime* (LR$_R$), say, one in which it is a criminal offense (1) to engage in sexual acts without the express consent of the other party, (2) to obtain that consent by proposing to violate a legal right of the other party, (3) to misrepresent or fail to disclose information about sexually transmitted diseases, (4) to engage in a sexual act with a party whose consent was first given when severely intoxicated, and so on. It is not important to define the precise contours of these two legal regimes. The point is that we are considering a choice between a (relatively) permissive and a (relatively) rigorous regime.

Which regime should we choose? I have suggested that we could model the choice along consequentialist lines, where we would calculate the costs and benefits associated with different sets of rules, or we could model the choice along contractualist lines, in which people would choose from behind a Rawlsian veil of ignorance. Suppose that we adopt the Rawlsian approach. To make progress on this issue, we must relax the veil. The contractors must know what life would be like for people under different sets of laws and norms, including the full range of information about the trade-offs between the costs and benefits of the two regimes. Here, as elsewhere, the contractors would know that there is no free and equal lunch. At the same time, the veil would be sufficiently thick to deprive them of information regarding their personal characteristics. They would not know whether they were male or female, a potential perpetrator or victim, or, say, their attitude toward sexual relations. They would not know whether *their* sexual lives would go better under one set of rules or another. I don't think we can say with any confidence what rules would be chosen under any of these models, but we might be able to say something about the sorts of benefits and costs they would have to consider.

On the assumption that LR_R would actually affect behavior in the desired direction, it would provide greater protection to the sexual autonomy of women and would promote an environment in which men come to consider "a woman's consent to sex significant enough to merit [their] reasoned attention and respect."[33] These are clear benefits. But there would be costs. Some of these costs would be endogenous to the legal system. LR_R may consume legal resources that would be better spent elsewhere. It may result in the prosecution or conviction of more innocent persons. LR_R may also generate some negative effects on the general structure of sexual and social relations. It may cause a decline in spontaneity and excitement in sexual relations. In addition, just as some persons enjoy the process of haggling over consumer transactions, some may enjoy the game of sexual negotiation, the haggling, bluffing, and concealment that have been a standard fixture of courtship. After all, whether coyness is biologically hard-wired or culturally driven, many women have long thought that it is better to (first) consent to sex after an initial indication of reluctance, lest they be viewed as too "easy" or "loose."[34] So B may suffer if A is too respectful of her initial reluctance. Finally, it is distinctly possible that some persons choose to become intoxicated precisely to render themselves less inhibited—the reverse of a standard Ulysses situation in which one acts *ex ante* to inhibit one's actions *ex post*.[35] So, if A were to comply with LR_R by refusing to have sexual relations with an intoxicated B, A would prevent B from doing precisely what B wanted to do.

Of course, to say that there is no free lunch does not mean that lunch isn't worth buying: The gains may be worth the costs. Whether that is so will depend, in part, on the way in which we aggregate the gains and costs. From a contractarian perspective, it is distinctly possible that we should give some priority to the interests of the worse off, that is, the potential victims of sexual offenses, rather than simply try to maximize the sum total of preference satisfaction or happiness or whatever. The weight of that priority will depend on the gravity of that violation, an issue that has not been settled. But I do not think we should be indifferent to numbers. If

LR$_R$ would work to the detriment of many and help but a few, that would make a difference. Still, here as elsewhere, we should be prepared to trade off considerable positive benefits to some persons in order to provide greater protection to those who would otherwise be harmed.

V. DECENT SEXUAL RELATIONS

Even if we were to expand the range of sexually motivated behaviors subject to criminal sanctions, the criminal law is a blunt instrument to be used relatively sparingly. There remains the question of what sort of behaviors should be regarded as indecent or seriously wrong. Is it seriously wrong for A to obtain B's consent to sexual relations by threatening to end a dating relationship? Is it less wrong if A is *warning* but not *threatening* B, that is, if A is not trying to manipulate B's behavior but is stating the truth, that he would not want to continue the relationship without sexual relations? Is it seriously wrong for A to falsely declare love in order to secure B's consent to sexual relations or to secure her consent while she is intoxicated?

I have no intention of trying to answer these questions in this essay. I do want to make a few remarks about the issues they present. First, there is no reason to think that the justified legal demands on our behavior are coextensive with the moral demands on our behavior. Just as we may have a (morally justified) legal right to engage in behavior that is morally wrong (for example, to give a lecture that the Holocaust is a hoax), we may have a morally justified legal right to produce another's consent to sexual acts in ways that are seriously wrong. Second, just as we might regard the principles of consent for the criminal law as the output of moral theorizing, we can regard the principles of consent for acting decently as the output of moral theorizing, although there would be a different mixture of benefits and costs. Third, this is not an issue without practical consequences. When millions of students are enrolled in sex education courses, it is a genuine question as to what principles we should teach them.

I think it fair to say that, at present, there is no consensus as to what constitutes immoral behavior in this arena. I believe that many people view the pursuit of sexual gratification in dating relationships along the lines of a "capitalist" model, in which all parties are entitled to try to press for the best deal they can get. On a standard (predominantly male) view of dating relationships, it is legitimate for A to seek B's consent to sexual relations, even if A believes B will come to regret that decision. Moreover, just as it is thought legitimate to misrepresent one's reservation price in a business negotiation (there is no assumption that one is speaking the truth when one says, "I won't pay more than $15,000 for that car"), one is entitled to misrepresent one's feelings or intentions. By contrast, in a fiduciary relationship, such as between physicians and patients, A has an obligation to act in the interests of his client rather than his own interests. A should not seek B's consent to a transaction if A believes it is not in B's interest to consent to that transaction.

It would probably be a mistake to apply a strong fiduciary model to sexual relations among competent adults. It might be argued that a paternalistic attitude toward another's sexual life would be rightly rejected as failing to respect the autonomy of the parties "to act freely on their own unconstrained conception of what their bodies and their sexual capacities are for."[36] This is all well and good as far as it goes, but it begs the question of how to understand autonomy, the pressures that it is reasonable for one to bring to bear on another's decision and whether one fails to respect another's autonomy when one fails to tell the truth and nothing but the truth about one's feelings, intentions, and other relationships. It may well turn out that some hybrid of these two models best captures A's moral responsibilities. Unlike the capitalist model, A must give considerable weight to B's interests, as well as his own. Unlike the fiduciary model, B's decision as to what serves her interests is in the driver's seat.

VI. WHEN SHOULD ONE CONSENT TO SEXUAL RELATIONS?

In this section, I want to open up a question that is frequently discussed among parties in enduring relationships but rarely mentioned in the academic literature: How should a couple deal with an asymmetrical desire for sexual relations? Let us assume that A desires sexual relations more frequently than B. Let us also assume that A and B agree that it is not permissible for A to have sexual relations with B when B does not consent. Their question—indeed, it is B's question—is whether she should consent to sexual relations when, other things being equal, she would prefer not to consent. In particular, they want to know if they could reasonably view the frequency of sexual relations or the distribution of satisfaction with their sexual lives as a matter to be governed by a principle of distributive justice. If, as Susan Moller Okin has argued, justice applies to some intrafamilial issues, such as the control of economic resources and the distribution of household labor, does justice also apply to sex?[37]

It might be thought that it is wrong to think that B should ever consent to sexual relations when she does not want sex. But this simply begs the question, for people's "wants" are complex and multifaceted. Consider the problem that has come to be known as the "battle of the sexes."

In one version of the problem, A and B both prefer to go to the movies together than to go alone, but each prefers to go to different types of movies. Their problem is to determine what movie they should see.[38] Although the "battle of the sexes" is usually used to exemplify a bargaining problem, I want to use the example to make a point about the character of one's "wants." For we can well imagine that A may not "want" to see B's preferred movie, other things being equal. Still, given that B really wants to see the movie and given that they most recently went to the movie that A preferred, A may genuinely want to see the movie that B prefers—all things considered.

It might be objected that "I want to do what you want to do" is fine for movies, but not sex. In this view, there are some "not wants" that are legitimate candidates for "all things considered wants," but the lack of a desire for sexual relations is not among them. In one variant of this view, sexual relations are radically different from other activities in which partners engage together because it would be self-defeating for partners to think that they are having sexual relations on this basis. A can enjoy the movie that he sees with B, although he knows that B would (otherwise) prefer to see something else, but A would not get satisfaction from sexual relations with B if A knows that B wants to have sexual relations only to satisfy or placate A's desire for sexual relations.

With some trepidation, I want to suggest that to think of sexual relations between partners in an enduring relationship as radically different from all other activities in which they engage "wildly misdescribes" their experience.[39] Sexual relations among such partners are simply not always viewed as sacred or endowed with greater mystery. But my point is not solely negative or deflationary. After all, to say that the most desirable form of sexual relations occurs within a loving relationship is also to say that sexual relations are a way of expressing affection and commitment, and not simply to express or satisfy erotic desire. It is, for example, entirely plausible that parties who have been fighting might engage in sexual relations as a way of demonstrating to themselves that the disagreement is relatively minor in the context of their relationship, that their love for each other is unshaken. In general, I see no reason to tightly constrain what count as legitimate reasons to want to engage in sexual relations—all things considered.

But what about distributive justice? Assume that A and B both understand that it is frustrating for A to forgo sexual relations when B does not desire sexual relations, whereas it is erotically unsatisfying for B to engage in sexual relations when she does not desire sexual relations—not awful or abhorrent, just unsatisfying. On some occasions, A would rather have sex than go to sleep, whereas B's utility function is the reverse. Given this situation, there are three possibilities: (1) A can absorb the burden of the asymmetry by forgoing sexual relations when B is not otherwise motivated to have sex; (2) B can absorb the burden of the asymmetry by consenting to have sexual relations whenever A desires to do so; or (3) A and B can share the burden of the asymmetry by agreeing that they will have sexual relations less often than A would (otherwise) prefer and more often than B would (otherwise) prefer. And B is trying to decide if she should choose (3). Note, once again, that the question is not whether B should consent to sexual relations that she does not want. Rather, she is trying to decide if she should want to have sexual relations—all things considered—when the things to be considered involve a commitment to fairness.

It might be objected that even if we do not tightly constrain the reasons that might legitimately motivate B to "want" to have sex with A, sexual relations lie beyond reasons based on justice or fairness. It might be maintained that a concern with fairness or justice arises only when interests conflict. As Hume remarked, justice has no place among married people who are "unacquainted with the *mine* and *thine*, which are so necessary and yet cause such disturbance in human society."[40] From this perspective, a conscious preoccupation with fairness in a marriage can be a symptom that the parties have failed to achieve the identity of interests that characterize a good marriage and may (causally) inhibit the formation of a maximally intimate relationship.[41] Love precludes a concern with justice, what Hume described as "the cautious, jealous virtue."[42]

I want to make several replies to this line of argument. First, and least important, there is obviously a limit to the identity of interests it is logically possible to achieve. If each party has an overall want to do what the other has a primary want to do, they will achieve an altruistic draw ("I want to do what you want to do." "But I want to do what you want to do."). And if each has an overall want to do what the other has an overall want to do, there will be no wants for the overall wants to get hold of.

Second, if we think that a good marriage is characterized by an identity of interests, this still leaves open the question as to how married partners should respond to the asymmetry of desire for sexual relations. Just as A might say, "I wouldn't want to have sexual relations if B doesn't want to," B might say, "If A wants to have sexual relations, then I want to have sexual relations." So if we reject the argument from distributive justice because it assumes that the interests of the parties conflict, there is no reason to think that the parties will settle on (1) rather than (2) or (3).

Third, I think it both unrealistic and undesirable to expect that the desires or interests of persons in the most successful intimate relationships will fully coincide. It is relatively, although not absolutely, easy for married partners not to distinguish between "mine" and "thine" with respect to property. It is much more difficult to achieve a communal view with respect to activities. Do loving spouses not care at all how many diapers they change? To which movies they go? Where they locate? Are they no longer loving if they do care? Indeed, it is not clear that it is even desirable for people to strive for a relationship in which their interests are so completely merged. It might be thought that a good marriage represents a "union" of autonomous individuals who do and should have goals and aspirations that are independent of their relationship.

From this perspective, a couple's concern with fairness simply reflects the fact that their desires are not identical, that they do not see why this fact should be denied or regretted, and that they want to resolve these differences in a fair way. As Susan Moller Okin puts it (albeit in a different context), "Why should we suppose that harmonious affection, indeed deep and long-lasting love, cannot co-exist with ongoing standards of justice?"[43] Indeed, I would go further. It might be argued that it is not merely that love can coexist with justice, but that to love another person is to want to be fair to them, or, more precisely, to want not to be unfair to them, for to love someone is typically to want to be more than fair to them, to be generous.

I have not actually argued that the distribution of satisfaction with one's sexual life in a enduring relationship is an appropriate topic for distributive justice. Although I have argued against several objections to the view that sexual relations are beyond the scope of justice, it is possible that other arguments would work. Moreover, even if the distribution of satisfaction with one's sexual life is an appropriate topic for a principle of justice, I make no suggestions here as to what the substance of a theory of justice in sexual relations would look like. It is entirely possible that such a theory would dictate that the parties choose something like (1) rather than (3) (I take it that (2) is a nonstarter). I only want to suggest that the topic may belong on the table.

Study Questions

1. What does Wertheimer mean when he calls consent "morally transformative"? Why does he claim that consent will *be* morally transformative, all things considered, only when certain conditions are met? What are these conditions?

2. Wertheimer discusses both sayings, that "no" means "no" and that "yes" means "yes." What do these expressions mean, literally-speaking? What do they mean when particular people use them in particular contexts? Compare what Wertheimer says about these two expressions with what Alan Soble says about them (below, chapter 29). Are there are significant differences?

3. The legal philosopher Jeffrie Murphy believes that women's abhorrence to being raped is due to cultural conditioning and that, as a result, if we did not teach women certain things about sex,

they would not experience being raped as such a grave harm. To the contrary, Wertheimer claims, women's abhorrence is "hard-wired," that is, is due to women's biology as molded by natural and sexual selection. Who do you think is right here, and why? And what difference does it make, philosophically, legally, or politically? Is the spiritual and psychological repugnance of a strict Orthodox Jew to pork biological or cultural? Does it matter, if someone shoves a piece of bacon, the forbidden meat, into his or her mouth?

4. Is it morally wrong for a person A to say falsely to another person B "I love you" just so A can induce B to engage in sex? Should it be legally culpable fraud or deception? Is it morally wrong for a person A to say truly to another person B, "Have sex with me or find yourself some other boyfriend [girlfriend]" just so A can induce B to engage in sex? Should it be legally culpable coercion? Might that threat be, in some circumstances, morally suspicious exploitation (see Thomas Mappes, chapter 16)? When?

5. In many marriages and relationships between two people, one person desires sexual activity from or with the other person more frequently than the second desires it with the first. Also, in many marriages and relationships one person desires a specific type of sexual activity that the second person finds distasteful or even immoral and prefers not to do. How would you propose to solve such conflicts—without suggesting that the two people get divorced or split up? What helpful suggestions does Wertheimer make in his essay?

Notes

1. See Alan Wertheimer, *Coercion* (Princeton, N.J.: Princeton University Press, 1987) and *Exploitation* (Princeton, N.J.: Princeton University Press, 1996).

2. I borrow this phrase from Heidi Hurd's remarks at the conference at the University of San Diego Law School, which gave rise to this symposium.

3. For example, it may be wrong for a physician to accede to a beggar's request to have his leg amputated so that he can enhance his success as a beggar.

4. "You have never left the city, even to see a festival, nor for any other reason except military service; you have never gone to stay in any other city, as people do; you have had no desire to know another city or other laws; we and our city satisfied you. So decisively did you choose us and agree to be a citizen under us." Plato, "Crito," in *The Trial and Death of Socrates*, trans. G. M. A. Grube (Indianapolis: Hackett, 1975).

5. "[E]very man that hath any possession or enjoyment of any part of the dominions of any government doth thereby give his tacit consent, and is as far forth

obliged to obedience to the laws of that government, during such enjoyment, whether this his possession be of land to him and his heirs for ever, or a lodging only for a week; or whether it be barely travelling freely on the highway . . ." John Locke, *Second Treatise Of Government*, ch. 8 (1690).

6. "Can we seriously say, that a poor person or artisan has a free choice to leave his country, when he knows no foreign language or manners, and lives, from day to day, by the small wages which he acquires? We may as well assert that a man, by remaining in a vessel, freely consents to the dominion of the master; though he was carried on board while asleep, and must leap into the ocean and perish, the moment he leaves her." David Hume, *Of the Original Contract* (1777).

7. Harry Frankfurt, "Coercion and Moral Responsibility," in *Essays on Freedom of Action*, ed. T. Honderich (London: Routledge & Kegan Paul, 1973), 65.

8. As Jeremy Waldron has put it, "[T]he question is . . . not what 'harm' really means, but what reasons of principle there are for preferring one conception to another . . . the question is not simply which is the better conception of harm, but which conception answers more adequately to the purposes for which the concept is deployed." *Liberal Rights: Collected Papers 1981-91* (Cambridge, UK: Cambridge University Press, 1993). For a somewhat different, view, see Frederick Schauer, "The Phenomenology of Speech and Harm," *Ethics* 103 (1993): 635–53.

9. *Vokes v. Arthur Murray, Inc.*, 212 So.2d 906 (1968) at 907.

10. See "Sexual Exploitation in Psychotherapy," chap. 6 in Wertheimer, *Exploitation*.

11. See *State v. Rusk*, 289 Md. 230, 424 A.2d 720 (1981). The defendant had also intimidated the prosecutor by taking the keys to her car, disregarded her statement that she did not want to have sexual relations with him, and was said to have "lightly choked" her.

12. *Director of Public Prosecutions v. Morgan* (1975), 2 All E.R. 347.

13. Donald A. Dripps, "Beyond Rape: An Essay on the Difference between the Presence of Force and the Absence of Consent," *Columbia Law Review* 92, no. 7 (November 1992), 1780–1809, esp. 1797.

14. Indeed, it might be thought that this case is, in one way, more serious than those in which force is used to overcome the victim's resistance, namely, that it requires the victim to act inauthentically.

15. See Catharine MacKinnon, *Feminism Unmodified* (Cambridge, Mass.: Harvard University Press, 1987), 5–6.

16. See Richard A. Posner, *Sex and Reason* (Cambridge, Mass.: Harvard University Press, 1992), 384.

17. For a discussion of nonexperiential harm, see Joel Feinberg, *Harm to Others: The Moral Limits of the Criminal Law* (New York: Oxford University Press, 1984), chap. 2.

18. Stephen J. Schulhofer, "Taking Sexual Autonomy Seriously: Rape Law and Beyond," *Law and Philosophy* 11 (1992): 35–94, esp. 70.

19. Dripps, "Beyond Rape," 1796n3.

20. Donald A. Dripps, "Force, Consent, and the Reasonable Woman," in *In Harm's Way: Essays in Honor of Joel Feinberg*, ed. J. L. Coleman and A. Buchanan (Cambridge, UK: Cambridge University Press, 1994), 231–54, esp. 235. McGre-

gor says that she borrows the notion of "border crossings" from Robert Nozick's *Anarchy, State and Utopia* (New York: Basic Books, 1974).

21. I think it no objection to the commodity (or any other) view of the law of sexual crimes that it "wildly misdescribes" the victim's experience. Robin West, "Legitimating the Illegitimate: A Comment on *Beyond Rape*," *Columbia Law Review* 93 (April 1993), 1442–48, esp. 1448. The question is whether a view provides a coherent framework for protecting the rights or interests that we believe ought to be protected. Indeed, it is an advantage of a "property" theory that it provides a basis for critiquing the traditional law of rape. That A takes B's property without B's consent is sufficient to show that A steals B's property. Force or resistance is not required.

22. See Jeffrie G. Murphy, "Some Ruminations on Women, Violence, and the Criminal Law," in Coleman and Buchanan, *In Harm's Way*, 214.

23. Robin Wright, "Feminists, Meet Mr. Darwin," *New Republic* (November 1994): 37. The evolutionary logic of nonconsensual sex is different for men. It is physically difficult to accomplish, and "the worst likely outcome for the man (in genetic terms) is that pregnancy would not ensue . . . hardly a major Darwinian disaster."

24. This is obviously true on a retributive theory of punishment, in which the level of punishment is related to the seriousness of the offense. But it is also true on a utilitarian theory, for the more serious the harm to the victim, the greater "expense" (in punishment) it makes sense to employ to deter such harms.

25. Murphy, "Some Ruminations on Women," 216n22.

26. Wertheimer, *Coercion*.

27. This is derived from a case introduced by Schulhofer, "Taking Sexual Autonomy Seriously," 70n18.

28. C. L. Muehlenhard and J. L. Schrag, "Nonviolent Sexual Coercion," in *Acquaintance Rape: The Hidden Crime*, ed. A. Parrot and L. Bechhofer (New York: Wiley, 1991), 115–28, esp. 119.

29. Don Dripps has suggested to me that case (5) is a variant on prostitution. In the standard case of prostitution, A proposes to pay B with A's money. In this case, A proposes to pay B with B's money.

30. As Stephen Schulhofer says, because there are "few pervasively shared intuitions" with regard to what constitutes serious misrepresentation as distinct from puffing or "story telling," the decisions as to "whether to believe, whether to rely and whether to assume the risk of deception . . . are often seen as matters to be left to the individual." "Taking Sexual Autonomy Seriously," 92n18.

31. It is less clear—and informal intuition (and pumping of friends) has done little to help—whether women would regard sexual relations while unconscious as worse than or not as bad as forcible sexual relations. One might think that it is worse to consciously experience an assault on one's bodily and sexual integrity, but it might also be thought that it is better to know what is happening to oneself than not to know.

32. I say "first" indication, because B could consent while sober to what she subsequently consents to while intoxicated.

33. Susan Estrich, *Real Rape* (Cambridge, Mass.: Harvard University Press, 1987), 98.

34. See the discussion of coyness in Robert Wright, *The Moral Animal* (Gloucester, Mass.: Peter Smith, 1994).

35. "Here are the keys to my car; don't let met drive home if I'm drunk." See, e.g., Thomas C. Schelling, "The Intimate Contest for Self-Command," in *Choice and Consequence* (Cambridge, Mass.: Harvard University Press, 1984) chap. 3.

36. Schulhofer, "Taking Sexual Autonomy Seriously," 70n18.

37. Susan Moller Okin, *Justice, Gender, and the Family* (New York: Basic Books, 1989).

38. See Brian Barry, *Theories of Justice* (Berkeley: University of California Press, 1989), 116–17.

39. With apologies to Robin West.

40. David Hume, *A Treatise of Human Nature*, bk. III, sec. II.

41. I thank Pat Neal and Bob Taylor for pressing me on this point.

42. David Hume, *An Enquiry Concerning the Principles of Morals*, Sec. III, pt. I, par. 3.

43. Okin, *Justice, Gender, and the Family*, 32n37.

Chapter 20

THE HARMS OF CONSENSUAL SEX

Robin West

In earlier chapters several lines of thought were encountered that opposed the consent standard of sexual libertarians and liberals. Some opposition came from the conservative strands of liberal theory—in particular, the Kantian view that consent is not sufficient when the participants still treat each other as mere means, and the Thomistic Natural Law view that marriage and procreation are also required for sexual activity to be morally permissible. In this essay, **Robin West** *finds fault with the consent standard from a very different (feminist) perspective. She argues that consensual (but unwanted) sex often harms a woman's autonomy in more subtle ways than do rape, assault, and harassment. West provides a compelling picture of the often unhappy circumstances under which much, though not all, everyday heterosexual activity occurs. Even when a woman employs her freedom and rationality in agreeing to sex, if she is consenting to sex that she does not genuinely desire, she may be undermining that same freedom and rationality. A strong consent standard, on West's view, is thereby an arrow in patriarchy's quiver. But West is not an uncritical feminist either. She concludes by questioning whether feminist-liberal reforms of rape laws do not have the unintended consequence of masking (by "legitimating") these subtle kinds of damage, and whether the radical feminist mantra that all heterosexual penetration is perpetration of illicit sex trivializes these subtle harms.*

West is professor of law at Georgetown University Law Center, where she teaches jurisprudence, torts, law and literature, and feminist legal theory. She is the author of *Narrative, Authority, and Law* (University of Michigan Press, 1994), *Progressive Constitutionalism* (Duke University Press, 1995), *Caring for Justice* (New York University

318   Robin West

Press, 1997), and *Re-Imagining Justice: Progressive Interpretations of Formal Equality, Rights, and the Rule of Law* (Ashgate/Dartmouth 2003).

Reprinted, with the permission of Robin West and The American Philosophical Association, from *The American Philosophical Association Newsletters* 94:2 (1995), pp. 52–55.

Are consensual, non-coercive, non-criminal, and even non-tortious, heterosexual transactions ever harmful to women? I want to argue briefly that many (not all) consensual sexual transactions are, and that accordingly we should open a dialogue about what those harms might be. Then I want to suggest some reasons those harms may be difficult to discern, even by the women sustaining them, and lastly two ways in which the logic of feminist legal theory and practice itself might undermine their recognition.

Let me assume what many women who are or have been heterosexually active surely know to be true from their own experience, and that is that some women occasionally, and many women quite frequently, consent to sex even when they do not desire the sex itself, and accordingly have a good deal of sex that, although consensual, is in no way pleasurable. Why might a woman consent to sex she does not desire? There are, of course, many reasons. A woman might consent to sex she does not want because she or her children are dependent upon her male partner for economic sustenance, and she must accordingly remain in his good graces. A woman might consent to sex she does not want because she rightly fears that if she does not her partner will be put into a foul humor, and she simply decides that tolerating the undesired sex is less burdensome than tolerating the foul humor. A woman might consent to sex she does not want because she has been taught and has come to believe that it is her lot in life to do so, and that she has no reasonable expectation of attaining her own pleasure through sex. A woman might consent to sex she does not want because she rightly fears that her refusal to do so will lead to an outburst of violent behavior some time following—only if the violence or overt threat of violence is very close to the sexual act will this arguably constitute a rape. A woman may consent to sex she does not desire because she *does* desire a friendly man's protection against the very real threat of non-consensual violent rape by other more dangerous men, and she correctly perceives, or intuits, that to gain the friendly man's protection, she needs to give him, in exchange for that protection, the means to his own sexual pleasure. A woman, particularly a young woman or teenager, may consent to sex she does not want because of peer expectations that she be sexually active, or because she cannot bring herself to hurt her partner's pride, or because she is uncomfortable with the prospect of the argument that might ensue, should she refuse.

These transactions may well be rational—indeed in some sense they all are. The women involved all trade sex for something they value more than they value what they have given up. But that doesn't mean that they are not harmed. Women who engage in unpleasurable, undesired, but consensual sex may sustain real injuries to their sense of selfhood, in at least four distinct ways. First, they may sustain injuries to their capacities for self-assertion: the "psychic connection," so to speak, between pleasure, desire, motivation, and action is weakened or severed. *Acting* on the basis of our own felt pleasures and pains is an important component of forging our own way in the world—of "asserting" our "selves." Consenting to *un*pleasurable sex—acting in spite of displeasure—threatens that means of self-assertion. Second, women who consent to undesired sex many injure their sense of self-*possession*. When we consent to undesired penetration of our physical bodies we have in a quite literal way constituted ourselves as what I have elsewhere called "giving selves"—selves who cannot be violated, because they have been defined as (and define themselves as) being "for others." Our bodies to that extent no longer belong to ourselves. Third, when women consent to undesired and unpleasurable sex because of their felt or actual dependency upon a partner's affection or economic status, they injure their sense of autonomy: they have thereby neglected to take whatever steps would be requisite to achieving the self-sustenance necessary to their independence. And fourth, to the extent that these unpleasurable and undesired sexual acts are followed by contrary to fact claims that they enjoyed the whole thing—what might be called "hedonic lies"—women who engage in them do considerable damage to their sense of integrity.

These harms—particularly if multiplied over years or indeed over an entire adulthood—may be quite profound, and they certainly may be serious enough to outweigh the momentary or day-to-day benefits garnered by each individual transaction. Most debilitating, though, is their circular, self-reinforcing character: the more thorough the harm—the deeper the injury to self-assertiveness, self-possession, autonomy, and integrity—the greater the likelihood that the woman involved will indeed *not* experience these harms as harmful, or as painful. A woman utterly lacking in self-assertiveness, self-possession, a sense of autonomy, or integrity will not experience the activities in which she engages that reinforce or constitute those qualities *as harmful*, because she, to that degree, lacks a self-asserting, self-possessed self who *could* experience those activities as a threat to her selfhood. But the fact that she does not experience these activities as harms certainly does not mean that they are not harmful. Indeed, that they are not felt as harmful is a consequence of the harm they have already caused. This phenomenon, of course, renders the "rationality" of these transactions tremendously and even tragically misleading. Although these women may be making rational calculations in the context of the particular decision facing them, they are, by making those calculations, sustaining deeper and to some degree unfelt harms that undermine the very qualities that constitute the capacity for rationality being exercised.

Let me quickly suggest some reasons that these harms go so frequently unnoticed—or are simply not taken seriously—and then suggest in slightly more detail some ways that feminist legal theory and practice may have undermined their recognition. The first reason is cultural. There is a deep-seated U.S. cultural tendency to equate the legal with the good, or harmless: we are, for better or worse, an anti-moralistic, anti-authoritarian, and anti-communitarian people. When combined with the sexual revolution of the 1960s, this provides a powerful cultural explanation for our tendency to shy away from a sustained critique of the harms of consensual sex. Any suggestion that legal transactions to which individuals freely consent may be harmful, and hence *bad*, will invariably be met with skepticism—*particularly* where those transactions are sexual in nature. This tendency is even further underscored by more contemporary post-mortem skeptical responses to claims asserting the pernicious consequences of false consciousness.

Second, at least our legal-academic discourses, and no doubt academic-political discourses as well, have been deeply transformed by the "exchange theory of value," according to which, if I exchange A for B voluntarily, then I simply must be better off after the exchange than before, having, after all, agreed to it. If these exchanges *are* the source of value, then it is of course impossible to ground a *value* judgment that some voluntary exchanges are harmful. Although stated baldly this theory of value surely has more critics than believers, it nevertheless in some way perfectly captures the modern zeitgeist. It is certainly, for example, the starting and ending point of normative analysis for many, and perhaps most, law students. Obviously, given an exchange theory of value, the harms caused by consensual sexual transactions simply fade away into definitional oblivion.

Third, the exchange theory of value is underscored, rather than significantly challenged, by the continuing significance of liberal theory and ideology in academic life. To the degree that liberalism still rules the day, we continue to valorize individual choice against virtually anything with which it might seem to be in conflict, from communitarian dialogue to political critique, and continue to perceive these challenges to individual primacy as somehow on a par with threats posed by totalitarian statist regimes.

Fourth, and perhaps most obvious, the considerable harms women sustain from consensual but undesired sex must be downplayed if the considerable pleasure men reap from heterosexual transactions is morally justified—*whatever* the relevant moral theory. Men do have a psychosexual stake in insisting that voluntariness alone ought be sufficient to ward off serious moral or political inquiry into the value of consensual sexual transactions.

Let me comment in a bit more detail on a further reason why these harms seem to be underacknowledged, and that has to do with the logic of feminist legal theory, and the efforts of feminist practitioners, in the area of rape law reform. My claim is that the theoretical conceptualizations of sex, rape, force, and violence that underscore both liberal and radical legal feminism undermine the effort to articulate the harms that might be caused by consensual sexuality. I will begin with liberal feminism and then turn to radical feminism.

First, and entirely to their credit, liberal feminist rape law reformers have been on the forefront of efforts to stiffen enforcement of the existing criminal sanction against rape, and to extend that sanction to include non-consensual sex, which presently is not cognizable legally as rape but surely should be. This effort is to be applauded, but it has the almost inevitable consequence of valorizing, celebrating, or, to use the critical term, "legitimating" consensual sexual transactions. If rape is bad *because* it is non-consensual—which is increasingly the dominant liberal-feminist position on the badness of rape—then it seems to follow that *consensual* sex must be good because it is consensual. But appearances can be misleading, and this one certainly is. That non-consensual transactions—rape, theft, slavery—are bad because non-consensual does *not* imply the value, worth or goodness of their consensual counterparts—sex, property, or work. It only follows that consensual sex, property, or work are not bad in the ways that non-consensual transactions are bad; they surely may be bad for some other reason. We need to explore, in the case of sex (as well as property and work), what those other reasons might be. Non-consensuality does not exhaust the types of harm we inflict on each other in social interactions, nor does consensuality exhaust the list of benefits.

That the liberal-feminist argument for extending the criminal sanction against rape to include non-consensual sex *seems* to imply the positive value of consensual sex is no doubt in part simply a reflection of the powers of the forces enumerated above—the cultural, economic, and liberal valorization of individualism against communal and authoritarian controls. Liberal feminists can obviously not be faulted for that phenomenon. What I want to caution against is simply the ever-present temptation to *trade* on those cultural and academic forces in putting forward arguments for reform of rape law. We need not trumpet the glories of consensual sex *in order* to make out a case for strengthening the criminal sanction against coercive sex. Coercion, violence, and the fear under which women live because of the threat of rape are sufficient evils to sustain the case for strengthening and extending the criminal law against those harms. We need not and should not supplement the argument with the unnecessary and unwarranted celebration of consensual sex—which, whatever the harms caused by coercion, does indeed carry its own harms.

Ironically, radical feminist rhetoric—which *is* aimed at highlighting the damage and harm done to women by ordinary, "normal" heterosexual transactions—*also* indirectly burdens the attempt to articulate the harms done to women by consensual heterosexual transactions, although it does so in a very different way. Consider the claim, implicit in a good deal of radical feminist writing, explicit in some, that "all sex is rape," and compare it for a moment with the rhetorical Marxist claim that "all property is theft." Both claims are intended to push the reader or listener to a reexamination of the ordinary, and both do so by blurring the distinction between consent and coercion. Both seem to share the underlying premise that that which is coerced—and perhaps *only* that which is coerced—is bad, or as a strategic matter, is going to be perceived as bad. Both want us to re-examine the value of that which we normally think of as good or at least unproblematic because of its apparent consensuality—heterosexual transactions in the first case, property transactions in the second—and both do so by putting into doubt the reality of that apparent consensuality.

But there is a very real difference in the historical context and hence the practical consequences of these two rhetorical claims. More specifically, there are two pernicious, or at least counter-productive, consequences of the feminist claim which are not shared, at least to the same degree, by the Marxist. First, and as any number of liberal feminists have noted, the radical feminist equation of sex and rape runs the risk of undermining parallel feminist efforts in a way not shared by the Marxist equation of property and theft. Marxists are for the most part not engaged in the project of attempting to extend the existing laws against *theft* so as to embrace non-consensual market transactions that are currently not covered by the laws against larceny and embezzlement. Feminists, however, *are* engaged in a parallel effort to extend the existing laws against rape to include all non-consensual sex, and as a result, the radical feminist equation of rape and sex is indeed undermining. The claim that all sex is in effect non-consensual runs the real risk of "trivializing," or at least confusing, the feminist effort at rape reform so as to include all truly non-consensual sexual transactions.

There is, though, a second cost to the radical feminist rhetorical claim, which I hope these comments have by now made clear. The radical feminist equation of rape and sex, no less than the liberal rape reform movement, gets its rhetorical force by trading on the liberal, normative-economic, and cultural assumptions that whatever is coercive is bad, and whatever is non-coercive is morally non-problematic. It has the effect, then, of further burdening the articulation of harms caused by consensual sex by forcing the characterization of those harms into a sort of "descriptive funnel" of non-consensuality. It requires us to say, in other words, that consensual sex is harmful, if it is, only because or to the extent that it shares in the attributes of non-consensual sex. But this might not be true—the harms caused by consensual sex might be just as important, just as serious, but nevertheless *different* from the harms caused by non-consensual sex. If so, then women are disserved, rather than served, by the equation of rape and sex, even were that equation to have the rhetorical effect its espousers clearly desire.

Liberal feminist rape reform efforts and radical feminist theory both, then, in different ways, undermine the effort to articulate the distinctive harms of consensual sex; the first by indirectly celebrating the value of consensual sex, and the latter by at least rhetorically denying the existence of the category. Both, then, in different ways, underscore the legitimation of consensual sex effectuated by non-feminist cultural and academic forces. My conclusion is simply that feminists could counter these trends in part by focusing attention on the harms caused women by consensual sexuality. Minimally, a thorough-going philosophical treatment of these issues might clear up some of the confusions on both sides of the "rape/sex" divide, and on the many sides of what have now come to be called the intra-feminist "sex wars," which continue to drain so much of our time and energy.

Study Questions

1. In arguing that the liberal's consent standard does not adequately protect women, is West's position ultimately paternalistic, and thus also injurious to women's autonomy? That is, in claiming that more than a woman's agreement must be in place to allow her to avoid unwanted sex, are we not robbing her of the freedom to consent to sex on her own terms? Compare West's position with Antioch's "Sexual Offense Policy" (chapters 29 and 30), which has also been criticized for reducing autonomy paternalistically, even as it aims at promoting autonomy.

2. It is known that some women apply various kinds of pressures on men (and women) to engage in sexual activity, without that pressure necessarily amounting to force or coercion that would make these sexual acts rape or nonconsensual. (See, for example, Peter Anderson and Cindy Struckman-Johnson, eds., *Sexually Aggressive Women: Current Perspectives and Controversies* [New York: Guilford, 1998].) Does this consensual sex harm men? When and how? Might there be a difference between men and women

in their ability to withstand the consequences of unwanted but consensual sex?

3. What if one partner in a couple desires to engage in sex more than the other partner, but both desire sex in general? This scenario seems rather the rule than the exception in many partnerships. What are the implications of it for West's position? Try to oppose the conclusions reached by Alan Wertheimer about this scenario (chapter 19) to the position found in West.

4. Is desire a more reliable moral criterion than consent? Granted, there are difficulties specifying what the consent standard demands, but what does West's no-harm standard mean in practice? What are the conceptual and normative differences between West's view and that of Robin Morgan, who focuses on desire: "rape exists any time sexual intercourse occurs when it has not been initiated by the woman, out of her own genuine affection and desire. . . . How many millions of times have women had sex 'willingly' with men they didn't want to have sex with? . . . How many times have women wished just to sleep instead or read or watch the Late Show? . . . Most of the decently married bedrooms across America are settings for nightly rape" ("Theory and Practice: Pornography and Rape," in *Going Too Far: The Personal Chronicle of a Feminist* [New York: Random House, 1977], 163–69, at 165–66)?

5. Does the analysis West provides of the background cultural assumptions responsible for the consent standards currently in force in sexual morality and the law add to or diminish the case for legalizing prostitution? Note that Yolanda Estes' objections to prostitution (chapter 23)—its psychological harmfulness, for example—are meant to apply to those cases in which the woman *does* consent.

Chapter 21

TWO VIEWS OF SEXUAL ETHICS: PROMISCUITY, PEDOPHILIA, AND RAPE

David Benatar

David Benatar *attempts to build a disjunctive dilemma surrounding two popular philosophical attitudes about sexuality. On one view (the "casual" philosophy of sex), sexual activity has intrinsic worth as a source of, in particular, pleasure; on the other view (the "significance" philosophy of sex), sexual activity has substantial instrumental value as an expression of love and commitment. If sexual activity has intrinsic worth as a source of pleasure, then casual sex is perfectly permissible but, at least in principle, sometimes that value, the pleasure, will outweigh the disvalue, the harm, done to unwilling people during rape or done to children in acts of pedophilia. On the other hand, if the value of sexual activity lies in its significance (through love or commitment) and not precisely in its pleasure, then rape and pedophilia are wrong, but casual sex and even mild promiscuity are also wrong. Given that both consequents are false—because rape and pedophilia are paradigm cases of morally wrong sexual activity; and because casual sex, in the liberal West at least, largely escapes moral notice, let alone reprobation—these two popular philosophical attitudes are unacceptable as stated. The "casual" view has no grounds to prohibit, absolutely, sexual acts that are immensely pleasurable for one person yet harmful for another, while the "significance" view cannot morally bless what many people in fact both engage in and approve of: sex without love. Benatar proceeds to ask whether there is some hybrid or intermediate philosophical position that is sufficiently permissive to allow casual sex and is also sufficiently restrictive to condemn rape and pedophilia. Because the child molester is contemporary* *culture's boogeyman, the embodiment of the darkest fears of many people, Benatar's frank discussion of the source of our abhorrence of pedophilia is valuable.*

Benatar is professor of philosophy at the University of Cape Town, South Africa, and the author of *Better Never to Have Been: The Harm of Coming into Existence* (Oxford University Press, 2006). He has also edited *Ethics for Everyday* (McGraw-Hill, 2002) and *Life, Death, and Meaning: Key Philosophical Readings on the Big Questions* (Rowman & Littlefield, 2004).

Reprinted, with the permission of David Benatar and the journal, from *Public Affairs Quarterly* 16, 3 (July 2002): 191–201.

The sexual revolution did not overthrow taboos about sex, but rather only restricted the number of practices regarded as taboo. Some sexual behaviors that were formally condemned are now tolerated or even endorsed. Others continue to be viewed with the opprobrium formerly dispensed to a broader range of sexual conduct. Promiscuity, for example, is widely accepted, but rape and pedophilia continue to be reviled.

On the face of it, this cluster of views—accepting promiscuity but regarding rape and pedophilia as heinous—seems perfectly defensible. I shall argue, however, that the view of sexual ethics that underlies an acceptance of promiscuity is inconsistent with regarding (1) rape as worse than other forms of coercion or assault, or (2) (many) sex acts with willing children as wrong at all. And the view of sexual ethics that would *fully* explain the wrong of rape and pedophilia would also rule out promiscuity. I intend this argument neither as a case against promiscuity nor as either a mitigation of rape or a partial defense of pedophilia. My purpose is to highlight an inconsistency in many people's judgments. Whether one avoids the inconsistency by extending or limiting the range of practices one condemns, will depend on which underlying view of the ethics of sex one accepts.

There are many views about the ethics of sex, but not all of these bear on the issues at hand. Consider, for instance, the view that a necessary condition of a sexual activity's being morally acceptable is that it carry the possibility of procreation.[1] While this view would be directly relevant to the practice of contraception, it would provide no way of morally judging promiscuity, pedophilia, or rape per se. Under some conditions, all of these practices would have procreative possibility.[2] Under others, none of them would. I shall restrict my attention to two views of sexual ethics that have special relevance to the three sexual practices I am considering.

TWO VIEWS OF SEXUAL ETHICS

The first of these is the view that for sex to be morally acceptable, it must be an expression of (romantic) love. It must, in other words, signify feelings of affection that are commensurate with the intimacy of the sexual activity. On this view a sexual union can be acceptable only if it reflects the reciprocal love and affection of the parties to that union. We might call this the significance view (or, alternatively, the love view) of sex, because it requires sex to signify love in order for it to be permissible.

On an alternative view of sexual ethics—what we might call the *casual view*—sex need not have this significance in order to be morally permissible. Sexual pleasure, according to this view, is morally like any other pleasure and may be enjoyed subject only to the usual sorts of moral constraints. A gastronomic delight, obtained via theft of a culinary delicacy, would be morally impermissible, but where no general moral principle (such as a prohibition on theft) applies, there can be no fault with engaging in gourmet pleasures. Having meals with a string of strangers or mere acquaintances is not condemnable as "casual gastronomy," "eating around," or "culinary promiscuity." Similarly, according to the casual view, erotic pleasures may permissibly be obtained from sex with strangers or mere acquaintances. There need not be any love or affection. (Nor need there always be pleasure. Just as a meal or a theatre performance might not be pleasurable and is not for that reason morally impermissible, so sex is not, nor ought, always to be pleasurable.)

Both the significance view and the casual view are moral claims about when people *may* engage in sex. They are not descriptive claims about when people *do* engage in sex. Clearly both kinds of sex *do* occur. Sometimes sex does reflect love. Sometimes it does not.

IMPLICATIONS OF THE TWO VIEWS

A sexually promiscuous person is somebody who is casual about sex—somebody for whom sex is not (or need not be) laden with romantic significance. (As promiscuity is obviously a matter of degree, for the most promiscuous people sex need not even be *tinged* with romantic significance.) This is not to say that the sexually promiscuous will have sex with simply anybody. Even the promiscuous can exercise some discretion in their choice of sexual partners just as the gastronomically "promiscuous" may be discriminating in the sort of people with whom they may wish to dine. The sexually promiscuous person is not one who is entirely undiscriminating about sexual partners, but rather somebody for whom romantic attachments are not a relevant consideration in choosing a sexual partner. It is thus clear why promiscuity is frowned upon by advocates of the significance view of sex. The promiscuous person treats as insignificant that which ought to be significant.

The significance view also has an explanation of why pedophilia is wrong. Children, it could be argued, are unable to appreciate the full significance that sexual activity should have.[3] This is not to suggest that children are asexual beings, but rather that they may lack the capacity to understand how sex expresses a certain kind of love. Having sex with a child is thus to treat the child as a mere means to attaining erotic pleasure without consideration of the mental states of which the provision of that pleasure should be an expression. Even if the child is sexually aroused, that arousal is not an expression of the requisite sorts of feelings. If the child is beyond infancy, the experience, in addition to being objectifying, may be deeply bewildering and traumatizing. The significance view of sex also provides an explanation of the special wrong of rape. On this view, raping people—forcing them to have sex—is not like forcing them to engage in other activities, such as going to the opera or to dinner. It is to compel a person to engage in an activity that should be an expression of deep affection. To forcibly strip it of that significance is to treat a vitally important component of sexual activity as though it were a mere trifle. It thus expresses extreme indifference to the deepest aspects of the person whose body is used for the rapist's gratification.

In defending promiscuous or casual sex, it has often been observed that not everybody thinks that sex must be an expression of love or affection. Many people, it is said, take the casual view of sex. For them, as I have said, sex is just another kind of pleasure and is permissible in the absence of love or affection. It is quite clear why this casual view does indeed entail the acceptability of promiscuous sex. What is often not realized, however, is that this view of sexual ethics leaves without adequate support the common judgments that are made about pedophilia and rape. I consider each of these two practices in turn.

If sex is morally just like other (pleasurable) activities and bears no special significance, why may it not be enjoyed with children? One common answer is that sex (with an adult)[4] can be harmful to a child. In the most extreme cases, including those involving physical force or those in which an adult copulates with a very small child, physical damage to the child can result. But clearly not all pedophilic acts are of this kind. Many, perhaps most, pedophilic acts are non-penetrative and do not employ physical force. Psychological harm is probably more common than physical damage. It is not clear, however, as a number of authors writing on this topic have noted, to what extent that harm is the result of the sexual encounter itself and to what extent it is the result of the secrecy and taboo that surrounds that sexual activity.[5] Insofar as a thorough embracing of the casual view of sex would eliminate those harms, the defender of this view cannot appeal to them in forming a principled objection to sexual interaction between adults and children. Because a society in which there were no taboos on pedophilia would avoid harm resulting from taboos on such activities and would simultaneously be inclusive of the pedophile's sexual orientation, it has everything to recommend it for defenders of the casual view.[6] At the most, advocates of this view can say that the current psychological harms impose temporary[7] moral constraints on sex with those children who, given their unfortunate puritanical upbringing or circumstances, would experience psychological trauma. Even such children may not be damaged by every kind of sexual interaction with an adult. For example, there is reason to believe that, where the child is a willing participant, the harm is either significantly attenuated or absent.[8]

Here it might be objected that although a child may sometimes appear to be a willing participant in sexual conduct with an adult, it is impossible for a child to give genuine consent to sexual activity.[9] For this reason, it might be argued, it is always wrong to engage in sexual relations with a child. Now, while this claim is entirely plausible on the significance view of sexual ethics, one is hard-pressed to explain how it is compatible with the casual view. What is it about sex, so understood, that a child is unable to consent to it? On this view, sex need carry no special significance and thus there is nothing that a child needs to understand in order to enter into a permissible sexual encounter. In response, it might be suggested that what a child needs to understand are the possible health risks associated with (casual) sex. That response, however, will not suffice to rule out all that those opposed to pedophilia wish to rule out. First, some sexual activities—most especially the noninvasive ones—do not carry significant health risks. Second, where children themselves are not thought competent to evaluate the risks of an activity, it is usually thought that a parent or guardian may, within certain risk limits, make the assessment on the child's behalf. Thus a parent may decide to give a child a taste of alcohol, allow a child to read certain kinds of books, or permit a child to participate in a sport that carries risks. If sex need be no more significant than other such activities, it is hard to see why its risks (especially when, as a result of safe sex, these are relatively small) and not those of the other activities (even when the latter are greater) constitute grounds for categorically excluding children and invalidating the consent which they or their parents give.

There is another consent-related objection that might be raised against pedophilia.[10] It might be argued that given the differences between adults and children, it is not possible for an adult and a child to understand one another's motives for wanting to have sex. The mutual unintelligibility of their motives makes it impossible for each party to know even roughly what the encounter means to the other and the absence of this information compromises the validity of the consent. Although this objection, like the previous one, is thoroughly plausible on the significance view, it lacks force on the casual view. Notice that the absence of mutual intelligibility of motives is not thought to be an objection to those activities with children, such as playing a game, that are not thought to carry the significance attributed to sex by the significance view. A child might be quite oblivious that the adult is playing the game only to give the child pleasure and that the adult may even be losing the game on purpose in order to enhance the child's pleasure or to build the child's sense of self-esteem. Yet, this is not thought to constitute grounds for invalidating a child's ability to consent to game playing with adults. The need for some mutual intelligibility of motive arises only if sex is significant.

Nor is it evident, on the casual view (unless it is coupled with a child-liberationist position), why children need consent at all. If a parent may pressure or force a child into participating in a sport (on grounds of "character-building"), or into going to the opera (on grounds of "learning to appreciate the arts"), why may a parent not coerce or pressure a child into sex? Perhaps a parent believes that treating sex as one does other aspects of life forestalls neurosis in the child and that gaining sexual experience while young is an advantage. If the evidence were sufficiently inconclusive that reasonable people could disagree about whether children really did benefit from an early sexual start, then those defenders of the casual view who also accept paternalism toward children would have to allow parents to decide for their children.

Whether or not interference with a child's freedom is justified, few people think that it is acceptable to interfere with the freedom of adults by, for example, forcing them to take up sport, go to the opera, or eat something (irrespective of whether it would be good for them). Those who accept this, even if they have the casual view of sexual ethics, have grounds for finding rape (of adults) morally defective. To rape people is to force them to do something that they do not want to do. Rape is an unwarranted interference with a person's body and freedom. The problem, for the defenders of the casual view is, that it need be no more serious an interference than would be forcing somebody to eat something, for example. Thus, although the casual view can explain why rape is wrong, it cannot explain why it is a special kind of wrong. One qualification needs to be added. Perhaps a proponent of the casual view could recognize that rape is especially wrong for those who do not share the casual view—that is, for those who believe (mistakenly, according to the casual view) that sex ought to be significant. A suitable analogy would be that of forcing somebody to eat a pork sausage. The seriousness of such an interference would be much greater if the person on whom one forced this meal were a vegetarian (or a Jew or a Muslim) than if he were not. A particular violation of somebody's freedom can be either more or

But ~~Sex~~ Rape is
about Power Not Sex

less significant, depending on that person's attitudes. Although some may be willing to accept that rape is especially wrong only when committed against somebody who holds the significance view of sex, many would not. Many feminists, for example, have argued at length for the irrelevance, in rape trials, of a woman's sexual history. But if the casual view is correct, then her sexual history would be evidence—although not conclusive evidence—of her view of sexual ethics. This in turn would be relevant to determining how great a harm the rape was (but not to *whether* it was rape and thus to whether it was harmful). Raping somebody for whom sex has as little significance (of the sort under consideration) as eating a tomato would be like forcing somebody to eat a tomato. Raping somebody for whom sex is deeply significant would be much worse. Although a significance view of sex might also allow such distinctions between the severity of different rapes, it can at least explain why rape of *anybody* is more serious than forcing somebody to eat a tomato.

CHOOSING BETWEEN THE VIEWS

Is there any way of choosing between the significance and casual views of sex? Some might take the foregoing reflections to speak in favor of or against one of the views. Those who are convinced that promiscuity is morally permissible may be inclined to think that the casual view must be correct because it supports this judgment. Others, who believe that pedophilia is wrong and that rape is a special kind of evil and is unlike other violations of a person's body or autonomy, may think that the significance view is correct given that it can support these judgments.

There are other factors that are also relevant to evaluating each of these views of sexual ethics. Consider first those who speak in favor of the significance view. This view fits well with judgments most people make about forms of intimacy that, although not sexual practices themselves, are not unrelated to the intimacies of sex: (1) casually sharing news of one's venereal disease (a) with a mere acquaintance, or (b) with one's spouse or other close family member; (2) undressing (a) in the street, or (b) in front of one's spouse in the privacy of one's bedroom. Very few people would feel exactly the same about (a) as about (b) in either of these examples. This would suggest that most people think that intimacies are appropriately shared only with those to whom one is close, even if they disagree about just how close one has to be in order to share a certain level of intimacy. The significance view seems to capture an important psychological feature about humans. Although descriptive psychological claims do not entail normative judgments, any moral view that attempted to deny immutable psychological traits characteristic of all (or almost all) humans would be defective.

But are these psychological traits really universal or are they rather cultural products, found only among some peoples? There are examples of societies that are much less restrictive about sex (including sex with children) than is ours, just as there are societies in which there are many more taboos than in ours pertaining to food and eating. It is too easy to assume that the way we feel about sex and food is the way all people do. If so, and if others are better off for their more open views of sex, then the defender of the casual view may have a message of sexual liberation that would be worth heeding.[11] This is not to say that it would be an easy matter (even for an individual, let alone a whole society) to abandon a significance view and thoroughly embrace the casual view. But if the casual view is the preferable one, then even if it would be difficult to adopt it would nonetheless be a view to which people ought to strive. One way to do this would be to rear children with the casual view.

Whether viewing sex as significant is characteristic of all humanity or only of certain human cultures is clearly an empirical issue that psychologists, anthropologists, and others would be best suited to determine. This matter cannot be settled here. In the absence of such a determination and of a convincing argument for one or the other view of sexual ethics, the appropriate response is agnosticism (of the theoretical even if not the practical form). Neither form of agnosticism would permit one to follow *both* views—the one for the pedophilia and rape issues and the other for the promiscuity issue. At least at the theoretical level, the choices we make should be consistent if they are to avoid the comfortable acquiescence to whatever happen to be the current mores. Agnosticism about the correct view of sex, like agnosticism on any other issue, is not to be confused with indifference. One may care deeply about an issue while realizing that the available evidence is insufficient to make a judgment on it. Caring deeply, however, should not stand in the way of a dispassionate assessment of the evidence. There is a great danger that in matters pertaining to current sexual taboos, clear thinking will be in short supply.

Hybrids of the two views may be possible. For instance, it may be thought that sex is not quite like other pleasures, but neither need it be linked to the deepest forms of romantic love. On one such view, it might be sufficient that one *like*[12] (rather than love) somebody in order to copulate. However, no such mixed view would resolve our problem. Any view that took a sufficiently light view of sex that would justify promiscuity would have difficulty ruling out all pedophilia or classifying rape as the *special* wrong it is usually thought to be.

Nor do I think that a non-hybrid intermediate view will be able to drive a moral wedge between promiscuity, on the one hand, and rape and pedophilia, on the other. Such an intermediate view would (as the casual view does) deny that sex must be an expression of romantic affection, but (in common with the significance view) deny that sex is like other pleasures. Although I obviously cannot anticipate every possible way in which such a view might be developed, I find it hard to imagine how any version could distinguish promiscuity from rape and pedophilia. Consider two versions of an allegedly intermediate view that have been put to me.

The first of these[13] is that although sex need not be an expression of romantic affection, it is unlike other pleasures in that it is intimate or private. The latter part of this claim might be understood as being either descriptive or normative. The descriptive claim is that most people prefer to engage in sex (i) with intimates[14] or (ii) away from the view of others. The normative claim is that people *ought* to engage in sex only (i) with intimates or (ii) away from the view of others. If the basis for (some or other of) these claims is that sex is or ought to be a deep expression of a romantic affection, then the view under discussion is either support for or a disguised version of the significance view rather than an alternative intermediate view. I cannot think of other reasons why sex is morally permissible only *between intimates*, but perhaps there is some such reason why sex is or ought to be *private*. If there is, then there would be an intermediate view between the significance and casual views. But what would be wrong, on this intermediate view, with *private* sex between an adult and a willing child? And why would coerced private sex be worse than other kinds of coerced activities in private? I suspect that any plausible answer to these questions would have to appeal to the normative significance of sex as an expression of affection, and any such appeal could not lead to a special condemnation of rape and all pedophilia without also implying a condemnation of promiscuity.

The second version of an allegedly non-hybrid intermediate view that has been suggested to me is that sex is unlike other pleasures because it is "personally involving ([that is,] psycho-dynamically complex)" in ways that other pleasures are not.[15] However, it seems that any interpretation of the view that sex is personally involving would be, or would lend support to, a significance view of sex. It would surely be inappropriate, at least as a moral ideal, to engage in personally involving behaviors with those (such as mere acquaintances) with whom personal involvement (at the relevantly complex or deep level) is not really possible. If that is so, then I cannot see how the second non-hybrid intermediate view can succeed in driving a wedge between promiscuity on the one hand, and rape and pedophilia on the other.

The above conclusions should obviously be extremely troubling to those who approve of promiscuity but who abhor pedophilia and rape. My deliberations show, however, that this should provide little cause for self-satisfaction on the part of those who condemn promiscuity along with rape and all pedophilia. Their moral judgments about these practices may be consistent but it remains an open question whether they are consistently right or consistently wrong. Which it is will depend on which of the rival views of sexual ethics is better. Until that matter is resolved, adherents of both the significance view and the casual view have cause for unease.

Study Questions

1. Defend the "casual" view against the charge, leveled by Benatar, that it is incompatible with the claim that sexual relations stemming from an adult that have a child as partner are always wrong. Try to do so without cutting back on the moral permissibility of sex without love.

2. "Raping a person for whom sexual activity has merely the significance of eating a tomato would be like forcing someone to eat a tomato." Is this analogy psychologically apt or a misleading piece of rhetoric? Explain your answer. Pay attention, in your deliberations, to the issue of the evidentiary status of a claimant's sexual history in a rape trial (e.g., whether she has had a wildly promiscuous lifestyle or has spent many years working as a prostitute).

3. Benatar writes, "Because a society in which there were no taboos on pedophilia would avoid harm resulting from taboos on such activities and would simultaneously be inclusive of the pedophile's sexual orientation, it has everything to recommend it for defenders of the casual view." Is there any rationale for the mention of *sexual orientation* in this context? How could Benatar's point be made without employing this concept? What *is* the "sexual orientation" of which he speaks?

4. Benatar dismisses intermediate philosophies of sex that invoke privacy, intimacy, or the "personally involving" nature of sexuality. Relying on views of sexual ethics expressed elsewhere in this volume (for example, Alan Wertheimer, Robin West), try to demarcate an intermediate view distinct from these that meets his objections.

5. Benatar closes by posing the question: Which of the rival views is better? What does "better" mean here? Would an explication or definition of "better" depend on which of the rival views one had prior commitments to? Or is there an independent or theory-neutral standard of "better" to which we might appeal in addressing this question?

NOTES

An earlier version of this paper was presented at a meeting of the Society for the Philosophy of Sex and Love at the Eastern Division meeting of the American Philosophical Association on December 30, 2001. The author is grateful to the University of Cape Town's Research Committee, as well as the International Science Liaison of the (South African) National Research Foundation for providing funding that enabled him to attend and participate in this meeting.

1. My own view is that if the possibility of procreation has anything to do with the moral acceptability of sex, then the *absence* rather than the presence of such a possibility is a necessary condition for sex's moral acceptability. The foundation for this admittedly unusual view is my argument that coming into existence is always a harm and therefore to bring somebody into existence is always to inflict a harm. (See my "Why It Is Better Never to Come Into Existence," *American Philosophical Quarterly* 34, no. 3 (July 1997), pp. 345–355.) It follows that it is procreative rather than non-procreative sex that bears the burden on moral justification.

2. Sexual intercourse with a pre-pubescent child has no procreative possibility. Those opposed to pedophilia, at least in our society, include under the rubric of "pedophilia" not only sex with such children, but also with pubescent children, where procreation is a possibility. I assume, then, that the procreative condition is not the grounds on which they oppose pedophilia.

3. Adherents of the significance view need not take all pedophilia to be wrong. They might think that children (beyond a certain age) *can* understand the full significance of sex. I am thus claiming only that the significance view has a way of arguing that pedophilia is wrong, not that it has to argue in that way.

4. It is interesting that many of those who take pedophilia to be harmful do not have the same reprobation for sex between two people both of whom are (in the relevant sense) children.

5. Alfred Kinsey et al., *Sexual Behavior in the Human Female* (Philadelphia: W. B. Saunders Co., 1953), pp. 120–121; Robert Ehman, "Adult-Child Sex," in *Philosophy and Sex* (New Revised Edition), ed. Robert Baker and Frederick Elliston (Buffalo, N.Y.: Prometheus Books, 1984), p. 436; Igor Primoratz, *Ethics and Sex* (London: Routledge, 1999), p. 138. A commentator on my paper when I presented it a conference claimed that there is much evidence to suggest that the harm does not result from the taboo. In support of this claim, she cited Anna Luise Kirkengen's *Inscribed Bodies: Health Impact of Childhood Sexual Abuse* (Dordrecht: Kluwer, 2001). I, however, am unable to find any support for her claim in this work. The book does deal with the adverse affects of sexual interactions with children. However, the question of whether it is the sexual interactions themselves or the taboos against them that cause harm is a specialized question that, as far as I can tell, is not addressed in this book. I mention the source in fairness to my commentator and for the benefit of those readers who wish to examine it for themselves.

6. Allen Buchanan has argued, in the context of a different debate, that the "morality of inclusion" requires that cooperative frameworks be made more inclusive where this is possible without unreasonable cost. (See his "The Morality

of Inclusion," *Social Philosophy and Policy* 10, no. 2 (June 1996): pp. 233–257.) Notice that even those ways of satisfying pedophilic preferences that do not involve actual children—such as child pornography that is either synthesized (that is, without using real models or actors) or is produced by adults being represented as children—are also abhorred, even where adult pornography is not. This suggests that the common abhorrence of pedophilia is not fully explained by the harm it is believed to do to the children involved.

7. That is, until the taboos can be eliminated.

8. T. G. M. Sandfort, "The Argument for Adult-Child Sexual Contact: A Critical Appraisal and New Data," in *The Sexual Abuse of Children: Theory and Research*, vol. 1, ed. William O'Donohue and James H. Geer (Hillsdale, N.J.: Lawrence Erlbaum Associates, 1992); Bruce Rind, Philip Tromovitch, and Robert Bauserman, "A Meta-Analytic Examination of Assumed Properties of Child Sexual Abuse Using College Samples," *Psychological Bulletin* 124, no. 1 (1998), pp. 22–53.

9. See, for example, David Finkelhor, "What's Wrong With Sex Between Adults and Children: Ethics and the Problem of Sexual Abuse," *American Journal of Orthopsychiatry* 49, no. 4 (1979): 692–697.

10. This objection was raised by an anonymous reviewer for *Public Affairs Quarterly*.

11. Of course, such benefits would have to be offset against the risks of sexually transmitted diseases, or steps would have to be taken within a sexual life governed by the casual view to minimize such risks.

12. In this context, "like" cannot mean "sexually attracted to" because that would be too weak to differentiate it from the pure hedonist view. Instead it would have to mean something like "have psychological affections-less-than-love for."

13. I am grateful to Raja Halwani for putting this to me and for suggesting that I raise and respond to the possibility of a non-hybrid intermediate view.

14. This appears not to be true of the promiscuous unless one stipulates that anybody with whom one has sex is thereby an intimate.

15. This view was suggested to me by an anonymous reviewer for *Public Affairs Quarterly*.

Chapter 22

VIRTUE ETHICS, CASUAL SEX, AND OBJECTIFICATION

Raja Halwani

*We hold the so-called sexual "player" and the "slut" or "tramp" up for a special kind of enmity, because these men and women seem to enjoy to an ill-advised extreme what many of us, truth be told, enjoy at least on occasion (even if only on occasion): casual sex, that is, sexual activity without promises, strings, or plans for the future. (More than a third of men recently surveyed approve of sexual relations without an emotional connection or commitment, though only half as many women do so. Is this difference the sociological result of a "double standard" moral ideology, or is it, more provocatively, the underlying foundation of that ideology?) At some point, as some philosophers, theologians, and psychologists worry, a person's attraction to and engaging in casual sex come to mold or define one's character. Regardless, that is, of whether causal sex is in itself morally suspicious, we can raise important questions about its consistency with leading a virtuous, flourishing life of human excellence. In this essay written from the perspective of virtue theory, **Raja Halwani** focuses on what we can learn about the characters, the moral personalities, of practitioners of casual sex; indeed, we can learn about the complexities of virtue theory itself by considering the test case of casual sex. Halwani arrives at a perhaps surprisingly benign, liberal judgment about casual sex. Laying out the conditions in which casual sex does not run afoul of virtue-theoretical considerations, Halwani argues that one of the purported defects of casual sex, that it involves sexual partners in noxious Kantian objectification, is not as serious as we might have supposed.*

Halwani did his graduate work at Syracuse University and is associate professor of philosophy at the School of the Art Institute of Chicago. He is the author of *Virtuous Liaisons: Care, Love, Sex, and Virtue Ethics* (Open Court, 2003) and has edited *Sex and Ethics: Essays on Sexuality, Virtue, and the Good Life* (Palgrave, 2007).

Little has been written philosophically about casual sex. In any case, casual sex is not usually considered morally good, even if there is agreement that its practitioners tend to find it pleasurable. I shall discuss the ethics of casual sex, arguing that from the point of view of virtue whether casual sex is immoral depends on the case, but that in general it is not morally wrong in itself. I also discuss objectification, a phenomenon that is thought to find a natural home in casual sex, concluding that it does not deserve a sweeping negative moral judgment; it, too, requires case-sensitive judgments.

I. What Is Casual Sex?

It is difficult to define "casual sex" if we understand this to mean the provision of necessary and sufficient conditions (Halwani 2006). Casual sex is sexual activity that occurs outside the context of a love relationship. Usually, but not invariably, the parties who engage in it do so with the sole intention of deriving sexual pleasure from the act. Typical examples include two people picking each other up in a bar for the purpose of sex, people meeting through the Internet for sex, and anonymous encounters in gay bath houses and straight swingers' clubs ("Plato's Retreat" in New York City). Note some departures. First, the parties to a casual sexual encounter may not be motivated solely by sexual pleasure. Some do it for the money, as in sex between a prostitute and client and sex between pornography actors. Second, people sometimes engage in casual sex without intending to do so. Two people might pick each other up in a bar, proceed to have sex, yet they intended (or hoped) that it would lead to a relationship. As it happens, the sex does not lead to a relationship, so they end up having casual sex despite their intentions.

Note also that casual sex is not promiscuity.[1] Promiscuity has a built-in temporal and quantitative requirement lacking in the former, namely, that a person engages in sex (which might not be casual in the usual sense) multiple times over a particular period of time. (Specifying the number and the duration of the period is difficult.) Casual sex is not like that; one can do it even only once in one's life (or a lot). Second, some sexual practices fit the above characterization of casual sex, but calling them "casual" seems bizarre: rape, bestiality, and necrophilia. If it is incorrect to label these "casual sex," then more needs to be done to fix the definition. I leave these issues open, focusing on paradigmatic instances of casual sex.

II. Virtue Ethics

Virtue ethics is often construed as a moral theory independent of, and perhaps rivaling, other theories, such as consequentialism and Kantian ethics.[2] Most virtue ethicists mine the writings of the ancient Greek philosophers, especially Aristotle, to develop a plausible version.[3]

Virtues and vices are character traits that dispose their possessor, the agent, to act according to their dictates (so to speak). On an Aristotelian view, the virtues are infused with wisdom, a form of practical intelligence that allows the agent to differentiate between what is right or proper to do, and what is wrong or improper to do. The virtues incline their agents not only to behave rightly, thereby judging rightly how to proceed in a particular situation, but also to exhibit, when applicable, the proper emotions.

Consider courage. According to Aristotle, this virtue allows its agent to handle fear and dangerous situations properly.[4] He claims that the courageous agent feels the right amount of fear when in danger; otherwise he would be either rash or cowardly (*NE* 1115b17–20). The goods for the sake of which the agent faces fear must be worthwhile (*NE* 1115a10–15). Overcoming one's fear and stepping into the bathroom despite the presence of a cockroach does not count as being courageous—the good at stake is trivial. By contrast, overcoming fear of retribution and reprisals and speaking up in a crowded and hostile room in defense of an innocent victim would count as being courageous. Aristotle also requires (*NE* 1105a30–1105b1) that the agent must act for the right reason or out of the right motive (this is also required by Kant). To be virtuous, the agent must speak up *because* an innocent victim must be defended and an injustice stopped, not because he is motivated by anticipated rewards for doing so.

Thus the virtuous agent is one who makes the right decision about what to do in a particular situation, makes this decision for the right reason, and feels the right kind and amount of any associated emotion.[5] Not all virtuous actions require the display of emotion, however. Some virtues have no necessary connection to emotions, for example, magnanimity and magnificence (Hursthouse 1980–1981, 58). And some virtues deal with desires, rather than emotions, as is the case with temperance. (This does not mean that emotions are never experienced along with temperate action: realizing that my hunky neighbor lusts after me as I lust after him, I strip for the ensuing sexual activity feeling not only desire but also joy and gratitude.)

III. Casual Sex and Virtue

A virtue ethics approach is neither inherently hostile to nor inherently in favor of sexual behavior. Aristotle's views on sex are found mostly in his treatment of temperance—the virtue that best expresses the proper attitudes and actions towards bodily desires (Halwani 2003 [chap. 3], 2007a; Young 1988). Whether a sexual action or desire is permissible or worthwhile depends on the object of the action or desire, much like whether fear is appropriate depends on its object (*NE* 1118b25). One question, then, is: Are people's desires for casual sex permissible or worthwhile? Is there anything wrong with desiring to have casual sex?

Further, assuming that desires for casual sex are morally permissible, ought they be acted on? The *type* of desire, say, a desire for heterosexual, vanilla sex, might be morally impeccable, yet acting on it in a particular case (having sex with my best friend's spouse) might not be. There might be types of casual sex such that desiring them is wrong and indicative of a lack of virtue. For example, rape is wrong; if it is casual sex, then it is wrong casual sex, and both desiring it and acting on the desire would be wrong. Similar reasoning applies to sex with children. Moreover, if sex with animals or with corpses is wrong, and it is casual sex, then it would be wrong casual sex, and so desiring it would be wrong. But these cases are not exhaustive. Indeed, they are not even the types of casual sex that first come to mind, which include one-night stands, anonymous sexual encounters, and swinger sex. What seems to be wrong about rape, pedophilia, and so forth, is something other than the fact that they are casual. They involve coercion, manipulation, deception, and harm, to name a few moral faults. In these cases, desire indicates a defective character.

If we focus on the usual cases of casual sex, they seem not to include these faults.[6] If two adults pick each other up in a bar with the intention and the knowledge that they are to have casual sex, what might be wrong? Setting objectification aside for a moment, and assuming—*contra* Kant[7]—that sexual desire is not inherently morally suspicious, it would seem that nothing is wrong with desiring casual sex or acting on the desire as long as, from a virtue-centered perspective, two conditions are satisfied (beyond that the type of casual sex desired must avoid the standard wrong-making features).

The first condition is one on which the advocates of virtue ethics must insist, given virtue theory's inclusion of character and motives under the moral umbrella: the agent's desire for casual sex should not consume his or her life. That is, desires should not be so strong or numerous that they overshadow other important aspects of life. Further, there might be something especially pernicious about letting sexual desire take control of one's life.[8] The first condition is bound to be controversial. Why should no single activity take over one's life, if that activity is worthwhile? And if there is nothing morally wrong or vicious in general with a worthwhile activity taking control of one's life, why be suspicious of sex? Perhaps when it comes to casual sex the idea is that an agent's life being consumed by it is hard to defend, because sex is not sufficiently worthwhile to justify sacrificing other things. But casual sex is not special here, for life-consuming sex between a loving couple would perhaps not redeem such lives.

There is a tradition in philosophy and theology, which includes Plato, Augustine, and even John Stuart Mill, that doesn't view sexual pleasure as valuable. The pleasures and goods of sex, though intense, are brief and tend to vanish (as opposed to, say, the pleasures and goods of reading a book). One can fondly remember sexual encounters, and can even dwell on these memories, but this is not worthwhile, if the activities that one dwells on are not worthwhile to begin with. One can manifest excellence when it comes to sex, but this, too, amounts to little if the activity at which one excels is not worthwhile.

I think this view is largely correct. Although sex is pleasurable, it is not the sort of activity to which devoting one's life would be good. It is not an activity that ordinarily enriches the agent or leaves its mark on humanity. Here casual sex might be especially vulnerable, since one cannot redeem it even on the grounds that one meets interesting people and thereby enriches one's life (as is often said about taxi drivers). The meetings tend to be fleeting; they involve superficial conversations (if any) between strangers; one's partner (and oneself) may well be dull and shallow. Casual sex seems not to merit letting one's life revolve around it, let alone letting it consume one's life. However, the argument has limits: if casual sex and the desire for it are not all-consuming, they could satisfy the first condition.

The second condition is another one on which advocates of virtue ethics would insist: what motivates the parties is subject to moral assessment, and casual sex must be engaged in for the right reason. Sometimes those who are motivated by desire for sexual pleasure have other motives that actually account for their behavior. (Similarly, one might desire casual sex yet for some virtuous reason not engage in it.) One's motives or reasons must be morally permissible or commendable. Having casual sex with X in order to spite Y, to make Y jealous, or to exact revenge on Y are morally pernicious motives. Morally permissible motives might include making money, engaging in leisurely activity, and wanting sexual pleasure. Morally commendable motives go beyond what is expected of people, for example, having casual sex with X out of compassion for X, or having sex with X so that X knows what to do on X's wedding night.

An Aristotelian virtue ethicist would also consider the role of casual sex in a flourishing—well-lived, *eudaimon*—life. The concept of a flourishing life is central to Aristotle's ethics since it explains why people should be virtuous (*NE* 1097a15–1098a20). Casual sex might not consume one's life, might be done for the right reasons, and might not involve the usual wrong-making features. Still, could it contribute to a flourishing life?

Sexual activity is often experienced as an urge that, if not satisfied, leaves the agent agitated; it is generally pleasurable; in this and other ways it is an important source of leisure; and it often functions as a release, whereby the agent is able, afterward, to attend more freely and less anxiously to other matters. Consider, in this light, an agent who has a healthy sexual drive but who either has no room for a romantic commitment in her life or who, for some good reason, does not desire such a commitment. She prefers to pursue activities and projects central to her life. She might then opt to conduct her sexual life by engaging in casual sex, meeting sexual partners in bars, online, or having one or two "fuck buddies." Such a sex life helps the agent flourish in the ways described above, i.e., casual sex allows her to avoid the agitation of unsatisfied desire, it refreshes her for a return to her work, and so forth.

Now consider a couple, X and Y, who decide to jettison sexual fidelity. They might do so because their sex has become boring or because they desire sexual variety. Extramarital sexual behavior should be conducted cautiously, because it can lead to jealousy and insecurity that endangers the relationship X and Y desire to continue to have. Still, if conducted wisely, it might lead to enriching their sexual lives without detracting from their lives and pursuits. It might even strengthen their love, allowing them to see how valuable they are to each other and how much they want to be with each other.[9] And their casual sex may make their lives more pleasant. If properly and wisely engaged in, casual sex can enrich an otherwise *eudaimon* life by making it more pleasant and allowing the agents to pursue their life-projects more comfortably.

Finally, consider people who are not especially virtuous, but are not vicious, either. Because the virtues are necessary for flourishing, according to Aristotle, these people are not living their lives well. Furthermore, they might have very little going for them under a philosophical (perhaps elitist) notion of what it is to live a worthwhile life: they are not astronauts, Proust scholars, or Piet Mondrians. They might be slow-witted or otherwise have bland personalities. Yet if they are physically attractive, the availability of casual sex might be something that makes their lives better. Casual sex would help them lead enjoyable, even if not flourishing, lives.

IV. Objectification

To objectify a person is to treat him or her only as an object. For example, a person treats another as an object if the first uses the second as a chair while reading the paper. If objectification is always morally wrong and is an essential feature of casual sex, casual sex is always wrong. It would not avoid one of the standard wrong-making characteristics of acts. Further, it would be tainted to the extent that the desire for casual sex included the vicious motive of objectifying one's partner. Objectification poses a problem for anyone who thinks that casual sex is morally permissible.

Why assume that objectification is always morally wrong? Its moral wrongness cannot simply be read off from the definition; it is not obvious why treating an entity that is not an object (in particular, a person) only as an object constitutes conclusive grounds for moral condemnation. Something else must be added, to the effect that the person does not merit object-like treatment in virtue of some characteristic he has that morally blocks object-like treatment. So, in treating the person only as an object, one is trespassing this moral boundary. For persons, it might be their rationality, sophisticated desires and mental structures, hopes, wishes, happiness, capacity for flourishing or *eudaimonia*, or their affinity to God that morally elevates them above objects. Note that any of these features—not only rationality—could be the basis on which persons can legitimately demand nonobjectifying treatment. Objectification, then, though it has its natural home and origin in Kantian ethics, is a concept that fits well with other moral frameworks, including virtue ethics. If the feature specified cannot do the job of morally elevating us above objects (or animals), those who think objectification is always morally wrong will have to find other arguments (Soble 2002, chap. 2). I shall not pursue this approach.

Why assume that objectification is an essential feature of casual sex? In typical cases of casual sex, two people engage in sex only for sexual pleasure. In doing so, we might argue, they use each other—treating each other as objects, as sophisticated dildos or plastic vaginas—for the purpose of pleasure. Even when one party has other reasons or motives (money), there is still objectification, for X uses Y to fulfill that purpose. This argument need not rely on the implausible assumption that in typical cases of casual sex the parties intend to objectify each other. Even if X does not intend to objectify Y, X still does so in and by using Y for sexual pleasure.

The defender of casual sex can adopt two strategies. First, it can be argued that although objectification is an essential feature of casual sex, objectification is not always wrong. Second, it can be argued that objectification is not an essential feature of casual sex, and that whether casual sex objectifies depends on the particular case. I adopt the second strategy.

How can a particular casual sex act not be objectifying? If objectification is to treat someone who is not an object merely as an object, attending to the phenomenology involved in casual sex helps us see how.[10]

Casual sex partners do not usually think of each other as mere objects. A woman who picks up a man in a bar does so precisely because she thinks him a man, not a cleverly constructed robot or a penis with some sort of body attached to it. A gay man who sucks another's penis through a glory hole does so precisely because he thinks the penis is attached to a man, a man whom he likely saw earlier and was attracted to. Thus, the parties to casual sex usually desire interaction with other persons, not objects. On its own, this fact means little, for even as we know that our casual sexual partner is a person, we can nonetheless proceed to objectify him or her. But the fact is still important in reminding us that casual sexual interaction is close to many other types of human interaction, sexual and nonsexual. In casual sex, as elsewhere, we are aware of the humanity of others, and we usually attempt to respect their wishes, desires, and wants. Paying the grocer for the chewing gum, in a civil fashion, is a form of respect: I respect his wishes to be treated as a seller and kindly, not merely someone to be abused and robbed. This is no less true in casual sex; in typical cases, the partners attend to each other's sexual needs, desires, and wishes. Indeed, even when X complies with Y's demand, "Yes! Use me like a lemon sucked dry," X would not be objectifying Y, for in treating Y as nothing but a body part, X is doing Y's bidding. The operative phrase is "doing Y's bidding," and it is hard to see how abiding by Y's wishes and desires one is objectifying Y, that is, treating Y *merely* as an object.

Note that this argument does not deny that objectification occurs in some cases of casual sex, in which, say, one partner treats the other as a piece of meat. Such cases are unlikely to be frequent, since the used person, realizing that he or she is being used in selfish ways, opts out of the activity (unless he or she is unable or afraid to), and since such behavior is largely confined to deranged individuals. Note also that this argument does not deny that in casual sex the focus is on sex itself and the body of one's partner, rather than on some purportedly more substantial feature. Indeed, few things can disrupt the mood of casual sex act as well as intellectual conversation. But it does not follow that objectification is occurring, unless it also follows (which I cannot see that it does) from my focusing on a dancer's body that I am objectifying her, or focusing on a chef's hands as he swiftly dices an onion is objectification. If so, objectification is not an essential feature of casual sex, and casual sex cannot be sweepingly faulted on this score.

Perhaps the defense of casual sex has gone through so easily because we have been employing a superficial definition of objectification. As argued by Martha Nussbaum (1995), objectification may be more complex, and treating someone as an object can take many forms and have different meanings. If so, a defense of casual sex should take this complexity into account. Of the seven senses of "objectification" Nussbaum lists, however, only two pose difficulties; the other five—denial of autonomy, inertness, violability, ownership, and denial of subjectivity—do not. On the contrary, what typically occurs during casual sex is the opposite. In taking into account my partner's sexual desires, I consider him to have autonomy, self-determination, and agency. Furthermore, I do not consider him to be violable, for I attribute to him boundaries and integrity in two ways: first, by not treating him contrary to his desires and, second, precisely by treating him in accordance with his desires. I also, for the same reasons, do not treat him as an owned object. Finally, in taking his sexual desires into account, I certainly do not treat him "as something whose experience and feelings . . . need not be taken into account" (257).

This leaves us with two objectifications, instrumentality and fungibility. Instrumentality is a problem only if the person is treated merely as a tool (which Nussbaum acknowledges, 265). But people frequently use each other as tools (students use teachers for educational purposes; teachers use students for career purposes). In interactions with each other, if we use each other as tools but also, in doing so, act in accordance with each other's wishes and desires, it seems that objectification disappears. Since in casual sex the partners typically do this, instrumentalization, understood as the *mere* use of another as a tool, is not a problem.

Fungibility—the treatment of something or someone "as interchangeable (a) with other objects of the same type, and/or (b) with objects of other types" (Nussbaum 1995, 257)—is an interesting type of objectification. When we objectify someone, he would make perfect sense were he to say, "I demand that I not be treated this way," given that we ought not to objectify people. However, fungibility does not license such reactions. Suppose I enter a coffee shop, do not like the selection, and go somewhere else. In doing so, I treat the owner of the store as fungible with other coffee shop owners. Yet for him to protest that I have wronged him in this treatment would be silly. Similarly, if I go to a bar in search of casual sex, no one can demand that I pick him or her up. In considering people as "interchangeable with other objects of the same type" I do nothing wrong. When objectification is wrong, others can demand of objectifiers that they, the objectified, not be objectified. This seems out of place regarding fungibility. Unless I have preexisting obligations, no one can demand of me that I purchase coffee from his shop rather than another shop or that I have sex with him instead of someone else.

Does this argument show that fungibility is morally innocuous objectification, or that fungibility is not objectification, period? If objectification is always morally wrong, as I have presumed, then fungibility cannot be objectification, because not all cases of treating people as fungible are morally wrong. We can add that in permissible fungibility—buying and selling merchandise, selecting hotels for vacationing, picking up people in bars, hiring people for jobs—those making the choices treat others in a fungible way, but they do not treat them as objects, because both the selected and rejected people have made the choice to compete with others for special attention, whether this attention be economic, sexual, academic, etc. The respectful treatment of others that occurs here nullifies objectification.

The reason why fungibility seems wrong is that it is like treating people like pens or paper cups, discarding one and using another for our own purposes. But this indicates that fungibility is wrong when it occurs with actions that are otherwise wrong, in which case fungibility itself is not the problem,[11] or when it occurs in special relationships. For example, were I to own five slaves whom I treated like pens, consigning each to the trash bin when they ceased to be useful, I would be treating them fungibly. The wrongness here, however, stems from my treating them as objects to begin with, not the resulting fungibility. If I kidnap my neighbor's child and bring them a child from the local shelter, declaring "Have this one. He'll do," the wrongness is fungibility, but only because I acted, wrongly, as if no special relationship had existed between parent and child, that is, as if any child of a certain age would for them be an adequate substitute. Now, if I were in a bar cruising for a one-night stand, eyeing potential sexual partners, I would be treating them as fungible; I view them, individually, as interchangeable with other men in general or with other men of a particular sort, say, thirty-something Indian or Pakistani men ("of the same type"). But since none of them can rightly demand of me that I sleep with him, and since I cannot sexually impose myself on any one of them or demand of any one of them that he sleep with me, in treating them as fungible I not only do not do them wrong, I do not objectify them. So fungibility, when it comes to casual sex, should be stricken from the list of possible ways to objectify others.

I have argued that virtue ethics morally permits casual sex in some cases but not in others. Virtue ethics also allows that an otherwise flourishing life can be enriched by casual sex. Moreover, objectification in casual sex is much less frequent than thought; it requires morally nasty behavior in which casual sexual partners do not usually engage.

Study Questions

1. If it is true, as a number of surveys have been quick to remind us, that three-quarters of all men think about sex every day (every ten seconds?), at what point is it accurate or fair to conclude that a person's desires for sex have become consuming, or *too* consuming? Do those judgments make any sense, or *how* could we fashion them to make sense?

2. Suppose the sexual player disagrees with the claim made in the essay that "sex is not so worthwhile to justify sacrificing other things for its sake." Can you imagine what sort of reasonable grounds the player might offer? How would you defend Halwani's virtue ethics against the player's arguments?

3. Halwani suggests that my abiding by or acceding to your sexual wishes and needs is sufficient for my avoiding objectifying you, even if, or especially when, you wish to be sexually objectified (see Alan Goldman's similar sentiment, in chapter 5). Is it possible to rely either on Thomas Mappes's (chapter 16) or Immanuel Kant's (as presented by Alan Soble in chapter 18) notions of impermissible sexual use to rebut this view?

4. Virtue ethics expects people to exhibit appropriately virtuous emotions, but at least for some emotions (joy and grief) this is asking a lot of us. What emotional responses can any theory reasonably expect of people with respect to sexual attraction and romantic love? Try to develop this inquiry into a criticism of Halwani's views.

5. The list of dominant virtues changes over time; the central virtues of courage and temperance for the Greeks were, it is plausible to say, supplanted by faith and charity for the Christians. Further, the range of behaviors and motives exemplary of any particular virtue is acknowledged by Aristotle to be relative to a mean discernible by the person of practical wisdom. Given these vicissitudes, might Halwani's conclusion, that casual sex is on the whole a positive phenomenon, have to be qualified? That is, might it be true only for liberal societies? If so, is this a drawback to his approach?

Notes

The author thanks Alan Soble for comments on earlier drafts, and many students with whom I discussed these issues, especially David Cordero, Elliot Layda, Nora Mapp, Will Megson, and Carissa Ann Owen.

1. One essay whose title claims to "revisit" casual sex is about promiscuity (Kristjansson 1998). For more on casual sex and promiscuity, see Anscombe 1972; Ellis 1986; Elliston 1975; Halwani 2003 (chap. 3), 2006, and 2007b.
2. See Foot 2001 and Hursthouse 1999.
3. Not all do. See Swanton 2003 for a Nietzschean version of some virtues.
4. *Nicomachean Ethics* (henceforth *NE*).

5. Not all virtue ethicists agree; see Driver 2001, especially chap. 5, for an account not requiring right motives.

6. There might be manipulation, such as using cosmetics to conceal wrinkles, but this does not seem to be morally objectionable (Baumrin 1984, 301).

7. Kant argued that sexual acts were objectifying in virtue of the nature of sexual desire (*Lectures on Ethics*, 162–70). On Kant, see Mappes 2002 [in this volume, chap. 16]; Denis 1999, 2007; Soble 2007b [in this volume, chap. 18].

8. See Dent 1984, especially chap. 2 and 5; Carnes 1983; Soble 2007a, 241–47.

9. This case indicates that wedding sex to love or intimacy is not necessary, as some (Finnis 1994; Scruton 1986, chap. 11) have maintained.

10. See Scruton 1986, especially chap. 5, 6, and 11, for a similar argument that has a different conclusion.

11. Nussbaum seems to accept this point about fungibility, unwittingly, when she states, "the suspicion remains that there may . . . be some connection between the spirit of fungibility and a focus on these superficial aspects of race and class and penis size, which do in a sense dehumanize, and turn people into potential instruments" (287). The problem here is dehumanization and instrumentalization, not fungibility.

References

Anscombe, G. E. M. 1972. "Contraception and Chastity." *The Human World* 7, 9–30.

Aristotle. 1999. [ca. 330 BCE] *Nicomachean Ethics*. Trans. Terence Irwin, 2nd ed. Indianapolis, Ind.: Hackett.

Baumrin, Bernard. 1984. "Sexual Immorality Delineated." In Robert Baker and Frederick Elliston, eds., *Philosophy and Sex*, 2nd ed. Buffalo, N.Y.: Prometheus, 300–11.

Carnes, Patrick. 1983. *The Sexual Addiction*. Minneapolis, Minn.: Compcare.

Denis, Lara. 1999. "Kant on the Wrongness of 'Unnatural Sex.'" *History of Philosophy Quarterly* 16: 225–48.

———. 2007. "Sex and the Virtuous Kantian Agent." In Raja Halwani, ed., *Sex and Ethics: Essays on Sexuality, Virtue, and the Good Life*. New York: Palgrave Macmillan, 37-48.

Dent, N. J. H. 1984. *The Moral Psychology of the Virtues*. Cambridge: Cambridge University Press.

Driver, Julia. 2001. *Uneasy Virtue*. Cambridge: Cambridge University Press.

Ellis, Anthony. 1986. "Casual Sex." *International Journal of Moral and Social Studies* 1: 157–69.

Elliston, Frederick. 1975. "In Defense of Promiscuity." In Robert Baker and Frederick Elliston, eds., *Philosophy and Sex*, 1st ed. Buffalo, N.Y.: Prometheus, 223–43.

Finnis, John. 1994. "Law, Morality, and 'Sexual Orientation.'" *Notre Dame Law Review* 69: 1049–76.

Foot, Philippa. 2001. *Natural Goodness*. New York: Oxford University Press.

Halwani, Raja. 2003. *Virtuous Liaisons: Care, Love, Sex, and Virtue Ethics*. Chicago: Open Court.

———. 2006. "Casual Sex." In Alan Soble, ed., *Sex from Plato to Paglia: A Philosophical Encyclopedia.* Westport, Conn.: Greenwood Press, 136–42.

———. 2007a. "Sexual Temperance and Intemperance." In Raja Halwani, ed., *Sex and Ethics: Essays on Sexuality, Virtue, and the Good Life.* New York: Palgrave Macmillan, 122–33.

———. 2007b. "Casual Sex, Promiscuity, and Temperance." In Raja Halwani, ed., *Sex and Ethics: Essays on Sexuality, Virtue, and the Good Life.* New York: Palgrave Macmillan, 215–25.

Hursthouse, Rosalind. 1980–1981. "A False Doctrine of the Mean." *Proceedings of the Aristotelian Society* 81: 57–72.

———. 1999. *On Virtue Ethics.* New York: Oxford University Press.

Kant, Immanuel. [ca. 1780] *Lectures on Ethics.* Trans. Louis Infield. Indianapolis, Ind.: Hackett, 1963.

Kristjansson, Kristjan. 1998. "Casual Sex Revisited." *Journal of Social Philosophy* 29: 97–108.

Mappes, Thomas. 2002. "Sexual Morality and the Concept of Using Another Person." In Thomas Mappes and Jane Zembaty, eds., *Social Ethics: Morality and Social Policy,* 6th ed. Boston, Mass.: McGraw-Hill, 157–64.

Nussbaum, Martha. 1995. "Objectification." *Philosophy and Public Affairs* 24: 249–91.

Plato. [ca. 380 BCE] *Symposium.* Trans. Alexander Nehemas and Paul Woodruff. Indianapolis, Ind.: Hackett, 1989.

Scruton, Roger. 1986. *Sexual Desire: A Moral Philosophy of the Erotic.* New York: Free Press.

Soble, Alan. 2002. *Pornography, Sex, and Feminism.* Amherst, N.Y.: Prometheus.

———. 2007a. "Concealment and Exposure: A Mostly Temperate and Courageous Afterword." In Raja Halwani, ed., *Sex and Ethics: Essays on Sexuality, Virtue, and the Good Life.* New York: Palgrave Macmillan, 229–52.

———. 2007b. "Sexual Use." In this volume, chapter 18.

Swanton, Christine. 2003. *Virtue Ethics: A Pluralistic View.* New York: Oxford University Press.

Young, Charles. 1988. "Aristotle on Temperance." *Philosophical Review* 97: 521–42.

PART 4

USE, OBJECTIFICATION, AND CONSENT—APPLIED TOPICS

Chapter 23

PROSTITUTION: A SUBJECTIVE POSITION

Yolanda Estes

In this essay, **Yolanda Estes** *draws on the views of the German philosophers Immanuel Kant and Johann Gottlieb Fichte, as well as on her own experiences, in developing a transcendental, phenomenological, and empirical account of prostitution that implies that prostitution is psychologically damaging and morally wrong. Even if the prostitute fully consents to the sexual activity, Estes argues, that does nothing to block the psychological damage or the immorality. Thus Estes offers an alternative to more common liberal defenses of prostitution.*

Estes is associate professor of philosophy at Mississippi State University, where she specializes in German idealism and ethics. Her publications include *Marginal Groups and Mainstream American Culture*, coedited with Arnold Lorenzo Farr, Patricia Smith, and Clelia Smyth (Lawrence: University Press of Kansas, 2000). She is completing *Fichte and the Atheism Dispute (1798–1800)*, coedited with Curtis Bowman (London: Ashgate).

Reprinted, revised, with permission of the journal, from Yolanda Estes, "Moral Reflections on Prostitution," *Essays in Philosophy* 2, 2 (2001), published online at www .humboldt.edu/~essays/estes.html.

I will argue that prostitution is morally wrong, socially destructive, and personally harmful, because it proffers a monetary substitute for mutual desire and concern and thereby defies the limits of respectful sexual relations.[1] Although other definitions might be apt in other contexts, I define prostitution, for the purposes of this essay, as the performance, for money, of a sexual act involving physical contact. My argument will consider prostitution from a subjective position, which approach can enhance the study of prostitution but does not preclude examining prostitution from other perspectives.[2] I begin by refining the notion of prostitution I am using and by discussing several useful meanings of subjectivity. I then turn to examining in more detail the transcendental (section 2), the phenomenological (section 3), and the empirical (section 4) subject of prostitution.

1. Prostitution and the Prostitute as Subject

Prostitution requires two elements: one person (the prostitute) willing to exchange sexual service for money, or its tangible equivalent, and another person (the client) willing to exchange money, or its equivalent, for sex. In each act of prostitution, money is the prostitute's primary motivation.[3] Money would be secondary only if she were willing to engage in that particular sexual act without receiving it. She engages in the act for reasons other than her own sexual desire and, hence, without expressing an authentic interest in relating to her client sexually. Sexual gratification is the client's primary motivation.[4] It would be secondary only if he were willing to give the prostitute money without their engaging in sex. His indifference to her lack of sexual desire is obvious insofar as he accepts her terms. The prostitute and the client understand each other's motives and goals.

Transcendental philosophy distinguishes between the transcendental standpoint and the empirical standpoint.[5] Transcendental philosophers, such as Immanuel Kant and Johann Gottlieb Fichte, use abstraction to isolate the transcendental conditions necessary for empirical reality from experience. The idea of the transcendental subject is what remains after the philosopher has abstracted from the characteristics of personality, or empirical subjectivity.[6] The transcendental subject may be viewed in light of its theoretical or its practical capacity (as a will). Herein, the transcendental subject is the prostitute as a moral agent considered apart from her empirical subjectivity.

A phenomenology is a description. A description can be philosophical (a report of events isolated by reflection), actual (a report of real events), or conjectural (a study of possible events). Philosophical phenomenology, such as that employed by Edmund Husserl, has a venerable role in the history of philosophy and has exerted a profound influence on contemporary philosophy.[7] It requires a philosophical reduction of experience similar to the abstraction from experience employed by the transcendental philosopher. Actual and conjectural phenomenology involves a sustained focus on specific features of experience but requires a less rigorous and complete reduction than philosophical phenomenology. The phenomenological subject is the perspectival center of such a phenomenology. Herein, the phenomenological subject is the prostitute treated as the protagonist of a conjectural description of prostitution.

Empirical accounts are based in actual experience. Empirical reports assume many forms; one possible form is a study of an individual's behavior. Such a report can be drawn from our observations of a subject or from a subject's self-report, narrative, or story. The empirical subject is an individual personality, replete with contingent characteristics such as a history that unfolded within a specific spatiotemporal context. Herein, the empirical subject is a prostitute regarded as an individual with a personal history that includes prostitution.

2. Transcendental Subjectivity

Transcendental philosophy identifies human subjectivity and dignity with a self-determining will that expresses itself through the limited willing activity of embodied individuals. The individual knows itself as a subject only by means of mutual recognition within a particular social context.[8] Moreover, each person's subjectivity is partly determined by her or his choices with regard to sexual expression and their mode of integrating sex, gender, and sexuality within their life as a whole.[9]

All sexual activities express subjectivity, but not all sexual activities involve mutual recognition. Some reflect one person's attempt to determine or dominate the other, by receiving her recognition, without deferring to her influence or acknowledging her will and, thus, without incurring an obligation to her. Moral subjects must eschew such actions, because they stand under a moral law that states, in the words of Immanuel Kant, "Act in such a way that you always treat humanity, whether in your own person or in the person of another, never simply as a means, but always at the same time as an end."[10] This principle demands both the preservation and the active promotion of humanity as an end in itself.[11] Consequently, moral subjects have duties to adopt the rational ends of all human beings with regard to their greater moral perfection, general human development, and self-determined projects.[12] All their relations, including the sexual, must exhibit mutual respect.

Mutually respectful sex occurs within a context of reciprocal consent, desire, and concern. It requires that potential sexual partners give explicit, or at least implicit, expression of their willing participation in the sexual act. But whether verbal or not, consent alone provides no immunity to moral reproach.[13] Insofar as one shows regard for a potential sexual partner, one cannot ignore her desires.[14] While one need not accommodate every sexual desire of the other, one ought to take their desires and aversions into account. Human beings suffer when they engage in unwelcome activities, just as they suffer when their wishes are disappointed. Distress is, sometimes, unavoidable or morally necessary, such as when our desires and aversions are unreasonable or morally objectionable. Still, inflicting unnecessary pain is morally wrong. Moreover, one should exhibit concern—moral regard—for the other's interests, needs, and general well-being.

Without mutual consent, mutual desire, and mutual concern, potentially pleasing sexual acts become mere corporal intrusions that obscure the distinction between a human or person's body and an arational, nonconscious thing. Other standards might be necessary to determine that a sexual encounter is morally right, personally satisfying, or prudent, but respect for persons in a sexual context requires that these minimal criteria be fulfilled. Prostitution fails to satisfy them, because its motives preclude mutual respect. In the prostitute's case, she intends to use her body as tool for exploiting the client's desire. In the client's case, he intends to treat her as a thing on which to sate his appetite.[15] Each participant expects to be viewed and treated as a mere means to the other's goals. Each eschews full recognition of the other, thereby eliminating the possibility of being recognized. Such behavior cannot be construed as something other than an affront to humanity in oneself and others. Consequently, prostitution is wrong by transcendental moral standards. It is questionable also according to other moral standards, insofar as it is detrimental to human well-being and destructive of human virtues.

3. Phenomenological Subjectivity

The prostitute's consent to engage in sexual relations need not express her sentiments; indeed, the client has every reason to suspect it does not. Sex is an exploration wherein one is permitted to fail, but her role forbids this luxury. The bargain demands she exclude her sexual identity from the encounter. Overt indifference might insulate her individual subjectivity, but he expects more than a skilled automaton. Disclosure of her desires and interests might allow the client to glimpse her subjectivity. But precisely that situation exceeds and violates the scope of their agreement. A compromise more aptly safeguards both her individual subjectivity and professional persona; thus, she might best present a semblance of sexual desire by means of various theatrical devices. Some prostitutes—wives and girlfriends, too—learn these dramatic devices well and employ them effectively (as if they had read Thomas Nagel's essay on the intentionality of sexual interactions, which allows one person to arouse another by feigning her own arousal).[16] Others, by comparison, are amateurs at carrying out, or unsuited to, pretense.

The prostitute's sexual activity evokes physical, emotional, and intellectual reactions that threaten to undermine the illusion of reciprocity. Every visible response must address the client's desires and wishes. Her repugnance must not blatantly force itself upon him; any disgust she experiences must not be a clue that it was invoked by her sensing him. Her pleasure must appear to him as the satisfaction that he demands and he thinks he has elicited. But her yielding to any sensations that might arise in their sexual activity, responding either with frank displeasure or with genuine arousal, to what is happening in and to her body, jeopardizes the integrity of her relationship with the client, others, and herself. To avoid this danger, to attend to the client's pleasure without succumbing to her own responses, she must *detach* herself from the bodily events without, for all that, *losing control* over her body. No mean feat.

The prostitute attempts to annihilate her presence within the sexual act by extinguishing her reaction to it. Mindful of the risk posed by intense feelings that are otherwise likely to occur, she estranges herself from her body, presenting a phantom of the sensibility that she forbids herself to possess. When the illusion dissolves, she expects to reintegrate her alienated self with her prostituted flesh, but the residue of her actions taints both her self and her flesh. It is not difficult to imagine that, as a result, she becomes conditioned to respond similarly to all sexual stimulation.

The client's own set of conflicting demands mirrors the prostitute's self-fragmentation. He wants more than the prostitute's artifice and the stimulation of his genitals that he bought: he also expects the hidden subject to recognize his subjectivity. That, however, requires that he acknowledges hers as well. Genuine interest in her personality or personhood would compromise their bargain. As a result, his demands are contradictory, which precludes a happy coincidence of his desires. Further, his attempt to obtain recognition from her without incurring any obligation in return deepens her dissolution. Any endeavor on his part to reunite the pieces, to undo her fragmentation, in order to secure her recognition of him would have to involve pressure or coercion and hence would mimic rape or, at least, involuntary seduction.

Attempts of the client to coax the prostitute to drop her guard produce an illusion of trust, understanding, and mutual recognition. Indeed, the need to maintain this illusion might inspire him to manifest courtesy by making a determined effort to give her pleasure and to avoid causing her distress. Outward appearances make his attempted seduction of a reluctant mistress look like considerate lovemaking. Alternatively, his efforts to provoke a genuine sexual and emotional response by denigrating her may allow him to feel that he commands her body and soul. Exhibiting his disregard for her needs and desires perpetuates this semblance of control. Again from outward appearances, his assault might look like sexual brutishness that resembles rape in every respect, except that she had earlier consented.

Obviously, he might do something else to try to reach her, but unless he forgoes his original objectives, anything he does is destined to fail. Honest savagery denies her subjectivity overtly, but feigned tenderness undercuts it surreptitiously. On the one hand, brutality threatens her composure, but on the other hand, tenderness compels her to view him as a person. Her task might be easier if he presented her with the option of viewing him precisely as an animal, neither as a human rapist nor human lover, as an animal that completes its biologically fixed natural act without human emotion but with only lowly, crude, instinctual, unreflective emotion. By evading his various possible attempts to engage her, rebuffing his expressions of either intimidation or compassion, she repudiates his capacity to touch her.

One can easily imagine that she resents these attempts to engage her. In other contexts, she would be touched, by interacting with those to whom she is bound by complex patterns of attraction and obligation. But how dare this presumptuous client, who in a business deal paid for a service, attempt to arouse her! By what imagined right does he pretend to recognize her humanity, seeking illegitimately to integrate himself "compassionately" within a life and emotional structures she has carefully isolated from their encounter? How dare the client, who bought her compliance or obedience, attempt to hurt, anger, or shame her in order to evoke and steal the sentiments she will not and cannot sell? When the job is done, she may well turn aside from the encounter as from any loathsome chore. Perhaps she will be able to regain some of her lost integration, but she has powerful reasons to be cognitively and emotionally confused and to doubt the veracity or reliability of her self-perception. She likely can only disown its reports and ignore its advice.

One can also credibly imagine that he feels cheated. While expecting to purchase sex, he hoped, moreover, to buy sex with a woman, albeit one over whom he had temporary control.[17] However, she denied him what he most desired: her recognition of his subjectivity through a true—if brief—surrender of body and soul. He sought to control her sexual expression without, at the same time, stifling her candid spontaneity. He yearned for her to get caught up in the sexual moment despite herself. He tried to elicit genuine responses, ordinarily the predictable outcome of standard sexual maneuvers. It is conceivable that he did, to some extent, penetrate her defenses. But even if he did, he—unless especially unobservant, or stupid, or the perennial optimistic—should suspect the authenticity of her responses to his ministrations. Predictable responses to standard sexual maneuvers can be genuine, even if caused by textbook techniques; but the cognitive and emotional complexity of human sexual interactions prevents all genuine responses from being predictable.

4. Empirical Subjectivity

Some years ago, after I presented a paper on prostitution, someone in the audience asked, "Do you think a prostitute could understand a paper like this?" All that I recall of my reply was that it was neither pointed nor candid. A better response would have been, "Yes, because a prostitute wrote it." I refused to provide that forthright answer because doing so might have shamed my friends and family, endangered my position or advancement as a tenure-track (untenured) assistant professor in a conservative university, triggered accusations of histrionics, or attracted intrusions into my personal life.[18] Although I still fear my story might grieve various intimates, I can now manage threats to my station, integrity, and privacy.

For about five years, I financially supported a man and myself and, later, our infant children, by engaging in prostitution. I did so, in the first instance, because I lacked the degrees, experience, and skills necessary to obtain lawful employment. Second, I was in a destructive relationship with a controlling person who enjoyed depending on me economically and sabotaged my efforts to enter a more socially conventional occupation. Third, the inelastic needs of my children and the demands of their father made it difficult to work regular hours in a normal job. To be sure, a misguided combination of pride and self-loathing also pointed me toward a path that promised to confirm my sexual worth, deny my human value, and diminish my personality.[19]

Among the prostitutes I knew, some were drug addicts who sold their bodies to support their habits; others used drugs in order to tolerate prostitution. Many, though, refrained entirely from drugs. Of these women, a few had abusive or simply weak lovers who lived off their earnings. But other prostitutes lived independently, using, investing, or squandering their money as they pleased. Histories of childhood abuse and psychological disorders—not altogether consistently with the testimony offered by working women during, for example, the Minneapolis and other hearings—seemed, in my estimate, no more common among prostitutes than among scholars and students. These women had diverse interests, characters, and histories, yet they were similar with regard to their financial needs. They differed from other people, who also have financial needs, only insofar as twists and turns in their personal histories made prostitution seem more viable to them than other ways of having an income.[20] None wanted to continue plying the trade any longer than necessary to get as much money as they thought they needed.

My initiation to prostitution was neither remarkable nor complicated. After a period of unemployment and homelessness, I answered a newspaper advertisement and found myself employed, thereby solving my immediate financial problems through gainful, if disreputable, work. I worked for massage parlors, escort agencies, dating clubs, and houses specializing in the more unusual sexual proclivities. Anyone who wants to learn about the services available in such establishments can read factual or fictitious accounts abundantly available in popular periodicals, pulp novels, and scholarly journals.[21]

Most of my clients had wives or steady girlfriends, others had occasional lovers, and a few had no prospects in sight. I never met a client who wanted only to talk. Each client wanted something different sexually, but they all wanted the impossible. Did they ever touch me, reach me, penetrate me? Had it been within my power, none would have been successful. But I felt and sometimes expressed compassion, empathy, and even amity; and I felt and sometimes expressed revulsion, anger, and even dread. Regardless of my response, each client left a psychic residue.

I cannot recall the names or faces of all my clients. But afterward, I walked home with a pocketful of money—earned by selling what was mine alone—content in my self-sufficiency. I remember grinding my teeth as I distracted myself with visions of castrating, disemboweling, and mutilating the oaf currently on top of me. I remember hearing semi-hysterical laughter spilling from a sensitive, intelligent man, whose highly specific sexual tastes probably frustrated his pursuit of accommodating lovers and partners. I remember shameful tears running down my face as a client, who I could have desired in another context, touched me in a manner that I would have desired in another context. He said, "I don't think you're cut out for this line of work."

I was, in fact, not cut out for prostitution, but not because of shame, pain, or fear, which visit every walk of life. I was not cut out for it because, and only eventually, I refused to be witness of my own cowardice, inauthenticity, and fragmentation. Cowardice made prostitution seem a viable choice, because being a prostitute seemed less humbling, laborious, and horrifying than becoming someone better. Prostitution allowed me to nourish an inequitable relationship rather than taking actions that would result in its demise. It let me support my children and myself rather than first or immediately building a sustainable life for us. It permitted me to engage in needless bravado and sacrifice rather than confronting my own timidity and weaknesses. It required not that I be active and a full subject, but only that I endure, assume an object-like status, and embrace passive acceptance, false obedience, and alienated execution.[22]

5. Conclusion

The experiences of other prostitutes differ from mine. We can learn by listening to their stories. Likewise, empirical accounts that rely on different methodologies, such as those involving quantifiable data or historical research, enhance our comprehension of prostitution. We should take special care that the prostitutes themselves are not lost among the statistics and documents. Although I stand fast by my conclusions, I do not intend that my descriptions—even of my own experience—be accepted uncritically. I expect that my observations and reflections be recognized as containing hard-earned insights that deserve serious and respectful consideration.

A conjectural phenomenology requires a degree of abstraction. Ideally, the writer maintains a clear distinction between the phenomenological subject and herself. In practice, the description is always somewhat corrupted by the writer's experience. This fact should keep us alert to the dangers of trying to view any situation from another person's perspective, but it in no manner negates the value of such accounts for the study of prostitution or any other phenomenon. Indeed, since many subjects are unwilling or unable to describe their position (or they have not been asked to do so), conjectural phenomenology might be essential to understanding.[23]

As a former prostitute, a scholar, and an idealist, I have explained why I think prostitution is personally harmful, socially destructive, and morally wrong. I hope to have persuaded readers to view prostitution as a problematic activity. Sexuality is an essential aspect of subjectivity, so a human being risks losing herself if she allows her body to serve as an expendable tool. Likewise, sexual relations are woven into the very fabric of human society, which prostitution strains beyond reasonable endurance. If prostitution does not utterly denigrate, it certainly threatens, the humanity of everyone it touches.

Study Questions

1. Is it possible that Estes's counterfactual claim about the motives of the typical female prostitute does not apply to other women or to some gay male prostitutes? That is, might their primary goal be money even when they would have participated in these particular sexual encounters anyway? Or even if they thoroughly enjoy the sex they are paid for?

2. Estes speaks throughout of the prostitute as a woman and the client as a man. Even if it is true that most acts of prostitution are

heterosexual in this way, does the sex/gender of the client and the prostitute matter to her account of the phenomenology she describes? Why or why not?

3. Why does Estes's complex phenomenological description of the prostitute-client business bargain not also apply to other purely business relationships to which, by both law and morality, we have no objections? Is there something ontologically or anthropologically special about sex? If so, what is it? Consider, among other examples suggested by your own imagination, hair cutting, podiatry and proctology, tax and legal advising, and various kinds of "noncontact" sex work—in all of which the provider of the service must suppress his or her emotional responses and engage in pretense. Indeed, is it not nearly impossible to avoid the suppression of emotion and pretense in most of personal and social life?

4. Recall Greta Christina's attempt to define "sex" and how that task was influenced by her own sexual experiences (chapter 2). Is the closeness of Christina and Estes to the phenomena they observe, discuss, and analyze a methodological advantage, or does it make their accounts suspicious in some way? Note Estes's own doubts near the end of her essay.

5. Estes denies—in contrast to, for example, Thomas Mappes (chapter 16)—that the consent of two adults is sufficient, *ceteris paribus*, for making their sexual interaction morally permissible. What are her reasons for this claim? Are they better or worse than the reasons provided by Mappes for the alternative, liberal position? Similarly, what seems to divide Martha Nussbaum's liberal defense of sex work (chapter 24) from Estes's condemnation of it?

Notes

The author is grateful to Michael Goodman, the editor of *Essays in Philosophy*, for allowing us to republish parts of "Moral Reflections on Prostitution," and to Alan Soble for his helpful comments.

1. The idea that a "monetary substitute for mutual desire" is deeply objectionable can be found in such disparate writers as Bertrand Russell ("The intrusion of the economic motive into sex is . . . disastrous"; *Marriage and Morals* [London: Allen and Unwin, 1929], 121), and Robin Morgan, "Theory and Practice: Pornography and Rape," in her *Going Too Far: The Personal Chronicle of a Feminist* (New York: Random House, 1977), 163–69, at 165–66.

My argument in this essay is fairly simple; most scholars and lay people should understand it easily. Nonetheless, the argument presupposes certain ideas, principles, and knowledge that do not normally make their way into contemporary discussions of prostitution. For this reason, I urge the reader to become acquainted with the sources to which I refer. In light of this, see my "Moral Reflections on Prostitution," *Essays in Philosophy* 2, 2 (2001), and Clelia Smyth Anderson and Yolanda Estes, "The Myth of the Happy Hooker: Kantian Moral Reflections on a Phenomenology of Prostitution," in Stanley G. French, Wanda Teays, and Laura M. Purdy, eds., *Violence against Women: Philosophical Perspectives* (Ithaca, N.Y.: Cornell University Press, 1998), 152–58.

2. There are many approaches to the study of prostitution. On the origins of prostitution and the need for a theory of prostitution, see Alison M. Jaggar, "Prostitution," in Alan Soble, ed., *The Philosophy of Sex*, 1st edition (Totowa, N.J.: Rowman & Littlefield, 1980), 348–68. For a comparison of prostitution in different societies, see Laurie Shrage, "Should Feminists Oppose Prostitution?" *Ethics* 99, 2 (1989): 347–61 (reprinted in Alan Soble, ed, *The Philosophy of Sex*, 4th edition [Lanham, Md.: Rowman and Littlefield, 2002], 435–50), and her *Moral Dilemmas of Feminism: Prostitution, Adultery, and Abortion* (New York: Routledge, 1994), 99–161. For a discussion of prostitution and marriage in patriarchal-capitalist society, see Carole Pateman, *The Sexual Contract* (Stanford, Calif.: Stanford University Press, 1988), 189–218. For a discussion of the need for prostitutes to become subjects within discourse on prostitution, see Shannon Bell, *Reading, Writing, and Rewriting the Prostitute Body* (Bloomington, Ind.: Indiana University Press, 1994). For a critique of liberal/libertarian defenses of prostitution, see Evelina Giobbe, "Confronting the Liberal Lies about Prostitution," in Alison M. Jaggar, ed., *Living with Contradictions: Controversies in Feminist Social Ethics* (Boulder, Colo.: Westview, 1994), 120–26, and Carole Pateman, "Sex and Power," *Ethics* 100, 2 (1990): 398–407.

3. I cannot here thoroughly explore why she prostitutes herself for money. I consider the issue in section 4, below, as well as in "The Myth of the Happy Hooker" and "Moral Reflections on Prostitution" (note 10).

4. Why he buys the prostitute's services in order to obtain sexual gratification also exceeds the scope of this essay, but it is certainly worthy of discussion. See "Moral Reflections on Prostitution" (section IV), where I suggest that men seek prostitutes, in part, to avoid the inconvenience of sexual relations with another subject; obtaining sex from a lover in a relationship, instead, burdens him with responsibilities that he prefers to avoid.

5. For a remarkably clear explanation of this distinction in Kant's philosophy, see Henry E. Allison, *Kant's Transcendental Idealism*, revised ed. (New Haven, Conn.: Yale University Press, 2004). For an equally clear explanation of this distinction in Johann Gottlieb Fichte's philosophy, see Daniel Breazeale, "The 'Standpoint of Life' and the 'Standpoint of Philosophy' in the Jena *Wissenschaftslehre*," in Albert Mues, ed., *Transzendentalphilosophie als System: Die Auseinandersetzung zwischen 1794 und 1806* (Hamburg, Ger.: Felix Meiner, 1989), 81–104.

6. See Fichte, "First Introduction to the *Wissenschaftslehre*," in Daniel Breazeale, ed. and trans., *Introductions to the Wissenschaftslehre and Other Writings, 1797–1801* (Indianapolis, Ind.: Hackett, 1994), 7–14.

7. See Husserl, *Cartesian Meditations*, trans. Dorion Cairns (The Hague, Hol.: Martinus Nijhoff, 1960), 151.

8. It is well-known that "mutual recognition" figured prominently also in the philosophy of G. W. F. Hegel; see his 1807 *Phenomenology of Spirit*, trans. Arnold V. Miller (Oxford: Clarendon Press, 1977), paragraphs 178–96. Fichte introduced his notion of recognition through his doctrine of the *Aufforderung*, or summons. For discussions of the summons in Fichte's idealism, see Robert R. Williams, "Recognition, Right, and Social Contract," in Daniel Breazeale and Tom Rockmore, eds., *Rights, Bodies, and Recognition* (Hampshire: Ashgate, 2006), 26–43; Robert R. Williams, *Recognition: Fichte and Hegel on the Other* (Albany, N.Y.: SUNY Press, 1992); and Robert R. Williams, "Sartre's Strange Appropriation of Hegel," *Owl of Minerva* 23, 1 (Fall, 1991): 5–14. For my account of the summons, see "Intellectual Intuition, the Pure Will, and the Categorical Imperative in the Later Jena *Wissenschaftslehre*," in Daniel Breazeale and Tom Rockmore, eds., *New Essays on Fichte's Later Jena Wissenschaftslehre* (Evanston, Ill.: Northwestern University Press, 2002), 209–25.

9. Contrary to popular belief, German philosophers in the modern period were quite cognizant of the finite, carnal nature of humans. See Karl Ameriks and Dieter Sturma, eds., *The Modern Subject: Conceptions of the Self in Classical German Philosophy* (Albany, N.Y.: SUNY Press, 1995), and Frederick Neuhouser, *Fichte's Theory of Subjectivity* (Cambridge: Cambridge University Press, 1990). For my discussion of the relation between bodies, species, genders, and subjectivity in Fichte's philosophy, see "Society, Embodiment, and Nature in J. G. Fichte's Practical Philosophy," in Cheryl Hughes, ed., *Environmental Philosophy as Social Philosophy* (Charlottesville, Va.: Philosophy Documentation Center, 2004), 123–34.

10. *Groundwork of the Metaphysic of Morals*, trans. H. J. Paton (New York: Harper and Row, 1964), 96.

11. Note Fichte's demand: "[D]emonstrate just as much concern for the well-being of each of your neighbors as you do for your own well-being; love your neighbor as yourself" (*The System of Ethics*, ed. and trans. Daniel Breazeale and Günter Zöller [Cambridge: Cambridge University Press, 2006], 268).

12. Kant, *Groundwork*, 96–97; see Fichte, *System of Ethics*, 222. For how mutual sexual desire can degenerate into the will to dominate or submit to the other, see Jean-Paul Sartre, "Concrete Relations with Others," in his *Being and Nothingness: An Essay on Phenomenological Ontology*, trans. Hazel E. Barnes (New York: Philosophical Library, 1956).

13. Regarding the insufficiency of consent for mutual respect, Fichte says: "[N]o human being can demand the sacrifice of a human character. Therefore, a man can accept his wife's submission only under those conditions on which alone she can submit herself to him; otherwise he would not be treating her as a moral being but as a mere thing.—Even if a woman were to offer herself on other conditions, the man could not accept her subjugation, and in this case the legal principle, 'no wrong happens to a person who is treated in accordance with his own will,' does not hold." (*System of Ethics*, 314). For a contemporary Kantian account of sexual morality according to which treating the other an as end requires not only the other's consent but also attending to the other's sexual desires, see Alan Goldman, "Plain Sex" (in this volume, chap. 5).

14. For Fichte's discussion of the primary importance of feminine sexual desire in social and moral relations, see *System of Ethics*, 312, and his *Foundations of Natural Right: According to the Principles of the Wissenschaftslehre*, ed. Frederick Neuhouser, trans. Michael Baur (Cambridge: Cambridge University Press, 2000), 265–75, 284–85. See also Lance Byron Richey, "Fichte, Johann Gottlieb," in Alan Soble, ed., *Sex from Plato to Paglia: A Philosophical Encyclopedia*, vol. 1 (Westport, Conn.: Greenwood, 2006), 347–53.

15. He tries to make her into "a thing on which another satisfies his appetite, just as he satisfies his hunger on a steak" (Kant, *The Philosophy of Law*, trans. W. Hastie, in John Arthur, ed., *Morality and Moral Controversies* [Englewood Cliffs, N.J.: Prentice Hall, 1993], 254). For additional remarks by Fichte on prostitution, see *System of Ethics*, 251, and *Foundations of Natural Right*, 268, 287, 289–90. Russell, too, made the point: "Morality in sexual relations . . . consists essentially of respect for the other person, and unwillingness to use that person solely as a means of personal gratification. . . . [P]rostitution sins against this principle" (*Marriage and Morals*, 153).

16. "Sexual Perversion" (in this volume, chap. 3).

17. On men's presumption to be in control in heterosexual relations of all sorts, see Carole Pateman, "What's Wrong with Prostitution," in Jaggar, ed., *Living with Contradictions*, 131; John Stuart Mill, "The Subjection of Women," in Alice Rossi, ed., *Essays on Sex Equality* (Chicago, Ill.: University of Chicago Press, 1970), 141; and Fichte, *Science of Right*, 419–45.

18. For similar reasons—when I was a graduate student—my good friend and fellow student, Clelia Smyth (formerly Clelia Smyth Anderson) agreed to co-author "The Myth of the Happy Hooker."

19. For some illumination of this claim, see my "Confessions of a Refugee: My Life as a Loner, Rebel, and Renegade," in Yolanda Estes, Arnold Lorenzo Farr, Patricia Smith, and Clelia Smyth, eds., *Marginal Groups and Mainstream American Culture* (Lawrence, Kan.: University Press of Kansas, 2000), 193–208.

20. See Sunny Carter, "A Most Useful Tool," in Jaggar, ed., *Living with Contradictions*, 112–16. Carter's account of why she became a prostitute—to care for her seriously ill son—is honest and well-written.

21. See, for example, Anne McClintock, "Maid to Order: Commercial S/M and Gender Power," in Pamela Church Gibson and Roma Gibson, eds., *Dirty Looks: Women, Pornography, Power* (London: BFI Publishing, 1993), 207–31.

22. On complicity, cowardice, and endurance, see Fichte, *System of Ethics*, 191–93, 256–57. On mutual respect, self-respect, and despair, see 302–3.

23. Consider, for example, subjects determined not to relive and revisit traumatic events or to reveal secrets, and those rendered voiceless due to age, species, or impairment.

Chapter 24

"WHETHER FROM REASON OR PREJUDICE": TAKING MONEY FOR BODILY SERVICES

Martha C. Nussbaum

In this provocative essay, **Martha C. Nussbaum** *offers an interesting approach to understanding prostitution by drawing analogies between the prostitute and other kinds of workers: the factory laborer, domestic servant, nightclub singer, philosophy professor, masseuse, and her hypothetical "colonoscopy artist." One of Nussbaum's points is that most people sell their bodies, or the use of them, for money, and we do not usually object to this circumstance in itself. Although Nussbaum does express doubts about the coherence of the moral criticism of prostitution, her focus here is largely legal: she attempts to refute, at length, seven arguments that have been proffered for the continuing criminalization of prostitution.*

Nussbaum, a leading writer in the philosophy of love and sexuality, is Ernst Freund Professor of Law and Ethics at the University of Chicago and the author of *The Fragility of Goodness* (Cambridge University Press, 1986); *Sex and Social Justice* (Oxford University Press, 1999); *Upheavals of Thought: The Intelligence of Emotions* (Cambridge University Press, 2001); and *Hiding from Humanity: Disgust, Shame, and the Law* (Princeton University Press, 2004). Among her many significant journal articles are "Objectification," *Philosophy and Public Affairs* 24, no. 4 (1995): 249–91; and (with Kenneth Dover), "Platonic Love and Colorado Law: The Relevance of Ancient Greek Norms to Modern Sexual Controversies," *Virginia Law Review* 80, no. 7 (1994): 1515–1651, which contains much about John Finnis (see chapter 9).

Nussbaum, Martha C. "'Whether from Reason or Prejudice': Taking Money for Bodily Services," from *Sex and Social Justice* (New York: Oxford University Press, 1999), pp. 276–98; original version published in *Journal of Legal Studies* 27, 2 (1998), pp. 693–724. Reprinted with the permission of Martha C. Nussbaum and the University of Chicago Press. © 1998 by The University of Chicago. All rights reserved.

Taking leave of Binod, Durga slowly, deliberately walks towards the shack of Sukhlal the contractor, who stared at her even yesterday and flashed ten-rupee notes.

What else can one do, she argues to herself, except fight for survival? The survival of oneself, one's loved ones, and the hopes that really matter.
—Manik Bandyopadhyay, "A Female Problem at a Low Level" (1963)

If the story is about the peasant wife selling her body, then one must look for the meaning of that in the reality of peasant life. One can't look at it as a crisis of morality, in the sense one would in the case of a middle-class wife.
—Manik Bandyopadhyay, *About This Author's Perspective*

I. Body Sellers

All of us, with the exception of the independently wealthy and the unemployed, take money for the use of our body. Professors, factory workers, lawyers, opera singers, prostitutes, doctors, legislators—we all do things with parts of our bodies, for which we receive a wage in return.[1] Some people get good wages and some do not; some have a relatively high degree of control over their working conditions and some have little control; some have many employment options and some have very few. And, some are socially stigmatized and some are not.

The stigmatization of certain occupations may be well founded, based on convincing, well-reasoned arguments. But it may also be based on class prejudice, or stereotypes of race or gender. Stigma may also change rapidly, as these background beliefs and prejudices change. Adam Smith, in *The Wealth of Nations*, tells us that there are "some very agreeable and beautiful talents" that are admirable as long as no pay is taken for them, "but of which the exercise for the sake of gain is considered, whether from reason or prejudice, as a sort of publick prostitution." For this reason, he continues, opera singers, actors, and dancers must be paid an "exorbitant" wage, to compensate them for the stigma involved in using their talents "as the means of subsistence." "Should the publick opinion or prejudice ever alter with regard to such occupations," he concludes, "their pecuniary recompence would quickly diminish."[2] Smith was not altogether right about the opera market,[3] but his discussion is revealing for what it shows us about stigma. Today few professions are more honored than that of opera singer, and yet only two hundred years ago, that public use of one's body for pay was taken to be a kind of prostitution. Looking back at that time, we now think that the judgments and emotions underlying the stigmatization of singers were irrational and objectionable, like prejudices against members of different classes and races. (I shall shortly be saying more about what I think those reasons were.) Nor do we see the slightest reason to suppose that the unpaid artist is a purer and truer artist than the paid artist. We think it entirely right and reasonable that high art should receive a high salary. If a producer of opera should take the position that singers should not be paid, on the grounds that receiving money for the use of their talents involves an illegitimate form of commodification and even market alienation of those talents, we would think that this producer was a slick exploiter, out to make a profit from the ill treatment of vulnerable and impressionable artists.[4] On the whole we think that far from cheapening or ruining talents, the presence of a contract guarantees conditions within which the artist can develop her art with sufficient leisure and confidence to reach the highest level of artistic production.[5]

It is widely believed, however, that taking money or entering into contracts in connection with the use of one's sexual and/or reproductive capacities is genuinely bad. Feminist arguments about prostitution, surrogate motherhood, and even marriage contracts standardly portray financial transactions in the area of female sexuality as demeaning to women and as involving a damaging commodification and market alienation of women's sexual and reproductive capacities.[6] The social meaning of these transactions is said to be both that these capacities are turned into objects for the use and control of men and also that the activities themselves are being turned into commodities, and thereby robbed of the type of value they have at their best.

One question we shall have to face is whether these descriptions of our current judgments and intuitions are correct. But even if they are, what does this tell us? Many things and people have been stigmatized in our nation's history, often for very bad reasons. An account of the actual social meaning of a practice is therefore just a door that opens onto the large arena of moral and legal evaluation. It invites us to raise Adam Smith's question: Are these current beliefs the result of reason or prejudice? Can they be defended by compelling moral arguments? And, even if they can, are these the type of moral argument that can properly be a basis for a legal restriction? Smith, like his Greek and Roman Stoic forebears, understood that the evaluations that ground emotional responses and ascriptions of social meaning in a society are frequently corrupt—deformed by self-interest, resentment, and mere unthinking habit. The task he undertook, in *The Theory of Moral Sentiments*, was to devise procedures and strategies of argument through which one might separate the rationally defensible emotions from the irrational and prejudiced. In so proceeding, Smith and the Stoics were correct. Social meaning does no work on its own: It offers an invitation to normative moral and political philosophy.

My aim in this essay will be to investigate the question of sexual "commodification" by focusing on the example of prostitution.[7] I argue that a fruitful debate about the morality and legality of prostitution should begin from a twofold starting point: from a broader analysis of our beliefs and practices with regard to taking pay for the use of the body, and from a broader awareness of the options and choices available to poor working women. The former inquiry suggests that at least some of our beliefs about prostitution are as irrational as the beliefs Smith reports about singers; it will therefore help us to identify the elements in prostitution that are genuinely problematic. Most, though not all, of the genuinely problematic elements turn out to be common to a wide range of activities engaged in by poor working women, and the second inquiry suggests that many of women's employment choices are so heavily constrained by poor options that they are hardly choices at all. I think that this should bother us—and that the fact that a woman with plenty of choices becomes a prostitute should not bother us provided there are sufficient safeguards against abuse and disease, safeguards of a type that legalization would make possible.

It is therefore my conclusion that the most urgent issue raised by prostitution is that of employment opportunities for working women and their control over the conditions of their employment. The legalization of prostitution, far from promoting the demise of love, is likely to make things a little better for women who have too few options to begin with.[8] The really helpful thing for feminists to ponder, if they deplore the nature of these options, will be how to promote expansion in the option set, through education, skills training, and job creation. These unsexy topics are not common themes in U.S. feminist philosophy, but they are inevitable in any practical project dealing with prostitutes and their female children.[9] This suggests that at least some of our feminist theory may be insufficiently grounded in the reality of working-class lives and too focused on sexuality as an issue in its own right, as if it could be extricated from the fabric of poor people's attempts to survive.

II. Stigma and Wage Labor

Why were opera singers stigmatized? If we begin with this question, we can move on to prostitution with expanded insight. Although we can hardly provide more than a sketch of the background here, we can confidently say that two common cultural beliefs played a role. First, throughout much of the history of modern Europe—as, indeed, in ancient

Greece—there was a common aristocratic prejudice against earning wages. The ancient Greek gentleman was characterized by "leisure"— meaning that he did not have to work for a living. Aristotle reproved the Athenian democracy for allowing such base types as farmers and crafts- men to vote, because, in his view, the unleisured character of their daily activities and their inevitable preoccupation with gain would pervert their political judgment, making them grasping and small-minded.[10] The fact that the Sophists typically took money for their rhetorical and philo- sophical teaching made them deeply suspect in the eyes of such aristo- crats.[11] Much the same view played a role in the medieval Church, where it was controversial whether one ought to offer philosophical instruction for pay.[12] Bernard of Clairvaux, for example, held that taking fees for ed- ucation is a "base occupation" (*turpis quaestus*). (Apparently he did not think this true of all wage labor but only where it involved deep spiritual things.)

Such views about wage labor remained closely linked to class privilege in modern Europe and exercised great power well into the twentieth century. Any reader of English novels will be able to produce many ex- amples of the view that a gentleman does not earn wages, and that some- one who does is too preoccupied with the baser things in life, and there- fore base himself. Such views were a prominent source of prejudice against Jews, who, not having the same land rights as Christians, had no choice but to earn their living. Even in this century, in the United States, Edith Wharton shows that these attitudes were still firmly entrenched. Lily Bart, impoverished heroine of *The House of Mirth* (1905), is dis- cussing her situation with her friend Gus Trenor. He praises the invest- ment tips he has gotten from Rosedale, a Jewish Wall Street investments expert whose wealth has given him entry into the world of impoverished aristocrats who both use and despise him. Trenor urges Lily to encour- age Rosedale's advances: "The man is mad to know the people who don't want to know him, and when a fellow's in that state, there is nothing he won't do for the first woman who takes him up." Lily dismisses the idea, calling Rosedale "impossible" and thinking silently of his "intrusive per- sonality." Trenor replies: "Oh, hang it—because he's fat and shiny and has a shoppy manner! . . . A few years from now he'll be in it whether we want him or not, and then he won't be giving away a half-a-million tip for a dinner!" In the telling phrase "a shoppy manner," we see the age-old aristocratic prejudice against wage work, so deeply implicated in stereo- types of Jews as pushy, intrusive, and lacking in grace.

To this example we may add a moment in the film *Chariots of Fire* when the Jewish sprinter hires a professional coach to help him win. This in- troduction of money into the gentlemanly domain of sport shocks the head of his college, who suggests to him that as a Jew he does not un- derstand the true spirit of English athletics. Genteel amateurism is the mark of the gentleman, and amateurism demands, above all, not earning or dealing in money. It may also imply not trying too hard, as if it were really one's main concern in life, but this attitude appears to be closely related to the idea that the gentleman does not need the activity because he has his living provided already; so the rejection of hard work is a corollary of the rejection of the tradesman. (Even today in Britain, such attitudes have not totally disappeared; people from aristocratic backgrounds frequently frown on working too hard at one's scholarly or athletic pursuits, as if this betrays a kind of base tradesmanly mentality.)

What is worth noting about these prejudices is that they do not attach to activities themselves, as such, but, rather, to the use of these activities to make money. To be a scholar, to be a musician, to be a fine athlete, to be an actor even, is fine—so long as one does it as an amateur. But what does this mean? It means that those with inherited wealth[13] can perform these activities without stigma, and others cannot. In England in the nineteenth century, it meant that the gentry could perform those activities, and Jews could not. This informs us that we need to scrutinize all our social views about money making and alleged commodification with extra care, for they are likely to embed class prejudices that are unjust to working people.

Intersecting with this belief, in the opera singer example, is another: that it is shameful to display one's body to strangers in public, especially in the expression of passionate emotion. The anxiety about actors, dancers, and singers reported by Smith is surely of a piece with the more general anxiety about the body, especially the female body, that has been a large part of the history of quite a few cultures. Thus, in much of India until very recently (and in some parts still), it is considered inappropriate for a woman of good family to dance in public; when Rabindranath Tagore included middle-class women in his theatrical productions early in the twentieth century, it was a surprising and somewhat shocking move. Similarly in the West: The female body should be covered and not displayed, although in some respects these conditions could be relaxed among friends and acquaintances. Female singers were considered unacceptable during the early history of opera; indeed, they were just displacing the *castrati* during Smith's lifetime, and they were widely perceived as immoral women.[14] Male actors, singers, and dancers suffered too; and clearly Smith means to include both sexes. Until very recently such performers were considered to be a kind of gypsy, too fleshy and physical, unsuited for polite company. The distaste was compounded by a distaste for, or at least a profound ambivalence about, the emotions that it was, and is, the business of these performers to portray. In short, such attitudes betray an anxiety about the body, and about strong passion, that we are now likely to think irrational, even though we may continue to share them at times; certainly we are not likely to think them a good basis for public policy.

When we consider our views about sexual and reproductive services, then, we must be on our guard against two types of irrationality: aristocratic class prejudice and fear of the body and its passions.

III. Six Types of Bodily Service

Prostitution is not a single thing. It can only be well understood in its social and historical context. Ancient Greek *hetairai*, such as Pericles' mistress Aspasia, have very little in common with a modern call girl.[15] Even more important, within a given culture there are always many different types and levels of prostitution: In ancient Greece, the *hetaira*, the brothel prostitute, the streetwalker; in modern America, the self-employed call girl, the brothel prostitute, the streetwalker (and each of these at various levels of independence and economic success). It is also evident that most cultures contain a continuum of relations between women and men (or between same-sex pairs) that have a commercial aspect—ranging from the admitted case of prostitution to cases of marriage for money, going on an expensive date when it is evident that sexual favors are expected at the other end, and so forth. In most cultures, marriage itself has a prominent commercial aspect: The prominence of dowry murder in contemporary Indian culture, for example, testifies to the degree to which a woman is valued, above all, for the financial benefits one can extract from her family.[16] Let us, however, focus for the time being on contemporary America (with some digressions on India), on female prostitution only, and on explicitly commercial relations of the sort that are illegal under current law.

It will be illuminating to consider the prostitute by situating her in relation to several other women who take money for bodily services:

1. A factory worker in the Perdue chicken factory, who plucks feathers from nearly frozen chickens.

2. A domestic servant in a prosperous upper-middle-class house.

3. A nightclub singer in middle-range clubs, who sings (often) songs requested by the patrons.

4. A professor of philosophy, who gets paid for lecturing and writing.

5. A skilled masseuse, employed by a health club (with no sexual services on the side).

6. A person whom I'll call the "colonoscopy artist": She gets paid for having her colon examined with the latest instruments, in order to test out their range and capability.[17]

By considering similarities and differences between the prostitute and these other bodily actors, we will make progress in identifying the distinctive features of prostitution as a form of bodily service.

Note that nowhere in this comparison am I addressing the issue of child prostitution or nonconsensual prostitution (e.g., young women sold into prostitution by their parents, forcible drugging and abduction, etc.). Insofar as these features appear to be involved in the international prostitution market, I do not address them here, although I shall comment on them later. I address only the type of choice to be a prostitute that is made by a woman over the age of consent, frequently in a situation of great economic duress.

The Prostitute and the Factory Worker

Both prostitution and factory work are usually low-paid jobs, but in many instances a woman faced with the choice can (at least over the short haul) make more money in prostitution than in this sort of factory work. (This would probably be even more true if prostitution were legalized and the role of pimps thereby restricted, though the removal of risk and some stigma might at the same time depress wages, to some extent offsetting that advantage for the prostitute.) Both face health risks, but the health risk in prostitution can be very much reduced by legalization and regulation, whereas the particular type of work the factory worker is performing carries a high risk of nerve damage in the hands, a fact about it that appears unlikely to change. The prostitute may well have better working hours and conditions than the factory worker; especially in a legalized regime, she may have much more control over her working conditions. She has a degree of choice about which clients she accepts and what activities she performs, whereas the factory worker has no choices but must perform the same motions again and again for years. The prostitute also performs a service that requires skill and responsiveness to new situations, whereas the factory worker's repetitive motion exercises relatively little human skill[18] and contains no variety.

On the other side, the factory worker is unlikely to be the target of violence, whereas the prostitute needs—and does not always get—protection against violent customers. (Again, this situation can be improved by legalization: Prostitutes in the Netherlands have a call button wired up to the police.) This factory worker's occupation, moreover, has no clear connection with stereotypes of gender—though this might not have been the case. In many parts of the world, manual labor is strictly segmented by sex, and more routinized, low-skill tasks are given to women.[19] The prostitute's activity does rely on stereotypes of women as sluttish and immoral, and it may in turn perpetuate such stereotypes. The factory worker suffers no invasion of her internal private space, whereas the prostitute's activity involves such (consensual) invasion. Finally, the prostitute suffers from social stigma, whereas the factory worker does not—at least among people of her own social class. (I shall return to this issue, asking whether stigma too can be addressed by legalization.) For all these reasons, many women, faced with the choice between factory work and prostitution, choose factory work, despite its other disadvantages.

The Prostitute and the Domestic Servant

In domestic service as in prostitution, one is hired by a client and one must do what that client wants, or fail at the job. In both, one has a limited degree of latitude to exercise skills as one sees fit, and both jobs require the exercise of some developed bodily skills. In both, one is at risk of enduring bad behavior from one's client, although the prostitute is more likely to encounter physical violence. Certainly both are traditionally professions that enjoy low respect, both in society generally and from the client. Domestic service on the whole is likely to have worse hours and lower pay than (at least many types of) prostitution, but it probably contains fewer health risks. It also involves no invasion of intimate bodily space, as prostitution (consensually) does.

Both prostitution and domestic service are associated with a type of social stigma. In the case of domestic service, the stigma is, first, related to class: It is socially coded as an occupation only for the lowest classes.[20] Domestic servants are in a vast majority of cases female, so it becomes coded by sex. In the United States, domestic service is very often racially coded as well. Not only in the South, but also in many parts of the urban North, the labor market has frequently produced a clustering of African-American women in these low-paying occupations. In my home in suburban Philadelphia in the 1950s and 1960s, the only African Americans we saw were domestic servants, and the only domestic servants we saw were African American. The perception of the occupation as associated with racial stigma ran very deep, producing difficult tensions and resentments that made domestic service seem to be incompatible with dignity and self-respect. (It need not be, clearly, and I shall return to this.)

The Prostitute and the Nightclub Singer

Both of these people use their bodies to provide pleasure, and the customer's pleasure is the primary goal of what they do.[21] This does not mean that a good deal of skill and art is not involved, and in both cases it usually is. Both have to respond to requests from the customer, although (in varying degrees depending on the case) both may also be free to improvise or to make suggestions. Both may be paid more or less and have better or worse working conditions, more or less control over what they do.

How do they differ? The prostitute faces health risks and risks of violence not faced by the singer. She also allows her bodily space to be invaded, as the singer does not. It may also be that prostitution is always a cheap form of an activity that has a higher better form, whereas this need not be the case in popular vocal performance (though of course it might be).[22] The nightclub singer, furthermore, does not appear to be participating in, or perpetuating, any type of gender hierarchy—although in former times this would not have been the case, singers being seen as "a type of publick prostitute" and their activity associated, often, with anxiety about the control of female sexuality. Finally, there is no (great) moral stigma attached to being a nightclub singer, although at one time there certainly was.

The Prostitute and the Professor of Philosophy

These two figures have a very interesting similarity: Both provide bodily services in areas that are generally thought to be especially intimate and definitive of selfhood. Just as the prostitute takes money for sex, which is commonly thought to be an area of intimate self-expression, so the professor takes money for thinking and writing about what she thinks—about morality, emotion, the nature of knowledge, whatever— all parts of a human being's intimate search for understanding of the world and oneself. It was precisely for this reason that the medieval thinkers I have mentioned saw such a moral problem about philosophizing for money: It should be a pure spiritual gift, and it is degraded by the receipt of a wage. The fact that we do not think that the professor (even one who regularly holds out for the highest salary offered) thereby alienates her mind, or turns her thoughts into commodities—even when she writes a paper for a specific conference or volume—should put us on our guard about making similar conclusions in the case of the prostitute.

There are other similarities: In both cases, the performance involves interaction with others, and the form of the interaction is not altogether controlled by the person. In both cases there is at least an element of producing pleasure or satisfaction (note the prominent role of teaching evaluations in the employment and promotion of professors), although in philosophy there is also a countervailing tradition of thinking that the goal of the interaction is to produce dissatisfaction and unease. (Socrates would not have received tenure in a modern university.) It may appear at first that the intimate bodily space of the professor is not invaded—but we should ask about this. When someone's unanticipated argument goes into one's mind, isn't this both intimate and bodily (and far less consensual, often, than the penetration of prostitute by customer)? Both performances involve skill. It might plausibly be argued that the professor's involves a more developed skill, or at least a more expensive training—but we should be cautious here. Our culture is all too ready to think that sex involves no skill and is simply "natural," a view that is surely false and is not even seriously entertained by many cultures.[23]

The salary of the professor, and her working conditions, are usually a great deal better than those of (all but the most elite) prostitutes. The professor has a fair amount of control over the structure of her day and her working environment, although she also has fixed mandatory duties, as the prostitute, when self-employed, does not. If the professor is in a nation that protects academic freedom, she has considerable control over what she thinks and writes, although fads, trends, and peer pressure surely constrain her to some extent. The prostitute's need to please her customer is usually more exigent and permits less choice. In this way, she is more like the professor of philosophy in Cuba than like the U.S. counterpart[24]—but the Cuban professor appears to be worse off, because she cannot say what she really thinks even when off the job. Finally, the professor of philosophy, if a female, both enjoys reasonably high respect in the community and also might be thought to bring credit to all women in that she succeeds at an activity commonly thought to be the preserve only of males. She thus subverts traditional gender hierarchy whereas the prostitute, while suffering stigma herself, may be thought to perpetuate gender hierarchy.

The Prostitute and the Masseuse

These two bodily actors seem very closely related. Both use a skill to produce bodily satisfaction in the client. Unlike the nightclub singer, both do this through a type of bodily contact with the client. Both need to be responsive to what the client wants, and to a large degree take direction from the client as to how to handle his or her body. The bodily contact involved is rather intimate, although the internal space of the masseuse is not invaded. The type of bodily pleasure produced by the masseuse may certainly have an erotic element, although in the type of "respectable" masseuse I am considering, it is not directly sexual.

The difference is primarily one of respectability. Practitioners of massage have fought for, and have to a large extent won, the right to be considered dignified professionals who exercise a skill. Their trade is legal; it is not stigmatized. And people generally do not believe that they degrade their bodies or turn their bodies into commodities by using their bodies to give pleasure to customers. They have positioned themselves alongside physical therapists and medical practitioners, dissociating themselves from the erotic dimension of their activity. As a consequence of this successful self-positioning, they enjoy better working hours, better pay, and more respect than most prostitutes. What is the difference, we might ask? One is having sex, and the other is not. But what sort of difference is this? Is it a difference we want to defend? Are our reasons for thinking it so crucial really reasons, or vestiges of moral prejudice? A number of distinct beliefs enter in at this point: the belief that women should not have sex with strangers; the belief that commercial sex is inherently degrading and makes a woman a degraded woman; the belief that women should not have to have sex with strangers if they do not want to, and in general should have the option to refuse sex with anyone they do not really choose. Some of these beliefs are worth defending and some are not. (I shall argue that the issue of choice is the really important one.) We need to sort them out and to make sure that our policies are not motivated by views we are not really willing to defend.

The Prostitute and the Colonoscopy Artist

I have included this hypothetical occupation for a reason that should by now be evident: It involves the consensual invasion of one's bodily space. (The example is not so hypothetical, either: Medical students need models when they are learning to perform internal exams, and young actors do earn a living playing such roles.)[25] The colonoscopy artist uses her skill at tolerating the fiber-optic probe without anesthesia to make a living. In the process, she permits an aperture of her body to be penetrated by another person's activity—and, we might add, far more deeply penetrated than is generally the case in sex. She runs some bodily risk, because she is being used to test untested instruments, and she will probably have to fast and empty her colon regularly enough to incur some malnutrition and some damage to her excretory function. Her wages may not be very good—for this is probably not a profession characterized by what Smith called "the beauty and rarity of talents," and it may also involve some stigma given that people are inclined to be disgusted by the thought of intestines.

And yet, on the whole, we do not think that this is a base trade, or one that makes the woman who does it a fallen woman. We might want to ban or regulate it if we thought it was too dangerous, but we would not be moved to ban it for moral reasons. Why not? Some people would point to the fact that it does not either reflect or perpetuate gender hierarchy, and this is certainly true. (Even if her being a woman is crucial to her selection for the job—they need to study, for example, both male and female colons—it will not be for reasons that seem connected with the subordination of women.) But surely a far greater part of the difference is made by the fact that most people do not think anal penetration by a doctor in the context of a medical procedure is immoral,[26] whereas lots of people do think that vaginal or anal penetration in the context of sexual relations is (except under very special circumstances) immoral, and that a woman who goes in for that is therefore an immoral and base woman.

IV. Sex and Stigma

Prostitution, we now see, has many features that link it with other forms of bodily service. It differs from these other activities in many subtle ways, but the biggest difference consists in the fact that it is, today, more widely stigmatized. Professors no longer get told that selling their teaching is a *turpis quaestus*. Opera singers no longer get told that they are unacceptable in polite society. Even the masseuse has won respect as a skilled professional. What is different about prostitution? Two factors stand out as sources of stigma. One is that prostitution is widely held to be immoral; the other is that prostitution (frequently at least) is bound up with gender hierarchy, with ideas that women and their sexuality are in need of male domination and control, and the related idea that women should be available to men to provide an outlet for their sexual desires. The immorality view would be hard to defend today as a justification for the legal regulation of prostitution, and perhaps even for its moral denunciation. People thought prostitution was immoral because they thought nonreproductive and especially extramarital sex was immoral; the prostitute was seen, typically, as a dangerous figure whose whole career was given over to lust. But female lust was (and still often is) commonly seen as bad and dangerous, so prostitution was seen as bad and dangerous. Some people would still defend these views today, but it seems inconsistent to do so if one is not prepared to repudiate other forms of nonmarital sexual activity on an equal basis. We have to grant, I think, that the most common reason for the stigma attaching to prostitution is a weak reason, at least as a public reason: a moralistic view about female sexuality that is rarely consistently applied (to premarital sex, for example), and that seems unable to justify restriction on the activities of citizens who have different views of what is good and proper. At any rate, it seems hard to use the stigma so incurred to justify perpetuating stigma through criminalization unless one is prepared to accept a wide range of laws that interfere with chosen consensual activities, something that most feminist attackers of prostitution rarely wish to do.

More promising as a source of good moral arguments might be the stigma incurred by the connection of prostitution with gender hierarchy.

But what is the connection, and how exactly does gender hierarchy explain pervasive stigma? It is only a small minority of people for whom prostitution is viewed in a negative light because of its collaboration with male supremacy; for only a small minority of people at any time have been reflective feminists, concerned with the eradication of inequality. Such people will view the prostitute as they view veiled women, or women in *purdah*: with sympathetic anger, as victims of an unjust system. This reflective feminist critique, then, does not explain why prostitutes are actually stigmatized and held in disdain—both because it is not pervasive enough and because it leads to sympathy rather than to disdain.

The way that gender hierarchy actually explains stigma is a very different way, a way that turns out in the end to be just another form of the immorality charge. People committed to gender hierarchy and determined to ensure that the dangerous sexuality of women is controlled by men, frequently have viewed the prostitute, a sexually active woman, as a threat to male control of women. They therefore become determined either to repress the occupation itself by criminalization or, if they also think that male sexuality needs such an outlet and that this outlet ultimately defends marriage by giving male desire a safely debased outlet, to keep it within bounds by close regulation. (Criminalization and regulation are not straightforwardly opposed; they can be closely related strategies. Similarly, prostitution is generally conceived as not the enemy but the ally of marriage: The two are complementary ways of controlling women's sexuality.) The result is that social meaning is deployed in order that female sexuality will be kept in bounds carefully set by men. The stigma attached to the prostitute is an integral part of such bounding.

A valuable illustration of this thesis is given by Alain Corbin's valuable and careful study of prostitutes in France in the late nineteenth century.[27] Corbin shows that the interest in legal regulation of prostitution was justified by the alleged public interest in reining in and making submissive a dangerous female sexuality that was always potentially dangerous to marriage and social order. Kept in carefully supervised houses known as *maisons de tolérance*, prostitutes were known by the revealing name of *filles soumises*, a phrase that most obviously designated them as registered, "subjugated" to the law, but that also connoted their controlled and confined status. What this meant was that they were controlled and confined so that they themselves could provide a safe outlet for desires that threatened to disrupt the social order. The underlying aim of the regulationist project, argues Corbin (with ample documentation), was "the total repression of sexuality."[28] Regulationists tirelessly cited St. Augustine's dictum: "Abolish the prostitutes and the passions will overthrow the world; give them the rank of honest women and infamy and dishonor will blacken the universe" (*De ordine* 2.4.12). In other words, stigma has to be attached to prostitutes because of the necessary hierarchy that requires morality to subjugate vice, and the male the female, seen as an occasion and cause of vice. Bounding the prostitute off from the "good woman," the wife whose sexuality is monogamous and aimed at reproduction, creates a system that maintains male control over female desire.[29]

This attitude to prostitution has modern parallels. One instructive example is from Thailand in the 1950s, when Field Marshal Sarit Thanarat began a campaign of social purification, holding that "uncleanliness and social impropriety . . . led to the erosion of social orderliness. . . ."[30] In theory, Thanarat's aim was to criminalize prostitution by the imposition of prison terms and stiff fines; in practice, the result was a system of medical examination and "moral rehabilitation" that shifted the focus of public blame from the procurers and traffickers to prostitutes themselves. Unlike the French system, the Thai system did not encourage registered prostitution, but it was similar in its public message that the problem of prostitution is a problem of "bad" women, and in its reinforcement of the message that female sexuality is a cause of social disruption unless tightly controlled.

In short, sex hierarchy causes stigma, commonly, not through feminist critique but through a far more questionable set of social meanings, meanings that anyone concerned with justice for women should call into question. For it is these same meanings that are also used to justify the seclusion of women, the veiling of women, the genital mutilation of women. The view boils down to the view that women are essentially immoral and dangerous and will be kept in control by men only if men carefully engineer things so that they do not get out of bounds. The prostitute, being seen as the uncontrolled and sexually free woman, is in this picture seen as particularly dangerous, both necessary to society and in need of constant subjugation. As an honest woman, a woman of dignity, she will wreck society. As a *fille soumise*, her reputation in the dirt, she may be tolerated for the service she provides (or, in the Thai case, she may provide an engrossing public spectacle of "moral rehabilitation").

All this diverts attention from some very serious crimes, such as the use of kidnapping, coercion, and fraud to entice women into prostitution. For these reasons, international human rights organizations, such as Human Rights Watch and Amnesty International, have avoided taking a stand against prostitution as such and have focused their energies on the issue of trafficking and financial coercion.[31]

It appears, then, that the stigma associated with prostitution has an origin that feminists have good reason to connect with unjust background conditions and to decry as both unequal and irrational, based on a hysterical fear of women's unfettered sexuality. There may be other good arguments against the legality of prostitution, but the existence of widespread stigma all by itself does not appear to be among them. As long as prostitution is stigmatized, people are injured by that stigmatization, and it is a real injury to a person not to have dignity and self-respect in her own society. But that real injury (as with the comparable real injury to the dignity and self-respect of interracial couples, or of lesbians and gay men) is not best handled by continued legal strictures against the prostitute and can be better dealt with in other ways (e.g., by fighting discrimination against these people and taking measures to promote their dignity). As the Supreme Court said in a mixed-race custody case, "Private biases may be outside the reach of the law, but the law cannot, directly or indirectly, give them effect."[32]

V. Criminalization: Seven Arguments

Pervasive stigma itself, then, does not appear to provide a good reason for the continued criminalization of prostitution, any more than it does for the illegality of interracial marriage. Nor does the stigma in question even appear to ground a sound *moral* argument against prostitution. This is not, however, the end of the issue. There are a number of other significant arguments that have been made to support criminalization. With our six related cases in mind, let us now turn to those arguments.

(1) *Prostitution involves health risks and risks of violence.* To this we can make two replies. First, insofar as this is true, as it clearly is, the problem is made much worse by the illegality of prostitution, which prevents adequate supervision, encourages the control of pimps, and discourages health checking. As Corbin shows, regimes of legal but regulated prostitution have not always done well by women: The health checkups of the *filles soumises* were ludicrously brief and inadequate.[33] But there is no reason why one cannot focus on the goal of adequate health checks, and some European nations have done reasonably well in this area.[34] The legal brothels in Nevada have had no reported cases of AIDS.[35] Certainly risks of violence can be far better controlled when the police are the prostitute's ally rather than her oppressor.

To the extent to which risks remain an inevitable part of the way of life, we must now ask what general view of the legality of risky undertakings we wish to defend. Do we ever want to rule out risky bargains simply because they harm the agent? Or do we require a showing of harm to others (as might be possible in the case of gambling, for example)? Whatever position we take on this complicated question, we will almost certainly be led to conclude that prostitution lies well within the domain of the legally acceptable, for it is certainly far less risky than boxing, another activity in which working-class people try to survive and flourish by subjecting their bodies to some risk of harm. There is a stronger case for paternalistic regulation of boxing than of prostitution, and externalities (the glorification of violence as example to the young) make boxing at least as morally problematic and probably more so. And yet I would not defend the criminalization of boxing, and I doubt that very many Americans would either. Sensible regulation of both prostitution and boxing, by contrast, seems reasonable and compatible with personal liberty.

In the international arena, many problems of this type stem from the use of force and fraud to induce women to enter prostitution, frequently at a very young age and in a strange country where they have no civil rights. An especially common destination, for example, is Thailand, and an especially common source is Burma, where the devastation of the rural economy has left many young women an easy mark for promises of domestic service elsewhere. Driven by customers' fears of HIV, the trade has focused on increasingly young girls from increasingly remote regions. Human rights interviewers have concluded that large numbers of these women were unaware of what they would be doing when they left their country and are kept there through both economic and physical coercion. (In many cases, family members have received payments, which then become a "debt" that the girl has to pay off.)[36] These circumstances, terrible in themselves, set the stage for other forms of risk and/or violence. Fifty to seventy percent of the women and girls interviewed by Human Rights Watch were HIV positive; discriminatory arrests and deportations are frequently accompanied by abuse in police custody. All these problems are magnified by the punitive attitude of the police and government toward these women as prostitutes or illegal aliens or both, although under both national and international law trafficking victims are exempt from legal penalty and are guaranteed safe repatriation to their country of origin. This situation clearly deserves both moral condemnation and international legal pressure, but it is made worse by the illegality of prostitution itself.

(2) *The prostitute has no autonomy; her activities are controlled by others.* This argument[37] does not distinguish prostitution from very many types of bodily service performed by working-class women. The factory worker does far worse on the scale of autonomy, and the domestic servant no better. I think this point expresses a legitimate moral concern. A person's life seems deficient in flourishing if it consists only of a form of work that is totally out of the control and direction of the person herself. Marx rightly associated that kind of labor with a deficient realization of full humanity and (invoking Aristotle) persuasively argued that a flourishing human life probably requires some kind of use of one's own reasoning in the planning and execution of one's own work.[38] But that is a pervasive problem of labor in the modern world, not a problem peculiar to prostitution as such. It certainly does not help the problem to criminalize prostitution—any more than it would be to criminalize factory

work or domestic service. A woman will not exactly achieve more control and "truly human functioning" by becoming unemployed. What we should instead think about are ways to promote more control over choice of activities, more variety, and more general humanity in the types of work that are actually available to people with little education and few options. That would be a lot more helpful than removing one of the options they actually have.

(3) *Prostitution involves the invasion of one's intimate bodily space.* This argument[39] does not seem to support legal regulation of prostitution, provided that as the invasion in question is consensual—that is, that the prostitute is not kidnapped, or fraudulently enticed, or a child beneath the age of consent, or under duress against leaving if she should choose to leave. In this sense prostitution is quite unlike sexual harassment and rape, and far more like the activity of the colonoscopy artist—not to everyone's taste, and involving a surrender of bodily privacy that some will find repellant—but not for that reason necessarily bad, either for self or others. The argument does not even appear to support a moral criticism of prostitution unless one is prepared to make a moral criticism of all sexual contact that does not involve love or marriage.

(4) *Prostitution makes it harder for people to form relationships of intimacy and commitment.* This argument is prominently made by Elizabeth Anderson, in defense of the criminalization of prostitution.[40] The first question we should ask is, Is this true? People still appear to fall in love in the Netherlands and Germany and Sweden; they also fell in love in ancient Athens, where prostitution was not only legal but also, probably, publicly subsidized.[41] One type of relationship does not, in fact, appear to remove the need for the other—any more than a Jackie Collins novel removes the desire to read Proust. Proust has a specific type of value that is by no means found in Jackie Collins, so people who want that value will continue to seek out Proust, and there is no reason to think that the presence of Jackie Collins on the bookstand will confuse Proust lovers and make them think that Proust is really like Jackie Collins. So, too, one supposes, with love in the Netherlands: People who want relationships of intimacy and commitment continue to seek them out for the special value they provide, and they do not have much trouble telling the difference between one sort of relationship and another, despite the availability of both.

Second, one should ask which women Anderson has in mind. Is she saying that the criminalization of prostitution would facilitate the formation of love relationships on the part of the women who were (or would have been) prostitutes? Or, is she saying that the unavailability of prostitution as an option for working-class women would make it easier for romantic middle-class women to have the relationships they desire? The former claim is implausible, because it is hard to see how reinforcing the stigma against prostitutes, or preventing some poor women from taking one of the few employment options they might have, would be likely to improve their human relations.[42] The latter claim might possibly be true (though it is hardly obvious), but it seems a repugnant idea, which I am sure Anderson would not endorse, that we should make poor women poorer so that middle-class women can find love. Third, one should ask Anderson whether she is prepared to endorse the large number of arguments of this form that might plausibly be made in the realm of popular culture—and, if not, whether she has any way of showing how she could reject those as involving an unacceptable infringement of liberty and yet allowing the argument about prostitution that she endorses. For it seems plausible that making rock music illegal would increase the likelihood that people would listen to Mozart and Beethoven; that making Jackie Collins illegal would make it more likely that people would turn to Joyce Carol Oates; that making commercial advertising illegal would make it more likely that we would appraise products with high-minded ideas of value in our minds; that making television illegal would improve children's reading skills. What is certain, however, is that we would and do utterly reject those ideas (we do not even seriously entertain them) because we do not want to live in Plato's *Republic*, with our cultural options dictated by a group of wise guardians, however genuinely sound their judgments may be.[43]

(5) *The prostitute alienates her sexuality on the market; she turns her sexual organs and acts into commodities.*[44] Is this true? It seems implausible to claim that the prostitute alienates her sexuality just on the grounds that she provides sexual services to a client for a fee. Does the singer alienate her voice, or the professor her mind? The prostitute still has her sexuality; she can use it on her own, apart from the relationship with the client, just as the domestic servant may cook for her family and clean her own house.[45] She can also cease to be a prostitute, and her sexuality will still be with her, and hers, if she does. So she has not even given anyone a monopoly on those services, far less given them over into someone else's hands. The real issue that separates her from the professor and the singer seems to be the degree of choice she exercises over the acts she performs. But is even this a special issue for the prostitute, any more than it is for the factory worker or the domestic servant or the colonoscopy artist—all of whom choose to enter trades in which they will not have a great deal of say over what they do or (within limits) how they do it? Freedom to choose how one works is a luxury, highly desirable indeed, but a feature of few jobs that nonaffluent people perform.

As for the claim that the prostitute turns her sexuality into a commodity, we must ask what that means. If it means only that she accepts a fee for sexual services, then that is obvious, but nothing further has been said that would show us why this is a bad thing. The professor, the singer, the symphony musician—all accept a fee, and it seems plausible that this is a good state of affairs, creating spheres of freedom. Professors are more free to pursue their own thoughts now, as money makers, than they were in the days when they were supported by monastic orders; symphony musicians playing under the contract secured by the musicians' union have more free time than nonunionized musicians, and more opportunities to engage in experimental and solo work that will enhance their art. In neither case should we conclude that the existence of a contract has converted the abilities into things to be exchanged and traded separately from the body of the producer; they remain human creative abilities, securely housed in their possessor. So, if to "commodify"' means merely to accept a fee, we have been given no reason to think that this is bad.

If, on the other hand, we try to interpret the claim of "commodification" using the narrow technical definition of "commodity" used by the Uniform Commercial Code,[46] the claim is plainly false. For that definition stresses the "fungible" nature of the goods in question, and "fungible" goods are, in turn, defined as goods "of which any unit is, by nature or usage of trade, the equivalent of any other like unit." Although we may not think that the soul or inner world of a prostitute is of deep concern to the customer, she is usually not regarded as simply a set of units fully interchangeable with other units.[47] Prostitutes are probably somewhat more fungible than bassoon players but not totally so. (Corbin reports that all *maisons de tolérance* standardly had a repertory of different types of women, to suit different tastes, and this should not surprise us.) What seems to be the real issue is that the woman is not attended to as an individual, not considered a special, unique being. But that is true of many ways people treat one another in many areas of life, and it seems implausible that we should use that kind of disregard as a basis for criminalization. It may not even be immoral, for surely we cannot deeply know all the people with whom we have dealings in life, and many of those dealings are just fine without deep knowledge. So our moral question boils down to the question, Is sex without deep personal knowledge always immoral? It seems to me officious and presuming to use one's own experience to give an affirmative answer to this question, given that people have such varied experiences of sexuality.

In general, then, there appears to be nothing baneful or value debasing about taking money for a service, even when that service expresses something intimate about the self. Professors take a salary, artists work on commission under contract—frequently producing works of high intellectual and spiritual value. To take money for a production does not turn either the activity or the product (e.g., the article or the painting) into a commodity in the baneful sense in which that implies fungibility. If this is so, there is no reason to think that a prostitute's acceptance of money for her services necessarily involves a baneful conversion of an intimate act into a commodity in that sense. If the prostitute's acts are, as they are, less intimate than many other sexual acts people perform, that does not seem to have a great deal to do with the fact that she receives money, given that people engage in many intimate activities (painting, singing, writing) for money all the time without loss of expressive value. Her activity is less intimate because that is its whole point; it is problematic, to the extent that it is, neither because of the money involved nor because of the nonintimacy (which, as I have said, it seems officious to declare bad in all cases) but because of features of her working conditions and the way she is treated by others.

Here we are left with an interesting puzzle. My argument about professors and painters certainly seems to imply that there is no reason, in principle, why the most committed and intimate sex cannot involve a contract and a financial exchange. So why doesn't it, in our culture? One reply is that it quite frequently does, when people form committed relationships that include an element of economic dependence, whether one-sided or mutual; marriage has frequently had that feature, not always for the worse. But to the extent that we do not exchange money for sex, why don't we? In a number of other cultures, courtesans, both male and female, have been somewhat more common as primary sexual partners than they are here. Unlike quite a few cultures, we do not tend to view sex in intimate personal relationships the way we view an artist's creation of a painting, namely, as an intimate act that can nonetheless be deliberately undertaken as the result of an antecedent contract-like agreement. Why not? I think there is a mystery here, but we can begin to grapple with it by mentioning two features. First, there is the fact that sex, however prolonged, still takes up much less time than writing an article or producing a painting. Furthermore, it also cannot be done too often; its natural structure is that it will not very often fill up the entire day. One may therefore conduct an intimate sexual relationship in the way one would wish, not feeling that one is slighting it, while pursuing another line of work as one's way of making a living. Artists and scholars sometimes have to pursue another line of work, but they prefer not to. They characteristically feel that to do their work in the way they would wish, they ought to spend the whole day doing it. So they naturally gravitate to the view that their characteristic mode of creative production fits very well with contract and a regular wage.

This, however, still fails to explain cultural differences. To begin to grapple with these we need to mention the influence of our heritage of romanticism, which makes us feel that sex is not authentic if not spontaneous, "natural," and to some degree unplanned. Romanticism has exercised a far greater sway over our ideas of sex than over our ideas of artistic or intellectual production, making us think that any deal or antecedent arrangement somehow diminishes that characteristic form of expression.

Are our romantic ideas about the difference between sex and art good, or are they bad? Some of each, I suspect. They are problematic to the extent that they make people think that sex happens naturally, does not require complicated adjustment and skill, and flares up (and down) uncontrollably.[48] Insofar as they make us think that sex fits badly with reliability, promise keeping, and so forth, these ideas are certainly subversive of Anderson's goals of "intimacy and commitment," which would be better served, probably, by an attitude that moves sex in intimate personal relationships (and especially marriages) closer to the activity of the artist or the professor. On the other hand, romantic views also promote Anderson's goals to some degree, insofar as they lead people to connect sex with self-revelation and self-expression rather than prudent concealment of self. Many current dilemmas concerning marriage in our culture stem from an uneasy struggle to preserve the good in romanticism while avoiding the dangers it poses to commitment. As we know, the struggle is not always successful. There is much more to be said about this fascinating topic. But since (as I've argued) it leads us quite far from the topic of prostitution, we must now return to our primary line of argument.

(6) *The prostitute's activity is shaped by, and in turn perpetuates, male dominance of women.*[49] The institution of prostitution as it has most often existed is certainly shaped by aspects of male domination of women. As I have argued, it is shaped by the perception that female sexuality is dangerous and needs careful regulation; that male sexuality is rapacious and needs a "safe" outlet; that sex is dirty and degrading, and that only a degraded woman is an appropriate sexual object.[50] Nor have prostitutes standardly been treated with respect, or given the dignity one might think proper to a fellow human being. They share this with working-class people of many types in many ages, but there is no doubt that there are particular features of the disrespect that derive from male supremacy and the desire to lord it over women, as well as a tendency to link sex to (female) defilement that is common in the history of Western European culture. The physical abuse of prostitutes and the control of their earnings by pimps—as well as the pervasive use of force and fraud in international markets—are features of male dominance that are extremely harmful and do not have direct parallels in other types of low-paid work. Some of these forms of conduct may be largely an outgrowth of the illegality of the industry and closely comparable to the threatening behavior of drug wholesalers to their—usually male—retailers. So there remains a question of how far male dominance as such explains the violence involved. But in the international arena, where regulations against these forms of misconduct are usually treated as a joke, illegality is not a sufficient explanation for them.

Prostitution is hardly alone in being shaped by, and reinforcing, male dominance. Systems of patrilineal property and exogamous marriage, for example, almost certainly do more to perpetuate not only male dominance but also female mistreatment and even death. There probably is a strong case for making the giving of dowry illegal, as has been done since 1961 in India and since 1980 in Bangladesh[51] (though with little success), for it can be convincingly shown that the institution of dowry is directly linked with extortion and threats of bodily harm, and ultimately with the deaths of large numbers of women.[52] It is also obvious that the dowry system pervasively conditions the perception of the worth of girl children: They are a big expense, and they will not be around to protect one in one's old age. This structure is directly linked with female malnutrition, neglect, noneducation, even infanticide, harms that have caused the deaths of many millions of women in the world.[53] It is perfectly understandable that the governments of India, Bangladesh, and Pakistan are very concerned about the dowry system, because it seems very difficult to improve the very bad economic and physical condition of women without some structural changes. (Pakistan has recently adopted a somewhat quixotic remedy, making it illegal to serve food at weddings—thus driving many caterers into poverty.) Dowry is an institution affecting millions of women, determining the course of almost all girl children's lives pervasively and from the start. Prostitution as such usually does not have either such dire or such widespread implications. (Indeed, it is frequently the product of the dowry system, when parents take payment for prostituting a female child for whom they would otherwise have to pay dowry.) The case for making it illegal on grounds of subordination seems weaker than the case for making dowry, or even wedding feasts, illegal, and yet these laws are themselves of dubious merit and would probably be rightly regarded as involving undue infringement of liberty under our constitutional tradition. (It is significant that Human Rights Watch, which has so aggressively pursued the issue of forced prostitution, takes no stand one way or the other on the legality of prostitution itself.)

More generally, one might argue that the institution of marriage as most frequently practiced both expresses and reinforces male dominance. It would be right to use law to change the most inequitable features of that institution—protecting women from domestic violence and marital rape, giving women equal property and custody rights and improving their exit options by intelligent shaping of the divorce law. But to rule that marriage as such should be illegal on the grounds that it reinforces male dominance would be an excessive intrusion upon liberty, even if one should believe marriage irredeemably unequal. So, too, I think, with prostitution: What seems right is to use law to protect the bodily safety of prostitutes from assault, to protect their rights to their incomes against the extortionate behavior of pimps, to protect poor women in developing countries from forced trafficking and fraudulent offers, and to guarantee their full civil rights in the countries where they end up—to make them, in general, equals under the law, both civil and criminal. But the criminalization of prostitution seems to pose a major obstacle to that equality.

Efforts on behalf of the dignity and self-respect of prostitutes have tended to push in exactly the opposite direction. In the United States, prostitutes have long been organized to demand greater respect, though their efforts are hampered by prostitution's continued illegality. In India, the National Federation of Women has adopted various strategies to give prostitutes more dignity in the public eye. For example, on National Women's Day, they selected a prostitute to put a garland on the head of the prime minister. Similarly, UNICEF in India's Andhra Pradesh has been fighting to get prostitutes officially classified as "working women" so that they can enjoy the child-care benefits local government extends to that class. As with domestic service, so here: Giving workers greater dignity and control can gradually change both the perception and the fact of dominance.

(7) *Prostitution is a trade that people do not enter by choice; therefore the bargains people make within it should not be regarded as real bargains.* Here we must distinguish three cases. First is the case in which the woman's entry into prostitution is caused by some type of conduct that would otherwise be criminal: kidnapping, assault, drugging, rape, statutory rape, blackmail, a fraudulent offer. Here we may certainly judge that the woman's choice is not a real choice, and that the law should take a hand in punishing her coercer. This is a terrible problem currently in developing countries; international human rights organizations are right to make it a major focus.[54]

Closely related is the case of child prostitution. Child prostitution is frequently accompanied by kidnapping and forcible detention; even when children are not stolen from home, their parents have frequently sold them without their own consent. But even where they have not, we should judge that there is an impermissible infringement of autonomy and liberty. A child (and, because of clients' fears of HIV, brothels now often focus on girls as young as ten)[55] cannot give consent to a life in prostitution; not only lack of information and of economic options (if parents collude in the deal) but also absence of adult political rights makes such a "choice" no choice at all.

Different is the case of an adult woman who enters prostitution because of bad economic options: because it seems a better alternative than the chicken factory, because there is no other employment available to her, and so on. This too, we should insist, is a case in which autonomy has been infringed but in a different way. Consider Joseph Raz's vivid example of "the hounded woman," a woman on a desert island who is constantly pursued by a man-eating animal.[56] In one sense, this woman is free to go anywhere on the island and do anything she likes. In another sense, of course, she is quite unfree. If she wants not to be eaten, she has to spend all her time and calculate all her movements in order to avoid the beast. Raz's point is that many poor people's lives are nonautonomous in just this way. They may fulfill internal conditions of autonomy, being capable of making bargains, reflecting about what to do, and so on. But none of this counts for a great deal, if in fact the struggle for survival gives them just one unpleasant option, or a small set of (in various ways) unpleasant options.

This seems to me the truly important issue raised by prostitution. Like work in the chicken factory, it is not an option many women choose with alacrity, when many other options are on their plate.[57] This might not be so in some hypothetical culture, in which prostitutes have legal protection, dignity and respect, and the status of skilled practitioner, rather like the masseuse.[58] But it is true now in most societies, given the reality of the (albeit irrational) stigma attaching to prostitution. But the important thing to realize is that this is not an issue that permits us to focus on prostitution in isolation from the economic situation of women in a society generally. Certainly it will not be ameliorated by the criminalization of prostitution, which reduces poor women's options still further. We may grant that poor women do not have enough options, and that society has been unjust to them in not extending more options while nonetheless respecting and honoring the choices they actually make in reduced circumstances.

How could it possibly be ameliorated? Here are some things that have actually been done in India, where prostitution is a common last-ditch option for women who lack other employment opportunities. First, both government and private groups have focused on the provision of education to women, to equip them with skills that will enhance their options. One group I recently visited in Bombay focuses in particular on skills training for the children of prostitutes, who are at especially high risk of becoming prostitutes themselves unless some action increases their options. Second, nongovernmental organizations have increasingly focused on the provision of credit to women, in order to enhance their employment options and give them a chance to "upgrade" in the domain of their employment. One such project that has justly won international renown is the Self-Employed Women's Association (SEWA), centered in Ahmedabad in Gujarat, which provides loans to women pursuing a variety of informal-sector occupations,[59] from tailoring to hawking and vending to cigarette rolling to agricultural labor.[60] With these loans, they can get wholesale rather than retail supplies, upgrade their animals or equipment, and so forth. They also get skills training and, frequently, the chance to move into leadership roles in the organization itself. Such women are far less likely to need to turn to prostitution to supplement their income. Third, they can form labor organizations to protect women employed in low-income jobs and to bargain for better working conditions—once again making this work a better source of income and diminishing the likelihood that prostitution will need to be selected. (This is the other primary objective of SEWA, which is now organizing hawkers and vendors internationally.) Fourth, they can form groups to diminish the isolation and enhance the self-respect of working women in low-paying jobs; this was a ubiquitous feature of both government and nongovernment programs I visited in India, and a crucial element of helping women deliberate about their options if they wish to avoid prostitution for themselves or their daughters.

These four steps are the real issue, I think, in addressing the problem of prostitution. Feminist philosophers in the United States do not write many articles about credit and employment;[61] they should do so far more. Indeed, it seems a dead end to consider prostitution in isolation from the other realities of working life of which it is a part, and one suspects that this has happened because prostitution is a sexy issue and getting a loan for a sewing machine appears not to be. But feminists had better talk more about getting loans, learning to read, and so forth if they want to be relevant to the choices that are actually faced by working women, and to the programs that are actually doing a lot to improve such women's options.

VI. Truly Human Functioning

The stigma traditionally attached to prostitution is based on a collage of beliefs most of which are not rationally defensible, and which should be especially vehemently rejected by feminists: beliefs about the evil character of female sexuality, the rapacious character of male sexuality, and the essentially marital and reproductive character of "good" women and "good" sex. Worries about subordination more recently raised by feminists are much more serious concerns, but they apply to many types of work poor women do. Concerns about force and fraud should be extremely urgent concerns of the international women's movement. Where these conditions do not obtain, feminists should view prostitutes as (usually) poor working women with few options, not as threats to the intimacy and commitment that many women and men (including, no doubt, many prostitutes) seek. This does not mean that we should not be concerned about ways in which prostitution as currently practiced, even in the absence of force and fraud, undermines the dignity of women, just as domestic service in the past undermined the dignity of members of a given race or class. But the correct response to this problem seems to be to work to enhance the economic autonomy and the personal dignity of members of that class, not to rule off-limits an option that may be the only livelihood for many poor women and to further stigmatize women who already make their living this way.

In grappling further with these issues, we should begin from the realization there is nothing per se wrong with taking money for the use of one's body. That's the way most of us live, and formal recognition of that fact through contract is usually a good thing for people, protecting their security and their employment conditions. What seems wrong is that relatively few people in the world have the option to use their body, in their work, in what Marx would call a "truly human" manner of functioning, by which he meant (among other things) having some choices about the work to be performed, some reasonable measure of control over its conditions and outcome, and also the chance to use thought and skill rather than just to function as a cog in a machine. Women in many parts of the world are especially likely to be stuck at a low level of mechanical functioning, whether as agricultural laborers or as factory workers or as prostitutes. The real question to be faced is how to expand the options and opportunities such workers face, how to increase the humanity inherent in their work, and how to guarantee that workers of all sorts are treated with dignity. In the further pursuit of these questions, we need, on balance, more studies of women's credit unions and fewer studies of prostitution.

Study Questions

1. In explaining why prostitution is stigmatized, Nussbaum points out that it is commonly believed to be immoral. She then argues that "it seems inconsistent to do so [that is, object to prostitution morally] if one is not prepared to repudiate other forms of non-marital sexual activity on an equal basis." Can you construct a moral position according to which prostitution is morally wrong yet noncommercial casual sex is morally permissible? Or is prostitution morally wrong, since casual or promiscuous sex, as Nussbaum argues elsewhere, is itself morally questionable? (See her "Objectification," *Philosophy and Public Affairs* 24, no. 4 (1995): 249–91; reprinted in Alan Soble, ed., *Philosophy of Sex*, 3rd edition, 283–321, and 4th edition, 381–419.)

2. Nussbaum considers the claim, which could be used to support the criminalization of prostitution, that the acts of the prostitute "under contract express not her own valuations but the will of her customer." Nussbaum replies that in this regard the prostitute is

in the same situation as most workers, that is, lack of control is a "pervasive problem of labor" in our society and others. What do you think of the alternative reply that many prostitutes firmly set the ground rules before they engage in sex with their clients and thereby do not succumb to "the will of [the] customer"? Is it possible that at least some prostitutes have more control over the conditions of their work than many wage laborers? (See, for example, H. E. Baber, "How Bad Is Rape?" *Hypatia* 2, no. 2 (1987): 125–38, reprinted in Alan Soble, ed., *Philosophy of Sex*, 4th ed. [Lanham, Md.: Rowman & Littlefield, 2002], 303–16.)

3. Is there not anything significant and morally relevant about sexual activity that might distinguish it from all the other examples of work, discussed by Nussbaum, in which people sell their bodies or the use of them? If not, why (as David Benatar might ask; see chapter 21) is rape considered to be such a morally atrocious act? If prostitution should not be stigmatized, as Nussbaum argues, does that provide any reason for lessening the stigmatization of rape or of being raped?

4. Is the analogy between prostitution and Nussbaum's "colonoscopy artist" a good or fair one? How would you respond to someone who said, "The anus is not a sex organ, unlike the vagina; an inanimate instrument is not a body part, unlike the penis of a living male human being; and the purpose of colonoscopy artistry, for the consumer, is not the same as the purpose of prostitution, for the consumer"?

5. If Nussbaum is right that prostitution should be decriminalized, ceteris paribus, does this imply that the making of pornography should not be subject to criminal or civil sanctions?

Notes

Both epigraphs to this chapter are translated from the Bangali by Kalpana Bardhan, in *Women, Outcastes, Peasants, and Rebels: A Selection of Bengali Short Stories* (Berkeley: University of California Press, 1990). Bandyopadhyay (1908–56) was a leading Bengali writer who focused on peasant life and issues of class conflict.

The author is grateful to students in her seminar on sexual autonomy and law for all that their discussions contributed to the formulation of these ideas, to Sibyl Schwarzenbach and Laurie Shrage for discussions that helped her think about how to approach this topic, and to Elizabeth Anderson, Gertrud Fremling, Richard Posner, Mark Ramseyer, Eric Schliesser, Elizabeth Schreiber, Stephen Schulhofer, Alan Soble, and Cass Sunstein for valuable comments on an earlier draft of this essay.

1. Even if one is a Cartesian dualist, as I am not, one must grant that the human exercise of mental abilities standardly requires the deployment of bodily skills. Most traditional Christian positions on the soul go still further: Aquinas, for example, holds that souls separated from the body have only a confused cognition and cannot recognize particulars. So my statements about professors can be accepted even by believers in the separable soul.

2. Adam Smith, *The Nature and Causes of the Wealth of Nations*, I.x.b.25. Elsewhere, Smith points out that in ancient Greece acting was "as creditable . . . as it is discreditable now" (*Lectures on Rhetoric and Belles Lettres* ii.230).

3. He expresses the view that the relevant talents are not so rare, and that when stigma is removed, many more people will compete for the jobs, driving down wages; this is certainly true today of acting, but far less so of opera, where "the rarity and beauty of the talents" remains at least one dominant factor.

4. Such arguments have often been used in the theater; they were used, for example, in one acting company of which I was a member, in order to persuade actors to kick back their (union-mandatory) salaries to the owners. This is fairly common in theater, where the union is weak and actors are so eager for employment that they are vulnerable to such arguments.

5. The typical contract between major U.S. symphony orchestras and the musicians' union, for example, guarantees year-round employment to symphony musicians, even though they do not play all year; this enables them to use summer months to play in low-paying or experimental settings in which they can perform contemporary music and chamber music, do solo and concerto work, and so forth. It also restricts hours of both rehearsal and performance during the performing season, leaving musicians free to teach students, attend classes, work on chamber music with friends, and in other ways to enrich their work. It also mandates blind auditions (i.e., players play behind a curtain)—with the result that the employment of female musicians has risen dramatically over the past twenty or so years since the practice was instituted.

6. See Elizabeth Anderson, *Value in Ethics and Economics* (Cambridge, Mass.: Harvard University Press, 1993); and Anderson, "Is Women's Labor a Commodity?" *Philosophy and Public Affairs* 19 (1990): 71–92; Margaret Jane Radin, *Contested Commodities: The Trouble with the Trade in Sex, Children, Bodily Parts, and Other Things* (Cambridge, Mass.: Harvard University Press, 1996); and Radin, "Market-Inalienability" *Harvard Law Review* 100 (1987): 1849–1937; Cass R. Sunstein, "Neutrality in Constitutional Law (With Special Reference to Pornography, Abortion, and Surrogacy)," *Columbia Law Review* 92 (1992): 1–52; and Sunstein, *The Partial Constitution* (Cambridge, Mass.: Harvard University Press, 1993), 257–90. For contrasting feminist perspectives on the general issue of contract, see Jean Hampton, "Feminist Contractarianism," in *A Mind of One's Own: Feminist Essays on Reason and Objectivity* (Boulder, Colo.: Westview, 1993), 227–55; Susan Moller Okin, *Justice, Gender, and the Family*, ed. L. Antony and C. Witt (New York: Basic Books, 1989).

7. I use this term throughout because of its familiarity, although a number of international women's organizations now avoid it for reasons connected to those in this essay, preferring the term "commercial sex worker" instead. For one recent example, see *Report of the Panel on Reproductive Health, National Research Council, Reproductive Health in Developing Countries: Expanding Dimensions, Building Solutions,*

ed. Amy O. Tsui, Judith N. Wasserheit, and John G. Haaga (Washington, D.C.: National Academy Press, 1997), 30, stressing the wide variety of practices denoted by the term "commercial sex" and arguing that some studies show economic hardship as a major factor but some do not.

8. Among feminist discussions of prostitution, my approach is close to that of Sibyl Schwarzenbach, "Contractarians and Feminists Debate Prostitution," *New York University Review of Law and Social Change* 18 (1990–1): 103–29, and to Laurie Shrage, "Prostitution and the Case for Decriminalization," *Dissent* (Spring 1996): 41–45 (in which Shrage criticizes her earlier view expressed in "Should Feminists Oppose Prostitution?" *Ethics* 99 [1989]: 347–61).

9. To give just one example, the Annapurna Mahila Mandal project in Bombay offers job training and education to the daughters of prostitutes, in a residential school setting; they report that in five years they have managed to arrange reputable marriages for 1,000 such girls.

10. Aristotle, *Politics*, III.5 and VII.9–10.

11. See Plato, *Apology* 19D–20C, *Protagoras* passim, *Gorgias* passim.

12. I have profited here from reading an unpublished paper by Dan Klerman, "Slavery, Simony and Sex: An Intellectual History of the Limits of Monetary Relations."

13. Or those supported by religious orders.

14. Mrs. Elizabeth Billington, who sang in Arne's *Artaxerxes* in London in 1762, was forced to leave England because of criticisms of her morals; she ended her career in Italy. Another early *diva* was Maria Catalani, who sang for Handel (d. 1759), for example, in *Samson*. By the time of the publication of *The Wealth of Nations*, female singers had made great headway in displacing the *castrati*, who ceased to be produced shortly thereafter. For Smith's own attitudes to the female body, see *The Theory of Moral Sentiments* I.ii.1.3, where he states that as soon as sexual passion is gratified it gives rise to "disgust," and leads us to wish to get rid of the person who is their object, unless some higher moral sentiment preserves our regard for (certain aspects of) this person. "When we have dined, we order the covers to be removed; and we should treat in the same manner the objects of the most ardent and passionate desires, if they were the objects of no other passions but those which take their origin from the body." Smith was a bachelor who lived much of his life with his mother and did not have any lasting relationships with women.

15. Aspasia was a learned and accomplished woman who apparently had philosophical and political views; she is said to have taught rhetoric and to have conversed with Socrates. On the other hand, she could not perform any of the functions of a citizen, both because of her sex and because of her foreign birth. On the other hand, her son Pericles was subsequently legitimated and became a general. More recently, it has been doubted whether Aspasia was in fact a *hetaira*, and some scholars now think her a well-born foreign woman. But other *hetairai* in Greece had good education and substantial financial assets; the two women recorded as students in Plato's Academy were both *hetairai*, as were most of the women attested as students of Epicurus, including one who was apparently a wealthy donor.

16. See chapter 3 of my *Sex and Social Justice* (New York: Oxford University Press, 1999).

17. As far as I know, this profession is entirely hypothetical, though not by any means far-fetched. It is clear, at any rate, that individuals' abilities to endure colonoscopy without anesthesia and without moving vary considerably, so one might well develop (or discover) expertise in this area.

18. It is probably, however, a developed skill to come to work regularly and to work regular hours each day.

19. Consider, for example, the case of Jayamma, a brick worker in Trivandrum, Kerala, India, discussed by Leela Gulati, *Profiles of Female Poverty* (Delhi: Hindustan Publishing Corp., 1981) and whom I met on March 21, 1997, when she was approximately sixty-five years old. For approximately forty years, Jayamma worked as a brick carrier in the brick-making establishment, carrying heavy loads of bricks on her head all day from one place to another. Despite her strength, fitness, and reliability, she could never advance beyond that job because of her sex, whereas men were quickly promoted to the less physically demanding and higher-paying tasks of brick molding and truck loading.

20. Indeed, this appears to be a ubiquitous feature: In India, the mark of "untouchability" is the performance of certain types of cleaning, especially those dealing with bathroom areas. Mahatma Gandhi's defiance of caste manifested itself in the performance of these menial services.

21. This does not imply that there is some one thing, pleasure, varying only by quantity, that they produce. With Mill (and Plato and Aristotle), I think that pleasures differ in quality, not only in quantity.

22. This point was suggested to me by Elizabeth Schreiber. I am not sure whether I endorse it: It all depends on whether we really want to say that sex has one highest goal. Just as it would have been right, in an earlier era, to be skeptical about the suggestion that the sex involved in prostitution is "low" because it is nonreproductive, so too it might be good to be skeptical about the idea that prostitution sex is "low" because it is nonintimate. Certainly nonintimacy is involved in many noncommercial sexual relationships and is sometimes desired as such.

23. Thus the *Kama Sutra*, with its detailed instructions for elaborately skilled performances, strikes most Western readers as slightly comic, because the prevailing romantic ideal of "natural" sex makes such contrivance seem quite unsexy.

24. We might also consider the example of a skilled writer who writes advertising copy.

25. See Terri Kapsalis, *Public Privates: Performing Gynecology from Both Ends of the Speculum* (Durham: Duke University Press, 1997); and Kapsalis, "In Print: Backstage at the Pelvic Theater," *Chicago Reader*, April 18, 1997, 46. While a graduate student in performance studies at Northwestern, Kapsalis made a living as a "gynecology teaching associate," serving as the model patient for medical students learning to perform pelvic and breast examinations.

26. The same goes for vaginal penetration, according to Kapsalis: She says that the clinical nature of the procedure more than compensates for "society's queasiness with female sexuality."

27. Alain Corbin, *Women for Hire: Prostitution and Sexuality in France after 1850*, trans. Alan Sheridan (Cambridge, Mass.: Harvard University Press, 1990).

28. Ibid., 29. Representative views of the authors of regulationism include the view that "[d]ebauchery is a fever of the senses carried to the point of delirium; it leads to prostitution (or to early death) . . ." and that "[t]here are two natural sisters in the world: prostitution and riot." Ibid., 373.

29. For a more general discussion of the relationship between prostitution and various forms of marriage, see Richard Posner, *Sex and Reason* (Cambridge, Mass.: Harvard University Press, 1992), 130–33.

30. Sukanya Hantrakul, "Thai Women: Male Chauvinism à la Thai," *The Nation*, November 16, 1992, cited with further discussion in Asia Watch Women's Rights Project, *A Modern Form of Slavery: Trafficking of Burmese Women and Girls into Brothels in Thailand* (New York: Human Rights Watch, 1993).

31. See *A Modern Form of Slavery: The Human Rights Watch Global Report on Women's Human Rights* (New York: Human Rights Watch, 1995), 196–273, esp. 270–73. The pertinent international human rights instruments take the same approach, including the International Covenant on Civil and Political rights, the Convention on the Elimination of All forms of Discrimination against Women, and the Convention for the Suppression of Traffic in Persons and the Exploitation of the Prostitution of Others.

32. *Palmore v. Sidoti*, 466 U.S. 429 (1984).

33. See Corbin, *Women for Hire*, 90: In Paris, Dr. Clerc boasted that he could examine a woman every thirty seconds, and estimated that a single practitioner saw 400 women in a single twenty-four-hour period. Another practitioner estimated that the average number of patients per hour was fifty-two.

34. For a more pessimistic view of health checks, see Posner, *Sex and Reason*, 209, pointing out that they frequently have had the effect of driving prostitutes into the illegal market.

35. See Richard Posner, *Private Choices and Public Health: The AIDS Epidemic in an Economic Perspective* (Cambridge, Mass.: Harvard University Press, 1993), 149, with references.

36. See *Human Rights Watch Global Report*, 1–7.

37. See Anderson, *Value in Ethics and Economics*, 156: "Her actions under contract express not her own valuations but the will of her customer."

38. This is crucial in the thinking behind the "capabilities approach" to which I have contributed in *Women, Culture, and Development* and other publications. For the connection between this approach and Marx's use of Aristotle, see Martha C. Nussbaum, "Aristotle on Human Nature and the Foundations of Ethics," in *World, Mind, and Ethics: Essays on the Philosophy of Bernard Williams*, ed. J. E. J. Altham and R. Harrison (Cambridge: Cambridge University Press, 1993).

39. Made frequently by my students, not necessarily to support criminalization.

40. Anderson, *Value in Ethics and Economics*, 150–58; Anderson pulls back from an outright call for criminalization, concluding that her arguments "establish the legitimacy of a state interest in prohibiting prostitution, but not a conclusive case for prohibition," given the paucity of opportunities for working women.

41. See K. J. Dover, *Greek Homosexuality*, 2nd ed. (Cambridge, Mass.: Harvard University Press, 1978); and David Halperin, "The Democratic Body," in *One Hundred Years of Homosexuality and Other Essays on Greek Love* (New York: Routledge, 1990). Customers were all males, but prostitutes were both male and fe-

male. The evidence that prostitution was publicly funded is uncertain because it derives from comic drama, but it is clear that both male and female prostitution enjoyed broad public support and approval.

42. For a similar point, see Radin, "Market-Inalienability," 1921–25; and *Contested Commodities*, 132–36; Anderson refers to this claim of Radin's, apparently as the source of her reluctance to call outright for criminalization.

43. I would not go quite as far as John Rawls, however, in the direction of letting the market determine our cultural options. He opposes any state subsidy to opera companies, symphony orchestras, museums, and so on, on the grounds that this would back a particular conception of the good against others. I think, however, that we could defend such subsidies, within limits, as valuable because they preserve a cultural option that is among the valuable ones, and that might otherwise cease to exist. Obviously much more argument is needed on this entire question.

44. See Radin, "Market-Inalienability"; and Anderson, *Value in Ethics and Economics*, 156: "The prostitute, in selling her sexuality to a man, alienates a good necessarily embodied in her person to him and thereby subjects herself to his commands."

45. On this point, see also Schwarzenbach, "Contractarians," with discussion of Marx's account of alienation.

46. See Richard Epstein, "Surrogacy: The Case for Full Contractual Enforcement," *Virginia Law Review* 81 (1995): 2327.

47. Moreover, the UCC does not cover the sale of services, and prostitution should be classified as a service rather than a good.

48. It is well known that these ideas are heavily implicated in the difficulty of getting young people, especially young women, to use contraception.

49. See Shrage's earlier article; Andrea Dworkin, "Prostitution and Male Supremacy," in *Life and Death* (New York: The Free Press, 1997).

50. An eloquent examination of the last view, with reference to Freud's account (which endorses it) is in William Miller, *The Anatomy of Disgust* (Cambridge, Mass.: Harvard University Press, 1997), chap. 6.

51. The Dowry Prohibition Act of 1961 makes both taking and giving of dowry illegal; in Bangladesh, demanding, taking, and giving dowry are all criminal offenses. See chapter 3 in *Sex and Social Justice*.

52. It is extremely difficult to estimate how many women are damaged and killed as a result of this practice; it is certainly clear that criminal offenses are vastly underreported, as is domestic violence in India generally, but that very problem makes it difficult to form any reliable idea of the numbers involved. See Indira Jaising, *Justice for Women* (Bombay: The Lawyers' Collective, 1996); and chapter 3 in *Sex and Social Justice*.

53. See Amartya Sen and Jean Drèze, *Hunger and Public Action* (Oxford: Clarendon Press, 1989), 52; and chapter 1 in *Sex and Social Justice*. Kerala, the only Indian state to have a matrilineal property tradition, also has an equal number of men and women (contrasted with a 94 : 100 sex ratio elsewhere), and 97 percent both male and female literacy, as contrasted with 32 percent female literacy elsewhere.

54. See, for example, *A Modern Form of Slavery: Trafficking of Burmese Women; Human Rights Watch Global Report*, 1296–373; Amnesty International, *Human Rights Are Women's Right* (London: Amnesty International, 1995), 53–6.

55. See *Human Rights Watch Global Report*, 197, on Thailand.

56. Joseph Raz, *The Morality of Freedom* (Oxford: Clarendon Press, 1986), 374.

57. See Posner, *Sex and Reason*, 132n43 on the low incidence of prostitution in Sweden, even though it is not illegal; his explanation is that "women's opportunities in the job market are probably better there than in any other country."

58. See Schwarzenbach, "Contractarians."

59. An extremely high proportion of the labor force in India is in the informal sector.

60. SEWA was first directed by Ela Bhatt, who is now involved in international work to improve the employment options of informal-sector workers. For a valuable description of the movement, see Kalima Rose, *Where Women Are Leaders: The SEWA Movement in India* (Delhi: Sage Publications, 1995).

61. But see, here, Schwarzenbach and Shrage (op. cit.). I have also been very much influenced by the work of Martha Chen, *A Quiet Revolution: Women in Transition in Rural Bangladesh* (Cambridge, Mass.: Schenkman, 1983); Chen, "A Matter of Survival: Women's Right to Work in India and Bangladesh," in *Women, Culture, and Development*, ed. M. Nussbaum and J. Glover (Oxford: Clarendon Press, 1995); and Bina Agarwal, *A Field of One's Own: Gender and Land Rights in South Asia* (Cambridge: Cambridge University Press, 1994); and also "Bargaining and Gender Relations: Within and Beyond the Household," FCND Discussion Paper No. 27, Food Consumption and Nutrition Division, International Food Policy Research Institute, Washington, D.C.

Chapter 25

PORNOGRAPHY AS
EMBODIED PRACTICE

Joan Mason-Grant

*The writings of Andrea Dworkin and Catharine MacKinnon are well
known for their forceful criticism of pornography. In this essay, which summarizes some of the central arguments in her* Pornography Embodied:
From Speech to Sexual Practice *(Rowman & Littlefield, 2004),* **Joan
Mason-Grant** *revisits some of the themes found in Dworkin and MacKinnon. In particular, Mason-Grant argues that pornography should not be
understood as "speech," that examining pornography as a vehicle for the expression of ideas leads us astray from comprehending pornography and its
relationship to a socialized sexuality in an illuminating and potentially liberating way. Pornography, she claims, is better understood as an "embodied
practice," as something that shapes pernicious, women-subordinating forms
of sexuality.*

Mason-Grant teaches part-time in the interdisciplinary Social Justice and Peace Studies program at King's University College of the University of Western Ontario. Her interest in the relationship between embodied personal know-how and dominant social
systems has now extended from sexuality into the realm of food, with a focus on understanding and transforming our practices within the global food system.

We live in interesting times, sexually speaking. We in the West often
think of ourselves as sexually liberated, and in many ways we are.
In school, we talk openly about AIDS and other sexually transmitted diseases, and teach our children how to put condoms on bananas. We talk

directly about birth control, at least in those educational contexts not yet
recuperated by feverishly fearful moral conservatives. Women are now
recognized as beings with sexual desires and capable of sexual autonomy. Homosexual relationships are on the way to being brought into the
fold of socially and legally recognized love relationships. Victorian skirts
have been lifted, so to speak, and the sexual revolution appears to have
taken hold in a rollicking, widespread, open embrace of sexuality. Still,
all is not well in the land of sexual liberation. The bodies of women and
children, and some men, have been re-commodified to an extent that is
disturbing. Rigid gender scripts have been reinstated to an astonishing
degree through this commodification. And, as is predictable in capitalist economies, the commodification process has been accompanied by
an interesting discourse about "choice" and "liberation," buzzwords that
often mask underlying power relations that systematically deny certain
groups of people the experience of real choice or real liberation.

The debate over pornography contains all these contradictions. In
this essay, I seek to open a space, in the context of the pornography debate, for a critical exploration of the widespread assumption that the
pervasiveness of pornography is a sign of liberation, and I seek to do so
by challenging the long-held conceptualization of pornography as
speech.

In the realm of pornography (I speak of the readily accessible, heterosexual mainstream of pornography),[1] the road to sexual liberation
has been opened up almost exclusively by appeal to the idea of "freedom
of speech." One of the tasks in this essay is to explain how pornography
has come to be seen as "speech" and thereby found its protection not
only from law but from social critique generally. I believe the well-
entrenched "liberal" idea that pornography is speech has shut down
fruitful critical discussion of the material role of mainstream pornography in our sexual lives.

As a counterpoint to this understanding of pornography, I revisit the
fundamentals of the much maligned (and, I believe, much misunderstood) analysis of pornography first worked out by Andrea Dworkin and
then taken up by Catherine MacKinnon.[2] The crux of this analysis is the
claim that pornography is not merely the representation or expression
of ideas, that is, "speech," but a *material practice* of subordination.
Dworkin and MacKinnon are most well known, infamously perhaps, for
their construction in 1992 of a civil rights ordinance that attempted to
codify their conceptualization of pornography within the law. Their aim
was to shift the legal response to pornography from the paternalistic
criminal code of a patriarchal state to the realm of civil litigation so that
individuals who believed themselves to have been "subordinated"
through pornography's material practices—its production, distribution,
or consumption—could seek redress from those who materially profit

from the subordination. In my view, ironically, the ordinance and the legal debate it generated have actually consolidated and strengthened the general view, even among radical thinkers, that pornography is speech. In the wake of this debate, the innovative conceptual substance of the Dworkin-MacKinnon analysis of pornography has been distorted, obscured, often rendered virtually unrecognizable and, what is most frustrating, left undeveloped. The constructive aim of this essay is to bring critical awareness back to the core insight of that analysis—that pornography is a series of irreducibly embodied *practices* that work quite differently from political speech—and to begin to elaborate the concept of pornography as a practice in order to better understand how mainstream pornography contributes to a profoundly impoverished, overly objectifying and, yes, subordinating sexual know-how.

The Legal Question and the Speech Paradigm

Before I proceed, I feel compelled to state a couple of things categorically: First, I am opposed to state censorship (so was Andrea Dworkin).[3] Second, I do not think *looking* at pornography "causes" violence. This oversimplified characterization of the relationship between pornography and subordination is a symptom of the speech paradigm, which I critique in this essay. I feel called to state these facts clearly in advance of my argument because contemporary discussion of pornography tends to get absorbed into an over-determined conservative-versus-liberal binary opposition that has an astonishing power to prevent people from hearing what is actually being said.

The key reason for this rigid binary construction of the pornography debate is the preoccupation with the legal question of whether the state should have prohibitive laws regarding pornography.[4] Whenever the issue of pornography arises, it comes with the baggage of age-old questions about the extent of state intervention in and control of individual lives in matters of morality. In the case of pornography, the long-standing "conservative" view is that public communication of and about explicit sexuality is a threat to community moral standards. In this view, the state is understood to be the guardian of the moral fabric of society; laws proscribing and prohibiting "obscenity" are therefore justified. By contrast, the "liberal" view is that the expression of explicit sexuality is, at worst, merely offensive and, at best, a healthy release of sexual desire from the regulative confines of repression; in either case, liberals think that the use of pornography is none of the state's business. So a limit on repressive state or institutional power is taken to be essential to individual freedom and self-determination. Since the constitutionally based guarantee to freedom of speech has been effectively established as a limit to state power, especially in the United States, "freedom of speech" is universally aligned with emancipatory values.

The dominance of the legal question in the pornography debate has put in place a number of false dichotomies, composed of several false alignments: Those who are procensorship, conservative, antisex, antipornography are lined up against those who are anticensorship, liberal, prosex, propornography. The frigid and uptight side has to face off with those who are liberal and open and sexually liberated, and those who have a stake in keeping state power at bay have come to have a stake in the conceptualization of pornography as "speech." This makes it politically difficult to admit the possibility that the practices of pornography (production, distribution, and consumption) work quite differently from political speech, that they might be realms of systemic oppression as powerful and damaging as, though different in nature than, the oppression sometimes wielded by the state, and that the freedoms granted by constitutional guarantees to free speech may, in fact, exacerbate those oppressions, profoundly restricting the real autonomy and self-determination of entire groups of people. These are insights integral to the analysis of pornography Dworkin and MacKinnon developed. However, the dominance of the speech paradigm, girded up by fear of state oppression, has made it strangely difficult for critics of their work to assess these ideas on their own terms.

Pornography as Speech: Ronald Dworkin

A central premise of my argument is that the speech paradigm predominates in contemporary debate over pornography. I use the phrase "speech paradigm" to mean the general view of communication that takes political speech as its model. Ronald Dworkin[5] offers an argument that I take to be a well-formulated example of a liberal defense of pornography as speech that tacitly accepts the speech paradigm as a way to conceptualize pornography.

Ronald Dworkin's arguments[6] coincide with current First Amendment law in the United States regarding pornography and, I submit, with a significant range of public discourse and sentiment. The legal orientation and the popular sentiment I have in mind was expressed quite clearly, for example, in the Oliver Stone movie *The People vs. Larry Flynt*:

> At the heart of the First Amendment is the recognition of the fundamental importance of the free flow of ideas. Freedom to speak one's mind is not only an aspect of individual liberty, but essential to the quest for truth and the vitality of society as a whole. In the world of debate about public affairs, many things done with motives that are less than admirable are nonetheless protected by the First Amendment.[7]

The movie depicts the legal challenges of Larry Flynt, publisher of *Hustler* magazine, in fighting for First Amendment protection against applications of obscenity law. The power of the film lies in the antihero figure of Flynt, who is at once the object of our disgust (for there is little in the film that recommends him as a person of good character) and a kind of flag-bearer for the principle of free speech in a liberal democracy.

Ronald Dworkin's defense of Larry Flynt's right, even responsibility, to speak would look like this: Ronald Dworkin and others in society may not like Larry Flynt or the content of *Hustler*, but to constrain Flynt's liberty to publish *Hustler* is to limit his freedom *on the basis that his way of life is inherently less worthy than others*. The intriguing aspect of Ronald Dworkin's argument is that it derives from the principle of *equality* and not, as one might expect of a liberal, the principle of individual liberty. Equality, for Ronald Dworkin, is a matter of treating people's suffering and frustration with equal concern and *treating people's differing views about the good life with equal respect in the law*. His arguments about pornography tend to emphasize the latter aspect of this principle of equality over the former, which he calls the "right to moral independence." To preserve the principle of equality, the State must refrain from enforcing a certain conception of the good life and suppressing others. Laws censoring or otherwise prohibiting pornography would be laws enforcing a certain conception of the good life and, thereby, would violate the right of equality. So even if the public overwhelmingly called for the prohibition of pornography (a utilitarian justification for censorship laws) the principle of equality would trump this majority preference. On this argument, the right to publish, buy, and read pornography is understood to both derive from and protect equality.

Are there any circumstances in which the right to moral independence might be overridden? In his early discussions of pornography Ronald Dworkin considers only moralist criticisms or concerns about pornography that express preferences about the good life. In his later writings on the subject, he responds to the feminist argument that pornography is "not a moral issue"[8] but a question of harm. Ronald Dworkin allows that speech can justifiably be limited if it can be shown to constitute *a clear and present danger* or *cause* harm, that is, limited *if* certain forms of pornography could be shown to "significantly increase the danger that women will be raped or physically assaulted." However, he dismisses this possibility as academic speculation because, in his estimation, there has been no persuasive evidence of such a causal link between pornography and violence. He does consider the further claim that pornography "denies [women] the right to be their own masters by recreating them, for politics and society, in the shapes of male fantasy" and that it thereby produces a climate in which women cannot exercise their liberty because they "are perceived and understood unauthentically."[9] He acknowledges

that this is a potentially powerful argument, for the systematic reconstruction of women's public identity may infringe on their capacity to fulfill their responsibility to express their views. However, he quickly dis-
penses with this argument by first reducing it to the narrowly causal claim
that pornography is largely responsible for, rather than a core practice
of, this subordinating reconstruction of identity and then arguing that
this seems "strikingly implausible."

> Sadistic pornography is revolting, but it is not in general circulation, except
> for its milder, soft-porn manifestations. It seems unlikely that it has re-
> motely the influence over how women's sexuality or character or talents are
> conceived by men, and indeed by women, that commercial advertising and
> soap operas have. Television and other parts of popular culture use sexual
> display and sexual innuendo to sell virtually everything, and they often
> show women as experts in domestic detail and unreasoned intuition and
> nothing else. The images they create are subtle and ubiquitous, and it
> would not be surprising to learn, through whatever research might estab-
> lish this, that they indeed do great damage to the way women are under-
> stood and allowed to be influential in politics. Sadistic pornography,
> though much more offensive and disturbing, is greatly overshadowed by
> these dismal cultural influences as a causal force.[10]

Having conceded the strength of the argument that women's positive
liberty might be infringed by the systematic reconstruction of their public identity, and having recognized the force of these other forms of cultural expression, Ronald Dworkin might as easily have concluded not
only that pornography is subordinating to women but that these other
forms of expression also deserve effective intervention. It might seem
that the extent to which contempt for women saturates society would
count as unacceptable "suffering and frustration" under the "right to
equal concern" feature of the principle of equality. In short, he could
conclude that this systemic sexism violates the principle of equality on all
fronts. He does not.

Ideal versus Substantive Systems:
Equality, Social Power, and Speech

Ronald Dworkin's arguments about pornography are focused on the legal question of whether a prohibitive policy toward pornography can be
justified. My interest here is not in the legal question. As I indicated, I
am opposed to state censorship. Rather, my interest is in how the argument over pornography undertaken within this particular theater of law
commits Ronald Dworkin, and many other liberals, to certain scripts
about the nature of equality, social power, and speech and, by implica-

tion, about the *nature* of pornography. Because the tyranny of state power preoccupies Ronald Dworkin, he seems unable to seriously engage on its own terms the idea that pornography is a material practice that may be subordinating.

I maintain that Ronald Dworkin cannot move in this direction because he works within a particular framework involving abstract conceptions of equality, social power, and speech. Ronald Dworkin's project is idealist and normative. He is concerned to elaborate an *ideal* system, that is, a system of principle that constitutes a liberal political theory within which specific political decisions can be justified. In this formal project, the abstract principle of equality defines the system. Because he derives specific liberties such as free speech from the principle of equality, he assumes that equality is always already a constitutive feature of this system. The integrity of the system, its coherence and consistency, is of utmost concern.

Herein lies a fundamental conceptual and methodological conflict with the approach to questions of equality undertaken by social critics such as Dworkin and MacKinnon. They are concerned first and foremost with *substantive* systems—social systems, economic systems, meaning systems—that operate on the ground, as it were, in the messy negotiations of everyday life. Substantive systems are not made up of abstract principles. They are made up of people engaged in concrete practices with one another, people who understand themselves and others in terms of socially and politically charged categories. Dworkin and MacKinnon presume that substantive equality does not in fact exist even in our liberal society that holds equality as a cherished, constitutionally enshrined principle. So their approach to analyzing issues of equality is contextual and diagnostic; their task is to understand *how* sex/gender *in*equality works in such a social context, how it is lived out in everyday life, and why so many people do not perceive it as inequality.

Differing concepts of social power are intertwined with the notions of equality in these different approaches. For Dworkin and MacKinnon, equality is an irreducibly substantive matter: If it does not exist in the concrete practices of social life, this is because of an imbalance in social power. As MacKinnon writes, "In this approach, an equality question is a question of the distribution of power. . . . The question of equality, from the standpoint of what it is going to take to get it, is at root a question of hierarchy."[11]

It might be said that Ronald Dworkin also sees equality as a question of the distribution of social power, for the principle of equality properly adhered to prevents social inequality from seeping into policy making. But for him, social power is characterized quite narrowly as the power of one group (the majority preference) to enforce its conception of the good life on others (those in the minority) through the mechanism of state power. In his work, the problem of social power metamorphoses into the problem of state power. Dworkin and MacKinnon, by contrast, are concerned with actual disparities in social power.

Finally, these contesting notions of equality and social power manifest themselves in, and shed light on, differing conceptions of speech tacitly at work in these competing arguments. Ronald Dworkin states that pornography is no different than "speech directly advocating that women occupy inferior roles."[12] He apparently takes the analogy between pornography and such speech to be self-evident, for he offers no argument for it. Like political speech, the words and images of pornography represent ideas, or express a point of view. While pornography may indeed be powerful enough to provoke or excite certain feelings, such as disgust, it nonetheless depends, like any other speech, on "mental intermediation" for its effects.[13] The principle of the right to moral independence requires that people be allowed to *make up their own minds* about its rightness or wrongness, truth or falsity.

In this view, words and images are understood to be conveyors of ideas that, in the "marketplace of ideas," can be expressed and contemplated, offered and tested out, like so many heads of lettuce or widgets, by independent, fully mature, rational consumers and then accepted or rejected on their merits. Here, "thought" is presumed to be conscious, considered, and rational, and "ideas" and "meanings" are decidedly immaterial. This is the dominant way of understanding "speech" in contemporary liberalized countries. As Dworkin notes: "The general view . . . is that writers think up ideas or words and then other people read them and all this happens in the head, a vast cavern somewhere north of the eyes. It is all air, except for the paper and ink, which are simply banal. Nothing happens."[14]

Within this conceptual framework, words and images are passive conveyors of ideas. They can represent, refer, or connote, but they do not themselves "do" anything. People do things. The ideas represented or expressed in words and images cannot be said to be "ours" unless or until we consciously accept them. They may offend our sensibilities, they may give us a stomachache, but they do not shape our consciousness, or seep into our own way of thinking or acting, unless and until we (consciously) adopt them as our own. Words and images are thus safely at a distance from action by the process of mental intermediation, which is, of course, presumed to be private, personal, and internal.

On this way of looking at things, the claim that pornography is itself subordinating is prima facie implausible. Yet, this is precisely the claim that theorists such as Dworkin and MacKinnon seem to want to press:

> Pornography contains ideas, like any other social practice. But the way it works is not as a thought or through its ideas as such, at least not in the way

thoughts and ideas are protected as speech. Its place in abuse requires understanding it more in active than in passive terms, as constructing and performative rather than as merely referential or connotative.[15]

The model of speech tacitly ascribed to by Ronald Dworkin may work fine for political speech. But in the Dworkin-MacKinnon analysis, pornographic practices are critically different from someone explicitly asserting that women are inferior to men. Making sense of this difference requires understanding that the entire system of pornographic practices, including the use of pornographic materials for sex, consists in a series of embodied, material practices that contribute to the making and unmaking of meanings about sexuality, gender, race, ability, class, sexual power, control, self-esteem, and so on.

Pornography: Systemic Practices of Subordination

As indicated, the approach of Dworkin and MacKinnon is diagnostic, part of a critical investigation into extant inequalities manifested in phenomena ranging from economic and political inequality to harassment, child sexual assault, sexual violence, and femicide. Pornography emerges in their investigations not as the causal root of these inequalities but as a "core constitutive practice"[16] of gender inequality and "a major social force for institutionalizing . . . second class status for women."[17] As Dworkin writes,

> Pornography originates in a real social system in which women are sexually colonized and have been for hundreds of centuries. Pornography—whether as a genre or as industry or as aid to masturbation—originates in that system, flourishes in that system, and *has no meaning or existence outside that system.*[18]

On this approach, "pornography" is inadequately understood if reduced to the materials, the words and images, typically presumed to be denoted by the term. Rather, pornographic materials can be understood only within the context of a vast network of related and mutually constitutive material practices, including the production and consumption of pornography. The production of pornographic materials involves material activities among human beings, especially in modern pornography, which requires the bodies of real women and men. The pornography industry is linked to the modeling industry and is tied also to prostitution, sexual slavery, and sex tourism. Many, not all, women are coerced behind the scenes to perform in pornographic scenes they are not comfortable doing and to show themselves enjoying them. Many women report taking drugs or dissociating to get through this work. In short, pornography production makes use of the sexual relations of power that it is in the business of depicting as sexy. Similarly, the consumption of pornographic materials also occurs in materially real contexts, amidst sexual relations of power. For example, in addition to being used as sexual arousal or masturbation material, pornography also is used as a blueprint for sexual activity between partners, or as a tool in sex crimes ranging from the production of child pornography to sexual assault and sexual murder. It is also used in the workplace, to intimidate women. The key point, here, is that the social relations performed in pornographic materials are already at work in the world—in the production of the materials, in the structure of the sex industry, in modes of sexual practice—and they are legitimated and further entrenched when they are enacted through sexual activity involving the use of pornographic materials.

So pornographic materials exemplify a social logic that is already real in the world. What is this social logic?[19] On Dworkin and MacKinnon's analysis, mainstream heterosexual pornography fuses the eroticization of domination and subordination with the social construction of gender, race, class, and ability. Always primed for sex, the female or feminized performer is offered not as a fully developed character but as cunt, ass, tits—the object of desire. Her looked-at, freely displayed body parts are the catalyst to masculine arousal. More than this, female carnality is presented as the irresistible source of masculine desire, exerting a sexual "I must" that grips males from within, compelling them to act. This power of female sexuality over male desire explains the central eroticized dynamic of mainstream pornography: The sexual actor gendered "male" must pursue and conquer the actor gendered "female" who, while always prepared to be "taken," often coyly or aggressively resists. This dynamic restores masculine control, at once explaining and excusing male sexual dominance as a response to an insistent itch. This gendered dynamic is racialized within pornographic materials: the darker skinned the female actor, the more carnal and untamed her sexual desire tends to be (and the less valuable her life); the darker skinned the masculine actor, the more powerful his ability to overcome. Disabled women are hypersexualized, their particular disability offered as the fetishized vehicle of their compliance or their masochism. The sexual dynamic in mainstream pornography is one of overt or implied struggle, involving either flight and capture or, more subtly, resistance and subduing and possession. The resolution of the sexual tension, the closing act of the performance, is male ejaculation, the male spent and satisfied. Mainstream heterosexual pornography presents these relations in narrowly conceived scripts that are repeated over and over. They can thus be seen as regulative norms that establish what counts as normal and perverse, sexy and asexual, identifying the paths of access to social viability as a sexual actor.

Dworkin and MacKinnon emphasize the interrelatedness of all the practices of pornography, from the conditions of its production and distribution to its consumption. However, their claims about the consumption of pornography have drawn the sharpest resistance, principally because of the dominance of the speech paradigm. Discussion about the use of pornographic materials for sex routinely bumps up against the legal defense of pornography as speech and, as a result, tends to be protected from critical scrutiny by all, save conservative moralists. However, on Dworkin and MacKinnon's analysis, the use of pornography is nothing like engaging in political speech. Rather, the use of pornographic materials *is* sexual activity—a performed, *embodied practice.* Dworkin writes, "Pornography happens. . . . The man's ejaculation is real."[20] Similarly, MacKinnon argues:

> Pornography is masturbation material. It is used as sex. It therefore is sex. . . . With pornography, men masturbate to women being exposed, humiliated, violated, degraded, mutilated, dismembered, bound, gagged, tortured, and killed. . . . What is real here is not that the materials are pictures, but that they are part of a sex act. The women are in two dimensions, but the men have sex with them in their own three-dimensional bodies, not in their minds alone. Men come doing this.[21]

On this account, the consumption of pornographic materials is not adequately conceptualized as a disembodied, cognitive, contemplative, information-processing activity. Rather, it is a material activity, distinctly sexual and irreducibly embodied. While it involves representations, it is not "reading about" sex, as though the sex were elsewhere. *It is sex.* In using mainstream, mass-market pornographic materials for sex, consumers *bodily experience* inequality, the objectification of the female body, violence, and brutality as pleasureful, erotic, and orgasmic.

We Become What We Practice Being: The Practice Paradigm

In place of the dominant speech paradigm, we need an alternative "practice paradigm" that better captures and elaborates more complexly the embodied activity of using pornographic materials for sex. In *Pornography Embodied*, I work out a phenomenological account of the relationship between routinized bodily practices and the formation of our practical know-how. Too involved to reproduce here, I can nonetheless provide a summary of its central points. I draw on the work of Drew Leder who, in *The Absent Body*, provides a complex and dynamic account of corporeality that shows how the social and organic are intertwined phenomenologically.[22] His account links the production of agency—our ability to act intelligibly in the world—with the bodily practices in which we engage.

As he describes it, the structure of our practices is incorporated at the level of the lived body and sedimented in the form of tacit personal know-how. This account links our capacity for functional competence to the tacitness of our practiced bodies. The knowledge acquired through the process of incorporation is not propositional knowledge or abstract ideas, but a robustly practical, functional know-how. The process of incorporation operates over time and below the level of conscious awareness. The value of this account for understanding the use of pornography for sex is that it suggests how the reiterative enactment of certain repetitive scripts of sexuality works at the level of personal experience, explains why we are often unaware of these processes, and makes them available to critical scrutiny.

Sexual desire is often thought of as belonging to an essentially presocial, inherent, or "given" realm. Like hunger, sexual desire seems to be a force that grips us from within, exerting an "I must," demanding satisfaction. Arising from the organic dimension of our being, hunger and sexual desire are experienced as belonging to a realm outside personal mastery and quite apart from social influence. A fundamental implication of the account of incorporation referred to above is that it is a mistake to conclude from the experiential fact that processes and powers of the organic body exceed our direct control that they are uninfluenced by our activities and practices. Through the ongoing processes of incorporation characteristic of our embodied beings, the social norms that structure our practices become intertwined with the organic, and agency and personal know-how are so constituted. For example, a moment's reflection makes clear that the yearnings driven by hunger *are* shaped by the systemic norms of eating practices. Do you yearn for Kraft dinner when you are hungry? Or beans and rice, or raw fish, or whale blubber, or venison, or home-cooked organic veggie stew? The trajectory taken by our desire for food is intimately bound up with the social norms and practices through which we have learned about eating. Sexual desire is only a different kind of hunger. It is surely organic, arising as part of our biological being. But it takes shape within the social context in which we come to maturity as sexual beings.[23]

Importantly, the social norms of eating and of sex are not principally communicated to us as ideas or opinions. They are modeled, performed, acted out, rehearsed, from our earliest days. The notion of incorporation suggests that, over time, that which is repetitively acted out—practiced—seeps into one's organismic ground, coming to shape not only our habits, but our desires and yearnings, and our personal know-how. Incorporation happens not in a flash, but over time, through a bodily history of structured repetition. This suggests that, as a given form of sexuality is acted out, rehearsed, it seeps into our organismic ground, shaping sexual desire and pleasure, shaping perception and expectation, and thereby shaping the way one interacts sexually with others.

The Use of Pornography and the Cultivation of Sexual Know-how

Andrea Dworkin calls pornography a form of *sexual pedagogy*. The use of pornographic materials for sex is very often the sexual activity that first unlocks the mysterious and urgent world of sexuality to young people who are newly sexually alive and curious. Dworkin says that pornography is "exceptionally effective precisely because it is not just mental; it is physiologically real to [its users], and they learn in their bodies about women from the pornography in a way that it doesn't matter what they think. They can think one thing, but what they do is something else."[24] This "learning in their bodies" is aptly captured by the account of incorporation outlined above. Using the framework of this account, we can now fruitfully ask just what sort of sexual know-how the use of mainstream heterosexual pornography for sex cultivates.

If the use of mainstream heterosexual pornography is a practice routinely engaged in as one comes to sexual maturity, its users will *experience* sexual desire, arousal, and satiation in its terms. That is, their desire and pleasure will plausibly become calibrated to the values of gendered, racialized, and classed dominance, subordination, and objectification that mainstream pornography makes available as sex. The transgressive quality of using pornography for sex intensifies this experience, making the social logic that is the vehicle of sexual arousal seem not just normal but *natural*; in a world where sexual desire and pleasure are typically regarded as unanalyzable brute facts, whatever feels sexy must *naturally be* sexy. Sexual pleasure becomes an indicator of some underlying human nature: If domination and subordination feel good, they must be a natural part of human nature. Of course, the social relations that predominate in mainstream pornography are not limited to mainstream pornography. They are also pervasive in the larger culture. Surely the cultural prevalence of these norms bolsters rather than mitigates the force of mainstream pornography that, in turn, consolidates their normalizing force.

The corporeal practice of using pornographic materials for sex thus consists in a kind of erotic rehearsal of the social logic they contain.[25] The norms of sexuality thus experienced, supported and reiterated by other cultural practices, become incorporated into the functional base of one's sexual agency. Over time, they become the tacit basis of a personal sexual know-how that is experienced as natural and normal. In this way, mainstream pornography contributes to what one sexually knows how to do, shaping perceptions and expectations of oneself and others.

In fact, this analysis leads to the observation that it is not just the content of pornography that is concerning but the very situation of using pornographic materials as a way of practicing sex. The catalyst to sexual arousal in pornography is a two-dimensional, anonymous "other," and the key mode of interaction is voyeurism. That is, in using pornography, one is "having sex" with or in relation to, a two-dimensional rather than a three-dimensional "other." Despite the apparent realism of modern porn—real bodies, real orifices—the figures in pornography are completely unburdened by character or relationship development; the performers are reduced to their essential sexual parts: genitals or breasts. This provides the users of pornography an ease of access to sex objects that are otherwise either off limits or more complicated to access when they are attached to fully human, flesh-and-blood beings. Further, the only sense engaged in the "interaction" with the sexual other of pornography is vision. Now, there is nothing wrong with "looking" as a part of sexual interaction. But I worry that the prevalence of "looking" as a predominant form of sexual practice, instituted in pornography, establishes voyeurism as a predominant way of interacting sexually with others. This strips the situation of the mutuality of perception and concern demanded in respectful relationships with flesh-and-blood others, especially relationships involving intimate bodily interaction.

So what pornography does is to provide an opportunity, over and over, to have sex with another without actually having to directly interact with, or be accountable to, the sexual other. Indeed, the "reality" of the other (a photograph, a video) presents a real person who apparently *loves* being merely an object of arousal. In the routine use of porn, the cycle of erotic desire, arousal, and satiation is organized arrogantly, with exclusive concern for the needs, desires, and involvement of the user. Now, thinking again of the explorations of youth, if the use of porn for sex routinely precedes sex in the flesh with fully human others, it makes sense to me that such users will be practiced in an objectifying, self-absorbed form of sexuality without ever having had to attend to the needs, desires, feelings, or interests of another.

Here the link to a good deal of prostitution and sex tourism is obvious. For example, research on the travel postings to the World Sex Guide from Western men returning from Thailand make clear how much of their sexual experience there is dependent on their ability to view the women they fuck as merely objects, merely commodities they buy. These postings reveal a thoroughgoing market mentality. They provide extensive information about money, quantified descriptions of the sexual activity, and advice about how to be on guard against the possibility of being overcharged or robbed. And it's not that sex tourists don't know about the context of poverty in which the trade thrives in Thailand. But this is represented, in good business fashion, as an opportunity for getting the most bang for the buck.

Revolutionizing Practice

There is a deep irony in the contemporary sex scene. The sexual practice of using mainstream, mass-market pornography for sex, which many are inclined to think of as "sexually liberated," is, in fact, a repetitive rehearsal of an exceedingly impoverished sexual script. There is little that is creative, expressive, fully human or "free" down this road. If this were the only objection, we could just ignore pornography like we ignore a bad book. But the analysis offered here also shows that, insofar as this script serves as a widespread training ground for sexual know-how, it is likely to perpetuate subordinating forms of sexuality.

The cultivation of sexual know-how is a powerful process—intimate and personal. Our sexual desires and our ways of being sexual are formed under conditions we are rarely encouraged to scrutinize and in which we come to have a great personal stake. Thrown into the normalized relations of sexuality predominant in this culture, we are somewhat at their mercy as we mature into sexually alive persons. The nature of incorporation illuminates the intransigence of our learned sexual know-how; we all come to have a deeply personal stake in practices that may not only be impoverished, but subordinating. While it's true that we *experience* sexual desires as innate, as "just the way I am," it is possible to critically unpack these desires, ask of them where they came from and whether they may be rooted in social relations that are subordinating. Such a process can be authentically liberating, opening the possibility of reshaping our desire by actually leaving off some practices, and cultivating others. This is not easy work. Revolutionizing practice needs the cultural support of a community of people with the courage, maturity, and creativity to engage these issues openly, to disrupt entrenched ways of talking about them, and to take up the challenge of looking below the level of everyday conscious awareness into our own habitual sexual practices.

Study Questions

1. In her opening paragraph, Mason-Grant says that people in the Western world are sexually liberated in many ways, and gives this example: "Women are now recognized as beings with sexual desires and capable of sexual autonomy." Do you find this historical claim ("now," as opposed to earlier times) to be accurate? It

implies that there had been a time or times when women were not recognized as having sexual desires. Can you provide reasons to think the claim true or false? If you think the claim true, can you point to the dates around which women were (finally) recognized in the West as having sexual desires? Consider, in marshaling evidence for and against Mason-Grant's claim, Western literature, e.g., the Old Testament, Sappho's fragments, ancient Greek mythology (Zeus, Hera, Tiresias), the Roman poets (Ovid, Catallus), the writings of the Church Fathers (Augustine, Aquinas), Chaucer's *Canterbury Tales*, and Boccaccio's *Decameron*.

2. In her essay, Mason-Grant uses the expressions "real choice," "real liberation," and "real autonomy." Are you clear about the difference between, say, "real" liberation and "fake" liberation? What is accomplished substantively (or rhetorically) by attaching "real" to these words? Is "real" in these expressions being used the same way it is used by Mason-Grant in her expressions "real bodies," "real orifices," "real women," and "real persons"? What is a "fake" orifice or a "fake" person?

3. As Mason-Grant states several times, she is opposed to state censorship of pornography or its state-enforced legal prohibition. Yet the MacKinnon-Dworkin ordinance, as Mason-Grant points out, was meant to open up legal space for individual *civil* action against the producers, distributors, and consumers of pornography. Does Mason-Grant defend this legal tactic or is she sympathetic to it? Is this tactic in effect backhanded legal regulation of pornography? Does not resorting to civil courts still rely on state interference, which Mason-Grant claims to disdain?

4. One of MacKinnon's criticisms of pornography reproduced by Mason-Grant is that "With pornography, men masturbate to women being exposed, humiliated, violated, degraded, mutilated, dismembered, bound, gagged, tortured, and killed." Mason-Grant, too, seems to emphasize this sort of brutal pornography in her essay. Is this type of pornography representative of the genre, or have some critics of it exaggerated its extent among sexual materials? Is the type of man who masturbates to this sort of pornography representative of men? If brutal pornography is a very small part of the genre, and if the type of man who enjoys it is relatively uncommon, what happens to the case against pornography advanced by MacKinnon and Mason-Grant?

5. Mason-Grant claims that "the social norms of . . . sex are . . . modeled, performed, acted out, rehearsed, from our *earliest* days," which implies—even if we ignore specifically Freudian ideas

about events from infancy and very early childhood being the determinants of sexuality—that our sexualities are already being laid down well before we go to school or church, well before we read, watch television, and so forth (the same for food and eating). Yet she also claims that "the use of pornographic materials for sex is very often the sexual activity that first unlocks the mysterious and urgent world of sexuality to young people," that is, that exposure to pornography well beyond our "earliest days" is a significant element in the formation of our (or boys' and men's) sexualities. Do you sense a contradiction here or, at least, a puzzle? What *is* the empirical psychological or sociological evidence that pornography is "very often," as she claims, implicated in the formation of the awakening sexuality of teenagers? Is her claim true to your own experiences? (An exercise: page through Mason-Grant's *Pornography Embodied*, including the bibliography, for empirical evidence for her claims about pornography's influence on sexuality.)

Notes

1. Much is made about the inability to define precisely what is meant by "pornography." The drive to define precisely is a legalistic project. In my work, I am interested in practical know-how. Most any person familiar with the cultural conventions of where they live could go out and buy "pornography" or readily find it on the Internet without suffering any deep definitional anxieties. The analysis of this essay and the book on which it is based focuses on mainstream, mass-market pornography that is widely available and principally targeted to men or heterosexual couples.

2. Andrea Dworkin's work on pornography includes *Woman Hating* (New York: E. P. Dutton, 1974); *Pornography: Men Possessing Women* (New York: E. P. Dutton, 1979); *Intercourse* (New York: Free Press, 1987); and *Letters from a War Zone* (Brooklyn, N.Y.: Lawrence Hill Books, 1993). Catherine MacKinnon's work includes, most prominently, *Feminism Unmodified: Discourses on Life and Law* (Cambridge, Mass.: Harvard University Press, 1987) and *Only Words* (Cambridge, Mass.: Harvard University Press, 1993).

3. Andrea Dworkin, "Against the Male Flood: Censorship, Pornography and Equality," in *Letters from a War Zone*, 272.

4. See the Appendix in my *Pornography Embodied* for a detailed account of this legal history.

5. To avoid confusion between the two Dworkins, I will use "Dworkin" by itself to denote Andrea Dworkin and I will use Ronald Dworkin's full name when referring to him.

6. See Ronald Dworkin, *Taking Rights Seriously* (Cambridge, Mass.: Harvard University Press, 1977); "Do We Have a Right to Pornography?" in his *A Matter of Principle* (Cambridge, Mass.: Harvard University Press, 1985); "Liberty and

Pornography," *New York Review of Books* 38, no. 4 (August 15, 1991): 12–15; "The Coming Battles over Free Speech," *New York Review of Books* 39, no. 11 (June 11, 1992): 55–58, 61–64; and "Women and Pornography," *New York Review of Books* 40, no. 17 (October 21, 1993): 36–42.

7. Oliver Stone, Janet Young, and Michael Hausman, producers, *The People vs. Larry Flynt* (Columbia Pictures, 1996). The quotation is a paraphrased version of Chief Justice Rehnquist's court decision in *Hustler Magazine v. Falwell*, 485 US 46 (1988).

8. MacKinnon, "Not A Moral Issue," in *Feminism Unmodified*, 146–62. Ronald Dworkin focuses his critique entirely on MacKinnon's work, virtually ignoring the conceptual groundwork laid by Dworkin.

9. Ronald Dworkin, "Liberty and Pornography," 14.

10. Ronald Dworkin, "Liberty and Pornography," 14.

11. MacKinnon, "Difference and Dominance: On Sex Discrimination," in *Feminism Unmodified*, 40.

12. Ronald Dworkin, "Liberty and Pornography," 14.

13. The phrase is Judge Easterbrook's. See *American Booksellers Association, Inc. v. Hudnut*, 771 F2d 323 (1985), 328.

14. Dworkin, "Against the Male Flood," 255.

15. MacKinnon, *Only Words*, 21.

16. MacKinnon, "Not A Moral Issue" and "Francis Biddle's Sister: Pornography, Civil Rights, and Speech," in *Feminism Unmodified*, 149 and 173, respectively.

17. MacKinnon, "On Collaboration," in *Feminism Unmodified*, 201.

18. Dworkin, *Letters from a War Zone*, 237.

19. See chapter one of *Pornography Embodied* for a detailed explication of this analysis.

20. Dworkin, *Pornography*, xxxviii (1989 reprint).

21. MacKinnon, *Only Words*, 21.

22. Drew Leder, *The Absent Body* (Chicago: University of Chicago Press, 1990).

23. Despite the misunderstandings of some, this analysis fits with the constructivism of both Dworkin and MacKinnon. Both theorists ascribe to a "general theory of sexuality" in which sexuality is not considered to be "an inborn force inherent in individuals" but "social and relational, constructing and constructed of power." MacKinnon writes, "[Desire] is taken for a natural essence or presocial impetus but is actually *created* by the social relations, the hierarchical relations, in question. This process *creates the social beings we know as women and men*, as their relations create society" (MacKinnon, "Desire and Power," in *Feminism Unmodified*, 49–54, at 49).

24. Andrea Dworkin, in Cindy Jenefsky, *Without Apology: Andrea Dworkin's Art and Politics* (Boulder, Colo.: Westview Press, 1998), 58.

25. While we can talk of a predominant social logic within mainstream pornography, this social logic is not all-determining. All systems of meaning harbor constitutive instabilities, hence the possibility of change. I discuss this at length in chapter five of *Pornography Embodied*.

Chapter 26

TALK DIRTY TO ME

Sallie Tisdale

Sallie Tisdale's *"bornographical" essay, "Talk Dirty to Me," is as personal and sincere an apologia for pornography as one will find in print, and it lays down a powerful rebuttal to Mason-Grant's radically feminist approach to the nature and value of pornography in our erotomaniacal culture. "Talk Dirty to Me" traces the development of the ever-more-complex messages Tisdale received when her body was provoked by what her mind reproved. Without denying the feelings of shame and disgust she felt at times while watching pornography, Tisdale confronts the fact that the genre is also, at the same time, exciting. Because it "maps the limit of [the viewer's] shame," pornography can be used to explore the "deeply psychological" aspects of one's own sexuality and, through the resulting self-awareness and recognition, to liberate oneself from a measure of that shame. Now that pornography's preferred medium has shifted to an easily accessible internet, you, Dear Reader (not to mention your daughters and sons), will see an array of video-streamed sexual acts unimagined by most people in Tisdale's generation. It is that much more important that we have authors as honest as she is, and essays as uncompromising as this one, to help us make sense of the experience.*

Tisdale, a prolific author with wide interests and skills, has written *The Sorcerer's Apprentice: Tales of the Modern Hospital* (Henry Holt, 1986), *Harvest Moon: Portrait of a Nursing Home* (Henry Holt, 1987), *The Best Thing I Ever Tasted: The Secret of Food* (Riverhead, 2000), and *Women of the Way: Discovering 2,500 years of Buddhist Wisdom* (HarperSanFrancisco, 2006).

Once or twice a month I visit my neighborhood adult store, to rent a movie or buy a magazine. I am often the only woman there, and I never see another woman alone. Some days there may be only a single clerk and a few customers; at other times I see a dozen men or more: heavyset working men, young men, businessmen. In their midst I often feel a little strange, and sometimes scared. To enter I have to pass the flashing lights, the neon sign, the silvered windows, and go through the blank, reflecting door.

It takes a certain pluck simply to enter. I can't visit on days when I am frail or timid. I open the door feeling eyes on me, hearing voices, and the eyes are my mother's eyes, and, worse, my father's. The voices are the voices of my priest, my lover, my friends. They watch the little girl and chide her, a naïf no more.

I don't make eye contact. Neither do the men. I drift from one section of the store to the other, going about my business. I like this particular store because it is large and well-lit; there are no dark corners in which to hide or be surprised. The men give me sidelong glances as I pass by, and then drop their eyes back to the box in their hands. Pornography, at its roots, is about watching; but no one here openly watches. This is a place of librarian silences. As I move from shelf to shelf, male customers gather at the fringes of where I stand. I think they would like to know which movies I will choose.

In the large front room with the clerks are glass counters filled with vibrators, promising unguents, candy bowls filled with condoms. On the wall behind the counter where you ask for help are giant dildos, rubber vaginas, rubber faces with slit eyes, all mouth. Here are the more mainstream films, with high production values and name stars. Near the door are the straight movies, the standard hard core you can find these days in most urban video-rental stores. Here is the large and growing amateur section: suburban porn. Here is a small section of straight Japanese movies, a section of gay male films, and the so-called lesbian films, directed toward the male viewer: *Dildo Party* and *Pussy Licker*.

The first time I came here alone I dressed in baggy jeans and a pullover sweater, and tied my long hair up in a bun. After a while I was approached by a fat man with a pale, damp face and thinning hair.

"Excuse me," he said. "I'm not trying to come on to you or anything, but I can't help noticing you're, you know, female."

I could only nod.

"And I wonder," he continued, almost breathless, "if you like this stuff" —and he pointed at a nearby picture of a blonde woman in red lingerie. "You see, my girlfriend, she broke up with me, and I'd bought her all this stuff—you know, sex clothes—and she didn't like it." He paused. "I mean, it's out in the back of my truck right now. If you just want to come outside you can have it."

I turned my back in polite refusal, and left before it could grow completely dark outside. He didn't follow; I've never been approached there again.

Another day, when I asked for my movies by number, I didn't want the clerk to glance at the titles, and I tried to distract him with a question. I asked if any women still work here. He was young, effeminate, with a wispy mustache and loose, shoulder-length hair, and he apologized when he said no.

"Even though we're all guys now, we try to be real sensitive," he said, pulling my requests off the shelf without a glance. "If anyone gives you a hard time, let us know. You let us know right away, and we'll take care of it." He handed me my choices in a white plastic bag.

"Have a nice day."

Later. I am home, with my movies. I drink a glass of wine, my lover eats from a silver bowl of popcorn he put beside us on the couch. We are watching a stylish film with expensive sets and a pulsing soundtrack. The beautiful actresses wear sunglasses in every scene, and the wordless scenes shift every few minutes. Now there are two women together; now two women and an adoring man, a tool of the spike-heeled women. A few scenes later there is only one woman, blonde, with a luxuriant body. She reaches one hand slowly down between her legs and pulls a diamond necklace from between her vaginal lips, jewel by jewel. She slides it up her abdomen, across her breast, to her throat, and into her mouth.

Some of my women friends have never seen or read pornography—by which I mean expressions of explicit sex. That I don't find strange; it's a world of women which sometimes seems not to be about women at all. What is odd to me is that I know women who say they never think about it, that they are indifferent, that such scenes and stories seem meant for other people altogether. They find my interest rather curious, I suppose. And a little awkward.

The images of pornography are many and varied; some are fragmented and idealized. Some are crude and unflattering. I like the dreamy, psychedelic quality of certain scenes; I like the surprises in others, and I like the arousal, the heat which can be born in my body without warning, in an instant. I have all the curiosity of the anthropologist and the frank hope of the voyeur. Pornography's texture is shamelessness; it maps the limits of my shame.

At times I find it harder to talk about pornography than my own sexual experience; what I like about pornography is as much a part of my sexuality as what I do, but it is more deeply psychological. What I *do* is the product of many factors, not all of them sexually motivated. But what I *imagine* doing is pure—pure in the sense that the images come wholly from within, from the soil of the subconscious. The land of fantasy is the land of the not-done and the wished-for. There are private lessons there, things for me to learn, all alone, about myself.

I feel bashful watching; that's one small surprise. I am self-conscious, prickly with the feeling of being caught in the act. I can feel that way with friends, with my lover of many years, and I can feel that way alone. Suddenly I need to shift position, avert my eyes. Another surprise, and a more important one: These images comfort me. Pornography reflects the obsessions of the age, which is my age. Sex awakens my unconscious; pornography gives it a face.

When I was ten or eleven my brother shared his stolen *Playboy* with me. The pneumatic figurines seemed magnificent and unreal. Certainly they seemed to have nothing at all to do with me or my future. I was a prodigious reader, and at an early age found scenes of sex and lasciviousness in many books: *The French Lieutenant's Woman*, which granted sex such power, and William Kotzwinkle's *Nightbook*, blunt and unpredictable.

I was not *taught*, specifically, much of anything about sex. I knew, but I knew nothing that counted. I felt arousal as any child will, as a biological state. And then came adolescence: real kisses, and dark, rough fumblings, a rut when all the rules disappeared. Heat so that I couldn't speak to say yes, or no, and a boy's triumphant fingers inside my panties was a glorious relief, and an awful guilt.

I entered sex the way a smart, post-Sixties teenager should, with forethought and contraception and care. My poor partner: "Is that all?" I said out loud when it was over. Is that really what all the fuss was about? But the books and magazines seemed a little more complicated to me after that. I learned—but really just information. I had little enough understanding of sex, and very little wisdom.

At the age of twenty, when I was, happily, several months pregnant, the social work office where I was employed held a seminar on sexuality. We were determinedly liberal about the whole thing; I believe the point was to support clients in a variety of sexual choices. We were given a homework assignment on the first day, to make a collage that expressed our own sexuality. I returned the next morning and saw that my colleagues, male and female both, had all made romantic visions of candlelight and sunsets. I was the youngest by several years, heavy-bellied, and I had brought a wild vision of masked men and women, naked torsos, skin everywhere, darkness, heat.

I knew I was struggling, distantly and through ignorance, with a deep shame. It was undirected, confusing; for years I had been most ashamed of the shame itself. Wasn't sex supposed to be free, easy? What was wrong with me, that I resisted? Why did I feel so afraid of the surrender, the sexual depths? And yet I was ashamed of what I desired: men and women both. I wanted vaguely to try . . . *things*, which no one spoke about; but surely people, somewhere, did. I was ashamed of all my urges, the small details within the larger act, the sudden sounds I made. I could hear that little voice: *Bad girl. Mustn't touch.*

I was a natural feminist; I knew the dialectic, the lingo. And all my secrets seemed to wiggle free no matter what, expand into my unfeminist consciousness. I didn't even know the words for some of what I imagined, but I was sure of this: Liberated women didn't even *think* about what I wanted to do. My shame was more than a preoccupation with sex—everyone I knew was preoccupied with sex. It was more than being confused by the messy etiquette of the 1970s, more than wondering just how much shifting of partners I should do. It was shame for my own unasked-for appetites, which would not be still.

I was propelled toward the overt—toward pornography. I needed information not about sex but about sexual parameters, the bounds of the normal. I needed reassurance, and blessing. I needed permission.

Several years ago, now in my late twenties, I began to watch what I at first called "dirty movies" and to read what were undoubtedly dirty books: *The Story of O* and *My Secret Life*. I went with the man I was living with, my arm in his and my eyes down, to a theater on a back street. It was very cold and dark inside the movie house, so that the other patrons were only dim shadows, rustling nearby. The movie was grainy, half-blurred, the sound muddy, the acting awful. At the same time I felt as though I'd crossed a line: There was a world of sexual material to see, and I was very curious to see it. Its sheer mass and variety reassured me. I couldn't imagine entering this world alone, though, not even for a quick foray into the screened-off section of the local video store, behind the sign reading OVER 18 ONLY. There were always men back there, and only men.

Watching, for the first time, a man penetrate another woman was like leaving my body all at once. I was outside my body, watching, because she on the screen above me was me; and then I was back in my body very much indeed. My lust was aroused as surely and uncontrollably by the sight of sex as hunger can be roused by the smell of food. I know how naive this sounds now, but I had never quite believed, until I saw it, that the sex in such films was *real*, that people fucked in front of cameras, eyes open. I found it a great shock: to see how different sex could be, how many different things it could mean.

Not all I felt was arousal. There are other reasons for a hurried blush. A woman going down on a man, sucking his cock as though starving for it, the man pulling away and shooting come across her face, the woman licking the come off her lips. I felt a heady mix of disgust and excitement, and confusion at that mix. Layers peeled off one after the other, because sometimes I disliked my own response. I resist it still, when something dark and forbidden emerges, when my body is provoked by what my mind reproves.

Inevitably, I came across something awful, something I really hated. The world of pornography is indiscriminate; boundaries get mixed up. Some stories are violent, reptilian, and for all their sexual content aren't about sex. I was reminded of a story I had found by accident, a long time ago, in a copy of my father's *True* magazine. I was forbidden to read *True*, for reasons unexplained. Before I was caught at it and the magazine taken away, I had found an illustration of a blood-splattered, nearly naked woman tied to a post in a dim basement, and had read up to the place in the text where the slow flaying of her legs had begun. It was gothic and horrible, and haunted me for years. Of course, I make my own definitions, everyone does; and to me that sort of thing has nothing to do with pornography. It *is* obscene, though, a word quite often applied to things that have nothing to do with sex. Pornography is sex, and sex is consensual, period. Without consent, the motions of sex become violence, and that alone defines it for me.

I realize this is not the opinion of conservative feminists such as the lawyer Catharine MacKinnon, who believes that violence, even murder, is the end point of all pornography. Certainly a lot of violent material has sexual overtones; the mistake is assuming that anything with sex in it is primarily about sex. The tendency to assume so says something about the person making the assumption. One important point about this distinction is that the one kind of material is so much more readily available than the other: *True* and slasher films and tabloids are part of the common culture. My father bought *True* at the corner tobacco store. Scenes of nothing but mutual pleasure are the illicit ones.

I fall on a line of American women about midway between the actresses whose films I rent and the housewife in Des Moines who has never seen such a film at all. My female friends fall near me, to either side, but most of them a little closer to Des Moines. The store I frequent for my books and films reflects the same continuum: For all its blunt variety, that store is clean, well-lit, friendly, and its variety of materials reflects a variety of hoped-for customers. There are many places I will not go, storefronts and movie houses that seem to me furtive and corrupt. Every society has its etiquette, its rules; so does the world of pornography.

I am deep into thinking about these rules; my cheeks are bright and my palms damp, and the telephone rings. Without thinking I plunge my caller into such thoughts. I chatter a few minutes into a heavy, shifting silence, and then suddenly realize how ill-bred I must seem. Out here, in the ordinary world, such things are not talked about at all. It's one definition of pornography: whatever we will not talk about.

I know I break a rule when I enter the adult store, whether my entrance is simply startling or genuinely unwelcome. The sweaty-lipped man with lingerie wouldn't, couldn't approach me in a grocery store or even a bar. Not like that, and perhaps not at all. Pornography degrades the male vision of women in this way. When I stand among the shelves there I am standing in a maze of female images, shelf after shelf of them, hundreds of naked women smiling or with their eyes closed and mouths open or gasping. I am just one more image in a broken mirror, with its multiple reflections of women, none of them whole.

I am still afraid. These days I am most aware of that fear as a fear of where I will and will not go, what I think of as *possible* for me. But, oh— I'm curious. I can be so curious. A while ago I recruited two friends, one man and one woman, and the three of us went to a peep show together like a flying wedge, parting the crowds of nervy young men, them jostling each other with elbows in the ribs, daring each other, *g'wan*. We changed bills for quarters, leaned together in the dim hallways, elbowed each other in the ribs—*g'wan*. There were endless film loops in booths for singles, various movie channels from which to choose in booths for two people, tissues provided, and a live show. One minute for twenty-five cents, and the signs above each booth flashing on and off, on and off again in the dark, from a green VACANT to a red IN USE and back again.

I pulled a door shut and disappeared into the musky dark; I could hear muffled shouts from the young men in booths on either side. The panel slid up on my first quarter to a brightly lit, mirrored room with three women, all simulating masturbation. The one in the center was right in front of me, and she caught my eye and grinned at me, in black leather just like her. I think she sees few women in the booths, and many men.

Men—always the Man who is the standard-bearer for what is obscene and forbidden. That Man, the one I fear whether I mean to or not, in elevators and parking lots and on the street, is the man who will be inflamed by what he sees. I fear he will be *persuaded* by it, come to believe it, learn my fantasy and think I want him to make it come true. When I haven't the temerity to go through one of these veiled doors, it's because I am afraid of the men inside: afraid in a generic, unspoken way, afraid of Them.

Susan Sontag, exhaustively trying to prove that certain works of pornography qualify as "literature"—a proof almost laughably pointless, I think—notes its "singleness of intention" as a point against its inclusion. I am interested in literature, pornographic and otherwise, by my responses to any given piece; and my responses to pornography are layered and complex and multiple.

Some pieces bore me: They are cheesy or slow, badly written or mechanical. Others disturb me by the unhappiness I sense, as though the actors and actresses wished only to be somewhere else. There are days when I am saturated and feel weary of the whole idea. Sometimes I experience a kind of ennui, a *nausea* from all that grunting labor, the rankness of the flesh. I get depressed, for simple enough reasons. I rented a movie recently that opened with a scene of two naked women stroking each other. One of the women had enormous breasts, hard balloons filled with silicone riding high on her ribs and straining the skin. She looked mutilated, and the rest of the movie held no interest for me at all.

I wish for more craft, a more artful packaging. I tire of browsing stacks of boxes titled *Fucking Brunettes* and *Black Cocks and Black Cunts* and *Monumental Knockers*. The mainstream films, with their happy, athletic actors, can leave me a little cold. That's how I felt watching a comfortable film called *The Last Resort*. The plot, naturally, is simple: A woman with a broken heart accompanies her friends, a couple, to a resort. Over the next twenty-four hours she has vigorous sex with a waiter, a cook (he in nothing but a chef's hat and apron), a waitress, a waitress and a maintenance man together. The other guests cavort cheerfully, too. I found it all so earnest and wholesome. A friend and fellow connoisseur deplores these films where everyone has a "penis-deflatingly good time squirting sperm about with as much passion as a suburban gardener doing his lawn." These movies are too hygienic. They're not dirty enough.

And now women are making films for women viewers. The new films by and for lesbians can be nasty and hot. But the heterosexual films, heavy on relationships and light on the standard icons of hard core, seem ever so soft to me. (They're reminiscent of those social worker collages.) They're tasteful and discreet. I'm glad women have, so to speak, seized the means of production. I'm glad women are making pornographic films, writing pornographic books, starting pornographic magazines; I'm happier still when the boundaries in which women create expand. I don't believe there are limits to what women can imagine or enjoy. I don't want limits, imposed from within or without, on what women can see, or watch, or do.

Any amateur psychologist could have a field day explaining why I prefer low-brow, hard-core porn to feminine erotica. I've spent enough time trying to explain things to myself: why I prefer *this* to *that*. There are examples of pornography, films and stories both, that genuinely scare me. They are no more bizarre or extreme than books or movies that may simply excite or interest me, but the details affect me in certain specific ways. The content touches me, just there, and I'm scared, for no reason I can explain, or excited by a scene that repels me. It may be nothing more than sound, a snap or thwack or murmur. And I want to keep watching those films, reading those books; when I engage in my own fears, I learn about them. I may someday master a few. When I happen upon such scenes, I try to look directly. Seeing what I don't like can be as therapeutic as seeing what I do.

Feminists against pornography (as distinct from other anti-pornography camps) hold that our entire culture is pornographic. In a pornographic world all our sexual constructions are obscene; sexual materials are necessarily oppressive, limited by the constraints of the culture. Even the act of viewing becomes a male act—an act of subordinating the person viewed. Under this construct, I'm a damaged woman, a heretic.

I take this personally, the effort to repress material I enjoy—to tell me how wrong it is for me to enjoy it. Anti-pornography legislation is directed at me: as a user, as a writer. Catharine MacKinnon and Andrea Dworkin—a feminist who has developed a new sexual orthodoxy in which the male erection is itself oppressive—are the new censors. They are themselves prurient, scurrying after sex in every corner. They look down on me and stake a finger: *Bad girl. Mustn't touch.*

That branch of feminism tells me my very thoughts are bad. Pornography tells me the opposite: that *none* of my thoughts are bad, that anything goes. Both are extremes, of course, but the difference is profound. The message of pornography, by its very existence, is that our sexual selves are real.

Always, the censors are concerned with how men *act* and how women are portrayed. Women cannot make free sexual choices in that world; they are too oppressed to know that only oppression could lead them to sell sex. And I, watching, am either too oppressed to know the harm that my watching has done to my sisters, or—or else I have become the Man. And it is the Man in me who watches and is aroused. (Shame.) What a misogynistic worldview this is, this claim that women who make such choices cannot be making free choices at all—are not free to make a choice. Feminists against pornography have done a sad and awful thing: *They* have made women into objects.

I move from the front of the adult store I frequent to the back. Here is the leather underwear, dildos of all sizes, inflatable female dolls, shrink-wrapped fetish magazines. Here are movies with taboo themes—older movies with incest plots, newer ones featuring interracial sex, and grainy loops of nothing more than spanking, spanking, spanking. Here are the films of giant breasts, or all-anal sex, food fights, obese actresses, and much masturbation. This is niche marketing at its best.

In the far back, near the arcade booths, are the restraints, the gags and bridles, the whips and handcuffs, and blindfolds. Here are dildos of truly heroic proportions. The films here are largely European, and quite popular. A rapid desensitization takes me over back here, a kind of numbing sensory overload. Back here I can't help but look at the other customers; I find myself curious about which movies each of *them* will rent.

Women who have seen little pornography seem to assume that the images in most films are primarily, obsessively, ones of rape. I find the opposite theme in American films: that of an adolescent rut, both male and female. Its obsession is virility, endurance, lust. Women in modern films are often the initiators of sex; men in such films seem perfectly content for that to be so.

Power fantasies, on the other hand, are rather common for men and women both. I use the term "power" to describe a huge continuum of images: physical and psychological overpowering of many kinds, seduction and bondage and punishment, the extremes of physical control practiced by S&M enthusiasts. The word "rape" for such scenes is inappropriate; the fact of rape has nothing to do with sex, or pornography. Power takes a lot of forms, subtle, overt. Out of curiosity I rented a German film called *Discipline in Leather*, a film, I discovered, without sex, without nudity. Two men are variously bound, chained, laced, gagged, spanked, and ridden like horses by a Nordic woman. "Nein!" she shouts. "Nicht so schnell!" The men lick her boots, accept the bridle in cringing obeisance. I found it laughably solemn, a Nazi farce, and then I caught myself laughing. This is one of many similar films, and I never want to laugh at the desires of another. A lot of people take what I consider trifling or silly to be terribly important. I want never to forget the bell curve of human desire, or that few of us have much say about where on the curve we land. I've learned this from watching porn: By letting go of judgments I hold against myself, and my desires, I let go of judgments about the desires and the acts of others.

I recently saw a movie recommended by one of the clerks at the adult store, a send-up called *Wild Goose Chase*. In the midst of mild arousal, I found a scene played for laughs, about the loneliness taken for granted in the pornographic world. The actor is Joey Silvera, a good-looking man with blond hair and startling dark eyes. In this film he plays a detective; the detective has a torrid scene with his secretary, who then walks out on him. He holds his head in his hands. "I don't need her," he mumbles. "I got women. I got my *own* women!" He stands and crosses to a file cabinet. "I got plenty of women!" He pulls out a drawer and dumps it upside down, spilling porn magazines in a pile on the floor. He crawls over them, stroking the paper cunts, the breasts, the pictured thighs, moaning, kissing the immobile faces.

The fantasies of power are shame-driven, I think: When I envision my own binding, my submission, I am seeing myself free. Free of guilt, free of responsibility. So many women I've known have harbored these fantasies, and grown more guilty for having them. And so many of those women have been strong, powerful, self-assured. Perhaps, as one school of feminist thought says, we've simply "eroticized our oppression." I know I berated myself a long while for that very thing, and tried to make the fantasies go away. But doing so denies the fact of my experience, which includes oppression and dominance, fear and guilt, and a hunger for surrender. This is the real text of power fantasies: They are about release from all those things. A friend who admits such dreams herself gave me

Pat Califia's collection of dominance stories, *Macho Sluts.* I opened at random and was rooted where I stood: The stories are completely nasty, well written, and they are smart. "I no longer thought about the future," one character says, spread-eagle and bound in front of mirrors during sex. "I did not exist, except as a response to her touch. There was nothing else, no other reality, and no whim of my own will moved me." Such dreams transcend mere sex and enter, unexpectedly, the world of relationship. I could not read such stories, watch such films, with anyone but a lover. I couldn't act them out except with the person whom I trusted most of all.

It was only last year when I stopped making my lover go with me to the adult store. I make myself go alone now, or not at all; if I believe this should be mine for the choosing, then I want to get it myself. Only alone will that act of choosing be a powerful act. So I went yesterday, on a Wednesday in the middle of the morning, and found a crowd of men. There was even a couple, the young woman with permed hair and a startled look, like a deer caught in headlights. She kept her hands jammed in the pockets of her raincoat, and wouldn't return my smile. There was an old man on crutches huddled over a counter, and a herd of clerks, playing bad, loud rock music. I was looking for a few specific titles, and a clerk directed me to the customers' computer, on a table in the amateur section. It's like the ones at the library, divided by title, category (fat girl, Oriental, spanking, hetero, and so on), or a particular star.

The big-bellied jovial clerk came over after a few minutes.

"That working for you?" he sang out. "I tell you, I don't know how the hell that works."

I tell him I'm looking for a movie popular several years ago, called *Talk Dirty to Me.*

"Hey, Jack," he yells. "We got *Talk Dirty to Me?*" In a few minutes four clerks huddle around me and the computer, watching me type in the title, offering little suggestions. From across the store I can still hear the helpful clerk. "Hey, Al," he's shouting. "Lady over there wants *Talk Dirty to Me.* We got that?"

I still blush; I stammer to say these things out loud. Sex has eternal charm that way—a perpetual, organic hold on my body. I am aroused right now, writing this. Are you, dear reader? Do you dream, too?

A friend called this story my "accommodation," as though I'd made peace with the material. I have never had to do that. I have always just been trying to make peace with my abyssal self, my underworld. Pornography helps; that's simple. I became sexual in a generation that has explored sex more thoroughly and perhaps less well than any before. I live with myself day to day in a sex-drenched culture, and that means living with my own sex. After exposing myself truly to myself, it's surprisingly easy to expose myself to another.

I want not to accommodate to pornography but to claim it. I want to be the agent of sex. I want to *own* sex, as though I had a right to these depictions, these ideas, as though they belonged to us all. The biggest surprise is this one: When I am watching—never mind what. I am suddenly restless, shifting, crossing my legs. And my perceptive lover smiles at me and says, "You like that, don't you? See—*everyone* does that."

Study Questions

1. In arguing against feminists who oppose pornography, Tisdale concedes, "Certainly a lot of violent material has sexual overtones; the mistake is assuming that anything with sex in it is primarily about sex." Does Joan Mason-Grant make this assumption? Given Tisdale's further concession (which should please Mason-Grant), her fear that "men will be *persuaded* by it, come to believe it, learn my fantasy and think I want him to make it come true," is the assumption one made by Tisdale herself? Why or why not?

2. Some of the substantive and polemical power of "Talk Dirty to Me" seems to stem from the fact that its author is a woman. Why is this true, if it is? Why couldn't a male author as easily admit to finding in pornography a means of self-discovery? Would this explanation of his motives or the value he finds in pornography be seen as a smokescreen?

3. "Seeing what I don't like can be as therapeutic as seeing what I do." This claim summarizes much of Tisdale's positive appreciation of pornography. How plausible is it? Can mere images act as therapy and help us "master a few of [our fears]"? How else, besides watching pornographic movies, has Tisdale treated her fears and liberated herself from shame, assuming she has done these things? Is watching pornography necessary to achieve these goods?

4. Tisdale finds her "sexual self" vindicated in pornography, yet observes that some of her friends are "indifferent" to it. What does this say of their sexual selves, of Tisdale's sexual self, and even of the notion of a "sexual self"? What should we say about Greta Christina's "sexual self" (see chapter 2), on the basis of her own sexual autobiography?

5. Pornography is sex, says Tisdale. Explore the senses in which this claim rings true, and in which it seems false. On what sense(s) does Tisdale's argument hang? Consider, too, Catharine Mac-

Kinnon's claims, "whatever sexually arouses a man is sex" and "inequality is sex . . . humiliation is sex . . . debasement is sex . . . intrusion is sex" (*Toward a Feminist Theory of the State* [Cambridge, Mass.: Harvard University Press, 1989], 211).

Note

The essay reprinted here was published in *Harper's* in February 1992. Tisdale later gave her thoughts on sex more complete treatment in *Talk Dirty to Me: An Intimate Philosophy of Sex* (New York: Doubleday, 1994). See the review by James Wolcott, "Position Papers," *The New Yorker* (21 November 1994), 115–19. Be sure not to miss the color comic of Tisdale in a pornography store (115). Readers' letters of reply to her *Harper's* essay, as well as her responses to them, appeared in the May 1992 issue of that magazine (4–7, 72–73, and 76–78).

Chapter 27

PORNOGRAPHY AND THE SOCIAL SCIENCES

Alan Soble

One question that has arisen and been dealt with abundantly by scholars of pornography is whether the consumption of pornography by its users has a tendency to encourage them to carry out the sexual acts that they see or read about in pornographic materials and to cause harm to other people in the process. This essay by **Alan Soble** *is a philosophical, not empirical, approach to the question. He does not attempt to answer "yes" or "no" to the causal question, but to explore, by engaging in some philosophy of science, what the causal thesis means or asserts, how we might go about trying to answer the question, what counts and does not count as (good) evidence, and what difficulties might arise in trying to answer it. The causal question of the effect of the consumption of pornography on behavior is especially recalcitrant to reliable investigation because the subjects to be studied, the users of pornography, are human beings, and notorious epistemological problems operate here that are absent from or avoidable in the natural sciences. In particular, it has often been claimed that research in the social sciences is inevitably value-laden in various ways (or at various levels in the research enterprise), and this infection by moral or other normative presuppositions makes the purported results of social scientific research vulnerable to powerful criticisms and objections. Regardless of whether this global philosophical view is tenable (although he hints that he thinks it is true), Soble shows how, at least in this one significant case, research into the causal effects of pornography is indeed value-laden. Only some, but not all, of these value commitments can be eliminated from pornography research.*

Reprinted with permission from *Social Epistemology* 2, no. 2 (1988): 135–44. The publisher's website is http://www.tandf.co.uk/journals. This paper is a commentary on Augustine Brannigan and Sheldon Goldenberg, "Social Science versus Jurisprudence in Wagner: the Story of Pornography, Harm, and the Law of Obscenity in Canada," *Social Epistemology* 2, no. 2 (1988): 107–16. Unless otherwise indicated, all quoted material is from this essay. (See also their response, "Neither All the King's Horses Nor All the King's Men," *Social Epistemology* 3, no. 1 [1989]: 54–69.)

Augustine Brannigan and Sheldon Goldenberg have written a provocative essay about social scientific attempts to establish a connection between exposure to pornography and actions and attitudes harmful to women. Regarding laboratory experiments designed to demonstrate aggressive behavior after exposure to pornography, they argue that these laboratory results cannot be extrapolated to real life because the aggression found in laboratory experiments is neither the kind nor the amount of aggression that threaten women in real life, and because it should not be assumed that the responsiveness of laboratory subjects to pornography is the same as the responsiveness of ordinary consumers. Brannigan and Goldenberg offer similar arguments intended to undermine the significance of laboratory studies of the influence of pornography on attitudes. I will argue that these objections are not as powerful as Brannigan and Goldenberg make them out to be.

While demolishing, to their own satisfaction, some of the evidence suggesting that pornography contributes to violence against women, Brannigan and Goldenberg impugn the intellectual honesty not only of jurists who rely uncritically on the results of behavioral research, but also of the social scientists who provide those results. The conclusion that pornography contributes to harms against women is, according to Brannigan and Goldenberg, "contrived"; it is arrived at by a selective and misleading interpretation of the data. Further, the experimental designs employed by some social scientists already assume to be true that which is supposed to be tested or discovered. Brannigan and Goldenberg claim that "the current ideological opposition to pornography has come to dominant the interpretation of the . . . research in this area," and they call for a "formal and impartial scientific reexamination" of the whole field of pornography research. I fear, however, that the demand for a "formal and impartial scientific" assessment of the evidence is a demand that social science be value free, in which case the demand incorporates a naive view of the epistemological foundations of the social sciences.

1. The Causal Status of Pornography

I spent most of the summer of 1985 in Atlanta, Georgia, a city I was visiting for the first time. Since I had recently finished writing a book on pornography,[1] naturally I was curious about the state of porn in Atlanta, wondering how this blossoming Sun Belt metropolis compared with New York, Los Angeles, and other U.S. porn centers. Walking through the downtown area, I found no adult book stores, and there were none listed in the Yellow Pages. I wandered into no hard-core porn movie theaters. Eventually, I came across maybe six stores in the entire city that stocked *Playboy*, *Penthouse*, and of course, *Players*. But I didn't see any sexually explicit material, *Hustler*, or SM/BD pornography. Why? In the early 1980s (a couple of lawyers told me) a zealous Baptist district attorney ran the porn business out of town. That was surprising enough. What was more surprising was the mid-summer announcement, in the local newspaper, that in 1984 Atlanta ranked #1 among cities in the country for rapes per capita.[2] Furthermore, Atlanta was #1 in rape both in 1980, when porn could still be found in the city, and in 1984, when there was no porn. And I thought it noteworthy that neither New York (#34) nor Los Angeles made it into the top fifteen rape cities; and that Kansas City and Dallas did—hardly the porn connoisseur's choice for a place to go shopping.

I was surprised by this news because Robin Morgan's thesis that "pornography is the theory, rape is the practice,"[3] or, less flamboyantly, that the consumption of pornography by men increases their willingness to rape women, or that the use of pornography aggravates sexual hostility and aggression, seemed to be falsified by the Atlanta "experiment." But not exactly. *If* "porn is the theory, rape is the practice" means that the consumption of pornography is *sufficient* for the occurrence of rape, then what I discovered in Atlanta is, logically speaking, irrelevant. To refute the thesis understood in this sense, one should look for a city (or ten?) that has lots of porn but no rape. The Atlanta "experiment," in which there is no porn but lots of rape, shows only that the presence of porn is *not necessary* for the occurrence of rape. Who, however, would have asserted otherwise? No one.[4] Recall that Brannigan and Goldenberg make heavy weather over the fact that in laboratory settings, at least, a movie of an eye operation, or even noise, has much the same effect on aggression as exposure to pornography. This observation is defused of its rhetorical punch when we acknowledge that no one ever claimed that pornography was *necessary* for rape.[5] Brannigan and Goldenberg argue that *if* the laboratory results are taken at face value, and we want to reduce the frequency of rape, than we should be prepared to censor noise and surgical films. This conclusion is not the *reductio ad absurdum* that Brannigan and Goldenberg believe it to be. First, it is not obviously true that the right to make or be bombarded by noise overrides the right of women to be safe in their persons. Second, we could censor pornography but not noise on the grounds that in the attempt to reduce the frequency of rape we should focus on the more easily eliminable causal factors.

The claim that exposure to pornography is sufficient for the occurrence of rape is as false as the claim that it is necessary; no one asserts it, and that is not the intended meaning of Morgan's thesis or its variants. The fact that a man can buy some pornography, take it home, look at it, masturbate with it, and then go right to sleep and not commit a rape, shows that the most we could assert is that *given* the presence of factors A, B, and C, and/or the absence of factors D, E, and F, the additional factor of exposure to pornography will lead to rape or sexual aggression (i.e., that pornography may be sufficient "relative" to other fixed factors). The failure to recognize that if pornography is a cause of rape or sexual aggression at all, it is a causal factor that operates only in the context of other factors, yields careless and avoidable errors in reasoning about the connection between pornography and sexual aggression. For example, imagine someone arguing that (1) lots of women buy or rent, and masturbate while watching, pornographic videotapes, (2) these women do not rape men (or other women), and *therefore*, (3) the consumption of pornography by men cannot be a factor leading *them* to commit rape. The argument is weak because there may be other social or psychological factors operating on men and not on women (and/or operating on women and not on men) which, when interacting with exposure to pornography, do lead to sexual aggression by men. Similarly, the fact that women who go to bars in order to watch men dance in the nude find the exhibition amusing and are not caused to become sexually aggressive, does not mean that men who go to bars in order to watch women dance in the nude are not encouraged to express sexual aggression.

This point is elementary, and Brannigan and Goldenberg implicitly recognize it when they say that the aggression found in laboratory studies "is always an *interaction* effect and is *not* solely attributable to the film." Yet Brannigan and Goldenberg ignore their own good advice and trade on exactly this sort of fallacy when presenting one of their major criticisms of behavioral research on pornography. They write:

> The metatheory has also been invoked to confine the design to studies of male-female aggression. In certain early experiments male aggression towards male . . . targets was higher than against female targets. Also, Zillmann . . . found that aggression enhancement increased intra-female aggression. Does this mean that erotica causes men to bugger or assault other men? and women to rape other women? Since the metatheory presupposes that the lab aggression is a proxy for sexual aggression, male targets and female subjects are dropped from later studies, obviating such paradoxical extrapolations.[6]

The argument, it seems to me, is this. Some experimenters found that exposure to pornography in laboratory studies increased aggression in males against other males and in females against other females. But these facts are ignored by the experimenters, and later experimental designs do not involve tests for these effects, because for the experiments to acknowledge their existence is to admit that the laboratory studies of the influence of pornography on males cannot be employed to support the claim that in real life the consumption of pornography by males contributes to their sexual aggression. If the laboratory studies do show that in real life pornography leads men to be sexually aggressive toward women, then the laboratory studies also show that in real life pornography induces men to aggress sexually against men and encourages women to sexually assault women. (Call this conditional "Q.") But the experimenters do not want to draw that conclusion; after all, it is false that women aggress sexually against other women, and the conclusion is inconsistent with the experimenters' ideological opposition to pornography. Hence, to protect their ideological commitments, the experimenters conveniently forget the embarrassing facts they themselves discovered. Brannigan and Goldenberg are wrong to assume, however, that the conditional Q is true; at least, they have given us no reason to think it is true. In real life there may very well be other causal factors present (or absent), in addition to exposure to pornography, that permit pornography to induce male-female sexual aggression but put a clamp on some forms of male-male and female-female aggression. Clearly, Brannigan and Goldenberg want to argue that because the female-female aggression in response to pornography in the laboratory cannot be extrapolated to the real world, neither can the male-female aggression. But this claim commits a version of the fallacy described above.

Brannigan and Goldenberg might object here that they assert only that *the experimenters* in question believe the conditional Q. Because the experimenters hold Q, *they* have reason to exclude female-female studies from later designs; the experimenters, not Brannigan and Goldenberg, commit the fallacy. I think, to the contrary, that Brannigan and Goldenberg themselves assert Q. The tone and wording of the quoted passage (and of the passage in my note 6) support this view. Indeed, the experimenters criticized by Brannigan and Goldenberg might have *rejected* Q; their doing so even suggests a quite different and not dishonest reason for their excluding female-female studies from later experimental designs: laboratory studies of female sexual responsivity and aggressiveness are less extrapolatable to real life than studies of males, because women in our society fall under a myriad of social and sexual regulations and prohibitions that men escape. Of course, the claims that women fall under more social regulations than men, and that these regulations operate on women in real life but do not reach into the laboratory setting, may be false. (There may be regulations on the aggressiveness of men that operate in real life and do not reach into the laboratory, or are suspended in that context.) But if believing that laboratory studies of male-female aggression can be more easily extrapolated to real life than studies of female-female aggression is the reason the experimenters dropped female-female studies, the experimenters are hardly the ideological villains Brannigan and Goldenberg make them out to be. Furthermore, Brannigan and Goldenberg and the experimenters they criticize now have something tangible to debate, viz., the truth of Q and its grounds; it is no longer convincing for Brannigan and Goldenberg to rely on the mere charge that the experimenters are dishonest.

In light of the fact that Morgan's thesis is not intended to mean that exposure to pornography is literally sufficient for the occurrence of rape, the Atlanta 'experiment' is, after all, logically relevant. The thesis urges the legal censorship of pornography, or some other technique for reducing its availability, *in order to* lower the frequency of rape, on the grounds that *given* other social and psychological factors the consumption of pornography contributes to rape. Understood in this way, the thesis implies that if the other factors are held constant, the frequency of rape will within limits vary directly with the availability or consumption of pornography. The thesis, then, is prima facie refuted by both the Danish "experiment," in which an increase in the availability of pornography has not been matched by any increase in rape, and by the Atlanta "experiment," in which a decrease in the availability of pornography has not been matched by a drop in the frequency of rape.

Why do I say "prima facie" refuted? If Denmark and Atlanta are the only geographical areas in which the direct variation of rape with pornography fails, then these "experiments" tell us nothing valuable about the pornography-rape connection. Finding one bona fide blade of grass that is blue surely proves that "all blades of grass are green" is false. But because Morgan's thesis is that when A, B, and C are present and/or D, E, and F are absent, the frequency of rape follows the availability of pornography, a handful of counterexamples carries little weight. If the thesis is therefore difficult to refute, beyond a reasonable doubt, it is just as difficult to confirm. Even if we discovered a perfect correlation between the availability of pornography and the frequency of rape, *that* would hardly be enough evidence to allow us to conclude, beyond a reasonable doubt, that pornography was a causal factor in rape. As has been mentioned by many people already, a macroscopic correlation between the availability of pornography and the occurrence of rape, if one exists, is explainable by invoking a third phenomenon that independently causes both, in which case eliminating pornography will have no effect, contrary to the intention of Morgan's thesis, on the frequency of rape. The most obvious candidate for this phenomenon is "the culture of male dominance," which simultaneously causes or allows a society to have pornography and encourages men to commit rape.[7] Even here we need to be careful: We must have a way of defining "culture of male dominance" independently of the facts that such a society contains pornography and tolerates or encourages rape; otherwise the explanation will be circular. But "exhibits a high frequency of rape" is one of the primary characteristics defining "culture of male dominance."

There are, of course, other problems. In Atlanta, I said, the availability of pornography declined between 1980 and 1984 while the frequency of rape remained high. But did the availability of pornography really decline? Should we count *Playboy, Penthouse,* and *Players* as genuinely pornographic, as a large bulk of that category? (*This* question explains why I wrote, above, that the blue specimen was a bona fide blade of grass.) Pornography, then, might not have declined much between 1980 and 1984. Is that *enough* pornography to account for the continuing rate of rape? Is it sexually explicit enough, or violent enough, to contribute to rape? Or perhaps all the hard-core pornography bought through 1980 was still in the possession of its Atlanta owners (or traded) and still at work in 1984. Or perhaps pornography was still available to Atlantans who went on shopping trips to South Carolina or Alabama, or who ordered it through the mail from California. Or perhaps the effects of the pornography that existed before and during 1980 in Atlanta were persisting into 1984. Do totally nude female dancers count as a kind of pornographic genre? If so, Atlanta is hardly porn-free. It has no live or video peep shows, but there are a half-dozen bars in center city, and several others in the outer regions, that offer nude entertainment. How many privately owned VCRs are there in Atlanta, and how many imported pornographic videotapes? Is this *enough* pornography to sustain the claim that Atlanta is *not* porn-free and the thesis that rape there is connected with the consumption of pornography?

Some of these questions are empirical, others are conceptual. All these questions must be answered before the Atlanta "experiment" can be employed in the assessment of Morgan's thesis. Our question now is, Can the social sciences answer *these* questions? Can the social sciences confirm or refute, beyond a reasonable doubt, the thesis that the consumption of pornography is a significant causal factor in sexual aggression? Can the social sciences accurately fill in the *A, B, C, D, E,* and *F* of Morgan's thesis? Or demonstrate that there is nothing to fill in, or no point in doing so? One common answer goes like this: the social sciences, given the hard work, the cleverness, the patience, and the objectivity of its investigators, plus some good luck, can surely answer the empirical questions. In the process of testing hypotheses and interpreting the evidence, however, the investigators must make sure that their own values (including their ideological viewpoints, their political leanings, etc.) do not play any role, for that would prevent, as much as laziness would prevent, the social sciences from arriving at justified (or "valid") empirical conclusions. Regarding the conceptual questions, operational definitions of some concepts are possible and partially solve the problem. Or perhaps in some cases it is especially obvious how a concept should be defined. At the very least, values should be excluded also from definitions; and as long as experimenters are up front about their conceptual assumptions, their empirical claims can be objectively assessed. (*This* is what I'm going to count as grass; given that definition, here are the empirical facts.)

Brannigan and Goldenberg complain that the experimenters' ideological opposition to pornography has adversely affected not only the conclusions drawn when the experimenters interpret the data, but also the experimental designs employed to test hypotheses. Such research, then, is hardly trustworthy.[8] Brannigan and Goldenberg call for a "formal and impartial scientific" assessment of the pornography–sexual aggression research. Both their complaint and their recommendation imply that Brannigan and Goldenberg presuppose the general picture of proper procedure in the social sciences that I have just outlined. Further evidence is provided by Brannigan's apparent espousal of the standard fact-value distinction:

> Public inquiries into obscenity tend to oscillate . . . between what is democratic and political versus what is rational and scientific. Democratic forums sample public opinion and popular morality regarding sexual fiction and entertainment. Rationalist forums are preoccupied with the effects of pornography measured scientifically.[9]

The implication is that the democratic forum, and morality or values in general, should not be permitted to interfere with the rational assessment of the scientific evidence or to play any other epistemological role in the social sciences. On the question of how social scientists should approach conceptual matters, Brannigan and Goldenberg are less explicit. Let's examine their handling of conceptual issues; doing so will illustrate the logical fact that social science, contrary to the standard picture, cannot be the value-free enterprise Brannigan and Goldenberg want it to be.

2. Conceptual Analysis and Value Judgments

One of Brannigan and Goldenberg's major criticisms of the research investigating the effects of pornography on sexual aggression focuses on an experimental design which, they argue, tells us nothing about real life. Male subjects who are angered by a female confederate, and who are then exposed to pornography, retaliate against the same confederate by administering shocks in a bogus learning experiment. The problems with using the fact that previously angered mates administer shocks to females after being exposed to pornography, to defend Morgan's thesis or its variants, are legion. The male subjects in the laboratory are not exposed to pornography in the way in which pornography is consumed in real life by voluntary or confirmed users. Delivering electrical shocks to a female in a learning experiment is a far cry from real-life sexual aggression. The shocks are administered to exactly that person who had earlier deliberately provoked the male subject. And so on. Of course the experimenters bear the burden of proof; they must give us good reasons for accepting the proposition that laboratory aggression is a reliable proxy for real-life sexual aggression. (Just as the biologist must not simply assume, but give us good reasons for thinking, that an in vitro nerve preparation appreciably replicates the normal, intact functioning of the tissue.) Perhaps the most that the experimenters are entitled to conclude is that if a man is unjustly provoked and angered by a woman, after which event he takes a brief look at some pornography, he will punish that same woman for having angered him. If so, we are left wondering whether we have learned anything at all about the influence of pornography on rape, sexual assault, wife-beating, and other aggressions carried out against women.

But granting the victory to Brannigan and Goldenberg is premature. It seems quite perverse for them to complain that laboratory aggression in the form of the administration of electrical shocks in a bogus learning experiment cannot be considered a proxy for sexual aggression in real life. After all, for the experimenters to have given angered males the opportunity in the laboratory to carry out a real-life type of *sexual* aggression against the confederate female would have been morally and pragmatically preposterous. When attempting to discover whether exposure to pornography contributes to the occurrence of sexual aggression against women, *some* nonsexual aggression or another must be studied in the laboratory. Surely Brannigan and Goldenberg are not about to assert that because laboratory studies are for moral or pragmatic reasons restricted to measuring nonsexual aggression, experimenters will *never* have a reliable proxy for real-life sexual aggression. To assert that would be to assert that social psychology is absolutely powerless to investigate Morgan's thesis, and would be to deny that a "formal and impartial scientific" examination will eventually answer "yes" *or* "no" to the question of a pornography–sexual aggression link in real life.

There is a huge difference, or course, between the answers "no" and "not yet proven" (or, in the words of Brannigan and Goldenberg, 'far from well established') to the question "Does exposure to pornography contribute to harms done to women?" The latter answer is compatible with "maybe" and even with an eventual "yes." I just argued that Brannigan and Goldenberg believe that a "no" answer can, in principle, be given eventually by social science; they have not criticized social science per se (they apparently think Milgram's social psychology has merit), but only the way it is carried out by some researchers. I suspect there is another reason Brannigan and Goldenberg must insist that a "no" answer is eventually achievable. In order to claim persuasively that anti-pornography legislation is unnecessary, the answer "no" is much more effective than "not yet proven." Because rape is one of the most horrible crimes, legislatures—without embarrassment, without having to apologize, and without violating Constitutional provisions (in the United States, at least)—may assume that there is just enough evidence for a pornography–sexual aggression link (even though the thesis is "not yet proven") and place the burden of proof on those who deny that exposure to pornography contributes to harms done to women. (Further, to assert that social science is *incapable* of answering the question is to give legislatures carte blanche.) To defend their own legislative goals, then, Brannigan and Goldenberg must suppose that a "no" answer is achievable. But a "no" answer presupposes that there is some laboratory non-sexual aggression that is a reliable proxy for real-life sexual aggression, and that experiments utilizing this measure will find no effect of exposure to pornography.

Regardless of exactly why Brannigan and Goldenberg believe that a "no" answer is possible, a major weakness of their paper is that while criticizing other experimenters for not utilizing a reliable proxy, they are totally silent on the crucial question of what that proxy would be. To claim, as Brannigan and Goldenberg do, that the administration of electrical shocks during a bogus learning experiment is either not *at all* a proxy for sexual aggression in real life, or is an *inadequate* proxy, is to make a conceptual claim: that some types of laboratory aggression are *not similar enough* to real-life sexual aggression. But to assert this is to assert, implicitly, that one has *some* idea of what kind of laboratory aggression would be similar enough to real-life sexual aggression to count as a proxy. Yet, having entered the arena of conceptual dispute, Brannigan and Goldenberg's failure to propose a reliable proxy abandons the conceptual issue, rather than resolves it.

Note that Brannigan and Goldenberg also do not explain in any great detail *why* the administration of electrical shocks in bogus learning experiments is not an adequate proxy for real-life sexual aggression. Why are the studies defective, or why is pornography off the hook, if pornography only encourages men in real life to aggress against women in ways that are roughly similar in type to administering electrical shocks in a bogus learning experiment (e.g., by being especially tough on women during driving examinations, or by grading their school examinations too critically, or even by passing a negative judgment on women's submissions to professional journals)? After all, some of the experimenters criticized by Brannigan and Goldenberg claim that it is the *violence* in violent pornography, and not the pornographic dimension per se, that contributes to real-life aggression; if so, the laboratory aggression measured may be a quite adequate proxy.[10] Part of the problem is that Brannigan and Goldenberg understand the concept "sexual aggression" rather narrowly, in terms of aggression carried out with and/or on sexual and quasi-sexual organs or in the process of a sexual act. But "sexual aggression" can be conceived less narrowly as aggression carried out by a member of one sex (e.g., males) against a member of the other sex (e.g., females) *in virtue* of the fact that the object of aggression is a member of the other sex. Aggression motivated at least in part by the sexual difference is a kind of sexual aggression even if it does not include or is not constituted by a sexual act. Morgan, I take it, would be quite happy to have her thesis tested by employing this conception of sexual aggression. Brannigan and Goldenberg never tell us why their implicit notion of sexual aggression is the *right* one or *superior* to a broader definition. That perhaps Donnerstein et al. mean exactly what Brannigan and Goldenberg mean by "sexual aggression" is irrelevant. If, unbeknownst to them, the broader notion of "sexual aggression" helps Donnerstein et al. by making it more likely that their laboratory aggression is a decent proxy for real-life sexual aggression, that fact could be acknowledged by Brannigan and Goldenberg in the interest of an "impartial" assessment of the evidence.

As a result of overlooking the broader conception of sexual aggression, Brannigan and Goldenberg have also overlooked that there *are* real-life scenarios which are similar enough to the laboratory design they criticize. Suppose a man is angered by his wife (say, he comes home from work exhausted and she pesters him to take her out for dinner), and he mentally retreats from what he perceives to be unjustified nagging by flipping through a glossy sex magazine. The research implies that under these conditions the husband is likely to act aggressively toward his wife. Of course the husband cannot punish her by administering electric shocks—unless he keeps a cattle prod in the closet for such occasions—but perhaps he slaps her (harder or more often than he would have without looking at pornography), or screams at her, or even forces her into sexual activity. Clearly, this scenario is not a very pretty picture, and something is already very wrong with the marriage, or with him or her, that contributes to his aggression. But the laboratory experiments only claim to show that the presence of pornography may make things worse than they would have been. Even if the studies do not provide a convincing case for censorship (after all, if the husband drank a beer instead of flipping through a sex magazine, that might very well have had the same effect, and we are not ready to inaugurate a new Prohibition), they nonetheless might have some scientific validity in either explaining or predicting additional amounts of violence.

The way in which Morgan defines "rape" does indeed make it much easier to confirm the thesis that exposure to pornography causally contributes to rape; one of her examples of a rape according to her broad definition is a situation in which a woman, under an ordinary sort of pressure from her husband (e.g., his pleading), agrees to have sex with him even though she prefers to watch television.[11] Despite the absurdity of this view, it has the virtue of alerting us to the point that all social science investigations into the connection between pornography and rape are unavoidably value-laden. Suppose we define "rape" as it is commonly defined: x has raped y if x has had sexual contact with y in the absence of y's genuine consent. Then, whether a rape has occurred, or whether we should classify x's act as a rape, depends exquisitely on how we understand "genuine consent." And *that* is not a matter of empirical fact, but of values. Both confirmation *and* refutation of the thesis that exposure to pornography contributes to rape presuppose that we can define "rape," and doing that presupposes in turn that we have made a value judgment as to when consent is and is not genuine. Underneath all social science research in this area, then, is a value judgment—an "ideological" belief about the nature of consent.

Liberal and feminist values, we know, are different from conservative and nonfeminist values, and these different values influence the criteria to be used in classifying acts as rape. Here we have a case, typical of the social sciences, in which values operate not merely at the level of the interpretation or legal use of data, but at the deeper epistemological level of the composition—indeed, the existence—of data.[12] If we were to leave it up to the democratic forum to resolve the value dispute over "genuine consent" (and, pray tell, where else to go?), Brannigan's neat dichotomy between popular morality and the rationality of science goes down the tubes. Take note that the values (the "ideology") that Brannigan and Goldenberg wish to exclude at the level of interpretation are precisely the values operating within the evidential foundation. Therefore, even if Brannigan and Goldenberg are successful in eliminating the values at one level in the name of a "formal and impartial" assessment *of* the evidence, those values will remain *in* the evidence to haunt them, utterly impervious to the demand for impartiality. I do not mean to suggest that ideology should rule supreme at the level of the interpretation and political use of the data; that sort of tomfoolery is eliminable. The point is that while it is correct to object to "ideological opposition" interfering at the level of interpretation, it is *futile* and even self-defeating to object to "ideological opposition" operating at the deeper epistemological level; either "ideological opposition" *or* "ideological approval" must, for logical reasons, inform the values that are necessarily present in the constitution of the evidence. At least we have a more accurate picture of social science and can continue to practice it, realizing openly that the values are there, rather than pretend they aren't there by promulgating a misleading picture of social science as value-free.

Study Questions

1. Consider Robin Morgan's famous saying that "pornography is the theory, rape is the practice." Try to construct a handful of different meanings for this doctrine, and then assess the likely truth-value for each. Is the claim similar to "utilitarianism is the theory, capitalistic economics is the practice"? Come up with other "theory-practice" analogies in trying to understand Morgan's claim.

2. In note 8, Soble describes a disagreement he has with the philosopher of law Joel Feinberg over the explanation of a possible correlation between the availability of pornography and the occurrence of rape. What are the two sides of this debate, and who do you think is closer to the truth (and why)? Of what relevance is the fact that in Japan, for example, violent pornography (especially images of women in bondage) is abundantly available, yet rape occurs much less frequently there than in the United States?

3. Make a list of possible problems that could arise in extrapolating the results of laboratory research in the social sciences to real-world scenarios. To what extent and in what ways might these problems be adequately solved? Do the natural sciences (think about, for example, biomedical experiments on mice in a laboratory or on human cell cultures) face similar troubles?

4. What are the normative concepts that, according to Soble, are necessarily employed in research that studies the causal effects of pornography? Is it possible to give these terms firm and objective definitions in order to minimize the value-infection of this social scientific research? Are any "operational" definitions available that would solve these problems?

5. Go back and review the essays by Robin West on the harmfulness of consensual sex (chapter 20), Yolanda Estes on the harmfulness of prostitution (chapter 23), and Joan Mason-Grant on pornography (chapter 25). Try to find claims in these essays that employ value-laden terms or concepts in what otherwise appear to be factual or empirical statements about sex. Do the problems revealed by Soble pop up in these three essays?

Notes

The author gratefully acknowledges the financial support of the National Endowment for the Humanities during the summer of 1985 and the conscientious typing of Jeannie Shapley.

1. Soble, A. *Pornography: Marxism, Feminism, and the Future of Sexuality*, Yale University Press, New Haven (1986).

2. *The Atlanta Journal*, 21 July, 1985, p. 1B; 23 July, 1985, p. 8A.

3. Morgan, R. 'Theory and practice: pornography and rape', in L. Lederer (ed), *Take Back the Night*, Morrow, New York (1980), pp. 134–40. It may not be necessary to remark that Morgan means "theory" and "practice" in the standard sense, in which theory precedes practice and is accountable for it, rather than in the Marxist or Hegelian sense, in which theory *follows* practice and largely only rationalizes it (the Owl of Minerva, etc.).

4. Susan Brownmiller's history of rape amply documents that the occurrence of rape does not require the consumption of pornography—even as she argues that in the US today pornography contributes to the occurrence of rape. See Brownmiller, S. *Against Our Will: Men, Women, and Rape*, Simon and Schuster, New York (1975), pp. 390–95.

5. The social science experts quoted by the *Atlanta Journal* had no trouble finding other explanations for the city's high rape rate: long, hot summers (like Los Angeles?); the large number of single persons and singles' bars (again, like LA?); and the city's "culture of mate dominance" (unlike *where*, exactly?).

6. Brannigan's accusation of intellectual dishonesty is more direct in his "The politics of pornography research: some reflections on Meese and criminogenic obscenity" ([1986], p. 14, typescript): "My thesis is that an *ideological* opposition to pornography has dominated the interpretation of the behavioural research . . . These experiments appear to be premised on the porn-rape-link metatheory. The heightened levels of aggression detected by psychologists in the lab are interpreted selectively in accord with this supposition. However, this requires the selective exclusion of some of the lab evidence. For example, in some Donnerstein studies males exposed to *explicit* erotica aggress more against other males than males exposed to *aggressive* pornography. Does this mean erotica makes men want to bugger or to beat up other men, while aggressive pornography does not? Some studies by Zillmann focus on aggression between female subjects and female targets. Is this an indication of lesbian rape-proclivity among female porn consumers? Most of the experimentalists began to drop the same-gender targets in order to obviate the problem of extrapolating selectively to cross-gender situations in the real world. The resulting designs reinforce the notion that only females are 'victimized' and only by pornography-inflamed males, just as in the metatheory."

7. Joel Feinberg has proposed that the culture of male dominance explains both the existence of men who commit rape and of violent pornography, in *Offense to Others*, Oxford University Press, New York (1985), pp. 152–53. Feinberg's microscopic hypothesis is less plausible. On his view, the culture of male dominance produces 'macho' men who both consume violent pornography and com-

mit rape (hence the macroscopic correlation), and these men would commit rape even if they never took a look at violent pornography. I have doubts, however, that the "macho" male buys pornography, violent or tame, and sits at home masturbating with it. Why not suppose, instead, that our culture of male dominance is not monolithic? It produces both 'macho' males who rape (but do not consume pornography) and less 'macho' or non-macho males who consume violent and tame pornography (but do not rape). This microscopic explanation, which also preserves the macroscopic correlation between pornography and rape, is suggested in my *Pornography* (1986), pp. 16–17, 81–85 (see note 1). Feinberg assumes that violent pornography appeals only or primarily to 'macho' males, who find welcome confirmation of their attitudes in this pornography, while I assume that violent pornography appeals only or primarily to "regular" males—it allows them to fantasize a sexual world that they believe is beyond their power to create. "Macho" males have no need to create that world by fantasy because they recognize no such limits to their power. (I sent a reprint of this essay, soon after it was published, to Professor Feinberg [University of Arizona]; I was pleasantly surprised to receive a handwritten note from him telling me that the essay was the "most reasonable" thing he had read on the topic and that he agreed with this endnote. His kind letter made my day, for many days.)

8. The experimenters criticized by Brannigan and Goldenberg can probably turn the tables, saying something like: "Well, now, who's calling the kettle black? You protest *too* vigorously, in your many papers on the subject, that we have not shown any connection between pornography and sexual aggression. It is therefore abundantly clear that you have found a convenient and respectable avenue for voicing your own ideological approval of pornography."

9. "The politics of pornography research" (1986), p. 1, typescript (see note 6).

10. Similarly, the common feminist claim that rape is not a "sexual" act but an act of violence suggests that *because* the laboratory aggression measured is not sexual, it is a perfectly good proxy for real-life aggression. But this feminist claim generates a problem: if pornography *is* "sexual" and rape is not a sexual act, then ordinary nonviolent pornography is not the kind of item that could instigate rape. To solve this problem some feminists deny that even ordinary pornography is "sexual." See my *Pornography*, pp. 14–20 (see note 1).

11. Morgan (1980), p. 137 (see note 3).

12. For the long argument and other examples, see my "The political epistemology of 'masculine' and 'feminine,'" in M. Vetterling-Braggin (ed), *"Femininity," "Masculinity," and "Androgyny,"* Littlefield, Adams, Totowa, N.J. (1982), pp. 99–127.

Chapter 28

POWER, SEX, AND
FRIENDSHIP IN ACADEMIA

Deirdre Golash

*The morality and prudence of sexual relationships between teachers and students has been a provocative topic in the academy that has stirred up plenty of emotional reactions and outbursts, not to mention administrative directives, sometimes faculty-supported, sometimes resisted, some ill-conceived, others sensible and reasonable. (We are speaking here of university and college settings, not high school.) In this essay, **Deirdre Golash** approaches the issue, as it should be, calmly and logically, providing plausible and clearly stated reasons for finding both teacher-student friendships and teacher-student sexual relationships morally problematic, if not disturbing. Much of her position (but not all; she has other worries) turns on recognizing a power imbalance between teacher and student, an imbalance that cannot be fully eradicated even when there is an appreciable level of trust and good communication between the parties involved. And if we assume, as many moral philosophies do, let alone the law, that sexual and other relationships, even business transactions, should be grounded in fully voluntary consent between (as a precondition) parties not exhibiting substantial inequality, then we have what appear to be good reasons for objecting to teacher-student relations—as well as to prostitution, pedophilia, exploitative employers, and other phenomena.*

Golash is professor of justice, law, and society at American University and the author of *The Case against Punishment* (New York University Press, 2005).

Reprinted with the permission of the author and the journal from the online journal *Essays in Philosophy* 2, no. 2 (January 2001), www.humboldt.edu/~essays.

It is uncontroversial that a threat by a professor to lower a student's grade if she refuses a sexual encounter is morally unacceptable (and legally constitutes sexual harassment). In contrast, it seems to many that a fully voluntary sexual relationship between professor and student is permissible. In this paper, I argue that the entanglement of personal and professional relationships makes almost any sexual offer by a professor to a student morally problematic.

I. Sexual Offers

Much discussion has focused on the question of whether consent can ever be truly voluntary, given power differentials between professor and student.[1] Larry May brings a new level of complexity to the discussion by focusing instead on how the offer itself changes the dynamics between the two. He argues that an offer by a male professor[2] to improve a student's grade if she engages in sex with him would constitute a "coercive offer," in the sense that it makes the student worse off in the post-offer than in the pre-offer situation. The student is worse off, May suggests, because she can no longer think of herself simply as a student, but must also consider herself a sex object in her relations with the professor. The well is poisoned, and the pre-offer situation can never be recovered. But a parallel phenomenon can also occur on a more subtle level. Suppose that the professor simply suggests to the student that she have sex with him, making no mention of a connection with grading. Assuming that the student is not sexually attracted to the professor, she will, I think, be overwhelmed, confused, and more than a little upset. Following May's analysis, we can see that the introduction of sex into the educational context has irredeemably poisoned the well; there is no going back to the pre-offer situation, and the student must now see herself, through the professor's eyes, as a sex object as well as a student. She may well suspect that the way she treats the offer will affect the professor's attitude toward her, and her grade as well—even if she assumes that there was no intent on the part of the professor to tie the offer to grading.

Now, let us carry the situation one step further. Suppose that the professor explicitly says to the student that he realizes his offer may raise issues about grading, and that he wants to reassure her that how she responds to his offer will have no effect on his grading practices. Nicholas Dixon has suggested that such reassurances will normally reduce doubts about the voluntariness of her consent to a low enough level that the presumption in favor of allowing her to choose her own relationships should prevail.[3] But it seems to me that the professor's words do not change the situation at all. The fact that he has power over the student's grade remains, as does the fact that he has now introduced sexual possibilities into the situation. Indeed, I would say there are no words the professor can say that will succeed in removing the situation from that context, or in mitigating the well-poisoning effect.

This, I think, is part of a more general problem concerning dual, and incompatible, roles. My personal experience as a law student with a Ph.D. in philosophy is an example. In my private relations with law school faculty members whose age, education, and social status would otherwise have made them my peers, I found my second role as a law student immensely constraining. For example, how should one interpret an invitation to "stop by (my office) any time"? Does it indicate a genuine interest in conversation, or is it merely the required politeness of a faculty member to a student? Conversely, how should one respond to remarks such as, "Students always want more than I am willing to give them"—a remark that would be commonplace among peers but if made to a "student" would be a pointed indication to ask for less. What is most interesting about this type of role conflict is that there is no reassurance that can be offered—in words at least—that will abolish the conflict.

There is always the issue of what role the words are being spoken in. The power relationship often requires the polite pretense that one considers the less powerful person one's equal, or at least that one is willing to provide all the time, interest, and consideration that the person wishes. At the same time, the peer relationship presupposes a degree of frankness about the negative aspects of one's attitudes toward students that crosses over into deliberate insult in the teacher-student role. Often, time and the development of trust will mitigate these problems, as they did in my case. Nevertheless, at the end of my third year of law school, I still managed to cross the invisible line by making an extremely negative comment about one faculty member to another. The professor, who I by then considered a close personal friend (and who, I later learned, thoroughly agreed with my assessment of his colleague), responded with evident agitation, "You can't say that to me!" My role as a student precluded him from giving the response of agreement that he would have given a peer; but the honesty required by friendship precluded the response of disagreement he would have given a more typical student.

If communication problems of this level of complexity can arise in simple friendships, then how much more acute they must be where sexual offers—or sexual relationships—are involved. Suppose that the student accepts the professor's sexual proposition. In view of the fact that they are both aware of his control over her grade, how should he interpret her acceptance? How can he ever be sure that she accepted his offer because she wanted to, independent of her desire for a better grade? He cannot ask her, because of course she will respond in either case that she is accepting because she is attracted to him. It is not exactly that the circumstances are not compatible with voluntariness, but rather that the circumstances do not permit uncluttered communication, so that he cannot know whether her acceptance is voluntary or not.

It may be argued that there are always power inequalities in sexual situations. One partner is, almost necessarily, more powerful than the other—whether the power arises from differentials in need for the other, or in degree of attraction, or whether they arise from external circumstances as, typically, wage-earning ability. Communication is thus always contaminated by one partner's greater desire to please the other, and one may accede to conditions that one does not really want to accept. (Indeed, this is the foundation of the famous feminist claim that "sex is seldom truly voluntary.") The more powerful partner would seem then always to be in the same position as the professor—unable to know whether acceptance is voluntary or not.

Here I think the question becomes one of what kinds of trade-offs are morally permissible. Where the proposed trade-off is morally unproblematic, the partner's use of the power resulting from control over the desired good to obtain consent to sex will not make that acceptance involuntary. It may well be, for example, that a man is much more strongly attracted to a woman than she to him; this creates a power differential, but it is not objectionable on that account for her to offer to have sex with him (purely in exchange for sex). There is a continuum of such trades, with sex for sex, love for love at one end.

A trade-off of sexual performance for increased time and attention is commonplace (though it is obviously not ideal, and has also been criticized by some feminists). The trade-off of sex for financial security—further along the continuum—is also common; we would be better off if social institutions made it less so.[4] But it is abundantly clear that a trade of grades for sex is not morally permissible—in part because others rely on the idea that this kind of trade will not be made, and that grades will be assigned for academic performance. Thus, the implicit possibility that the student's response to the offer will affect her grade may impermissibly influence her response. Yet, interestingly, it is because such a trade is not seen as utterly fantastic that the offer situation is contaminated; the student is likely to find it at least somewhat plausible that the professor would offer higher grades for compliance.

Now I do think that it is possible, and that it does happen, that professor and student become sufficiently good friends that these communication problems are superseded. There can be a gradual development of trust between two people who know each other well, and they may eventually arrive at a level of honesty where a sexual offer may be made and not misinterpreted. It is, however, important to attend to the nuances of the situation. Normally, overt sexual offers are preceded by a testing of the waters, perhaps on both sides.

Particularly where one fears rejection, one proceeds gradually—through increasingly personal conversation, discussions of past relationships, perhaps abstract discussions of sex and sexuality. The potential for the professor who is courting a student to misinterpret the signals given here is immense. The student who is made mildly uncomfortable by personal conversation is not likely to cut it off with a short reply. Having accepted the personal conversation, she will then find it more difficult to express her discomfort at increasingly personal revelations. Her need to maintain the goodwill of the professor can be a strong motive to dissemble. Misinterpretation of signals is of course always possible; but it is significantly more likely under such circumstances. Is it wrong, then, for the professor to make the offer even when he believes a sufficient level of honesty has been reached? I think the only possible answer is that it is wrong to make the offer if it will in fact be misinterpreted.

Here, as elsewhere in moral life, one treads on hazardous ground in trusting one's judgment about another person's beliefs. This is simply a feature of the human condition. If, for example, the professor, believing that he has developed a friendship with the student in which trust and honesty are possible, makes a sexual offer with appropriate disclaimers about grading, and she accepts the offer, but then later tells him that she felt pressured into acceptance, the fault is his. If he was in fact wrong about her perception of the relationship, then the facts were such that he should not have made the offer at all. He is not excused by the reasonableness of his belief that she shared his perceptions, because the situation is inherently ambiguous, and because he can avoid the moral hazard by not making the offer.

II. Sex and Friendship

But suppose that the professor and student have in fact developed a relationship in which trust and honesty have superseded the communication problem. And suppose that the professor and student go on to have a fully voluntary sexual relationship. Here I agree with Dixon that this relationship still raises serious issues—not with regard to their duties to each other, but with regard to their duties to third parties. Assuming the most sincere good faith on all sides, how will it be possible for the professor to give a fair evaluation of the student's work after the development of an intimate relationship? If the professor does indeed have power over the student, that power is premised upon his ability to help or harm her career through his evaluation of her work. If that evaluation is at all subjective, it is simply too much to hope that his perceptions will not be colored by the state of their personal relations—and despite his sincere efforts to avoid such coloring.

It may be argued that, once such a close and trusting relationship has developed, little is added by sexual involvement; objectivity is already compromised. Moreover, friendships of comparable depth may develop independently of sexual attraction, as between heterosexuals of the same gender. It would therefore seem that the same problem with respect to professional objectivity arises in any professor-student friendship, as Peter Markie has suggested.[5] It seems to me, however, that such friendships are substantially less problematic than sexual relationships.

In the case of a non-sexual friendship, it is easier to distance oneself from the emotions associated with it and to regard the student's work objectively; that is, to "forget" while reading it that it is the work of that particular person. In a typical sexual relationship[6] (at least in the early stages), the emotions aroused are qualitatively more overwhelming and more difficult to compartmentalize. Compare the feelings that one has for a lover before, as opposed to after, the first few sexual encounters. Another way to compare the depths of these feelings is to consider the emotions aroused on departure of the friend or lover to live far away. In the case of the friend, these feelings may well be non-trivial; but they are again qualitatively different from the truly overwhelming feelings aroused by the departure of one's lover in similar circumstances.

It is nevertheless true that in the case of deep friendships there are also significant issues about objectivity and one's duty to third parties. Would it be better if, as Markie suggests, professors took care not to form such relationships with their students? Here, there are countervailing values to be weighed. These friendships have a value of their own that cannot be dismissed. There are few enough people one encounters in life with whom such relationships are possible; restricting them further seems intolerable. And it appears plausible that some loss of objectivity in grading is a small price to pay for such an important aspect of human flourishing. Furthermore, particularly in the case of individually supervised graduate students, the trade off is not quite so simple. A certain depth of involvement with the student on a personal level may spur the professor to put an extraordinary amount of effort into aspects of teaching such as providing paper comments, entering into lengthy discussions, etc. These efforts unambiguously serve the teaching purpose. Fortunately, the effort put into teaching activities of this kind is not a fixed quantity, such that effort expended on one student must be taken away from another; friendship is a human good precisely because it serves to increase the total effort that one is willing to expend on others. It would thus seem that there are reasons to encourage such relationships even from the point of view of furthering education.

Markie argues that such friendships are morally objectionable because the professor has an obligation to treat all his students equally, which he violates precisely in providing better instruction to his friend. Even if all the other students receive the consideration that is due them, Markie argues, providing more than is due to students selected on the basis of friendship is comparable to giving each of them an extra ten points on exams otherwise fairly graded. Being a friend of the professor, he suggests, is not an appropriate criterion for the distribution of teaching effort. But it seems to me there is a significant difference between awarding unearned points on an exam and providing the help that enables a student to earn those points. Let us suppose that all of the students have received an amount of help that fully satisfies the normal obligations of a professor to his students. Let us further suppose that some of the students receive no additional help, but some are wealthy enough to hire personal tutors, others have parents who are particularly knowledgeable in the subject, and still others have friends who are willing to help them. While it is true that none of these differences among the students—wealth or knowledgability of parents or friends—is by itself an appropriate criterion for awarding more points, it is also true that there is nothing objectionable in students' obtaining any of these kinds of help in order to earn additional points. Similarly, if the professor has fully met all of his obligations to the other students, he may then turn to helping his friends, as friends, gain the knowledge that will enable them to earn the additional points, whether in his own class or in someone else's. It seems to me there is no important difference between this case and the case in which the student receives that help from any other friend.[7]

Evaluation tasks such as grading and writing letters of recommendation raise different problems. As Markie points out, the student who is the friend of a professor will enjoy advantages beyond those of possible loss of objectivity—such as the simple fact that the professor will know more about the student who is his friend than about other students. It does not follow, however, that refraining from becoming friends is the required course of action, particularly in view of the significant goods that friendship can produce. Other steps can instead be taken to preserve fairness to others. These might consist, depending on the circumstances, of revealing (e.g., in letters of recommendation or to other members of the dissertation committee) the nature of his relationship with the student, turning over evaluation and recommendation tasks to others, deferring more than usual to the views of others with respect to the student's progress, or using blind grading procedures. On the part of the student, it might mean choosing, where possible, to enroll in someone else's class, or refraining from any discussion of grading. Where the student is on any kind of academic borderline, greater caution is appropriate. It may thus be possible for the student to reap the benefits of enhanced instruction that she might receive from any knowledgeable friend without obtaining an unfair advantage over other students in various kinds of evaluations.

Most of the advantages, fair and unfair, of friendship between professor and student, and the measures that can be taken to minimize the latter, are also applicable to (non-casual) sexual relationships. There are, however, several important differences. First, the level of interest and attention in a friendship that is about to ripen into a sexual relationship is, perhaps, already as high as one could wish, with respect to its ability to foster better teaching. Secondly, non-sexual friendship is obviously a matter of degree; there is a smooth continuum of increasingly friendly relations that cannot be sharply differentiated at the point where it becomes a truly intimate friendship. Thus a rule that one should not develop intimate friendships would be impractical; the rule would have to be that one should have no friendships at all with students. (This, indeed, is Markie's position.) Contrastingly, in the case of sexual relationships, there is a very clear line to be crossed, and one that it is always possible to avoid crossing. Given the marked increase in feeling that exactly results from crossing that particular line, it would seem that here is a good place to draw it. Finally, a sexual relationship is more volatile than a non-sexual friendship; it is both more likely to rupture badly and more likely to leave a disruptive emotional aftermath. These considerations are, I think, sufficient to make sexual relationships significantly more problematic than even the closest friendships.

It thus seems to me that it is almost always the morally better course for a professor to refrain from making a sexual offer to any student over whom he has, or expects to have, power. Where a sexual relationship develops after the formal professor-student relationship is terminated, it must be in the knowledge—on both sides—that the professor thereby forfeits some of his say over the student's career. To a lesser degree, this latter is also true where professor and student are friends rather than lovers; but even a close friendship is significantly less problematic than a sexual relationship.

Study Questions

1. Grant that there is a power imbalance between a teacher and a student that means that the student's participation in a sexual relationship cannot be *fully* voluntary. How often in our dealings with other people is our consent or participation *fully* or perfectly voluntary?—yet this is not always a reason to object to or prohibit these interactions. Why insist on the criterion "fully" between teachers and students? Suppose we could rank situations in terms of to what degree participation deviated from being fully voluntary. Would those that deviated only slightly be less morally objectionable than those that deviated greatly? On this continuum, where are teacher-student sexual interactions?

2. Golash focuses on scenarios in which the teacher explicitly or implicitly makes the first move, or makes his desires and intentions known to the student. Would anything in her account have to be changed if we took into account students who make the first move, who flirt and initiate a sexual relationship, who try to seduce the teacher, or who are convinced they want to marry *this* professor and so must take steps to arrange that? What about sexually aggressive women students who undertake a project of hooking up sexually with professors, perhaps in part to exert power or to feel powerful? Some women students can be as sexually predatory as lecherous professors. Would arguments based on power imbalances be irrelevant in these cases? If so, what would the morally significant considerations be?

3. Some teacher-student sexual relationships and/or friendships eventually lead to marriages, some of which are as successful as marriages in general. Is the possible elimination of these marriages an acceptable price some people would have to pay if all teacher-student relationships were socially scorned or prohibited?

4. Is it fair to assume that in the teacher-student relationship, it is the teacher who has all the power or the most important, efficacious, type of power? In a relationship between an older, already physically compromised man and a young, beautiful woman, the teacher might have the power of the grade, but she has her own, perhaps more subtle, powers that can be just as efficacious. Where does the balance of power lie? Similarly, suppose that the student in the teacher-student relationship is as old as, or nearly as old as, the teacher himself? Might this, in some cases, undermine the possibility of a noxious power imbalance?

5. Consider Golash's essay from the perspective of this passage from Slavoj Zizek's *The Plague of Fantasies* (London: Verso, 1997, p. 72): "Sexuality as such . . . always involves a relationship of power: there is no neutral symmetrical sexual relationship/exchange, undistorted by power. The ultimate proof is the dismal failure of the 'politically correct' endeavour to free sexuality of power: to define the rules of 'proper' sexual rapport in which partners should indulge in sex only on account of their mutual, purely sexual, attraction, excluding any 'pathological' factor (power, financial coercion, etc.): if we subtract from sexual rapport the element of 'asexual' (physical, financial . . .) coercion, which distorts the 'pure' sexual attraction, we may lose sexual attraction itself. . . . [T]he very element which seems to bias and corrupt pure sexual rapport . . . may function as the very phantasmic support of

sexual attraction." If Zizek is right, the insistence on fully voluntary participation in the absence of inequality of power threatens
sexuality itself, or at least the excitement and pleasure often attached to sex. Do you agree?

Notes

An earlier version of this paper was presented as a response to a paper by Larry
May at the American Section of the International Association for Philosophy of
Law and Social Philosophy, Lexington, Kentucky, October 1996. I am indebted
to the conference participants, and to an anonymous reviewer for *Essays in Philosophy*, for their comments.

1. See., e.g., Nicholas Dixon, "The Morality of Intimate Faculty-Student Relationships," *Monist* 79, no. 4 (1996): 521–26; Thomas Mappes, "Sexual Morality
and the Concept of Using Another Person," in Thomas Mappes and Jane Zembaty, eds., *Social Ethics: Morality and Social Policy*, 4th ed. (New York: McGraw-Hill,
1992), 211–12 [in this volume, chap. 16].
2. Larry May, *Masculinity and Morality* (Ithaca, N.Y.: Cornell University Press,
1998), chap. 6. May draws this example from a lawsuit, *Alexander v. Yale University*, 459 F. Supp. 1 (D. Conn. 1977), 631 F.2d 178 (2d Cir. 1980). I have adhered
throughout to the male professor–female student example, not merely for sim-
plicity but also because, as a result of social attitudes too well known to require
recital, this is by far the most common occasion for a sexual offer. My observations would, I think, apply to other gender combinations, at least insofar as the
same imbalance of power obtains.
3. Dixon, "Morality," 523–25.
4. For a discussion of the subtle harms that are done by engaging in sex which
one does not desire for itself, see Robin West, "The Harms of Consensual Sex,"
APA Newsletters 94, no. 2 (1995): 52–55 [in this volume, chap. 20].
5. Peter Markie, "Professors, Students, and Friendship," in Steven M. Cahn,
ed., *Morality, Responsibility, and the University: Studies in Academic Ethics* (Philadelphia, Pa.: Temple University Press, 1990), 134–49.
6. In referring to a "typical sexual relationship," I mean to exclude the sort of
case in which one or both parties engage in sex without emotional involvement.
To the extent that I may be wrong about what is typical, my remarks will apply to
a smaller set of cases. But it is improbable that the parties can both achieve the
depth of honesty discussed here and avoid emotional involvement.
7. It may be argued that the professor has special knowledge of his own
course requirements and grading proclivities that other helpers would not have.
But I think for this to make a significant difference his standards would have to
be so idiosyncratic as to be indefensible. He would of course be obligated not to
offer improper kinds of help such as advance notice of exam questions, etc.

Chapter 29

ANTIOCH'S "SEXUAL OFFENSE POLICY": A PHILOSOPHICAL EXPLORATION

Alan Soble

*People, both young and old, are not always candid with others about their sexual intentions and desires: whether they have any, what they are, what strings might be attached. Some of this lack of full disclosure is due to embarrassment and feelings of vulnerability; some of it might amount to manipulative deception. In any event, withholding information and engaging in pretense seem to violate the moral requirement (found in Immanuel Kant and John Stuart Mill) that people who want to engage in sexual activity with each other must provide "free and informed consent." In order to abide by the principle, people must (among other things) avoid miscommunication. For example, some women occasionally offer what is known as "token resistance" to a man's sexual requests. Men are aware of this, and as a result do not always know whether a woman's "no" is genuine or pretend, whether it means "never" or "not right this second." Further, men for various reasons often try to read a woman's silence as a "yes." What are needed are reliable ways of indicating that one does or does not consent to sexual activity, and reliable ways of discerning whether someone else has or has not consented. Because consent can come in many forms—it might be explicit or implicit, verbal or nonverbal—indicating one's consent, or its absence, and discerning the consent of another is often difficult. In this essay, **Alan Soble** discusses a proposal for overcoming such problems: a standard of consent (embraced, for example, by the policy of Antioch University) that requires consent, before and during sexual activity, to be both verbally explicit and to be continuously repeated. Soble does not deny that mutual consent is a necessary condition for* *morally permissible sexual interactions. What he does is explore philosophically the rationale, the implications, and the advantages and disadvantages of Antioch University's standard of consent.*

Reprinted, slightly revised, from *Journal of Social Philosophy* 28, no. 1 (1997): 22–36, with the permission of Blackwell Publishing, Oxford, UK © 1997, *Journal of Social Philosophy*.

She: For the last time, do you love me or don't you?
He: I DON'T!
She: Quit stalling, I want a *direct* answer.
  —Jane Russell and Fred Astaire[1]

"When in Doubt, Ask"

Consider this seemingly innocuous moral judgment issued by philosopher Raymond Belliotti:

"teasing" without the intention to fulfill that which the other can reasonably be expected to think was offered is immoral since it involves the nonfulfillment of that which the other could reasonably be expected as having been agreed upon.[2]

This might be right in the abstract; provocative and lingering flirtatious glances sometimes can reasonably be taken as an invitation to engage in sex; hence brazenly flirting and not fulfilling its meaning, or never intending to fulfill its meaning, is, like failing to honor other promises or invitations, ceteris paribus a moral defect—even if not a mortal sin.[3] Abstractions aside, however, how are we to grasp "can *reasonably* be taken as"? A woman's innocent, inquisitive glance might be taken as a sexual invitation by an awfully optimistic fellow, and he and his peers might judge his perception "reasonable." This is why Catharine MacKinnon says that to use

reasonable belief as a standard without asking, on a substantive social basis, to whom the belief is reasonable and why—meaning, what conditions make it reasonable—is one-sided: male-sided.[4]

Similarly, a man's innocent, inquisitive glance might be taken as a sexual leer by an anxiously sensitive woman, and she and her peers might judge this perception "reasonable."

But Belliotti writes as if all were well with the slippery concept of "reasonable":

Although sexual contracts are not as formal or explicit as corporation agreements the rule of thumb should be the concept of reasonable expectation. If a woman smiles at me and agrees to have a drink I cannot reasonably assume . . . that she has agreed to spend the weekend with me.[5]

I suppose not. But why not? We do not now have in our culture a convention, a practice like the display of colored hankies, in which a smile before an accepted drink has that meaning. But nothing intrinsic to the action prevents its having, in the proper circumstances, that very meaning. And an optimistic fellow might say that the *special* sort of smile she, or another he, gave him constituted a sexual invitation. Belliotti continues his example:

On the other hand if she did agree to share a room and bed with me for the weekend I could reasonably assume that she had agreed to have sexual intercourse.

This is not true for many American couples as they travel through foreign lands together. Or maybe in accepting the invitation to share a room or sleeping car she agreed only to snuggle. Cues indicating the presence and kind of sexual interest are fluid; at one time in the recent past, a woman's inviting a man to her apartment or room carried more sexual meaning than it does now—even if that meaning still lingers on college campuses and elsewhere.[6] To forestall such objections, Belliotti offers these instructions:

If there is any doubt concerning whether or not someone has agreed to perform a certain sexual act with another, I would suggest that the doubting party simply ask the other and make the contract more explicit. . . . [W]hen in doubt assume nothing until a more explicit overture has been made.[7]

What could be more commonsensical than this? But it is wrong. The man who thinks it reasonable in a given situation to assume that the woman has agreed to have sex will not have any doubt and so will have no motive to ask more explicitly what she wants. His failure to doubt, or his failure to imagine the bare possibility of doubting, whether the other has consented to engage in sex is brought about by the same factors that determine, for him, the reasonableness of his belief in her consent. It is silly to suggest *"when* in doubt, ask," because the problem is that not enough doubt arises in the first place, that is, the brief look is taken too readily as reasonable or conclusive evidence of a sexual invitation. A man touches the arm of a woman who briefly glanced at him; she pulls away abruptly; but he is not caused to have doubts about her interest. Even if he does not take her resistance as further evidence of her desire, the reasonableness, for him, of his belief that her earlier glance was intentionally sexual is enough to prevent doubt from taking root when it should—immediately.

"'No' Means 'No'"

According to Susan Estrich, a man who engages in sex with a woman on the basis of an unreasonable belief in her consent should be charged with rape; only a genuinely reasonable belief in her consent should exculpate an accused rapist. Estrich (perhaps utilizing MacKinnon's point) wants it to be legally impossible for a man accused of rape to plead that he believed that the woman consented, when that belief was unreasonable, even though *he* thought it was reasonable. Estrich realizes that "reasonable belief" is a difficult notion. Still, she heroically proposes that "the reasonable man in the 1980s should be the one who understands that a woman's word is deserving of respect, whether she is a perfect stranger or his own wife." The reasonable man "is the one who . . . understands that 'no means no.'"[8] The man pawing the arm of the woman who pulls abruptly away—the physical equivalent of "no"—had better immediately doubt the quality of his belief in her sexual interest. At the psychological level, this man might not doubt that she is sexually interested in him; Estrich's normative proposal is that he is to be held liable anyway, because he *should* be doubtful. Beyond this crude sort of case, I think Estrich means that, for the reasonable man, a woman's qualified locution ("Please, not tonight, I think I'd rather not"; "I don't know, I just don't feel like it") is not an invitation to continue trying, but means "no." The woman's wish is expressed softly because she is tactful or frightened or because this is the language of women's culture that she has learned to speak. For the reasonable man, her "I'm not sure I want to" is either a tactful "no" or a request to back off while she autonomously makes up her own mind.

As congenial as Estrich's proposal is, she muddies the water with a tantalizing piece of logic:

> Many feminists would argue that so long as women are powerless relative to men, viewing a "yes" as a sign of true consent is misguided. . . . [M]any women who say yes to men they know, whether on dates or on the job, would say no if they could. I have no doubt that women's silence sometimes is the product not of passion and desire but of pressure and fear. Yet if yes may often mean no, at least from a woman's perspective, it does not seem so much to ask men, and the law, to respect the courage of the woman who does say no and to take her at her word.[9]

Estrich's reasoning seems to be: if something as antithetical to "no" as "yes" can mean "no," then surely something as consistent with "no," "no" itself, means "no." This argument has a curious consequence. If "yes" can mean "no," at least from a woman's *own* perspective (the woman who consents for financial reasons but whose heart and desire are not wrapped up in the act; a woman who agrees, but only after a barrage of pleading),[10] then it will be difficult to deny that "no" spoken by some women can mean "maybe" or even "yes." From the perspective of some women, "no" can mean "try harder to convince me" or "show me how manly you are." Charlene Muehlenhard and Lisa Hollabaugh have reported that some women occasionally say "no" but do not mean it; 39.3 percent of the 610 college women they surveyed at Texas A&M University indicated that they had offered "token resistance" to sex "even though [they] had every intention to and [were] willing to engage in sexual intercourse."[11] Susan Rae Peterson partially explains these findings: "typical sexual involvement includes some resistance on the part of women . . . because they have been taught to do so, or they do not want to appear 'easy' or 'cheap.'"[12]

Men cannot always tell when a woman's resistance is real or token, serious or playful; men are, moreover, often insensitive, even callous, as to what a woman does intend to communicate; and, after all, Muehlenhard and Hollabaugh's figure is only 39 percent and not 99 percent. For these reasons, as well as her own, Estrich's proposal is a wise suggestion. Men, and the courts, should always assume, in order to be cognitively, morally, and legally safe, that a woman's "no" means "no"—*even in those cases when it does or might not.* A man who takes "no" as "no" even when he suspects that a woman is testing his masculinity with token resistance is advised by Estrich to risk suffering a loss of sexual pleasure and a possible blow to his ego, in order to secure the greater good, for both him and her, of avoiding rape.

But if men are *always* to assume that "no" means "no," even though there is a nontrivial chance that it means "keep trying" or "yes," then Estrich, to be consistent, should permit men to assume that a woman's "yes" *always* means "yes"—even though, on her view, a woman's "yes" sometimes means "no."[13] If, instead, Estrich wants men to sort out when a woman's "yes" really means "yes" and when it does not, in order that he be able to decide whether to take the "yes" at its face value and proceed with sex, she should propose some workable procedure for men to follow. Yet her description of the reasonable man mentions only what his response to "no" should be, and not what his response to "yes" should be. Encouraging women to abandon the token resistance maneuver, to give up saying "no" when they mean "maybe" or "yes," is helpful. But it will not take theorists of sex, or men in the presence of an apparently consenting woman, very far in deciphering when "yes" means "no."[14]

The Antioch Policy

I propose that we understand Antioch University's "Sexual Offense Policy" as addressing the issues raised in our discussion of Belliotti and Estrich. The policy's central provisions are these:[15]

A1. "Consent must be obtained verbally before there is any sexual contact or conduct."

A2. "[O]btaining consent is an ongoing process in any sexual interaction."

A3. "If the level of sexual intimacy increases during an interaction . . . the people involved need to express their clear verbal consent before moving to that new level."

A4. "The request for consent must be specific to each act."

A5. "If you have had a particular level of sexual intimacy before with someone, you must still ask each and every time."

A6. "If someone has initially consented but then stops consenting during a sexual interaction, she/he should communicate withdrawal verbally and/or through physical resistance. The other individual(s) must stop immediately."

A7. "Don't ever make any assumptions about consent."

In an ethnically, religiously, economically, socially, and sexually diverse population, there might be no common and comprehensive understanding of what various bits of behavior mean in terms of expressing interest in or consenting to sex. In the absence of rigid conventions or a homogeneous community, a glance, either brief or prolonged, is too indefinite to be relied on to transmit information; an invitation to come to one's room, or sharing a room, or a bed, on a trip might or might not have some settled meaning; clothing and cosmetics in a pluralistic culture are equivocal. (Young men, more so than young women, take tight jeans and the absence of a bra under a top to signal an interest in sex.)[16] Because physical movements and cues of various kinds can be interpreted in widely different ways, sexual activity entered into or carried out on the basis of this sort of (mis)information is liable to violate someone's rights or otherwise be indecent or offensive. Antioch therefore insists that consent to sexual activity be verbal (A1) instead of merely behavioral.[17] Following this rule will minimize miscommunication and the harms it causes and will encourage persons to treat each other with Kantian respect as autonomous, or self-determining, agents.

Further, bodily movements or behaviors of a sexual sort that occur in the early stages of a sexual encounter can also be ambiguous and do not necessarily indicate a willingness to increase the intensity of, or to prolong, the encounter (hence A2, A3). Verbal communication is supposed to prevent misunderstandings rooted in indefinite body language; we should not assume consent to continue the encounter on the basis of expressions of desire (lubrication, groans) or failures to resist an embrace. None of these bodily phenomena—reacting with sexual arousal to a touch; not moving away when intimately touched—necessarily means that the touched person welcomes the touch or wants it to continue. There are times when one's body responds with pleasure to a touch but one's mind disagrees with the body's judgment; Antioch's insistence on verbal consent after discussion and deliberation is meant to give the mind decisive and autonomous power. Similarly, the request for, and the consent to, sexual contact must be not only *verbally explicit*, but also *specific* for any sexual act that might occur (A4). Consenting to and then sharing a kiss does not imply consent to any other sexual act; the bodily movements that accompany the sexual arousal created by the kiss do not signal permission to proceed to some other sexual activity not yet discussed (A3, A4).

One provision of the Antioch policy (A7) is a rebuttal of Belliotti's advice, that "when in doubt, ask." Antioch demands, more strictly than this, that the potential sexual partners entertain *universal* doubt and therefore *always* ask. Doubt about the other's consent must be categorical rather than hypothetical: not Belliotti's "when in doubt, assume nothing," but a Cartesian "doubt!" and "assume nothing!" To be on the cognitive, moral, and legal safe side, to avoid mistakes about desire or intention, always assume "no" unless a clear, verbal, explicit "yes" is forthcoming (Al, A3, A4). If this rule is followed, men no longer have to worry about distinguishing a woman's mildly seductive behavior from her "incomplete rejection strategy,"[18] about which men and boys are often confused; in the absence of an explicit "yes" on her part, he is, as demanded by Estrich, respectfully to assume "no." There's still the question of how a man is to know, when obvious consent-negating factors are lacking (for example, she's had too much alcohol), whether a woman's "yes" truly means "yes." Antioch's solution is to rely on explicit, probing verbal communication that must occur not only before but also during a sexual encounter (A3, A5). The constant dialogue, the "ongoing process" (A2) of getting consent in what Lois Pineau calls "communicative sexuality,"[19] is meant to provide the man with an opportunity to assess whether the woman's "yes" means "yes," to give her the opportunity to say a definite even if tactful "no," and to clear up confusions created by her earlier or current silence or passive acquiescence. At the same time, there is to be no constant badgering—especially not under the rubric of "communicative sexuality"—of a woman by a man in response to her "no." A man's querying whether a woman's "no" really means "no" is to disrespect her "no" and fails to acknowledge her autonomy. It is also to embark on a course that might constitute verbal coercion.[20]

It is illuminating to look at the Antioch policy from the perspective of the sadomasochistic subculture, in particular its use of "safe words." A set of safe words is a language, a common understanding, a convention jointly created in advance (hence a Cartesian foundation) of sex by the partners, to be used during a sexual encounter as a way to say "yes," "more," or "no," or to convey details about wants and dislikes, without spoiling the erotic mood. Thus the use of safe words attempts to achieve some of the goals of Antioch's policy without the cumbersome apparatus of explicit verbal consent at each level of sexual interaction (A3, A4). And a tactful and ingenious safe word can gently accomplish an Antiochian withdrawal of consent to sex (A6). But there is a major difference between sadomasochism and Antiochian sex: a sadomasochistic pair wants the activities to proceed smoothly, spontaneously, realistically, so one party grants to the other the right to carry on as he or she wishes, subject to the veto or modifications of safe words, which are to be used sparingly, only when necessary, as a last resort; the couple therefore eschews Antiochian constant dialogue. In dispensing with the incessant chatter of ongoing consent to higher levels of sexual interaction (A2, A3), the sadomasochistic pair violates another provision (A7): consent is assumed throughout the encounter in virtue of the early granting of rights. No such prior consent to sex into an indefinite future is admissible by Antioch.[21]

Pleasure

Does Antioch's policy make sex less exciting? Does it force a couple to slow down, to savor each finger and tooth, when they would rather be overwhelmed by passion? Sarah Crichton criticizes the Antioch policy on the grounds that "it criminalizes the delicious unexpectedness of sex—a hand suddenly moves to here, a mouth to there."[22] But this consideration is not decisive. One goal of the policy is to decrease the possibility that a person will unexpectedly experience (that is, without being warned by being asked) something unpleasant that he or she does not want to experience: a mouth sucking on the wrong toe, a finger too rudely rammed in the rectum. The risk of undergoing unwanted acts or sensations is especially great with strangers, and it is in such a context that the requirement that consent be obtained specifically for each act makes the most sense. Sometimes we do not want the unexpected but only the expected, the particular sensations we know, trust, and yearn for. So there is in the Antioch policy a trade-off. We lose the pleasure, if any, of the unexpected, but we also avoid the unpleasantness of the unexpected. This is why Crichton's point is not decisive. Perhaps for the young, or for those people more generally who do not yet know what they like sexually, verbal consent to specifically described touches or acts might make less sense. But in this case, too, there are reasons to insist, for the sake of caution, on such consent.

Julia Reidhead also attempts to rebut the objection that Antioch's policy begets dull sex.[23] She claims that the policy gives the partners a chance to be creative with language, to play linguistically with a request to touch the breast or "kiss the hollow of your neck" and to "reinvent [sex] privately." But Antioch thinks that sexual language needs to be less, rather than more, private; more specific, not less.[24] Hence Reidhead's praise for Antioch's policy misses its point: common linguistic understandings cannot be assumed in a heterogeneous population. To encourage the creative, poetic use of language in framing sexual requests to proceed to a new level of sex is to provoke the misunderstandings the policy was designed to prevent. Thus, when Reidhead queries, "What woman or man on Antioch's campus, or elsewhere, wouldn't welcome . . . 'May I kiss the hollow of your neck,'" Reidhead's homogenizing "or elsewhere" betrays an insensitivity to the cultural and social differences and their linguistic and behavioral concomitants that Antioch is trying to overcome.

Reidhead defends Antioch also by arguing that vocalizing creatively about sex before we do it is a fine way to mix the pleasures of language with the pleasures of the body. Indeed, the pleasures of talk are themselves sensual and sexual: "Antioch's subtle and imaginative mandate is an erotic windfall: an opportunity for undergraduates to discover that wordplay and foreplay can be happily entwined." Reidhead is right that talking about sex can be sexy and arousing, but wrong that this fact is consistent with the Antioch policy and one of its advantages. This cutesy reading of communication as itself sex almost throws Antioch's procedure into a vicious regress: if no sexual activity is permissible without prior consent (A1), and consent must be verbal or spoken, then if a request for sexual activity is constructed to be a sexually arousing locution, it would amount to a sexual act and hence would be impermissible unless it, in turn, had already received specific consent (A1, A4). So Y's consent to nonverbal sexual activity must be preceded by X's verbal request for that activity *and* by X's verbal request to utter that sexual or sexually arousing verbal request. Further, to try to get consent for the sexual act of kissing the neck by talking sensually about kissing the neck is to employ the pleasure elicited by one sexual act to bring about the occurrence of another sexual act. But obtaining consent for a sexual act by causing even mild sexual pleasure with a seductive request is to interfere with calm and rational deliberation—as much as a shot or two of whiskey would. This is why Antioch insists (A3) that between any two sexual levels there must be a pause, a sexual gap, that makes space for three things: a thoughtful, verbal act of request, deliberations about whether or not to proceed, and then either consent or denial. A well-timed hiatus respected by both parties provides an obstacle to misreadings; the demands of Augustinian bodily perturbations are to be checked while the mind (re)considers.

Body Talk

But the body should not be dismissed altogether. When two people in love embrace tightly, eyes glued to each other's eyes, bodies in contact pulsating with pleasure, they often do know (*how*, is the mystery) without explicit verbalization, from the way they touch each other and respond to these touches, that each wants and at least implicitly, if not explicitly, consents to the sex that is about to occur. Other cases of successful communication—in and out of sexual contexts—are explicit and specific without being verbal. So even if the truth of the particular claim that the mouth can say "no" while the body exclaims an overriding "yes" is debatable or doubtful, the general idea that the body sometimes does speak a clear language, seems fine. Maybe this is why Antioch, even though it requires a verbal "yes" for proceeding with sex (A1), allows a *nonverbal* "no" to be sufficient for *withdrawing* consent (A6). Nonverbal behavior can have a clear meaning after all. Certain voluntary actions, even some impulsive, reflex-like, bodily movements, do mean "no," and about these there should be no mistake, in the same Estrichian way that about the meaning of the simple verbal "no" there should be no mistake. But if such bodily motions can be assumed or demanded to be understood in a pluralistic community—*pulling away when touched means "no"*—then some voluntary behaviors and involuntary bodily movements must reliably signal "yes."

According to the policy, a verbal "yes" replaces any possible bodily movement or behavior as the one and only reliable sign that proceeding with sexual activity is permissible. If I ask, "may I kiss you?" I may not proceed on the basis of your bodily reply, for example, your pushing your mouth out at me, or your groaning and opening your mouth invitingly, because even though it seems obvious to me what these behaviors mean ("yes"), I might be making an interpretive mistake: I see your open mouth as presented "invitingly" because I have with undue optimism deceived myself into thinking that is what you mean. So I must wait for the words, "yes, you may kiss me,"[25] about which such interpretive unclarity is not supposed to arise (else the problem Antioch set for itself is unsolvable). The verbal "yes," *after* communicative probing, is Antioch's Cartesian foundation. But can the ambiguities of the verbal be cleared up by language itself? How much communicative probing is *enough?* This question creates a hermeneutic circle that threatens to trap Antioch's policy. Her "yes," repeated several times under the third-degree interrogation that comprises communicative sex, can always be probed more for genuineness, if I wanted to *really* make sure. But, losing patience, she shows her "yes" to be genuine when she grabs me or plants a kiss on my lips. The body reasserts itself.

My continuing to probe her "yes" over and over again, to make sure that her heart and desire are wrapped up in the act to which she is apparently consenting (must I ask her whether she realizes that her agreement might have been engineered for my benefit by "compulsory heterosexuality"?), is a kind of paternalism. The robust respect that Antioch's policy fosters for a woman's "no" is offset by the weaker respect it fosters for her "yes." Hence conceiving of the Antioch policy not as attempting to foster respect for the autonomy of the other, but as simply attempting to prevent acquaintance rape (that is, harmful actions), is more accurate. At best, the relationship between Antioch's policy and the autonomy of potential sexual partners is unclear. One Antioch student, Suzy Martin, defends the policy by saying that "it made me aware I *have* a voice. I didn't know that before."[26] Coming in the mid-1990s from a college-age woman, the kind of person we expect to know better, this remark is astonishing. In effect, she admits that what Antioch is doing for her, at such an advanced age, is what her parents and earlier schooling should have done long ago, to teach her that she has a voice. Thus Antioch is employing an anti-autonomy principle in its treatment of young adults—in loco parentis—that my college generation had fought to eliminate.

Consent

The policy lays it down that previous sexual encounters between two people do not relax or change the rules to be followed during their later encounters (A5); the casual sex of one-night stands and that of ongoing relationships are governed by the same rules or standards. Nor does a person's sexual biography (for example, reputation) count for anything. No historical facts allow "assumptions about consent" (A7). Indeed, in requiring consent at each different level of a single sexual encounter, Antioch applies the same principle of the irrelevance of history to each sub-act within that encounter. Earlier consent to one sub-act within a single encounter creates no presumption that one may proceed, without repeating the procedure of obtaining explicit and specific consent, to later sub-acts in the same encounter, in the same way that a sexual encounter on Friday night does not mean that consent can be assumed for a sexual encounter on the following Saturday night. The history of the relationship, let alone the history of the evening, counts for nothing.[27] The Antioch policy, then, implies that one cannot consent in advance to a whole night of sex, but only to a single atomistic act, one small part of an encounter. Similarly, in denying the relevance of the historical, Antioch makes both a Pauline and a Kantian marriage contract impossible.[28] In such marriages, one consents at the very beginning, in advance, to a whole series of sexual acts that might make up the rest of one's sexual life; consent to sex is presumed continuously after the exchange of vows and rings; each spouse owns the body and sexual powers of the other; and marital rape is conceptually impossible, replaced by a notion of fulfilling the "marriage debt." In rejecting the possibility of such an arrangement, even if voluntary and contractual, Antioch cuts back on a traditional power of consent: its ability to apply to an indefinite, open future. For Antioch, consent is short-lived; it dies an easy death, and must always be replaced by a new generation of consents.

Antioch also cuts back on the power of consent by making it not binding: one can withdraw consent at any time during any act or sub-act (A6). Nothing in the policy indicates that the right to withdraw is limited by the sexual satisfaction or other expectations of one's partner. Any such qualification would also run counter to the policy's spirit. This is a difference between Antioch's policy and Belliotti's libertarianism, according to which breaking a sexual promise is at least a prima facie moral fault. It is also contrary to the indissolubility of Pauline marriage. But that Antioch would be indulgent about withdrawing consent makes sense, given Antioch's distrust of the historical. Consenting is an act that occupies a discrete location in place and time; it is a historical event, and that it has occurred is a historical fact; thus consent is itself precisely the kind of thing whose weight Antioch discounts. Consenting to a sexual act does not entail, for Antioch, that one ought to perform the act, and not even that one has a prima facie duty to do so; the act need not take place because the only justification for it to occur is the act of consenting that has already receded into the past and has become a mere piece of impotent history. When consent into the future, today for tomorrow, is ruled out, so too is consent into the future, now for ten seconds from now. Then how could consent have the power to legitimize any subsequent sexual act? An air of paradox surrounds the policy: it makes consent the centerpiece of valid sexual conduct, yet its concept of consent is emaciated. Of course, as Carole Pateman says, "unless refusal of consent or withdrawal of consent are real possibilities, we can no longer speak of 'consent' in any genuine sense."[29] But that withdrawing consent must be possible does not entail that we have carte blanche permission to do so. My guess is that Belliotti is right, that withdrawing consent to an act to which one has consented is prima facie wrong. The logical possibility that consent is binding in this way is necessary for taking consent seriously in the first place as a legitimizer of sexual activity.

Still, if X has promised a sexual act to Y, but withdraws consent and so reneges, it does *not* follow from Belliotti's libertarianism that Y has a right to compel X into compliance.[30] Nor does it follow from the terms of Pauline or Kantian marriage, in which the spouses consent to a lifetime of sexual acts. Neither the fact that each person has a duty, the marriage debt, to provide sexual pleasure for the other whenever the other wants it, nor the fact that in such a marriage the one initial act of consent makes rape conceptually impossible, imply that a spurned spouse may rightfully force himself or herself upon the other. Pauline marriage is, in principle, egalitarian; the wife owns the husband and his ability to perform sexually as much as he owns her capacity to provide pleasure. In patriarchal practice, however, the man expects sexual access to his wife in exchange for economic support, and even if rape is conceptually impossible he might still extract or enforce the marriage debt: "if she shows unwillingness or lack of inclination to engage with him in sexual intercourse, he may wish to remind her of the nature of the bargain they struck. The act of rape may serve conveniently as a communicative vehicle for reminding her."[31] But neither violence nor abuse are legitimated by the *principles* of Pauline marriage; perhaps their possibility explains why Paul admonishes the spouses to show "due benevolence" to each other (I Corinthians 7:3).[32]

Finally, Antioch's policy also does not permit "metaconsent," or consent about (the necessity of) consent. Consent, in principle, should be able to alter the background presumption, in the relationship between two people, *from* "assume 'no' unless you hear an explicit 'yes'" *to* "assume 'yes' unless you hear an explicit 'no,'" or *from* "don't you dare try without an explicit go-ahead" *to* "feel free to try but be prepared for a 'no.'" This power of consent is abolished by Antioch's making history irrelevant; consent to prior sexual acts creates no presumption in favor of "yes" tonight (A5). Further, to give consent into the future allows one's partner to make a prohibited assumption (A7). There is no provision in the policy that empowers a couple to jettison the policy by free and mutual consent; here is another way Antioch's policy does not foster autonomy. In Pauline marriage, by contrast, one act of consent, the marriage vow, has the power to change presumptions from "no" to an ongoing "yes." Such is the power of consent for Paul, that it both applies to the future and is binding: we make our bed and then lie in it. Antioch's notion of consent has freed us from such stodgy concerns.

Study Questions

1. Provide examples both of consent and of refusals of consent that are (1) verbal and explicit, (2) verbal and implicit, (3) nonverbal and explicit, and (4) nonverbal and implicit. Is being "vocal" or "spoken" either necessary or sufficient for consent to be "verbal"?

2. Does it follow from the claim that a person's "no" in response to a sexual overture should always be taken as a firm "no" (even if it might be merely token resistance) that a person's "yes" may always be taken as a firm "yes"? Regardless, what are the merits of the latter claim? (Consult Alan Wertheimer, chapter 19.)

3. What does the sentence "Yes, let's have sex!" mean? How is it the same as, and how is it different from, "Yes, let's go to the movies!"? (How well can these questions be answered by taking "referential opacity" into account?)

4. Is it ever morally wrong to retract consent to sexual activity? In what circumstances? Why or why not? If and when it is wrong, when would it be a serious moral fault? Consider how morally wrong it is to break different kinds of promises. (Again, see also Alan Wertheimer's essay, chapter 19.)

5. Is "wanted" or "desired" sexual activity the same as "consensual" sexual activity? Is "unwanted" or "not desired" sexual activity the same as "nonconsensual" sexual activity?

Notes

Assistance in carrying out the research for and the writing of this essay was provided by the Research Support Scheme of the Open Society Institute (grant 1520/706/94). The earliest version of this paper was presented as a seminar at the philosophy department of the Budapest Technical University, May 1994. (Travel to Budapest was made possible by grants from the International Research and Exchanges Board and the Hungarian Ministry of Culture and Education.) A later version was presented on February 24, 1995, as a "Current Research in Philosophy" colloquium at Tulane University; and one more version was read at the Eastern Division meetings of the American Philosophical Association, December 30, 1995.

1. This is the epigraph to chap. 9 of Susan Haack's *Evidence and Inquiry* (Oxford: Blackwell, 1993), 182. Professor Haack thanks David Stove for supplying it.

2. Raymond Belliotti, "A Philosophical Analysis of Sexual Ethics," *Journal of Social Philosophy* 10, no. 3 (1979): 8–11, at 11.

3. According to John Sabini and Maury Silver ("Flirtation and Ambiguity," chap. 6 of their *Moralities of Everyday Life* [New York: Oxford University Press, 1982], 107–23, at 116n11), "Flirtation . . . offers no commitment and gives no right to claim abuse. To claim you were teased is to claim [that the other] went beyond flirting to committing. Of course, the disappointed one may be inclined to see a tease in a flirt." That is indeed the problem.

4. Catharine MacKinnon, *Toward a Feminist Theory of the State* (Cambridge, Mass.: Harvard University Press, 1989), 183; see 181.

5. Raymond Belliotti, "A Philosophical Analysis of Sexual Ethics," 9.

6. See T. Perper and D. Weis, "Proceptive and Rejective Strategies of U.S. and Canadian College Women," *Journal of Sex Research* 23, no. 4 (1987): 455–80, at 462.

7. Belliotti repeats the "when in doubt, ask" advice in his essay "Sex" (in Peter Singer, ed., *A Companion to Ethics* [Oxford: Blackwell, 1991], 315–26, at 325) and in his treatise *Good Sex: Perspectives on Sexual Ethics* (Lawrence: University Press of Kansas, 1993), 106–107. See my book note on *Good Sex*, in *Ethics* 105, no. 2 (1995): 447–48.

8. Susan Estrich, *Real Rape* (Cambridge, Mass.: Harvard University Press, 1987), 97–98.

9. Estrich, *Real Rape*, 102.

10. These examples are like Robin West's (who might not approve of my use of them), in "The Harms of Consensual Sex," *American Philosophical Association Newsletters* 92, no. 2 (1995): 52–55, at 53; in this volume, chap. 20. I am not sure that the examples capture what Estrich's brief remark, that some women who say "yes" would say "no" if they could, means. She makes the point, elsewhere, this way: "many women who say 'yes' are not in fact choosing freely but are submitting because they feel a lack of power to say 'no'" ("Rape," in Patricia Smith, ed., *Feminist Jurisprudence* [New York: Oxford University Press, 1993], 158–87, at 177).

11. Charlene Muehlenhard and Lisa Hollabaugh, "Do Women Sometimes Say No When They Mean Yes? The Prevalence and Correlates of Token Resistance to Sex," *Journal of Personality and Social Psychology* 54, no. 5 (1988): 872–79.

12. Susan Rae Peterson, "Coercion and Rape: The State as a Male Protection Racket," in Mary Vetterling-Braggin, Frederick A. Elliston, and Jane English, eds., *Feminism and Philosophy* (Totowa, N.J.: Littlefield, Adams, 1977), 360–71, at 365. See also Muehlenhard and Hollabaugh, "Do Women Sometimes Say No When They Mean Yes?" on the wide variety of reasons women have for carrying out this sometimes "rational" strategy (875, 878).

Rae Langton suggests that men's failure to take a woman's "no" as "no" is an effect of pornography on men ("Speech Acts and Unspeakable Acts," *Philosophy and Public Affairs* 22, no. 4 [1993]: 293–330, at 324–25). This thesis is surprising, because in most pornography women are portrayed as active seekers of sexual activity, as eschewing the traditional games, and not as reluctant participants. Consistent with men's fantasies, women's favorite word in pornography, it seems, is yes or an equivalent. Still, Langton supposes that because women as portrayed in pornography rarely say "no," men who learn "the rules of the [sexual] game" from pornography do not learn to recognize refusals for what they are. But do men learn about sex (only, mostly, or at all) from pornography? Do men really (and stupidly) take the fact that women rarely say "no" in pornography to mean that the real women in their presence do not mean "no" when they do say it? (For more on Langton on pornography, see my "Bad Apples: Feminist Politics and Feminist Scholarship," *Philosophy of the Social Sciences* 29, no. 3 [1999]: 354–88, sect. V.) Beatrice Faust proposes an alternative way, more plausible than Langton's, in which pornography might have an effect:

> Many nonviolent rapes are simply results of scrambled signals between the sexes. Pornography is relevant to this category of rape, since it reinforces the belief that women respond to sex exactly as men do. (*Women, Sex, and Pornography* [New York: Macmillan, 1980], 132.)

Women in pornography energetically seek sexual encounters and respond to the sexual advances of others without hesitation; they are portrayed as being as much interested in sex for its own sake, as eager to consent, and as easily aroused as men are (or as men think men are). Men who believe that women are as quick-triggered as men are might have difficulty comprehending a woman's unwillingness to proceed directly from a long kiss to more intimate sexual touches; a man, being already aroused and wanting to proceed, might assume that she is just as aroused and hence also wants to proceed—despite her pauses or silence. But men, especially when young, likely assimilate the sexuality of women to their own not in virtue of pornographic portrayals of sexually assertive women, but out of simple sexual inexperience.

Indeed, boys discover that "no" does not always mean "no" when they are young (i.e., pre-pornographically). Boys detect the maneuver in girls who say "no" but soon show they do not mean it; these girls say "no" only because they have been pushed by their mothers to say "no," even though pushed by their mothers, without complete success, to mean it. Muehlenhard and Hollabaugh's research shows that the phenomenon extends beyond grade school into college and strongly suggests that mechanisms other than pornography are at work. If we are worried, as we should be, about where college-age men get the idea, or have it reinforced, that a woman's "no" does not always mean "no," we might want to consider the effects of Muehlenhard's publication itself, which let a popular cat out of the scholarly bag. Men can read "39.3%" in print in a refereed, respected journal, which must be a more persuasive documentation of women's artifice than the fantasy world of pornography. Robin Warshaw and Andrea Parrot ("The Contribution of Sex-Role Socialization to Acquaintance Rape," in Andrea Parrot and Laurie Bechhofer, eds., *Acquaintance Rape: The Hidden Crime* [New York: John Wiley, 1991], 73–82) claim that "men's social training tells them . . . that women who say 'no' don't really mean it" (75) and "men are socialized to believe . . . that women do not mean 'no' when they say 'no'" (80). But if men discover that "no" does not always mean "no" *firsthand*, from women who say "no" but do not mean it, it is a conceptual disaster to point an accusing causal finger at "socialization" or "social training."

13. Carole Pateman turns this around: "if 'no,' when uttered by a woman, is to be reinterpreted as 'yes,' then . . . why should a woman's 'yes' be more privileged, be any the less open to invalidation" ("Women and Consent," *Political Theory* 8, no. 2 [1980]: 149–68, at 162)—that is, if men do not take "no" as "no," they have no right to take "yes" as "yes."

14. Stephen Schulhofer ("The Gender Question in Criminal Law," in Jeffrie G. Murphy, ed., *Punishment and Rehabilitation*, 3rd edition [Belmont, Calif.: Wadsworth, 1995], 274–311, at 308–309) discusses some cases in which "yes" does not mean "yes": the man obtains a woman's consent through fraud or deception. Estrich does not seem to have this sort of case in mind. Maybe she agrees with MacKinnon's point about the indistinguishability in patriarchy of rape and consensual sex, or with her rhetorical skepticism: "What is it reasonable for a man to believe concerning a woman's desire for sex when heterosexuality is compulsory?" (MacKinnon, *Toward a Feminist Theory of the State*, 183). "Nothing" is the implied answer; he may never assume that "yes" means "yes."

15. I quote from a copy of the policy and its introduction sent to me in 1994 by the Office of the President, Antioch University. The numbering of the provisions is my own. The policy was intended to be gender-neutral and sexual orientation-neutral, allowing the possibility of gay or lesbian acquaintance rape and a woman's raping a man.

16. Jacqueline D. Goodchilds and Gail L. Zellman, "Sexual Signaling and Sexual Aggression in Adolescent Relationships," in Neil M. Malamuth and Edward Donnerstein, eds., *Pornography and Sexual Aggression* (Orlando, Fla.: Academic Press, 1984), 233–43, at 236. In any event, "males have a more sexualized view of the world than females, attributing more sexual meaning to a wide range of behaviors" (239).

17. At least seven times in the policy and its introduction, it is stated that consent to sexual activity must be verbal. Only once does the policy depart from this formula: "the person with whom sexual contact/conduct is initiated is responsible to express verbally and/or physically her/his willingness or lack of willingness." Because the bulk of the policy insists that consent be verbal, I discount this one awkward and *possibly* contradictory sentence.

The policy also says, "If sexual contact . . . is *not* mutually and simultaneously initiated, then the person who initiates sexual contact . . . is responsible for getting the verbal consent of the other individuals(s) involved" (italics added). From the statement that when mutual and simultaneous initiation is absent, verbal consent is required, it does not follow (nor does the policy ever assert) that when mutual and simultaneous initiation is present, verbal consent can be dispensed with. To claim otherwise—that is, to deny on the basis of that sentence that the Antioch policy always requires verbal consent—is to commit an elementary logical fallacy. (I think this mistake is made by Eva Feder Kittay, "AH! My Foolish Heart: A Reply to Alan Soble's 'Antioch's "Sexual Offense Policy": A Philosophical Exploration,'" *Journal of Social Philosophy* 28, no. 2 [1997]: 153–59, at 154. See also note 25, below. [Kittay's essay is chapter 30 in this volume.]) At any rate, if we are to construe the Antioch policy as an interesting and novel approach to the problems we are discussing, we should not read it as asserting that "mutual and simultaneous initiation" cancels the need for verbal consent. The aroused and optimistic person who subjectively has no doubt that the other person is consenting, but is mistaken about that, is a version of the aroused and optimistic person who assumes that his initiation is reciprocated mutually and simultaneously by the other, but is similarly mistaken. Thus the good intentions of the Antioch policy would fall prey to the same psychological and moral delusions that undermine Belliotti's principle, "when in doubt, ask."

18. Perper and Weis, "Proceptive," 476.

19. For Lois Pineau, a man "cannot know, except through the practice of communicative sexuality, whether his partner has any sexual reason for continuing the encounter"—or any other reason for doing so ("Date Rape: A Feminist Analysis," *Law and Philosophy* 8 [1989]: 217–43, at 239). The essays in Leslie Francis's anthology *Date Rape* (University Park: Penn State University Press, 1996) explore both the Antioch policy and Pineau's essay. See also, on Antioch's policy, Bruno Leone, ed., *Rape on Campus* (San Diego, Calif.: Greenhaven Press, 1995).

20. Is a man's badgering a woman for sex "coercion"? Charlene Muehlenhard and Jennifer Schrag think so: "We define verbal sexual coercion as a woman's consenting to unwanted sexual activity because of a man's verbal arguments, not including verbal threats of physical force" ("Nonviolent Sexual Coercion," in Parrot and Bechhofer, *Acquaintance Rape*, 115–28, at 122). Muehlenhard and Schrag describe ways in which they think "women are coerced into having unwanted sexual intercourse," ways that are "more subtle" than being violently raped (115). Among the things listed that coerce women into unwanted sexual intercourse are "compulsory heterosexuality" (116–17), "status coercion" (119), "verbal sexual coercion" (122–23), and "discrimination against lesbians" (121). In agreement with Muehlenhard, Mary Koss uses the expression "sexually coercive men" to refer to those who obtain sex "after continual discussions and arguments" or by false avowals of love (Mary P. Koss and Kenneth E. Leonard, "Sexually Aggressive Men: Empirical Findings and Theoretical Implications," in Malamuth and Donnerstein, *Pornography and Sexual Aggression*, 213–232, at 216). For discussion, see Neil Gilbert, "Realities and Mythologies of Rape," *Society* (May/June 1992): 4–10, at 7; and Alan Wertheimer, "Consent and Sexual Relations," in this volume, chapter 19.

21. Pineau proposes that consensual sadomasochism be admissible by law, if "the court has a right to require that there be a system of signals whereby each partner can convey to the other whether she has had enough" ("Date Rape," 242). The safe words of consensual sadomasochism apparently fulfill the requirements of communicative sexuality (see her note 23).

22. Sarah Crichton, "Sexual Correctness: Has It Gone too Far?" in Susan J. Bunting, ed., *Human Sexuality 95/96* (Guilford, Conn.: Dushkin, 1995), 208–11, at 209.

23. Julia Reidhead, "Good Sex" [letter], *The New Yorker* (January 10, 1994), 8.

24. Antioch, however, does very little to make specific the "specific" of clause A4. Thus the policy is vulnerable to wisecracks. The scene is that *X* and *Y* are sitting on a couch, face-to-face.

X: May I kiss you?
Y. Of course. Go ahead.
[Y makes Y's mouth available; X slides X's tongue deeply into Y's oral cavity. Y pulls sharply away.]
Y: I didn't say you could *French* kiss me!

25. According to the Policy, "Consent must be clear and verbal (i.e., saying: yes, I want to kiss you also)."

26. Quoted by Jennifer Wolf, in "Sex By the Rules," *Glamour* (May 1994), 256–59, 290, at 258.

27. According to the Model Anti-Pornography Law drafted by Catharine MacKinnon and Andrea Dworkin (see "Symposium on Pornography: Appendix," *New England Law Review* 20, no. 4 [1984–85]: 759–77; sec. 3.1, 760), that a woman is or has been a prostitute outside of the making of an item of pornography means nothing in deciding whether she has been coerced into making this particular item of pornography. The historical fact of earlier or concurrent prostitution cannot be used as evidence by the defendant to show that her acts of prostitution in the making of this item of pornography were entered into by her free consent. The Model Law, in making history irrelevant, resembles the Antioch policy.

28. For St. Paul, see I Corinthians 7:4, "The wife hath not power of her own body, but the husband: and likewise also the husband hath not power of his own body, but the wife." And here is Immanuel Kant's definition of marriage: "Sexual union in accordance with principle is *marriage* (*matrimonium*), that is, the union of two persons of different sexes for lifelong possession of each other's sexual attributes" (*The Metaphysics of Morals* [1797], trans. Mary Gregor [Cambridge: Cambridge University Press, 1996], 62). For discussion of Kant on marriage, see my "Sexual Use," in this volume, 259–88, especially section 5, 278–82.

29. Pateman, "Women and Consent," 150.

30. Some teenagers (of both sexes) think that male anger and even assault are justified by a girl's apparently reneging on a sexual deal; see Goodchilds and Zellman, "Sexual Signaling," 237, 241–42.

31. Carolyn Shafer and Marilyn Frye, "Rape and Respect," in Mary Vetterling-Braggin et al., *Feminism and Philosophy*, 333–46, at 342.

32. Pope Paul VI makes the same point: "It is in fact justly observed that a conjugal act imposed upon one's partner without regard for his or her condition and lawful desires is not a true act of love, and therefore denies an exigency of right moral order in the relationships between husband and wife" ("Humanae Vitae," in Robert Baker and Frederick Elliston, eds., *Philosophy and Sex*, 2nd ed. [Buffalo, N.Y.: Prometheus, 1984], 167–83, at 173).

Chapter 30

AH! MY FOOLISH HEART:
A REPLY TO ALAN SOBLE'S
"ANTIOCH'S 'SEXUAL OFFENSE
POLICY': A PHILOSOPHICAL
EXPLORATION"

Eva Feder Kittay

*Alan Soble read an early version of his "Antioch's 'Sexual Offense Policy':
A Philosophical Exploration" (chapter 29) at the Eastern Division meetings of the American Philosophical Association on December 30, 1995; it
was later published in the* Journal of Social Philosophy. *At the APA
meeting,* **Eva Feder Kittay** *was the commentator; she, too, published her
talk in the same journal. In this lively rejoinder, Kittay defends the Antioch policy against the "pleasure," "body talk," and "consent" objections
raised by Soble.*

Kittay is professor of philosophy at the Stony Brook campus of the State University of
New York. She is the editor of *The Subject of Care: Feminist Perspectives on Depen-
dency* (with Ellen K. Feder; Rowman & Littlefield, 2002) and the *Blackwell Guide to
Feminist Philosophy* (with Linda Alcoff; Blackwell, 2006).

"AH! My Foolish Heart: A Reply to Alan Soble's 'Antioch's "Sexual Offense Policy"':
A Philosophical Exploration,'" *Journal of Social Philosophy* 28, no. 2 (1997):
153–59. Reprinted with the permission of Eva Feder Kittay and Blackwell Publishing,
Oxford, UK.

A sexual code occupies an uneasy position at the intersection of the public and private, the communal and intimate, the codifiable and spontaneous, the articulate and ineffable. And sexual conduct is located at the troubling interface of pleasure and offense; passion and power; freedom and submission; desire as an individual drive and desire as the epiphany of mutuality—the desiring of the other's desire. How do we regulate sexual conduct? How can any code legislate sexual desire or successfully thwart abusive sexuality? Here the wise say that only fools do tread. Since Antioch announced its "Sexual Offense Policy," Antioch has, in the eyes of the media and some retro (and not so retro) feminists and academics, worn a dunce cap. Is it well deserved?

After a clear, and seemingly sympathetic, discussion of the code that includes much of the motivation for the policy, Alan Soble weighs in with the wise. On three grounds: pleasure, body talk, and consent.[1]

Upon first learning of the "Sexual Offense Policy," my romantic heart declared this was a silly, foolish code—though my feminist mind urged a more cautious judgment. To have to verbally consent to each level (and just what is a level anyway?) of sexual intimacy? each time? even with a partner with whom one had been intimate many times before? Many of us lose the capacity of articulate speech at these moments. Are we to be deprived of our hearts' desire since, unlike Molly Bloom, we don't utter an ecstatic "Yes! yes! yes!" at the appropriate moment?

Reading the harrowing accounts of date rapes recounted by Robin Warshaw,[2] I kept wondering if a code such as Antioch's would help in any of these cases. And if it would not, what *was* the point? Being on sabbatical, I was unable to canvass my classes for the student point of view. Fortunately, I had some private college-aged informants, my twenty-year-old son, his girlfriend (whom I questioned separately), and their friends. I also queried colleagues who had discussed the code with their students. There seemed to be a rather interesting response that came up again and again: "The code is silly, but I wouldn't mind it being there. It would be a way of opening up discussion on these issues." Only one young man I spoke to said it would encourage him to only have sex with himself—he always would know that the answer was "yes."

Taking a closer look at the code, I noticed some interesting phrases that are omitted in Alan Soble's summary. In the seven-point discussion of consent, the first point justifies Soble's claim that "verbal 'yes' . . . is Antioch's Cartesian foundation":[3]

1. For the purpose of this policy, "consent" shall be defined as follows: "the act of willingly and verbally agreeing to engage in a specific sexual contact or conduct."[4]

And yet the next point has an antecedent clause that implies that verbal consent is not *always* demanded:

> 2. If sexual contact and/or conduct is not mutually and simultaneously initiated, then the person who initiates sexual contact/conduct is responsible for getting the verbal consent of the other individual(s) involved.[5]

"*If* sexual contact and/or conduct is *not mutually* and *simultaneously* initiated . . ." So, if my partner and I simultaneously are seized with the desire to kiss, we don't need to say a thing as our mouths spontaneously move toward each other. And if I am as passionately unbuttoning my partner and my partner unbuttons me, we can both remain undisturbed in our inarticulate bliss.

Therefore, contrary to Soble's reading, we are not always obliged to obtain verbal consent, not forced to "mix the pleasures of language with the pleasures of the body"[6] *if* the sex is mutually initiated.

Now consider the fourth point:

> 4. The person with whom sexual contact/conduct is initiated is responsible to express verbally and/or *physically* his/her willingness or lack of willingness when *reasonably* possible (emphasis mine).[7]

To express verbally or *physically* willingness or unwillingness, when *reasonably* possible. Aha! If the initiator asks, I can respond physically, I don't have to utter "yes" or even moan. And if the noninitiator is in a swoon of delight and tongue-tiedness, the whole sexual encounter can go on with a minimal amount of question and answer. But, if there is any ambiguity at all, the code protects both the noninitiator and the initiator alike by defining responsibilities for each.

Now this begins to sound less absurd. Under the heading of "Body Talk" Soble writes: "According to the policy, a verbal 'yes' replaces all bodily movements as the only reliable sign that proceeding with sex is permissible. If I ask, 'may I kiss you?' I may not proceed on the basis of your bodily reply, e.g., you push your mouth out at mine and open it invitingly. . . ."[8] A verbal yes may be the only fully *reliable* sign, but it's not at all clear from the passages cited above that the code *proscribes* sex based on such "body talk," or that it construes heeding (affirmative) body talk—in limited and unambiguous circumstances—as sexual offense.

Soble furthermore insists that the verbal "yes" is only a yes after sufficient probing. The probing requirement isn't explicit in the code, but arises from the possibility that women, because of their socialization to be cooperative and nonconfrontational, may say "yes" when they mean "no." Rather than explicitly calling for the sort of probing Soble envisions, the code sets out a clear set of responsibilities for both initiator and noninitiator: The initiator is responsible for obtaining verbal consent;

the noninitiator is responsible for responding verbally or physically whenever possible, As Soble points out, this privileges the physical withdrawal over the physical assent since consent is, both by definition and by explicit statement, verbal. But it also opens the window, when there is no ambiguity in the situation, for the sexual activity to respond to body talk.

Two things are learned from considering the passages omitted in Soble's summary.

First: There are allowances for the body language so often more in tune with the heightened sexual state than articulate speech. Perhaps this is a contradiction in the policy. Or perhaps the policy only starts to make sense in a context where there is a great deal of discussion that helps to clarify its intent and purpose.

Second: The noninitiator has a responsibility in this interaction, along with the initiator. A young woman socialized in a stereotypical feminine way has a responsibility to work her way out of such constricting socializing influences. If the policy is more educative and preventative than proscriptive and punitivie, as it declares itself to be, "The educational aspects of this policy are intended to prevent sexual offenses and ultimately to heighten community awareness,"[9] then this code serves to encourage previously unassertive partners to be more assertive and to encourage overly assertive partners to rein in their overbearing behavior. Rather than undermining autonomy and acting paternalistically in loco parentis, Antioch encourages autonomy in the form of more responsible and responsive sexuality.

These considerations mark a considerable change in my first reaction to the Antioch code. The clincher came when I located Antioch College on a websurfing night and read the home page addressed to prospective students: "Antioch believes it should be a single cohesive community based on principles of democracy and citizenship. . . . Because Antioch students are considered equal members of the community, they participate in major decision-making committees at the College and have responsibility for student organizations and activities on campus." Although many student handbooks read like this, Antioch has always had a very strong tradition of taking such words seriously. As Alan Guskin, President of Antioch at the time the policy was first formulated, writes,[10] and as discussions with Antioch alumnae confirmed,[11] the policy was arrived at through intensive campus discussion among students and faculty. Even more significant, the code is reviewed each year and each year students elect whether to retain it, modify it, or discard it.

This contextualization of the code is, I believe, crucial to evaluating it. If this policy were handed down from on high by the administration to a reluctant student body that had to puzzle its way through the sorts of unclarities and paradoxes Soble highlights, then I would continue to

[handwritten margin note: Antioch comes from a very liberal community]

share his skepticism. Likewise, if this policy were to be adopted outside of a specific and close community in which the code serves as a prod to discussing consensual sex, then again, we should be swayed by Soble's arguments. Although there is a sense in which the policy is, as Matthew Silliman declares in the title of an article, "a community experiment in communicative sexuality,"[12] the policy is also a product of an understanding of a *particular* community. How does contextualizing the policy to the Antioch community help?

Consider first the question of pleasure. Those who mutually initiate sex, at all levels, can have pleasure non-interruptus. But when one initiates sex, then a verbal consent is necessary. Can the verbal question and the consent be less intrusive to the romance than it seems at first? Soble says no, because sexy speech (as MacKinnon likes to remind us) is already sex. So either we have a non-sexy way of asking or we have an infinite regress. When I raised this point with the president of the Alumni Association, he responded that the permissibility of making the request a part of the sexual encounter is part of the social contract which established the code in the first place. That is to say, in the numerous workshops and discussions around the policy, the permissibility of this initiatory level of sexual contact is established. It forms part of the background condition and is not explicitly stated in the code.[13] Take the Antioch out of "Antioch's Sexual Offense Policy" and you have a different policy. Of course, this understanding of the policy leaves the door open to a lascivious and unwanted sexual invitation of, say, a faculty member to a student. Such a sexual invitation/question has all the power imbalances in place that can, at worst, make refusal difficult, and, at best, be shocking and highly offensive to the more vulnerable party. Such a possibility exposes a limitation of the policy and the need for more than a code to ensure fully consensual sex. But it doesn't vitiate the usefulness of the code.[14]

Second, consider the question of "body talk." We have already seen that in the situation in which all partners are mutually initiating at all points in the encounter, they can speak, moan, groan, or remain silent—as long as everything is completely clear to both. For the rest of the cases, Soble argues that not only do we have to ask and reply, but the initiator has to probe for a sincere "yes." This, he suggests, is because the Antioch policy does not sufficiently respect the ways in which the body talks, not only in sexual affairs, but in all matters. This argument is premised on a sexual scenario of a "yes" meaning a "no," one common enough. Soble directs us to a Texas A&M study in which 39 percent of college women polled indicated that they have offered token "resistance" when they *intended* to engage in sex.[15] However, within a community that affirms the sexual offense policy in question each year anew, where the policy becomes the prod to open discussion of matters sexual, and where the responsibility for learning to say no when you mean no is understood as part of the educative purpose of the code, the probing is *de trop*. The demand for verbal consent is not about a disregard for body talk (when affirmative) but about setting forth the conditions for a communication sufficiently *unambiguous* to minimize the dangers and harm of date rape. So contextualized, Soble's claim that "the robust respect that Antioch's policy fosters for a woman's 'no' is offset by the weaker respect it fosters for her 'yes'" is false.

Finally let us consider the question of consent. It is true that "Antioch cuts back on a traditional power of consent, its ability to apply to an indefinite, open future."[16] But perhaps that is just right, when it comes to matters of sexual desire. A Pauline marriage, after all, makes marital rape an oxymoron, and any woman who has been raped by her husband will tell you that there is nothing oxymoronic about her trauma. Antioch's policy, however, is not meant to govern long-term relationships or marriages, Pauline or otherwise. In the context of the Antioch College, the code applies to an undergraduate population that does not, in general, have many long-term relationships. Probably most sexual encounters are first-, second-, third-time contacts.[17] It is to these transient relations that the policy is directed. In this context it is inappropriate to think that consent applies to "an indefinite, open future." This is not to say that a marriage or long-term relation in which one could not make a transition from "assume 'no' unless you get a 'yes'" to "assume 'yes' unless you get a 'no'" would be a sad affair.

Soble, however, raises a more difficult issue with respect to consent. He points out that Antioch cuts back on the power of consent by making it not binding: I agree to have so much sex with you and while halfway through I change my mind and want you to stop. Am I immoral? Is the policy fostering the immorality of the tease in countering the immorality of the rapist? If I agree to a sexual act in bad faith, then I am a tease. But if I agree in good faith, and if in the midst of the experience I find it unpleasant or unexciting and so ask my partner to stop, I am not *teasing* but responding to something important to my own self-respect. To continue sex past the point of my own desiring is to experience myself as a mere object for another's use. "But," says my partner, "you consented and you are obliged to let me continue." Why doesn't that work? There is a feature of sexuality that is not amenable to a notion of consent. Consent within policies or codes are generally understood through the model of contract: I voluntarily agree to a specified such and such, and you forming your expectations based on the agreement hold me to the contractual terms.

The contractual model, however, is inappropriate in many intimate domains. Consent in these contexts is less an agreement binding into the future that will override itinerant desires than the expression of a willing, wanting, desiring self that seeks fulfillment with and through another. So-called "surrogate mothering" falls into this category. If a birth mother gives up the child she has born as a gift, that is one thing; if she gives it up for payment, that is quite another. A contractual relation demands the action of an agreed-to giving, whether or not the desire to give continues to be present at the moment, past the time the contract is signed. If I promise you a gift and don't deliver on the promise, I will disappoint you, but you will not have a claim on that gift. While you can accuse me of breaking my promise, you cannot make a claim to that gift. The strong sense that surrogacy ought not to be bound to contract in the same way other transactions are arises from the nature of the act as a gift, that is a giving to which we attach a desire to give another satisfaction through our own actions. Sexual contact has a similar nature. If the sexual contact is not desired at that moment, then one makes of oneself a sexual object and not a sexual agent. One makes oneself into a thing, and the other who insists on the sexual act makes of the partner a means only, a means to one's own pleasure regardless of the desire of the partner.

Barbara Herman in a fascinating article argues that Kant's view of sexuality is remarkably akin to that of some radical feminists, in particular, Andrea Dworkin and MacKinnon. Kant's resolution to the problem of sexual love, which makes of the other an object of one's own sexual desire without regard to human nature but to sex alone, is marriage:

> The sole condition on which we are free to make use of our sexual desire depends upon the right to dispose over the person as a whole—over the welfare and happiness and generally over all the circumstances of that person . . . [I obtain these rights over the whole person (and so have the right of sexual use of that person)] only by giving the person the same rights over myself.[18]

But why not say instead: A sexual encounter with another, which has the recognition of the other's desire (and so the other's sexual agency) as a *sine qua non*, is the sole way in which we can engage in sex without reducing the other to an object—whether in marriage or in a one-night stand. In that case, consent cannot be understood on the contractual model, but on a model of mutual desiring, a desiring which must be alive at each moment. This, I believe, stands behind the model of communicative sex as better sex that is advocated by Lois Pineau.[19] To the extent that the Antioch policy's demand for consent is understood contractually, it will be a limitation of the policy. But if the policy is used as an educative tool, accompanied by discussion about its meaning and intent, then it can serve to instruct and train young persons for sexual encounters that promote mutuality and respect. In so doing, it can foster both good sex and the autonomy of the one who initiates and the one who responds.

Now I have made a full 180-degree turnabout from my first reactions to the policy. Of course, it seems that some things might be lost: That surprise (not yet consented to) touch that thrills beyond measure; the awakening of ardor through a kiss by someone who never before moved you; and doubtless much else. Then again it would also be fun to drive without seatbelts and road signs, and with only a watchful eye. But even with the road signs there are too many car accidents. Best to keep the seatbelts on.

Maybe the policy seen in context is not so foolish after all. And perhaps it reaches me that I do well to listen to my feminist mind before allowing my foolish heart the last word.

Study Questions

1. Kittay claims that verbal consent is not required, according to the Antioch policy, when the sexual interaction is mutually and simultaneously initiated. How often does that happen, or is it abundantly likely that one person makes a beginning overture to the another?

2. What are the disagreements between Soble (chapter 29) and Kittay on what the Antioch policy states? Are these disagreements important or trivial to the main issues they discuss? See, especially, notes 17 and 25 in Soble's essay.

3. Why does Kittay go with her "head" instead of her "foolish" heart? Does her view pose a problem for that strain in feminist epistemology that attributes to women's emotions a distinct and crucial cognitive role?

4. Kittay claims that the Antioch policy was meant to apply only to brief or short-term sexual liaisons, that is, casual if not promiscuous sexual activity on college campuses. If true, does this fact make you take Antioch's policy less seriously, more seriously, or neither?

5. Some critics of campus sex policies think that such policies are patronizing toward students and paternalistic, undercut student autonomy, and infantalize especially women students. Do you share any of these worries? Why or why not?

Notes

This paper was first delivered as a commentary to Alan Soble's "Antioch's 'Sexual Offense Policy': A Philosophical Exploration," Dec. 1995, at the Eastern Division APA Meetings.

1. Alan Soble, "Antioch's 'Sexual Offense Policy': A Philosophical Exploration," *Journal of Social Philosophy* 28, no. 1 (Spring 1997): 22–36. Reprinted as chapter 29, in this volume. All quotations and page references are to the 1997 original.

2. Robin Warshaw, *I Never Called It Rape: The Ms. Report on Recognizing, Fighting and Surviving Date Rape* (New York: Harper & Row, 1988).

3. Soble, "Antioch," 27.

4. Antioch College, "The Antioch College Sexual Offense Policy," in *Date Rape: Feminism, Philosophy, and the Law,* ed. Leslie Francis (University Park: Pennsylvania University Press, 1992), 135–154, at 140.

5. Antioch, "Policy," 140.

6. Soble, "Antioch," 28.

7. Antioch, "Policy," 140.

8. Soble, "Antioch," 29.

9. Antioch, "Policy," 139.

10. Alan E. Guskin, "The Antioch Response: Sex, You Just Don't Talk About It," in Francis, *Date Rape: Feminism, Philosophy, and the Law,* 155–66.

11. My discussions included one with Eric Bates, president of Antioch's Alumni Association.

12. "The Antioch Policy, a Community Experiment in Communicative Sexuality" in Francis, *Date Rape: Feminism, Philosophy, and the Law,* 167–76.

13. Personal Communication with Eric Bates.

14. There is, however, a clause in the "Consent" discussion which covers situations of intimidation and coercion used for obtaining the verbal consent: "7. If someone verbally agrees to engage in specific contact or conduct, but it is not of her/his own free will due to any of the circumstances stated in (a) through (d) below, then the person initiating shall be considered in violation of this policy if: . . . (d) the person initiating has forced, threatened, coerced, or intimidated the other individual(s) into engaging in sexual contact and/or sexual conduct." Antioch College, "The Antioch College Sexual Offense Policy," in Francis, *Date Rape: Feminism, Philosophy, and the Law,* 141.

15. This study is cited in Soble, "Antioch," 24.

16. Soble, 31.

17. This point is emphasized in Guskin, "Antioch Response," 1996.

18. Kant, *Lectures on Ethics,* p. 167, quoted in Barbara Herman, "Could It Be Worth Thinking about Kant on Sex and Marriage?" in Anthony and Witt, eds., *A Mind of One's Own: Feminist Essays on Reason and Objectivity* (Boulder: Westview Press, 1993, p. 60.

19. Lois Pineau, "Date Rape: A Feminist Analysis," in Francis, *Date Rape: Feminism, Philosophy, and the Law,* 1–26.

SUGGESTED READINGS

General

Abramson, Paul R., and Steven D. Pinkerton, eds. *Sexual Nature/Sexual Culture.* Chicago: University of Chicago Press, 1995.

Alexander, W. M. "Philosophers Have Avoided Sex." *Diogenes* 72 (Winter 1970): 56–74. Reprinted in *The Philosophy of Sex,* edited by Alan Soble, 3–19. 2nd ed. Savage, Md.: Rowman & Littlefield, 1991.

———. "Sex and Philosophy in Augustine." *Augustinian Studies* 5 (1974): 197–208.

Ariès, Philippe, and André Béjin, eds. *Western Sexuality: Practice and Precept in Past and Present Times.* New York: Blackwell, 1985.

Atkinson, Ronald. *Sexual Morality.* London: Hutchinson, 1965.

Atkinson, Ti-Grace. *Amazon Odyssey.* New York: Links Books, 1974.

Baker, Robert, and Frederick Elliston, eds. *Philosophy and Sex.* 1st ed. Buffalo, N.Y.: Prometheus, 1975. 2nd ed. 1984.

Baker, Robert B., Kathleen J. Wininger, and Frederick A. Elliston, eds. *Philosophy and Sex.* 3rd ed. Amherst, N.Y.: Prometheus, 1998.

Beemyn, Brett, and Mickey Eliason, eds. *Queer Studies: A Lesbian, Gay, Bisexual, and Transgender Anthology.* New York: New York University Press, 1996.

Belliotti, Raymond. *Good Sex: Perspectives on Sexual Ethics.* Lawrence: University Press of Kansas, 1993.

Blackburn, Simon. *Lust: The Seven Deadly Sins.* New York: Oxford University Press, 2004.

Brundage, James A. *Law, Sex, and Christian Society in Medieval Europe.* Chicago: University of Chicago Press, 1987.

Bullough, Vern L., and Bonnie Bullough. *Sexual Attitudes: Myths and Realities.* Amherst, N.Y.: Prometheus, 1995.

Bullough, Vern L., and Bonnie Bullough, eds. *Human Sexuality: An Encyclopedia.* New York: Garland, 1994.

Buss, David M. *The Evolution of Desire.* New York: Basic Books, 1994.

Califia, Pat. *Public Sex: The Culture of Radical Sex.* Pittsburgh, Pa.: Cleis Press, 1994.

Carr, David. "Freud and Sexual Ethics." *Philosophy* 62, no. 241 (1987): 361–73.

Colker, Ruth. "Feminism, Sexuality, and Authenticity." In *At the Boundaries of Law,* edited by Martha A. Fineman and Nancy S. Thomadsen, 135–47. New York: Routledge, 1991.

———. "Feminism, Sexuality, and Self: A Preliminary Inquiry into the Politics of Authenticity." *Boston University Law Review* 68, no. 1 (1988): 217–64.

Davis, Murray. *Smut: Erotic Reality/Obscene Ideology.* Chicago: University of Chicago Press, 1983.

Devine, Philip E., and Celia Wolf-Devine, eds. *Sex and Gender: A Spectrum of Views.* Belmont, Calif.: Wadsworth, 2003.

Diamond, Jared. *Why Is Sex Fun? The Evolution of Human Sexuality.* New York: Basic Books, 1997.

Duggan, Lisa, and Nan D. Hunter. *Sex Wars: Sexual Dissent and Political Culture.* New York: Routledge, 1995.

Dworkin, Andrea. *Intercourse.* New York: Free Press, 1987.

Eadie, Jo, ed. *Sexuality: The Essential Glossary.* London: Arnold, 2004.

English, Deirdre, Amber Hollibaugh, and Gayle Rubin. "Talking Sex: A Conversation on Sexuality and Feminism." *Socialist Review* 11, no. 4 (1981): 43–62.

Epstein, Louis M. *Sex Laws and Customs in Judaism.* New York: Ktav, 1967. First published 1948.

Farley, Margaret. "Sexual Ethics." In *Encyclopedia of Bioethics,* edited by Warren Reich, 2365–75. Revised ed., vol. 5. New York: Simon & Schuster Macmillan, 1995.

Feder, Ellen K., Karmen MacKendrick, and Sybol S. Cook, eds. *A Passion for Wisdom: Readings in Western Philosophy on Love and Desire.* Upper Saddle River, N.J.: Prentice Hall, 2004.

Firestone, Shulamith. *The Dialectic of Sex: The Case for Feminist Revolution.* New York: Bantam Books, 1970.

Foucault, Michel. *The Care of the Self.* Vol. 3, *The History of Sexuality.* New York: Vintage, 1986.

———. *An Introduction.* Vol. 1, *The History of Sexuality.* New York: Vintage, 1976.

———. *The Use of Pleasure.* Vol. 2, *The History of Sexuality.* New York: Pantheon, 1985.

Fuchs, Eric. *Sexual Desire and Love: Origins and History of the Christian Ethic of Sexuality and Marriage.* Translated by Marsha Daigle. New York: Seabury, 1983.

Garry, Ann. "Why Are Love and Sex Philosophically Interesting?" *Metaphilosophy* 11, no. 2 (1980): 165–77.

Gilbert, Paul. *Human Relationships: A Philosophical Introduction.* Oxford, UK: Blackwell, 1991.

Gruen, Lori, and George F. Panichas, eds. *Sex, Morality, and the Law.* New York: Routledge, 1997.

Gudorf, Christine E. *Body, Sex, and Pleasure: Reconstructing Christian Sexual Ethics.* Cleveland, Ohio: Pilgrim Press, 1994.

Hunter, J. F. M. *Thinking about Sex and Love.* New York: St. Martin's, 1980.

Irigaray, Luce. *This Sex Which Is Not One.* Translated by Catherine Porter. Ithaca, N.Y.: Cornell University Press, 1985. First published 1977.

Jackson, Stevi, and Sue Scott, eds. *Feminism and Sexuality: A Reader.* New York: Columbia University Press, 1996.

Jeffreys, Sheila. *Anticlimax: A Feminist Perspective on the Sexual Revolution.* New York: New York University Press, 1990.

Jordan, Mark D. *The Ethics of Sex.* Oxford, UK: Blackwell, 2002.

Jung, Patricia Beattie, Mary E. Hunt, and Radhika Balakrishnan, eds. *Good Sex: Feminist Perspectives from the World's Religions.* New Brunswick, N.J.: Rutgers University Press, 2001.

Kalbian, Aline. *Sexing the Church: Gender, Power, and Contemporary Catholic Ethics.* Bloomington: Indiana University Press, 2005.

Kuefler, Mathew, ed. *The History of Sexuality Sourcebook.* Peterborough, Ont.: Broadview Press, 2007.

Laqueur, Thomas. *Making Sex: Body and Gender from the Greeks to Freud.* Cambridge, Mass.: Harvard University Press, 1990.

Laumann, Edward O., John H. Gagnon, Robert T. Michael, and Stuart Michaels. *The Social Organization of Sexuality: Sexual Practices in the United States.* Chicago: University of Chicago Press, 1994.

Lebacqz, Karen, ed., with David Sinacore-Guinn. *Sexuality: A Reader.* Cleveland, Ohio: Pilgrim Press, 1999.

Leidholdt, Dorchen, and Janice C. Raymond, eds. *The Sexual Liberals and the Attack on Feminism.* New York: Teachers College Press, 1990.

LeMoncheck, Linda. *Loose Women, Lecherous Men: A Feminist Philosophy of Sex.* New York: Oxford University Press, 1997.

MacKinnon, Catharine A. *Feminism Unmodified: Discourses on Life and Law.* Cambridge, Mass.: Harvard University Press, 1987.

Maglin, Nan Bauer, and Donna Perry, eds. *"Bad Girls"/"Good Girls": Women, Sex, and Power in the Nineties.* New Brunswick, N.J.: Rutgers University Press, 1996.

Marcuse, Herbert. *Eros and Civilization: A Philosophical Inquiry into Freud.* Boston: Beacon Press, 1966. First published 1955.

Marietta, Don E., Jr. *Philosophy of Sexuality.* Armonk, N.Y.: M. E. Sharpe, 1997.

Money, John. *The Adam Principle: Genes, Genitals, Hormones, and Gender: Selected Readings in Sexology.* Buffalo, N.Y.: Prometheus, 1993.

Nagel, Thomas. *Concealment and Exposure and Other Essays.* Oxford, U.K.: Oxford University Press, 2002.

Nelson, James B. *Embodiment: An Approach to Sexuality and Christian Theology.* Minneapolis, Minn.: Augsburg, 1978.

Nelson, James B., and Sandra P. Longfellow, eds. *Sexuality and the Sacred: Sources for Theological Reflection.* Louisville, Ky.: Westminster John Knox, 1994.

Nozick, Robert. "Sexuality." In *The Examined Life*, 61–67. New York: Simon & Schuster, 1989.

Nye, Robert A., ed. *Sexuality.* Oxford, UK: Oxford University Press, 1999.

Pagels, Elaine. *Adam, Eve, and the Serpent.* New York: Vintage, 1988.

Paglia, Camille. *Sexual Personae: Art and Decadence from Nefertiti to Emily Dickinson.* New Haven, Conn.: Yale University Press, 1990.

Posner, Richard A. *Sex and Reason.* Cambridge, Mass.: Harvard University Press, 1992.

Primoratz, Igor. *Ethics and Sex.* London: Routledge, 1999.

——, ed. *Human Sexuality.* Aldershot, UK: Dartmouth, 1997.

Punzo, Vincent. *Reflective Naturalism: An Introduction to Moral Philosophy.* New York: Macmillan, 1969.

Radakovich, Anka. *Sexplorations: Journeys to the Erogenous Frontier.* New York: Crown, 1997.

Ranke-Heinemann, Uta. *Eunuchs for the Kingdom of Heaven: Women, Sexuality and the Catholic Church.* New York: Penguin, 1990.

Reeve, C. D. C. *Love's Confusions.* Cambridge, Mass.: Harvard University Press, 2005.

Richter, Alan. *Dictionary of Sexual Slang*. New York: John Wiley & Sons, 1993.

Robinson, Paul. *The Freudian Left: Wilhelm Reich, Geza Roheim, Herbert Marcuse*. New York: Harper and Row, 1969.

———. *The Modernization of Sex: Havelock Ellis, Alfred Kinsey, William Masters and Virginia Johnson*. New York: Harper and Row, 1976.

Rogers, Eugene F. Jr., ed. *Theology and Sexuality: Classic and Contemporary Readings*. Oxford, UK: Blackwell, 2002.

Rubin, Gayle S. "Thinking Sex: Notes for a Radical Theory of the Politics of Sexuality." In *Pleasure and Danger: Exploring Female Sexuality*, edited by Carole S. Vance, 267–319. London: Routledge and Kegan Paul, 1984.

Rubin, Lillian B. *Erotic Wars: What Happened to the Sexual Revolution?* New York: Farrar, Straus and Giroux, 1990.

Russell, Bertrand. *Marriage and Morals*. London: Allen and Unwin, 1929.

Scruton, Roger. *Sexual Desire: A Moral Philosophy of the Erotic*. New York: Free Press, 1986.

Seidman, Steven. *Embattled Eros*. New York: Routledge, 1992.

Shelp, Earl E., ed. *Conceptual Roots*. Vol. 1, *Sexuality and Medicine*. Dordrecht: Reidel, 1987.

———. *Ethical Viewpoints in Transition*. Vol. 2, *Sexuality and Medicine*. Dordrecht: Reidel, 1987.

Singer, Irving. *The Goals of Human Sexuality*. New York: Schocken Books, 1973.

———. *Sex: A Philosophical Primer*. Lanham, Md.: Rowman & Littlefield, 2001.

Soble, Alan. "Philosophy of Sex." In *Encyclopedia of Philosophy*, edited by Donald Borchert, 521–32. 2nd ed., vol. 7. New York: Macmillan/Thomson, 2006.

———. *The Philosophy of Sex and Love: An Introduction*. St. Paul, Minn.: Paragon House, 1998.

———. *Sexual Investigations*. New York: New York University Press, 1996.

———, ed. *Eros, Agape, and Philia*. St. Paul, Minn.: Paragon House, 1989. Reprinted 1999.

———, ed. *Sex from Plato to Paglia: A Philosophical Encyclopedia*. Westport, Conn.: Greenwood, 2006.

———, ed. *The Philosophy of Sex: Contemporary Readings*. 1st ed. Totowa, N.J.: Rowman & Littlefield, 1980. 2nd ed., Savage, Md.: Rowman & Littlefield, 1991. 3rd ed., Lanham, Md.: Rowman & Littlefield, 1997. 4th ed., Lanham, Md.: Rowman & Littlefield, 2002.

———, ed. *Sex, Love, and Friendship*. Amsterdam: Rodopi, 1997.

Solomon, Lewis D. *The Jewish Tradition, Sexuality, and Procreation*. Lanham, Md.: University Press of America, 2002.

Solomon, Robert C., and Kathleen M. Higgins, eds. *The Philosophy of (Erotic) Love*. Lawrence: University Press of Kansas, 1991.

Stafford, J. Martin. *Essays on Sexuality and Ethics*. Solihull, UK: Ismeron, 1995.

Stein, Edward, ed. *Forms of Desire*. New York: Routledge, 1992.

Stewart, Robert M., ed. *Philosophical Perspectives on Sex and Love*. New York: Oxford University Press, 1995.

Stimpson, Catharine R., and Ethel Spector Person, eds. *Women: Sex and Sexuality*. Chicago: University of Chicago Press, 1980.

Stuart, Elizabeth, and Adrian Thatcher, eds. *Christian Perspectives on Sexuality and Gender*. Grand Rapids, Mich.: Eerdmans, 1996.

Swidler, Arlene, ed. *Homosexuality and World Religions.* Valley Forge, Pa.: Trinity Press, 1993.

Thurber, James, and E. B. White. *Is Sex Necessary?* New York: Harper and Brothers, 1929.

Tiefer, Leonore. (1995) *Sex Is Not a Natural Act and Other Essays.* 2nd ed. Boulder, Colo.: Westview, 2004.

Trevas, Robert, Arthur Zucker, and Donald Borchert, eds. *Philosophy of Sex and Love: A Reader.* Upper Saddle River, N.J.: Prentice-Hall, 1997.

Vance, Carole S., ed. *Pleasure and Danger: Exploring Female Sexuality.* London: Routledge and Kegan Paul, 1984.

Verene, Donald, ed. *Sexual Love and Western Morality.* 1st ed. New York: Harper and Row, 1972. 2nd ed. Boston: Jones and Bartlett, 1995.

Weeks, Jeffrey. *Invented Moralities: Sexual Values in an Age of Uncertainty.* New York: Columbia University Press, 1995.

———. *Sexuality and Its Discontents.* London: Routledge and Kegan Paul, 1985.

Weeks, Jeffrey, and Janet Holland, eds. *Sexual Cultures: Communities, Values and Intimacy.* New York: St. Martin's, 1996.

Whiteley, C. H., and Winifred M. Whiteley. *Sex and Morals.* New York: Basic Books, 1967.

Wilson, Edward O. "Sex." In *On Human Nature,* 125–54. Cambridge, Mass.: Harvard University Press, 1978.

Wilson, John. *Love, Sex, and Feminism: A Philosophical Essay.* New York: Praeger, 1980.

Wojtyla, Karol [Pope John Paul II]. *Love and Responsibility.* New York: Farrar, Straus and Giroux, 1981.

Conceptual Analysis

Benn, Piers. "Is Sex Morally Special?" *Journal of Applied Philosophy* 16, no. 3 (1999): 235–45.

Boswell, John. "Revolutions, Universals, and Sexual Categories." *Salmagundi* nos. 58–59 (Fall 1982/Winter 1983), 89–113.

De Cecco, John P. "Definition and Meaning of Sexual Orientation." *Journal of Homosexuality* 6, no. 4 (1981): 51–67.

Diorio, Joseph A. "Feminist-constructionist Theories of Sexuality and the Definition of Sex Education." *Educational Philosophy and Theory* 21, no. 2 (1989): 23–31.

Farrell, Daniel M. "Jealousy." *Philosophical Review* 89, no. 4 (October 1980): 527–59.

———. "Jealousy and Desire." In *Love Analyzed* edited by Roger E. Lamb, 165–88. Boulder, Colo.: Westview, 1997.

Fausto-Sterling, Anne. *Sexing the Body: Gender Politics and the Construction of Sexuality.* New York: Basic Books, 2000.

Frye, Marilyn. "Lesbian 'Sex.'" In *Willful Virgin: Essays in Feminism 1976–1992,* 109–19. Freedom, Calif.: Crossing Press, 1992.

Giles, James. *The Nature of Sexual Desire.* Westport, Conn.: Praeger, 2004.

———. "Sartre, Sexual Desire, and Relations with Others." In *French Existentialism: Consciousness, Ethics, and Relations with Others,* edited by James Giles, 155–73. Amsterdam: Rodopi, 1999.

———. "A Theory of Love and Sexual Desire." *Journal for the Theory of Social Behavior* 24, no. 4 (1995): 339–57.

Gray, Robert. "Sex and Sexual Perversion." *Journal of Philosophy* 75, no. 4 (1978): 189–99.

Jacobsen, Rockney. "Arousal and the Ends of Desire." *Philosophy and Phenomenological Research* 53, no. 3 (1993): 617–32.

Klein, Fritz, Barry Sepekoff, and Timothy Wolf. "Sexual Orientation: A Multi-Variable Dynamic Process." *Journal of Homosexuality* 11, nos. 1–2 (1985): 35–50.

Koertge, Noretta. "Constructing Concepts of Sexuality: A Philosophical Commentary." In *Homosexuality/Heterosexuality: Concepts of Sexual Orientation*, edited by David McWhirter, Stephanie Sanders, and June Reinisch, 387–97. New York: Oxford University Press, 1990.

Martin, Christopher F. J. "Are There Virtues and Vices That Belong Specifically to the Sexual Life?" *Acta Philosophica* 4, no. 2 (1995): 205–21.

Moore, Gareth. "Sexual Needs and Sexual Pleasures." *International Philosophical Quarterly* 35, no. 2 (1995): 193–204.

Morgan, Seiriol. "Sex in the Head." *Journal of Applied Philosophy* 20, no. 1 (2003): 1–16.

Padgug, Robert. "Sexual Matters: On Conceptualizing Sexuality in History." *Radical History Review* 20 (Spring/Summer 1979): 3–23.

Randall, Hilary E., and E. Sandra Byers. "What Is Sex? Students' Definitions of Having Sex, Sexual Partner, and Unfaithful Sexual Behaviour." *Canadian Journal of Human Sexuality* 12, no. 2 (2003): 87–96.

Ruddick, Sara. "Better Sex." In *Philosophy and Sex*, edited by Robert Baker and Frederick Elliston, 280–99. 2nd ed. Buffalo, N.Y.: Prometheus, 1984.

Sanders, Stephanie, and June Reinisch. "Would You Say You 'Had Sex' If . . . ?" *Journal of the American Medical Association* 281, no. 3 (January 20, 1999): 275–77.

Shaffer, Jerome A. "Sexual Desire." *Journal of Philosophy* 75, no. 4 (1978): 175–89. Reprinted in *Sex, Love, and Friendship*, edited by Alan Soble, 1–12. Amsterdam: Rodopi, 1997.

Shrage, Laurie. "Do Lesbian Prostitutes Have Sex with Their Clients? A Clintonesque Reply." *Sexualities* 2, no. 2 (1999): 259–61.

Solomon, Robert. "Sexual Paradigms." *Journal of Philosophy* 71, no. 11 (1974): 336–45.

Sullivan, John P. "Philosophizing about Sexuality." *Philosophy of the Social Sciences* 14, no. 1 (1984): 83–96.

Taylor, Roger. "Sexual Experiences." *Proceedings of the Aristotelian Society* 68 (1967–1968): 87–104. Reprinted in *The Philosophy of Sex*, edited by Alan Soble, 59–75. 1st ed. Totowa, N.J.: Rowman & Littlefield, 1980.

Thomas, Keith. "The Double Standard." *Journal of the History of Ideas* 20, no. 2 (1959): 195–216.

Sexual Perversion

Baltzly, Dirk. "Peripatetic Perversions: A Neo-Aristotelian Account of the Nature of Sexual Perversion." *The Monist* 85, no. 1 (2003): 3–29.

Bullough, Vern L., and Bonnie Bullough. *Sin, Sickness, and Sanity: A History of Sexual Attitudes*. New York: Garland, 1977.

Conrad, Peter, and Joseph W. Schneider. *Deviance and Medicalization: From Badness to Sickness*. St. Louis, Mo.: Mosby, 1980. Expanded ed. Philadelphia, Pa.: University Press, 1992.

Davidson, Arnold. "Conceptual History and Conceptions of Perversions." In *Philosophy and Sex*, edited by Robert B. Baker, Kathleen J. Wininger, and Frederick A. Elliston, 476–86. 3rd ed. Amherst, N.Y.: Prometheus, 1998.

———. "Sex and the Emergence of Sexuality." *Critical Inquiry* 14, no. 1 (1987): 16–48.

Denis, Lara. "Kant on the Wrongness of 'Unnatural' Sex." *History of Philosophy Quarterly* 16, no. 2 (1999): 225–48.

De Sousa, Ronald. "Norms and the Normal." In *Freud: A Collection of Critical Essays*, edited by Richard Wollheim, 196–221. Garden City, N.Y.: Anchor Books, 1974.

Freud, Sigmund. "Three Essays on the Theory of Sexuality." In *The Standard Edition of the Complete Psychological Works of Sigmund Freud*, translated and edited by James Strachey, 125–45. Vol. 7. London: Hogarth Press, 1953–74. First published 1905.

Gates, Katharine. *Deviant Desires: Incredibly Strange Sex*. New York: Juno Books, 2000.

Gert, Bernard. "A Sex Caused Inconsistency in DSM-III-R: The Definition of Mental Disorder and the Definition of Paraphilias." *Journal of Medicine and Philosophy* 17, no. 2 (1992): 155–71.

Gert, Bernard, and Charles M. Culver. "Defining Mental Disorder." In *The Philosophy of Psychiatry: A Companion*, edited by Jennifer Radden, 415–25. New York: Oxford University Press, 2004.

Gray, Robert. "Sex and Sexual Perversion." *Journal of Philosophy* 75, no. 4 (1978): 189–99.

Humber, James. "Sexual Perversion and Human Nature." *Philosophy Research Archives* 13 (1987–1988): 331–50.

Irvine, Janice M. *Disorders of Desire: Sex and Gender in Modern American Sexology*. Philadelphia, Pa.: Temple University Press, 1990.

———. "Reinventing Perversion: Sex Addiction and Cultural Anxieties." *Journal of the History of Sexuality* 5, no. 3 (1995): 429–50.

Kadish, Mortimer R. "The Possibility of Perversion." *Philosophical Forum* 19, no. 1 (1987): 34–53. Reprinted in *The Philosophy of Sex*, edited by Alan Soble, 93–116. 2nd ed. Savage, Md.: Rowman & Littlefield, 1991.

Kaplan, Louise J. *Female Perversions: The Temptations of Emma Bovary*. New York: Anchor Books, 1991.

Ketchum, Sara Ann. "The Good, the Bad, and the Perverted: Sexual Paradigms Revisited." In *The Philosophy of Sex*, edited by Alan Soble, 139–57. 1st ed. Totowa, N.J.: Rowman & Littlefield, 1980.

Kupfer, Joseph. "Sexual Perversion and the Good." *The Personalist* 59, no. 1 (1978): 70–77.

Levinson, Jerrold. "Sexual Perversity." *The Monist* 86, no. 1 (2003): 30–54.

Levy, Donald. "Perversion and the Unnatural as Moral Categories." *Ethics* 90, no. 2 (1980): 191–202. Reprinted (revised and expanded) in *The Philosophy of Sex*, edited by Alan Soble, 169–89. 1st ed. Totowa, N.J.: Rowman & Littlefield, 1980.

Neu, Jerome. "Freud and Perversion." In *The Cambridge Companion to Freud*, 175–208. Cambridge, UK: Cambridge University Press, 1991.

———. "What Is Wrong with Incest?" *Inquiry* 19, no. 1 (1976): 27–39.

Priest, Graham. "Sexual Perversion." *Australasian Journal of Philosophy* 75, no. 3 (1997): 360–72.

Primoratz, Igor. "Sexual Perversion." *American Philosophical Quarterly* 34, no. 2 (1997): 245–58.

Rosen, Raymond C., and Sandra R. Leiblum, eds. *Case Studies in Sex Therapy.* New York: Guilford Press, 1995.

Slote, Michael. "Inapplicable Concepts and Sexual Perversion." In *Philosophy and Sex*, edited by Robert Baker and Frederick Elliston, 261–67. 1st ed. Buffalo, N.Y.: Prometheus, 1975.

Soble, Alan. "Kant and Sexual Perversion." *The Monist* 86, no. 1 (2003): 57–92.

———. "Paraphilia and Distress in DSM-IV." In *The Philosophy of Psychiatry: A Companion*, edited by Jennifer Radden, 54–63. New York: Oxford University Press, 2004.

Solomon, Robert. "Sex and Perversion." in *Philosophy and Sex*, edited by Robert Baker and Frederick Elliston, 268–87. 1st ed. Buffalo, N.Y.: Prometheus, 1975.

Spiecker, Ben, and Jan Steutel. "Paedophilia, Sexual Desire and Perversity." *Journal of Moral Education* 26, no. 3 (1997): 331–42.

Steele, Valerie. *Fetish: Fashion, Sex and Power.* New York: Oxford University Press, 1996.

Szasz, Thomas S. "The Product Conversion—From Heresy to Illness." In *The Manufacture of Madness: A Comparative Study of the Inquisition and the Mental Health Movement*, 160–79. New York: Harper and Row, 1970.

Vannoy, Russell. "The Structure of Sexual Perversity." In *Sex, Love, and Friendship*, edited by Alan Soble, 358–71. Amsterdam: Rodopi, 1997.

Masturbation

Bennett, Paula, and Vernon A. Rosario, eds. *Solitary Pleasures: The Historical, Literary, and Artistic Discourses of Autoeroticism.* New York: Routledge, 1995.

Budapest, Zsuzsanna E. "Self-Blessing Ritual." In *Womanspirit Rising: A Feminist Reader in Religion*, edited by Carol P. Christ and Judith Plaskow, 269–72. San Francisco, Calif.: Harper and Row, 1979.

Burger, John R. *One-Handed Histories: The Eroto-Politics of Gay Male Video Pornography.* New York: Haworth, 1995.

Cornog, Martha, ed. *The Big Book of Masturbation: From Angst to Zeal.* San Francisco, Calif.: Down There Press, 2003.

Dodson, Betty. "How I Became the Guru of Female Sexual Liberation." In *Personal Stories of "How I Got Into Sex": Leading Researchers, Sex Therapists, Educators, Prostitutes, Sex Toy Designers, Sex Surrogates, Transsexuals, Criminologists, Clergy, and More. . .*, edited by Bonnie Bullough, Vern L. Bullough, Marilyn A. Fithian, William E. Hartman, and Randy Sue Klein, 122–30. Amherst, N.Y.: Prometheus, 1997.

———. *Liberating Masturbation: A Meditation on Self-Love.* New York: Betty Dodson, 1978.

Elders, M. Joycelyn. "The Dreaded M Word: It's Not a Four-Letter Word." *Nerve* (June 26, 1997), www.nerve.com/dispatches/elders/mword [accessed November 16, 2006].

Engelhardt, H. Tristram, Jr. "The Disease of Masturbation: Values and the Concept of Disease." *Bulletin of the History of Medicine* 48 (Summer 1974): 234–48. Reprinted in *Contemporary Issues in Bioethics*, edited by T. Beauchamp and L. Walters, 109–13. Encino, Calif.: Dickenson, 1978.

Fortunata, Jacqueline. "Masturbation and Women's Sexuality." In *The Philosophy of Sex*, edited by Alan Soble, 389–408. 1st ed. Totowa, N.J.: Rowman & Littlefield, 1980.

Francis, John J. "Masturbation." *Journal of the American Psychoanalytic Association* 16, no. 1 (1968): 95–112.

Groenendijk, Leendert F. "Masturbation and Neurasthenia: Freud and Stekel in Debate on the Harmful Effects of Autoeroticism." *Journal of Psychology and Human Sexuality* 9, no. 1 (1997): 71–94.

Haynes, James. "Masturbation." In *Human Sexuality: An Encyclopedia*, edited by Vern Bullough and Bonnie Bullough, 381–85. New York: Garland, 1994.

Jordan, Mark D. "Masturbation, or Identity in Solitude." In *The Ethics of Sex*, 95–104. Oxford, UK: Blackwell, 2002.

Laqueur, Thomas. *Solitary Sex: A Cultural History of Masturbation.* New York: Zone Books, 2003.

Kielkopf, Charles. "Masturbation: A Kantian Condemnation." *Philosophia* 25, nos. 1–4 (1997): 223–46.

Moore, Gareth. "Natural Sex: Germain Grisez, Sex, and Natural Law." In *The Revival of Natural Law: Philosophical, Theological and Ethical Responses to the Finnis-Grisez School*, edited by Nigel Biggar and Rufus Black, 223–41. Aldershot, UK: Ashgate, 2000.

Neu, Jerome. "An Ethics of Fantasy?" *Journal of Theoretical and Philosophical Psychology* 22, no. 2 (2002): 137–57.

Sarnoff, Suzanne, and Irving Sarnoff. *Sexual Excitement/Sexual Peace: The Place of Masturbation in Adult Relationships.* New York: M. Evans, 1979.

Satlow, Michael L. "'Wasted Seed': The History of a Rabbinic Idea." *Hebrew Union College Annual* 65 (1994): 137–69.

Soble, Alan. "Kant and Sexual Perversion." *The Monist* 86, no. 1 (2003): 57–92.

Tiefer, Leonore. "Review of Suzanne Sarnoff and Irving Sarnoff, *Sexual Excitement/Sexual Peace: The Place of Masturbation in Adult Relationships.*" *Psychology of Women Quarterly* 8, no. 1 (1983): 107–9.

Computers and the Internet

Adeney, Douglas. "Evaluating the Pleasures of Cybersex." *Australasian Journal of Professional and Applied Ethics* 1, no. 1 (1999): 69–79.

Ben-Ze'ev, Aaron. *Love Online: Emotions on the Internet.* Cambridge, UK: Cambridge University Press, 2004.

Collins, Louise. "Emotional Adultery: Cybersex and Commitment." *Social Theory and Practice* 25, no. 2 (1999): 243–70.

Cooper, Al, ed. *Cybersex: The Dark Side of the Force.* New York: Brunner-Routledge, 2000.

———. *Sex and the Internet: A Guide Book for Clinicians.* New York: Brunner-Routledge, 2002.

Hughes, Donna M. "The Use of New Communications and Information Technologies for Sexual Exploitation of Women and Children." *Hastings Women's Law Journal* 13, no. 1 (2002), 129–48.

Levy, Neil. "Virtual Child Pornography: The Eroticization of Inequality." *Ethics and Information Technology* 4, no. 4 (2002): 319–23.

Maheu, Marlene M., and Rona B. Subotnik. *Infidelity on the Internet: Virtual Relationships and Real Betrayal.* Naperville, Ill.: Sourcebooks, 2001.

Portmann, John. "Chatting Is Not Cheating." In *In Defense of Sin*, 223–41. New York: Palgrave, 2002.

Homosexuality

Baird, Robert M., and M. Katherine Baird, eds. *Homosexuality: Debating the Issues.* Amherst, N.Y.: Prometheus, 1995.

Ball, Carlos A. *The Morality of Gay Rights: An Exploration in Political Philosophy.* New York: Routledge, 2003.

Bersani, Leo. "Is the Rectum a Grave?" *October* no. 43 (Winter 1987): 197–222.

Boswell, John. *Christianity, Social Tolerance, and Homosexuality.* Chicago: University of Chicago Press, 1980.

———. *Same-Sex Unions in Premodern Europe.* New York: Villard, 1994.

Bradshaw, David. "A Reply to Corvino." In *Same Sex: Debating the Ethics, Science, and Culture of Homosexuality*, edited by John Corvino, 17–30. Lanham, Md.: Rowman & Littlefield, 1997.

Calhoun, Cheshire. "Separating Lesbian Theory from Feminist Theory." *Ethics* 104, no. 3 (1994): 558–81.

Callahan, Sidney. "Why I Changed My Mind: Thinking about Gay Marriage." *Commonweal* (April 22, 1994): 6–8.

Card, Claudia. *Lesbian Choices.* New York: Columbia University Press, 1995.

Colter, Ephen Glenn, Wayne Hoffman, Eva Pendleton, Alison Redick, and David Serlin, eds. *Policing Public Sex: Queer Politics and the Future of AIDS Activism.* Boston: South End Press, 1996.

Corvino, John. "Homosexuality and the Moral Relevance of Experience." In *Ethics in Practice*, edited by Hugh LaFollette, 241–50. 2nd ed. Oxford, UK: Blackwell, 2001.

———, ed. *Same Sex: Debating the Ethics, Science, and Culture of Homosexuality.* Lanham, Md.: Rowman & Littlefield, 1997.

Crompton, Louis. *Homosexuality and Civilization.* Cambridge, Mass.: Harvard University Press, 2003.

Dean, Craig R. "Fighting for Same Sex Marriage." In *Gender Basics*, edited by A. Minas, 275–77. Belmont, Calif.: Wadsworth, 1993.

Dover, Kenneth. *Greek Homosexuality*. Updated and with a new postscript. Cambridge, Mass.: Harvard University Press, 1989. First published 1978.

Dreger, Alice Domurat. *Hermaphrodites and the Medical Invention of Sex*. Cambridge, Mass.: Harvard University Press, 1998.

Elliston, Frederick. "Gay Marriage." In *Philosophy and Sex*, edited by Robert Baker and Frederick Elliston, 146–66. 2nd ed. Buffalo, N.Y.: Prometheus, 1984.

Eskridge, William N. Jr. *The Case for Same-Sex Marriage: From Sexual Liberty to Civilized Commitment*. New York: Free Press, 1996.

Finnis, John M. "Law, Morality, and 'Sexual Orientation.'" *Notre Dame Law Review* 69, no. 5 (1994): 1049–76.

———. "Natural Law and Unnatural Acts." In *Human Sexuality*, edited by Igor Primoratz, 5–27. Aldershot, UK: Dartmouth, 1997.

Freeman, M. D. A. "Not Such a Queer Idea: Is There a Case for Same Sex Marriages?" *Journal of Applied Philosophy* 16, no. 1 (1999): 1–17.

Garber, Marjorie. *Vice Versa: Bisexuality and the Eroticism of Everyday Life*. New York: Simon & Schuster, 1995.

Glick, Elisa. "Feminism, Queer Theory, and the Politics of Transgression." *Feminist Review* 64 (Spring 2000): 19–45.

Halperin, David M. *One Hundred Years of Homosexuality*. New York: Routledge, 1990.

Hamer, Dean, and Peter Copeland. *The Science of Desire*. New York: Simon & Schuster, 1994.

Herdt, Gilbert. *Sambia Sexual Culture: Essays from the Field*. Chicago: University of Chicago Press, 1999.

Jung, Patricia, and Ralph Smith. *Heterosexism: An Ethical Challenge*. Albany: State University of New York Press, 1993.

Koppelman, Andrew. "The Decline and Fall of the Case against Same-sex Marriage." *University of St. Thomas Law Journal* 2, no. 1 (2004): 5–32.

———. *The Gay Rights Question in Contemporary American Law*. Chicago: University of Chicago Press, 2002.

———. "Homosexual Conduct: A Reply to the New Natural Lawyers." In *Same Sex: Debating the Ethics, Science, and Culture of Homosexuality*, edited by John Corvino, 44–57. Lanham, Md.: Rowman & Littlefield, 1997.

———. *Same Sex, Different States: When Same-sex Marriages Cross State Lines*. New Haven, Conn.: Yale University Press, 2006.

LeVay, Simon. *Queer Science*. Cambridge, Mass.: MIT Press, 1996.

———. *The Sexual Brain*. Cambridge, Mass.: MIT Press, 1993.

Levin, Michael. "Homosexuality, Abnormality, and Civil Rights." *Public Affairs Quarterly* 10, no. 1 (1996): 31–48.

———. "Why Homosexuality Is Abnormal." *The Monist* 67, no. 2 (1984): 251–83.

Mayo, David. "An Obligation to Warn of HIV Infection?" In *Sex, Love and Friendship*, edited by Alan Soble, 447–53. Amsterdam: Rodopi, 1997.

Mohr, Richard D. "The Case for Gay Marriage." *Notre Dame Journal of Law, Ethics, and Public Policy* 9 (1995): 215–39.

———. *Gay Ideas*. Boston: Beacon Press, 1992.

———. *Gays/Justice*. New York: Columbia University Press, 1988.

———. *The Long Arc of Justice: Lesbian and Gay Marriage, Equality, and Rights*. New York: Columbia University Press, 2005.

———. *A More Perfect Union.* Boston: Beacon Press, 1994.

Moore, Gareth. "Natural Sex: Germain Grisez, Sex, and Natural Law." In *The Revival of Natural Law: Philosophical, Theological and Ethical Responses to the Finnis-Grisez School*, edited by Nigel Biggar and Rufus Black, 223–41. Aldershot, UK: Ashgate, 2000.

———. *A Question of Truth: Christianity and Homosexuality.* New York: Continuum, 2003.

Murphy, Timothy F. "Homosexuality and Nature: Happiness and the Law at Stake." *Journal of Applied Philosophy* 4, no. 2 (1987): 195–204.

———, ed. *Gay Ethics: Controversies in Outing, Civil Rights, and Sexual Science.* Binghamton, N.Y.: Haworth, 1994.

Nussbaum, Martha. "Platonic Love and Colorado Law: The Relevance of Ancient Greek Norms to Modern Sexual Controversies." *Virginia Law Review* 80, no. 7 (1994): 1515–1651.

Prager, Dennis. "Homosexuality, the Bible, and Us—A Jewish Perspective." *The Public Interest* no. 112 (Summer 1993): 60–83.

Quinn, Carol, ed. [Issue on Same-Sex Marriage] *American Philosophical Association Newsletter on Philosophy and Lesbian, Gay, Bisexual, and Transgender Issues* 4, no. 1 (Fall 2004).

Reamer, Frederic G., ed. *AIDS & Ethics.* New York: Columbia University Press, 1991.

Rich, Adrienne. "Compulsory Heterosexuality and Lesbian Existence." In *Blood, Bread and Poetry*, 23–75. New York: W. W. Norton, 1986.

Richards, David A. J. *Women, Gays, and the Constitution: The Grounds for Feminism and Gay Rights in Culture and Law.* Chicago: University of Chicago Press, 1998.

Robinson, Paul. *Gay Lives: Homosexual Autobiography from John Addington Symonds to Paul Monette.* Chicago: University of Chicago Press, 1999.

Ruse, Michael. *Homosexuality: A Philosophical Inquiry.* New York: Blackwell, 1988.

Schaff, Kory. "Kant, Political Liberalism, and the Ethics of Same-Sex Relations." *Journal of Social Philosophy* 32, no. 3 (2001): 446–62.

Snyder, Jane M. *Lesbian Desire in the Lyrics of Sappho.* New York: Columbia University Press, 1997.

Soble, Alan. "Kant and Sexual Perversion." *The Monist* 86, no. 1 (2003): 57–92.

Stafford, J. Martin. "Love and Lust Revisited: Intentionality, Homosexuality and Moral Education." *Journal of Applied Philosophy* 5, no. 1 (1988): 87–100.

———. "The Two Minds of Roger Scruton." *Studies in Philosophy and Education* 11 (1991): 187–93.

Stein, Edward. *The Mismeasure of Desire: The Science, Theory, and Ethics of Sexual Orientation.* Oxford, UK: Oxford University Press, 2001.

———. "The Relevance of Scientific Research about Sexual Orientation to Lesbian and Gay Rights." *Journal of Homosexuality* 27, nos. 3–4 (1994): 269–308.

Storms, Michael D. "Theories of Sexual Orientation." *Journal of Personality and Social Psychology* 38, no. 4 (1980): 783–92.

Strasser, Mark. *Legally Wed.* Ithaca, N.Y.: Cornell University Press, 1997.

———. *On Same-Sex Marriage, Civil Unions, and the Rule of Law: Constitutional Interpretation at the Crossroads.* Westport, Conn.: Praeger, 2002.

Sullivan, Andrew. *Love Undetectable: Reflections on Friendship, Sex, and Survival.* New York: Knopf, 1998.

———. *Virtually Normal: An Argument about Homosexuality.* New York: Knopf, 1995.

———, ed. *Same-Sex Marriage: Pro and Con.* New York: Vintage, 2004.

Thomas, Laurence M., and Michael E. Levin. *Sexual Orientation and Human Rights.* Lanham, Md.: Rowman & Littlefield, 1999.

Vacek, Edward. "A Christian Homosexuality?" *Commonweal* (December 5, 1980): 681–84.

Wardle, Lynn D., Mark Strasser, William C. Duncan, and David Orgon Coolidge, eds. *Marriage and Same-Sex Unions: A Debate.* Westport, Conn.: Praeger, 2003.

Weithman, Paul J. "Natural Law, Morality, and Sexual Complementarity." In *Sex, Preference, and Family: Essays on Law and Nature,* edited by David M. Estlund and Martha C. Nussbaum, 227–46. New York: Oxford University Press, 1997.

Williams, Craig A. *Roman Homosexuality: Ideologies of Masculinity in Classical Antiquity.* New York: Oxford University Press, 1999.

Wittig, Monique. *The Lesbian Body.* [*Le Corps Lesbien*] Trans. David Le Vay. Boston: Beacon Press, 1973.

Contraception and Abortion

Anscombe, G. E. M. "Contraception and Chastity." *The Human World* no. 7 (1972): 9–30. Reprinted (along with criticisms and a rebuttal) in *Ethics and Population,* edited by Michael Bayles, 134–53. Cambridge, Mass.: Schenkman, 1976.

———. "You Can Have Sex without Children." In *Ethics, Religion and Politics,* 82–96. Minneapolis: University of Minnesota Press, 1981.

Beis, Richard H. "Contraception and the Logical Structure of the Thomist Natural Law Theory." *Ethics* 75, no. 4 (1965): 277–84.

Boonin-Vail, David. "A Defense of 'A Defense of Abortion': On the Responsibility Objection to Thomson's Argument." *Ethics* 107, no. 2 (1997): 286–313.

Brake, Elizabeth. "Fatherhood and Child Support: Do Men Have a Right to Choose?" *Journal of Applied Philosophy* 22, no. 1 (2005): 55–73.

Cahill, Lisa Sowle. "Grisez on Sex and Gender: A Feminist Theological Perspective." In *The Revival of Natural Law: Philosophical, Theological and Ethical Responses to the Finnis-Grisez School,* edited by Nigel Biggar and Rufus Black, 242–61. Aldershot, UK: Ashgate, 2000.

Callahan, Joan C. "The Fetus and Fundamental Rights." *Commonweal* (April 11, 1986): 203–7. Reprinted, revised, in *The Ethics of Abortion: Pro-Life vs. Pro-Choice,* edited by Robert M. Baird and Stuart E. Rosenbaum, 249–62. Rev. ed. Buffalo, N.Y.: Prometheus, 1993.

Callahan, Sidney. "Abortion and the Sexual Agenda." *Commonweal* (April 25, 1986): 232–38. Reprinted in *The Ethics of Abortion: Pro-Life vs. Pro-Choice,* edited by Robert M. Baird and Stuart E. Rosenbaum, 111–21. Rev. ed. Buffalo, N.Y.: Prometheus, 1993, and in *Philosophy of Sex,* edited by Alan Soble, 3rd ed. (151–64) and 4th ed. (177–90).

Cohen, Carl. "Sex, Birth Control, and Human Life." In *Philosophy and Sex,* edited by Robert Baker and Frederick Elliston, 185–99. 2nd ed. Buffalo, N.Y.: Prometheus, 1984.

Corea, Gena. *The Mother Machine: Reproductive Technologies from Artificial Insemination to Artificial Wombs.* New York: Harper and Row, 1986.

Diorio, Joseph A. "Contraception, Copulation Domination, and the Theoretical Barrenness of Sex Education Literature." *Educational Theory* 35, no. 3 (1985): 239–54.

Dworkin, Ronald. *Life's Dominion: An Argument about Abortion, Euthanasia, and Individual Freedom.* New York: Knopf, 1993.

Finnis, John M. "Law, Morality, and 'Sexual Orientation.'" *Notre Dame Law Review* 69, no. 5 (1994): 1049–76.

———. "Natural Law and Unnatural Acts." In *Human Sexuality*, edited by Igor Primoratz, 5–27. Aldershot, UK: Dartmouth, 1997.

Geach, Mary. "Marriage: Arguing to a First Principle in Sexual Ethics." In *Moral Truth and Moral Tradition: Essays in Honour of Peter Geach and Elizabeth Anscombe*, edited by Luke Gormally, 177–93. Dublin: Four Courts Press, 1994.

Grisez, Germain, Joseph Boyle, John Finnis, William E. May, and John C. Ford. *The Teaching of "Humanae Vitae": A Defense.* San Francisco, Calif.: Ignatius Press, 1988.

Hull, Richard T., ed. *Ethical Issues in the Reproductive Technologies.* Amherst, N.Y.: Prometheus, 2005. First published 1990.

John Paul II (Pope). "Evangelium Vitae." *Origins* 24, no. 42 (1995): 689–727.

Lowe, Pam. "Contraception and Heterosex: An Intimate Relationship." *Sexualities* 8, no. 1 (2005): 75–92.

Martin, Christopher F. J. "Are There Virtues and Vices That Belong Specifically to the Sexual Life?" *Acta Philosophica* 4, no. 2 (1995): 205–21.

Murphy, Timothy F. "Abortion and the Ethics of Genetic Sexual Orientation Research." *Cambridge Quarterly of Healthcare Ethics* 4, no. 4 (1995): 340–50.

Nicholson, Susan T. *Abortion and the Roman Catholic Church.* Knoxville, Tenn.: Religious Ethics, 1978.

Noonan, John T. *Contraception: A History of Its Treatment by the Catholic Theologians and Canonists.* Enlarged ed. Cambridge, Mass.: Harvard University Press, 1986.

Paden, Roger. "Abortion and Sexual Morality." In *Sex, Love, and Friendship*, edited by Alan Soble, 229–36. Amsterdam: Rodopi, 1997.

Paul VI (Pope). "Humanae Vitae." *Catholic Mind* 66 (September 1968): 35–48. Reprinted in *Philosophy and Sex*, edited by Robert Baker and Frederick Elliston, 167–83. 2nd ed. Buffalo, N.Y.: Prometheus, 1984.

Pius XI (Pope). "On Christian Marriage" ("Casti connubii"). *Catholic Mind* 29, no. 2 (1931): 21–64.

Shrage, Laurie. *Moral Dilemmas of Feminism: Prostitution, Adultery, and Abortion.* New York: Routledge, 1994.

Silverstein, Harry. "On a Woman's 'Responsibility' for the Fetus." *Social Theory and Practice* 13, no. 1 (1987): 103–19.

Smith, Holly M. "Intercourse and Moral Responsibility for the Fetus." In *Abortion and the Status of the Fetus*, edited by W. B. Bondeson, H. T. Engelhardt Jr., S. F. Spicker, and D. H. Winship, 229–45. Dordrecht: Reidel, 1983.

Soble, Alan. "More on Abortion and Sexual Morality." In *Sex, Love, and Friendship*, 239–44. Amsterdam: Rodopi, 1997.

Solomon, Robert. "Sex, Contraception, and Conceptions of Sex." In *Thirteen Questions in Ethics*, edited by G. Lee Bowie, Meredith W. Michaels, and Kathleen Higgins, 95–107. 2nd ed. Fort Worth, Tex.: Harcourt Brace, 1992.

Teichman, Jenny. "Intention and Sex." In *Intention and Intentionality: Essays in Honour of G. E. M. Anscombe*, edited by Cora Diamond and Jenny Teichman, 147–61. Ithaca, N.Y.: Cornell University Press, 1979.

Thomson, Judith Jarvis. "A Defense of Abortion." *Philosophy and Public Affairs* 1, no. 1 (1971): 47–66.

Watt, E. D. "Professor Cohen's Encyclical." *Ethics* 80 (1970): 218–21.

Whitehead, Mary Beth, and Loretta Schwartz-Nobel. *A Mother's Story: The Truth about the Baby M Case.* New York: St. Martin's Press, 1989.

Wilcox, John T. "Nature as Demonic in Thomson's Defense of Abortion." *The New Scholasticism* 63, no. 4 (1989): 463–84.

Willis, Ellen. "Abortion: Is a Woman a Person?" In *Beginning to See the Light*, 205–11. New York: Knopf, 1981. Reprinted in *Powers of Desire: The Politics of Sexuality*, edited by Ann Snitow, Christine Stansell, and Sharon Thompson, 471–76. New York: Monthly Review Press, 1983, and in *Philosophy of Sex*, edited by Alan Soble, 3rd ed. (165–69) and fourth ed. (191–95).

Wilson, George B. "Christian Conjugal Morality and Contraception." In *Population Ethics*, edited by Francis X. Quinn, 98–108. Washington, D.C.: Corpus, 1968.

Wolf-Devine, Celia. "Abortion and the Feminine Voice." *Public Affairs Quarterly* 3, no. 3 (1989): 81–97. Reprinted in *The Problem of Abortion*, edited by Susan Dwyer and Joel Feinberg, 160–74. 3rd ed. Belmont, Calif.: Wadsworth, 1997, and in *Sex and Gender: A Spectrum of Views*, edited by Philip E. Devine and Celia Wolf-Devine, 163–72. Belmont, Calif.: Wadsworth, 2003.

Zaner, Richard M. "A Criticism of Moral Conservatism's View of *In Vitro* Fertilization and Embryo Transfer." *Perspectives in Biology and Medicine* 27, no. 2 (1984): 201–12.

Sex, Love, and Marriage

Anapol, Deborah M. *Love without Limits: The Quest for Sustainable Intimate Relationships.* San Rafael, Calif.: IntiNet Resource Center, 1992.

Barash, David P., and Judith Eve Lipton. *The Myth of Monogamy: Fidelity and Infidelity in Animals and People.* New York: Henry Holt, 2001.

Brake, Elizabeth. "Justice and Virtue in Kant's Account of Marriage." *Kantian Review* 9 (March 2005): 58–94.

Brophy, Brigid. "Monogamy." In *Don't Never Forget: Collected Views and Reviews*, 28–31. London: Jonathan Cape, 1966.

Carr, David. "Chastity and Adultery." *American Philosophical Quarterly* 23, no. 4 (1986): 363–71.

Cicovacki, Predrag. "On Love and Fidelity in Marriage." *Journal of Social Philosophy* 24, no. 3 (1993): 92–104.

Clark, Elizabeth A. "'Adam's Only Companion': Augustine and the Early Christian Debate on Marriage." *Recherches Augustiniennes* 21 (1986): 139–62.

Collins, Louise. "Emotional Adultery: Cybersex and Commitment." *Social Theory and Practice* 25, no. 2 (1999): 243–70.

Denis, Lara. "From Friendship to Marriage: Revising Kant." *Philosophy and Phenomenological Research* 63, no. 1 (2001): 1–28.

Diorio, Joseph. "Sex, Love, and Justice: A Problem in Moral Education." *Educational Theory* 31, nos. 3–4 (1982): 225–35. Reprinted in *Eros, Agape, and Philia*, edited by Alan Soble, 273–88. St. Paul, Minn.: Paragon House, 1989.

Ellis, Albert. *The Civilized Couple's Guide to Extramarital Adventure*. New York: Wyden, 1972.

Finnis, John M. "The Good of Marriage and the Morality of Sexual Relations: Some Philosophical and Historical Observations." *American Journal of Jurisprudence* 42 (1997): 97–134.

Francoeur, Robert T., Martha Cornog, and Timothy Perper. *Sex, Love, and Marriage in the 21st Century: The Next Sexual Revolution*. San Jose, Calif.: toExcel, 1999.

Geach, Mary. "Marriage: Arguing to a First Principle in Sexual Ethics." In *Moral Truth and Moral Tradition: Essays in Honour of Peter Geach and Elizabeth Anscombe*, edited by Luke Gormally, 177–93. Dublin: Four Courts Press, 1994.

Gregor, Thomas. "Sexuality and the Experience of Love." In *Sexual Nature/Sexual Culture*, edited by P. Abramson and S. Pinkerton, 330–50. Chicago: University of Chicago Press, 1995.

Gregory, Paul. "Against Couples." *Journal of Applied Philosophy* 1, no. 2 (1984): 263–68.

———. "Eroticism and Love." *American Philosophical Quarterly* 25, no. 4 (1988): 339–44.

Halwani, Raja. "Virtue Ethics and Adultery." In *Ethics for Everyday*, edited by David Benatar, 226–39. Boston: McGraw-Hill, 2002.

Higgins, Kathleen Marie. "How Do I Love Thee? Let's Redefine a Term." *Journal of Social Philosophy* 24, no. 3 (1993): 105–11.

Lesser, A. H. "Love and Lust." *Journal of Value Inquiry* 14, no. 1 (1980): 51–54.

Lodge, David. "Sick with Desire." *New York Review of Books*, July 5, 2001, 28–32.

Marquis, Don. "What's Wrong with Adultery?" In *What's Wrong? Applied Ethicists and Their Critics*, edited by David Boonin and Graham Oddie, 231–38. New York: Oxford University Press, 2005.

Martin, Mike W. "Adultery and Fidelity." *Journal of Social Philosophy* 25, no. 3 (1994): 76–91.

McMurtry, John. "Sex, Love, and Friendship." In *Sex, Love, and Friendship*, edited by Alan Soble, 169–93. Amsterdam: Rodopi, 1997.

Palmquist, Stephen. "Kant, Sexism, and the Ethics of Polygamy." Hong Kong : Hong Kong Baptist University, 2005, www.hkbu.edu.hk/~ppp/srp/arts/KSEP .htm [accessed December 18, 2006].

Rapaport, Elizabeth. "On the Future of Love: Rousseau and the Radical Feminists." *Philosophical Forum* 5, nos. 1–2 (1973–1974): 185–205.

Rubin, Roger H. "Alternative Lifestyles Revisited, or Whatever Happened to Swingers, Group Marriages, and Communes?" *Journal of Family Issues* 22, no. 6 (2001): 711–16.

Shrage, Laurie. *Moral Dilemmas of Feminism: Prostitution, Adultery, and Abortion*. New York: Routledge, 1994.

Small, Meredith F. *What's Love Got to Do with It? The Evolution of Human Mating*. New York: Anchor, 1995.

Stafford, J. Martin. "Love and Lust Revisited: Intentionality, Homosexuality and Moral Education." *Journal of Applied Philosophy* 5, no. 1 (1988): 87–100.

———. "On Distinguishing between Love and Lust." *Journal of Value Inquiry* 11, no. 4 (1977): 292–303.

Steinbock, Bonnie. "Adultery." In *The Philosophy of Sex*, edited by Alan Soble, 187–92. 2nd ed. Savage, Md.: Rowman & Littlefield, 1991.

Taylor, Richard. *Having Love Affairs*. Buffalo, N.Y.: Prometheus, 1982.

———. *Love Affairs: Marriage and Infidelity*. Amherst, N.Y.: Prometheus, 1997.

Vannoy, Russell. "Can Sex Express Love?" In *Sex, Love, and Friendship*, edited by Alan Soble, 247–57. Amsterdam: Rodopi, 1997.

———. *Sex Without Love: A Philosophical Exploration*. Buffalo, N.Y.: Prometheus, 1980.

Vernallis, Kayley. "Bisexual Monogamy: Twice the Temptation but Half the Fun?" *Journal of Social Philosophy* 30, no. 3 (1999): 347–68.

Walsh, Anthony. "Love and Sex." In *Human Sexuality: An Encyclopedia*, edited by Vern Bullough and Bonnie Bullough, 369–73. New York: Garland, 1994.

Wasserstrom, Richard. "Is Adultery Immoral?" In *Philosophy and Sex*, edited by Robert Baker and Frederick Elliston, 93–106. 2nd ed. Buffalo, N.Y.: Prometheus, 1984.

Wreen, Michael J. "What's Really Wrong with Adultery." In *The Philosophy of Sex*, edited by Alan Soble, 179–86. 2nd ed. Savage, Md.: Rowman & Littlefield, 1991.

Kantian Sexual Ethics

Anderson, Clelia Smyth, and Yolanda Estes. "The Myth of the Happy Hooker: Kantian Moral Reflections on a Phenomenology of Prostitution." Pp. 152–58 and 231–33 in Stanley G. French, Wanda Teays, and Laura M. Purdy, eds., *Violence against Women: Philosophical Perspectives*. Ithaca, N.Y.: Cornell University Press, 1998.

Baker, Robert B. "'Pricks' and 'Chicks': A Plea for 'Persons.'" Pp. 45–64 in Robert B. Baker and Frederick A. Elliston, eds., *Philosophy and Sex*, 1st ed. Buffalo, N.Y.: Prometheus, 1975; reprinted as pp. 281–97 in Robert B. Baker, Kathleen J. Wininger, and Frederick A. Elliston, eds., *Philosophy and Sex*, 3rd ed. Amherst, N.Y.: Prometheus, 1998, along with "'Pricks' and 'Chicks': A Postscript after Twenty-Five Years," 297–305.

Baron, Marcia. "Love and Respect in the *Doctrine of Virtue*." Pp. 29–44 in Nelson Potter and Mark Timmons, eds., *Kant's Metaphysics of Morals. Southern Journal of Philosophy* 35, supp., 1997.

Baumrin, Bernard. (1975) "Sexual Immorality Delineated." Pp. 300–11 in Robert B. Baker and Frederick A. Elliston, eds., *Philosophy and Sex*, 2nd ed. Buffalo, N.Y.: Prometheus, 1984.

Belliotti, Raymond. *Good Sex: Perspectives on Sexual Ethics*. Lawrence, Kan.: University Press of Kansas, 1993.

Bencivenga, Ermanno. "Kant's Sadism." *Philosophy and Literature* 20, no. 1 (1996): 39–46.

Brake, Elizabeth. "Justice and Virtue in Kant's Account of Marriage." *Kantian Review* 9 (March 2005): 58–94.

Brecht, Bertolt. "On Kant's Definition of Marriage in *The Metaphysic of Ethics*." In *Poems 1913–1956*, edited by John Willett and Ralph Manheim, with Erich

Fried, 312. Rev. ed. Translated by John Willett. New York: Methuen, 1987. First published 1938.

Cooke, Vincent M. "Kant, Teleology, and Sexual Ethics." *International Philosophical Quarterly* 31, no. 1 (1991): 3–13.

Denis, Lara. "From Friendship to Marriage: Revising Kant." *Philosophy and Phenomenological Research* 63, no. 1 (2001): 1–28.

———. "Kant on the Wrongness of 'Unnatural' Sex." *History of Philosophy Quarterly* 16, no. 2 (1999): 225–48.

Freud, Sigmund. "On the Universal Tendency to Debasement in the Sphere of Love." In *The Standard Edition of the Complete Psychological Works of Sigmund Freud*, vol. 11, edited and translated by James Strachey, 177–90. London: The Hogarth Press, 1953–1974. First published 1912.

Gregor, Mary J. *Laws of Freedom: A Study of Kant's Method of Applying the Categorical Imperative in the Metaphysik der Sitten.* New York: Barnes and Noble, 1963.

Hampton, Jean. "Defining Wrong and Defining Rape." In *A Most Detestable Crime: New Philosophical Essays on Rape*, edited by Keith Burgess-Jackson, 118–56. New York: Oxford University Press, 1999.

Haslanger, Sally. "On Being Objective and Being Objectified." In *A Mind of One's Own: Feminist Essays on Reason and Objectivity*, edited by Louise Antony and Charlotte Witt, 85–125. Boulder, Colo.: Westview, 1993.

Herman, Barbara. "Could It Be Worth Thinking about Kant on Sex and Marriage?" In *A Mind of One's Own: Feminist Essays on Reason and Objectivity*, edited by Louise Antony and Charlotte Witt, 49–67. Boulder, Colo.: Westview, 1993.

Kant, Immanuel. *Lectures on Ethics.* Trans. Peter Heath. Ed. Peter Heath and J. B. Schneewind. Cambridge, UK: Cambridge University Press, 1997. First published ca. 1762–1794.

———. *The Metaphysics of Morals.* Trans. Mary Gregor. Cambridge, UK: Cambridge University Press, 1991, 1996. First published 1797–1798.

Kielkopf, Charles. "Masturbation: A Kantian Condemnation." *Philosophia* 25, nos. 1–4 (1997): 223–46.

Korsgaard, Christine M. "Creating the Kingdom of Ends: Reciprocity and Responsibility in Personal Relations." *Philosophical Perspectives* 6, *Ethics* (1992): 305–32.

Langton, Rae. "Love and Solipsism." In *Love Analyzed*, edited by Roger E. Lamb, 123–52. Boulder, Colo.: Westview, 1997.

———. "Sexual Solipsism." *Philosophical Topics* 23, no. 2 (1995): 149–87.

LeMoncheck, Linda. *Dehumanizing Women: Treating Persons as Sex Objects.* Totowa, N.J.: Rowman & Allanheld, 1984.

Madigan, Timothy. "The Discarded Lemon: Kant, Prostitution and Respect for Persons." *Philosophy Now* 21 (Summer/Autumn 1998): 14–16. Reprinted in *Prostitution: On Whores, Hustlers, and Johns*, edited by James E. Elias, Vern L. Bullough, Veronica Elias, and Gwen Brewer, 107–11. Amherst, N.Y.: Prometheus, 1998.

Morgan, Seiriol. "Dark Desires." *Ethical Theory and Moral Practice* 6, no. 4 (2003): 377–410.

Moscovici, Claudia. *From Sex Objects to Sexual Subjects.* New York: Routledge, 1996.

Mosser, Kurt. "Kant and Feminism." *Kant-Studien* 90, no. 3 (1999): 322–53.

Nussbaum, Martha C. "Objectification." *Philosophy and Public Affairs* 24, no. 4 (1995): 249-91. Reprinted in *Philosophy of Sex*, edited by Alan Soble 3rd ed. (283–321), and 4th ed. (381–419). Revised in her *Sex and Social Justice*, 213–39. New York: Oxford University Press, 1999.

O'Neill, Onora. "Between Consenting Adults." *Philosophy and Public Affairs* 14, no. 3 (1985): 252–77. Reprinted in *Constructions of Reason: Explorations of Kant's Practical Philosophy*, 105–25. Cambridge, UK: Cambridge University Press, 1989.

———. "Kantian Ethics." In *A Companion to Ethics*, edited by Peter Singer, 175–85. Oxford, UK: Blackwell, 1991.

Sample, Ruth. "Sexual Exploitation and the Social Contract." *Canadian Journal of Philosophy*, "Feminist Moral Philosophy," supp. vol. 28 (2003): 189–217.

Sartre, Jean-Paul. *Being and Nothingness: An Essay on Phenomenological Ontology.* Translated by Hazel E. Barnes. New York: Philosophical Library, 1956. First published 1943.

Schaff, Kory. "Kant, Political Liberalism, and the Ethics of Same-Sex Relations." *Journal of Social Philosophy* 32, no. 3 (2001): 446–62.

Singer, Irving. "Benign Romanticism: Kant, Schlegel, Hegel, Shelley, Byron." In *The Nature of Love*, vol. 2: *Courtly and Romantic*, 376–431. Chicago: University of Chicago Press, 1984.

———. "The Morality of Sex: Contra Kant." *Critical Horizons* 1, no. 2 (2000): 175–91. Reprinted in *Explorations in Love and Sex*, 1–20. Lanham, Md.: Rowman & Littlefield, 2001, and in *The Philosophy of Sex*, edited by Alan Soble, 4th ed., 259–72.

Soble, Alan. "Kant and Sexual Perversion." *The Monist* 86, no. 1 (2003): 57–92.

Sparshott, Francis. "Kant without Sade." *Philosophy and Literature* 21, no. 1 (1997): 151–54.

Waldron, Jeremy. "When Justice Replaces Affection: The Need for Rights." *Harvard Journal of Law and Public Policy* 11, no. 3 (1988): 625–47.

Virtue Ethics

Carr, David. "Two Kinds of Virtue." *Proceedings of the Aristotelian Society* 84 (1984–1985), 47-61.

Geach, Peter T. *The Virtues.* Cambridge, UK: Cambridge University Press, 1977.

Halwani, Raja. "Virtue Ethics and Adultery." *Journal of Social Philosophy* 29, no. 3 (1998): 5–18. Reprinted in *Ethics for Everyday*, edited by David Benatar, 226–39. Boston: McGraw-Hill, 2002.

———. *Virtuous Liaisons: Care, Love, Sex, and Virtue Ethics.* Chicago: Open Court, 2003.

———, ed. *Sex and Ethics: Essays on Sexuality, Virtue, and the Good Life* (New York: Palgrave, 2007).

Martin, Christopher F. J. "Are There Virtues and Vices That Belong Specifically to the Sexual Life?" *Acta Philosophica* 4, no. 2 (1995): 205–21.

Morgan, Seiriol. "Dark Desires." *Ethical Theory and Moral Practice* 6, no. 4 (2003): 377–410.

Putman, Dan. "Sex and Virtue." *International Journal of Moral and Social Studies* 6, no. 1 (1991): 47–56.

Casual Sex and Promiscuity

Birkhead, Tim. *Promiscuity: An Evolutionary History of Sperm Competition.* Cambridge, Mass.: Harvard University Press, 2000.

Ellis, Anthony. "Casual Sex." *International Journal of Moral and Social Studies* 1, 2 (1986): 157–69.

Elliston, Frederick. "In Defense of Promiscuity." Pp. 223–43 in Robert Baker and Frederick Elliston, eds., *Philosophy and Sex,* 1st ed. Buffalo, N. Y.: Prometheus, 1975.

Groneman, Carol. *Nymphomania: A History.* New York: Norton, 2000.

Kristjánsson, Kristján. "Casual Sex Revisited." *Journal of Social Philosophy* 29, no. 2 (1998): 97–108.

Lehrman, Sally. "The Virtues of Promiscuity." *AlterNet* (July 22, 2002), www .alternet.org/story.html?StoryID=13648 [accessed December 17, 2006].

Wolf, Naomi. *Promiscuities: The Secret Struggle for Womanhood.* New York: Random House, 1997.

Rape and Date Rape (and Consent)

Anderson, Peter B., and Cindy Struckman-Johnson, eds. *Sexually Aggressive Women: Current Perspectives and Controversies.* New York: Guilford, 1998.

Archard, David. "'A Nod's as Good as a Wink': Consent, Convention, and Reasonable Belief." *Legal Theory* 3, no. 3 (1997): 273–90.

———. *Sexual Consent.* Boulder, Colo.: Westview, 1998.

Baber, H. E. "How Bad Is Rape?" *Hypatia* 2, no. 2 (1987): 125–38. Reprinted in *Philosophy of Sex,* edited by Alan Soble, 303–16. 4th ed. Lanham, Md.: Rowman & Littlefield, 2002.

Belliotti, Raymond. "A Philosophical Analysis of Sexual Ethics." *Journal of Social Philosophy* 10, no. 3 (1979): 8–11.

Bogart, John H. "On the Nature of Rape." *Public Affairs Quarterly* 5 (1991): 117–36. Reprinted in *Philosophical Perspectives on Sex and Love,* edited by Robert M. Stewart, 168–80. New York: Oxford University Press, 1995.

Burgess, Ann Wolbert, ed. *Rape and Sexual Assault: A Research Handbook.* New York: Garland, 1985.

Burgess-Jackson, Keith. *Rape: A Philosophical Investigation.* Aldershot, UK: Dartmouth, 1996.

———, ed. *A Most Detestable Crime: New Philosophical Essays on Rape.* New York: Oxford University Press, 1999.

Calhoun, Laurie. "On Rape: A Crime against Humanity." *Journal of Social Philosophy* 28, no. 1 (1997): 101–9.

Card, Claudia. "Rape as a Weapon of War." *Hypatia* 11, no. 4 (1996): 5–18.

Davis, Michael. "Setting Penalties: What Does Rape Deserve?" *Law and Philosophy* 3, no. 1 (1984): 61–110.

Doniger, Wendy. "Sex, Lies, and Tall Tales." *Social Research* 63, no. 3 (1996): 663–99.

Estrich, Susan. "Rape." In *Feminist Jurisprudence,* edited by Patricia Smith, 158–87. New York: Oxford University Press, 1993.

———. *Real Rape: How the Legal System Victimizes Women Who Say No.* Cambridge, Mass.: Harvard University Press, 1987.

Francis, Leslie P., ed. *Date Rape: Feminism, Philosophy, and the Law.* State College: Pennsylvania State University Press, 1996.

French, Stanley G., Wanda Teays, and Laura M. Purdy, eds. *Violence against Women: Philosophical Perspectives.* Ithaca, N.Y.: Cornell University Press, 1998.

Hampton, Jean. "Defining Wrong and Defining Rape." In *A Most Detestable Crime: New Philosophical Essays on Rape,* edited by Keith Burgess-Jackson, 118–56. New York: Oxford University Press, 1999.

Hasday, Jill. "Contest and Consent: A Legal History of Marital Rape." *California Law Review* 88 (October 2000), 1373–1505.

Hickman, Susan, and Charlene L. Muehlenhard. "By the Semi-Mystical Appearance of a Condom: How Young Women and Men Communicate Sexual Consent in Heterosexual Situations." *Journal of Sex Research* 36, no. 3 (1999): 258–72.

Hurd, Heidi. "The Moral Magic of Consent." *Legal Theory* 2, no. 2 (1996): 121–46.

Husak, Douglas. "The Complete Guide to Consent to Sex: Alan Wertheimer's *Consent to Sexual Relations.*" *Law and Philosophy* 25, no. 2 (March 2006), 267–87.

Husak, Douglas N., and George C. Thomas III. "Date Rape, Social Convention, and Reasonable Mistakes." *Law and Philosophy* 11, no. 1 (1992): 95–126.

———. "Rapes without Rapists: Consent and Reasonable Mistake." *Noûs,* Supp. 11 (2001), 86–117.

Kennedy, Duncan. "Sexual Abuse, Sexy Dressing, and the Eroticization of Domination." 126–213 In *Sexy Dressing Etc.: Essays on the Power and Politics of Cultural Identity.* Cambridge, Mass.: Harvard University Press, 1993.

Leone, Bruno, ed. *Rape on Campus.* San Diego: Greenhaven, 1995.

McGregor, Joan. *Is It Rape? On Acquaintance Rape and Taking Women's Consent Seriously.* Aldershot, U.K.: Ashgate, 2005.

Muehlenhard, Charlene L., and Lisa C. Hollabaugh. "Do Women Sometimes Say No When They Mean Yes? The Prevalence and Correlates of Women's Token Resistance to Sex." *Journal of Personality and Social Psychology* 54, no. 5 (1988): 872–79.

Muehlenhard, Charlene L., Irene G. Powch, Joi L. Phelps, and Laura M. Giusti, "Definitions of Rape: Scientific and Political Implications." *Journal of Social Issues* 48, no. 1 (1992): 23–44.

Muehlenhard, Charlene L., and Jennifer L. Schrag. "Nonviolent Sexual Coercion." In *Acquaintance Rape: The Hidden Crime,* edited by Andrea Parrot and Laurie Bechhofer, 115–28. New York: John Wiley, 1991.

Murphy, Jeffrie. "Some Ruminations on Women, Violence, and the Criminal Law." In *In Harm's Way: Essays in Honor of Joel Feinberg,* edited by Jules Coleman and Allen Buchanan, 209–30. Cambridge, UK: Cambridge University Press, 1994.

Paglia, Camille. *Sex, Art, and American Culture.* New York: Vintage, 1992.

Parrot, Andrea, and Laurie Bechhofer, eds. *Acquaintance Rape: The Hidden Crime.* New York: John Wiley, 1991.

Pineau, Lois. "Date Rape: A Feminist Analysis." *Law and Philosophy* 8 (1989): 217–43.

Primoratz, Igor. "Sexual Morality: Is Consent Enough?" *Ethical Theory and Moral Practice* 4, no. 3 (2001): 201–18.

Reitan, Eric. "Date Rape and Seduction: Towards a Defense of Pineau's Definition of 'Date Rape.'" *Southwest Philosophy Review* 20, no. 1 (2004): 99–106.

———. "Rape as an Essentially Contested Concept." *Hypatia* 16, no. 2 (2001): 43–66.

Remick, Lani Anne. "Read Her Lips: An Argument for a Verbal Consent Standard in Rape." *University of Pennsylvania Law Review* 141, no. 3 (1993): 1103–51.

Schulhofer, Stephen J. "The Gender Question in Criminal Law." In *Punishment and Rehabilitation*, edited by Jeffrie Murphy, 274–311. 3rd ed. Belmont, Calif.: Wadsworth, 1995.

———. *Unwanted Sex: The Culture of Intimidation and the Failure of Law*. Cambridge, Mass.: Harvard University Press, 1998.

Shields, William, and Lea Shields. "Forcible Rape: An Evolutionary Perspective." *Ethology and Sociobiology* 4, no. 3 (1983): 115–36.

Soble, Alan. "In Defense of Bacon." *Philosophy of the Social Sciences* 25, no. 2 (1995): 192–215. Reprinted, revised, in *A House Built on Sand: Exposing Postmodernist Myths about Science*, edited by Noretta Koertge, 195–215. New York: Oxford University Press, 1998.

Sommers, Christina Hoff. *Who Stole Feminism? How Women Have Betrayed Women*. New York: Simon & Schuster, 1994.

Thornhill, Randy, and Craig Palmer. *A Natural History of Rape: Biological Bases of Sexual Coercion*. Cambridge, Mass.: MIT Press, 2000.

Warshaw, Robin. *I Never Called It Rape: The Ms. Report on Recognizing, Fighting, and Surviving Date and Acquaintance Rape*. New York: Harper and Row, 1988.

Pedophilia (and Consent)

Adler, Amy. "The Perverse Law of Child Pornography." *Columbia Law Review* 101 (March 2001): 209–73.

Califia, Pat. "A Thorny Issue Splits a Movement." *Advocate* (October 30, 1980): 17–24, 45.

Ehman, Robert. "Adult-Child Sex." In *Philosophy and Sex*, edited by Robert Baker and Frederick Elliston, 431–46. 2nd ed. Buffalo, N.Y.: Prometheus, 1984.

———. "What Really Is Wrong with Pedophilia?" *Public Affairs Quarterly* 14, no. 2 (2000): 129–40.

Finkelhor, David. "What's Wrong with Sex between Adults and Children?" *American Journal of Orthopsychiatry* 49, no. 4 (1979), 692–97.

Frye, Marilyn. "Critique [of Robert Ehman]." In *Philosophy and Sex*, edited by Robert Baker and Frederick Elliston, 447–55. 2nd ed. Buffalo, N.Y.: Prometheus, 1984. Reprinted, revised, as "Not-Knowing about Sex and Power," in her *Willful Virgin*, 39–50. Freedom, Calif.: Crossing Press, 1992.

Kershnar, Stephen. "The Moral Status of Harmless Adult-Child Sex." *Public Affairs Quarterly* 15, no. 2 (2001): 111–32.

Levy, Neil. "Virtual Child Pornography: The Eroticization of Inequality." *Ethics and Information Technology* 4, no. 4 (2002): 319–23.

Primoratz, Igor. "Pedophilia." *Public Affairs Quarterly* 13, no. 1 (1999): 99–110.

Spiecker, Ben, and Jan Steutel. "A Moral-Philosophical Perspective on Paedophilia and Incest." *Educational Philosophy and Theory* 32, no. 3 (2000):
283–91.

———. "Paedophilia, Sexual Desire and Perversity." *Journal of Moral Education* 26,
no. 3 (1997): 331–42.

Sexual Harassment

Altman, Andrew. "Making Sense of Sexual Harassment Law." *Philosophy and Public Affairs* 25, no. 1 (1996): 36–64.

Christensen, Ferrel M. "'Sexual Harassment' Must Be Eliminated." *Public Affairs
Quarterly* 8, no. 1 (1994): 1–17.

Crosthwaite, Jan, and Graham Priest. "The Definition of Sexual Harassment."
Australasian Journal of Philosophy 74, no. 1 (1996): 66–82.

Dershowitz, Alan M. "The Talmud as Sexual Harassment." In *The Abuse Excuse
and Other Cop-outs, Sob Stories, and Evasions of Responsibility*, 251–53. Boston: Little, Brown, 1994.

Dodds, Susan M., Lucy Frost, Robert Pargetter, and Elizabeth W. Prior. "Sexual
Harassment." *Social Theory and Practice* 14, no. 2 (1988): 111–30.

Gallop, Jane. *Feminist Accused of Sexual Harassment*. Durham, N.C.: Duke University Press, 1997.

Hajdin, Mane. *The Law of Sexual Harassment: A Critique*. Selinsgrove, Pa.: Susque-
hanna University Press, 2002.

———. "Sexual Harassment and Negligence." *Journal of Social Philosophy* 28, no. 1
(1997): 37–53.

———. "Sexual Harassment in the Law: The Demarcation Problem." *Journal of Social Philosophy* 25, no. 3 (1994): 102–22.

Hughes, John C., and Larry May. "Sexual Harassment." *Social Theory and Practice*
6, no. 3 (1980): 249–80.

Kenrick, Douglas T., Melanie R. Trost, and Virgil L. Sheets. "Power, Harassment,
and Trophy Mates: The Feminist Advantages of an Evolutionary Perspective."
In *Sex, Power, Conflict: Evolutionary and Feminist Perspectives*, edited by David M.
Buss and Neil M. Malamuth, 29–53. New York: Oxford University Press, 1996.

Klatt, Heinz-Joachim. "Regulating 'Harassment' in Ontario." *Academic Questions*
8, no. 3 (1995): 48–58.

Landau, Iddo. "Is Sexual Harassment Research Biased?" *Public Affairs Quarterly*
13, no. 3 (1999): 241–54.

LeMoncheck, Linda, and Mane Hajdin. *Sexual Harassment: A Debate*. Lanham,
Md.: Rowman & Littlefield, 1997.

LeMoncheck, Linda, and James P. Sterba, eds. *Sexual Harassment: Issues and Answers*. New York: Oxford University Press, 2001.

MacKinnon, Catharine A. *Sexual Harassment of Working Women*. New Haven,
Conn.: Yale University Press, 1979.

McBride, William L. "Sexual Harassment, Seduction, and Mutual Respect: An
Attempt at Sorting It Out." In *Feminist Phenomenology: Contributions to Phenome-
nology*, vol. 40, edited by Linda Fisher and Lester Embree, 249–66. Dordrecht:
Kluwer, 2000.

Paludi, Michele A., ed. *Sexual Harassment on College Campuses: Abusing the Ivory Power.* Revised ed. Albany: State University of New York Press, 1990.

Patai, Daphne. *Heterophobia: Sexual Harassment and the Future of Feminism.* Lanham, Md.: Rowman & Littlefield, 1998.

Paul, Ellen Frankel. "Sexual Harassment as Discrimination: A Defective Paradigm." *Yale Law and Policy Review* 8, no. 2 (1990): 333–65.

Robinson, Paul. "'Dear Paul': An Exchange between Student and Teacher." In *Opera, Sex, and Other Vital Matters,* 219–37. Chicago: University of Chicago Press, 2002.

Roiphe, Katie. *The Morning After: Sex, Fear, and Feminism on Campus.* New York: Little, Brown, 1993.

Sanday, Peggy Reeves. *A Woman Scorned: Acquaintance Rape on Trial.* New York: Doubleday, 1996.

Stan, Adele M., ed. *Debating Sexual Correctness.* New York: Delta, 1995.

Superson, Anita M. "A Feminist Definition of Sexual Harassment." *Journal of Social Philosophy* 24, no. 1 (1993): 46–64.

Tuana, Nancy. "Sexual Harassment: Offers and Coercion." *Journal of Social Philosophy* 19, no. 2 (1988): 30–42.

Wall, Edmund, ed. *Sexual Harassment: Confrontations and Decisions.* Buffalo, N.Y.: Prometheus, 1992.

Prostitution

Anderson, Clelia Smyth, and Yolanda Estes. "The Myth of the Happy Hooker: Kantian Moral Reflections on a Phenomenology of Prostitution." In *Violence against Women: Philosophical Perspectives,* edited by Stanley G. French, Wanda Teays, and Laura M. Purdy, 152–58, 231–33. Ithaca, N.Y.: Cornell University Press, 1998.

Christina, Greta, ed. *Paying for It: A Guide by Sex Workers for Their Clients* (Oakland, Calif.: Greenery Press, 2004).

"Code of Ethics for Prostitutes." *Coyote Howls* 5, no. 1 (1978): 9.

Davidson, Julia O'Connell. "Prostitution and the Contours of Control." In *Sexual Cultures: Communities, Values and Intimacy,* edited by Jeffrey Weeks and Janet Holland, 180–98. New York: St. Martin's, 1996.

Delacoste, Frédérique, and Priscilla Alexander, eds. *Sex Work: Writings by Women in the Sex Industry.* 1st ed. Pittsburgh, Pa.: Cleis Press, 1987.

Elias, James E., Vern L. Bullough, Veronica Elias, and Gwen Brewer, eds. *Prostitution: On Whores, Hustlers, and Johns.* Amherst, N.Y.: Prometheus, 1998.

Ericsson, Lars O. "Charges against Prostitution: An Attempt at a Philosophical Assessment." *Ethics* 90, no. 3 (1980): 335–66.

Garb, Sarah H. "Sex for Money Is Sex for Money: The Illegality of Pornographic Film as Prostitution." *Law and Inequality* 13, no. 2 (1995): 281–301.

Green, Karen. "Prostitution, Exploitation and Taboo." *Philosophy* 64 (1989): 525–34.

Jaggar, Alison. "Prostitution." In *The Philosophy of Sex,* edited by Alan Soble, 259–80. 2nd ed. Savage, Md.: Rowman & Littlefield, 1991.

Marshall, S. E. "Bodyshopping: The Case of Prostitution." *Journal of Applied Philosophy* 16, no. 2 (1999): 139–50.

Nagle, Jill, ed. *Whores and Other Feminists.* New York: Routledge, 1997.

Overall, Christine. "What's Wrong with Prostitution? Evaluating Sex Work." *Signs* 17, no. 4 (1992): 705–24.

Pateman, Carole. "Defending Prostitution: Charges against Ericsson." *Ethics* 93 (1983): 561–65.

———. "Sex and Power." *Ethics* 100, no. 2 (1990): 398–407.

———. *The Sexual Contract.* Stanford, Calif.: Stanford University Press, 1988.

Primoratz, Igor. "What's Wrong with Prostitution?" *Philosophy* 68 (1993): 159–82.

Shrage, Laurie. "Is Sexual Desire Raced? The Social Meaning of Interracial Prostitution." *Journal of Social Philosophy* 23, no. 1 (1992): 42–51.

———. *Moral Dilemmas of Feminism: Prostitution, Adultery, and Abortion.* New York: Routledge, 1994.

———. "Prostitution and the Case for Decriminalization." *Dissent* (Spring 1996), 41–45.

———. "Should Feminists Oppose Prostitution?" *Ethics* 99, no. 2 (1989): 347–61.

Stewart, Robert M. "Moral Criticism and the Social Meaning of Prostitution." In *Philosophical Perspectives on Sex and Love,* 81–83. New York: Oxford University Press, 1995.

Pornography

Adler, Amy. "The Perverse Law of Child Pornography." *Columbia Law Review* 101 (March 2001): 209–73.

Allen, Amy. "Pornography and Power." *Journal of Social Philosophy* 32, no. 4 (2001): 512–31.

Assiter, Alison, and Avedon Carol, eds. *Bad Girls and Dirty Pictures.* London: Pluto Press, 1993.

Baird, Robert M., and Stuart E. Rosenbaum, eds. *Pornography: Private Right or Public Menace?* Buffalo, N.Y.: Prometheus, 1991.

Baldwin, Margaret. "The Sexuality of Inequality: The Minneapolis Pornography Ordinance." *Law and Inequality: A Journal of Theory and Practice* 2, no. 2 (1984): 629–53.

Beauvoir, Simone de. "Must We Burn Sade?" Translated by Annette Michelson. In Austryn Wainhouse and Richard Seaver, comps., *The Marquis de Sade: The 120 Days of Sodom and Other Writings,* 3–64. New York: Grove Press, 1966. First published 1951–1952.

Berger, Fred R. "Pornography, Sex, and Censorship." *Social Theory and Practice* 4, no. 2 (1977): 183–209. Reprinted in *The Philosophy of Sex,* edited by Alan Soble, 322–47. 1st ed. Totowa, N.J.: Rowman & Littlefield, 1980.

Berns, Walter. "Dirty Words." *Public Interest* no. 114 (Winter 1994): 119–25.

Brod, Harry. "Pornography and the Alienation of Male Sexuality." *Social Theory and Practice* 14, no. 3 (1988): 265–84. Reprinted in *The Philosophy of Sex,* edited by Alan Soble, 281–99. 2nd ed. Savage, Md.: Rowman & Littlefield, 1991.

Brown, Beverley. "Pornography and Feminism: Is Law the Answer?" *Critical Quarterly* 34, no. 2 (1992): 72–82.

Burger, John R. *One-Handed Histories: The Eroto-Politics of Gay Male Video Pornography.* New York: Haworth Press, 1995.

Burstyn, Varda, ed. *Women against Censorship.* Vancouver: Douglas and McIntyre, 1985.

Butterworth, Dianne. "Wanking in Cyberspace: The Development of Computer Porn." In *Feminism and Sexuality: A Reader,* edited by Stevi Jackson and Sue Scott, 314–20. New York: Columbia University Press, 1996.

Carse, Alisa L. "Pornography: An Uncivil Liberty?" *Hypatia* 10, no. 1 (1995): 156–82.

Caught Looking, Inc., eds. *Caught Looking: Feminism, Pornography, and Censorship.* East Haven, Conn.: Long River Books, 1992.

Chancer, Lynn S. "From Pornography to Sadomasochism: Reconciling Feminist Differences." *Annals of the American Academy of Political and Social Science* 571, no. 1 (2000): 77–88.

Christensen, Ferrel M. "The Alleged Link between Pornography and Violence." In *The Handbook of Forensic Sexology: Biomedical and Criminological Perspectives,* edited by J. J. Krivacska and J. Money, 422–48. Amherst, N.Y.: Prometheus, 1994.

———. "Cultural and Ideological Bias in Pornography Research." *Philosophy of the Social Sciences* 20, no. 3 (1990): 351–75.

———. *Pornography: The Other Side.* New York: Praeger, 1990.

Cohen, Joshua. "Freedom, Equality, Pornography." In *Justice and Injustice in Law and Legal Theory,* edited by Austin Sarat and Thomas R. Kearns, 99–137. Ann Arbor: University of Michigan Press, 1996.

Cornell, Drucilla, ed. *Feminism and Pornography.* Oxford, UK: Oxford University Press, 2000.

Dworkin, Andrea. *Life and Death.* New York: Free Press, 1997.

———. *Pornography: Men Possessing Women.* New York: Perigee, 1981.

Dworkin, Andrea, and Catharine A. MacKinnon. *Pornography and Civil Rights: A New Day for Women's Equality.* Minneapolis, Minn.: Organizing Against Pornography, 1988.

Dworkin, Ronald. "Women and Pornography." *New York Review of Books,* October 21, 1993, 36–42; reply to letter, *New York Review of Books,* March 3, 1994, 48–49.

Dwyer, Susan, ed. *The Problem of Pornography.* Belmont, Calif.: Wadsworth, 1995.

Easton, Susan M. *The Problem of Pornography: Regulation and the Right to Free Speech.* London: Routledge, 1994.

Ferguson, Frances. *Pornography, the Theory: What Utilitarianism Did to Action.* Chicago: University of Chicago Press, 2004.

Garry, Ann. "Pornography and Respect for Women." In *Philosophy and Women,* edited by Sharon Bishop and Marjorie Weinzweig, 128–39. Belmont, Calif.: Wadsworth, 1979.

———. "Sex, Lies, and Pornography." In *Ethics in Practice: An Anthology,* edited by Hugh LaFollette, 344–55. 2nd ed. Malden, Mass.: Blackwell, 2002.

Gibson, Pamela Church, and Roma Gibson, eds. *Dirty Looks: Women, Pornography, Power.* London: BFI Publishing, 1993.

Gubar, Susan, and Joan Hoff, eds. *For Adult Users Only: The Dilemma of Violent Pornography*. Bloomington: Indiana University Press, 1989.

Hill, Judith M. "Pornography and Degradation." *Hypatia* 2, no. 2 (1987): 39–54.

Hoffman, Eric. "Feminism, Pornography, and Law." *University of Pennsylvania Law Review* 133, no. 2 (1985): 497–534.

Hornsby, Jennifer. "Disempowered Speech." *Philosophical Topics* 23, no. 2 (1995): 127–47.

———. "Speech Acts and Pornography." *Women's Philosophical Review* 10 (November 1993), 38–45.

Hunter, Nan D., and Sylvia A. Law. "Brief Amici Curiae of Feminist Anticensorship Task Force et al., in *American Booksellers Association v. Hudnut*." In *Feminist Jurisprudence*, edited by Patricia Smith, 467–81. New York: Oxford University Press, 1993.

Itzin, Catherine, ed. *Pornography: Women, Violence and Civil Liberties*. Oxford, UK: Oxford University Press, 1992.

Jacobson, Daniel. "Freedom of Speech Acts? A Response to Langton." *Philosophy and Public Affairs* 24, no. 1 (1995): 64–79.

Jarvie, Ian C. "Pornography and/as Degradation." *International Journal of Law and Psychiatry* 14 (1991): 13–27.

———. *Thinking about Society: Theory and Practice*. Dordrecht: Reidel, 1986.

Kaite, Berkeley. *Pornography and Difference*. Bloomington: Indiana University Press, 1995.

Kappeler, Susanne. *The Pornography of Representation*. Minneapolis: University of Minnesota Press, 1986.

Kimmel, Michael S., ed. *Men Confront Pornography*. New York: Crown, 1990.

Kipnis, Laura. *Bound and Gagged: Pornography and the Politics of Fantasy in America*. New York: Grove Press, 1996.

———. "(Male) Desire and (Female) Disgust: Reading Hustler." In *Cultural Studies*, edited by Lawrence Grossberg, Cary Nelson, and Paula A. Treichler, 373–91. New York: Routledge, 1992.

Kittay, Eva Feder. "Pornography and the Erotics of Domination." In *Beyond Domination*, edited by Carol C. Gould, 145–74. Totowa, N.J.: Rowman & Allanheld, 1984.

Langton, Rae. "Love and Solipsism." In *Love Analyzed*, edited by Roger E. Lamb, 123–52. Boulder, Colo.: Westview, 1997.

———. "Sexual Solipsism." *Philosophical Topics* 23, no. 2 (1995): 149–87.

———. "Speech Acts and Unspeakable Acts." *Philosophy and Public Affairs* 22, no. 4 (1993): 293–330.

———. "Subordination, Silence, and Pornography's Authority." In *Censorship and Silencing: Practices of Cultural Regulation*, edited by R. C. Post, 261–83. Los Angeles, Calif.: Getty Research Institute, 1998.

———. "Whose Right? Ronald Dworkin, Women, and Pornographers." *Philosophy and Public Affairs* 19, no. 4 (1990): 311–59.

Lynn, Barry W. "'Civil Rights' Ordinances and the Attorney General's Commission: New Developments in Pornography Regulation." *Harvard Civil Rights-Civil Liberties Law Review* 21, no. 1 (1986): 27–125.

MacKinnon, Catharine A. *Only Words*. Cambridge, Mass.: Harvard University Press, 1993.

———. "Pornography Left and Right." In *Sex, Preference, and Family: Essays on Law and Nature*, edited by David M. Estlund and Martha C. Nussbaum, 102–25. New York: Oxford University Press, 1997.

———. "Sexuality, Pornography, and Method: 'Pleasure under Patriarchy.'" *Ethics* 99, no. 2 (1989): 314–46.

———. "Vindication and Resistance: A Response to the Carnegie Mellon Study of Pornography in Cyberspace." *Georgetown Law Journal* 83 (1995): 1959–67.

MacKinnon, Catharine A., and Andrea Dworkin, eds. *In Harm's Way: The Pornography Civil Rights Hearings*. Cambridge, Mass.: Harvard University Press, 1997.

McCormack, Thelma. "If Pornography Is the Theory, Is Inequality the Practice?" *Philosophy of the Social Sciences* 23, no. 3 (1993): 298–326.

McGowan, Mary Kate. "Conversational Exercitives and the Force of Pornography." *Philosophy and Public Affairs* 31, no. 2 (2003): 155–89.

Morgan, Robin. "Theory and Practice: Pornography and Rape." In *Going too Far: The Personal Chronicle of a Feminist*, 163–69. New York: Random House, 1977.

Parent, W. A. "A Second Look at Pornography and the Subordination of Women." *Journal of Philosophy* 87, no. 4 (1990): 205–11.

Rea, Michael C. "What Is Pornography?" *Noûs* 35, no. 1 (2001): 118–45.

Richlin, Amy, ed. *Pornography and Representation in Greece and Rome*. New York: Oxford University Press, 1992.

Rimm, Marty. "Marketing Pornography on the Information Superhighway: A Survey of 917,410 Images, Descriptions, Short Stories, and Animations Downloaded 8.5 Million Times by Consumers in over 2000 Cities in Forty Countries, Provinces, and Territories." *Georgetown Law Journal* 83 (1995): 1849–934.

Russell, Diana E. H. "Pornography and Rape: A Causal Model." *Political Psychology* 9, no. 1 (1988): 41–73. Revised in *Making Violence Sexy: Feminist Views on Pornography*, edited by D. E. H. Russell, 120–50. New York: Teachers College Press, 1993.

———, ed. *Making Violence Sexy: Feminist Views on Pornography*. New York: Teachers College Press, 1993.

Saul, Jennifer. "On Treating Things as People: Objectification, Pornography, and the History of the Vibrator." *Hypatia* 21, no. 2 (2006): 45–61.

———. "Pornography, Speech Acts, and Context." *Proceedings of the Aristotelian Society* (2005–2006), 229–48.

Segal, Lynne, and Mary McIntosh, eds. *Sex Exposed: Sexuality and the Pornography Debate*. New Brunswick, N.J.: Rutgers University Press, 1993.

Skipper, Robert. "Mill and Pornography." *Ethics* 103, no. 4 (1993): 726–30.

Soble, Alan. "Bad Apples: Feminist Politics and Feminist Scholarship." *Philosophy of the Social Sciences* 29, no. 3 (1999): 354–88.

———. "The Mainstream Has Always Been Pornographic." *Bridge* 12 (October–November 2004): 33–36.

———. "Pornography: Defamation and the Endorsement of Degradation." *Social Theory and Practice* 11, no. 1 (1985): 61–87.

———. *Pornography: Marxism, Feminism, and the Future of Sexuality*. New Haven, Conn.: Yale University Press, 1986.

———. *Pornography, Sex, and Feminism*. Amherst, N.Y.: Prometheus, 2002.

Stark, Cynthia A. "Is Pornography an Action? The Causal vs. the Conceptual View of Pornography's Harm." *Social Theory and Practice* 23, no. 2 (1997): 277–306.

Stoltenberg, John. *Refusing to Be a Man: Essays on Sex and Justice.* Portland, Ore.: Breitenbush, 1989.

Strossen, Nadine. *Defending Pornography: Free Speech, Sex, and the Fight for Women's Rights.* New York: Scribner, 1995.

Tong, Rosemarie. "Feminism, Pornography, and Censorship." *Social Theory and Practice* 8 (1982): 1–17.

———. "Women, Pornography, and the Law." In *The Philosophy of Sex,* edited by Alan Soble, 301–16. 2nd ed. Savage, Md.: Rowman & Littlefield, 1991.

Tucker, Scott. "Gender, Fucking, and Utopia: An Essay in Response to John Stoltenberg's *Refusing to Be a Man.*" *Social Text* 27 (1990): 3–34.

Turley, Donna. "The Feminist Debate on Pornography: An Unorthodox Interpretation." *Socialist Review* 16, nos. 3–4 (1986): 81–96.

Vadas, Melinda. "A First Look at the Pornography/Civil Rights Ordinance: Could Pornography Be the Subordination of Women?" *Journal of Philosophy* 84, no. 9 (1987): 487–511.

———. "The Manufacture-for-Use of Pornography and Women's Inequality." *Journal of Political Philosophy* 13, no. 2 (2005): 174-93.

———. "The Pornography/Civil Rights Ordinance v. the BOG: And the Winner Is . . . ?" *Hypatia* 7, no. 3 (1992): 94–109.

Valverde, Mariana. "Beyond Gender Dangers and Private Pleasures: Theory and Ethics in the Sex Debates." *Feminist Studies* 15, no. 2 (1989): 237–54.

Ward, David. "Should Pornography Be Censored?" In *Classic Philosophical Questions,* edited by James A. Gould, 504–12. New York: Prentice Hall, 1995.

Williams, Linda. *Hard Core: Power, Pleasure, and the "Frenzy of the Visible."* Berkeley: University of California Press, 1989.

———. "Second Thoughts on Hard Core: American Obscenity Law and the Scapegoating of Deviance." In *Dirty Looks: Women, Pornography, Power,* edited by Pamela Church Gibson and Roma Gibson, 46–61. London: BFI Publishing, 1993.

Sadomasochism

Airaksinen, Timo. *The Philosophy of the Marquis de Sade.* London: Routledge, 1995.

Bartky, Sandra Lee. "Feminine Masochism and the Politics of Personal Transformation." *Women's Studies International Forum* 7, no. 5 (1984): 323–34.

Califia, Pat. "Feminism and Sadomasochism." *Heresies* 12 ["Sex Issue"] nos. 3–4 (1981): 30–34. Reprinted in *Feminism and Sexuality: A Reader,* edited by Stevi Jackson and Sue Scott, 230–37. New York: Columbia University Press, 1996.

———. *Macho Sluts.* Los Angeles: Alyson Books, 1988.

———. *Public Sex: The Culture of Radical Sex.* Pittsburgh, Pa.: Cleis Press, 1994.

———, ed. *The Lesbian S/M Safety Manual.* Boston: Lace Publications, 1988.

Card, Claudia. "Review Essay: Sadomasochism and Sexual Preference." *Journal of Social Philosophy* 15, no. 2 (1984): 42–52.

Chancer, Lynn S. "From Pornography to Sadomasochism: Reconciling Feminist Differences." *Annals of the American Academy of Political and Social Science* 571, no. 1 (2000): 77–88.

———. *Sadomasochism in Everyday Life: The Dynamics of Power and Powerlessness.* New Brunswick, N.J.: Rutgers University Press, 1992.

Corvino, John. "Naughty Fantasies." *Southwest Philosophy Review* 18, no. 1 (2002): 213–20.

Cross, Patricia A., and Kim Matheson. "Understanding Sadomasochism: An Empirical Examination of Four Perspectives." *Journal of Homosexuality* 50, nos. 2–3 (2006): 133–66.

Fitzpatrick Hanly, Margaret Ann, ed. *Essential Papers on Masochism*. New York: New York University Press, 1995.

Gebhardt, Paul. "Fetishism and Sadomasochism." In *Sex Research: Studies from the Kinsey Institute*, edited by M. Weinberg, 156–66. New York: Oxford University Press, 1976.

Hopkins, Patrick D. "Rethinking Sadomasochism: Feminism, Interpretation, and Simulation." *Hypatia* 9, no. 1 (1994): 116–41. Reprinted in *The Philosophy of Sex*, edited by Alan Soble, 189–214. 3rd ed. Lanham, Md.: Rowman & Littlefield, 1997.

———. "Simulation and the Reproduction of Injustice: A Reply." *Hypatia* 10, no. 2 (1995): 162–70.

Kenney, Shawna. *I Was a Teenage Dominatrix: A Memoir*. New York: Retro Systems Press, 1999.

Linden, Robin Ruth, Darlene R. Pagano, Diana E. H. Russell, and Susan Leigh Star, eds. *Against Sadomasochism: A Radical Feminist Analysis*. East Palo Alto, Calif.: Frog in the Well, 1982.

Mann, Jay, and Natalie Shainess. "Sadistic Fantasies." *Medical Aspects of Human Sexuality* 8, no. 2 (1974): 142–48.

Noyes, John K. *The Mastery of Submission: Inventions of Masochism*. Ithaca, N.Y.: Cornell University Press, 1997.

Reik, Theodor. *Masochism in Sex and Society*. Translated by M. H. Beigel and G. M. Kurth. New York: Grove Press, 1962.

Sade, The Marquis de. *Justine, Philosophy in the Bedroom, and Other Writings*. Translated by Richard Seaver and Austryn Wainhouse. New York: Grove Press, 1965.

Samois, ed. *Coming to Power: Writings and Graphics on Lesbian S/M*. 1st ed,. Palo Alto, Calif.: Up Press, 1981. 2nd ed., Boston: Alyson Publications, 1982.

Shattuck, Roger. *Forbidden Knowledge: From Prometheus to Pornography*. San Diego: Harcourt Brace, 1996.

Vadas, Melinda. "Reply to Patrick Hopkins." *Hypatia* 10, no. 2 (1995): 159–61. Reprinted in *The Philosophy of Sex*, edited by Alan Soble, 215–17. 3rd ed. Lanham, Md.: Rowman & Littlefield, 1997.

Weinberg, Thomas S., ed. *S&M: Studies in Dominance & Submission*. Amherst, N.Y.: Prometheus, 1995.

INDEX

ABOUT THE EDITORS

Alan Soble, who has taught the philosophy of sex (and love, sometimes) more than fifty times in his career, is Professor Emeritus and University Research Professor of the University of New Orleans, from which he retired in 2007, eighteen months after the flooding caused by Hurricane Katrina and the collapse of the levees destroyed his home. Now teaching the philosophy of sex and love and other courses as an adjunct at several schools, he is the editor of the two-volume *Sex from Plato to Paglia: A Philosophical Encyclopedia*. Some of his journal articles and book chapters have been reprinted abroad, translated into German, Hungarian, Portuguese, French, Italian, and Chinese. After Katrina, his daughters scattered: Rebecca Jill (b. 1969) has been spending time in the Middle East, including Turkey, and (for vacations) Bulgaria, while Rachel Emőke (b. 1993) resettled in Milwaukee. Soble has been called, at various times, "insufferable" and a "buffoon," accolades the accuracy of which can be confirmed or refuted by visiting his web site, fs.uno.edu/asoble, or by perusing his contributions to Amherst College's question-and-answer web site, AskPhilosophers.org, for which he serves as a panelist.

Nicholas Power is associate professor of philosophy at the University of West Florida (in Pensacola, Florida) and has published on the philosophy of science and of mind as well as evolutionary theory. Now teaching courses in the philosophy of sex and love, of science, and of mind, and chairing a department of philosophy and religious studies, he received his dissertation from Temple University, hails originally from Kilkenny, Ireland, the city of Berkeley and Swift, and shares their scatalological outlook. His two daughters, Hannah (b. 1992) and Molly (b. 1998), don't.